The Child's Story Bible

◆

CATHERINE F. VOS

Revised by
Marianne Catherine Vos Radius

WILLIAM B. EERDMANS
255 JEFFERSON AVE. S.E.
GRAND RAPIDS, MICH. 49503

"*Let*
the little children
come to Me," He said.
"Do not forbid them, for
the kingdom of heaven be-
longs to just such as they
are." Then Jesus took the
little children in His arms,
and laid His hands on
their heads and
blessed them.

PUBLISHER'S NOTE

The Child's Story Bible by Catherine F. Vos has been a family favorite for decades; it has been read and reread in countless homes and has gone through numerous editions and reprintings.

Originally published in 1934, this classic story Bible is here being issued in a special fiftieth-anniversary edition. The text is that of the most recent revision by Marianne Catherine Vos Radius, readily understood by today's children. The illustrations, however, are the classic artworks that appeared in the early editions. An attractive new format and durable binding make the book as practical as it is beautiful.

It is our hope that this much-loved work will continue to instruct and delight not only those children and families for whom it is already a classic but also those now discovering it for the first time.

THE CHILD'S STORY BIBLE
by CATHERINE F. VOS
Entire contents, including illustrations,
Copyright © 1935, 1949, 1958, 1966, and 1977 by
WM. B. EERDMANS PUBLISHING COMPANY
Grand Rapids, Michigan

Vol. I, November, 1934
Vol. II, October, 1935
Vol. III, October, 1936
One-volume edition, April, 1940
Second edition, August, 1949
Third edition, May, 1958
Fourth edition, December, 1966
Paperback edition, November, 1977
Fifth edition, July, 1983

ISBN 0-8028-5011-1

Printed in the United States of America

PREFACE TO THE REVISED EDITION

These stories have a family history. They were first told by my grandmother to my mother when she was a little girl. Later my mother told them to me, as I was to tell them to my daughter. I hope that someday she will tell them to her children.

When my brothers and I grew old enough to want to read the Bible stories for ourselves, my mother searched through the bookstores for a Bible storybook which would be both faithful to the inspired Word of God and successful in conveying the dramatic excitement and human warmth of these most wonderful of all stories. When she finally despaired of ever finding such a book, she sat down with simple determination to write one.

It was a labor of many years. It was still being written when I was sent off to Calvin College in Grand Rapids, where my father had been a professor of theology, and where the roots of our family lay. When I came home to Princeton for vacations, I would find my mother still busy with her Bible storybook. Day after day she carried her Bible, her pencil, and her notebook to the upstairs porch where she could have a measure of privacy from the busy confusion of family life. With the unreflecting carelessness of youth, I accepted this as just one of the things my mother did. Like her gardening, and her visiting the aged and the sick, it lay outside my own circle of interests. It was not until I myself had written many Bible stories for Sunday school papers that I fully realized the monumental task my mother had assigned herself.

The National Union of Christian Schools and the William B. Eerdmans Publishing Company undertook the publication of her manuscript as a joint venture of faith. The book appeared first in three volumes. My mother did not live to see it in its later one-volume form.

This new edition has been revised to conform more closely to our modern idiom, and to incorporate the many archaeological discoveries of the past thirty years which have corroborated and confirmed the Biblical account. Although the book has been shortened somewhat, mainly by the elimination of some repetition, in order to make the volume more easy to handle, every effort has been made to preserve my mother's style, and especially to remain absolutely faithful to the Bible as the inspired and infallible Word of God. Dates and the spelling of names and places are based on *The New Bible Dictionary,* edited by J. D. Douglas. The Bible text, where it is directly quoted, is the King James Version.

It would be impossible to say in how many ways my husband has helped me in this task which has been a family undertaking for over a year. He and I together join in the hope that this book may make some small contribution to the nurture of God's children.

And these words, which I command thee this day, shall be in thine heart: And thou shalt teach them diligently unto thy children, and shalt talk of them when thou sittest in thine house, and when thou walkest by the way, and when thou liest down, and when thou risest up (Deut. 6:7).

—MARIANNE CATHERINE VOS RADIUS

Dedication

To my dear Mother in heaven
who told me these stories
when I was a little child
in much the same way
in which I have written them
in this book

CONTENTS

Old Testament

PART I: CREATION

PART II: WANDERING

PART III: LAWS

PART IV: SETTLEMENT

New Testament

PART VIII: SAVIOUR

PART IX: THE EARLY CHURCH

LIST OF ILLUSTRATIONS

Old Testament

2: THE LAW GIVEN ON MT. SINAI.

3: ADAM AND EVE DRIVEN FROM EDEN

IN THE BEGINNING GOD

GOD IS AND WAS Long, long ago — nobody knows how long ago — this world on which we live, this big ball that we call earth, was not here. The earth did not exist. There was nothing but emptiness, wide empty space. That was before the beginning of the first things, before the beginning of time.

Yet there was something in that long, long ago. God was there. When did God begin? And who made God? *No one made God.* And God did not begin. God has always been. Forever and ever and ever, God has lived. God never had a beginning, and His life will never end.

PART I Creation

If you were to take a cup and dip water out of the big, wide, and deep ocean, you could dip and dip and dip, but you could never dip the ocean dry. Your mind is like a little cup, and God's life is like the big, deep ocean. You cannot dip the ocean dry with a cup. And you and I, with our little minds, cannot understand God's life, which never began, and will never, never end.

God is eternal. Someday the sun and the moon and the stars and the earth on which we live will all grow old, just as your clothes grow old and wear out. But God will be the same as He was — today, yesterday, long, long ago, and tomorrow. His life will go on and on forever.

God is also very great. He can do many things which men cannot do. You and I can be in only one place at a time. If we want to be in some other place, we have to go there. But God is in heaven, and at the same time He is everywhere upon earth. If we go into the deepest dark mines, God is there. If we fly up into the clouds of the sky, God is there.

God also knows everything. He sees us always and everywhere. He knows everything we do, hears every word we speak, and even knows the thoughts we have in our minds. We cannot hide from God. If we do wrong, God knows it, even if we have not told anyone. He knows, too, when we love Him, and trust Him, and try to please Him, even if no one else knows.

Long ago someone said: "Thou God seest me" (Genesis 16:13). That is a good line to remember.

God is even more wonderful. He knows everything that is *going* to happen in the world. We do not know what will happen tomorrow. But God knows. He knows what is going to happen tomorrow, and next week, and next year, and always, till the very end of the world. God also knows what will happen after the world has passed away. For every-

1

thing that has ever happened and everything that will ever happen is part of God's great plan.

And God is good. He is perfectly good, so that He cannot do anything wrong. Everything that God does is right.

Most wonderful of all, God is love. He loves you more than anyone in the world loves you. He loves you more than even your father and your mother love you. It was God who gave you a father and a mother to love you and take care of you.

Your father and your mother, much as they love you, cannot take care of you all the time. Sometimes they have to go away. At night they must sleep. But God is always near you, and He is always taking care of you. God never sleeps. All night long, when you are sleeping, God is watching over you and taking care of you. God takes care of you all day long too.

It is God who made you. He made you because He wanted to love you. God wants you to love Him too.

God lives in heaven. Heaven is more beautiful than any place you have ever seen. It is more beautiful than anything you can imagine. It is beautiful because God is there. There is a wonderful river in heaven called the River of the Water of Life, with water as clear as crystal. There is no dark night in heaven, but always bright, beautiful day. The glory of God makes heaven brighter than the sun.

There is no sickness nor sadness in heaven, but all is joy and happiness. There are no tears. There is no crying. There is no death.

With God in heaven are the beautiful angels, thousands and thousands of them. With Him, too, are all the people who loved and trusted God while on earth. And there is a place there for us, if we love God, and if our sins are forgiven for Jesus' sake.

THE ANGELS, GOOD AND BAD   God made the beautiful angels to live with Him in heaven. There are very many angels, so many that we cannot count them — ten thousand times ten thousand, and thousands of thousands. The angels are bright like the light. They are much stronger than men, and can do things that men cannot do. They go wherever God sends them. They can fly down from heaven to this earth.

These angels love God and are happy. They spend all their time with God, loving and praising Him, and doing whatever He wants them to do. Some are called archangels, because they are much greater than the rest. God has let us know the names of a few. One of them is the great archangel Gabriel, who stands in God's holy presence. God sent him down to earth several times, with messages from God to man. It was the archangel Gabriel who told Mary that God was going to send the baby Jesus to her.

Sometimes God sends angels down to earth to help people who are in trouble. An angel once opened the prison door to let God's servant Peter out. The Bible tells of more than twenty times that God sent angels down to earth with messages to men.

But long ago there were some angels in heaven who turned away from being good. Instead of loving God, they began to hate Him. They became wicked. The name of the leader of these wicked angels is Satan. Many other angels listened to Satan, and rebelled against God.

God cannot have anything wicked

in His beautiful heaven. So God threw the wicked angels out of heaven. Now they are no longer called angels. They are called demons.

The demons hate everything that is good. Most of all they hate God. And they do not want us to love God and to go to heaven to live with Him after we die. They try all they can to make us hate God, as they do. They want us to lie and steal, to be disobedient, quarrelsome, and cruel.

But the demons are afraid of God. God is much stronger than Satan and all his demons. They fear and tremble before God. So we do not need to be afraid of them. We should love and trust God, as the good angels do, and try in every way to please Him. Let us pray to God always. He will take care of us. He will make us strong to do what is good.

Chapter 2
HOW THE WORLD BEGAN
GENESIS 1

"In the beginning God created the heavens and the earth." *Created* means "made out of nothing."

When a man builds a house, he must first have wood, nails, glass, and many other things. If he does not have something out of which to make it, he cannot build a house. But God made the world out of nothing at all.

God made the world in a most wonderful way. When God began to make the world, He did not have to work hard and long, as a man has to work when he makes a house. All God had to do was simply to speak, and the world began.

God did not make the world all at once as we see it now. At first land and water, air and sky were all mixed up, without any shape. Over it all was darkness — deep, deep darkness, without a ray of light.

Then God said, "Let there be light," and there was light. And God saw the light, that it was good, and God divided the light from the darkness. And God called the light day, and the darkness He called night. That was the first day.

It is God who still makes the daylight come every morning, so that we can get up out of our beds to work and play. It is God, too, who sends the darkness every night, so that we can sleep quietly and rest our tired bodies. We need never be afraid of the darkness, because it is God's darkness. He made it, and He will not let anything hurt us.

God made the air and the blue sky with the soft, white clouds floating in it on the second day. The earth and the water were still mixed up. After He made the air and the blue sky, God said, "Let the waters under the heavens be gathered together into one place, and let the dry land appear."

The waters obeyed God. They separated themselves from the earth and ran down the hills into the valleys and out into the sea. So the deep places of the earth were filled with water, and the big oceans began to appear. The land — the hills and the

3

mountains — stood up high and dry above the oceans. And God called the dry land earth, and the gathering together of the waters He called seas. And God saw that it was good.

Now there was light, and the beautiful blue sky. There were hills, valleys, plains, brooks, rivers, and oceans. The world was ready for something to grow on it. Then God commanded the earth to bring forth grass and vegetables and fruit trees.

As soon as God said it, the bare earth began to grow green with beautiful grass. All kinds of vegetables began to grow. Peaches, apples, oranges, cherries — all these delicious fruits were also created by God at this time. And God made the first roses and lilies and all the other bright-colored flowers which make the world very beautiful. And God saw that it was good. And there was evening, and there was morning, the third day.

Next God made the great and glorious sun to flood the earth with beautiful sunshine and make the earth warm, so that all the flowers, fruits, and plants could grow. God also made the silver moon to shine in the dark night when the sun has gone away. And God made the thousands and thousands of bright, twinkling stars that shine in the sky at night. God made all these to give light upon the earth, and to rule the day and the night, and to divide the light from the darkness. And God saw that it was good. And there was evening, and morning, the fourth day.

Now that the beautiful earth was clothed with grass and flowers and trees, and the warm sun was pouring down upon it, it was ready for some animals to live on it. The first living creatures that God made were fish and birds.

God filled the brooks and the rivers and the ocean with all kinds of fish — great whales and little minnows, and every other kind of fish that swims.

God made all the beautiful, sweet-singing birds at this time also. The earth, which till now had only heard such sounds as the humming of the winds and the dashing of the ocean waves, was full of sweet songs from the birds. And it was full of beauty, as the bright-colored birds, like lovely jewels, flitted to and fro among the branches of the trees. And there was evening, and there was morning, the fifth day.

And now we come to the sixth day. On that day God made the animals of every kind, and all creeping things. Lions and tigers began to live in the deep woods where there had been no animals at all before. Great herds of cows and sheep fed in the wide meadows. Goats and deer climbed over the high mountains. Rabbits ran about in the grass and made their homes in the ground. White bears trampled over the snow of the cold north. Hosts of chattering monkeys swung from the branches of the trees in hot regions. Soft purring kittens chased their tails and tumbled over each other in the grass. Huge elephants and tall giraffes, big animals and small ones — God made all of them on this day.

Chapter 3

THE FIRST MAN, ADAM
GENESIS 1, 2

There were now many animals, but there was not a man in all the wide world. Last of all, God made a man. God made the first man entirely grown up. It was a great deal better to make him grown up, because he was all alone in the world. If he had first been a little baby, he would not have been able to take care of himself. God called the man Adam.

God made man a body. He gave him eyes to see with, ears to hear with, and feet to walk with. Have you ever stopped to think how precious it is to be able to see the stars or to hear the waves against the seashore when you are camping or at a cottage? Or to see your mother or father, and to hear their voices, perhaps when you are afraid? These are truly wonderful gifts from God.

But God gave man a gift even more wonderful, something he did not give to the animals. The Bible tells us that God created man in his own image. When God created man, He meant him to love God and to think about Him and to serve Him. An animal cannot think about God or love Him or choose to serve Him. Only man is created in God's image.

The Bible says, "God formed man of the dust of the ground, and breathed into his nostrils the breath of life, and man became a living soul." This does not mean that God picked up a handful of dirt and made a man out of it. It means that man's body is made out of the same materials we find in the soil and the rocks.

After a man's body lies in the earth a long time, it turns back to dust, for it is made of dust.

When an animal dies, its body is dead, and that is the end of the animal. But when we die, this is not the end for us. We have been created in God's image, and the Bible promises that because we are special we will someday be made alive again, with glorious new bodies. All God's children will then be with their Heavenly Father and know Him and love Him and serve Him forever.

God did not give the angels bodies like ours. Angels are pure spirits, without bodies. God also is a spirit without a body.

God made both animals and man on that sixth day. And then He was finished with the making of the heavens and the earth and all that is in them. And God saw everything that He had made, and, behold, it was very good.

On the seventh day God rested. He blessed the seventh day, and rested from all His works that He had made. And He commanded that the seventh day should be a day of rest for man too, who was created in God's image. We do not have to work every day. On Sunday we may rest from our daily work. Sunday is a special day, set apart to worship God with His people, a day to sing His praise together in church, to talk to Him in prayer, and to listen as God talks to us in His Word, the Bible.

Chapter 4

THE FIRST WOMAN, EVE
GENESIS 2

Adam was the only human being in the world. Yet he was not alone. For in the evening, in the cool of the day, God came to him and talked to him.

At night Adam lay down on the cool grass to sleep. He had no house to live in, but he was not afraid, for none of the animals would hurt him. They were neither wild nor fierce.

God took care of Adam. God planted a garden, and He filled it with beautiful trees and plants whose fruit was delicious to eat. He put Adam in the garden to take care of it. The beautiful garden was called the Garden of Eden, or Paradise. Every plant was pleasant to look at, and every fruit was good to eat.

In the middle of the garden was a very wonderful tree called the Tree of Life. Whoever ate the fruit of that tree would live forever. There was another tree in the middle of the garden called the Tree of the Knowledge of Good and Evil. God said to Adam, "You may eat freely of every tree of the garden, but you must not eat the fruit of the Tree of the Knowledge of Good and Evil. For if you eat that fruit, you will surely die."

God had given Adam many wonderful gifts. The greatest of all these gifts was the love and the friendship of God Himself. Now God was testing Adam, to see whether Adam loved and trusted God in return. That was the reason for the strict command not to eat the fruit of the Tree of the Knowledge of Good and Evil.

God had made Adam good. Adam did not do anything wrong. He knew only about goodness; he did not know anything about wickedness. God did not want him to know anything about being wicked.

Adam was very happy in the Garden of Eden. Once in a while he was lonely, because there were no other people in the world. He had no wife, no children, no friends to talk to. But he loved the flowers and the trees.

God brought all the animals to Adam so that he could name them, and to see if he could make a friend or companion of any of them. Adam gave names to all the animals. Each animal kept the name that Adam gave it. But not one of them could understand what he said, or talk to him.

God said, "It is not good that the man should be alone. I will make a help meet for him." God caused Adam to fall into a deep sleep. While he was asleep God took out one of his ribs, and closed up the place from which He had taken it. God made that rib into a beautiful, sweet woman.

When Adam woke up, God brought the lovely woman to him. How surprised and pleased Adam was! Now he was not alone any more. Now he had someone to talk to and to love. Adam called her name Eve, and she became his wife. They wandered through the beautiful garden hand in hand, picking the delicious fruit, and taking care of God's garden together.

They did not have to wear clothes. They did not know anything about clothes. They went naked and were not ashamed, because they were as innocent as little babies. They did not yet know sin and shame.

Chapter 5

ADAM AND EVE DISOBEY GOD
GENESIS 3

Adam and Eve were happier than anyone else has ever been in the whole wide world. Why were they happier? They were happier because they were good. They loved God, and they loved each other, and they never wanted to do anything wrong.

There is something in my heart, and in yours, that makes us want to do wrong, because we have bad, sinful hearts. But when God made Adam and Eve, he gave them hearts that wanted to be good.

They were never sick. They were never very tired. When God made them, He gave them bodies that were always perfectly healthy and well. They never had to work hard, as we do now. All they had to do was to take care of the beautiful garden.

God also promised them a wonderful gift. He promised that if they obeyed his command not to eat of the fruit of the Tree of the Knowledge of Good and Evil, they would never die.

God made the first man and the first woman perfectly good, and perfectly strong and healthy. But think how much wickedness there is now in the world, and how much pain and suffering there is, and, worst of all, death! How did this sad change come about?

The wicked devil was once an angel in heaven. But he did not stay good and pure, as the other angels are. He became wicked, and God put him out of heaven as a punishment for his wickedness. The devil, being very wicked, hated God, and tried to fight against Him.

When he saw the beautiful new world that God had made, and Adam and Eve happy because they loved God, the devil wanted to spoil God's beautiful world, and make Adam and Eve wicked like himself. He knew that if Adam and Eve disobeyed God, they could not live in the beautiful garden, and walk and talk with God. Satan wanted the man and the woman to be as unhappy as he was himself.

So the devil disguised himself as a snake. The snake was the cleverest of all the animals God had made. Satan, hiding himself in the snake, came and talked to Eve.

"Did God really say you must not eat the fruit of any tree in the garden?" he asked.

Eve answered, "No, we may eat all the fruit in the garden, except the fruit of the Tree of the Knowledge of Good and Evil. God says if we eat the fruit of that tree, or touch it, we shall surely die."

Then the devil in the snake's body told Eve a wicked lie. He said, "You shall not surely die. God knows that the day that you eat the fruit of that tree your eyes shall be opened, and you shall be like God, knowing good and evil."

Would Eve believe Satan, or would she believe God? This was a test of whether she really loved and trusted God.

Eve went and looked at the tree. It was a beautiful tree. She thought the fruit would taste very good. She would like to be as wise as God, knowing both good and evil. She knew God had commanded them not to eat the fruit, or even to touch it. But she disobeyed God. She picked some of the fruit and ate it. She gave some of it to Adam. He disobeyed God too, and ate the fruit.

Now a horrible change came. No longer did the man and the woman want to be good. No longer did they love God and want to please Him! No longer did they love each other! Now they had angry and selfish feelings in their hearts. They began to want to do wicked things.

It was indeed true that the fruit of the tree would make them wise to know evil as well as good. Before this they knew only what it was to have good thoughts, and to do good things. Now at once they knew what it was to have wicked thoughts, and to do wicked things.

Now that they had eaten the forbidden fruit, they began to be ashamed that they were naked. Before this they had never thought of being ashamed. They took fig leaves and fastened them together. In this way they made themselves clothes, so that they would not be naked.

Chapter 6
THE TERRIBLE RESULT OF SIN
GENESIS 3

Adam and Eve no longer loved to have God come into the garden. They were afraid of God, because they knew that they had disobeyed Him. When they heard God walking in the garden in the cool of the day, they hid themselves among the trees.

God called to the man and said, "Where are you?" Adam answered, "I heard Thy voice in the garden, and I was afraid, because I was naked; and I hid myself." Then God said, "Who told you that you were naked? Have you eaten the fruit of the tree that I commanded you not to eat?"

And Adam, whose heart now was wicked, tried to lay all the blame on his wife. He said to God, "The woman that Thou gavest me to be with me, she gave me some of the fruit of the tree, and I ate it."

Then God said to the woman, "What is this that you have done?" And Eve laid the blame on the snake.

She said, "The snake persuaded me, and so I ate the fruit."

Then God said to the snake, "Because you have done this, you are cursed above all cattle, and above every beast of the field. You must crawl on your belly, and eat dust all the days of your life."

And the Lord made for Adam and for his wife garments of skins and clothed them.

Then God made a wonderful promise, a promise Adam and Eve did not deserve. He said, "I will put enmity between the serpent and the woman, between her children and the serpent's children. Satan shall bruise your heel, but a son of yours shall bruise his head." God meant that some day one of Eve's children would conquer Satan and crush his head. That child would be our Lord Jesus Christ.

Then God said to the woman that she would have a great deal of sickness. She would have pain and weariness, and her husband would rule over her. Her disobedience had brought sickness and pain and weariness to the world. Eve would never again know what it was to be perfectly well. And when she had children, they too would sometimes become sick and suffer pain.

God told Adam that because he had listened to the voice of his wife, and eaten the forbidden fruit, the ground would no longer grow fruits and vegetables by itself. After this Adam would have to work very hard to get enough to eat, until the sweat poured down from his face. Thorns and thistles would come up where Adam had planted seeds, because God had cursed the ground as a result of Adam's sin. All his life Adam would have to work, and in the end he would die, and his body would return to the dust.

What unhappiness they had brought upon themselves! They no longer wanted to be good, and to love God and each other. Their hearts were full of badness now. They became selfish, untruthful, angry. Instead of loving to think about God, and to talk to Him, they wanted to forget Him.

There was more sadness to come. For when God sent them little children, the children would be like their father and mother. They would have wicked hearts too. Adam and Eve were the parents from whom all the people in the world have come. If Adam and Eve had obeyed God, their hearts would have stayed clean and sinless, and all the people in the world would have had sinless hearts. But now we are all wicked because Adam and Eve disobeyed God. The Bible says, "There is none good, no not one."

Chapter 7
A LOSS AND A PROMISE
GENESIS 3

You remember that besides the Tree of the Knowledge of Good and Evil, there was another wonderful tree in the Garden of Eden. It was called the Tree of Life. Whoever ate of that tree would live forever. Now that Adam and Eve had become wicked, God would no longer let them stay in the Garden of Eden, for fear that they might eat of the Tree of Life, and live forever.

God drove Adam and Eve out of the Garden of Eden. To keep them from going back, He placed cherubim at the east of the garden to guard

the way to the Tree of Life, and a flaming sword which turned every direction. Cherubim are heavenly beings, or angels, who stand by the throne of God to serve Him.

When Adam and Eve were sent out of their home in the beautiful garden, they had to make a home for themselves. Things were not pleasant for them. They had to work hard to get enough to eat. Thorns and thistles began to grow. The trees were no longer full of delicious fruits for them to eat. They often felt tired and sick and unhappy. But what they missed most of all were those wonderful evenings when God came down to the garden, and walked and talked with the man and the woman. He had made. Oh, how they longed for those happy times of fellowship with God! How they wished that they had not disobeyed His command.

But now it was too late. They could not go back to the garden. A holy God cannot associate with sinners. And they could never go to live with God in heaven because of their wicked hearts. Neither can you and I go to heaven with a wicked heart. God is so pure and holy that He cannot allow the least bit of sinfulness in heaven.

Was it altogether too late? Were Adam and Eve and all their children lost in sin forever? Was there nothing they could do to pay for their sin?

No, there was nothing they could do. With wicked hearts like theirs they could never pay for their sin. But what is impossible for men is possible for God. The Bible tells us that with God all things are possible.

God loved the man so much that He promised that He Himself would make a way for Adam and Eve and their children once more to walk and talk with God. He would send a Saviour who would pay for their sin, who would bear their punishment in their place.

Adam and Eve did not know who the Saviour would be, or when and how He would come to help them. They had only the promise of God, and they had to trust blindly in that promise. But that was enough for them. Someday they were going to walk and talk with God again. For God Himself had said so.

You and I, however, know who the Saviour is. It is our Lord Jesus Christ, God's own Son. He came to earth on Christmas Day, and died on the cross on Good Friday, to pay for Adam's sin, and Eve's sin, and my sin, and yours, and the sins of all the people who have ever lived, or shall ever live, who put their trust in Him and love Him.

The whole Bible is the story of how God planned and prepared for the coming of His Son, and how the Saviour finally came to earth and died to pay for our sins. It is the story of how you and I, even though we have wicked hearts, can be forgiven, and once again walk and talk with God.

Chapter 8

THE FIRST CRIME

GENESIS 4

Sometime after Adam and Eve had been sent out of the Garden of Eden, something happened which showed that God still loved them. God sent them a present — the first baby that ever was born in the whole wide world! How surprised and pleased they were! They had never seen anything like it before. But Eve knew that it was God who had sent them their son.

Later God sent them another baby. They named the first boy Cain, and the second one Abel. And how they loved the two boys!

Cain and Abel did not have to go

to school, because there were no schools and no books. There was a great deal to learn, however. They had to find out much by themselves, because they had no one except their father and mother to tell them how to do anything.

They had to learn which animals were safe to play with, and which were wild and dangerous. The animals were not all mild and gentle, as they had been before Adam and Eve sinned. Some of them were fierce and bad.

Cain liked to dig in the ground. He found out that by gathering seeds, by planting them in the ground, by watering them, and by digging out the weeds, he could make fruits and vegetables grow. He enjoyed this, so he became a farmer.

Abel liked to play with the little lambs and goats. He learned how to lead them to the tenderest grass and the freshest water, and to drive away the fierce wolves and other animals which would have killed the sheep. So he became a shepherd.

But Cain and Abel had sinful hearts, like their father and mother. When Adam and Eve saw their little boys doing wicked things, fighting and quarreling, they must have been more sorry than ever that they had brought sin into the world. Of course, they taught their children about God. Abel learned to love God, and to trust in His promise.

By and by Cain and Abel grew up and became men. One day Cain brought a gift to the Lord. It was some of his fruits. It was only a gift of fruit; there was no real thanks in his heart. Abel brought a little lamb from his flock. He offered the lamb to God with true thankfulness and trust in God's promise. He knew that

he was sinful, and did not deserve the blessings of God.

God can see every man's heart. He is not interested in your gifts unless you bring them with a thankful and a trusting heart. God accepted Abel's gift, but He did not accept Cain's. When Cain saw that Abel's gift was accepted, but his was not, his face grew black with anger.

"Why are you angry?" God said to Cain. "If you bring an offering in the right spirit, your offering will be accepted too. Do not allow these angry thoughts to fill your mind. Sin is like a wild animal. It is always waiting to jump on you and choke you."

Cain did not listen to God's warning. He was jealous of his brother. One day, when he and Abel were in the field, Cain did a dreadful thing. He killed his brother. Abel's blood ran out and soaked the ground, making it red.

How sad Adam and Eve must have felt when they saw their son lying dead upon the ground. They had seen dead animals before, but no man had ever died. Just a short time ago Abel had been full of life, talking and running and working. Now he lay on the ground dead. And Adam and Eve knew it was their own sin which had brought death into the world. Oh, if only they had not disobeyed God!

Adam and Eve were not the only ones who saw Abel lying on the ground, dead. God saw it too. God spoke to Cain. "Where is your brother?" He asked. Cain told a wicked lie. He said, "I do not know. Am I my brother's keeper?"

God said, "The voice of your brother's blood is crying to Me from the ground. The ground which soaked up your brother's blood shall not grow

11

things for you any longer. You must go away, and become a homeless wanderer on the earth."

So Cain went away to a far country and lived a lonely life, far away from his father and mother. Cain took his wife with him when he left home. Adam and Eve must have had daughters, and Cain must have had one of them for his wife.

Soon Cain and his wife had a baby named Enoch. Enoch grew up and had a son named Irad. Irad also grew up and had children. And his children had children. After a while there was a son named Lamech who had three sons. He named them Jabal, Jubal, and Tubal-cain. Probably all of Cain's children were wicked like their father. But some of them were very clever.

Jabal was the first man to think of making a tent to live in. Jabal kept cows and sheep and goats, so that he would not have to go catch a wild one every time he wanted meat to eat or wool to make clothes of.

Jubal was also very clever. He was the first man to make a musical instrument. He found out how to make a whistle out of a piece of wood. After making many whistles of different sounds, he put them together and made a kind of organ. Then, too, he found out how to fasten strings over a piece of wood so that they would make musical sounds like a harp.

Tubal-cain found out something even more wonderful. He discovered how to make iron and copper red-hot until they were soft, and how to beat them into shapes such as knives, swords, plows, and pots. It was a great help to have good knives to cut with. Just think how hard it must have been to cut things with sharp stones or sticks!

When God made the world, He hid wonderful things in the earth for man to find and use. These three sons of Lamech quickly learned about some of them.

Chapter 9
WHAT THE FIRST MEN WERE LIKE
GENESIS 5

I have been telling you about wicked Cain and his descendants. What are descendants? Children, and grandchildren, and grandchildren's children, and so on — these we call descendants.

How dreadful it would have been if all the people in the world had come from wicked Cain! God would not permit such a thing to happen, however.

God gave Adam and Eve another son to take the place of Abel, whom Cain had killed. Eve was glad to have another baby. Abel was dead, and Cain had had to go far away so that she never saw him. Besides, he had caused them great sorrow. Eve called this new son Seth. She said, "God has given me another son to take the place of Abel, whom Cain killed."

Adam and Eve were a hundred and thirty years old when Seth was born. Yet Adam was a very young man

12

when he was a hundred and thirty years old. How is that possible?

God let Adam live a very, very long time. He was nine hundred and thirty years old before he died. He lived almost a thousand years! Adam had a great many children, both boys and girls, before he died.

Most of Adam's children lived a long time too. They also lived to be almost a thousand years old. Many of their children, in turn, lived almost a thousand years. The world was becoming full of people.

The man who lived the longest was Methuselah. He lived to be nine hundred and sixty-nine years old. He was the oldest man that ever lived.

Why did God let those first people live so long? The Bible does not tell us, but I shall tell you what I think. I think that those people were very much stronger than people are now. God had wanted men to live forever. Even after they had sinned, and God had told them that they must die sometime, they still had a great deal of strength. They did not wear out as soon as we do.

The Bible tells us that many of them were giants — "mighty men of renown," the Bible calls them. They lived longer, and many of them were much taller and stronger than we are. Probably they had better minds than we have, too.

I think, too, that God let them live very long so that they could have time to learn how to do things, and then teach their children. There was very much to learn. God had made man with a desire to learn, and with a mind keen and bright to think and plan. So the people on earth soon learned how to build houses. They learned how to make axes to cut down trees for lumber.

They learned about fire — how to make a fire and how to use it for cooking food. They had to make kettles to hold the food they cooked, and they found copper and iron to use for that. How they must have enjoyed discovering new wonders every day! And they taught all these things to their children and grandchildren.

Probably another reason the first people lived so long was so that they could teach their children and grandchildren about God. Adam, who had once talked with God in the garden, could tell them all about the wonderful first things.

For there was no Bible to read so that they might learn about God and His dear Son, Jesus, who was to come. After a while men learned to write. They learned to make the letters of the alphabet. But at first there were no books, and the only way things could be remembered was for fathers and mothers to tell their children all that they had learned from *their* parents and grandparents and even great-grandparents.

Adam lived to tell the story of creation to very many children and grandchildren and great-grandchildren.

Among all those early people there was one man who did not live as long as the others. That man was Enoch. Enoch lived to be three hundred and sixty-five years old. But he did not die.

What happened to him, then, if he did not die? Something very wonderful. Enoch loved God. He often talked to God in prayer, and he trusted in God's promise. He thought about God so much that it was as if God was very close to him. The Bible says, "Enoch walked with God."

God was pleased that Enoch loved Him and trusted Him. He did something very wonderful for Enoch. God took him straight up to heaven — took him with his body, without his having to pass through the experience of death, as all other people must. The Bible says, "And Enoch walked with God, and he was not found, for God took him." Now in heaven Enoch could always be with the God whom he so loved.

When we go to heaven, we shall see that saintly man of old.

Chapter 10
THE SECOND BEGINNING
GENESIS 6-8

BUILDING THE ARK I am sorry to say that though Enoch loved God, most of the people on earth did not. Here and there a single man turned to God for forgiveness, for help, for fellowship. But not many.

Most of them relied not on God but on their own strength and cunning. They took whatever they wanted, and hated and fought whoever got in their way. There was wickedness everywhere, such wickedness as you can hardly imagine. At last there was only one family left that served God. Noah still trusted God, and tried to do what was right. All of the rest of the human race were utterly corrupt.

God is a God of goodness. He cannot stand wickedness. God created man to have fellowship with Him. But it is not possible for a good God to have fellowship with such desperately wicked men. He decided to destroy them all, and start over again with Noah.

God told Noah to build a big ship, so that he and his wife and his sons and his sons' wives might be saved from the flood God was going to send on the earth. They were to take into the ship with them two of every kind of animal — beasts, and birds, and creeping things — to keep them alive, and to start a new world after the flood.

God told Noah just how to make the ship, or ark. He was to make it very large, so that there would be room for all the animals. It was to be four hundred and fifty feet long. Now suppose you take a ruler and measure four hundred and fifty feet on the sidewalk. Then you will see how very long the ark was. It was to be seventy-five feet wide. That is wider than most streets. It was to be forty-five feet high. That is as high as a high house.

It was to have three stories in it. We might call them a downstairs, an upstairs, and an attic. There were to be rooms in it, probably so that Noah could keep the different kinds of animals separate, which otherwise would fight and kill each other. There was to be a window in the ark, so that there would be plenty of air to breathe. There was also to be a door by which the animals and people could go in. Noah was to build it of very strong wood, and to cover it inside and outside with pitch to make it watertight.

God told Noah to take a great deal of food into the ark, of all kinds, so that he and his family and all the animals might have enough to eat

14

when the flood came. For the flood was going to last a long time.

It took Noah a long time to build the ark, more than a hundred years. While Noah was busy with it, he preached to the people. He warned them that if they did not turn away from their sins, God would punish them for all their wickedness. God would send a flood to drown them all. But the people laughed at Noah. They did not believe there was going to be a flood. They thought Noah was very foolish to build such a big ship on dry land when there was no sign of any flood.

Over and over Noah told his neighbors about the flood God was going to send. Over and over he warned them to change their wicked ways, to trust in God instead of in their own right arm. And this was God's amazing mercy extended this one last time even to these wicked men, urging them to repent. For God has no delight in the death of the wicked, but wishes, instead, that they should turn from their sins and live.

At last the boat was finished. The day of salvation was past. The terrible day of judgment had arrived. "Come into the boat," God said to Noah, "you and all your family. Take with you two of each of the animals, and a pair of each of the birds."

So Noah, and his wife, and his three sons, Shem, Ham, and Japheth and their wives, went into the ark.

Then was seen such a sight as has never been seen before or since. Noah did not have to go into the fields and woods to catch the animals. No, they came of their own accord, each one moved by the secret call of God, walking together two by two up the gangplank into the boat.

Here come the lions — the father lion and the mother lion — marching quietly along, and going right up into the ark. Here are two tall giraffes, and here come two big gray elephants, and there come two tigers with their beautiful striped coats. Two by two they march into the ark.

Ah! here come the birds, flying two by two, straight into the ark. There are two big eagles; and there are two ravens. See them come — a perfect cloud of birds of all kinds! Here are two big ostriches, lumbering along, and two brilliant peacocks.

And here come the creeping things — the snails, and toads, and lizards.

At last the long procession came to an end. Two of each kind of animal had come into the ark.

THE FLOOD When they were all safe in the ark, God Himself shut the door. Then God sent the rain. You have never seen rain like that! It did not come down in drops. It poured down. The Bible says, "God opened the windows of heaven, and the fountains of the great deep were broken up."

Soon all the land was covered with water. Still the rain came down in torrents from the sky, and great tidal waves rose up from the ocean and swept over the land with terrific force and swiftness, carrying everything before them. The flood rose higher and higher. The waters lifted the ark up, and it floated upon the waves. It rained for forty days and nights.

"And the waters prevailed exceedingly upon the earth, and all the high hills that were under the whole heaven were covered. And every living substance was destroyed which was upon the face of the ground, both man, and cattle, and the creeping things, and the birds of the heavens; and they were destroyed from the earth: and Noah only remained alive, and they that were with him in the ark."

At last, after forty days and nights, the rain stopped. Slowly the water began to go down, but still no land could be seen. For five months, whenever Noah and his family looked out of the window, they saw nothing but desolate water.

Then one day the ark struck something underneath. It was a high mountain called Ararat. The ark rested on the top of the mountain. The waters kept on going down. After three more months they could see the tops of other mountains from the window.

Noah waited forty days longer. Then he opened the window and sent a bird called a raven out of the ark. The raven, being a very strong bird, flew to and fro, and did not come back to the ark.

At the same time Noah sent out a dove to see if the waters had dried up from the earth. The little dove was not as strong as the raven. She could not keep on flying all the time without any rest. She could not find any place to perch that was not covered with water. The dove flew back again to the ark, and Noah put out his hand and took her back in.

Noah waited a week longer, and then he sent the dove out again. At evening she came back. In her beak she had a leaf that she had picked from some olive tree. Then Noah knew that the waters were going away from the earth.

He waited a week longer, and then he sent the dove out again. This time she did not come back at all. So Noah knew that she must have found some dry place to stay.

When Noah was six hundred and one years old, in the first day of the year, he took off the covering of the ark. He looked out and saw that the earth was dry. He stayed two months longer in the ark. Altogether Noah and his family stayed one year and ten days in their great boat.

GOD BLESSES NOAH   And God spoke to Noah, and told him to come out of the ark with all his family and all the animals. So Noah opened the door and stepped upon the solid earth of Mount Ararat.

Out flew the birds — so glad to be free! Down the steep sides of the mountain ran the animals. They spread out into the woods and fields below, each kind of animal finding the sort of place it liked best. There it could make its home, and have its little ones, and fill the earth again with animals.

The first thing that Noah and his family did after they came out of the ark was to kneel down and thank God for keeping them alive, and to promise that they would always trust Him, and try to live so as to please Him. Noah took stones and made an altar. On the altar he offered some animals as a gift to God. And God was pleased with Noah's gift.

So God blessed Noah and his sons, and told them to have a great many children, to fill the earth with people again.

God also gave them a further command. It was this: "Thou shalt not kill." God said to Noah, "Every living thing that moveth is meat for you. I have given it to you to eat. But whoever sheds man's blood, by man shall his blood be shed, for God made man in His own image."

God also made a covenant with Noah and with all the animals that had been in the ark. A covenant is a solemn promise. God's covenant was that He would never again send a flood to destroy all the people and animals in the world. "While the earth remaineth," God said, "seedtime and harvest, and cold and heat, and summer and winter, and day and night shall not stop."

God gave a sign to Noah, to reassure him when storms came again.

"I will set my rainbow in the clouds," God said, "and it shall be a sign of the covenant between Me and the earth." You have seen the beautiful rainbow many times. Whenever you see it, remember that this is God's sign that He still remembers His promise not to destroy the whole world again with a flood.

Chapter 11
THE STRANGE DIVISION OF MEN INTO NATIONS
GENESIS 10, 11

NOAH'S CHILDREN Now after the flood Japheth, Noah's son, and his wife made a home for themselves. By and by some little children were born to them, seven boys, and probably some girls. When the children grew up, they had children, and so on.

Shem and his wife had five sons and some daughters. Their sons and daughters grew up and were married and had children.

Ham and his wife had four boys and some girls. They also grew up and had children.

Soon the country began to be overspread with the children and grandchildren of Shem, Ham, and Japheth. From these three sons of Noah all the people that are now in the world have come.

Noah, Shem, Ham, and Japheth, and their children and grandchildren lived very long lives, but they did not live quite as long as Adam and his children had lived. Adam and his children and grandchildren lived almost a thousand years. Noah and his children lived to be six hundred years old. His grandchildren lived to be five hundred years old. After that people lived to

be four hundred years old, and then three hundred, and still later God cut down the life of man to one hundred and fifty years.

In one respect these early people were very different from us. They all spoke the same language, and everybody understood everybody else. Today some people speak English, and other people speak German. Some people speak French, and others speak Italian. The French cannot understand the Germans, and the Germans cannot understand the English, and the English cannot understand the Italians.

But in those days, the Bible tells us, all the people spoke one language, and everyone understood everyone else. Not even the wisest man in the world knows what that first language was which Noah and his children spoke.

THE TOWER OF BABEL As the number of people increased, they moved farther and farther away from the mountains of Ararat. Gradually they began to spread far and wide over the earth. As they traveled south and east, they came to a plain in the land of Shinar. This plain was very well watered, for it had the mighty Tigris River to the east, and the still greater Euphrates River on the west. The people thought this would be a good place to live. Here they built their homes.

In their pride they wanted to build a big city, with a tower so high that they could see it from a long distance. Then they would know in which direction the city was when they had traveled some distance away, and could easily find their way back. They thought this would keep them together, so they would not become scattered over the whole earth.

A great many workmen assembled to build the tower. They made bricks of mud and dried them in the sun. They built the tower of these bricks, using asphalt to hold them together. Asphalt is a kind of natural concrete which is found in the ground in some parts of that country. It is something like what is used to make our tar roads.

The people worked together busily. They shouted and called to one another. One man might call, "Bring me some bricks. I need more for this corner." Another would say, "I am ready for another pail of asphalt." With all their bustle, it was a very noisy place. And as they kept on building, the tower became higher and higher.

The Lord came down to see the city. He saw that the people had begun to build the tower, and now they would stop at nothing that they might want to do. God did not want them to stay in one city, all huddled together. He wanted them to spread over the big world which He had made for man.

You remember that all the people spoke the same language. But now God changed the speech of all the men, without their knowing it, so that they did not understand each other. Each one spoke an entirely different language from that which he had spoken before.

When one man called out, "Bring me some bricks," he was speaking a new language that no one in all the world had ever heard. The man he spoke to looked at him in astonishment and asked, "What did you say?" But he also was speaking a new language. Although they tried again and again, neither of them could understand the other.

Then the first man called to another and said, "Here, something is the matter with this man. I have asked him ever so many times to bring me some bricks, and he answers something I cannot understand at all. Will you bring them to me, please." But the other man only stared at him.

"What did you say?" he asked. "I cannot understand you." But he also, without knowing it, was speaking another language that nobody had ever heard. They shouted, and called, and tried to make each other understand, but it was no use. The louder they called, the less they understood each other. There was only a big noise and confusion.

They had to stop building the tower and the city. As they could not understand each other any longer, there was no use in trying to live together. So they all separated, and each went to live in a different place with his own family. They were scattered over the earth, just as God wanted them to be.

The name of the tower and of the

city was Babel. This means "confusion," because there was a very big mix-up when God confused the language of the people. Even to this day, when we hear a great confusion of noise, we call it a babel.

Chapter 12
ABRAHAM FOLLOWS GOD
GENESIS 12, 13

ABRAHAM LEAVES HOME After the flood people again increased in number. They were not as wicked as men had been before the flood. They remembered very well how dreadfully God had punished wickedness.

Now God began to prepare the world for the coming of that man whom He had promised. You remember that when God cursed the serpent for leading Eve into sin, He said that someday a child of Eve's would crush the head of the serpent.

Of course the serpent really was Satan. When God promised that someday a child of Eve's would crush the serpent's head, He meant to say that someday a man would be born who would defeat Satan. Satan had caused sin and death to come into the world, but someday one of Eve's children would again bring everlasting life by taking away the sin of the world.

That man is the very Son of God, our Saviour, Jesus Christ.

The first thing God did to make the world ready for the coming of the promised Saviour was to pick out one man, and separate him from all the other wicked people in the world, so that knowledge about God and trust in God would not be entirely lost again, as had nearly happened before the flood.

The man God chose was Abraham. His wife's name was Sarah. God told Abraham to leave his country and his family and friends, and to go to another country. He did not even tell him where that new country was. Abraham was simply to follow where God led, in trust.

God said to Abraham, "I will make of you a great nation. In you all the families of the earth shall be blessed." That wonderful blessing to all the families of the earth, including yours and mine, would come from Jesus, who would at last be born in Abraham's family.

Abraham did as God had commanded. He took his wife Sarah and his nephew Lot, whose own father was dead, and his servants, and left his own country to start out on that long journey to a country he did not know. He trusted God would take care of him and show him where to go. When Abraham said good-bye to his friends and relatives, it was forever. He never saw any of them again.

Abraham was not a young man when he set out on this strange journey. He was seventy-five years old. Sarah was ten years younger, but men and women did not age as rapidly then as they do now.

Although Abraham and his family lived in tents on this journey — and, indeed, continued to live in tents all the rest of their lives — Abraham

19

was a very rich man. He had a great many cows, oxen, sheep, donkeys, and camels. He had more than three hundred men-servants, and probably as many women-servants. The men-servants took care of the animals. The women-servants milked the cows, made the cheese and butter, cooked the meals for all that large family, and wove the sheep's wool into cloth to be made into clothes.

Sarah was a very beautiful woman. I am sure she had many pretty clothes to wear. She must have had beautiful golden bracelets for her arms, golden anklets for her feet, and golden rings for her fingers. With her rich clothes and sparkling jewels, she must have looked very attractive indeed.

At that time, of course, there were no cars or trains. Abraham could not travel quickly to this faraway country. He had to travel by camel. He and Sarah, and Lot and his wife, rode on finely harnessed camels. The servants rode on donkeys or walked. Most of the servants were married, and there were many little children among them — even little babies. These little ones had to be carried in their mothers' arms, while the mothers rode on donkeys. Big baskets were flung across the backs of the donkeys, one on each side, and the children who were too young to walk were put into these baskets and carried that way.

It seemed as if a whole village traveled along when Abraham began his journey to this faraway country which God was going to show him. Abraham was a true chieftain — a man who had many servants, and flocks, and herds.

LOT CHOOSES A HOME   After a very long trip Abraham and his family pitched their tents in a land called Canaan. There God appeared to Abraham and said, "I will give this land to your children." And there Abraham built an altar to the Lord.

The flocks and herds now scattered over a large part of the country. There were no fences, so the animals could wander around, eating as they went. Between the two of them, Abraham and Lot had so many sheep and cattle that the land could not take care of them. There was not enough grass for the animals to eat. As a result Abraham's servants and Lot's servants quarreled about the best pasture land.

Abraham said to Lot, "Let there be no quarreling, I pray you, between me and you, for we are brothers. Is not the whole land before you to choose from? If you wish to go to the left hand, I will go to the right hand. Or, if you go to the right, I will go to the left."

Lot lifted up his eyes. Toward the east he saw the beautiful Jordan River. All the country near the Jordan was very green and beautiful, because it had so many little streams and brooks running through it. It was so lovely that it reminded people of the Garden of Eden which God Himself had planted so long ago.

Selfishly, Lot chose that country. He thought he had made a good choice. But he really made a terrible mistake. For in that beautiful country were two of the most wicked cities that have ever been on this earth. These great wicked cities fascinated Lot. Every day he moved his tents nearer and nearer to them. At last he moved into the city of Sodom itself, and left the care of his flocks to his servants.

The Bible says that the men of Sodom were "wicked and sinners before the Lord, exceedingly." What a dreadful place for Lot to live! How could his children grow up loving and trusting God in this wicked city?

Chapter 13

GOD TALKS WITH ABRAHAM

GENESIS 13, 15, 16, 18

THE STORY OF A SLAVE After Lot had separated from Abraham, God said to Abraham, "Lift up now your eyes, and look from the place where you are, northward, and southward, and eastward, and westward. All the land which you see, I will give it to you and to your children forever."

But Abraham had not even one little child at this time. He was no longer young, and you know that people do not have children when they are old. Yet God promised that Abraham's children's children should be as many as the dust of the earth. Abraham knew that God is all-powerful, and he believed that God would do what He promised. He trusted in God's promise, even though it seemed impossible for it to happen.

This answer of faith is what God wants to see in all His children. If you truly love someone, you trust him; and that is exactly what God asks of you and me. He has loved us with a love so great that He was willing to give His own Son to die for our sins. He wants us to love Him in return and, because we love Him, to believe what He says, even if it seems impossible. For nothing is impossible to God.

But at another time, when God repeated His promise, Abraham could not help saying, "But Thou hast not given me any child at all." Then God

brought him out into the dark night. God said, "Look toward the sky, and count the stars, if you can. So many shall your children's children be. I have given this land to them, all the way from the great river Euphrates in the east to the River Nile in Egypt in the south." And Abraham believed God, and God counted it to him for righteousness. For Abraham was a sinner, just as you and I are. He had a wicked heart. But he was saved in the same way we must be saved, by trusting in the promise of God. For Jesus paid for the sins of all who trust in Him, and He gives all of them a new heart that loves God and wants to do what pleases Him.

Sarah, Abraham's wife, knew she was too old to have any children. She said to Abraham, "God has not given me any children. Perhaps you had better marry my maid Hagar. Maybe God will give her a child."

Abraham thought this was a good idea. Perhaps this was the way God planned to give him the long-promised child. So Abraham married Hagar.

But Sarah did not feel pleased about it later. For Hagar began to think she was now just as fine a lady as her mistress. She began to be rude to Sarah. Sarah complained to Abraham, "I have given you my

21

maid as wife, and now she despises me. The Lord judge between me and you."

Abraham answered, "She is your servant. Do with her as it pleases you." So Sarah treated Hagar harshly, and Hagar ran away, far off into the desert. The desert was not a safe place for Hagar. There were wild animals there, and wild robbers, too, sometimes. Hagar found a well of water and sat down by it. Water is very important in hot desert country.

But Hagar was not really alone. God saw her sitting by that well, frightened and lonely. He sent an angel down from heaven. The angel asked Hagar, "Where did you come from, Hagar? And where are you going?" Hagar said, "I am running away from the face of my mistress Sarah."

The angel said, "Go back to your mistress, and be obedient to her. You are going to have a baby boy. You must call his name Ishmael, because the Lord has heard your trouble." Now the name Ishmael means "God shall hear."

Hagar was very much comforted by the words of the angel. She knew now that God was taking care of her. She said, "Thou God seest me." And that is the name of the well Hagar sat beside that day.

Hagar went back home. Before long a little son was born to her. He was Abraham's son too. Abraham named him Ishmael, as the angel had directed. Abraham was eighty-six years old when his son Ishmael was born. Abraham thought that this was the son God had promised. And Hagar was very happy with her little boy.

A PROMISE   God talked to Abraham many times. One day when Ishmael was thirteen years old, and Abraham was ninety-nine, the Lord appeared to him again. Abraham was now a very old man — much too old to have children. His wife Sarah was eighty-nine years old.

Abraham was sitting at the door of his tent, resting himself. He lifted up his eyes and saw three persons coming toward him. Abraham stood up quickly, and went to meet them, and very politely bowed before them. He said, "My Lord, come and stay with me, I beg you. And let a little water be brought in a basin to wash your feet." In that very hot country people wore sandals on their feet, and their feet became very hot and dusty from walking on the burning sand. The first thing any polite host did was to wash the feet of his guests.

Abraham said to his visitors, "Come and rest yourselves under the shady tree. And I will bring a morsel of bread to refresh you."

The strangers answered, "Yes, do as you have said." Abraham told a servant to take some water and wash their feet. He himself hurried to Sarah's tent and said, "We have some visitors. Quickly bake some nice cakes for them." Then he ran to the herd of cattle and picked out a fine young calf. He gave it to one of the servants and told him, "Prepare it nicely as quickly as you can, and bring it to me for the visitors."

After the meat was prepared and the cakes were baked, Abraham took these, and some milk and butter, and set everything before his visitors, who started to eat.

Sarah did not come out to meet the visitors, for it was not the custom for women in that country to eat with strange men. So she stood in the tent door behind them, where she could hear what they said. She listened closely, for strange visitors were not very common. She wondered who they were, and why they had come.

One of the visitors asked, "Where is Sarah, your wife?" Abraham said, "She is in the tent." The visitor said, "Next year I shall give Sarah, your wife, a son." In a flash Abraham understood that these visitors were not ordinary men. One of them was God Himself. The other two were angels.

Sarah, standing in the tent door, heard what was said. She began to laugh unbelievingly. "Shall I have a baby," she said to herself, "when I am old, and my husband is old too?"

God said to Abraham, "Why did Sarah laugh? Is anything too hard for the Lord? Next year, at the appointed time, Sarah shall have a son." Then Sarah said, "I did not laugh," for she was afraid. But God said, "No, but you did laugh." For God knows all that we do and say, and even the secret thoughts of our hearts.

Chapter 14
SODOM AND GOMORRAH
GENESIS 18, 19

ABRAHAM PLEADS WITH GOD The two angels went on ahead, but the Lord stayed to talk to Abraham. He said, "Shall I hide from Abraham what I am about to do? Because the cry of the sin of Sodom and Gomorrah is very great, I will go down now to see whether they have done as wickedly as is reported."

At once Abraham thought of his nephew Lot living in Sodom. He drew near the Lord and asked, "Wilt Thou destroy the righteous together with the wicked? Perhaps there are as many as fifty righteous in the city. Wilt Thou not spare the city for the sake of fifty righteous?"

The Lord answered Abraham, "If I find fifty good people in Sodom, then I will spare the whole city for their sake." Abraham knew there were not fifty people who trusted God in wicked Sodom. He said, "Behold, now, I have taken it upon me to speak unto the Lord, I who am but dust and ashes. Perhaps there will be five less than fifty righteous. Wilt Thou destroy all the city for the lack of five?"

The Lord answered, "If I find forty-five good people there, I will not destroy it." Then Abraham spoke again, and said, "Maybe there will be forty found there." And God said, "I will not do it for the forty's sake."

Again Abraham said, "Oh, let not the Lord be angry, and I will speak. Perhaps there will be thirty found there." And the Lord said, "I will not do it if I find thirty there."

Then Abraham said, "Behold, now, I have taken it upon myself to speak unto the Lord. Maybe there will be twenty found there." God said, "I will not destroy it for the twenty's sake."

At last Abraham said, "Oh, let not the Lord be angry, and I will speak just this once more. Perhaps there will be ten found there." The Lord said, "I will not destroy it for the sake of ten."

Then the Lord went on His way.

Abraham hoped that ten people who loved and trusted God could be found in Sodom. There were Lot and his wife, and his two daughters who were married, and their husbands, and his two daughters who were not married. That made eight. Perhaps there might be two other good people in the whole city.

But there were not!

FIRE FROM HEAVEN In the evening the two angels came to the city of Sodom. Lot was sitting in the gate of the city. He saw the visitors, and stood up to greet them. He bowed with his face to the ground. This was the polite way to greet strangers at that time.

He said — for people were very hospitable in those days — "My lords, come to my house to stay tonight, and in the morning you can continue on your journey." At first the angels refused. But when Lot insisted, they went with him to his house.

That night the wicked people of the city, both young and old, came from every part of the city and crowded around Lot's house. "Where are the men that came to your house tonight?" they shouted. "Bring them out so we can hurt them."

Lot opened the door of his house, went out, and shut the door tightly behind him. He said to those wicked people, "I beg of you, do not do anything so wicked." But the people answered, "Stand back, or we will hurt you a great deal worse than we will hurt them. You are only a stranger here in our city. You are not a judge over us." And they pushed Lot so hard that they almost broke down the door.

Then the angels put their hands out of the door, pulled Lot inside, and shut the door again. And they made all the people outside blind, so that they could not find the door, no matter how they fumbled.

Inside, the angels said to Lot, "Get your married daughters and your sons-in-law, and leave the city at once with all your family. For the Lord has sent us to destroy this wicked city." Lot went to warn his sons-in-law, but they laughed at him. They did not believe that God would destroy Sodom.

Very early the next morning the angels said to Lot, "Get up! Take your wife and your two daughters who are here, and hurry. Otherwise you, too, will be destroyed." But Lot lingered. He hated to leave his home and the city. Surely he hated to leave his married daughters and their husbands too. Then the angels took him by the hand, and his wife and his two daughters — because God had mercy on them — and hurried them out of the city. They said to Lot, "Run for your life! Do not look behind you! Escape to the mountains, or you will be killed too."

Then the Lord rained fire and brimstone out of heaven upon the two wicked cities. He completely destroyed the cities, and all the wicked people who lived in them.

Lot's wife disobeyed the angel's command. She turned around and looked back to see what was happening. In one moment she was changed from a living woman into a pillar of salt.

Lot and his two daughters were saved. They escaped to the mountain and lived in a cave. Oh, poor Lot! His home was burned. His flocks and herds were destroyed. His wife was turned into a pillar of salt. He and his daughters lived in a bare cave. He was no longer a rich man. He had nothing at all left now.

I am sure he now wished that he had not thought so much about the beautiful cities, about getting rich and living in luxury. He wished he had thought more about trusting in God, and about living with other people who loved and trusted God, too.

Chapter 15
ABRAHAM SENDS ISHMAEL AWAY
GENESIS 21

The next year God fulfilled His promise that Sarah would have a son. He sent her a dear little baby boy, and told her to call him Isaac. Oh, how happy Sarah was that at last she had a baby of her very own! How happy Abraham was, too, that the long-promised child had come!

Abraham was one hundred years old when Isaac was born, and Sarah was ninety. God is able to do anything. He gave them a baby in their old age by His almighty power.

When Isaac was about three years old, his father gave a fine feast, or party, for him. Very many people were invited. Even the servants came to the feast. Little Isaac was dressed in his finest clothes. Everyone admired him and praised him.

There was one person who was not happy at the party. That person was Ishmael. Ishmael was a big boy now. He was seventeen years old. He had been the only son, the beloved son, for many years. I am afraid that now he was jealous of all the attention Isaac was getting. He began to tease his little brother and to make fun of him.

When Sarah saw this, she was very angry. She said to Abraham, "Send away this slave woman and her son. For the son of the slave woman shall not share the inheritance with my son Isaac." This made Abraham very sad. Ishmael was his son too, and he loved him.

God said to Abraham, "Do not be grieved. Do what Sarah says, for Isaac is the son who shall inherit the promises. But I will make a great nation out of Ishmael too, because he is your son."

Abraham got up very early the next morning. He gave Hagar some bread and a bottle of water to put on her shoulder. He kissed Ishmael, and sent both of them away into the desert. The bottle was only an animal skin filled with water, but it was very important, since in that dry country it is often hard to find water. People in the desert die if they cannot find anything to drink.

By and by all the water in the bottle was used up, and Ishmael began to suffer from thirst. He became too weak to walk any further. His mother laid him down under the shade of a little bush, and went a short distance away. She began to cry. She said, "Let me not see the death of the child!"

Ishmael was crying too, I think. Perhaps he was praying to God to take care of him, for his father had taught him to pray. God heard Ishmael's voice. God was not going to let Ishmael die. No! God was going to take very good care of Ishmael, because he was Abraham's son.

The angel of God called to Hagar out of heaven. "What is the matter, Hagar?" he said. "Do not be afraid! God has heard the boy's cry. Get up! Pick the boy up. I am going to make a great nation out of him."

God opened Hagar's eyes. What should she see but a fine well of water! Hagar went to the well and filled her bottle with water. She took it back to Ishmael. She lifted up the poor, weak boy and made him drink some water. Soon he felt much better, and could run about as before.

After this, Ishmael always lived in the desert. He learned to shoot with a bow and arrow. When he wanted some meat he could shoot a rabbit, or a bird. The well provided him with drinking water. Though he lived in the desert, God took care of him.

When he was grown up, his mother took a wife for him out of Egypt. God gave him twelve fine sons. They lived in the desert of Arabia, and there the descendants of Ishmael live to this day. They are called Arabs. They live in tents in the desert, and travel about from one place to another on camels. They also have splendid horses. Arabian horses are the finest in the world.

God kept His promise to Ishmael, for the Arabs are one of the great nations in the world today. There are many Arabs in the world now, and they are proud to count their descent from their first father, Abraham.

Chapter 16

GOD TESTS ABRAHAM
GENESIS 22

Ishmael had gone away, and he never came back. He stayed in the desert, where God took care of him, as He had said He would.

Isaac was the only son now. His father taught him many things about God. He taught him to pray. He taught him to trust in God's promise. Isaac learned while he was still young to love and trust God.

Abraham, his father, loved God very much. And God loved Abraham. God often spoke to him, and He called Abraham His friend. And Abraham loved Isaac very much. Perhaps he loved Isaac almost too much.

Did Abraham love his son Isaac better than he loved God? God wanted to know this. He put Abraham to a very hard test. God said to him, "Abraham!" Abraham answered, "Here I am."

"Take your son Isaac," God said, "your only son, whom you love, and go to the land of Moriah. Build an altar there on one of the mountains I will point out to you, and offer Isaac as a sacrifice to Me."

God wanted to see if Abraham really loved Him enough to do this. He wanted to know if Abraham trusted God's promise even when it seemed impossible for the promise to come true. You remember that long before this God had promised to make Abraham the father of many people. He had promised that all the nations of the world would be blessed through one of Abraham's children. And God had plainly said that this promise would come true through Isaac.

Abraham's heart shrank within him. His precious son, for whom he had waited so long! The one in whom all God's promises were to be fulfilled! How could God's promises come true if Isaac died? Abraham was torn with grief and with perplexity. He felt as if he was lost in a dark night and could not find his way. But there was one thing he knew. God was faithful. God does fulfill His promises. Abraham had experienced this in his own life. He clung to this truth. Somehow God's promises would come true, no matter what happened.

He got up early the next morning. He cut the wood he needed for the sacrifice, and he took some fire, perhaps in a pan, since at that time they did not have matches. Abraham rode on a donkey, because he was more than a hundred years old. He took two servants along to carry the wood.

After they had traveled three days, Abraham lifted up his eyes and saw Mount Moriah in the distance. He got down from the donkey. He made a little bundle of the wood, and tied it on Isaac's back, so that it would be easy to carry. He took the fire in his hand, and a knife.

He said to his servants, "Stay here with the donkey. I and the boy will go yonder to worship God, and will come back again to you." So they went, both of them together.

Isaac said to Abraham, "My father!" Abraham answered, "Here I am, my son." Isaac said, "I see the fire and the wood, but where is the lamb for the sacrifice?" And Abraham answered, "God will provide Himself a lamb for the burnt offering." So they went, both of them together.

At last they came to the place that God had told Abraham about. There Abraham built an altar. He laid the wood on top, all ready to burn. Then he took a rope and bound Isaac. Isaac was big and strong enough to struggle. Abraham could not have bound him against his will. But he did not fight against his father. Whatever happened, he was sure — as his father was sure — that God would take care of him.

Abraham placed Isaac on the altar. He took the knife in his hand, and raised his arm to kill his son. At that very moment an angel spoke to Abraham out of heaven. "Abraham, Abraham!" the angel said. Abraham answered, "Here I am." The angel said, "Lay not your hand upon the boy, and do him no harm. Now I know that you trust God because you have not held back your son, your only son, from Me."

Abraham untied Isaac. How happy he felt now! His boy had been given back to him, almost from the grave. He was happy, too, because he had trusted God, and obeyed Him. And Isaac felt happy too, you may be sure.

Just then Abraham saw a ram caught by his horns in a thicket. He took the ram and offered it to God as a burnt offering in the place of his son Isaac. Then the angel of the Lord called to Abraham out of heaven a second time. "Because you have done this thing," he said, "I will bless you, and multiply your children till they are as many as the stars of the heaven, and the sands of the seashore. And in you shall all the nations of the earth be blessed."

When you go to bed tonight, look up at the stars. Can you count them?

Of course you cannot. Can you count the grains of sand in a single handful? The people who have come from Abraham are as many as the stars in the sky and as the sands on the seashore.

God repeated this promise to Abraham five times. He has fulfilled that promise. God rewarded Abraham wonderfully for that act of trust in offering his son. The Jews are Abraham's children. Many of the races which lived during the time of Abraham have entirely died out. And even though the Jews have often been cruelly persecuted by their enemies, there are still millions of Jews in the world today.

Long after all this there was another Father who offered His Son in a sacrifice, and there was no one that day to stay His hand, to say, "Do not harm the boy." That Father was God Himself, and the Son who died for you and me — and for Abraham and Isaac — was our Lord Jesus. He was the Son of God, and He was the son of Abraham too. For He was the one whom God had promised to Adam and Eve, and to Abraham. He was the one in whom all the nations of the earth are blessed.

Chapter 17
REBEKAH
GENESIS 23, 24

AN ANSWER TO A PRAYER After Isaac had grown up, his mother Sarah died. Abraham did not have any place in which to bury her. Although God had often promised that the whole land of Canaan would belong to his family, he did not yet own any of it. He lived in a tent and wandered from one place to another.

Abraham went to some people of the country of Canaan and said to them, "I am a stranger among you, and I do not own any land. Be so kind as to let me buy a piece of land where I may bury my dead." The people were very kind, and after a good deal of politeness on both sides, they sold Abraham a field that had a cave in it, called the Cave of Machpelah. Here Abraham buried his wife Sarah.

After Sarah died, Abraham and Isaac were lonely. Abraham was a very old man. Isaac was forty years old, but he was not yet married. Abraham did not want him to marry any of the heathen women who lived near them. Before he died, Abraham wanted to see Isaac married to a woman who worshiped God, not heathen idols.

Abraham called his oldest servant, who ruled over all that he had. Abraham made him make a very solemn promise that he would not take a wife for Isaac from the Canaanite people living in the neighborhood. "Go to my country," Abraham said, "and take a wife for Isaac from among my relatives."

The servant started on his long journey through the hot, sandy country. He took ten camels with him. He took servants also, for safety's sake. In that time, and in that lonely country, it would not have been safe for one man to travel alone, even on a swift-footed camel. Besides, he hoped to bring Isaac's bride back with him.

At last, after several days of travel, he reached the place where Abraham's brother Nahor now lived. This city was called Haran. Outside the city was a well of water. In that dry country there was often only one well for a whole city. Every night the young girls of the city went out to the well, with tall pitchers balanced on their heads. They let down their pitchers into the well and drew water. Then they carried it home on their heads for the family to use.

When Abraham's servant came to Haran, he made his camels kneel down by the well. It was evening — just the time when the young girls always gathered around the well to draw water.

Abraham's servant believed in God. He had come safely on his journey and had reached the city to which Abraham had sent him. But he thought to himself, "How shall I be able to tell which young girl is the one God wants Isaac to have for his wife?" He kneeled down on the ground beside the well and bowed his head. He prayed, "O Lord God of my master Abraham, help me this day! When the daughters of the people of the city come down to draw water, and I say to one of them, 'Let down your pitcher, I pray you, that I may drink,' and she shall say, 'Drink, and I will give your camels drink also,' let that be the one whom Thou hast appointed as a wife for Isaac."

God often answers prayer almost before we have asked, and He did so this time. Before the servant had finished praying, a very beautiful girl named Rebekah came to the well. The servant thought, "Can this be the right one?" He ran to her and said, "Let me, I pray you, drink a little water out of your pitcher."

The girl said very politely, "Drink, my lord, and I will draw water for your camels also, till they have finished drinking." She took the pitcher down from her head and let him drink. Then she emptied the rest of the water into the drinking trough for the camels. She kept drawing water till all the camels had had a drink.

The servant was very much astonished to have her say and do just as he had prayed that she might. Had his prayer been answered so soon? When the camels had had enough water, he gave Rebekah a rich, gold ring which he had brought with him, and he put on her arms two beautiful gold bracelets.

Then he asked her, "Whose daughter are you? Is there room in your father's house for us to stay?"

She answered, "I am Nahor's granddaughter. We have plenty of room for you to stay with us, and straw and food for your camels." Nahor was Abraham's brother. When the servant heard this, he was so happy that he bowed his head down to the ground and worshiped, saying, "Blessed be the Lord God of my master Abraham, who has led me to the house of my master's family."

THE SERVANT'S STORY Now Rebekah had a brother named Laban. Rebekah ran home and told him what the man had said to her. When Laban heard this, and saw the rich ornaments the man had given her, he hurried to the well. He said to Abraham's servant, "Come, you blessed of the Lord. Why do you stand here? The house is all ready for you, and there is plenty of room for your camels."

So the servant came to Nahor's house. Laban unharnessed the camels and gave them food and bedding. Then he brought water to wash the feet of the servant and of the men who had come with him. He knew he must be tired and hungry after his long journey, and so he had supper made ready for him.

But Abraham's servant said to Laban and his family, "Before I eat anything, I must tell you why I have come." They were eager to listen. In those days there was no mailman to bring letters. People never heard about their friends who had gone away, unless some traveler brought news from them. Probably Abraham's relatives had not heard anything about him since he left home sixty years before.

They gathered around the servant to listen to the news he brought of their uncle Abraham. He said, "I am Abraham's servant. The Lord has blessed my master Abraham greatly. He is very rich, for God has given him flocks, herds, camels, donkeys, silver, gold, men-servants, and maid-servants.

"In his old age, God gave him one son, Isaac. Isaac will be very rich too, because Abraham has given everything that he has to his son.

"My master does not wish his son to marry a wife from the heathen Canaanites in the land where he lives. He made me swear a solemn oath to go to his father's country, to his own family, and to get a wife for his son from among them.

"I said to my master, 'Perhaps the woman will not be willing to come with me.' But my master said to me, 'The Lord whom I serve will send His angel with you to prosper your way.'

"I came this day to the well and said, 'O Lord God of my master Abraham, behold, I stand by the well of water. When a young girl comes to draw water, and I say to her, "Give me, I pray you, a little water to drink," and then she answers, "Drink, and I will draw water for your camels also," then, O Lord, let that be the woman the Lord has chosen for my master's son.'

"Before I had finished my prayer, I saw Rebekah coming, with her pitcher on her shoulder. She went down to the well and drew water. I said to her, 'Let me drink, I pray you.' And she hurried and let down her pitcher from her shoulder and said, 'Drink, and I will give your camels drink also.'

"I asked her, 'Whose daughter are you?' And she said, 'I am the grand-daughter of Nahor.' "

While the servant was speaking, they gathered around him, listening most eagerly to all he said. They were astonished to see how wonderfully God had made everything happen just as the servant had prayed it might. For Nahor's family, too, were worshipers of God.

The servant went on. "I gave her the golden ring, and put the bracelets on her arms. Then I bowed my head and worshiped the Lord of my master Abraham, who had led me in the right way to take my master's brother's daughter to be the wife of his son Isaac."

At last the servant asked, "I want you to tell me whether you will let Rebekah go back with me to be my master's son's wife."

Nahor's family said, "This thing comes from the Lord, and we must not hinder it. Behold, here is Rebekah. Take her, and go, and let her be your master's son's wife, as the Lord has spoken."

When Abraham's servant heard

this, he bowed down and thanked God for helping him in this wonderful way. Then he opened the packs on the backs of the camels. He brought out beautiful jewels of gold, and of silver, and some rich and handsome silk clothes. He gave these to Rebekah. He also gave valuable presents to her mother and her brother.

THE END OF THE JOURNEY In the morning the servant said, "Now I must return to my master." Rebekah's mother and her brother said, "Oh, do not be in such a hurry. Let her stay with us at least ten days."

He said, "Do not hinder me. Let me go back to my master."

"Well," they said, "we will call Rebekah and see what she says." So they called Rebekah and asked her, "Are you willing to go with this man right away?" And she said, "I will go."

So they said good-bye to Rebekah very affectionately, and blessed her. She did not go alone to her new home. She took her old nurse as a maid, and some girl friends as companions. Then she would not become homesick far away in a strange land. They all rode upon the camels that Abraham's servant had brought.

Abraham was a worshiper of God, and he had taught his son to worship God also. One evening Isaac took a walk in the fields so that he could quietly think about God and pray to Him. Looking up, he saw a cloud of dust in the distance. Very soon he saw that it was the camel train coming back.

Rebekah also saw Isaac walking in the fields, and she said to Abraham's servant, "What man is this walking in the field to meet us?" The servant said, "It is my master." Rebekah made her camel kneel down so that she could get off. She wanted to dress herself properly before she met the man who was to be her husband.

In that country it was not considered proper for a young lady to meet a strange man unless her face was covered with a veil. Rebekah wrapped herself from head to foot in a long veil. Only her beautiful eyes could be seen. She was now ready to meet her future husband.

In a few minutes the camels approached Isaac. When he saw the beautiful young girl whom the servant had brought with him, Isaac fell in love with her. He brought her home with him, and took her to the tent that had been his mother's. Soon they were married.

And Isaac felt comforted after the death of his mother Sarah.

The time finally came when Abraham, too, must die. He had had a long life of one hundred and seventy-five years. His sons, Isaac and Ishmael, buried him in the Cave of Machpelah, where Abraham had buried his wife Sarah.

Although Abraham lived long before the Bible was written, and in a country of heathen idol worshipers, he trusted all his life all the promises of God, and tried to do what God commanded. He was called the friend of God, and God loved him and talked to him. God made Abraham the father of the great nation of the Jews. Our Saviour, Jesus, was one of his descendants.

Abraham is in heaven now, and if we love and trust God, as Abraham did, we shall one day see him in heaven.

Chapter 18

JACOB BUYS THE BIRTHRIGHT
GENESIS 25

Isaac was forty years old when he married Rebekah. For twenty long years they had no little children to brighten their home. This was a great disappointment to them. Isaac prayed to God and asked Him to give them a child.

God heard Isaac's prayer, for He is a prayer-hearing and prayer-answering God. He gave them more than they had asked for — he gave them twin baby boys.

They named the first one Esau, which means "red." For when he was born, he was covered with soft red hair. The second one they called Jacob.

Although these boys were twins, they were not one bit alike. Esau had red hair and very hairy skin, but Jacob had soft, smooth skin. Nor were they alike in character. Esau was an outdoor kind of boy who loved sports, but Jacob was a home-loving boy who liked to stay in the tent with his mother.

Esau hunted wild animals. He shot them with his bow and arrow, and brought them home for the family to eat. Isaac was very fond of the tasty meat Esau prepared for him. He loved Esau more than Jacob, but Rebekah loved Jacob better.

One day Esau was out hunting in the fields, and Jacob was at home cooking some delicious vegetable soup. Esau came home tired out, and so hungry that he felt as if he would die of hunger. When he came into the tent, he smelled that delicious soup.

He said to Jacob, "Give me some of that good soup you are cooking, for I am about to die of hunger." Now Jacob ought to have been generous enough to give his hungry brother some of his soup; but Esau had something that Jacob wanted just as much as Esau wanted the soup. Jacob thought this would be a good chance to strike a bargain. Jacob wanted Esau's birthright.

Let me explain what a birthright is. It is the right which belongs to the oldest son in the family to have a larger share of his father's possessions when the father dies than any of the other sons, and to become the new head of the family. In our country each son is usually treated like the others. But even today in some countries the oldest son is favored.

Even though these two boys were twins, Esau was the older, and so the birthright belonged to him. Jacob was jealous of Esau. Isaac often talked to the two boys about God. Abraham too — for the twins were fifteen years old when grandfather Abraham died — had often told them his wonderful story. He told them how God had commanded him to leave his family and his country, and to go to a strange country, he did not even know where; how God had promised that this country should belong to his children's children, and that his children should be as many as the stars in the sky and the sands on the seashore.

Esau was not much interested in the things his grandfather was saying. But in Jacob's heart these stories sank down deep. Jacob thought it a pity that such a wonderful birthright belonged to Esau. Many times he wondered if he could not somehow snatch that birthright away from him.

Now he saw his chance. Esau was

4: THE DOVE RETURNS TO NOAH

5: JACOB OBTAINING THE BLESSING

faint with hunger. Jacob said to Esau, "Yes, I will give you some of my soup, if you will sell your birthright to me."

You would expect Esau to say, "What? Sell my birthright for a little bit of soup? No indeed!"

What he really did say was, "Here I am dying of hunger. What good will this birthright be to me? You may have it, only give me some soup!"

Jacob thought, "When Esau gets over being hungry, he will be angry, and refuse to keep the bargain." So he said, "First promise solemnly that you will give me the birthright." Impatiently, Esau promised, and reached for the dish of soup.

So Jacob bought the birthright which Esau valued so little.

Chapter 19
JACOB DECEIVES HIS FATHER
GENESIS 27

REBEKAH'S PLAN Isaac, you remember, was forty years old when he married Rebekah, and he was sixty years old before Jacob and Esau were born. His sons had now grown to be men forty years old, and Isaac was a hundred years old. His eyes were dim with old age, so that he was almost blind.

Isaac had inherited great riches from his father, and he became still richer. He had "possessions of flocks, and possessions of herds, and a great store of servants." He was a great and mighty prince in the country.

Isaac was a man who worshiped, loved, and trusted God. God had appeared to him once and had blessed him, giving him the same promise that He had given to his father Abraham.

His son Esau gave Isaac a good deal of trouble. Often he went out to visit the heathen Hittites who lived nearby. After a while he even married two Hittite wives. This was wrong. If he had children, his wives would be sure to bring them up to be heathen and to worship idols. Esau had not paid much attention to the teaching of his grandfather Abraham, or he would have known that God wanted his family to keep apart from the heathen.

Isaac, now a hundred years old and nearly blind, thought that it was almost time for him to die. One day he called his older son Esau to him. He said, "Behold, I am old, and I know not the day of my death. Now I want you to do something for me. I want you to go hunting, and get some meat, and prepare it the way I like it. Then bring it to me to eat, and I shall give you my blessing before I die."

I don't know whether Isaac knew that Esau had sold the birthright to Jacob. Perhaps even if he did know, he intended to give the blessing to Esau anyway, for Esau was the one he loved the best. Yet it was all going to turn out very differently from what Isaac and Esau expected.

Rebekah overheard Isaac speak to Esau. She loved Jacob more than Esau, and she wanted him to have the blessing. She called Jacob and told him what she had heard Isaac say to Esau. "Now, therefore, my son," she said, "obey my voice, and do what I command you. Go to the flock and fetch me two young goats. I shall prepare them, and make savory meat, just as your father loves it. You must take it to him, and he will give the blessing to you, instead of to Esau."

Jacob answered, "My father is blind and cannot see, but perhaps he will touch me. I have smooth skin, but Esau is hairy. When Father finds out that I am deceiving him, he will curse me instead of blessing me."

His mother said, "If he curses you, I will bear the curse instead of you. Only go and do what I have commanded you."

Jacob brought the two young goats, and his mother prepared the meat just as his father liked to have it cooked. Then Rebekah took one of Esau's best garments, and told Jacob to put it on. She fastened pieces of the young goat's hairy skin on his hands and on his smooth neck, so that Isaac might think he was Esau.

THE BLESSINGS Jacob took the meat and went in to his father. He said, "My father."

Isaac answered, "Here I am. Who are you, my son?"

Jacob answered, "I am Esau, your older son. I have done what you told me to do. Now come, and eat of the meat, so that you may bless me."

"How is it you found an animal so quickly?" Isaac asked in surprise. Jacob said, "Because the Lord your God brought it to me." (How he dared to tell this wicked lie, I cannot understand.)

Isaac was not quite satisfied. He was a little suspicious. It did not seem to him that the voice sounded like Esau's. He said, "Come here, so

that I may touch you and see if you are truly my son Esau." Jacob came near, and his father felt his hands, now covered with the hairy kidskin. He said, "The voice is Jacob's, but the hands are Esau's."

Isaac said, "Bring the meat to me. I shall eat of your meat, so that I may bless you." Jacob brought the delicious food to his father. And he brought him some wine. Poor blind Isaac ate and drank, thinking Esau was with him. After he had finished, he said, "Come near and kiss me, my son." Jacob came near and kissed his father.

Isaac smelled the smell of Esau's clothes. He said, "See, the smell of my son is as the smell of a field which the Lord has blessed. God give you the dew of heaven, and the fatness of the earth, and plenty of grain and new wine.

"Let peoples serve you, and nations bow down to you. Be lord over your brothers, and let your mother's sons bow down to you. Cursed be everyone that curses you, and blessed be everyone that blesses you."

As you can imagine, Jacob did not linger. Having received the blessing, he was in a hurry to leave. And he did not get away a minute too soon. For he had just left the tent when Esau arrived with the venison stew he had made.

Esau said, "Let my father now arise, and eat of my meat, that his soul may bless me." How startled old Isaac was! He cried out, "Who are you then?" And Esau said, "I am Esau, your son, your first-born."

Then Isaac shook and trembled with fear. For in a flash he saw that this was the doing of God Himself. Esau might be Isaac's favorite son, but it was for God, not Isaac, to choose who should inherit the blessing. He said sadly, "Your brother came and stole away your blessing. But it is God who has chosen him, and God will surely bless him."

Esau cried out with a bitter cry, "He took away my birthright, and now he has taken my blessing too! Have you not reserved a blessing for me too, my father? Bless me, even me also, my father!"

Then his father gave him a blessing too, but he could not take back the best blessing, which he had given to Jacob. He said, "Behold, the fatness of the earth shall be your dwelling, and the dew of heaven from above. By your sword shall you live, and you shall serve your brother. But when you break loose, then you shall shake his yoke from off your neck."

These blessings that Isaac gave to his two sons were not only for Jacob and Esau. They were meant also for their descendants. They foretold what would happen to the children of Jacob and Esau long after they themselves were dead. That was what made the blessings of such great importance.

Although Isaac intended to give the best blessing to Esau, and although it was wrong for Jacob to deceive his blind, old father, and to cheat his brother out of his birthright, yet God was ruling all this. It was God's will that Jacob should be the one to have both the birthright and the blessing. Not because Jacob deserved this, but only because God had chosen Jacob to inherit the promises.

Chapter 20
JACOB LEAVES HOME
GENESIS 27, 28

A HURRIED FLIGHT After the blessing had been given to Jacob, Esau hated Jacob for cheating him. He said in his heart, "My father is an old man. Very soon he will die. Then I will kill my brother."

Someone, probably one of the servants, told Rebekah about Esau's threats. She was now in great fear that some harm might come to Jacob. To save his life, she planned to send him away from home for a while, until the fierceness of Esau's anger had cooled.

She said to Jacob, "My son, Esau is so angry with you that he will kill you when your father dies. The best thing for you to do is to escape to my brother Laban in Haran. Stay there

a few days till your brother's anger has turned away, and he forgets what you have done."

Rebekah did not tell Isaac that she wanted to send Jacob away for safety's sake. She gave another reason. She said, "Jacob must not marry one of the heathen Hittites who live around here."

Isaac agreed with Rebekah. He called Jacob and said to him, "We do not want you to take a heathen wife, as your brother Esau has done. Now, you go to Haran, where your mother came from, and take a wife from one of the daughters of your mother's brother, Laban."

They did not give Jacob servants and camels to go with him, as Abraham had done when he sent his servant to bring back a wife for Isaac. They let him go alone and on foot. His father was a very rich man; he could easily have given his son both servants and camels. But most likely Rebekah had to send Jacob off quietly and quickly, for fear that Esau would follow him and kill him.

His mother told him before he started that as soon as Esau's anger had cooled down, she would send for him to come back. She could not keep that promise. Jacob never saw his mother again. When he said good-bye to her, it was forever.

His father blessed him and said to him, "May God Almighty bless you, and give you the blessing of Abraham, that you may inherit the land in which you are now a stranger."

So Jacob set out on his long and lonely journey. It was more than three hundred miles to Haran, where Jacob's uncle Laban lived. Many days he had to tramp over the hot and burning sands, and many a night he had to lie down on the bare ground and sleep under the open sky.

Jacob knew he had done wrong to deceive his old, blind father, and to steal his brother's blessing. He did not know whether he would ever see his father again, whether he would ever be able to throw himself at his father's feet and say, "Forgive me!" He did know that Esau was very angry with him, and would kill him if he caught him. Jacob was lonely, and he was homesick.

But Jacob was not really alone. God had been with him all the time. God was taking care of Jacob, even though Jacob did not deserve God's loving care.

JACOB'S DREAM   One night Jacob lay down on the ground to sleep, with only a stone for his pillow. While he was asleep, he forgot all about being tired and lonely, for he dreamed a most wonderful dream.

He saw a ladder. It was so long that it seemed to stand on the earth and reach to heaven. On the ladder he saw bright angels walking up and down. This beautiful sight filled Jacob's mind with wonder. At the top of the ladder stood God Himself.

God said to Jacob, "I am the Lord God of Abraham, and the God of Isaac your father. I am going to give the land that you are lying on to you and to your children.

"Your children's children shall be as many as the dust of the earth. They shall spread to the west and the east, to the north and the south. And in your children shall all the families of the earth be blessed.

"I will be with you, and will take care of you in every place where you go. And I will bring you back again to this land. For I will not leave you until I have done everything that I have promised."

When Jacob woke up, he said, "Surely the Lord is in this very place, and I did not realize it." And he was afraid, for he said, "How awesome this place is! This is the very house of God, and the gate of heaven."

Very early in the morning Jacob took the stone he had used for a pillow and set it up as a pillar. He wanted to remember the exact place where he had seen the angels going up and down, and where God had spoken to him directly from heaven. He had nothing to offer God but a little oil. He poured the oil on the stone, and named the place Bethel, which means "house of God."

Jacob made a vow, a solemn promise to God. This is what he said: "If God will be with me, and will keep me in the way that I go, and will give me food to eat and clothing to put on, so that I come back safely to my father's house, then the Lord shall be my God. This stone that I have set up shall be God's house, and of everything the Lord gives me I will surely give back a tenth to God."

Do you think that Jacob was lonely and unhappy now? No, indeed, he was most happy. He was filled with wonder that God should be so good to him when he did not deserve it. As he went on his way, he was thinking about that unexpected, wonderful dream.

He looked about him at the country that the Lord had said would someday belong to him and to his children. He thought about what the Lord had said, that his descendants should be as many as the dust of the earth.

He remembered that the Lord had said He would never leave him; that He would go with him all the way, and bring him back safely. He thought about the beautiful angels, as they went up and down the ladder.

Jacob had found a friend in God, and no one is unhappy who has God for his friend.

Chapter 21
JACOB MEETS RACHEL
GENESIS 29, 30

Jacob continued on his journey. At last he came to a place where there was a well in a field. There was a great stone upon the opening of the well. Three flocks of sheep were waiting to have water drawn for them.

Jacob asked the shepherds, "Where do you come from?" They said, "We come from Haran." Now that was where Jacob's uncle Laban lived. So Jacob asked them another question, "Do you know Laban?"

"Yes," they answered, "we know him." Then Jacob asked, "Is he well?" And they said, "He is well. Here comes his daughter Rachel now with her sheep."

When Jacob saw Rachel, the daughter of Laban, coming near to give water to her sheep, he rolled the stone from the well's mouth, and he watered the flock for her. Then Jacob told Rachel that he was her cousin Jacob, Rebekah's son, and he kissed her.

Rachel ran home and told her father that his sister's son had come. Laban ran out to meet Jacob. He kissed his nephew, and brought him to his home.

They were all very glad to see him, and Jacob stayed with them for about a month. Jacob helped Laban in whatever work had to be done. Then Laban said to Jacob, "If you will stay with me and help me, I will pay you wages. I don't want you to work for nothing. What shall I pay you?"

Laban had two daughters. The name of the older one was Leah, and the name of the younger one was Rachel. Leah was not very pretty, but Rachel was beautiful. Jacob already loved his beautiful cousin Rachel. He said to Laban, "If you will give me Rachel, your younger daughter, to be my wife, I will work for you for seven years."

Laban said, "Very well. I would rather give her to you than to a stranger. Stay here and work for me."

So Jacob served Laban seven years for Rachel, and they seemed to him only a few days, because he loved her so much. At the end of the seven years Laban gave a big wedding, and invited all the men of the place.

In those days the bride at a wedding wore a long veil that completely covered her. Laban deceived Jacob. Instead of giving him Rachel as his wife, Laban gave him his older daughter Leah. She was so covered up with her veil that Jacob did not know it was not Rachel. But when she took off her veil, he found he had married Leah.

Jacob went to Laban and said, "Why did you treat me this way? Did I not serve you for Rachel? Then why have you given me Leah instead?"

Laban said, "In this country it is not the custom to let the younger daughter get married before her older sister. If you want Rachel also, you may have her a week from now; but then you must work seven more years for her." So Jacob had to work seven years longer for Rachel, whom he loved.

God did not intend that a man should have more than one wife. Having two wives caused Jacob a great deal of trouble and led to much unhappiness. For Jacob loved Rachel much more than he loved Leah. This made Leah very sad.

When God saw that Jacob did not love Leah as much as Rachel, He gave Leah some children to comfort her. She received four little boys, one right after the other. That made her very happy, for at that time people wanted to have children more than they wanted anything else in the world. She named them Reuben, Simeon, Levi, and Judah. She thought that her husband Jacob would surely love her now that she was the mother of his four fine little boys.

God did not give Rachel any children. It made Rachel very unhappy to see her sister have four little boys, while she did not have any.

At last Rachel did just what Sarah, Abraham's wife, had done. She gave her maid-servant to Jacob for a wife. She thought, "Perhaps my maid Bilhah will have some babies, and then I can call them mine." Jacob married Rachel's maid Bilhah, and God sent Bilhah two little sons. Rachel called these two little boys her own, and she named them Dan and Naphtali.

When Leah saw what Rachel had done, she told Jacob to marry her servant Zilpah, too. She thought, "Perhaps in that way I can get still more children." Jacob married Zilpah, and Zilpah received two little boys. Leah called them hers, and she named them Gad and Asher. After this God sent Leah two more little boys of her own. She named them Issachar and Zebulun. She was very happy now, because she had six little sons of her own, and two of her handmaid's. After a while, Leah received a little girl, whom she named Dinah.

Last of all God sent Rachel a little baby boy. She was happier than she had ever been before. She named the baby Joseph. Jacob loved Joseph the best of all his sons, because he was the son of Rachel, whom he loved, and because he was the son of his old age.

Chapter 22

JACOB LEAVES HARAN SECRETLY
GENESIS 31

After Joseph was born, Jacob began to think that it was about time for him to go back to his own country. He had been away twenty years — a long, long time. He did not know whether his father and his mother were still alive. He had not heard from them during all those twenty years.

Jacob had served his uncle Laban fourteen years for his two wives, Leah and Rachel. Then he had served six years more for wages. Laban paid him in sheep and goats. He told Jacob he might have all the brown sheep and goats, and all the speckled and spotted ones. When the new little goats and lambs were born, a large number of them were brown and speckled and spotted. Jacob, of course, took those for his. So Jacob got a great many sheep and goats, and many camels and donkeys. He also had men-servants and maid-servants. He was a rich man.

Indeed, he was much richer than Laban. Laban began to be jealous of Jacob. He was not pleasant to Jacob as he had been before. About this time the Lord spoke to Jacob in a dream and said to him, "Go back to your own land, and I will be with you."

Jacob knew that if Laban found out he was going away, he would not like it. Perhaps he would not let him go. The only way he could leave was to go without letting Laban know.

It happened that Laban was going away for a few days to shear his sheep. Jacob thought that this was the time for him to leave. He got everything ready. His servants brought the camels, and Jacob put his wives and children on the backs of the animals. Joseph was only a baby. He had to be carried in his mother's arms, or perhaps in his nurse's arms when his mother was tired.

Jacob took all his household goods, and all his flocks and herds, to go back to the home of his father Isaac in Canaan. They took tents to sleep in at night, for they had a long journey of three hundred miles before them. It would take them at least a month to make this long journey, with all the young animals they had with them — the lambs and little goats, the baby donkeys and baby camels.

They started off secretly, when Laban had gone to shear his sheep. They had been gone for three days before someone told Laban that Jacob and his family had gone for good.

Laban and his brothers started after Jacob. They traveled for seven days before they caught up with him. I do not know what Laban planned to do to Jacob. But just then God appeared to Laban and told him to be very careful not to say anything threatening to Jacob.

The next day, when Laban met Jacob, he spoke very politely to him. The two of them set up a pillar and a heap of stones. Each made a promise that he would not go past that pillar to do harm to the other. Then Laban stayed all night with Jacob. In the morning Laban kissed his two daughters and his little grandchildren, and went back home to his own country, while Jacob went on.

Chapter 23

JACOB GOES HOME
GENESIS 32, 33, 35

GOD WRESTLES WITH JACOB Though it was twenty years since he had left home, Jacob was still afraid of his brother Esau. He was afraid that Esau might still kill him and his family.

He sent some men ahead, to find out if Esau was still angry with him. He told them to speak very politely and humbly to Esau. The messengers came back and told Jacob, "We saw your brother, and he is coming to meet you with four hundred men."

Then Jacob became very much afraid that Esau was coming to kill him and his wives and his little children. Jacob divided all those who were with him, and his camels and flocks and herds, into two groups, so that if Esau should come upon one company and kill them all, then perhaps the other company could escape.

Then Jacob did what all people should do when they are in trouble. He prayed to God, saying, "O God of my father Abraham, and God of my father Isaac, Thou hast said to me, 'Return unto your country, and I will be with you.' I am not worthy of all the mercies that Thou hast showed unto Thy servant, for I was all alone when I passed over this Jordan River before, and now I have become two bands. Save me, I pray Thee, from the hand of my brother Esau, for I am afraid of him, that he will come and smite me, and the mothers, and the children."

The next day Jacob gathered together a very fine present for Esau, to see if he could not please his brother. This was the present: two hundred she-goats and twenty he-goats; two hundred mother sheep and twenty rams; thirty mother camels, all of whom had baby camels with them; forty cows and ten bulls; and twenty donkeys and ten baby donkeys.

Was not that a fine present to give to Esau? Count all these animals, and you will see that there are five hundred and eighty animals — enough to stock a large farm. Jacob must have been a rich man to be able to give away so many animals. He gave the animals to his servants — one servant to drive each flock, and each flock by itself. These servants went ahead of him to meet Esau.

Jacob commanded the first servant, "When you meet my brother Esau, and he asks, 'Who are you? Where are you going? Whose animals are these?' then you must answer very politely, 'These belong to your servant Jacob. He has sent them as a present to my lord Esau. He himself is coming behind us.'" And Jacob commanded the second servant, who was driving the second flock, and the third, and all that followed, the same thing.

The flocks of animals started out. The second servant waited till the first one was perhaps a mile ahead, and then he started. This was to surprise Esau. He would think the first flock was the only present. When he saw the second flock coming over the hill, he would be surprised; and then when the others came he would be still more surprised.

There was a little river called the Jabbok in the place where they camped that night. After all the animals had crossed over the Jabbok, Jacob sent his two wives, and the two maid-servants, and his children after them.

But Jacob himself did not go over the brook. He stayed behind. Jacob must have been more afraid than he had ever been in all his life. He wanted to be all alone, so that he could pray to God for help.

That night a man came and wrestled with Jacob the whole night long. Jacob wrestled so hard that he almost overcame the man. When the stranger saw how hard Jacob wrestled, He touched the hollow of Jacob's thigh. This made Jacob's thigh out of joint, so that he became lame and could not wrestle very well. Then Jacob understood that it was the angel of the Lord who wrestled with him.

The heavenly visitor said, "Let me go, for it is almost day." But Jacob answered, "I will not let Thee go unless Thou bless me." Then the angel said to him, "What is your name?" And Jacob said, "My name is Jacob."

The angel said, "Your name shall be no more Jacob. Your name shall be Israel, because you have wrestled with God and men, and have won." Israel means "God strives." Then the visitor blessed Jacob.

Jacob called the name of that place Penuel, which means "the face of God." "For," said Jacob, "I have seen God face to face, and yet my life has been saved."

JACOB MEETS ESAU When the sun rose, Jacob crossed over the brook to join his family. He could not walk without limping on the leg where the Lord had touched the sinew of his thigh. He was lame all the rest of his life. But his lameness made him always remember that wonderful night when he had seen the Lord face to face.

After Jacob and his family had gone some distance, they saw a cloud of dust far off. Soon they saw that it was Esau and his company of men. Jacob and his family were badly frightened, you may be sure.

Jacob put the two handmaids and their children in front, then Leah and her children, and Rachel and Joseph last of all. In this way, if Esau meant to do them any harm, at least Rachel and Joseph might have a chance to escape.

Then Jacob himself went ahead of them all. He bowed himself right down to the ground — not once, but seven times — till he came near to his brother Esau.

Esau did not bow down to Jacob. He got down from his camel — and what do you think he did? He ran to Jacob, threw his arms around him, and kissed him. They both cried with joy to see each other. Both of them forgot they had ever been angry with each other. They remembered only that they were twin brothers.

After a while Esau noticed the women and children. He asked, "Who are these?" Jacob answered, "The children whom God has graciously given me." Then the two handmaids came near with their children, and bowed themselves low to Esau. Next Leah came near and bowed. And last of all Rachel and little Joseph came, and they, too, bowed low.

Esau asked, "What are all these flocks of animals that I have met on the way?"

Jacob said, "They are a present for my lord." Esau answered, "I have enough, my brother. Keep them for yourself." But Jacob said, "I pray you, accept my present." And he urged him until Esau accepted.

Esau suggested that he and Jacob should travel together. But Jacob was still somewhat afraid of Esau. He said, "My lord knoweth that the children are small, and there are many young animals in the flocks and herds also. Let my lord, I pray you, pass ahead of his servant, and I will follow more slowly."

So they parted. Esau went on to Mount Seir, the place where he lived. Jacob went into the land of Canaan, toward Hebron, where his father Isaac was still living, now a very old man.

But before Jacob reached Hebron, something very sad happened. His wife Rachel, whom he loved so dearly, became sick and died. Just before she died, God sent her another baby boy. His father called him Benjamin. It is no wonder that Jacob loved little Benjamin very much. Joseph and Benjamin were Rachel's children, and Jacob loved them because he had loved her.

They buried Rachel there, and Jacob set up a pillar to mark the grave. After this they came at last to Hebron, where Isaac lived.

Isaac was nearly a hundred and forty years old when Jacob went away, and Jacob had been gone for twenty years. His father was now about a hundred and sixty years old. He lived twenty years longer, and was able to talk to his grandchildren, Jacob's twelve sons and one daughter. He taught them about God, telling them about the wonderful promises that God had made to their great-grandfather Abraham and to Isaac himself.

At last Isaac's life ended. He was a hundred and eighty years old when he died. His sons, Jacob and Esau, buried him in the Cave of Machpelah, where Abraham and Sarah and Rebekah were buried.

A little town grew up near the pillar that marked Rachel's grave. The town was called Bethlehem. Do you know who was born in Bethlehem hundreds of years later? It was the great Son of Jacob, our Saviour, Jesus Christ.

Chapter 24
HOW JOSEPH WAS SOLD
GENESIS 37

Jacob lived now in the land of Canaan, where his father had lived. When Joseph was still a young boy, seventeen years old, the other brothers were grown-up men. They were shepherds, pasturing their father's flocks. Often they had to travel about to find enough grass for the animals.

Jacob loved Joseph more than all his other children because he was Rachel's son. He gave Joseph a coat of many beautiful colors. Probably it was made of silk, skillfully embroidered. When the older brothers saw that their father loved Joseph the most, they were jealous. They hated Joseph, and could not speak kindly to him.

Once Joseph dreamed a strange dream, which he told to his brothers. He said, "Listen, I pray you, to this dream of mine. We were in the field, binding the grain into bundles. And my bundle stood up straight, and all your bundles came and bowed down to mine."

His brothers were angry when they heard him say this. They said, "Do you think this dream means that you are going to rule over us?" And they hated him still more because of the dream.

Joseph dreamed another time. Again he told the dream to his father and his brothers. "This time," he said, "I dreamed that I saw the sun, the moon, and eleven stars, and they all came and bowed down to me."

The brothers became still more jealous. Jacob said to Joseph, "What is this that you have dreamed? Shall I and your mother and your brothers indeed come and bow down to you?" But his father wondered about this dream.

Joseph's wonderful dreams really did mean something. They came true many years later. But first many strange things happened to him.

Soon after these dreams, Joseph's brothers went to pasture their flocks in Shechem, a place quite far from Jacob's home. After they had been gone for some time, their father Jacob wanted to know how they were getting along. He called Joseph and said, "Go, I pray you, and see if all is well with your brothers, and with the flocks, and bring me word again."

When Joseph came to Shechem, he looked around for his brothers. There was no sign of them. At last a man found him wandering in the field and asked him, "What are you looking for?"

"I am looking for my brothers," Joseph said. "Can you tell me where to find them?"

"They were here," the man said, "but they have gone away. I heard them say, 'Let us go to Dothan.'" So Joseph went to Dothan. As his brothers saw him coming across the fields, thoughts filled their hearts.

They said to each other, "Here comes this dreamer. Let us kill him, and throw his body into some hole. Then we shall see what will become of his dreams. We will tell our father that a wild beast has eaten him."

Reuben, the oldest brother, was not so wicked and cruel as the others. He said, "Let us not kill him. Instead, let us just throw him alive into this dark hole." Reuben planned to take Joseph out of the water hole when the others were not around, and send him home to his father.

When Joseph came near, his brothers pounced on him. They took off his beautiful coat of many colors. Then they threw him into the empty, dark water hole. The sides were steep, so that Joseph could not climb out. He cried out in terror, "Help me! Let me out!" But the wicked brothers sat down to eat their dinner, just as if their brother were not crying and calling to them.

While they were eating, they saw a cloud of dust in the distance. Pretty soon they could see it was a group of camels and traders. The people were Ishmaelites on their way to Egypt. Their camels were loaded with spices and perfumes, which they were going to sell in Egypt.

Judah, one of the brothers, said to the others, "What good will it do us to kill our brother? Let us instead sell him as a slave to these Ishmaelites. After all, he is our brother!" The others thought this would be a good way to get rid of Joseph for good.

By this time the Ishmaelites were near. The brothers called to them to stop, because they had a young boy they wanted to sell as a slave. This did not seem strange to the Ishmaelites, for it was their custom to buy and sell slaves.

His brothers went to the dark hole and pulled Joseph up. Joseph thought

43

at first they were going to let him go free. How bitterly disappointed he must have been when he found out that he was going to be sold as a slave! Joseph begged his brothers to let him go home to his father, but they would not listen. The Ishmaelites paid twenty pieces of silver for Joseph. They put him on one of the camels and continued on their journey, carrying him farther and farther away from his home.

Reuben, the oldest brother, was not with the others when Joseph was sold. When he came back, intending to take Joseph out of the hole secretly and send him back to his father, he could not find Joseph. He was afraid that his brothers might have killed him.

He tore his clothes, as people did in those days when they felt very sad. He cried out, "The child is dead, and I, what shall I do?" He knew that his father would hold him responsible, because he was the oldest.

The brothers killed a goat, and dipped Joseph's many-colored coat in the blood. When they reached home, they showed the bloody coat to their father. They lied, "We found this coat. Look and see whether it is your son's."

Jacob knew that it was Joseph's coat. He cried out, "It is my son's coat! Some wild animal must have eaten him! Joseph has without doubt been torn into pieces!"

Jacob tore his clothes, and put sackcloth on his body. He mourned for Joseph so long that his sons and daughter began to be afraid he would never get over it. They tried to comfort him, but it was no use. He said, "I will go down to the grave to my son, mourning."

The wicked brothers added to their sin by not telling the truth to their poor old father. (Do you remember that Jacob himself once cruelly deceived his old father?) They let Jacob believe that Joseph had really been torn to pieces by a wild beast. This was acting a lie, which is just as bad as telling a lie.

Although Jacob did not know how wicked his sons were, God knew all about it.

Chapter 25

IN POTIPHAR'S HOUSE

GENESIS 39, 40

Joseph traveled with the Ishmaelites for many days. Finally, after a long journey through the hot desert, they came to the fertile land of Egypt. Here everything was beautiful and green, watered by the mighty Nile River.

Joseph was sold as a slave to a rich soldier named Potiphar, who was the captain of Pharaoh's guard. Pharaoh was the king of the land of Egypt. Of course, since Potiphar was one of his high officers, he lived in a very fine house and had many servants.

This was a strange life to Joseph. Before, he had been his father's favorite son, taking care of his father's sheep. Now he was only a slave in the beautiful home of a rich man. His life was changed in a more important way, too. Now he was in a heathen country, where God was not known. The Egyptian people worshiped the sun.

Joseph was only seventeen years old when he was taken down to Egypt. Did he forget the God of his fathers, Abraham, Isaac, and Jacob? Did he soon learn to worship idols? No, he never forgot God. He remembered what his father and his mother and his grandfather Isaac had taught him about God. He still prayed. He was in a strange land, as his great-grandfather Abraham had been. But, like Abraham, he trusted in God to take care of him.

Joseph must have learned his lessons about trusting God well as a little boy at home. He never had another chance to learn about God.

Joseph was not alone even though he was so far from home. God stayed with him and took care of him. God was planning everything that happened to Joseph. There was a reason why God allowed Joseph to be sold as a slave in a strange country. But Joseph did not find out what this reason was till many years later.

God prospered everything Joseph did. When Potiphar saw how everything Joseph did went well, he let Joseph manage the whole household.

Joseph became a handsome young man. His mother Rachel had been very beautiful, and Joseph looked much like her. He was so good-looking that Potiphar's wife fell in love with him. Of course, this was wrong, because she was a married woman. Joseph knew it was wrong, and he refused to listen to her.

When Potiphar's wicked wife found she could not make Joseph sin, she began to hate him. She told her husband lying stories about him. Of course, Potiphar believed his wife's stories. He threw Joseph into the prison where the king's prisoners were kept. There Joseph's feet were bound with iron chains.

It was hard for Joseph to be in prison for doing good instead of wrong; but God was taking care of Joseph all this time, and He had a wonderful plan for Joseph's life.

God made the keeper of the prison friendly to Joseph. Soon the jailer put him in charge of all the other prisoners, and trusted everything in the prison to him. The Lord was with Joseph here too, making everything that he did prosper.

While Joseph was in prison, two of the king's chief servants were sent there. They had done something to make the king angry. One of them was Pharaoh's chief butler, who waited on Pharaoh at the table. The other was Pharaoh's chief baker, who was in charge of all the king's kitchens. These two men were put under Joseph's care.

One night each of them dreamed a strange dream. When Joseph came to see them in the morning, they looked worried and sad, for there was no one to tell them what the dreams might mean. In Egypt, too, people thought that a dream was sent to them to foretell something that was going to happen.

Joseph said to them, "Understanding dreams belongs to God. Tell me what you dreamed, I pray you."

The chief butler said, "In my dream I saw a grape vine which had three branches, with blossoms and ripe grapes on them. Pharaoh's cup was in my hand, and I took the grapes and squeezed them into Pharaoh's cup, and gave the cup to Pharaoh to drink from."

Joseph said, "This is what your dream means. The three branches are three days. In three days Pharaoh will take you out of prison, and will make you his chief butler again. You will hand Pharaoh his cup, as you used to.

"Don't forget me, when things go well with you. Mention me to Pharaoh, and get me out of this prison. For I was stolen away out of the land of the Hebrews; and here also in Egypt I have done nothing for which they should put me into this dungeon."

When the chief baker saw that the meaning of the butler's dream was good, he told Joseph his dream. "I dreamed that I had three baskets on my head, and the top basket was filled with all kinds of baked foods for Pharaoh to eat. Then the birds came down and ate up all the food out of the basket."

Then Joseph said, "This is what your dream means. The three baskets are three days. In three days Pharaoh shall lift your head off from you, and shall hang you on a tree, and the birds shall eat your flesh."

Three days later Pharaoh had a birthday. He gave a feast to all his servants. He sent for the chief butler and the chief baker. He restored the chief butler to his position, as Joseph had said. The butler waited upon Pharaoh's table again, and gave Pharaoh his cup.

And Pharaoh hanged the chief baker, as Joseph had foretold.

But the chief butler did not remember Joseph. He forgot all about him.

Chapter 26
FROM PRISON TO PALACE
GENESIS 41

PHARAOH'S DREAM   Poor Joseph was in the dungeon. He was there two more years. Then God made something happen which brought a great change in Joseph's life.

The great king of Egypt himself had a dream. It was a very strange one. It was a double dream.

Pharaoh dreamed that he stood by the river. He saw seven very fine, fat cows coming up out of the river. They went into a meadow and began to graze. Then he saw seven thin, starved-looking cows coming up out of the river. The seven thin, starved-looking cows ate up the seven fat ones.

Pharaoh woke up. Before he could

think what this strange dream meant, he fell asleep again, and dreamed another dream.

This time he saw seven fine, fat ears of grain come up on one stalk. After them came seven thin ears, blasted by the east wind. And the seven thin ears ate up the seven fat ears. Again Pharaoh woke up and found it was a dream.

In the morning Pharaoh was much troubled about this dream. He called for all the magicians and wise men of Egypt to tell him what this dream meant. The wise men thought and thought. At last they shook their heads and said, "O great and mighty king, we cannot explain your dream."

Now there was great trouble in the court. No one could explain Pharaoh's dream.

Then the chief butler remembered Joseph. He said to Pharaoh, "Today I remember my faults. Pharaoh was angry with the chief baker and with me. He put us both in prison. While we were there, we each dreamed a dream. In the prison there was a young Hebrew. We told him our dreams, and he explained them to us. What he said came true. I was taken back as the king's chief butler, but the chief baker was hanged."

Then Pharaoh sent for Joseph. The messengers ran to the prison quickly. They told Joseph that Pharaoh wanted to see him. Joseph shaved himself and put on clean clothes. Then he went to the palace. Pharaoh said to him, "I have dreamed a dream, and no one in all my kingdom can explain it. I have been told that you understand dreams, and can explain them."

Joseph said, "It is not in me. God shall give Pharaoh an answer of peace." Then Pharaoh told his dream to Joseph. Joseph answered the great king, choosing his words carefully, because it is not polite to say *you* to a king. When he meant *you*, he had to say *Pharaoh*.

He said, "The two dreams are one dream. God has shown Pharaoh what He is going to do.

"The seven good cows and the seven fat ears of grain are seven years. And the seven thin cows and the seven empty ears of grain are seven years. There are coming seven years of wonderful harvests throughout the whole land of Egypt. In those plentiful years the earth will bring forth so much food that the people will not know what to do with it.

"But after the seven plentiful years, there will come seven years of terrible famine, when nothing at all will grow. The seven years of famine will be so severe that people will forget there ever were any years of rich harvests.

"The reason that Pharaoh dreamed the dream twice is that God will surely bring all this to pass, and very soon.

"Now let Pharaoh find a man who is wise, and let Pharaoh set him over the whole land of Egypt. When the seven plentiful years come, let this man gather up one-fifth of the food of these good years, and store it in barns. Then when the bad years come, there will be enough food to keep the people from starving."

JOSEPH'S REWARD Pharaoh was very much pleased with Joseph's advice. He said to his servants, "Where can we find another man as wise as this Joseph is? For the very Spirit of God is in him!"

Then Pharaoh said to Joseph, "Because God has showed you all this, there is no one so wise as you are. So I appoint you to be ruler over the land of Egypt. Whatever you decide will be done. Only in the throne itself will I be greater than you are."

Pharaoh took off his royal ring and put it on Joseph's hand. The ring had Pharaoh's seal on it, and this seal, stamped on any paper, would make it an official law. Pharaoh had his servants dress Joseph in beautiful clothes. And he put a heavy gold chain around Joseph's neck.

He gave Joseph a chariot, a horse-drawn cart, to ride in. There was only one chariot in the whole kingdom that was handsomer than Joseph's — and that was Pharaoh's own. Pharaoh appointed servants to run before Joseph's chariot and to cry to all the people, "Bow the knee!" All the people in the street must fall down on their knees till Joseph's chariot passed by, just as they did when Pharaoh's chariot passed.

Now that Joseph had become a great man, he must have a fine name too. The king named him Zaphnath-paaneah, which in the Egyptian language means "the man to whom secrets are revealed." Pharaoh gave Joseph a princess named Asenath for his wife.

Joseph lived in a beautiful palace. He had many servants, was dressed in rich clothing, and rode in the second best chariot in the kingdom. Wherever he went, he was treated with great respect.

Soon God gave him another blessing. God gave him two little sons. Joseph named the first one Manasseh, which means "forgetting." "For," he said, "God has made me forget all my troubles." The second boy he named Ephraim, which means "fruitful." He said, "God has made me fruitful in the land of my affliction."

Joseph was now thirty years old. Instead of being a Hebrew slave boy, he was an Egyptian prince. It was God who planned Joseph's life and made all these wonderful things happen to him. And God had a special reason for His plan.

Meanwhile the seven years of plenty came. The earth brought forth such bountiful harvests that the people could not use all the grain. No one had ever seen such rich harvests before. Joseph built big barns in which he stored the grain he gathered. He gathered so much food that it could not be counted. Around every city there were enormous granaries, filled to the roof with grain.

At last the seven years of plenty were ended, and the seven years of famine began. The famine was not only in Egypt, but in every land. When people planted their seed, nothing came up. In other lands the people had not known about the seven years of famine, and so they had not saved up anything during the seven years of plenty. Now they began to suffer from hunger.

But in the land of Egypt there was bread. When the fields would not grow any grain, the people cried to Pharaoh for food. He answered all of them, "Go to Joseph, and do whatever he tells you." Joseph opened the storehouses and sold grain to the Egyptians.

When the people in other countries heard that there was grain in Egypt, they came there to buy some. Everybody wanted some of the food Joseph had stored during the years of plenty.

Chapter 27
JOSEPH'S DREAMS COME TRUE
GENESIS 42

JOSEPH MEETS HIS BROTHERS Joseph was a young boy about seventeen years old when he was taken to Egypt by the Ishmaelites, and sold there as a slave to Potiphar. Now he was thirty-seven years old.

Meanwhile, what had been happening to his father and his brothers? His father was becoming an old man. All of his brothers, except Benjamin, were married, with wives and children of their own.

There was famine in the land of Canaan, as well as in other countries. Jacob and his family were in great distress because they did not have enough food. They did not know what to do. The brothers looked at each other and said, "What shall we do to get food? The little that we have will soon be gone, and then we and our little ones will starve."

But their father said to them, "Why are you looking so anxiously at each other? I have heard that there is food in Egypt. Go down there and buy us some, so that we do not starve." So Jacob's ten oldest sons went to Egypt to buy food. Benjamin did not go with them, for his father was afraid to let him go on a long journey, for fear he would meet with harm, as Joseph had. Now that Joseph was gone, Benjamin was all that Jacob had left of his beloved wife Rachel. So Jacob kept Benjamin at home.

One day, as Joseph was selling grain to all the men who came to buy, he looked up and saw ten men from his own country, the land of Canaan. They came, like the others, and bowed themselves before him with their faces to the earth. It was the custom for men in that country to bow in this manner before a great lord.

Suddenly Joseph saw that the ten men from Canaan were his own brothers. He knew them, for they looked the same as when he had seen them last, except that they were older. They wore the same kind of clothes. They also spoke Hebrew, and Joseph understood everything they said to each other.

Joseph suddenly remembered his boyhood dreams about the eleven bundles of grain which bowed down to his bundle, and the sun and moon and stars which bowed to him. Joseph saw that his dreams had come true at last.

But his brothers did not recognize him. How could they? He had been only a young boy when they had seen him last. They had sold him to be a slave, and I suppose they thought he was still a slave working for some master in Egypt. They did not expect to see him. And certainly they did not expect to see him as ruler of the kingdom of Egypt, the highest ruler except Pharaoh himself.

When they had sold him as a slave, he was dressed as a simple Hebrew shepherd boy. Now he was beautifully dressed as an Egyptian prince, with a heavy gold chain around his neck, and the king's ring on his finger.

Joseph did not tell them who he was. He wanted to find out if they had changed. Were they still as cruel as they had been when they sold him? So he did not speak to them in Hebrew, but in Egyptian. An interpreter translated what he said into Hebrew.

Joseph spoke roughly to them, to frighten them. "Where do you men come from?" he asked. They answered, "We come from the land of Canaan to buy food."

He said to his brothers, "No, no, you did not come here to buy food. You came as spies, to find out how your country can make war on us." The brothers were very much frightened. Spies were always hanged when they were caught. They answered very humbly, "No, no, my lord, we are not spies. We have come to buy food."

But Joseph acted as if he did not hear them. "I tell you," he said, "you are spies. You have come to make trouble." The brothers were terrified. They said, "My lord, we are your servants. We are all good men. We are brothers, the sons of one man. The youngest is still at home with our father, and one of us is dead."

Joseph said, "I will give you a chance to prove that what you say is true. If you really have a younger brother, as you say, send one of you back to get him, and bring him here, so that I can see if you speak the truth. By the life of Pharaoh, you shall not be allowed to leave Egypt unless your younger brother comes here first. I will keep you in prison till your youngest brother comes."

Joseph put all his brothers into prison for three days. It was good for the brothers to have this hard experience. It made them remember how cruel they had been to Joseph.

THE BROTHERS RETURN HOME After three days Joseph let the brothers out of prison. He said to them, "I will not keep you in prison, for I believe in God. I will keep only one of you here. The rest of you may go back and carry food to your families, for they may be starving. But when you need more food, you must bring your youngest brother along with you. Then I will know that you are speaking the truth."

This worried the brothers They knew that their father would not let Benjamin go, and they did not see how they could ever come back for more food. Their guilty consciences reminded them of how they had treated Joseph. They said to each other, "We are guilty concerning our brother. We saw the anguish of his soul, when he begged us to let him go, and we would not listen. That is why this trouble has come upon us." And Reuben — you remember it had been Reuben who had tried to save

Joseph from the others — said, "Did I not tell you not to sin against the boy? But you would not listen. Now his blood is required of us."

When Joseph heard them talking together, admitting their guilt, his heart was deeply touched. He loved them still. He could not keep from weeping for homesickness. He went into another room because he could not keep the tears from rolling down his cheeks.

Yet he did not want to tell them who he was. He knew they would soon have to come back again to buy grain. Then he would tell them who he was. How he longed to see Benjamin! Benjamin was his full brother; the others were only half-brothers. That is why he insisted that they must bring Benjamin when they came again.

Joseph wiped his tears away and went back to his brothers. He took Simeon and bound him before their eyes, and put him in prison. He commanded his servants to fill the brothers' sacks with grain. He did not want to take pay from his brothers; so he told his servants to put the money back into the sacks.

The brothers loaded their sacks of grain on their donkeys, and started on their homeward journey. On the way one of them opened his sack to give his donkey some food. He called to the others, "My money has been given back! Here it is in my sack!" Then their hearts failed them, and they were afraid. They said, "What is this that God has done to us?" For they knew that nothing can happen unless God sends it.

At last they reached home, where their old father was anxiously awaiting them. They told him all that had happened to them — that the ruler had accused them of being spies, that he had put Simeon in prison till they should come back for more food, and that they had to bring Benjamin with them. Then they emptied their sacks. How surprised each of the brothers was to find that his money was still in his sack!

Their poor father felt very sad when he listened to their story. He became most sorrowful when they said that they could not go back again unless their brother Benjamin went with them. "You are making me lose my children," he said. "Joseph is dead, and Simeon is in prison in Egypt. Now you want to rob me of Benjamin too. All these things are against me."

Then Reuben said to his father, "I myself will take care of Benjamin. I promise surely to bring him back to you safely. If I do not, you may kill my two sons." Reuben knew that his father would never kill his two little grandsons, but he hoped that if he made such a strong promise, his father would let Benjamin go.

But it did no good. Jacob only said, "No, Benjamin shall not go with you. Joseph is dead, and Benjamin alone is left of his mother. If anything happens to him, you will bring down my gray hairs with sorrow to the grave."

Chapter 28
BENJAMIN GOES TO EGYPT
GENESIS 43

The family of Jacob lived on the grain they had brought from Egypt. They hoped that the famine would stop soon. They did not know, as Joseph did, that the famine was going to last seven long years.

By and by they had eaten up almost all their food. Their father said to them, "Go again, and buy us a little food."

But Judah said to his father, "The man told us, 'You shall not see my face unless you bring your youngest brother with you.' If you will let Benjamin go with us, we will go down and buy more food. If you will not let Benjamin go, we will not go."

Poor old Jacob said, "Why did you treat me so badly as to tell the man that you had a younger brother?" They all answered, "The man asked us all about ourselves. He wanted to know if our father was still alive, and if we had another brother. How could we know that he would say, 'Bring your brother down'?"

Judah said, "Send him with me. I promise to take care of him. If I do not bring him back to you, I will bear the blame forever. Unless we go, both we, and you, and all our little ones will die of hunger. If we had not waited so long, we could have gone and come back by now."

Their father saw he would have to let Benjamin go. They had hardly enough food now to last till the brothers came back again. He said, "If it must be so, do this: take the man a present of the best fruits of the land — some honey, and spices, and nuts, and almonds; and take double money in your hand. Perhaps it was a mistake that your money was returned in your sacks. And take your brother. And God Almighty give you mercy before the man, that he may send back Simeon and Benjamin also."

So the brothers took the present, and the double money, and Benjamin, and soon they were on their way to Egypt.

When Joseph saw his brothers, and Benjamin with them, his heart leaped with joy. There he was — his own brother Benjamin! He told his servants to take the men to his home, and to prepare a fine feast, for they were to have dinner with him.

Joseph's brothers were very much alarmed when they were taken to his house. They said to each other, "It is because of the money that was returned in our sacks. He is going to use that for an excuse to make slaves of us all." They came near to the man in charge of Joseph's house and said, "O sir, the first time we were here, when we returned home we found every man's money in his sack. We have brought it back to you again. And we have also brought other money, to buy food. We cannot tell who put the money back in our sacks."

But the man said to them, "Peace be to you. Do not be afraid. Your God and the God of your father gave you treasure in your sacks. I had your money." Then he brought Simeon to them, out of prison. And he sent a servant to wash their hot, dusty feet, and to feed their donkeys.

When Joseph came in, they gave him the present they had brought, and they bowed themselves low before him. When Joseph saw his own brother Benjamin, he wanted to run and embrace him. But instead he asked them, "Is your father well, the old man of whom you spoke? Is he yet alive? And is this your youngest brother of whom you spoke to me?" And to Benjamin he said, "God be gracious to you, my son!"

Tears began to roll down Joseph's cheeks. He hurried into his bedroom, so that his brothers would not see him weeping. After a while he washed his face, and came out again, and said to his servant, "Bring the dinner on." The servant set three tables. The first one was for Joseph alone, because he was too important a man to eat with ordinary people. The second table was for the brothers. The third one was for the Egyptians, for they would not eat at the same table with Hebrews.

The servant seated the brothers according to their age, the oldest first, and then the next, and so on down to the youngest, who was seated last. This surprised the brothers, for they did not understand how he knew how old they were. Joseph sent good things to their table as they ate. When he sent food to Benjamin, however, he sent five times as much as to any of the others. The brothers began to enjoy themselves. But still Joseph did not tell them who he was.

Chapter 29
JOSEPH'S SILVER CUP
GENESIS 44, 45

After dinner was finished, Joseph commanded his servant to fill the sacks of the brothers with grain. "Put every man's money back into his sack," he told his servant, "and put my silver cup in the sack of the youngest brother."

As soon as it was light the next morning, the brothers started out for home. When they were not yet far away from the city, Joseph sent his servant after them. "Hurry," he said, "and as soon as you catch up to them, say to them, 'Why have you paid back evil for good? Why have you stolen my lord's silver cup? It was wrong of you to do this.'"

This was a test to see whether the brothers had really changed since they so cruelly sold Joseph into slavery. Would they give Benjamin up also, to save their own skins? Joseph had to know.

The servant hurried after the brothers. As soon as he caught up with them, he called out, "Why have you stolen my lord's silver cup, when he treated you so well?" The brothers were astonished. They answered, "God forbid that we should do such a thing! Didn't we bring back the money we found in our sacks before? Search our sacks. If you find any one of us has stolen the silver cup, he shall die, and we will all become my lord's slaves."

"No," the servant said, "only the one who has stolen the cup shall be my lord's slave. The rest of you may go home." Quickly each of the brothers took down his sack and opened it. The servant looked into every man's sack, beginning with the oldest, and going on until he reached the youngest. There, on the top of Benjamin's grain, they saw Joseph's silver cup!

The brothers were horrified. How could the cup have gotten into Benjamin's sack? It was as mysterious as the way in which the money had been returned on their first trip. In their distress they tore their clothes. They could not let Benjamin go back to become an Egyptian slave! They strapped the bags of grain on their donkeys. Then they turned around, and all of them together went back to Joseph's house.

They all fell down before Joseph on the ground. And Joseph said to them, "What have you done? Didn't you know I would surely find you out?" Judah answered, "What can we say to my lord? God has found out our sin. We will all be my lord's slaves."

But Joseph said, "God forbid that I should do such a thing! The one who stole my cup shall become my slave. The rest of you may go home in peace to your father."

Then Judah came near to Joseph and said, "Let your servant, I pray you, speak a word in my lord's ears. My lord asked his servants, 'Have you a father? Or a brother?' and when we said, 'We have a father, an old man, and a little brother, a child of his old age, and his brother is dead, and he alone is left of his mother, and his father loves him,' then you said, 'Bring him down to me.' And we said, 'The boy cannot leave his father, for if he should leave his father, his father would die.' And you said to your servants, 'Unless you bring your youngest brother with you, you shall not see my face again!'

"When our father said to us, 'Go again and buy us a little food,' we said, 'We cannot go unless our youngest brother go with us.' And our father said, 'You know that my wife had only two sons. And one is already gone from me, and surely some wild beast has torn him in pieces. If you take this boy also, and some mischief happens to him, you will bring my gray hairs down with sorrow to the grave.'

"Now, therefore, I pray you, my lord, let me stay a slave to my lord, instead of the boy! And let the boy go home with his brothers! For how can I go home to my father if the boy is not with me?"

Joseph could not stand it any longer. He did not want the Egyptians to see him weeping, so he commanded all of them to leave the room. Then he said to his brothers, "I am Joseph! Is my father still living?" And he wept aloud, so that the Egyptians heard it in the next room.

His brothers were so astonished that they could not answer him. Was this grand man their brother Joseph, whom they had sold into Egypt as a slave? They could hardly believe it.

Joseph said to them, "Come near to me. Do not be angry with yourselves that you sold me. For God sent me ahead of you to save your lives. Hurry now to my father and say to him, 'Thus says Joseph, "Come down to me. Do not wait. Bring your children, and your children's children, and all your flocks and herds. I will take care of you. For there are still five years of famine coming."'"

Joseph threw his arms around his own dear brother Benjamin. He hugged him and kissed him, the tears rolling down his cheeks. Then he kissed all his other brothers. At last the brothers began to believe what Joseph said. They were no longer afraid of him. They spent a long time talking to him.

Chapter 30
JACOB GOES TO EGYPT
GENESIS 45-47

THE GOOD NEWS The Egyptians in the next room wondered what all this meant. Why did they hear this sound of weeping? When they learned that the men were Joseph's brothers, there was great excitement among them. Soon the news reached Pharaoh's palace: "Joseph's brothers have come to Egypt!"

Pharaoh said to Joseph, "Tell your brothers to go back to the land of Canaan, and to bring your father and their families to this country. Take wagons out of the land of Egypt to carry your little ones, and your wives, and your father. Do not bother to bring all your household goods, for I will give you the best that there is in the land of Egypt."

Joseph had done so much for Egypt that Pharaoh was glad to be able to do something for Joseph.

So Joseph sent wagons along with his brothers, so that his aged father and all the women and little children could ride to Egypt. He gave them everything they needed for the journey. And he gave each brother a present of a suit of clothes. To Benjamin he gave five suits of clothes and three hundred pieces of silver. He sent along a present for his father too — ten donkeys loaded with delicious things to eat, and also ten donkeys loaded with grain and bread and meat for his father and his family to use on the journey.

How eager the brothers were to get back to their father and tell him the wonderful news! All the way home they kept saying, "What will Father say when we tell him?"

Far off in the land of Canaan poor old Jacob was sitting alone in his tent door. He was thinking of his dear boy Joseph, so long lost to him, and saying to himself, as he had said so many times before, "He was surely torn in pieces by some wild animal. Now Benjamin, too, is gone, and perhaps I shall never see him again."

He was praying, "God, bring back my boy. Do not let me lose him as I lost Joseph." Often when we look to God for help, He sends us an answer to our prayers that is even better than what we asked for.

As Jacob was straining his eyes to see if his sons were returning, he saw a cloud of dust in the distance. Soon he could make out the wagons and the donkeys. As soon as they were near enough, Benjamin jumped down from his donkey and ran ahead to his father. He kissed him, crying out, "Joseph is alive, and he is the ruler of all Egypt!" And then the older brothers came with the same story.

The shock was too much for Jacob. He almost fainted with excitement. How could this be? Joseph had been dead for many years. But his sons showed him all that Joseph had sent, and told him everything Joseph had said to them. When Jacob saw the wagons, and the donkeys loaded with presents, at last he believed it.

"It is enough," he said. "Joseph, my son, is still alive. I will go and see him before I die."

So Jacob got ready with all his family, and his household goods, and his flocks and his herds, to go down to Egypt to live. How large a family do you think he had? Jacob's wives, Leah and Rachel, were both dead, but he had eleven sons. Except Benjamin, all the brothers were married and had little children. If you counted their wives too, there were more than sixty people in the family.

This large family, with the servants who cared for the flocks and herds, made a great train of people traveling to Egypt. The wives and the children and Jacob himself rode in the wagons Joseph had sent. The men rode on the donkeys, and the servants walked, driving the sheep and cattle.

Soon they came to Beersheba, where Jacob's grandfather Abraham had prayed to God, and had planted a grove of trees. Jacob stopped there to offer sacrifices to God. He did not want to leave the land God had promised to his children unless he was sure that God would go with him.

That night God appeared to him and said, "I am the God of your father. Do not be afraid to go down to Egypt, for I will make a great nation out of you there. I will go with you to Egypt, and I will surely bring you back again."

This was a great comfort to Jacob, who was such an old man that he dreaded the long journey.

IN THE LAND OF EGYPT After they had traveled a week or two through the hot, sandy desert, and were approaching Egypt, Judah went ahead to lead the way.

When Joseph heard that his father and his brothers had come, he called for his chariot, and went out to meet them. At last he saw them coming in the distance. He made his horses go faster because he was so impatient. Then he jumped out of his chariot, ran to his father, threw his arms around him, and kissed him. He was so happy that tears rolled down his cheeks, as they sometimes do when we are very happy.

Joseph put his head down on his father's shoulder and wept for a long time. His father was just as happy as Joseph was. He said, "Now I am ready to die, because God has let me see your face, and you are still alive."

Joseph went to tell Pharaoh that his father and his brothers had come. He brought Jacob to the palace to see the king. Pharaoh was very polite to Jacob. He asked him, "How old are you?" That was the polite thing to say to very old men in those days.

Jacob answered, "The days of the years of my pilgrimage are a hundred and thirty years. Few and evil have been the days of the years of my life, and they have not attained unto the days of the years of my fathers, in the days of their pilgrimage."

Wasn't that a beautiful and dignified answer? Then Jacob blessed Pharaoh.

Pharaoh told Joseph that his father and his brothers might have the very best part of Egypt to live in. This was the land of Goshen. Joseph took his father and his brothers to their new home, and gave them food and everything they needed.

THE FAMINE Now the famine was very bad, so that the land of Egypt and all the land of Canaan fainted.

As long as the people had money, Joseph sold grain out of the king's granaries to all the people of Egypt. But by and by their money was all gone. What could they do now?

They came to Joseph and said, "Give us food, or we will die."

Joseph answered, "If your money is gone, bring your cattle, and your donkeys, and I will give you food in exchange for your animals." The

people sold all their animals to Joseph for food. In exchange he gave them enough food to last a whole year.

They came again the next year and said, "We are very poor. Our money is all gone, and we have sold our cattle to you. We have nothing left to buy food with except our bodies and our lands. If you will give us food, we will sell ourselves and our lands to be servants to Pharaoh."

So Joseph bought all the land of Egypt for Pharaoh, in exchange for food. Joseph did not drive a hard bargain. He gave the people food to eat, and he said to them that when better times came again, and they planted seed and it grew, they should give one-fifth of the harvest to Pharaoh, and four-fifths should be their own.

The people were grateful to Joseph for making things easy for them. They said to him, "You have saved our lives by your kindness. We will be Pharaoh's servants to pay for all this goodness."

At last the seven terrible years of famine were over, and once again the land of Egypt was green and beautiful, and the harvest was plentiful. But Jacob and his sons did not go back to the land of Canaan. They were happy and prosperous in Egypt, and they stayed there.

Chapter 31
THE DEATH OF JACOB
GENESIS 48, 49, 50

After the children of Israel had been in Egypt for seventeen years, the time came when Jacob must die. Someone told Joseph that his father was very sick. Joseph took his two young sons, Ephraim and Manasseh, and hurried to his father's bedside.

Jacob was so old that his eyes were dim. He said to Joseph, "Who are these?" And Joseph answered, "These are the two sons whom God has given me here in Egypt." Jacob said, "Bring them near to me, so that I may bless them."

Joseph brought the two boys to his father, and Jacob kissed them. He said, "I thought I would never see you again, and now God has been so good to me that He has even let me see your children." And Jacob laid his hands on the boys' heads and blessed them, saying, "The God before whom my fathers Abraham and Isaac did walk, the God who has fed me all my life long unto this day, the Angel who redeemed me from all evil, bless the boys. Let my name be named on them, and the name of my fathers, Abraham and Isaac, and let them grow into a multitude in the earth."

Old father Jacob knew that his time had come to die. He called all his twelve sons to his bedside to give them a blessing before he died. All his sons stood around him to hear his last words.

Reuben and Simeon, who had lived wild, violent lives, did not receive good blessings. But when Jacob came to Judah he gave him the promise of great things. He said that the kings of the children of Israel would come from Judah's children, and at last the greatest ruler of all would be born in Judah's family. That ruler is Jesus Christ. This prophecy of Jacob's is most important, because it promises the coming of our Saviour.

After he had finished blessing his children, Jacob said, "Do not bury me in Egypt, but take my body back to the land of Canaan, and bury me with my fathers, Abraham and Isaac."

When Jacob had said all these things he died, and his spirit returned to God.

When Joseph saw that his dear father was dead, he put his face down on his father's face, and kissed him several times, and cried.

Then Joseph commanded the Egyptians to embalm his father's body. This was never done to common people, but only to kings and great men. We today do not know how to embalm as the Egyptians embalmed. In some way they wrapped cloths dipped in spices around dead bodies, so that they would not decay, although they did dry up. Bodies treated in this way are called mummies. People digging in the sands of Egypt have found old coffins containing mummies which were buried more than four thousand years ago.

To honor Joseph, the whole land of Egypt mourned for Jacob for seventy days. Joseph asked Pharaoh, "I beg you, allow me to take my father's body back to Canaan, for my father made me swear a solemn oath to bury him there." And Pharaoh said, "Go, and bury your father, as he made you promise."

So Joseph took his father's body back to Canaan. Of course his eleven brothers went with him. They did not go alone, for the Egyptians wanted to show honor to Joseph's father. Therefore all the servants of Pharaoh and all the elders of the land of Egypt went along, with their fine chariots and horsemen. The people of the land of Canaan looked in wonder at the grand funeral procession as it went along.

After Joseph and his brothers had buried their father in the Cave of Machpelah, they all returned to Egypt, where they had left their wives and children.

Now that their father was dead, Joseph's brothers were very much afraid that Joseph would no longer be kind to them. They thought that he might at last punish them for selling him to be a slave.

One day they came to Joseph, saying, "Our father, before he died, told us to come and beg you to forgive us for all the wickedness that we did to you when you were a boy." And they fell down on their faces before Joseph.

Joseph's eyes filled with tears. He spoke kindly to them. "Do not be afraid. You meant to do me harm, but God meant it for good. It was God who sent me here to save many people from starving. Do not be afraid, for I will take care of you and your little ones."

Joseph and his brothers lived in Egypt all the rest of their lives. After some time, Joseph's two boys were married. They had children, and Joseph had the pleasure of playing with his own grandchildren, and with some of his great-grandchildren, for he lived to be an old man.

Before he died, Joseph said to the children of Israel, "I am going to die, but God will surely bring you out of this land to the land of Canaan again. When you go, I want you to carry my bones with you, and to bury them in the land of Canaan among my own people." He made them swear a solemn oath that they would certainly do this.

Joseph was a hundred and ten years old when he died. And they embalmed his body and put it in a coffin in Egypt.

Chapter 32

MOSES
EXODUS 1, 2

THE ISRAELITE SLAVES The children of Israel were now settled in the land of Egypt. They lived there for many, many years.

Joseph and all his brothers died. Another generation grew up and died, and another. The king who knew Joseph died, and he was followed by another Pharaoh; and he, by another. For the Egyptians called all their kings *Pharaoh*.

God gave many children to the Israelites so that, as the years passed by, they became a mighty nation. After four hundred years in the land of Egypt there were about two million of the children of Israel.

They had almost forgotten that they had ever lived in another land. They had almost forgotten about Joseph, and how he had saved the land of Egypt from starvation at the time of the terrible famine, when the Israelites had first come to Egypt. It was not strange that they had almost forgotten these things, for that time was almost as far away from them as the time of Columbus is from us.

But they had not entirely forgotten. Mothers still told their children bedtime stories of the boy Joseph who was sold into slavery by his cruel brothers, and of his wonderful rise to power, till he was next in power to Pharaoh himself. The fathers still told their sons about Abraham, and Isaac, and Jacob, and how God had often spoken to them, how He had promised to give them the land of Canaan, and how they had trusted in God's promise.

As one Pharaoh after another reigned, the Egyptians also forgot who Joseph was, and what he had done for the people of Egypt in the time of the terrible famine. There came to the throne a Pharaoh who knew nothing about Joseph. This new king saw the mighty nation of the Israelites living in the land of Egypt, right among the Egyptians. He said to his people: "Behold, the children of Israel are more and mightier than we are. If there should be a war, they might join with our enemies and fight against us. We must do something to prevent this."

Pharaoh made the children of Israel work hard. He was building two treasure cities, called Pithom and Rameses, and he made the Israelites work hard on these cities as slaves. He set taskmasters over the Israelites, with long whips in their hands. If they saw a man who was not working hard enough, they brought the cruel whip down on his back. But the more cruelly the Egyptians treated them, the more the Israelites multiplied

PART II
Wandering

and grew. This was because of God's promise to Abraham that his children's children should be as many as the sands on the seashore and as the stars in the sky. God was blessing the Israelites even in their great trouble.

When Pharaoh saw this, he thought of a still more cruel way to prevent the Israelites from becoming stronger. He commanded that whenever a little boy was born in any Israelite home, the baby must be thrown into the river. The little girls might live, because they could not grow up to be soldiers who would fight against the Egyptians.

A STRANGE CRADLE Now in those evil days, a beautiful baby boy was born to a father and mother among the Israelites. He was a fine baby, strong and well. His mother made up her mind to hide him, so that the Egyptian soldiers would not come and throw him into the Nile River. She did not tell anybody that she had a new baby. She hid him where none of the neighbors would see him. The minute he began to cry, she hushed him up very quickly.

But when he was three months old, she could not hide him any longer, for he cried so loudly that people could hear him even when they were outside the house. So she wove a little boat of reeds, which she covered on the outside with tar to stop up the cracks and to keep the water out. She lined it with a soft cloth, and put the baby in it. She carried the basket-boat down to the riverside and laid it gently in the bulrushes that grew near the river bank.

Then she went home, for she did not dare to stay there. She was afraid that someone would see her, and suspect that she had a baby hidden there. The baby had a sister, Miriam, who was about twelve years old. Miriam stood at a little distance to watch what would happen to the baby.

That very day Pharaoh's daughter went down to the river to bathe. She saw the little basket among the bulrushes. She had one of her maids bring it to her. When she opened it, she saw the beautiful baby, who began to cry. She felt sorry for the baby. "For," she said, "this is one of the Hebrew children." All her maids clustered around and looked at the baby. When he began to cry, they lifted him out of the basket and tried to soothe him.

The princess took him in her arms. The baby soon stopped crying, and smiled up into her face. When she saw that, she loved him, and determined to adopt him as her own son.

All this time Miriam had been watching from the bulrushes. When she saw the princess take the baby in her arms, she ran out and asked the princess, "Shall I go and call one of the Hebrew women to nurse the baby for you?"

"Yes, go," answered the princess. Little Miriam ran home very quickly and called her mother. Her mother hurried to the princess, who said to her, "I found this child in the bulrushes, and I am going to adopt him. Will you take him home and take care of him for me? I will pay you for it."

So the mother carried home her own baby, and took care of him for Pharaoh's daughter. The princess had some silk and linen clothes made for him, such as kings' sons wear. Every week his mother took him to Pharaoh's palace, so that the princess could see him. The princess gave him beautiful gold and silver toys, and everything that a little prince might like to have.

Although he was often taken to the palace, he lived with his mother till he was about four years old. He played with his brother Aaron, who was three years older than he was, and with Miriam. His mother carefully taught him about the true God — for the Egyptians worshiped idols. She told him about Abraham, and Isaac, and Jacob. "You must remember," she said, "that though Pharaoh's daughter has adopted you as her son, you are really an Israelite, not an Egyptian." She taught him about God very carefully, weighing every word, for she knew that she would never have another chance to tell him these important things.

At last he went to live with the princess in the palace. She hired the finest teachers in the land to teach him all the wisdom and learning of the Egyptians. Since he was a prince, he must be a wise man. The princess named him Moses, which means "drawn out." "For," she said, "I drew him out of the water."

It was a very good thing that Moses was taught all the learning of the Egyptians. God had a great work for Moses to do. God was already planning Moses' life.

A FLIGHT INTO THE DESERT One day, when Moses was forty years old, he went out to the place where the Egyptians were working. There he saw an Egyptian cruelly beat an Israelite slave.

Moses was angry. He looked this way and that. He did not see anyone near. He raised his arm and killed the Egyptian. He hid his body in the sand.

The next day he went out again to the place where the Hebrews were working. Two Hebrews were fighting with each other, and one of them was beating the other. Moses said to the man who was beating the other, "Why do you hurt him?" The man answered roughly, "Who made you a judge over us? Do you intend to kill me, as you killed that Egyptian?"

Moses was very much frightened. He thought nobody had seen him kill the Egyptian. When Pharaoh heard what he had done, he wanted to kill Moses. Moses ran for his life, far away into the desert.

At last he came to the land of Midian, which was so far away from Egypt that he knew Pharaoh could not find him. This was a hot, dry country. Moses sat down by a well to rest.

Now in that country there lived a man named Jethro. He had seven daughters. They watched the sheep in the fields, for Jethro had large flocks. These young girls brought their sheep to the well and let down their pitchers to draw up water for the sheep. They poured the water into a trough, so that the sheep could drink.

But some rough country fellows came around, who were also shepherds. They pushed the girls rudely away, and began to water their own sheep. When Moses saw this, he helped the girls draw water for their sheep.

When the girls came home, their father said to them, "How is it that you have come home so early today?" They answered, "There was a very kind man by the well, an Egyptian. He drove away the rough shepherds, and he helped us water our sheep."

Their father Jethro said to them, "Why did you not bring him home with you if he was so kind? Go

61

back, and invite him for supper."
So the girls went back to the well
and invited Moses to come and eat
supper with them. Moses came, and
he liked the family so much that he
stayed with them. After a while he
married one of the girls.

By and by he had a little son whom he named Gershom, which means "a stranger here." Soon after that, he had another little son. He named him Eliezer, which means "God is a help." "For," he said, "God has helped me when Pharaoh wanted to kill me."

Moses now kept the sheep for Jethro, his father-in-law.

Chapter 33
GOD CHOOSES MOSES
EXODUS 3-5, 7

THE BURNING BUSH Moses was no longer an Egyptian prince, dressed in fine clothes and living in a fine palace with many servants to wait on him. For many years he was a shepherd, wandering in the lonely desert from one green place to another, and sleeping under the stars at night. It was a very lonely life, for in that desert country there is very little grass, and he often had to lead his flock far away from home to find pasture for the sheep.

It is sometimes a good thing for people to be all alone by themselves. It gives them time to think about God.

One day Moses saw a strange sight in the desert. A bush was on fire. Moses watched it a long time, but the bush did not burn up. It just kept on burning. Moses said to himself, "I will go and see this great sight, why the bush is not burned up."

When Moses came near the bush, something still stranger happened. God called to him out of the bush. God said, "Moses! Moses!" Moses was surprised, but he answered, "Here I am."

God said, "Do not come any nearer. Take off your shoes, for the place on which you are standing is holy ground." In that country it is still the custom for people who go into a church or into any other holy place to take off their shoes, instead of taking off their hats, as men do here. So Moses took off his shoes, as God had commanded him.

A long, long time had passed since God had spoken to any man. The last time He had done so was when He had told Jacob not to be afraid to go to Egypt. How many years do you think had passed since then? More than four hundred years!

In those days the Bible had not yet been written. Fathers and mothers had to tell their children about God, and how He had spoken to Abraham, Isaac, and Jacob. They had to tell them about the promises God had made, how He had promised to send a Saviour, and how they must always trust not in themselves but in God's promises. They said to their children, "Always remember that we are not like the Egyptians, who worship the sun and all kinds of animals. We are Israelites, and we worship the true God, who made the heaven and the earth."

But the Israelites had lived so long among the idol-worshiping Egyptians, and it was so long since any message had come from God, that some of them had almost forgotten about the one true God.

God said to Moses, "I am the God

of your father, the God of Abraham, the God of Isaac, and the God of Jacob." Then Moses hid his face, for he was afraid to look at God. God said, "I have seen the affliction of my people in Egypt. I have heard their cry, and I know their sorrow. I am come down to deliver them from the Egyptians, and to bring them to a good land, flowing with milk and honey. Come now, I will send you to Pharaoh, to bring my people out of Egypt."

Moses said to God, "Who am I, that I should go to Pharaoh?"

God promised, "I will certainly be with you. And this shall be a sign to you: when you have brought forth the people out of Egypt, you shall serve God upon this mountain."

Moses knew that the children of Israel had almost forgotten that they had a God. He said, "When I come to the children of Israel, and say to them, 'The God of your fathers has sent me to you,' they will ask, 'Which God are you talking about?' What shall I say to them?"

God said to Moses, "Tell the children of Israel, 'The God of your fathers, the God of Abraham, the God of Isaac, and the God of Jacob has sent me.' This is My Name forever.

"Go to Pharaoh, and say to him, 'The Lord God of the Hebrews has met with us. Let us go a three days' journey into the wilderness to worship our God.' And I know that the king of Egypt will not let you go. But I will stretch out My arm and do wonders. And after that Pharaoh will let you go."

Moses did not want to go. Perhaps he was afraid of Pharaoh. Perhaps he was afraid he was not strong enough, or wise enough, to lead God's people. He kept thinking of excuses. He said, "The Israelites will not be-

lieve that the Lord has appeared to me."

Then the Lord asked, "What is that in your hand?" Moses said, "A rod." God said, "Throw it on the ground." Moses threw it on the ground. It turned into a big snake. Moses was afraid of the snake, and ran away from it. But the Lord said, "Take hold of its tail."

Moses believed that if God could turn a rod into a snake, He could also keep the snake from biting him. He obeyed God. He ran after the snake and caught it by the tail. It turned back into a rod again.

Then God said, "Put your hand into your bosom." Moses put his hand into his bosom, and when he drew it out it was as white as snow. Moses knew that his hand had the dreadful disease of leprosy. He looked at it with horror.

But God said to him, "Put your hand into your bosom again." Moses did so, and when he took it out, it was no longer white with leprosy, but brown and healthy just as it had been before.

"Now," said the Lord, "I have given you two signs. If they do not believe the first sign, they will believe the second one. If they do not believe that, take some water and pour it out upon the dry land, and it shall become blood."

But Moses did not want to go. "O my Lord," he said, "I cannot speak well. I am slow of speech." Then the Lord said, "Who made man's mouth? Was it not I, the Lord? Go now, and I will be with your mouth, and teach you what you shall say."

Still Moses objected. He said, "O my Lord, send someone else." Now God was angry with Moses' many excuses. He said, "I know your brother Aaron can speak. Tell him what I have told you. Let him do the speaking."

THE BEGINNING OF THE TASK Moses went to his father-in-law Jethro, and said to him, "I want to go back to Egypt to visit my family." Jethro said, "Go in peace."

God commanded Aaron, Moses' brother, to go into the desert to meet Moses. It was many, many years since Aaron had seen his brother Moses. When he met him in the desert, he was very glad to see him, and he kissed him.

Moses told Aaron all the things God had said to him. When they reached Egypt, they gathered together the chief men of the children of Israel. They told them what God had said, and showed them the signs of the snake and the leprosy. The people were very happy to know that God was going to deliver them from the cruel slavery in Egypt, and to take them back to the country He had promised to the children of Abraham, a country none of them had ever seen.

Then Moses and Aaron went to the palace of Pharaoh. It was the place where Moses had grown up, but the same king was no longer there. Moses and Aaron said to the king, "The Lord God of the Hebrews says, 'Let my people go, that they may hold a feast for Me in the wilderness.'"

Pharaoh looked with scorn at these two Israelites who dared to ask such a thing as that. He answered coldly, "Who is the Lord, that I should obey Him, to let Israel go? I don't know the Lord, and I won't let Israel go."

Then Pharaoh called the taskmasters and said to them, "Make the people work harder. They are lazy,

and this is why they say, 'Let us go and worship our God.'"

Now the bricks the Israelites made were made of clay. They had to make the clay wet, mix chopped straw with it, shape it into bricks, and then dry these in the hot Egyptian sun till they became hard. The straw afterwards rotted and turned into a sort of glue, which held the clay together. The taskmasters supplied the workers with straw to put into their bricks.

Pharaoh said to the taskmasters, "Do not give the people straw as you used to. Make them go out into the fields and gather straw for themselves. Yet they must make the same number of bricks as before." Of course, the people could not do this. The taskmasters beat them and asked, "Why have you not made as many bricks today as before and as you were told to make?"

The workers saw that they were in a bad way. They said to Moses and Aaron, "The Lord look upon you, and judge, because you have made Pharaoh hate us, and he is killing us with work."

So Moses said to the Lord, "Why did You send me to Egypt? It has only done harm and made Pharaoh angry with the people. You have not delivered them at all."

Then God said to Moses, "Now you shall see what I will do to Pharaoh. Soon he will drive the people out of his land. Go now, and tell Pharaoh to let the children of Israel go."

So Moses and Aaron went to Pharaoh. Aaron threw down Moses' rod, and it became a snake. Pharaoh called his wise men and magicians, and every one of them threw down his rod, and every rod became a

6: JOSEPH IN PRISON: INTERPRETING THE DREAMS

7: THE PASSOVER INSTITUTED

snake. But Moses' snake swallowed all the others. Still Pharaoh paid no attention to Moses and his miracle. Since his magicians could make their rods turn into snakes too, he would not believe Moses. In those olden times the magicians could do clever tricks, but they could not perform real miracles, as Moses did. But Pharaoh hardened his heart. He would not listen to God. He would not let the people go.

Chapter 34
A STUBBORN KING
EXODUS 7-11

GOD SENDS PLAGUES God said to Moses, "In the morning Pharaoh is going to the river. Meet him there." So Moses and Aaron met Pharaoh at the river's edge, and Moses said to Pharaoh, "The Lord God of the Hebrews sent me to say, 'Let My people go!' and you would not listen. Therefore thus says the Lord, 'Now you shall know that I am the Lord, for I will turn the water of your rivers into blood.'"

Aaron took Moses' rod and stretched out his arm over the Nile River, and over all the little rivers and lakes. Suddenly the water turned into blood. The fish in the river died, and the river smelled because of the dead fish.

The magicians of Egypt did the same with their enchantments. Perhaps they dropped a little red powder into some water to make it look like blood. And so Pharaoh did not pay any attention to Moses and Aaron. He refused to listen when God spoke to him. He just turned around and walked back to his palace.

The river water remained blood for a whole week. The Egyptian people could not drink it. They had to dig wells near the river to get a little good water to drink.

Then the Lord commanded Moses to go to Pharaoh again and say to him, "Thus says the Lord, 'Let My people go. And if you refuse to let them go, I will fill your land with frogs.'"

Then Aaron stretched out his hand, and great armies of frogs came up out of the river. They marched right up into the houses and into the king's palace, till all the houses were filled with frogs. They climbed on the chairs, so that when the people wanted to sit down, they first had to knock off the frogs. They climbed up on the beds, crawled under the pillows, and crept between the sheets. When anybody wanted to go to bed, he first had to shake out the frogs, and even that was no use, for just as soon as he was in bed he would feel them crawling over his face. It was almost impossible to walk without stepping on frogs. They hopped into the food and drink, and into the dough from which the women were making bread.

The magicians also produced some frogs, but that was only a trick. They could easily have picked up a few of them and hidden them in their clothes, and then pretended they had made them. For we know that no

65

man can create even one living frog. Only God can create life.

Now Pharaoh sent for Moses and Aaron. He said to them, "Pray to the Lord to take away the frogs, and I will let the people go." Pharaoh began to see that the God of the Hebrews was very powerful. So Moses and Aaron prayed to God to take away the frogs.

The Lord did so. The frogs died, all over Egypt. There were dead frogs everywhere — on the floors, in the beds, on the tables, all over the ground. Oh, it was horrible! The people gathered them up in heaps and dug holes to bury them, because of the smell of the dead frogs.

But when Pharaoh saw that the frogs were gone, he hardened his heart, and would not let the children of Israel go.

Then the Lord commanded Moses, "Tell Aaron to stretch out his rod, and to strike the dust of the ground, and it shall become lice on man and beast." Aaron did so, and soon every person and every animal was covered with crawling, biting lice. The people were almost crazy with the itching of their bodies. They scratched themselves until the blood came, but the lice were so thick that they could not get rid of them.

The magicians tried to produce lice, but they could not do it. They said to Pharaoh, "This is the finger of God!" But Pharaoh hardened his heart. He would not listen to all these God-sent warnings.

MORE EVILS VISIT EGYPT   Again God told Moses to rise up early in the morning, and go to meet Pharaoh at the river. There he must say to Pharaoh: "Thus says the Lord, 'Let My people go, that they may serve Me. If you will not let them go, I will send swarms of flies upon you. They will fill your houses, and even the ground will be covered with them. But I will make a difference between My people and the Egyptians. There shall be no flies in the houses of the Israelites. And then you will know that I am the Lord, and that I can do whatever I will on the earth.'"

The next day the Lord sent great swarms of flies into the house of Pharaoh, and into all the land of Egypt.

Everything and everybody was covered with flies. They flew into the people's faces, into their ears and eyes and noses, and even into their mouths.

Their soup was full of flies, and their bread and meat were black with them.

Even Pharaoh could stand it no longer. Again he called for Moses and Aaron and said to them: "Sacrifice to your God right here in Egypt. There is no need for you to go out into the wilderness."

But Moses said, "Oh, no! We can't do that! When we sacrifice, we kill sheep and oxen. The Egyptians worship these animals, and if they see us killing them, they will stone us. We will go a three days' journey into the wilderness, and there we will sacrifice as our God tells us to do."

"Well," said Pharaoh, "I will let you go, but do not go very far away."

"Very well," agreed Moses, "I shall pray the Lord to take away the flies tomorrow. But do not let Pharaoh tell lies any more and change his mind about letting the people go."

Moses left Pharaoh, and prayed to God to take away the flies. God took them away, so that not one was left.

But Pharaoh broke his promise again, and would not let the people go.

66

Again the Lord told Moses to go to Pharaoh's palace and to say to him that if he still refused to let the people go, God would send a dreadful sickness upon all Egypt's animals, and many of them would die. But He would not send any sickness upon the cattle of the Israelites, and none of them would die.

The next day the Lord sent the sickness to the animals. Almost all of the cattle of Egypt died.

Pharaoh sent some of his servants to find out if any one of the cattle of the children of Israel had died. He found that not one of their cattle lay dead.

But Pharaoh hardened his heart again, and he would not let the children of Israel go.

Now the Lord told Moses and Aaron to take some handfuls of ashes from the furnace, and throw them into the air in the sight of Pharaoh.

Moses and Aaron did as God had told them. Soon everybody in Egypt was covered with sore boils which made the people sick and miserable. The magicians could not even try their tricks, because they were so sick that they could not stand up.

Again the Lord told Moses to warn the king to let God's people go to serve Him. If he would not let them go, God would send all His plagues, so that Pharaoh would know that there is no other God like Him in all the earth. But Pharaoh was a cruel man. Even though all his people were suffering, he would not give in.

God let Pharaoh be so stubborn so that all the people of the earth might see the power of the Lord, and worship Him. Moses told Pharaoh this. Then he said that if he should refuse to let the people go, God would send a terrible rain of hail the next day. He warned the king to send his cattle

and servants into barns, or they would be killed by the hail.

All the servants of Pharaoh heard this warning too. They were not as stubborn as Pharaoh. They began to think that the God of the Hebrews was a very great God, much more powerful than their idols of wood and stone, which could not do anything at all.

The news that the God of the Hebrews was going to send a storm of hail soon spread over all the land of Egypt. All the people who feared the Lord made their servants and animals run under shelter. Those who did not fear the Lord left their servants and animals out in the fields.

Then the Lord sent a most fearful storm. Peal after peal of terrific thunder sounded. Rain came down in torrents, with hailstones so big that if one struck a man or a beast, he was instantly killed. Lightning flashed across the sky, and great balls of fire ran along the ground. All the trees were broken in pieces with the terrible force of the storm.

There had never been such a storm in Egypt before. It did not stop in half an hour, or an hour, as our storms generally do. It kept on and on without stopping.

But in the land of Goshen, where the children of Israel were, there was no hail at all.

The Egyptians were almost dying with fear as they crouched in their houses, and even Pharaoh was terrified. This was far worse than flies or sick animals. This surely came from Almighty God.

At last even Pharaoh's hard heart gave in, and he sent for Moses and Aaron. He said, "I have sinned this time. The Lord is righteous, and I and my people are wicked. It is enough. Pray to the Lord that there be no more thundering and hail. Then I will let you go."

Moses said, "As soon as I have gone out of the city, I will pray unto the Lord, and the thunder and hail will stop, so that you may know that the earth is the Lord's. But I know that you and your servants will not yet fear the Lord enough to do His will."

When Pharaoh saw that the thunder and hail were over, he and his servants immediately sinned still more. They would not let the children of Israel go.

What do you think the people of Israel, in the land of Goshen, thought of these wonders? They had been in the heathen land of Egypt four hundred and thirty years. They had almost forgotten that they had a God who was much more powerful than the heathen idols. They began to rejoice when they saw how wonderful their own God was. They began to trust in Him, and to believe His promises.

Another reason why God did all these wonderful things was so that His own people might know that He is the great God of the whole earth, and that anyone may turn to Him and worship Him.

PHARAOH WILL NOT GIVE IN   The Lord commanded Moses, "Go and talk to Pharaoh." So Moses and Aaron went to the palace and spoke to Pharaoh boldly, saying that if he would not let the people go, the Lord would send a plague of locusts. The locusts would fill all the houses, and eat all the growing things in the fields. Moses did not wait for Pharaoh to answer him, but turned his back. With his head high in the air, he walked out of the palace.

Pharaoh's servants said to their master, "How long shall this man torment us? Let the people go. Do you not know that Egypt is utterly ruined already?" Pharaoh said, "Very well, then, call the man back." Some servants ran after Moses and Aaron and told them to come back, for Pharaoh would let the people go.

When they returned, Pharaoh said to Moses and Aaron, "You may go. But which of the people do you want to go?" Moses replied, "We will go with our young and our old, with our sons and with our daughters, with our flocks and with our herds, for we want to give a feast to the Lord." Pharaoh insisted, "No, indeed, all of you can't go! The men may go, if they want to, but the rest must stay here." He was too proud to talk with them any longer. He turned his back and told his servants to drive them out of the palace.

So the Lord said to Moses, "Stretch out your hand for locusts to come over the country." Moses stretched out his hand, and the Lord brought an east wind for a whole day and a night. In the morning the wind brought the locusts. The locusts covered the earth, so that the people could not see the ground. They ate every green thing that the hail had left, just as God had warned.

Pharaoh called for Moses and Aaron in haste. He was very humble this time. "I have sinned against the Lord and against you. Now I pray you to forgive my sin, only this once, and entreat the Lord to take away this death."

Moses prayed to the Lord. The Lord brought a strong west wind, which carried all the locusts into the Red Sea. But still Pharaoh would not let the children of Israel go.

Once more the Lord spoke to Moses: "Stretch out your hand toward heaven, and there will be darkness over the land of Egypt — darkness so black that it may be felt as well as seen." Moses stretched forth his hand. There came thick darkness over all the land of Egypt.

When it is a dark night, there is always a little light from the moon or the stars, so that we can see a little, after our eyes are used to the darkness. But this Egyptian darkness was without a single ray of light. No matter how long the people stared, they could not see anything at all. They stayed just where they had been when the darkness came upon them. They dared not move.

After three days Pharaoh could stand it no longer. He called Moses and said to him: "Go and serve the Lord. Take your little ones along, but leave your flocks and your herds here." But Moses answered, "You must let us take our flocks and herds, because we need them for sacrifices and burnt offerings. Our cattle must go with us too. Not one of them shall be left behind."

Then Pharaoh became very angry. He lost his temper and shouted, "Get out of here, and don't come back, for if you do, I will surely kill you."

Moses said, "You have spoken well. I will see your face again no more. And now, thus says the Lord, 'About midnight I will go out in the midst of Egypt. And all the first-born in the land of Egypt shall die, from the first-born of Pharaoh that sits on the throne even to the first-born of the maid-servant that pounds the grain in the mill, and all the first-born of the animals. And there shall be a great cry throughout all the land of Egypt. But against the children of Israel shall not a dog move his tongue: that you may know that the Lord puts a difference between the Egyptians and Israel.'

"And all your servants, Pharaoh, shall come to me, and bow down to me, and say, 'Get out of Egypt, together with all the people that follow you!' And after that I will leave." And Moses went out from Pharaoh in great anger.

Chapter 35
THE CHILDREN OF ISRAEL LEAVE EGYPT
EXODUS 12

GETTING READY Moses and Aaron had to hurry. A very busy time was before them. They had to get the children of Israel ready to leave Egypt in a very short time. It was a big job to move so many people. Everything had to be ready, for when the time came, the Egyptians would hurry them out without giving them any time to get ready.

Moses and Aaron said to the people, "Let every one of you ask his neighbors to give him gold and silver jewels and fine clothes." This was to pay for the long years the Israelites had worked as slaves without pay. God did not want His people to be poor. They were going into a strange land where they would need money to buy food and other things.

Moses and Aaron said to the people, "Every family must take a lamb, and kill it in the evening. Collect the blood in a basin, and sprinkle the

69

sides and the top of the door with the blood of the lamb. Not one of you must go out of your houses from evening till morning. For the Lord will pass through the land in the night to smite the Egyptians. When the Lord sees the blood around your door, He will pass by your house, and will not let the destroyer come in.

"After you have done this, you must roast the lamb and eat it. Dress yourselves all ready for a journey, for you are going to leave Egypt in a great hurry. Put on your shoes and your coat, and fasten your belt, and take your walking stick in your hand."

The people in that hot country did not wear shoes or coats in the house. They put them on only when traveling. They wore a long coat, and when they were going to walk, they tucked it up with their belt, so that they could walk more easily.

What a day that was for the children of Israel! Getting ready to leave Egypt! Packing the baby's clothes in a little bundle, so that one of the children could carry it on his back! Packing some of the household goods on a donkey! Getting another donkey ready for dear old Grandmother to ride on, with one or two folded blankets for a saddle so that she would be comfortable!

Each of the children had to carry something. We can imagine the scene: "Here, Reuben, you are the oldest — you can carry this big bundle. Let me strap it on your shoulder. That is the easiest way to carry it. Miriam, here are your clothes and baby's, in this bundle. I think this won't be too heavy for you. Little Rachel can carry this bundle. Come here, Rachel, and let me strap it to your shoulders, so you won't lose it."

Toward evening all the families killed a lamb. They let the blood drop into a basin. Then the father sprinkled the sides and the top of the door with the blood. After this the people quickly made a fire to roast the lamb. They must eat it before they left that night.

The children of Israel had had a very busy day, but now everything was ready. Even the dough for the bread had been made, though they had not yet had time to put in the yeast which would raise the bread and make it light. In the land of Goshen all was quiet that evening. The people waited for God.

At midnight God passed through the land of Egypt and smote the first-born of every Egyptian family, from the first-born of Pharaoh who sat on the throne to the first-born of the prisoner who lay in the dungeon.

Pharaoh rose up in the night, and so did all the Egyptians. A terrible shriek arose from the palace. The crown prince was dead! In fear and grief the wicked king looked at his dead son. Shriek after shriek rose from the terrified Egyptians.

But in the land of Goshen no one had died. The Lord had passed over all the houses sprinkled with blood. In each of these houses a little lamb had died instead of the first-born.

Pharaoh called for Moses and Aaron in the middle of the night. He could not wait till morning. He cried out, "Start right away, and get away from here. Take everything with you, and go! Take your people and your flocks and your herds, and be gone, as fast as you can! Don't stop for anything!"

The Egyptian people ran into the Israelite houses and shouted, "Get out of our land as fast as you can! Go, or we shall all be dead men! Hurry! Get out of our country!"

"But we have to bake our bread

first," objected the Israelites. "Otherwise we won't have anything to eat on the way."

"No, no, don't wait for that! Take your dough with you, and bake it on the way, after you are out of Egypt." So Mother had to tie a cloth over her bread pan, and take the unbaked dough with her.

The Israelites asked their neighbors, "Will you give us jewels of silver and gold, and nice clothes, if we leave?" And the Egyptians answered, "Yes, yes! Take anything you want, only get out!" The Egyptians brought out their most beautiful gold chains, and gold earrings, and gold bracelets, and all their silver jewelry, and all their finest clothes, and heaped them upon the Israelites.

"Here, take them all," they said. "Only hurry! Go just as fast as you can! Don't wait a minute! We won't feel safe till you are out of our country!"

GOOD-BYE TO SLAVERY It was a good thing the Israelites had made everything ready. Now it took only a short time for two million people to start. They were all dressed for the journey, with everything already packed.

And they had had a good supper. The little lamb had been killed so that, by its blood, it could save the first-born. But it was God's kind thought to tell the people to roast the lamb and eat it before they started on their long journey. Now none of them would go hungry. God takes care of us, not only in big things, but in little things too.

The Bible tells us to cast our cares upon God, for He cares for us. It was God who had commanded Moses to tell the people to get everything ready beforehand, so that they could start quickly. God was kindly taking care of them in every way.

Moses gave the order to form a procession and march. He called out, "Ready! March!" and the journey began. Was there ever such a procession as that? Two million people, each family walking in its place. Of course, not all of them were walking. The old people and the small children had to ride. Their flocks and herds were in the procession too. Their household goods were loaded on donkeys.

They started at Rameses in the land of Goshen. They marched on until they were out of Egypt. Then the procession stopped. They removed folded tents from the backs of the donkeys, and set them up. Each family gathered twigs for a little fire, and made some stones very hot in the fire. Then they brushed off the ashes. They made little flat cakes from the dough they had brought with them, and laid the cakes on the hot stones to bake. There was no yeast in the dough because they had had to leave Egypt so suddenly. The bread tasted more like crackers than the bread we are used to. But it tasted very good to the hungry Israelites who had been walking all day.

There was one important thing the Israelites had taken along with them. It was Moses who had thought about it. They had brought the bones of Joseph with them. Joseph had been dead for three hundred and fifty years, but his body had been embalmed by the Egyptians. Now it was to be taken back to Canaan, as he had made his children promise.

How long had the children of Israel been in Egypt? They had been there just four hundred and thirty years since Jacob had come to Egypt with his family of seventy persons. When they marched out of Egypt, four hundred and thirty years later, they were about two million strong.

God commanded Moses to tell the children of Israel something very important. "This night," Moses said, "must never be forgotten, for in it the Lord has brought us out of Egypt.

"Every year from now on, when this night comes around, we must celebrate it, in remembrance of the wonderful way the Lord brought us out of Egypt. We must kill a lamb, roast it, and eat it. For we and our children and their children must remember that when the Lord passed through the land of Egypt to kill the first-born in every house, He passed over the houses where He saw the blood on the doorpost. The lamb died instead of the first-born.

"We shall call this night the Passover Night, and every year we shall eat the lamb in the very same way we ate it this night — with our shoes on, and our sticks in our hands, just as if we are going on a journey in a hurry. We shall eat bread without yeast in it, to help us to remember this night when we did not have time to put yeast in our bread before we hurried out of Egypt.

"And when our grandchildren ask us, 'What does this Passover mean?' we shall say, 'It is the Lord's Passover, to make us remember the night He smote the Egyptians, but passed over our houses.' "

God commanded the children of Israel to keep the Passover for a whole week of every year. They were to eat bread without yeast that entire week. On the last day of the week, they were to kill the lamb and eat it. This would help the children of Israel to remember how God had rescued them from slavery in Egypt. And it would also remind them of the Saviour whom God had promised to send someday. For the lamb could not really pay for the sins of the people. No, the lamb was just a sign, pointing forward to Jesus, who would be the real Lamb of God, and who would die so that everyone who trusts in Him can be forgiven.

Chapter 36
THE END OF THE EGYPTIANS
EXODUS 13-15

How were the children of Israel, who had never been out of Egypt, going to find their way in the wild desert? God Himself led them through the wilderness. He went before them in a pillar of cloud. At night the pillar glowed like fire. This pillar traveled in front of them night and day, to lead them in their journey. When God wanted the people to go on, the pillar of cloud moved ahead. When God wanted them to stop, the pillar of cloud stopped.

God led the people to the Red Sea, and there they stopped and pitched their tents by the shore of the sea.

After the children of Israel had been gone from Egypt for a few days, Pharaoh began to be sorry that he had let them go. Who would work for him now? Who would finish building his treasure cities if he had no slaves?

Pharaoh called for his chariot, and

he gathered all the chariots of Egypt. There was a driver in each chariot, and a captain to shoot arrows. Then Pharaoh and his army started out after the children of Israel.

The Israelites had not gone far, for most of them were walking. There were many little children who could not walk fast. And they had to let their flocks and herds eat the grass as they went along. So Pharaoh and his chariots soon came in sight of the Israelites camped on the shore of the Red Sea.

When the children of Israel saw the Egyptian army coming after them, they were terrified. They cried to the Lord to save them. They complained to Moses, "Was it because there were no graves in Egypt that you have brought us here, to die in this wilderness?"

Moses tried to calm them. "Don't be afraid," he said. "God will take care of you. Just stand still, and see how wonderfully God will save you. The Lord will do all the fighting, and you will only have to watch. For this is the last time you will ever see these Egyptians."

Then God said, "Tell the children of Israel to move forward." The Israelites began to pack up their goods in a great hurry. But they did not see where they could march. The big sea was ahead of them. They could not go that way, surely. On either side of them were mountains. And when they looked back, they saw the Egyptians coming nearer and nearer. Their hearts sank with fear.

But they did not need to be afraid. The pillar of cloud that was in front of them lifted up and moved behind them, between them and the Egyptians. The cloud was so dark on their side that the Egyptians could not see the Israelites at all. But on the side of the Israelites the cloud was bright and shining. It gave light to the Israelites all night, and made it easy for them to see.

Then Moses stretched out his arm over the Red Sea, and the Lord sent a strong east wind which blew all night. It blew so hard that the water was moved back, and stood up like a wall on each side. And the bottom of the sea was dry.

Moses gave the order to march forward. Between the walls of water the Israelites marched all night, till they came safely to the other shore.

When the Egyptians discovered what the Israelites were doing, they followed them between the walls of water, driving their chariots right into the path of the sea. They thought that if the Israelites could get through safely, they could follow. They could see for themselves that the bottom was quite dry!

Very early in the morning the Lord looked at the army of the Egyptians through the pillar of fire and cloud. The Lord made trouble for the Egyptians. Their chariot wheels began to fall off in the soft sand, so that they could not go fast. They began to say to each other, "Let us escape from here, for God is fighting for the Israelites!"

Then the Lord said to Moses, "Stretch out your hand over the sea, so that the water may come back again." Moses stretched out his hand, and the waters tumbled back again over the path. The Egyptians saw the water coming. "Look! Look!" they cried. "The water is coming back! We shall all be drowned!" They turned their chariots in a hurry. They whipped their horses to make them go faster, yelling and screaming.

It was no use. The water came rolling over the heads of the Egyptians, and covered them from sight. Where the Egyptians had been before, there was only the rolling, tossing sea.

Soon the restless waves began to cast up the bodies of the drowned Egyptians. The Israelites stared at their dead enemies on the sand. These Egyptians had treated them so cruelly for many years, but they could never harm the Israelites again.

The Israelites saw how wonderful, how great their God was, who had brought them out of Egypt with such mighty miracles. "We are free! We are free!" they shouted to each other. "The Egyptians can never trouble us any more!"

Then Moses and the Israelites sang a beautiful song of praise to God for saving them from the Egyptians. They were so happy and light-hearted that they felt like dancing and singing. Miriam, Moses' sister, took a timbrel and began to dance and sing. All the women did the same. They shook their jingling timbrels, and sang:

> I will sing unto the Lord, for He hath triumphed gloriously;
> The horse and his rider hath He thrown into the sea.

Oh, what a happy people, singing and dancing to the Lord! They were safe now, after all those hard years of slavery!

Would they ever forget how God had cared for them? Would they ever again be afraid of trouble or danger? I am sorry to say that they were weak, trembling, doubting people. They were much better at forgetting than remembering. And so, perhaps, they were quite like you and me.

Chapter 37
ISRAEL IN THE WILDERNESS
EXODUS 15-17

A HEAVENLY FOOD   After this happy time the children of Israel began their journey toward the land of Canaan. They soon came to the sandy desert of Shur. There were enough plants here for their animals to eat, but there were no brooks or springs where the people could get water to drink. For three days they found no water. Everyone was becoming very thirsty.

At last they came to a place called Marah. Here, to their delight, was running water. The people hastily filled their cups and water bottles with the precious water. But when they tasted it, it was so bitter that they could not drink it.

Oh, what a disappointment! They began to find fault with Moses. How quickly they had forgotten God's wonderful care! They said to Moses, "What shall we drink?" Moses prayed to the Lord, and God showed him a tree he must throw into the water. Moses cut down the tree and threw it into the water. It made the water sweet, so that the children of Israel could drink all they wanted.

Soon the children of Israel came to a lovely little oasis in the desert. It was a beautiful spot, fresh and green and shady. There were seventy tall, graceful palm trees, and there was plenty of water from twelve springs. What a comfort this oasis was, after the hot, dry, sandy desert! The Israelites camped near the waters. They stayed for quite a while in this oasis of Elim and rested from their journey.

But they had to move on again. They folded up their tents, packed their belongings, and started into the desert once more.

They were in another wild, rough desert country. It was called the desert of Sin.

After they had been journeying for a month and a half, they began to find fault with Moses about their food. They said, "We wish we had stayed in Egypt, and had died there instead of coming out into this desert! We had all the bread we wanted to eat there, and here we shall probably die of hunger."

The Lord heard their complaints and told Moses that that night He would give them meat to eat, and in the morning He would send them bread from heaven.

Just then the children of Israel noticed that the cloud, which always was before their camp, was shining with a brilliant light. It was the glory of the Lord! God had come to let the people know that He had heard their murmurings.

Toward evening great flocks of quails flew over the camp. The people caught many of them, and cooked them for their supper.

The next morning the ground was covered with heavy dew that looked like frost. After the dew had passed away, the children of Israel saw small white things upon the ground. They all came out of their tents and looked at it: *Manhu?* they asked, which means, "What is it?" Since no one knew, they gave it this name, or *manna*.

It looked like seed. They scooped it up in their hands and found that it tasted good.

Moses said to them, "This is the bread which the Lord promised to send you. Gather it up, as much as you need for today. Don't keep any of it until tomorrow, for it will come every day."

They gathered up as much as they wanted for that day. The sun became hot and melted what was left.

In spite of Moses' command, some of them did keep a part of it until the morning. When they came to look at it, it was wormy and bad-smelling. Moses was angry with them for not obeying.

On the sixth day Moses said to the people, "Gather twice as much today. Prepare what you need to eat today, and lay up the rest for tomorrow. Tomorrow is the Sabbath, and manna will not come on the Sabbath day."

The children of Israel had been in the heathen land of Egypt, where there was no Sabbath day. In heathen countries the people do not keep a day of rest, but work every day of the week. God wanted to teach the Israelites to keep the Sabbath holy, and not to work on that day, and so He sent no manna on the Sabbath.

But some of the people again disobeyed Moses, and did not save any manna for the Sabbath. On that morning they went out as usual to gather manna. Of course, there was none at all on the ground. The Lord said to Moses, "Tell those people that they *must* obey Me." After that, the people rested on the Sabbath.

Moses said, "The Lord wants us to fill a pot full of manna and to keep it forever, so that our children's children may see the bread with which the Lord fed us on our journey through the wilderness." They gathered a pot full of manna. God kept it from spoiling, and the children of Israel saved it for hundreds of years.

This wonderful heavenly bread tasted like honey cookies. Manna was white and round, and it looked like seed. For forty years the Lord fed the Israelites with manna, until they finally came to the land of Canaan.

THE FIRST BATTLE The children of Israel moved from the wilderness of Sin and pitched their tents in the highlands of Rephidim. They were now in a very rocky country, with mountains all around them.

Again there was no water for the people to drink. Again they scolded Moses about it. "Why did you bring us up out of Egypt?" they asked. "We and our children and our cattle will die of thirst." By this time the children of Israel should have learned that the Lord would take care of them.

Moses cried to the Lord, "What shall I do to this people? They are almost ready to stone me." The Lord answered that he should go to one of the rocks of the mountain and strike it with his rod, and water would come out of it. Moses did so, and a stream of clear, cool water poured out of the rock. Now the people could drink their fill.

In these mountains of Rephidim there lived some people called Amalekites. Do you remember that Esau married two heathen wives? The Amalekites were descendants of one of these wives of Esau. All the time that the children of Israel had been living in Egypt, the Amalekites had been dwelling in this wild, mountainous country. They were a wandering people. When they saw the great host of Israelites coming through their land, they wanted to fight. They hid behind rocks and shot arrows at the last of the great host, at those who lagged behind because they were too tired or too weak to keep up with the rest.

Moses called a young man named Joshua, and told him to choose a number of soldiers to fight with the Amalekites. Then Moses took Aaron and Hur, who was probably Moses' brother-in-law, and went to the top of a hill to pray. When Moses held up his hands in prayer, the Israelites drove back the Amalekites; but when Moses dropped his hands, then the Amalekites were stronger than the Israelites. Moses tried to hold up his hands, but they became so tired that he could not keep them up, no matter how hard he tried. When Aaron and Hur saw that Moses could not keep his hands up all the time, they found a big stone for him to sit on. Aaron went on one side of him to hold up his right hand, and Hur stood on the other side to hold up his left hand.

Aaron and Hur held up Moses' hands until the sun went down and the Israelites had won the victory. They were not victorious because of the hands Moses held up. It was God who defeated their enemies. But the hands Moses raised in prayer taught the Israelites that God hears our prayers, and that when we pray to Him for help, He will fight our battles for us, and win victories you and I would never be strong enough or good enough to win.

Chapter 38

GOD TALKS FROM MOUNT SINAI
EXODUS 19, 20, 24

THE CAMP After the Israelites had been traveling for three months, with the pillar of cloud leading the way, they came to some very high and rugged mountains, called the mountains of Sinai. Here the pillar of fire stopped. The children of Israel pitched their camp in the wilderness at the bottom of the Sinai mountains.

There were six hundred thousand tents spread out in every direction, as far as you could see. Each tent had a little space around it, so that the people could make a little fire to boil or roast their manna. From their tents the people could always see the pillar of cloud by day or the pillar of fire at night.

They stayed here almost a whole year, for God wanted to teach them many things. This was a quiet place, far away from other people, where they could give their whole attention to what God wanted them to do. The people of Israel had been in the heathen land of Egypt for four hundred and thirty years. In all those years no word had come to them from God. They had no Bible, as we have, in which they could read about God. Many of them had forgotten the true God, and had begun to worship idols.

But now God was going to teach them His law, so that they would know how to live in a way that was pleasing to Him. Moses was to write this law in a book, so that it could be read at any time. Now you see why it was so important that Moses had been adopted by Pharaoh's daughter, and had learned all the wisdom and learning of the Egyp-

tians. If he had been brought up as a little slave boy, he would never have known how to write down God's law for us. God had planned all this long before.

God told Moses that in three days He would speak to the people right from heaven, and the children of Israel would hear Him with their own ears, so that they would always remember this, and believe in God.

First of all the people had to get ready to hear God's voice. Moses put a fence all around the mountain. Not one person, not even an animal, must touch the mountain, because God Himself was there. If anyone did, he would have to die. All the people had to wash their clothes. This was a sign that their hearts were wicked, and needed to be washed and forgiven before they could meet with a holy God.

Early on the morning of the third day Mount Sinai was covered with thick clouds. Terrible thunderings pealed through the sky, and great streaks of lightning flashed through the clouds. The whole mountain shook and trembled, and its top was covered with smoke and flames, for God Almighty had come down upon the mountain.

The mighty trumpet of God sounded through the sky. When the Israelites heard the trumpet, they came trembling to the foot of the mountain. Louder and louder the trumpet pealed forth, until the very heavens resounded.

Then God Himself spoke out of the thunder, and the lightning, and the blazing fire — spoke to the Israelites, and to us. God spoke all these words, saying:

THE TEN COMMANDMENTS   I am the Lord thy God, who brought thee out of the land of Egypt, out of the house of bondage.

I. Thou shalt have no other gods before Me.

II. Thou shalt not make unto thee any graven image, nor any likeness of anything that is in heaven above, or that is in the earth beneath, or that is in the water under the earth; thou shalt not bow down thyself to them, nor serve them: for I, the Lord thy God, am a jealous God, visiting the iniquity of the fathers upon the children, upon the third and upon the fourth generation of them that hate Me; and showing lovingkindness unto thousands of them that love Me and keep My commandments.

III. Thou shalt not take the name of the Lord thy God in vain; for the Lord will not hold him guiltless that taketh His name in vain.

IV. Remember the Sabbath day to keep it holy. Six days shalt thou labor and do all thy work; but the seventh day is a Sabbath unto the Lord thy God; in it thou shalt not do any work, thou, nor thy son, nor thy daughter, thy manservant, nor thy maidservant, nor thy cattle, nor thy stranger that is within thy gates. For in six days the Lord made heaven and earth, the sea, and all that in them is, and rested the seventh day; wherefore the Lord blessed the Sabbath day and hallowed it.

V. Honor thy father and thy mother, that thy days may be long in the land which the Lord thy God giveth thee.

VI. Thou shalt not kill.

VII. Thou shalt not commit adultery.

VIII. Thou shalt not steal.

IX. Thou shalt not bear false witness against thy neighbor.

X. Thou shalt not covet thy neighbor's house, nor his wife, nor his manservant, nor his maidservant, nor his ox, nor his ass, nor anything that is thy neighbor's.

These are the Ten Commandments, God's law for man.

Could the Israelites keep this law? They thought they could. They promised they would do everything God told them to do. But even if they tried hard, they could not really keep God's law. You remember that we said that after Adam and Eve sinned, all their children were born with sinful hearts. They could not do what was pleasing to God, no matter how hard they tried.

Why did God give them a law they could not keep? God gave them this law to show them how sinful they really were. He wanted them to understand that they could never by themselves live the kind of life God required. He wanted them to discover how desperately they needed the Saviour whom God had promised to send. They must be sorry for their sins, and pray to God to forgive them. They must put their trust not in their own good deeds, but only in the promised Saviour. Then God would forgive them, for the sake of Jesus. And God forgives us too, all of us who trust in our Saviour, Jesus, whenever we do wrong and are sorry for it.

GOD TALKS TO MOSES   The people saw the thunder and the lightning, and they trembled with fear. They pushed back from the mountain in terror. They said to Moses, "You speak to us, and we will listen. But do not let God speak to us, or we will die."

So while the terrified people stood at a distance, Moses went up the mountain into the thick clouds to talk to God. There the Lord spoke to Moses, telling him what to say to the children of Israel.

After God had finished giving Moses directions about what he should tell the people, Moses came down from the mountain. He told the people what God had said. And the people answered, "All that God has said we will do." (How little they understood about the sin in their own hearts! And afterward, how quickly they forgot what they had promised!)

Moses wrote down in a book all that the Lord had said to him on the mountain. After he had written it down, he read it to the people.

After that, the Lord called Moses again to come up on the mountain. Moses said to the leaders of the tribes, "You must wait for me, till I come back. I will leave Aaron and Hur with you. If you have any troubles to settle, you go to them."

So Moses left the children of Israel, and climbed up the mountain till the people could not see him any more. He went into the thick cloud where God was.

All the people could see the glory of the Lord resting on the top of Mount Sinai. It was a shining brightness, as if the whole top of the mountain was on fire. Moses stayed up there with God a long time. He was gone forty days and forty nights.

Chapter 39
THE GOLDEN CALF
EXODUS 32-34

ISRAEL WORSHIPS THE IDOL   God gave Moses very careful directions about how to build a place in which God could be worshiped. This was to be a tent, because the Israelites were traveling all the time. They could not take a building of wood or stone with them on their journey. They called the place a tabernacle, which is the word in their language for tent. Aaron was to be the minister, or high priest, of the tabernacle.

Then God gave Moses two tablets of stone on which God had written the Ten Commandments with His own finger.

Moses was up on the mountain for forty days and forty nights. He had nothing to eat in all that time, but God kept him alive.

What were the children of Israel doing all this time? They waited at the foot of the mountain for Moses to come down again. They waited and waited, but he did not come back. At last they thought something must have happened to him. Perhaps they would never see him again!

Instead of praying to God to keep Moses safe, they came to Aaron and said, "Make us gods to go before us, for as for this man Moses, who brought us out of the land of Egypt, we do not know what has become of him."

You would expect Aaron to say,

"What! Make you a heathen idol! No, indeed! That would be a great sin. Only a month ago God Himself spoke to you out of heaven, and told you not to make idols or to worship them. He will be very angry if you do this."

Was that what Aaron said? No, that was what he should have said. What he did say was, "Break off your golden earrings, and bring them to me."

The children of Israel were very fond of jewelry. They had a great deal of it, for on that last night in Egypt the Egyptians had given them many beautiful jewels, to hurry them out of Egypt. All the men and women, and even little boys and girls, wore beautiful rings, earrings, and bracelets.

The Israelites took off their golden earrings and brought them to Aaron. He melted them in the fire and made a calf of gold. Then he said to the Israelites, "This is your god, O Israel, who brought you out of the land of Egypt."

It was wrong for Aaron to make the golden calf. It was even worse to lie and say that the golden calf had brought the Israelites out of Egypt. But this was not all. Aaron went still further. He made an altar before the calf and said, "Tomorrow we will have a feast unto the Lord." Did Aaron suppose that the God of heaven and earth would share a feast with a golden calf?

The next day all the people got up early. They brought oxen and sheep, and killed them, sacrificing them on the altar before the golden calf. Then they had a big feast. They ate and drank, and sang and danced, and had a good time.

In those days all the world was filled with idolatry. People wanted to have a god that they could see. They made images according to their own ideas, and called them gods. But no one has ever seen God. God is a spirit. He is so great that no one can see Him and live. The children of Israel knew this, for God had warned them just a month ago in the Ten Commandments.

Moses did not see the golden calf and the feasting, because of the thick cloud that was on the mountain. But God saw what the children of Israel were doing, because God sees everything at all times. God saw that, instead of trusting the God who had rescued them from slavery, and brought them out of Egypt with so many wonders, the Israelites were worshiping a calf of gold.

God was very angry because the people did not trust Him even after all He had done for them. He said to Moses, "I will destroy them, and make a great nation out of you."

Moses prayed to God, "Oh, Lord, do not be so angry, I beg of You. If You destroy these people, the Egyptians will say You have brought them out of Egypt just to kill them in the mountains. They will say the God of the Hebrews is not powerful enough to bring these people to the land You promised them. Remember the promise that You made to Abraham and Isaac and Jacob, that their children should be as many as the stars of heaven, and that You would give them the land of Canaan. O Lord, do not punish these people, even though they have deserved to be punished!"

When Moses prayed to the Lord so earnestly to forgive the sinning people, God turned away His fierce anger.

A BITTER LESSON   Moses went down

the mountain. In his hand he carried the two tablets of stone. God Himself had made the tablets, and had written the Ten Commandments on them with His own finger. We shall never know what those tablets of stone looked like.

As Moses went down the mountain, he heard the noise of the people. He could hear them before he could see them. He stopped and listened for a moment.

What was all that noise he heard at the foot of the mountain? Were the people having a war? Was it the noise of fighting that he heard? It was not a battle. It sounded more like singing. When he came a little lower, he saw the people dancing, and he saw the golden calf.

Now he knew why God was so angry.

Moses became angry too. In his anger Moses forgot that he held in his hands the precious tablets of stone on which God had written the Ten Commandments. He threw the tablets down the mountain, and they crashed in pieces on the rocks below.

Just as soon as he came to the bottom of the mountain, he took the golden calf and broke it in pieces. Even that was not enough. He put the pieces in a mill and ground them into a fine powder. He threw the powder into some water, and made the people drink it. He ground up the pieces so fine that the Israelites could not find even a little piece to keep.

Then he turned to Aaron. "Whatever made you do such a thing?" he asked. "Were the people threatening to kill you if you did not make it? You have made them sin a great sin."

Aaron said, "Do not be so angry, Moses. You know how the people are determined to have their own way. They said to me, 'Make us gods to go

before us, for we do not know what has become of this Moses.' So I said to them, 'Whoever has any gold, give it to me.' They gave me their gold, and I threw it in the fire, and this calf came out."

Moses knew that some of the people had been leaders in this wicked thing, and that they were the ones who deserved punishment. He knew, too, that some of the people had not wanted to join in worshiping the idol.

He stood in the gate of the camp, and called out to the people, "Who is on the Lord's side? Those who did not want to do this, come and stand by me." The whole tribe of Levi came and stood by Moses.

Moses said to them, "Every man of you take his sword, and go through the camp, and kill all those people who persuaded Aaron to make this calf." So the Levites took their swords, ran among the Israelites, and killed those who had trusted in the idol instead of in God. Three thousand people died that day.

Then Moses said to the people, "You have all been guilty of a great sin. But I will go to the Lord, and see if I can persuade Him to forgive you."

Moses went back up the mountain. He said to God, "Oh, this people have sinned a great sin, and have made themselves gods of gold. If Thou wilt only forgive them —!"

Moses was so overcome by the thought of how terrible it would be if God would not forgive them that he could not say another word, and he stopped right there.

After a little while he went on, "But if not, then blot me out of the book which Thou hast written!" You see that even then Moses knew that God keeps a book, and that He writes down in that book the names of all who trust in Him.

God answered Moses, "I will blot out of My book those who have sinned against Me. Go, now, and lead this people to Canaan. My presence shall go with thee." Then Moses said, "If Thy presence go not with us, do not lead us there."

Now God told Moses to make two tablets of stone like the first ones, and to bring them up to the mountain, and God would write on them the same words that were on the first tablets Moses had broken. Again Moses stayed on the mountain alone with God for forty days and forty nights. There have been many other men to whom God has spoken. But there has never been anyone else who has been alone with God in this way for forty days and forty nights. But to Moses it happened twice!

When God had finished telling Moses all the things he needed to know to teach and lead His people, Moses came down again from the mountain. He brought with him the two tablets of stone which he had made and on which God had written the Ten Commandments.

Moses had been so long in God's presence that his face shone with a heavenly glory, though he himself did not realize it. His face was so bright that he looked like an angel. When Aaron and the children of Israel saw his face, they were afraid of him and did not dare to come near to him.

So Moses put a veil over his face while he told the people what God had said. Afterward, when he went to talk to God again, he took the veil off. And the Lord spoke to Moses face to face, as a man speaks to his friend.

Chapter 40
THE TABERNACLE
EXODUS 35-40

BUILDING GOD'S HOUSE The people had sinned a great sin, and they had put a golden calf in the place of the one true God, who had led them out of slavery in Egypt. But though the people had forgotten their promise to serve God, God did not forget His promise to be their God, and to lead them and care for them. Though all of us are faithless, God is always faithful, and His promises are forever sure.

God graciously forgave the people their sins, and in His great goodness He set the people to work to build a house where they could worship God, the God no man can see, as God wishes to be worshiped. Moses called the people together and said to them, "We are going to build a house for the Lord. God Himself has shown me how it must be built. We shall need fine cloth, and gold, and silver, and brass, and precious jewels, and oil, and sweet spices. Anyone who wishes to give a gift to God may bring it to me."

The people were delighted that they were going to have a place where they could worship God. They brought their treasures gladly. God appointed two men to do the finest work. They were Bezaleel and Aholiab. God gave these two men skill and wisdom to make beautiful things out of gold and wood and precious stones. For God always gives His children whatever they need to do the work to which He calls them.

Soon there was great activity in the camp. The women wove curtains for God's house. And the men cut and carved wood, melted metal, and fitted the different pieces together. After the parts of the house itself had been made, the people made the furniture to go in the house; and then they made the clothes for the priests to wear.

God had appointed Aaron to be the high priest. And after he died, his sons would be priests, and their sons after them. Bezaleel and Aholiab made a beautiful long blue robe for Aaron, and they sewed little golden bells around the bottom, which tinkled when Aaron walked. Over the robe there was a sort of tunic, called an ephod, woven of blue and purple and scarlet and golden threads. From Aaron's neck there hung a square breastplate, with twelve precious stones set in it, each stone engraved with the name of one of the tribes of Israel. And on his head Aaron wore a golden crown with the words *Holiness to the Lord* engraved on it. Of course these beautiful clothes were not for everyday common use. They were only to be worn when Aaron served God in His house.

At last everything was ready, and the people set the tabernacle up.

WORSHIPING IN A TENT You remember that I told you that this house of God had to be in a tent, because the people were traveling, and needed a place of worship which they could take down and carry with them when they moved. What was it like to worship in a tent?

The worshipers themselves did not ever go into that part of the tabernacle that was the house of God. They stood outside in a large courtyard. There was a high fence around the courtyard, and linen curtains hung on the fence, so that the people were not distracted by the sights and sounds of the camp outside. God's sky itself was the roof, and there were no pews or benches. They did not sit down; they stood up instead.

There was a large brass basin in the courtyard, where Aaron and his sons could wash themselves before they went into the house of God. This was to remind them that they were sinful, and needed to be washed of their sins before they came near to God. You can never guess how this basin was made. It was made of the mirrors of the Israelite women. In those days they did not have glass mirrors, but they used mirrors of fine polished brass. The women were proud to give their mirrors to be used in the house of God. There was a large altar in the courtyard too, where sacrifices were offered.

The tabernacle itself, which was God's house, stood at one end of the large courtyard. The wooden supports, or tent poles, as we would call them, were all covered with gold. The cloth of the tent itself was fine linen, blue and purple and red, embroidered all over with the figures of cherubim. Cherubim are great winged angels whose task it was to guard the holy place. The cloth was hung on golden pins, and over it, to keep out the rain, was another cover of goatskins, the same material of which the tents of the people were made. Only the priests were allowed to go into the tent.

The tent itself was divided into two rooms, with a curtain, or veil, as it is sometimes called, hanging down to separate them. In the outer room, the Holy Place, there stood a seven-branched golden candlestick, which burned both day and night, to show that the worship of God never stopped. Opposite the candlestick was a golden table, and on it twelve loaves of fine bread, one for each of the twelve tribes of Israel, as a sign that it is God who provides us with our daily food, and that we depend on His goodness for all our needs. These twelve loaves of bread, which were changed every Sabbath, were called the showbread. In the center of this room there was a golden altar where incense was burned. The sweet smell of the incense stood for the prayers of God's people.

The inside room was called the Holy of Holies because it was here that God Himself dwelt. Here was the ark, a box made of wood and covered both inside and out with gold. Inside the ark were kept the stone tablets on which God Himself had written the Ten Commandments. The cover of the ark was the most important thing in the whole tabernacle. It was made of pure gold, and on it were two golden cherubim, facing each other, their wings stretched out to cover the center of the lid. This center was called the Mercy Seat, the place where God met with His people. The Mercy Seat was a good name for it, for it is only because of the mercy of God that it is possible for sinful people like you and me to meet a holy God. God showed His presence in His house by a glorious and dazzling light just above the Mercy Seat.

There were golden rings at the corners of the ark, and golden poles through the rings, so that it could be carried. When the Israelites moved from place to place, Aaron and his sons took down the veil and covered the ark with it. Then the ark, and the golden table, and the golden candlestick, and the altar of incense were carried on the shoulders of the Levites. For the Levites had been appointed by God to help the priests take care of the tabernacle. The curtains, and the poles, and all the other parts of the tabernacle were moved in wagons.

THE TABERNACLE IS DEDICATED After all these beautiful things had been set up, Moses took some holy oil and sprinkled a little upon each piece of furniture, to show that these things were holy, and were not to be used for anything else except the worship of God. Next Moses sprinkled the oil on Aaron and his sons, to show that they had been set apart forever as God's priests.

Last of all Moses put the show-bread on the golden table, lighted the seven lamps of the golden candlestick, and burned sweet-smelling incense on the altar of incense. When he had done all these things, a cloud covered the tabernacle, and a glorious light filled the Holy of Holies. The glory of God shone forth between the golden cherubim over the Mercy Seat.

From this time on the glory of the Lord always shone between the cherubim in the Holy of Holies, showing the people that God was right there among them. And the pillar of cloud now rested above the tabernacle.

Now that the tabernacle was set up, God did not call Moses to come up on Mount Sinai when He wished to speak to him. He talked to Moses from the tabernacle, and told him what He wanted the children of Israel to do.

When God wanted the Israelites to move on to some other place, the pillar of cloud lifted up from the tabernacle and moved in front of the people, leading them wherever God wanted them to go. As long as the pillar of cloud stayed on the tabernacle, the children of Israel rested, whether it was a day or a month or a year. When the cloud was lifted up, they traveled, knowing that God was leading them.

THE SACRIFICES Because all people constantly sin against God, Aaron, the high priest, offered sacrifices every morning and evening on the large brass altar in the courtyard of the tabernacle. A lamb was killed every morning and every evening. Its blood was poured out, and its body burned on the altar.

Nowadays we do not sacrifice animals to take away our sins. For we know that Jesus has come into the world, and that He has died on the cross to take away our sins. Jesus Himself was the great sacrifice. But Moses and the children of Israel lived long before the time of Jesus. They did not yet know about Him as we do. So God commanded that animals should be sacrificed, to teach the people that sin had to be paid for, and to point the people to the great Sin-Bearer, our Saviour Jesus, whom God had promised to send into the world.

When a man knew that he had sinned, and that he was guilty before God, he brought an animal — a bullock, or a sheep, or a goat. He put his hands on the head of the animal to show that he was putting his sins on it. Then Aaron and the priests killed the animal, and burned it on the altar. Thus an innocent animal, which had never done anything wrong, was killed instead of a sinful man. And God forgave the man's sin.

God did not forgive the man's sin *because* the animal had been killed — for no animal can ever pay for a man's sins. God forgave the man because Jesus was going to die for his sins. The animal was only a sign pointing to our Saviour, who would one day die Himself to pay for the sins of the world. God forgave the man's sin because He was going to send His own Son to pay the price of sin which you and I could never pay.

There were many other kinds of sacrifices. When the people wanted to thank God for something God had done for them, or when they wanted to ask His blessing, they brought gifts which were called peace offerings.

THE DAY OF ATONEMENT Once a year the Jews were to have a solemn fast day, called the Day of Atonement. On this day the children of Israel were not to work, but to rest, just as they did on the Sabbath. They were to spend the whole day thinking about their sins and being sorry for them. On this day they did not eat anything at all. Why not? It was to show that they were truly sorry for their sins; so sorry, so sick at

PART III
Laws

heart, so discouraged about their sinning and sinning and sinning again, that they could not even stand it to eat. Have you perhaps ever been so excited, or so afraid, or so unhappy, that you could not stand even the sight of food? The fasting on the Day of Atonement expressed the grief in the hearts of the Israelites, and it also helped them really to feel grieved. They saw with their eyes — or perhaps I should say they felt in their empty stomachs — how grieved they ought to be.

And then all the people assembled in the courtyard of the tabernacle. They brought with them two goats. The priests took off the beautifully embroidered clothes they usually wore in the tabernacle — as if they, too, were too grieved about their sins to wear their best clothes — and put on a plain white robe. Aaron took a little shovel filled with red-hot coals. Then he poured incense on the coals, and with this shovel in his hand he lifted the curtain or veil, and went into the Holy of Holies, where God was. The cloud of smoke of the incense rising from the burning coals covered the Mercy Seat, so that Aaron was not blinded by the sight of God's glory.

After this, Aaron sacrificed one of the two goats. He took the blood of this goat, and went again into the Holy of Holies where he sprinkled the blood on the Mercy Seat itself. This was the only time in the whole year that anyone was allowed to enter this holiest part of the tent; and the high priest was the only one who might go in, and he could go in only if he brought with him the blood of the sacrifice. By this, God taught His people that they were sinners, that a holy God cannot associate with sinners, that sin must be paid for, and that nothing less than blood, *life itself,* will pay this debt.

Then Aaron took the second goat, the live goat. He laid his hands on this goat, and, as he stood there in front of God's people, with his hands on the goat's head, he confessed all the sins which the people had committed in the past year, everything displeasing to God which Aaron himself or anyone else among the Israelites had done. Then a servant drove the goat away, out into the wilderness, and the goat took the sins of God's people away with it. This was a sign that God had forgiven the sins of the people forever.

After all this was over, Aaron took off his white robe, and left it in the Holy Place till the next year when the Day of Atonement came around again.

Chapter 42
ISRAEL'S FEASTS
LEVITICUS 23; NUMBERS 9

It was now a year since the Israelites had left Egypt. A whole year had passed since that dreadful night when God passed through the land of Egypt, and there was a dead child in every house which did not have blood on the door. Even the little children could remember that dreadful night.

God said to Moses, "Tell the children of Israel to keep the Passover." And so, in each tent, they killed a lamb, and ate it in a hurry, dressed as if ready for a journey, as they had that terrible night in Egypt. After that they ate bread without any yeast in it for a whole week, so that they would remember how they had been forced to leave Egypt in a hurry.

God appointed two other great feasts for the Israelites to celebrate every year. Fifty days after Passover they celebrated the Feast of Weeks. This was a harvest feast, something like our Thanksgiving Day, in which the people thanked God for the blessings He had given them.

Later in the year they celebrated the Feast of Tabernacles. Do you remember that I told you that tabernacle is the Hebrew word for *tent*?

In this feast the people cut down palm branches and made little booths from them. They lived in these booths for a whole week. This reminded them of the years they had lived in tents while they traveled from Egypt to the promised land. How the children loved this Feast of Tabernacles! What fun to live in a green tent for a week — to sleep there too, with only a few leaves between them and the stars! And to see on all sides of them other green tents where their little friends were sleeping! They kept the first day and the last day of this feast holy, so that all the people could meet together to praise the Lord.

Chapter 43
THE YEAR OF JUBILEE
LEVITICUS 25

God commanded that, after the people would be settled in Canaan, they should plow their land, and sow their seed, and reap their harvests for six years. The seventh year they should not plow or sow seed or gather harvests. They should let the land lie idle, so that it could have a rest. If they obeyed Him, God promised He would send them such a bountiful harvest in the sixth year that it would be enough for three years.

God appointed one year in every fifty to be a very special year, the Year of Jubilee. In this year, too, they should plant no crops; but the Year of Jubilee was more than a year of rest. It was a year of freedom. I shall explain.

When the children of Israel came into the land of Canaan, God gave each tribe a part of the land. And each tribe must divide its part into smaller pieces, a share for each family. That part was to be theirs forever. If a family became so poor that they had to sell their land, then, when the Year of Jubilee came around, the man who had bought it had to give it back. It must go back to the family that had first owned it, for God had given it to that family.

If any man should become so poor that he had to work for another man, the rich man could not make a slave of him. He had to treat him kindly, and he could not make him work for nothing. And when the Year of Jubilee came around, the poor man must be allowed to go free.

The Year of Jubilee was a great blessing to poor people. It came only once in fifty years, but the poor people looked forward to it. When fifty years had gone by, they listened for the sound of the trumpet. The trumpet resounded in the quiet air to proclaim liberty throughout all the land of Israel, and to all the people living in it.

Chapter 44
THE ISRAELITES CONTINUE THEIR JOURNEY
NUMBERS 10

It was now more than a year since the children of Israel had come out of Egypt. All this time they had been in the wilderness of Sinai. They had been very busy. God had given them His law to tell them how to live. And they had built the tabernacle where God could be worshiped.

One morning the Israelites saw that the pillar of cloud had moved from its place over the tabernacle. Oh, how excited the children were! "Look! Look!" they shouted. "The cloud has moved. We are going to travel again!"

Aaron and his two sons covered the ark and the holy furniture in the tabernacle, so that the Levites could carry it. Some of the Levites took down the curtains of the tabernacle, and others took down the tent poles and the silver sockets. They piled these all very carefully in wagons.

Meanwhile the people were packing their clothes and taking down their tents. "Come here, Daniel," said one of the fathers, "you must lead this calf. I will tie a rope around his neck. Jacob, you are big and strong. You must carry this little lamb. It is too small to walk."

At last all was ready. The children were dressed carefully, their sandals strapped tight to their feet. Everything was packed so that it would be easy to carry. The people were eagerly waiting for the blast of the trumpet, which was the signal to start.

Finally it came. Long and loud the trumpets sounded. Not a silvery, sweet tone like the one they heard on Sabbath days, but a loud alarm, a call to march.

The tribes always camped in regular order, with the tabernacle in the center. They were to march in the same way. Each tribe had a captain over it, and a flag of its own. How proud the young man was who was chosen to carry the flag at the head of his tribe!

The Levites who carried the ark and the holy furniture of the tabernacle on their shoulders marched in the center of the great procession. When the ark began to move, Moses said, "Rise up, O Lord, and let Thine enemies be scattered; and let them that hate Thee flee before Thee." In front of them went the pillar of cloud that changed into a pillar of fire at night.

The children of Israel marched for three days, stopping only to sleep at night. After three days the pillar of cloud stood still. Then they knew that God wanted them to stay there. The Levites stopped the wagons and set up the tabernacle. And Moses said, "Return, O Lord, unto the ten thousands of the thousands of Israel."

Chapter 45

THE GRUMBLING ISRAELITES
NUMBERS 11, 12

God kept sending the delicious manna every morning for the Israelites to eat. But instead of being thankful, they complained, saying, "We are tired of this manna. We have nothing to eat except manna all the day long. We want some meat. We want some fresh vegetables too. We remember the fish we ate in Egypt, and the cucumbers and the melons and the onions and the leeks and the garlic. Now we have nothing at all except this manna, and we are tired of it!"

Throughout the camp the people were feeling sorry for themselves. They were so discontented that they could not stand it to live on manna for the few weeks they were traveling, even though they knew they would soon come to a land where they could get all kinds of delicious things to eat. They stood in the doors of their tents with the tears rolling down their cheeks. No matter where Moses walked among the tents, he heard nothing but complaining.

Moses was not happy either. He was discouraged. He had had so much trouble with the people. They complained so much. They never seemed to be thankful for the blessings God sent. Moses began to feel it was too hard for him to have to manage all these people. They were forever finding fault. Now they said, "Give us meat. We are tired of this manna." Where could he get meat for so many people?

Moses was not the only one who was weary of the grumbling. God heard the discontented murmurs and saw the rebellious tears too. He was going to help Moses. He told him to pick out seventy of the best men among the children of Israel, and bring them to the door of the tabernacle. God would put some of the spirit that was in Moses upon these men, so that they might help Moses govern the people.

To the grumblers God would send so much meat that they would become sick of it, enough to last for a month. Moses was so astonished that he could hardly believe God. The Israelites numbered six hundred thousand men, without the women and children. Where could so much meat come from? Must they kill all their sheep and cattle? The Lord answered Moses, "Is My hand too short to do this? Now you shall see whether what I have said will happen or not."

Moses chose the seventy men, as God had commanded. God put in them some of the same spirit that was in Moses, so that they could help him rule. Moses ordered the seventy men to judge justly, and not to favor the rich above the poor.

Then the Lord sent a wind which brought quails from the sea. They came in such numbers that all the ground around the camp was covered with them. They flew so low that even the children could catch them.

The people stopped their work. All day and all night, and all the next day, they did nothing but catch quails. The birds were piled high around their tents. To keep them from spoiling, they spread the quails out on the sand. The air was so dry and the blazing sun so hot that the quails dried out like dried beef.

You could never guess how many quails they caught. The Bible says that even those who had caught the least had ten homers, or about sixty bushels. Sixty bushels of quails would last a family longer than four months, for no family could eat more than half a bushel a day. How wonderfully God had provided!

But God was angry that these people refused to learn to trust in His loving care. To teach them that they must believe His promises, God sent sickness to many of those who had rebelled, and some of the people died. For those who refuse to learn from God's kindness will have to learn in harder ways.

It would seem as if Moses had enough trouble with the rebellious Israelites, without having trouble in his own family besides. But his sister Miriam and his brother Aaron were jealous of him, because God had made Moses the leader of the people. Moses was a very meek man. He did not become angry. He did not say a word to Miriam and Aaron in protest.

But God was angry. He spoke suddenly to Moses and Aaron and Miriam, saying, "Come out, the three of you, to the tabernacle." Then God came down in the pillar of cloud, and stood in the door of the tabernacle. Moses and Aaron and Miriam could not see Him, but they could hear Him speak.

"If there is a prophet among you," God said, "I will speak to him in a vision, or in a dream. But to My faithful servant Moses I will speak mouth to mouth, openly, not in dreams, and he shall see My form. Why were you not afraid to speak against My servant Moses?"

When the pillar of cloud moved away from the tabernacle, Aaron was shocked to see that Miriam was as white as snow. She had the dreadful disease of leprosy. Aaron said to Moses, "We have been foolish, and have sinned. But, I pray you, do not lay this sin upon us. Do not let Miriam be as one who is dead, whose body is half wasted away."

Moses prayed to God, and said, "Heal her, O God, I beg You." God answered, "Let her be shut up outside the camp for seven days, and then she may be brought back again." So Miriam was shut up outside the camp for seven days. The Israelites waited for her, not traveling till she was well again and could go with them.

Chapter 46
SPIES SEARCH OUT THE LAND
NUMBERS 13, 14

THE SPIES SENT OUT After a while the pillar of cloud lifted again from the tabernacle, and the children of Israel continued their journey till they came to the wilderness of Zin. Here they were on the very border of Canaan, the promised land.

Now that the Israelites were so near to their new home, God commanded Moses to send out spies to discover who lived in the land, and how to go about taking it. Moses chose twelve men to be spies, one from each of the tribes.

"Go and spy out the land," Moses told them. "Find out whether the people that live there are strong or weak; whether there are few of them, or many; whether they live in the country, or in cities with strong stone walls. See whether the land is fruitful, whether there are forests, and bring us back some of the fruits of the land."

So the spies set out. They traveled from the south of the country all the way to the north and back again. As they came back, they cut down a bunch of grapes to show the children of Israel. The bunch was so big it took two men to carry it, hanging from a wooden pole. They also brought back some other fruits with them, figs and pomegranates. After forty days they arrived back in the camp.

When the people heard that the spies had come back, they crowded around to hear their report. "The land is a beautiful country," the spies said. "It is very fruitful, truly flowing with milk and honey. These grapes that we brought back will give you some idea of the fruits of Canaan.

"It is a lovely land, but — *we will never be able to conquer it!* The people who live there are very strong. They have cities which are fortified with high stone walls, and there are even giants. They are so big that when we saw them we felt like grasshoppers beside them."

When the people heard this, they lifted up their voices and wept bitter tears. "We wish that we had died in Egypt, or here in this desert," they said. "Why did God bring us so far only to be killed? Our women and our children will all be sold as slaves. Come, let us turn around, and go back to Egypt."

The Israelites were forgetting the most important thing of all. They were forgetting the promises of God.

Two of the spies, Joshua and Caleb, did not agree with this report. They were shocked that the people did not trust in God after He had brought them all this way, and had performed so many wonders for them.

"If God is with us, we do not have to be afraid," they told the Israelites. "He will bring us into Canaan, and will defend us against the people of the land."

But the Israelites refused to listen. They took up stones to throw at Caleb and Joshua.

THE ISRAELITES SENT BACK TO THE DESERT God heard the children of Israel crying in their tents, "We wish that we had died in Egypt, or in this wilderness!" He saw them pick up stones to throw at Joshua and Caleb. He was angry with these people who refused to learn to believe in Him. All at once God's glory shone forth from the tabernacle.

All the Israelites saw it. This was not the pillar of fire they saw every night. It was the presence of God shining forth in His terrible anger.

"How long will it be," God said, "before these people learn to trust Me? After all the wonders I have done among them, they still do not believe. They shall no longer be My people! Moses, I will make a nation out of your children instead."

Moses pleaded with God, as he had done before when the Israelites made the golden calf: "Then the

Egyptians will say, 'It was because the Lord was not able to bring the people into the land which He promised; that is why He killed them in the wilderness.' Forgive, I pray Thee, the sin of this people, according to the greatness of Thy mercy, as Thou hast spoken, saying, 'The Lord is longsuffering, and of great mercy, forgiving sin.'"

"I will forgive them," God said, "but not one of these people who have seen all My wonders and still do not trust Me, not one of them shall ever see the country I promised to their fathers. Instead they shall wander in the wilderness for forty years. They wished they had died in this wilder-

ness. I will give them their wish. They shall all die here. Only their little children, who they said would be slaves, only these little children shall ever see the land I promised to them. But Joshua and Caleb, who trusted in Me, they shall enter Canaan."

So the Israelites had to turn their back on the beautiful promised land that they had come so far to see. They had to wander forty years in the wilderness. They were not able to enter in because they did not trust in God. Only Caleb and Joshua and the little children ever saw the country that flowed with milk and honey.

Chapter 47
THREE MIRACLES
NUMBERS 16, 17, 20

THE MUTINY Their monotonous food was not the only thing the Israelites complained about. They complained about their leaders, Moses and Aaron, too. "They are no better than we are!" they said. "Why should they put on such airs? After all, all of us are God's people. We are all holy, aren't we?"

They were right about this, of course. All God's people are holy. But a person who belongs to God, who is one of "God's people," does not demand that he get his rights. If you are really God's child, you have given yourself completely to Him in trust. You trust Him for your daily needs, and you are willing to serve wherever He places you.

The Israelites were quite content to accept God's blessings, but they were

not yet ready to yield their lives to God, and to let Him choose where He wanted each one of them to serve.

Three men, Korah, Dathan, and Abiram, got together and decided not to obey Moses any longer. They gathered together two hundred and fifty men, and started a rebellion against Moses and Aaron. They had forgotten how often Moses had saved their lives. They had forgotten how twice before Moses had pleaded with God to have mercy on His sinning people and God had listened to his prayer.

"Tomorrow," Moses said to the rebels, "the Lord will show who are His, and who is holy. Let each one of the two hundred and fifty of you bring a censer tomorrow, with coals burning in it, and incense on the coals. Aaron also will bring a censer with burning coals and incense. Then God will choose which one of you He wishes to stand before all the people as His priest."

The next day Korah and his two hundred and fifty followers came with their censers to the entrance of the tabernacle. All the people of Israel came too. Suddenly the brilliant, dazzling glory of the Lord appeared above the tabernacle. God said to Moses and Aaron, "Separate yourselves from these people, that I may consume them in a moment." Moses and Aaron fell on their faces before the Lord. "O God," they prayed, "the God of all men, shall one man sin, and will You be angry with the whole congregation?" God answered, "Tell all the people to get away from the tents of Korah, Dathan, and Abiram."

Moses said to the people, "Depart, I pray you, from the tents of these wicked men. Touch nothing of theirs, or you may also be consumed in their sins." And then he added, "If these men die the common death of all men, then the Lord has not sent me to do all these works. But if the Lord makes a new thing, and the earth opens its mouth and swallows them, then you will understand that these men have provoked the Lord."

Just at that moment the earth opened with a great crack right where the rebels stood. Korah and the others went down into the crack, with their tents and everything that they had. The earth closed over them again, and they were gone. The terror-stricken people rushed away from that awful spot, for they were afraid the earth would swallow them up too.

This dreadful judgment of God did not fall on these men because they had spoken against Moses and Aaron. For it was not Moses who was leading the children of Israel. It was God. Moses was only a servant of God. Korah, Dathan, and Abiram had seen God's wonderful works. They had seen how God had rescued His people from cruel slavery in Egypt, how He had dried up the Red Sea so that they could pass through, how He had spoken to them right out of heaven on Mount Sinai, how He had fed them day by day with heavenly manna. And still they had not learned to trust God, to love Him, and to obey Him. God is just. He took away from among His people those who in their hearts hated God and who openly rebelled against Him.

Korah's children did not die with their sinful father. Later their descendants served in the temple, and some of our psalms are dedicated to them. Perhaps the psalmist was thinking of this terrible judgment of God when he wrote Psalm 85:

Turn us, O God of our salvation, and cause Thine anger toward us to cease.

Wilt Thou be angry with us forever? Wilt Thou draw out Thine anger to all generations?

Show us Thy mercy, O Lord, and grant us Thy salvation.

I will hear what the Lord will speak: for He will speak peace unto His people, and to His saints. But let them not turn again to folly.

GOD CHOOSES A PRIEST Because the children of Israel had grumbled so much against Moses and Aaron, God said that He would show them plainly whom He wanted to be His priest. God actually stooped down from heaven to show this to His people in a sign which even their dull eyes could see.

"Tell the children of Israel," God said to Moses, "to bring their rods, one rod for the prince of each of the twelve tribes. Write the name of the owner on each rod. Since Aaron is the prince of the tribe of Levi, put his name on the rod of Levi. Put all the rods in the tabernacle, in front of the golden ark where I meet with My people. And I will show these people whom I have chosen to serve as priest in My house."

Moses collected twelve rods, one for each of the princes of the twelve tribes of Israel. He laid them all in the Holy Place in front of the ark where God dwelt among His people.

The next morning all Israel assembled outside the tabernacle to hear whom God had chosen as priest. Moses went into the tent and brought out the rods. Eleven of the rods were exactly as they had been the evening before, dead, and dry, and lifeless. But the rod with Aaron's name on it had come alive. Though it was months, perhaps even years, since it had felt the life-giving sap of the tree from which it had been cut, this morning, by the almighty power of God, Aaron's rod had leaves on it, and almond flowers, and even ripe nuts. The other princes took up their rods again. Without a word they turned away and went back to their tents.

Then God said to Moses, "Put Aaron's flowering rod in the ark, so that children not yet born may see and know that I, God, am the one who chooses every man's work and every man's place. For unless they learn to trust their lives to My direction, they will surely die."

The Israelites wandered about in the desert until they came again to the desert of Zin. Here Miriam, the sister of Moses, died and was buried.

In this dry desert there was no water for the people to drink. Again they grumbled against Moses and Aaron. "Why did you bring us to this evil place?" they said. "There are no figs here, or grapes, or pomegranates, neither is there any water for us and our animals to drink."

Moses and Aaron went to the door of the tabernacle, and they fell on their faces. Suddenly the glory of the Lord appeared to them, and God said, "Gather the people together. Take your rod, and speak to the rock, and it will give forth water."

But Moses was angry. He was quite out of patience with this headstrong, complaining people. He lifted his rod and struck the rock violently, instead of speaking to it as God had commanded. He struck it twice. "Hear now, you rebels," he said in his anger, "shall I and my brother Aaron bring water out of this rock for you?"

A great stream of water burst out of the rock, enough for all the people and all their animals. But God was not pleased with what Moses had done. In his anger Moses had forgotten that he was the leader. He had forgotten that it was his task to show the people God's power, never his own power; to teach them to trust, not to set them an example of distrust and disobedience.

"Because you did not believe in Me," God said to Moses and Aaron, "you shall not lead this people into the land that I have given them." It was a bitter disappointment to Moses. After leading the people all those years through the dreary desert, he himself would not be allowed to enter the land of promise.

Chapter 48

THE DEATH OF AARON
NUMBERS 20

The children of Israel were now wandering in the desert of Zin. The people walked from one place to another, as far as the Red Sea, and back again to the mountains of Seir.

How tired and discouraged they became! How often they wished that they had trusted God when the spies brought back their report about the giants living in the land of Canaan! God had conquered all their enemies so far, and they should have believed that He would also help them to overcome the giants.

But it was useless now for them to wish that they had trusted God. They must go on wandering in this hot desert until they died. Not one of them would ever see the beautiful land of promise, except Joshua and Caleb.

But though they had forsaken God, He did not forsake them. He took wonderful care of them. Every day God sent them fresh manna to eat. They could eat it raw, or fry it, or boil it, or make cakes out of it and bake it. It was delicious any way they ate it.

How did they get new clothes when they needed them in that lonesome desert? Where could they buy new shoes when their old ones wore out? God provided for this too. For all those forty years their clothes and shoes never wore out, nor did their feet swell from walking so much on the hot sand.

One by one the old people died. The children grew up. God was leading them nearer and nearer to the promised land now. They had been in the desert for almost forty years.

This time they did not take the nearest way, by the south. They went around to the eastern side, and then they went north. So they came to the land of Edom.

Moses sent messengers to the king. They asked for permission to go through his country, promising not to harm the land or the people living there. But the king of Edom was afraid of this great crowd of Israelites. He did not trust them to keep their promise, and refused to let them go through his country.

God would not allow the Israelites to fight the Edomites because the Edomites were also children of Abraham, descended from Esau. God had given this country to them. So the Israelites did not pass through the country of Edom, but made a long journey around it.

At last they came to Mount Hor, on the eastern border of Moab. Aaron, the high priest, was now a very old man. God told Moses that this was the place where Aaron was to die.

"Take Aaron, and his son Eleazar," God said to Moses, "and bring them up into the mountain. And put Aaron's garments on Eleazar his son; for Aaron shall die on the mountain."

All the people saw them starting off. After they had said good-bye, they stood and watched their priest go up to die. They knew that he would never come back to them again.

While they watched him, tears rolled down their cheeks. Never again would they see his dear face, and his hands raised in blessing the tribes of Israel. Never again would they hear his sweet old voice saying,

8: THE WORSHIP OF THE GOLDEN CALF

9: CROSSING THE JORDAN

The Lord bless thee and keep thee.
The Lord make His face to shine
upon thee.
The Lord lift up His countenance
upon thee, and give thee peace.
At last the three men were out of sight, on the top of the mountain. Moses took off Aaron's beautiful high-priestly robes and put them on Eleazar. Moses and Eleazar tenderly kissed Aaron. And Aaron folded his hands; his eyes closed, and his soul went to live with God. Now Eleazar was the high priest.

The children of Israel mourned a whole month for Aaron.

Chapter 49
THE BRASS SNAKE
NUMBERS 21

Once more the people continued their journey. They were still traveling through the wilderness. Sad to say, they again complained, against God and against Moses.

"Why did you bring us out of Egypt to die in this wilderness?" they grumbled. "We have no bread to eat or water to drink here, and we loathe this light manna." Each man stood in front of his tent, complaining.

Then the Lord sent fiery snakes among the people. No matter where the people turned, or how they tried to escape, they could not get away, for the snakes were all over the camp. Many of the people were bitten, and soon they became hot and burning up with fever. Some of the Israelites died.

This time the people behaved better than their fathers had. They came to Moses in sorrow, saying, "We know that we have sinned, for we have spoken against the Lord, and against thee. Pray to the Lord that He take away the snakes."

Though the people had so often grumbled and complained and doubted God's care, though they had been so hard to lead all these years through the wilderness, still Moses loved them. He prayed to God to forgive them, and to take away the poisonous snakes.

God heard Moses' prayer. "Make a snake out of brass," God said to him, "and set it upon a pole where everyone can see it. Every person who has been bitten by the snakes, and who looks at the brass snake, trusting in My promise, shall not die but live."

So Moses made a brass snake, and he set it up on a high pole where all the people could see it. Whoever had been bitten, so that the venom of the snakes burned in his blood, was healed just by looking at the brass snake Moses had made.

Was the brass snake magic? Could it cure the deadly snake bite? No, it was just a piece of metal. It was God who cured the snake bites, God who forgave the sins of the people, God who gave them life instead of death. Only God can do these things.

But the brass snake was a test. It was a test of whether the people really trusted in God, and whether they were willing to obey His commands. Those who believed what God had promised, that they would be cured by looking at the brass snake, were healed. Those who did not believe, and refused to obey, died.

And the brass snake was a picture

— and a promise — of *how* God was going to save His people. The brass snake pointed to Someone else, who, long, long after this happened, was also going to be lifted up. It pointed to Jesus, our Saviour, who died on a cross so that you and I could be forgiven for our sins.

Chapter 50
GOD GIVES VICTORY
NUMBERS 21

All the older people were now dead except Moses and Joshua and Caleb. There was not one left of those who had sinned against God by refusing to trust in Him and to enter the promised land forty years ago.

The young children were now grown up. They must have trusted God more than their fathers and mothers did, for at one time when they reached a place where there was no water, they did not grumble as their parents had.

The Lord said to Moses, "Gather the people together, and I will give them water." Moses told the people to dig a well with their walking sticks. They dug a well, and the Lord filled it with water. The people made a song about this event, and often sang it.

They had now come to the land of Moab, where the Moabites and the Ammonites lived. These people were descendants of Lot, Abraham's nephew. God had given the land of Moab to Lot's descendants, and so the Israelites went around, not attempting to pass through.

They crossed the River Arnon and came to the country of the Amorites. These people were wicked heathen who worshiped a dreadful idol called Chemosh.

Moses sent messengers to Sihon, king of the Amorites, to ask permission to pass through his country, promising not to trample down the fields or eat the grapes in the vineyards. The Amorites had heard about the Israelites, and about their powerful God, who was probably more powerful even than Chemosh. "What shall we do?" they cried. "They will kill us all."

So Sihon gathered his army and came out to fight against Israel. The Israelites were all ready for them. They had six hundred thousand strong men ready to fight. Above all, they had God for their helper. And so the children of Israel won a glorious victory over the Amorites. There were many big cities with high walls. The Israelites destroyed all the cities, because of their wickedness.

All the cattle — the sheep and cows and donkeys and camels and goats — the children of Israel saved. God allowed them to take all these animals for themselves. And He gave them the houses of the Amorites, with the vineyards and olive orchards, and all the other good things they found there.

At last they were out of the dreary desert and living in a beautiful land.

Chapter 51

BALAAM DISPLEASES A FRIGHTENED KING
NUMBERS 22-25, 31

WHY THE KING WAS AFRAID After the children of Israel had conquered the Amorites, they settled for a time in the plains of Moab. This was a rich, grassy country with plenty of fine food for their flocks and herds.

In front of them was the Jordan River. Behind their camp were several mountains and high hills. One of these was called Pisgah, and another, Nebo. From the tops of these hills one could see the tents of the Israelites spreading out in every direction like a sea.

In the land where they now were, there lived a nation called the Midianites. These people did not always live in the same place. They were a wandering nation. Just now they were living in Moab under their king, Balak.

King Balak had been hearing about the children of Israel for many years. Time and again reports had reached him about the wonderful God of the Israelites, so much more powerful than Baal-peor, the god of the Midianites. Balak had heard about the dreadful plagues God had sent to Egypt, and how He had brought the Israelites through the Red Sea, and destroyed the Egyptian army. And now he heard how Sihon had fought against Israel, and how he and all his people had been killed. And here were these Israelites right in his own country! Balak was terribly frightened, and his princes were just as much afraid as he.

What should they do? It was no use to try to fight them. The God of the Israelites was very powerful, and He would surely help His people. No, they must think of some other way to drive out this great crowd of Israelites.

After Balak had thought and thought about what he should do, an idea came to him. As I said before, Balak and his people wandered from one place to another. They had once lived in the land of Assyria, where the mighty Euphrates River ran. In that country there was a man who claimed to be a prophet of the same God the Israelites worshiped. His name was Balaam.

Balaam was not an Israelite. We do not know how he found out about the true God. Perhaps, like King Balak, he had heard of the wonders God did in Egypt and at the Red Sea. Perhaps he thought it would be wonderful to be known as the prophet of a God like that. We do know that he did not really love God, and trust in His promises, and want to serve Him.

Balak sent messengers to ask Balaam to come to Moab and curse the people of Israel. For who would be so effective against these people as a prophet of their own God? The messengers brought rich presents as a reward for Balaam if he did as King Balak asked.

Balaam asked the messengers to stay all night. "I will have to find out," he said, "what the Lord says to me about this." That night God appeared to Balaam. "Who are these men with you?" God asked. "You shall not go with them, and you shall not curse the Israelites, for I have blessed them."

In the morning Balaam said to the

messengers, "You can go home again, for the Lord will not let me go with you."

The messengers returned to Balak. They said, "Balaam refused to come with us." Balak was desperate. He sent other messengers, more noble than the first ones. The messengers said to Balaam, "Let nothing prevent you from coming, for King Balak will promote you to great honor." But Balaam answered, "Even if Balak would give me his house full of silver and gold, I cannot do what God will not let me do."

Balaam wanted to go with the messengers, and earn the rich rewards that the king had promised him. But he knew that God did not want him to go. He was afraid to disobey God, but he hoped that perhaps God might have changed His mind.

"Stay overnight," he said to the messengers, "and I will see if the Lord has any further word for me." That night God told Balaam that he might go with the men. "But," God said, "only the word I tell you may you say."

The next morning Balaam saddled his donkey and went with the men.

AN ANIMAL TALKS God was angry with Balaam, because Balaam knew well enough that God did not want him to go. God sent an angel to stop Balaam in the way. The donkey saw the angel standing in the road, but Balaam, who pretended to be a prophet who saw better and further than ordinary men, did not see the angel. Perhaps his mind was too full of dreams of that house full of silver and gold which he hoped King Balak would give him.

The donkey was afraid of the angel. She turned aside out of the road into the field. Balaam struck the donkey to make her go back into the road.

Then the angel went and stood some distance further along the road, where there was a wall on each side. When the donkey came to this place, and saw the angel, she pushed herself just as close to the wall on one side as she could, to escape the angel. Balaam's foot was crushed against the wall.

Balaam was very angry with the donkey. He gave the animal a hard beating, for his foot hurt.

Then the angel went still further, and stood in a very narrow place along the road, where there was no room to turn either to the right or to the left. When the donkey saw the angel standing here, with a drawn sword in his hand, the terrified beast sat down on the road under Balaam.

Balaam was furiously angry. He laid blow after blow on the back of the poor animal. Then God opened the mouth of the donkey. "What have I done to you, that you have beaten me these three times?" the donkey asked. Balaam was so angry that he did not even notice that the donkey was talking as a man talks. He answered, "You have disobeyed me these three times. If I had a sword in my hand, I would kill you." Then the donkey answered, "Am I not your own donkey, on which you have ridden ever since you bought me? Did I ever do anything like this before?" And Balaam said, "No."

Then God opened Balaam's eyes. Now he, too, saw the angel standing in the road with a drawn sword in his hand. His guilty heart told him that the angel had come to punish him for disobeying God. He was very frightened, and he fell flat on his face.

The angel said, "Why have you beaten your donkey these three times? If she had not turned aside to save your life, surely I would have killed you, and let her live."

Balaam said very humbly to the angel, "I have sinned. I did not know that you were standing in the way against me. And now, if you wish me to, I will go back." But the angel said, "No, go with the men. But remember, you shall speak only the word that I give you."

King Balak was waiting anxiously at home. When he heard Balaam was coming, he went out to meet him. "Did I not earnestly send for you?" he said. "Why didn't you come? Don't you know I am able to promote you to great honor?"

Balaam answered, "Well, I am here now; but I have no power to say anything except the word God puts in my mouth." Balaam had not forgotten the angel and the drawn sword.

The next day King Balak took Balaam up on a high hill, so that he could see the tents of the Israelites spread out in every direction. Balaam said, "Build seven altars, and offer a bullock and a ram on each altar. Then you stand here by the sacrifices, and I will go a little further off. Perhaps the Lord will meet me, and I will tell you whatever He shows me."

Then God met Balaam and told him what to say to King Balak. The prophet returned to where the king and all his nobles waited to hear Balaam curse the Israelites. Balaam recited what God had told him, as if he were reciting poetry. This is part of what he said:

How shall I curse whom God hath not cursed?
Or how shall I defy whom the Lord hath not defied?
Who can count the dust of Jacob?
Or number the fourth part of Israel?

King Balak and his princes were astonished. For Balaam had not cursed the Israelites at all. Instead, he had blessed them. "I called you to curse my enemies, and you have blessed them instead," Balak said. Balaam answered, "Must I not be careful to say what the Lord has put in my mouth?"

King Balak said, "Come, I will take you to another place, and you shall not see all of them, but only a few." He took Balaam to the top of a high mountain called Pisgah. Again Balaam had Balak build seven altars, and offer a bullock and a ram on each altar. Perhaps he hoped that if they offered enough sacrifices, God might change His mind after all. Balaam went a little distance off to hear what God had to say to him. Then he came back to the altars where King Balak and his nobles were eagerly waiting to hear him curse the Israelites. He said:

God is not a man that He should lie,
Nor a son of man, that He should change His mind.
I have received command to bless them;
And He has blessed them, and I cannot change it.

How disappointed King Balak was! He said, "Do not curse them or bless them either. Don't say anything at all." And Balaam answered, "Did I not tell you that I must say whatever God tells me to say?"

BALAAM WORKS AGAINST GOD   Then Balak said, "Come to another place. Perhaps God will let you curse them from there." So they went to the top of another high mountain called Peor. Here also King Balak made

101

sacrifices to try to win the favor of the God of the Israelites. The Spirit of God came upon Balaam, and the man spoke as if he were in a dream or a trance:

How goodly are thy tents, O Jacob,
Thy tabernacles, O Israel! . . .
Blessed be everyone that blesseth thee,
And cursed be everyone that curseth thee.

King Balak was furious. He said, "I intended to promote you to great honors, but the Lord has kept you back from these honors. Go home as fast as you can. I sent for you to curse my enemies, and instead you have blessed them three times."

But Balaam was not finished. The Spirit of God was upon him, and he had to say what God told him, whether he wished to or not. He said, "I will tell you what will happen in the days to come:

There shall come forth a star out of Jacob,
And a king shall rise out of Israel."

Thus Balaam, though he did not want to do it, foretold the most marvelous thing that ever happened — the coming of Jesus Christ, the Saviour of the world.

Balaam was not a good man who loved and trusted God. He was disappointed that he did not get the rich rewards King Balak had offered him. He did a very wicked thing. He went to live among the Midianites. He said to them, "I will tell you how you can make the God of the Israelites angry with His people. Go and visit them. Invite them to your idol feasts. Get them to worship your god, Baal-peor. Then their God will be angry with them."

The Midianites did just what Balaam had suggested. They invited the Israelites to the feasts held in the honor of Baal-peor. When the Israelites worshiped the idol, God was angry, as Balaam had known He would be. God told Moses that the Israelites must go to war against the Midianites to punish them for teaching the people of God to worship their idol. So the Israelites fought with the Midianites, killing all the men and their five kings. They killed the wicked Balaam too. They burned all their cities and castles.

Chapter 52
THE LAST DAYS OF MOSES
NUMBERS 26, 32; DEUTERONOMY 3, 31, 33, 34

THE ISRAELITES NUMBERED AGAIN The people were camped now in the land of Moab. Just on the other side of the Jordan River was the city of Jericho. They were waiting till God would tell them to cross the river and enter the promised land.

Something else had to be done first. The Israelites had to be counted, to find out how many men there were over twenty years old who could fight. Soon they would cross over into Canaan where they would have to fight many battles with the fierce heathen who lived there.

In eleven of the tribes there were six hundred and one thousand, seven hundred thirty men able to fight. The Levites, who took care of God's tabernacle, were counted separately. There were twenty-three thousand of them.

Three of the tribes — Reuben, Gad, and half of Manasseh — liked the plains of Moab so well that they asked Moses if they could settle there, instead of in Canaan itself. The land of Moab was rich and fertile, and the grass grew green and thick. It was just the place for the large flocks of cows and sheep these tribes had.

Moses said they might settle there if they would promise to cross the Jordan with the rest of the Israelites and help them fight against the heathen in Canaan. They said they would do this if they might first build houses and cities to protect their wives and children, and shelters for their animals.

So Moses gave the fertile plains of Moab to the tribes of Reuben, Gad, and half the tribe of Manasseh.

MOSES SAYS GOOD-BYE Moses had been the leader of the children of Israel for forty years. Now he was an old man, and his work on earth was nearly done.

Not long before this, you remember, Moses had struck the rock to bring water out of it, instead of speaking to it, as God had commanded; and he told the Israelites that *he*, not God, would bring water out for them. That day God had said that Moses would not be allowed to finish his work of leading the Israelites to Canaan, and that Moses himself would not enter the country God had promised to His people.

This was a bitter disappointment to Moses. He begged God to let him cross the river so that he, too, could see the longed-for promised land.

God did not give Moses what he asked for. Instead, as He so often does, God gave Moses something much better than he had prayed for, and a home far lovelier than the land of Canaan.

"Be satisfied with what I have decided," God said to him. "Do not speak about this any more. Climb this mountain, and I will show you the land. Then you are to die here on this mountain. For you are not to cross this river."

Moses was concerned about what would happen to the children of Israel when he was no longer there to lead them. For Moses loved the people of Israel. He said to God, "Let the Lord choose a man to lead this people, so that they will not be as sheep which have no shepherd."

God said, "Take Joshua, and lay your hands on him, set him before all the people, and give him the commission of leading them."

Before Moses left, he called all the people together to remind them of many things they must not forget. The people listened carefully, for they knew that in a few days their beloved leader would be gone from them forever, and they would no longer hear his voice.

Moses wrote down all the laws of God, and gave the rolls to the priests to keep. He said to them, "Every seven years you must gather all the people together — the men, and the women, and the children too. You must read the law of God to them, so that they may learn to fear God, and may know how God wants them to live." And Moses told the fathers and mothers to tell their children about God and His law every day.

Moses wrote the first five books of the Bible. He did not write them by himself, but God told him what to write, for these books were to teach the Israelites, and all the world, about God. After he had written them, Moses gave these books to the Levites, and commanded that they should be put beside the sacred

103

ark in the inner room of the tabernacle, the Holy of Holies. This was the safest place for them.

Moses had two great works to do in his life. One was to lead the children of Israel from Egypt to Canaan. It was a very great task to lead two million people and all their great herds of cattle for forty years through hot desert lands. Moses could never have done it alone, but God helped him. When God calls any man to work for Him, He always gives him the necessary strength and wisdom.

The other great work Moses had to do was to write the first five books of the Bible. This task was important because these books are God's Word to man. The Bible tells us about God's wonderful, life-giving plan of salvation.

But now Moses' work was finished. He was a hundred and twenty years old, but he was still as strong and as well as a young man. His eyes were still clear and bright, and he could walk with a quick step. God had given Moses good health.

"Get you up into the mountain, and view the land I promised to My people, and die there," God said to Moses. Moses said a last good-bye to the people he loved, and to Joshua, on whose shoulders now fell the great responsibility of leading God's people. He raised his hands and blessed the people:

The eternal God is thy dwelling place,
And underneath are the everlasting arms. . . .
Happy art thou, O Israel.
Who is like unto thee,
A people saved by the Lord!

Then he climbed Mount Nebo. And God met him there. God showed Moses the promised land, all the way from the valley of Jericho to the Mediterranean Sea far to the west. Moses looked long at the beautiful country spread out before his eyes. He was happy to know that this land was where his people would soon be living in peace. His heart was filled with love to God for His goodness.

Then he lay down on that lonely mountain and died. God Himself buried his body there on Mount Nebo. To this day no man knows where his grave is.

But Moses himself went to live with God in a land far lovelier than Canaan, in that city prepared by God for all those who love and trust Him, the city where there is no sin or sorrow or parting or death. For God Himself is there among His people.

The children of Israel mourned for Moses for thirty days.

Chapter 53
CANAAN AT LAST
JOSHUA 1-5

RAHAB AND THE SPIES After the death of Moses, God spoke to Joshua and said, "Moses, My servant, is dead; now, therefore, arise, go over this Jordan to the land which I do give you. As I was with Moses, so I will be with you. Be strong and of good courage. Do not be afraid, for the Lord your God is with you wherever you go."

Joshua sent his officers to tell the people to cook a lot of food to take with them, for in three days they were going into the land of Canaan. Everyone was delighted. At last! At last! In three days they were going to enter the promised land!

All the housewives began to cook and bake. They still ate the daily manna from heaven, but now they had many other things to eat too, for did not the flocks and herds of the Midianites belong to them?

Just across the Jordan River was the big city of Jericho, with high stone walls around it, and big iron gates which were shut every night, so that no enemies could get in. This was the first town the Israelites would have to conquer. So Joshua sent two spies to Jericho, to find out the easiest way to get into the city.

The spies managed to get into the city secretly. After looking around, they went to the house of a woman called Rahab, with whom they stayed.

For a long time Rahab, as well as the other Canaanites, had been hearing wonderful stories of the power and the might of the God of the Israelites. Rahab did not wish to fight against this great God and His people, as the other Canaanites did. Although she had been a heathen all her life, there now came into her heart the thought that it would be better to take this great God for her own, and to try to help His people. Where did Rahab get this thought? It must have been put in her heart by God's Holy Spirit.

When the two spies came to her house, she took them upstairs to the flat roof of her house. She told them to lie down. Then she covered them over with the stalks of flax, which were piled on the roof to dry. The flax was like stiff hay. Rahab piled it carefully over the spies so they could not be seen.

But someone had seen the spies come into Jericho and go to Rahab's house. He ran to the king and said excitedly, "O king, do you know that two men of the Israelite people came into our city today? Surely they are spies."

The king sent soldiers in great haste to Rahab. They said, "Bring out those men who came to your

PART IV
Settlement

105

house, for they have come to spy out the city."

Rahab said, "Two men did come in here, but I did not know who they were. When it was dark, just before the gates of the city were shut, they left. I don't know where they went, but if you hurry after them, you can catch them."

The messengers did not stop to ask any more questions, or to search Rahab's house. They hurried away, hoping to catch the spies. As soon as they had left the city, the keepers shut the gates, so that no other spies could get in.

Then Rahab went up to the roof. She said to the men, "I know that the Lord has given you the land. Everyone here is afraid of you. We have heard how the Lord dried up the water of the Red Sea for you when you came out of Egypt, and what you did to the Amorites on the other side of the Jordan. When we heard these things, our hearts melted with fear. Not one of us has any courage left. For the Lord your God, He is God both in heaven above and on this earth beneath.

"Now promise me, by the name of your God, that since I have been kind to you, you will also be kind to me, and will save me and my father and mother and brothers and sisters alive, when you come into Jericho with your armies."

The men answered her, "Our life for yours, if you do not betray our secret."

Now the city wall was so thick that houses were built on top of it, and Rahab lived in one of these houses. Some of her windows looked out into the country.

Rahab said to the spies, "The gates are shut now, so you can't get out that way. I will let you down out of my window into the open country with this scarlet rope. Escape to the mountains, and hide yourself there for three days, till the men who are hunting for you have come back. Then you can safely return to your people."

The men said, "When we come here to conquer Jericho, you must fasten this bright red rope in your window where we can see it plainly. Bring your father and mother and sisters and brothers into your own house. We promise to save all your family alive. But you must not speak a word to anyone about all this."

So Rahab let the men down out of her window into the fields outside the town. They hid in the mountains for three days.

Afterward they went back to Joshua. They said, "Truly the Lord has delivered all the land into our hands, for all the people faint with fear because of us."

CROSSING THE RIVER The people had made everything ready. They had cooked and baked enough food to last for several days. Everything was packed and ready to go, except the tents in which they slept that last night.

Early in the morning the long procession formed. You remember that they always marched in regular order. This time the priests went first, carrying God's holy ark, the place where God Himself lived among His people.

The Jordan River is wild and turbulent. At this time of the year it was flooded with the spring rains, and overflowed all its banks. But just as soon as the feet of the priests stepped into the water, the river stopped flowing. The water piled up into a high wall further up the river. The water that had already flowed down drained

106

away, and the hot sun quickly dried up the bottom of the riverbed, so that the children of Israel could walk across.

The priests holding the ark on their shoulders stood in the middle of the riverbed. They did not move while the long, long procession of Israelites passed by them to the other side.

Joshua had picked out twelve men beforehand, a man from each tribe. Now he said to them, "Pass over before the ark of the Lord, your God, into the middle of the Jordan. Pick up, each one of you, a big stone, as heavy as you can lift, and carry it on your shoulder to the other side."

When all the people had passed over, Joshua commanded the priests to come up out of the riverbed. Just as soon as the priests stepped up on the bank of the other side of the river, the high wall of water gave way, and the water came roaring and tumbling down and filled the riverbed again.

The children of Israel were at last, after all their wanderings, at home in the land of Canaan, which had been promised to their fathers, Abraham, Isaac, and Jacob. They pitched their tents that night for the first time in their own country.

Joshua piled up the twelve stones the men had carried out of the river-bed and made a monument. He said to the Israelites, "When in time to come your children ask you, 'What do these stones here mean?' then you must tell them, 'The Lord our God dried up the water of the Jordan for us here, so that we passed over on dry ground.' And this monument will remind you that the hand of the Lord is mighty, and you must fear your God forever."

The Israelites rested here for a few days, because it was the time of the year for their Passover feast. They did not move until they had finished celebrating the Passover. The day after this feast the manna they had been eating for forty years stopped coming. They did not need it any longer, for there was plenty of food to be had in their own new country.

The people of the land heard about the way the God of the Israelites dried up the Jordan River so that His people could pass over, and they were terrified. Who could fight against a God so powerful?

These people, the Amorites and the Canaanites, were cruel, wicked heathen. They worshiped the idol Moloch, and burned their little children on his altar fires. For hundreds of years God had borne with them. But now at last the terrible day of judgment had arrived for these wicked people. God was going to use Israel to punish them.

Chapter 54
A VICTORY AND A DEFEAT
JOSHUA 6, 7

MARCHING AROUND JERICHO The camp of the Israelites was very near the city of Jericho. When the people of the city saw the Israelites coming upon them, they kept the city gates shut and locked, both day and night. No one was allowed to go out or come in.

If God had not helped the Israelites, they could never have entered the city. But the Lord told Joshua how the people might take the city.

Joshua arranged everything as God had commanded. The women and the children stayed in their camp at Gilgal. Only the men went to fight against Jericho. First came thousands of soldiers marching in regular order. Then came seven priests with seven trumpets. Four more priests followed, bearing God's ark on their shoulders. Last of all came other thousands of soldiers.

This procession marched around the city of Jericho. The priests blew their trumpets as they went, but the soldiers were perfectly quiet. They did not open their mouths to speak a single word.

It took a long time to march all around the big city. When they had done it once, the soldiers went home to their tents for that day.

The people of Jericho who had houses on the wall had their windows all barred and barricaded because they were afraid that the Israelites might shoot arrows through them. But wherever there was a little chink or crack, they peered down to see what the Israelites were doing. They saw the soldiers marching around the city, as still as mice, and the seven priests blowing horns. Then they saw them go home to their camp.

The next day they heard the trumpets again, and again they looked through their peepholes. Again they saw the Israelite soldiers marching silently around the city. Again they saw them go home to their camp without attacking the city.

This happened for six days. At first the people of Jericho were terribly frightened. "What are they going to do to us?" they asked. But after the same thing happened for six days, they were no longer frightened. They boasted, "Well, if they aren't going to do anything but march around the city, it won't hurt us very much."

On the morning of the seventh day the soldiers started very early. Today they were going to march around the city seven times, instead of only once. Six times they marched in perfect silence, except for the priests blowing their horns. But the seventh time all at once the priests blew a loud blast on their horns, and Joshua threw up his arms and cried, "Shout! for the Lord has given you the city!"

In an instant every man threw up his arms and shouted as loud as he could. At that very moment the walls fell down with a terrible crash. Jericho was wide open to the Israelite soldiers.

The people of Jericho were so surprised that they could do nothing to save themselves. The soldiers ran right into the city. With their swords and spears they killed all the people of Jericho — even all the oxen and sheep and donkeys. God had commanded them to destroy everything because of the great wickedness of the people.

Only Rahab and her family were saved. After this Rahab lived among the Israelites, and worshiped the true God for the rest of her life.

Although God had commanded the soldiers not to take any of the things they found in the city, one man, whose name was Achan, saw a very beautiful garment and a pile of silver and a big piece of gold which he wanted very much. He took them secretly back to his tent. He dug a hole in the ground inside the tent and hid them. He thought no one had seen him. He forgot that God sees everything we do.

The soldiers saved the silver and the gold, and the kettles of brass and iron. They put these things in the Lord's treasury in the tabernacle. They burned the city. The people of Jericho were so wicked that God did not want even their houses saved. I suppose that the houses were full of heathen idols and wicked pictures. God did not want the children of Israel to live in such houses.

After the capture of Jericho, the people saw that God was with Joshua, as He had been with Moses. And Joshua's fame spread throughout the country.

THE DEFEAT AT AI Near Jericho was a small town called Ai. Joshua sent some men to Ai to find out about the town. The men came back and said to Joshua, "Ai is just a small place. We can easily conquer it. It is not necessary for all the army to go there. Two or three thousand soldiers will be enough."

After such a glorious victory at Jericho, the Israelites thought it would be no trouble at all to conquer Ai. But things turned out differently. When the army of the Israelites attacked, the men of Ai killed thirty-six of them, and chased all the others back to their own camp.

When the people of Israel heard how their soldiers had been beaten by the men of Ai, they were very much frightened. Joshua tore his clothes and put dust on his head. The elders of Israel did the same. They fell on their faces before the ark of God.

Joshua said, "O Lord God, what shall I say, now that the Israelites have turned their backs before their enemies? For all the heathen people will hear that Israel has been beaten like this. They will not be afraid of us any longer. They will

fight us and kill us all. And what will they think about our God? They will think our God is not powerful at all."

The Lord said to Joshua, "Why are you lying on your face like this? Get up! Israel has sinned, and has stolen some of the things I commanded them not to touch, and has lied about it."

You see, Achan had *stolen* the silver and gold, for all the silver and gold belonged to the treasury of the Lord. None of the people had any right to it. For it was not the Israelite soldiers who had conquered the city, but God. Achan had lied, too, for he had hidden the beautiful garment and the silver and gold in the ground under his tent. He was trying to deceive Joshua and the people. He was trying to deceive God. And trying to deceive is lying even if we do not speak a word that is not true.

God can see what is in our hearts, even if we have not spoken aloud, and God knew that Achan was lying. "In the morning," God said, "you shall come before Me, according to your tribes, and families, and households; and I will show you the man who has taken the forbidden thing."

Early in the morning the priests sounded the trumpets. The tribes of Israel came up, one after another. God pointed out the tribe of Judah. Then all the families of Judah came, one after another, and God pointed out the family of the Zarhites. All the households of the Zarhites came up, one by one, and God pointed out the household of Zabdi. Then the members of Zabdi's family came up one at a time, and God pointed out Achan, Zabdi's grandson.

Joshua said to Achan, "My son,

confess your sin to God, and tell me what you have taken. Do not try to hide it from me." Then Achan said, "I have sinned against the Lord God of Israel. In Jericho I saw a beautiful garment and a lot of silver and a big piece of gold, and I took them. They are hidden in the ground underneath my tent."

Joshua sent a man to Achan's tent. There lay the garment and the gold and the silver. Joshua said to Achan, "Why have you troubled Israel? God will trouble you this day."

All Israel took Achan, his sons and his daughters, his oxen, his donkeys, his sheep, his tents, and all he had, together with the garment, the silver, and the gold, and they brought them to a nearby valley. There the people of Israel stoned Achan to death. Then the Israelites burned everything, and threw stones over the place where the ashes were, till there was a great heap of stones.

Did Achan go to heaven? No one but God can answer that question. But I think that perhaps he did, for Achan did confess his sin, and if we confess our sins and are sorry for them, "God is faithful and just to forgive us our sins."

Chapter 55
HOW TRICKERY OVERTHREW AI AND SAVED GIBEON
JOSHUA 8, 9

After this God said to Joshua, "Do not be afraid. Take the soldiers, and go to Ai, for I have given the city to you. This time you may keep for yourselves all the cattle and the treasures you find in the city."

Joshua chose thirty thousand brave soldiers. He sent them to Ai at night, so that no one would see them. He commanded them to go to the further side of the town, and to hide themselves. Another five thousand hid themselves on the west side of the city.

At daybreak Joshua took all the rest of the soldiers, and marched openly to the front of the city. The king of Ai saw these soldiers, but he did not know about the thirty thousand who were hiding behind the town, nor the five thousand hidden on the west side. He called every single man to come out of the town to fight the Israelites. There was not one man left in the city.

Joshua and all the soldiers with him pretended to be afraid. They fled, and the men of Ai ran after them. Then the Lord commanded, "Stretch out your spear toward the city."

The men in hiding were waiting for that signal. As soon as they saw Joshua stretch out his spear, they rose up from their hiding places and rushed toward the city. They had no trouble getting in, for the men of Ai had left the gates wide open.

The soldiers set fire to the city. When the men of Ai looked behind them, they saw the smoke of their city rising up to the sky. Joshua saw the smoke too. He knew that his thirty thousand brave soldiers had succeeded in getting into the city. He and his men no longer pretended to be afraid of the men of Ai. They turned around and began to fight.

The other Israelite soldiers came from near the burning city and began to attack the men of Ai from the back. The Israelites surrounded the enemy on every side. Not one escaped.

Not far from Ai was a large city called Gibeon. The people of Gibeon were just as much afraid of the Israelites as the people of Jericho had been. The elders of the city talked the matter over. What should they do about these Israelites? They had conquered Jericho and killed all its people. They had conquered Ai. Undoubtedly they would soon come to Gibeon. Their God, as everyone knew, had commanded them to destroy all the people of the land.

The Gibeonites knew that they must do something and do it quickly, or they would all be dead men While they were talking, someone thought of a plan to trick the Israelites.

They sent messengers to Joshua. The messengers put on very old, dirty, ragged clothes. They wore old shoes, and they put old, patched wineskins on their donkeys. They filled torn bags with dry, moldy bread. Dressed like this, they went to the camp at Gilgal to see Joshua. "We have come from a very far country," they said. "We want to make an alliance with you."

The Israelites were cautious. "How can we know," they answered, "that you do not live right here among us? We couldn't make an alliance with you then." For God had strictly forbidden the Israelites to make an alliance with any of the Canaanite peoples.

The Gibeonites said, "Your servants have come from a very far country. Even far off, where we live, the name of your God, and the wonders He did in Egypt, are known. Our people have sent us to make an alliance with a nation so favored as to have such a powerful God.

"When we left home, we took this bread hot out of the ovens; see how dry and moldy it is now! These wineskins were new when we started out; see how old and torn they are! Even our clothes and our shoes are worn out, because we have come such a long way. We want you to make an alliance with us, and to be our friends."

Joshua listened to the clever story of the Gibeonites. He even tasted the moldy bread they had brought. But he forgot one very important thing — he forgot to ask God what he should do. He made an alliance with the Gibeonites. He swore by the name of God Himself that the Israelites would be their friends.

Three days later the Israelites learned the truth. The Gibeonites lived next door. Gibeon was one of the wicked cities God had commanded them to destroy. Now they had sworn in God's name not to harm them. They could not take back their promise. A promise made in God's name is holy. Joshua called the leaders of Gibeon together.

"You have tricked us," he said. "We will not kill you, because we have promised in the name of our God. But you shall not get off free, either. From now on, as long as you live among us, you will have to work as servants for the house of our God. You will have to chop the wood for the sacrifices, and carry in the water for the priests to wash themselves."

So the Gibeonites saved their lives by their trick, but they became slaves to the Israelites.

111

Chapter 56

WHEN NIGHT WAS LATE
JOSHUA 10, 11

When the other cities in Canaan heard that Gibeon had surrendered to the Israelites, they were very angry. Five of the neighboring kings collected all their soldiers together, and set out to punish these traitors in their midst. The Gibeonites sent a frantic message to Joshua.

"Come and help us quickly," they said. Joshua collected his army together, and set out at once — for he *had* made an alliance with Gibeon. As they marched from Gilgal to Gibeon, God spoke to Joshua.

"Do not be afraid of these kings," He said, "for I have delivered them all into your hands. Not one of them shall be able to stand before you."

Joshua marched all night. He came upon the armies camped in front of Gibeon suddenly, before they expected him. There was a great battle, and the armies of the Canaanite kings fled in panic before the Israelites. The Lord helped Joshua by sending a terrible hailstorm from heaven upon the enemy. More of the enemy were killed by God's hail than by the Israelite soldiers.

After a while Joshua looked at the sun. It was beginning to go down. But the battle was not yet ended. Then Joshua prayed: "Sun, stand thou still upon Gibeon; and thou moon, in the valley of Ajalon." God granted Joshua's prayer, and made the day longer for him, so that he had time to defeat the enemy. That was the only time in the history of the world that the sun did not set at its usual time.

When the five kings saw that their soldiers could not stand against the soldiers of Israel, they themselves ran away and hid in a cave. Joshua heard about this and said, "Roll big stones before the opening of the cave, and set soldiers to guard it. The rest of you go on pursuing the enemy, for the Lord is giving us the victory over them."

The Israelite soldiers ran on, and that day they conquered all the armies of the five kings.

Still the soldiers of Israel went on, for many days more, capturing every city they came to. When at last they returned to the camp at Gilgal, they had conquered all the southern part of Canaan, from Kadesh-barnea to Gaza.

Then the northern Canaanite kings came together in the far north. Their armies were a great host, like the sands of the seashore. They had a large number of horses and chariots, while the Israelites did not have any horses or chariots for the battle.

The Lord said to Joshua, "Do not be afraid of them, for tomorrow about this time I will deliver them all up to you." So Joshua marched to the north, and came upon his enemies suddenly. The Lord delivered all that great host into the hands of the Israelites. The soldiers of Joshua pursued them to the city of Sidon, near the seacoast, and to Mizpeh in the east.

Of course the Israelites did not do all this in one day. It took a long time, for every city in the land except Gibeon fought against them, and every city was conquered. Joshua subdued thirty-one kings.

Joshua warned the Israelites that God did not give them the land of Canaan because they were so good that they deserved it. God destroyed those nations because of their great wickedness, just as He had once destroyed wicked people with a flood, and the sinners of Sodom and Gomorrah with fire. This is God's world, and He will surely punish all those who do wrong. But if we are sorry for our wrongdoing, and put our trust in our Lord and Saviour, Jesus, God will forgive us.

Chapter 57
DIVIDING THE LAND
JOSHUA 13-24; JUDGES 1

Although Joshua and the Israelites had not yet conquered the whole land of Canaan, Joshua began to divide the land. He parceled it out by lot, giving each tribe a piece according to the size of the tribe.

The tribe of Levi, who had been chosen to serve in God's house, was not given any land. Instead they were given forty-eight cities. Each city had a little land around it where the Levites could pasture their cattle, but no farmland.

Joshua also appointed six cities of refuge, where a man who had killed another man accidentally, not on purpose, might be safe from revenge. Three of these cities of refuge were on each side of the Jordan.

When all the land was conquered, Joshua called together the tribes of Reuben and Gad and the half-tribe of Manasseh and said to them, "You have kept your promise to help your brothers fight the Canaanites. Now you may go back to your homes and families on the other side of the Jordan. But do not forget to love the Lord your God, and to walk in His ways, and to serve Him with all your heart." And Joshua gave the tribes of Reuben and of Gad and the half-tribe of Manasseh a rich share of the spoils which had been captured in the fighting — silver and gold and brass and fine clothing and cattle.

The Israelites now had everything their hearts could wish. They had houses to live in that they had not built, rich vineyards and olive orchards which they had not planted, flocks and herds of animals which they had not raised, and much gold and silver and brass and iron.

Was it right for them to take all these things away from the heathen? Yes, but *only* because God told them they might. For many, many years God had given all these rich blessings to the heathen, but the heathen had not used them to serve God. They had used them for the worship of idols, and had sinned against God in every possible way. So God took these undeserved blessings away from them, and He gave their land to the Israelites, commanding them to worship Him.

Joshua was now very old. He had lived a hundred and ten years. Before he died, he called the people together. He was one of only two persons in all that great crowd of people who could remember what it had been like in Egypt. He spoke solemnly to the people. He reminded them of all that God had done for them. "It is the Lord your God who fought for you," he said. "There has not one thing failed of all the good things that God promised you. And now I am going the way of all the earth. Take heed, now, that you love the Lord your God." Joshua asked all the Israelites to promise solemnly to serve God. "As for me and my house," he said, "we will serve the Lord."

The people answered, "We will

113

serve the Lord our God, and we will obey His voice."

After Joshua died, the Israelites no longer had a leader. Some of the heathen people were still left in the land, and the Israelites knew that God wanted these people driven out. What should they do, now that they had no one to lead them in war?

They did exactly the right thing — they went to God and asked Him what they should do. God told them that the tribe of Judah should go out first to fight against the heathen Canaanites. The soldiers of Judah asked the tribe of Simeon to come with them. The Lord gave them a great victory.

After this victory, the tribes of Judah and Simeon went to fight against Hebron. This was where Abraham had lived many years earlier. Abra-

ham and Sarah, Isaac and Rebekah, Jacob and Leah were buried in the Cave of Machpelah, near Hebron.

But about six hundred years had passed since Abraham lived in Hebron. It was now the home of a terrible race of giants called Anakims. Since the tribes of Judah and Simeon trusted the Lord to help them, God gave them the victory. Hebron was given to Caleb, one of the two men who had spied out Canaan forty years before. You remember that Joshua and Caleb were the only two spies who trusted God, and so were allowed to enter the promised land.

Later Judah and Simeon went to fight against the cities of Gaza, Ashkelon, and Ekron, near the Mediterranean Sea. There were giants living there too, but Judah and Simeon defeated them with the help of God.

Chapter 58
JUDGES RULE ISRAEL
JUDGES 2, 3

Now that God had given them the promised land, did the children of Israel love and serve Him faithfully? As long as that first generation who had seen God's mighty works lived, they were faithful. But now Joshua, and Eleazar the priest, and all those who had crossed the Jordan and conquered the land with God's help, were gone. Their children had grown up and taken their place.

Then there began a sad story which was repeated over and over. Whenever God gave His people peace and prosperity, they forgot Him. They began to worship idols. Then God had to send them troubles to teach them how much they needed His help. He sent them war and famine, so that they would learn God could

not bless those who rebelled against Him.

In their trouble the Israelites remembered their God. They prayed to Him, and asked Him to forgive them, and to help them again. Patiently, over and over again, God forgave them for their sins. He drove away their enemies, and gave them peace. And then, after these hard lessons, for a time the people loved and trusted God. But soon they forgot again. They again worshiped idols, instead of the only true God. They trusted in their own strength, instead of in the promises of God. God had to send them troubles again. It seemed that they would never learn this lesson.

Some of the heathen people still

remained in Canaan. In the north, around the city of Sidon and in the Lebanon mountains, the Lord left some of the Canaanites. The children of Israel lived right among these heathen people, even marrying some of them. They forgot their own God, and worshiped the heathen idols. God let the king of Mesopotamia fight against them and conquer them. For eight years this heathen king ruled over them.

Not all the children of Israel had forgotten God, however. There were some who still trusted only in the Lord. They cried to God for help, and God sent them a deliverer. This was Othniel, Caleb's younger brother.

Othniel fought against the king of Mesopotamia and God gave him the victory. Othniel ruled Israel for forty years, until he died.

But after his death the children of Israel did evil again; and God permitted the king of Moab to come against them and to conquer them. Moab, as you remember, is on the other side of the Jordan River, east of the Dead Sea.

The king of Moab, whose name was Eglon, ruled over the children of Israel for eighteen years. At last the people realized how wicked they had been to forget God. They turned again to Him, praying Him to help them. God heard them and gave them a deliverer, Ehud, who lived in Benjamin.

The Israelites sent Ehud to King Eglon. Ehud carried a present for the king. But Ehud meant to do more than give him the present. Before he started, he made himself a very long, sharp, two-edged dagger. He fastened it carefully to his side, under his long cloak.

When Ehud reached Moab, he found the king sitting in a cool room which he had made for himself, for he was a very fat man. After giving the present to Eglon, Ehud said to him, "I have a secret message for you, O king."

King Eglon told all the people to go out of the room, so that he could talk to Ehud alone. Ehud came close to the king, as if he were going to whisper his message so that no one else could hear.

Again Ehud said, "I have a message from God for you." At the same instant, he quickly drew his sharp dagger, and thrust it right into King Eglon's body.

Ehud went softly out of the room, shutting the doors and locking them. He hurried as fast as he could, and escaped to his own country.

While Ehud had been making his escape, the servants of King Eglon were waiting for him to come out of his room. They wondered and wondered why he stayed there so long. They tried the doors and found that they were locked; so they thought that he must be taking a nap and had locked the doors so that he would not be disturbed. By and by they decided that something must be wrong. They shook the doors and called to him, but there was no answer. In the end, they found another key and opened the doors. Great was their horror to see their king lying dead upon the floor!

Meanwhile Ehud had gathered his army to go against the Moabites. Since their king was dead, the Moabites had no leader. When Ehud and his army came to fight against them, they easily gained the victory.

That was the end of the war with the Moabites. They did not trouble the Israelites again.

After this, the land of Israel had rest for eighty years.

Chapter 59

HOW DEATH CAME TO SISERA
JUDGES 4, 5

When Ehud was dead, the children of Israel did evil in the sight of the Lord again.

Then God allowed Jabin, who was king of the Canaanites far up in the north, to come down and make trouble for the Israelites. King Jabin had nine hundred chariots of iron. He oppressed the children of Israel for twenty years. Again they cried to God.

At that time Israel was ruled by a woman. The name of this woman judge was Deborah. She was a very wise and good woman. She lived in a tent under a fine palm tree. Whenever the people of Israel needed any advice, they came to Deborah.

God told her now to send for a soldier named Barak, to tell him that God wanted him to take ten thousand soldiers and go up north to fight with Sisera, the captain of Jabin's army. God promised to give Barak the victory over Sisera.

Barak was afraid. He said to Deborah, "I will go if you come with me. But if you do not come along, then I will not go."

Deborah was a brave woman. She said, "I will surely go with you. But you will not win honor by this journey, for God will give a woman the honor of defeating Sisera."

So Barak gathered together ten thousand soldiers and went to the north. Deborah went with him. When Sisera heard that Barak was coming to fight against him, he gathered his own army, and his nine hundred iron chariots, and marched out to meet him.

Deborah encouraged Barak. "Up!" she said to him, "for this is the day that the Lord has delivered Sisera into your hand. Has not the Lord Himself gone out before you?" And God defeated Sisera and all his iron chariots.

When Sisera saw that the battle was lost, he got down from his chariot and escaped on foot. He ran till he was almost exhausted. When he could not run another step, he came to a tent standing all by itself. A woman named Jael lived here.

Jael was a Kenite. Do you remember that after Moses had run away from Pharaoh, he lived in the desert? There he married a Kenite woman. Some of her relatives had come along with the Israelites to Canaan, and they now lived among them.

Jael saw Sisera coming. She stepped out of the tent. "Come in, and rest in my tent," she said. "Do not be afraid." Sisera staggered in and lay down on the floor. Jael covered him with a coat.

Sisera said, "I am so thirsty. Give me, I pray you, a drink of water." Jael brought him a drink of milk. Again he said to her, "Stand in the door of the tent. If anyone comes and asks, 'Is there anyone here?' you must say, 'No!'"

Sisera was so exhausted that he soon fell into a sound sleep. When she saw that he was fast asleep, Jael picked up a tent stake. Softly she stole up to him and hammered the stake right through his head into the ground. Sisera never woke up from that sleep.

Then Jael stood in the door of her tent. Soon Barak came running past, looking for Sisera. Jael went out to meet him. "Come with me," she said, "and I will show you the man you are looking for." She took him into the tent and showed him Sisera lying dead on the ground with the tent stake through his head. And that was how God defeated Sisera before the children of Israel.

Then Deborah and Barak sang a song, praising God for the great victory:

> *I will sing praise to the Lord.*
> *The Lord came down for me*
> *against the mighty.*

> *So let all thine enemies perish,*
> *O Lord.*
> *But let them that love Thee be*
> *as the sun*
> *When he goeth forth in his*
> *might.*

After this victory, the land had rest for forty years. Ehud had conquered the Moabites, and Deborah and Barak had defeated the Canaanites.

Chapter 60
GOD APPEARS TO GIDEON
JUDGES 6

By this time the children of Israel should have learned to forsake idols, and to worship the one true God. But they had not. After Deborah died, they again did evil in the sight of the Lord. This time the Lord let the Midianites oppress them.

The Midianites were a wandering people who did not live in one place. They were hated because they were thieves. The Israelites had had trouble with the Midianites before, you remember. That was just before they crossed the Jordan to come into the land of Canaan. The Midianite king Balak had called the prophet Balaam to curse the Israelites for him, but Balaam had blessed them instead.

Since that time the Midianites had increased to a very large nation. They were mean thieves. Instead of settling down in one spot to cultivate their own fields, they swooped down onto some weaker nation, stealing all their crops. Then they would move on to another place, and steal there.

This was how they treated the Israelites. They came into Canaan as many as a cloud of grasshoppers. They trampled the growing crops, stole whatever could be carried away, and burned everything that was not movable. The children of Israel became very poor, but they were too terrified to defend themselves, for the Midianites killed anyone who opposed them.

This went on for seven long years. The Midianites had driven the Israelites out of their homes. The people had to hide in caves and dens in the mountains. They were nearly starving. At last, in their misery, they remembered the former mercies of God. They cried to God to help them. And God heard their cries and took pity on them.

One of the Israelites was a young farmer named Gideon. One day he was threshing some wheat. He was working secretly, beating out the grain by hand in the winepress, for fear that the Midianites might discover him and steal his grain.

Suddenly a man he did not know appeared beside him, sitting underneath the oak tree. The stranger said, "The Lord is with you, you brave, strong man."

Gideon answered sadly, "If the Lord is with us, why have all these terrible things happened to us? Where are the wonders which our fathers have told us God did when He brought our nation out of Egypt? No, the Lord has forsaken us, and delivered us into the hands of our enemies, the Midianites."

Do you remember that Abraham once had a visitor whom he did not recognize? Do you remember that that visitor was God Himself? The stranger under the oak tree was God too, but Gideon, like Abraham, did not recognize Him at first.

And God said to Gideon, "Go in this your might, and save Israel from the Midianites. Have not I Myself sent you?"

Gideon was astonished. How should he, a poor farmer, save his people from the hosts of the Midianites? "How should I save Israel?" he asked. "My family is the poorest in our whole tribe, and I am the least important person in my father's house."

God said to him, "Surely I will go with you, and you shall conquer the Midianites as easily as if they were only one man."

Gideon hardly dared to believe that this was God Himself talking to him. Yet, who but God would speak like this? He said, "Show me a sign that it is really You. Do not leave till I have brought You a present." And God said, "I will wait till you come back."

Gideon went home. Quickly he prepared some meat and some little cakes of bread. He brought them to the oak tree.

"Take the meat and the cakes," God said, "and lay them on this rock, and pour out the broth over them." Gideon did this. Then the Lord touched the bread and the meat with the end of the rod He had in His hand. A fire burst out of the rock and burned up the bread and the meat. At the same time God Himself disappeared.

Then Gideon knew that it was truly God. He was afraid. He prayed, "O Lord, I am afraid, because I have seen Thee face to face." But God said to him, "Peace! Do not be afraid. You shall not die." And Gideon built an altar to God there.

The children of Israel had become so idolatrous that Gideon's own father worshiped idols. There was an altar to the heathen god Baal right in the village where Gideon lived. By the side of Baal's altar was an image of the goddess called Asherah. The people used to worship this image also.

That night God spoke to Gideon again. "Throw down the altar of Baal," God said, "and the Asherah that stands beside it. Build an altar to Me in its place, and offer a sacrifice to Me there."

Gideon knew the people of his village would try to stop him from doing this. So he waited till the next night to obey God's command. After it was dark, he took ten of his servants, and knocked down the altar of Baal and the image of the Asherah. Then he built an altar to the Lord and sacrificed an ox on it.

In the morning, when the people of the village saw what had happened, they were furious. Who had dared to do such a thing? Someone said, "It was Gideon." The people hurried to the house of Gideon's father. "Bring out your son," they ordered, "for he must die."

Gideon's father answered, "If Baal is a god, he can defend himself. He does not need you to save him!"

THE SWORD OF THE LORD AND OF GIDEON

THE SMALL ARMY   Then the Spirit of God came upon Gideon. He blew a trumpet, and sent messengers to the northern tribes of Manasseh and Naphtali and Asher and Zebulun. When the people heard that the true God had spoken to Gideon, they were ready to help him. Soon soldiers came flocking to his army, for they were anxious to fight against the Midianites, now that they had a leader.

The Midianites also were ready to fight. The valley of Jezreel soon was filled with them. There were more than one hundred and twenty thousand of them, three times as many as the Israelite soldiers.

Gideon wanted to be very certain that God was with him. "O God," he prayed, "if truly Thou art going to save Israel by me, give me, I pray Thee, a sign. Tonight I will lay a sheep's fleece on the ground. If the fleece alone is wet with dew in the morning, and the ground is dry, I will know that Thou goest with us." So Gideon spread the fleece, and in the morning the ground was dry, but when Gideon lifted the fleece, he found it was so wet that he wrung a big bowlful of water out of it.

Still Gideon was afraid. Once again he prayed, "O God, do not be angry with me, but give me one more sign. Tonight let the fleece be dry, and the ground wet." The next morning it was exactly as Gideon had asked. Now Gideon had to believe once and for all that God wanted him to lead the Israelites against the Midianites.

Early in the morning Gideon took his thirty-two thousand soldiers and pitched camp on the hillside, over-looking the valley of Jezreel, where the Midianites were camped.

"You have too many soldiers," God said to him. "If you fight this way, the Israelites will say, 'We won today in our own strength. We did not need God's help.' Tell every man in your army who is afraid to fight that he may go home again."

Gideon was amazed. How could he win a victory over the big Midianite army if some of his little army went back home? But though he did not understand, he did as God commanded. Twenty-two thousand of the Israelite soldiers went home. Gideon had only ten thousand left!

Then God spoke to Gideon again. "There are still too many soldiers in your army," He said. "Bring them down to the water pool, and there I will show you which soldiers to take and which to leave behind. Those that lap up the water from their hands, as a dog laps up a drink, put them by themselves. Those that get down on their hands and knees to drink, and drink directly from the pool, put them by themselves."

Again Gideon obeyed, though he did not understand. There were three hundred men who lapped the water from their hands, as a dog drinks. And God said, "By these three hundred men I will save you from the Midianites. Send everyone else home again."

THE END OF THE THIEVES   Now Gideon was camped on the mountainside, with a tiny army of just three hundred men. That night God said to him, "Take your servant with you, and go down to the Midianite camp.

119

There you will hear something that will give you new courage."

Gideon and his servant slipped down the hillside secretly in the dark, creeping very cautiously nearer to the camp of the Midianites. They heard two men talking together in a tent. "I had a dream," one of the men said. "I dreamed I saw a loaf of barley bread come tumbling down the hillside into our camp. It hit the tent and knocked it over, flat to the ground." His companion answered and said, "That loaf of bread in your dream is nothing else but the sword of Gideon, for the Lord has delivered all the host of Midian into his hand."

When Gideon heard this, he was not afraid any more. He bowed his head and said a short prayer of thanks to God. Then he and his servant crept cautiously back again into their own camp.

"Get up quickly," he said to his men. "God has delivered the Midianites into our hands." Gideon divided his three hundred men into three companies. To each man he gave a trumpet, a lighted torch, and an empty pitcher to hide it in. They were now all ready. In the middle of the night Gideon and his three hundred men slipped down the hillside without a sound.

They crept up to the very edge of the Midianite camp. One hundred men went on one side, another hundred on the other side, and the third hundred slipped behind the enemy camp. They were so quiet that not one of the sleeping Midianites woke up to give the alarm. That whole great host lay asleep.

Then all at once Gideon gave the signal. He lifted his trumpet to his lips, and in an instant there rang out in the still night the terrible war cry of a trumpet. Dashing his pitcher against the stones with a tremendous crash, he seized his torch and waved it furiously above his head, shouting, "The sword of the Lord and of Gideon!"

Instantly he was answered by three hundred trumpets blaring out defiance from every quarter; three hundred pitchers went crashing on the stones; three hundred flaring torches streamed out in the darkness; and from three hundred throats rang out the war cry: "The sword of the Lord and of Gideon!"

The dazed Midianites awoke with terror. They jumped up and rushed to their tent doors. On every side they saw streaming torches lighting up the faces of strange soldiers. On every side they heard the war cry of the trumpets and the shouts of the Israelite soldiers, "The sword of the Lord and of Gideon!"

Stupid with sleep and terror, they thought that a tremendous host had attacked them. Their one thought was to save themselves. In their confusion and fear, they seized their swords and spears and hit at everything around them. There was no time to get lights, and in the darkness they could not tell friend from enemy. They slashed frantically this way and that, killing each other in the terrible tumult.

That night one hundred and twenty thousand Midianite soldiers were killed, some by Gideon and his men, many others by their own panic-stricken countrymen. God had routed that enormous army by Gideon's tiny band of men. The Midianites came no more to steal and murder the Israelites. And God gave His people forty years of peace.

The men of Israel were so pleased with Gideon that they wanted to make him their king. But Gideon said, "I will not rule over you, nor shall my sons. God is your King."

Chapter 62
SAMSON
JUDGES 13-16

A HARD RIDDLE   After the death of Gideon the children of Israel served idols again. They forgot their own God, who had saved them so wonderfully from the Midianites. They worshiped instead the gods of the heathen peoples around them.

God was angry that His people were so faithless. This time He sent the Philistines to trouble them. The Philistines lived in the west near the shore of the Mediterranean Sea. Gath and Gaza and Lachish were Philistine cities.

It was now about eighty years since Gideon had died. Seven different judges had ruled, but now there was no law in the land. Every man did what he pleased, for these were wild, rough times. The Israelites had become almost like heathen people.

In these troubled days there was a man of the tribe of Dan whose name was Manoah. He and his wife had no child. One day, when Manoah's wife was alone, an angel of the Lord appeared to her. "You are going to have a son," the angel said. "He must be given to God from the day he is born. As a sign of this his hair must never be cut. When he grows up, he will begin to deliver Israel from the Philistines."

The next year the baby was born to Manoah and his wife. His father and mother called him Samson. As the boy grew up, he became very strong.

One day, as Samson was walking alone, he saw a lion. Samson took hold of the fierce animal and tore him to pieces with his bare hands.

Soon after this Samson fell in love with a Philistine woman. He told his parents that he wanted to marry her. His father objected, "Isn't there any woman among all your own people that you could marry? Do you have to choose a heathen Philistine?" But Samson refused to listen. At last his father and his mother gave in. They all went together to visit the Philistine woman.

It was a great mistake for Samson to marry this heathen woman. It caused him a great deal of trouble. But God used even Samson's sin to help His people.

As they were coming home from visiting the Philistine woman, Samson turned aside to look at the body of the lion he had killed. A swarm of bees had made a hive in the lion's skeleton. Samson took some of the honey and ate it, and he gave some to his father and his mother.

After a time Samson returned to the country of the Philistines, and he gave a fine wedding feast. Thirty young Philistine men were invited to the party, which lasted a whole week.

At this party everyone told riddles. Samson told a riddle about the lion

121

and the honey. He said to his guests that if they could guess his riddle before the party ended, he would give them thirty shirts and thirty robes. If they could not guess it by that time, they must give him thirty shirts and thirty robes.

They all agreed to this. Then Samson told them the riddle: "Out of the eater came forth food, and out of the strong came forth sweetness."

The young men guessed and guessed for three whole days, but they could not give the right answer. They began to be afraid they could never guess this riddle. They did not want to give Samson the thirty shirts and thirty robes they had promised.

On the last day of the party they came to Samson's wife. "You must tease your husband," they said, "to tell you the answer to that riddle, so that you can tell us. Otherwise we will burn you and all your family. Did you invite us to this party just to make us poor?" You see what wicked people they were!

Samson's wife said to him, "You do not love me at all! You hate me. You have given a riddle to my people and have not told me what the answer is."

Samson answered, "I have not told even my father and my mother. Why should I tell you?" But his wife kept tormenting him, saying over and over, "You do not love me at all, or you would tell me the answer."

At last Samson was so tired of her complaints that he told her the answer. She told the answer to the thirty young men. They came to Samson and boasted, "We know your riddle now. What is sweeter than honey, and what is stronger than a lion?"

Samson saw at once that his wife had given him away. He was very angry, but he had to keep his prom-ise. Where could he get thirty shirts and thirty robes? He did not have the money to buy them. So he went to the Philistine city of Ashkelon. He killed thirty Philistines, and gave their clothes to the young men.

That was a dreadful thing to do, but it helped the Israelites. God had told Samson's mother that Samson would begin to deliver His people from the Philistines. That was what God had given Samson his great strength for.

A ONE-MAN BATTLE   After this, Samson went home in a great rage. He left behind the wife who had be-trayed him. Since Samson did not seem to love her any more, her father gave her to another young man.

After a while Samson got over his anger. He went to see his wife, taking along a young goat as a present for her. His father-in-law would not let him in the house. He said to Samson, "I thought you hated her, so I gave her to another young man."

Samson said, "Now it is not my fault if the Philistines pay for this." He caught three hundred foxes. He turned them tail to tail and tied the two tails together with a piece of dry wood between them. Then he set the wood on fire, and let the foxes go into the grain fields of the Philis-tines. This set the grain on fire until the entire harvest was burned, and the vineyards and olive orchards were destroyed too.

When the Philistines saw their crops destroyed and their vineyards and olive orchards on fire, they were furious. "Who has done this?" they exclaimed. Someone answered, "It was Samson, because his father-in-law gave his wife to another man."

The Philistines could not pay Sam-son back because he was so strong. So they went to his father-in-law's house and burned Samson's wife and her father to death. Probably they set the house on fire at night when everyone was asleep.

Samson was still more angry when he heard that the Philistines had killed his wife and her father. To get revenge he picked a fight with the Philistines, and killed a great many of them. Finally, in disgust, he went back to his own country, and lived in a secret cave on the top of a high rock.

The Philistines soon came hunting for him. The men of Judah were very much afraid of these wild, rough Philistines. "What have you come here for?" they asked. The Philistines answered, "We have come to catch Samson, and bind him, and to get even with him for the way he has treated us."

When the men of Judah heard the Philistines wanted only Samson, and no one else, they themselves set out to find him. They knew that he was so strong that no single man, or even three or four of them, could catch him. So three thousand of them went together.

When they found him, they asked, "Why have you done all these things to the Philistines? Don't you see that you have only made trouble for us?" Samson answered, "I have treated them just as they treated me."

Then the men of Judah said, "We have come to tie you up, and to give you to the Philistines." Samson must have laughed to himself when he heard that all three thousand of them had come to bind him. But he let them tie both his arms and his legs with two new ropes, which they wound around and around him so that he could not get away. Then they carried him down to the Philistines.

More than a thousand Philistines were watching to see if the men of Judah could really catch and bind Samson. When they saw him securely tied up, they set up a loud shout of triumph.

Then the Spirit of the Lord came mightily upon Samson. He snapped those strong new ropes as if they were only threads burned in the fire. He saw the jawbone of a donkey lying on the ground. He made one leap and picked it up. Striking right and left, as fast as he could make his mighty arms fly, he dashed into the midst of the Philistines. The force of his blows was so great that the men who were struck fell down dead, one on top of another.

The Philistines scattered in every direction. They were in such a hurry that they stumbled over each other and fell. Samson easily caught up with them, and rained blows on their heads and shoulders, thick and fast.

At last he stopped, drew a long breath, and looked around him. All around there were heaps of dead men. Samson counted them. You will hardly believe it, but there were a thousand men in those great heaps. I don't think there has ever been another fight like this, where one man alone, without any of the usual weapons, killed a thousand men. It was God who gave Samson this great strength, so that he could deliver the Israelites from their enemies.

After the fight was over, Samson was so thirsty he thought he would die of thirst, or even that some of the Philistines might capture him in his weakness. He called upon God in his trouble, and God made a spring of delicious cool water bubble up out of a hollow place in the ground. If you ever visit that country, the people there will show you a spring which, they say, was the one God sent to take care of the man who trusted in Him.

Sometime after this, Samson went again to the city of Gaza in the country of the Philistines. Like most cities of that time, Gaza was a walled town with heavy gates.

Someone told the city rulers that Samson had come into the town that afternoon. They quickly closed and locked the city gates. "Now," they said, "we have caught him! He can-not get out. In the morning, when he tries to leave, we will kill him."

In the middle of the night Samson got up to go home. Finding the city gates locked and shut, he pulled up the posts that the gates were fastened to. He put the two heavy gates and the posts and the bar upon his shoulders. He carried them thirty miles away to his own country.

Chapter 63
SAMSON CAPTURED
JUDGES 16

DELILAH   Sometime later Samson went again to the country of the Philistines. He saw another Philistine woman with whom he fell in love. Her name was Delilah.

One day, when Samson was not around, the lords of the Philistines came to see Delilah. They said, "See if you can persuade him to tell you what it is that makes him so strong. Find out if there is any way in which we can bind him so that he cannot break the ropes. If you do this, we will, each of us, give you eleven hundred pieces of silver."

If Delilah had been a good woman, and if she had loved Samson, she would have refused. For she knew that if the Philistines caught Samson, they would torture and kill him. But she was not a good woman. She cared more for the hundreds of pieces of silver than she did for Samson.

When she was alone with him, she said to Samson, "Tell me where you get your great strength, and how you could be bound."

Samson did not tell her the truth. He said, "If they bind me with seven green bowstrings that were never dried, then I will be weak, just like other men."

Delilah told the lords of the Philistines what Samson had said. They brought her seven bowstrings that had never been dried. Then they themselves hid in another room. Delilah bound Samson with the strings and then she cried out, "The Philistines are upon you, Samson!"

Samson jumped up, threw out his arms, and broke the seven green strings as quickly as a thread is broken when it touches the fire.

Delilah saw that he had not told her the truth. Again she teased him to tell her the secret of his great strength. Samson said, "If they bind me with new ropes that have never been used, then I shall be as weak as other men."

So Delilah took some new ropes that had never been used, and she bound him with them. This time again she had hidden some Philistine men in another room. When Samson was securely tied, she cried, "Samson, the Philistines are coming!" Samson jumped up and threw out his arms. The new ropes broke like threads!

Delilah was provoked. "You have lied to me again," she said. "You are only making fun of me. Now tell me truly how you can be bound." Samson answered, "When you are weaving your cloth, you must weave the seven locks of my long hair into the web you are weaving."

While Samson lay down with his head close to the loom, Delilah began to weave. Back and forth her shuttle went, weaving Samson's long hair into her cloth. After she had woven his long hair securely into the cloth she cried out, "Samson, Samson, the Philistines are coming!"

Samson woke up and rushed out. He carried along with him, dragging it by his hair, the heavy loom and the pin and the beam. Delilah saw that he had tricked her again. He was just as strong as ever.

"How can you say you love me," she reproached him, "when you are telling me lies all the time? You have mocked me three times, and you have not really told me what makes you so strong."

Samson knew very well that he ought not to tell her. It was God who had given him his great strength, so he could help his countrymen overcome the cruel Philistines. If he told Delilah the secret, she would surely tell it to the lords of the Philistines.

THE CAPTIVE Day after day Delilah teased and tormented Samson to tell her what gave him his great strength. She wanted those eleven hundred pieces of silver each of the lords of the Philistines had promised to give her. She did not care what happened to Samson.

She kept at him till Samson was tired to death of her nagging. At last he could not stand it any longer. He said to her, "My hair has never been cut, for I have been dedicated to God since I was born. If my hair were cut, my strength would leave me, and I would be weak like other men."

Delilah knew instantly that he had told her the truth this time. She sent for the lords of the Philistines and said, "Come once more, for this time he has really told me the secret."

The lords of the Philistines came, and they brought along the money they had promised to pay Delilah for her treachery. She hid them in the house, and had another man ready too. She made Samson go to sleep with his head in her lap.

When she saw that he was sound asleep, she beckoned to the man. He came in very softly, and cut off the seven locks of Samson's long hair. Then Delilah called out loudly, "Samson, Samson, wake up! The Philistines are coming!"

Samson awoke out of his sleep. He said, "I will go out as I did the other times, and shake myself." He did not know that God had left him. He lost his great strength when he broke God's command that his hair should never be cut.

It did not take the Philistines long to catch him, for now he was as weak as other men. The first thing his cruel masters did was to put out his eyes! Then they took him down to Gaza — the very town whose gates he had once carried off. They bound him securely with brass chains and made him grind grain in the town's prison house.

Poor Samson! Now he was blind, and his strength was gone. All day long he was forced to walk around and around in a circle, turning the mill that ground the grain! But God had not left him forever. His hair began to grow again, and with it some of his strength returned.

One day the Philistines gave a great feast. It was to honor their god

Dagon, for they said, "Our god has delivered our enemy into our hands." The big feast was held in Dagon's temple. There was a great crowd of Philistines, some of them in the temple itself, and others, who could not get into the temple, sitting on the flat roof. They were eating and drinking and singing to celebrate their victory over their enemy Samson.

While they were having a good time, someone said, "Let us bring Samson out of prison, so that we can make fun of him." As poor, blind Samson stumbled along, led by a little boy, the people set up a shout of derision. If he fell over something he could not see, the people screamed with laughter.

After a time Samson asked the little boy who led him to put his hands on the pillars of the temple, so that he could lean against them to rest himself. Then he prayed from the depths of his heart: "O Lord, re-member me, I pray Thee, and strengthen me only this once, that I may be avenged of the Philistines for my two eyes."

He took hold of the two middle pillars which held up the roof, one with his right hand, and one with his left. Then he said, "Let me die with the Philistines!" He bowed himself, and pulled at the pillars with all his strength. The pillars creaked and staggered. Down they came with a mighty crash, bringing the roof with them. The three thousand people on the roof tumbled with shrieks and screams onto the great crowd of people who were below, crushing them.

Samson died with the Philistines. In his death he killed more of his enemies than he had in his life.

Poor Samson had a sad, unhappy life, but he helped Israel by destroying many of the Philistines. For a time after this they did not trouble the Israelites.

Chapter 64
RUTH'S CHOICE
RUTH

A SAD STORY You must not think that all the people forsook God to worship idols in the days of the judges. No, indeed; there were many who tried to obey God, and to live just as God had commanded them to. I am now going to tell you a story about some of these God-fearing people.

When the judges ruled, there lived in the land of Israel a man whose name was Elimelech. He was a good man, who truly worshiped God and would have nothing to do with idols. Elimelech was married to a sweet wife, Naomi, which means "pleasant." They had two sons, named Mahlon and Chilion, who had grown up to be fine young men. They were a very happy family living in Bethlehem, on the land that had been given to their forefathers when Joshua had divided the land of Canaan among the children of Israel.

After a time there came several bad years, when nothing would grow. So little rain fell that there was a famine in the land. Across the Jordan River, in the land of Moab, there was no famine.

Elimelech and his wife, after talking things over between themselves, thought it would be better to leave

Bethlehem for a time, and live in Moab until better times should come. They did not sell their own land in Bethlehem, for God did not allow any of the Israelites to sell their land. It always remained in the same family, descending from father to son. They probably rented their land to another farmer.

After Elimelech's family had lived in Moab for a time, Elimelech died. This was very sad for Naomi, but she still had her two sons, who were able to take care of her. By and by Mahlon and Chilion married two young women of Moab. Their names were Ruth and Orpah.

The two young women were heathen when they married Mahlon and Chilion. But when they lived in Naomi's family and saw the whole family worshiping the true God, and when they heard them telling about the wonderful acts of God, and when they saw how good Mahlon and Chilion were, and how sweet Naomi was, they made up their minds that they, too, would worship the true God.

At last, when they had been in Moab about ten years, a terrible calamity befell this family. First one of the sons died, and then the other. Poor Naomi had lost her husband and both of her sons. Ruth and Orpah were now widows, like Naomi.

Soon afterward, Naomi heard that God had sent plentiful rains to the land of Israel. The famine was over. She had lost her husband and her sons, and she longed to go back home so that she might at least be among her own people, her friends and relatives.

One day she told her two daughters-in-law that she had decided to go back again to Bethlehem, in the land of Judah. Ruth and Orpah said that they would go with her.

The three started to walk to Bethlehem. It was several days' journey. After they had gone some distance, Naomi said to her two daughters-in-law, "Thank you very much for walking so far with me. Now each of you had better go home to her mother's house. I pray that God will be kind to you, as you have been to me, and to my dead sons. May God give you other husbands so that you may be happy again."

Ruth and Orpah began to cry. They said, "No, but we will go on with you to your country."

Naomi said, "No, my daughters; it is better for you to go back to your own country. It makes me feel sad for your sakes that God has sent me so much trouble. Return to your home country."

Then both of them began to cry again. After a while, Orpah dried her eyes, kissed her mother-in-law good-bye, and started to go back to her native land.

Naomi suggested to Ruth, "See, your sister-in-law has gone back to her own people and her own gods. Now you had better return." But Ruth only cried harder. She threw her arms around her mother-in-law, holding her tight, and said, "Do not tell me to leave you. I love you, and I want to stay with you. Where you go I will go, where you live I will live; your people shall be my people, and your God shall be my God. Nothing but death will ever part us."

When Naomi saw that Ruth no longer wanted to be a heathen but that she truly wanted to become an Israelite, she stopped trying to persuade her to go back. The two went on together. They crossed the Jordan River and walked until they came to Bethlehem.

A HAPPY ENDING   You must remember that there was no mailman to deliver letters in those days. Probably the people of Bethlehem had heard very little about Elimelech and Naomi since they had left Bethlehem ten years earlier. When they saw the two women, Ruth and Naomi, walking into town one warm evening, they gathered around them; and when they saw the older lady looking sad and tired, they said, "Can this be Naomi, who left here ten years ago, so happy with her strong husband and her two fine sons?"

Naomi said, "Do not call me Naomi, but call me Mara." Now Naomi means "pleasant," but Mara means "bitter." "For," she said, "I have had bitter trouble since I left here. I went out with my husband and my two sons, but my husband and my sons are dead, and now I have come back alone."

Such bad news shocked the people. They were very kind to Naomi. They welcomed Ruth for Naomi's sake. So Ruth and Naomi went to live in the house where Naomi had lived with her family.

Ruth was not the only person who left the Canaanites to join the people of God. Do you remember Rahab who hid the spies when Joshua sent them to spy out the city of Jericho? And do you remember that when the soldiers destroyed the city, they saved Rahab and her family, and that she lived among the Israelites after that?

After a time Rahab married a fine Israelite man and had children. When they grew up, Rahab's children married Israelites and worshiped the true God. At the time of Ruth and Naomi, one of them, named Boaz, was a rich and important man in Bethlehem. He was a close relative of Naomi's husband.

It was just the time of the barley harvest when Ruth and Naomi returned. All the fields around Bethlehem were filled with reapers. As the reapers cut down the barley and tied it into bundles, working very fast to cover the whole field, some stalks of barley fell on the ground. The reapers did not pick up the fallen stalks. For long ago, in Moses' time, God had commanded that the fallen stalks should be left for the poor to gather up. They came behind the reapers, and gathered whatever barley had fallen to the ground. This was called gleaning.

When Ruth saw the other young women going out to glean barley behind the reapers, she said to Naomi, "Let me, too, go and glean." Naomi said, "Go, my daughter."

Ruth happened to choose Boaz' field in which to glean. Boaz had hired many reapers to harvest his field, and there were several young women gleaning behind them. One day Boaz came to see how his men were getting along. He said to them, "The Lord be with you!" They answered, "The Lord bless you!" Was that not a beautiful way in which to greet one another? Surely these people were true worshipers of God.

Boaz saw Ruth among the gleaners. He said to his overseer, "What young girl is this?"

"This is the Moabite girl who came back with Naomi," the man answered. "She asked me if she could glean after the reapers." Then Boaz said to Ruth, "Listen, my daughter. Don't go to glean in another field, but stay here. I will tell the young men to be kind to you, and also to give you water to drink whenever you are thirsty."

Ruth bowed low before Boaz and said, "Why are you so kind to me, a

10: GIDEON THE DELIVERER

11: THE CHILD SAMUEL

stranger?" Boaz said, "I have heard how good you have been to Naomi, and how you have left your own country to come to live here. The Lord will reward you for trusting yourself under His wings." Perhaps Boaz was thinking of how Rahab had been welcomed by God's people when she, too, was a stranger.

At lunchtime Boaz invited Ruth to sit down with the workers, and he passed her some of the food. After she had gone back to the fields, Boaz said to his reapers, "Let her glean wherever she wants, and purposely let some of the stalks fall from the bundles for her."

Ruth gleaned until evening. Then she took her barley home to her mother-in-law. Naomi asked her, "Where did you glean today?" "The name of the man is Boaz," Ruth answered. Naomi said, "Blessed is the Lord, who has not stopped being kind both to the living and the dead. This man is a cousin of ours."

So Ruth gleaned in Boaz' fields till the end of the barley harvest, and after that through all the wheat harvest.

It was the custom at that time among the Israelites that when a man died and left no children, someone who was a near relative should marry his widow. When Boaz saw the beautiful Ruth gleaning day after day in his fields, he fell in love with her. He asked her to become his wife.

Ruth married Boaz and went to live in his beautiful house. This made Naomi very happy. By and by a little son was born to Ruth and Boaz. They called him Obed.

Naomi took the baby boy in her arms, and she was comforted for all the sad experiences she had had. All her neighbors came to see the baby. They said, "Blessed be the Lord, who, in your old age, has given you this child to love — this child of your daughter-in-law, who is better to you than seven sons!"

The child, when he grew up, was the grandfather of great King David. In the course of time, from his family came Jesus, our Saviour.

Chapter 65
SAMUEL IS GIVEN TO GOD
I SAMUEL 1-3

HANNAH'S PRAYER In Israel there lived a man named Elkanah. He had two wives, as a great many people in those days had. As often happened, Elkanah's having two wives caused trouble in the family. One wife, Peninnah, had a number of children; the other wife, Hannah, whom Elkanah loved more, had no children.

In those days every woman wanted very much to have many children. It was considered a disgrace for her not to have any. Hannah's disappointment was worse because Peninnah was very proud of her fine family. She was always boasting about her children, while poor Hannah had none. Hannah became very unhappy. Many times she went off all by herself and cried bitterly because God had not given her any children.

Elkanah was a good man, who brought up his family to love and trust God. Every year he took his wives and children to Shiloh to worship the Lord at the tabernacle.

Even there Peninnah made fun of Hannah, for Peninnah was jealous because her husband loved Hannah more. Poor Hannah could not keep her tears from falling when she heard Peninnah's taunts. Elkanah tried to comfort her; he could not bear to see her so unhappy. "Never mind, Han-

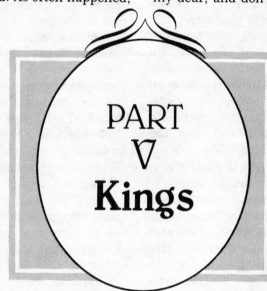

PART
V
Kings

nah," he said. "Don't cry any more. Don't you know that I love you more than ten sons could? Dry your eyes, my dear, and don't grieve. Come, eat your dinner."

But Hannah had made up her mind what to do. After dinner she went to the tabernacle of the Lord. There she saw the priest, Eli, sitting on a seat by the door of the tabernacle.

Hannah was in great bitterness of spirit. She prayed to God, weeping as she did so: "O Lord, if Thou wilt look on my grief, and remember me, and give me a son, then I will give him back to Thee, to serve Thee all the days of his life, and as a sign of my promise, his hair shall never be cut."

Hannah prayed earnestly from her heart, but not out loud. Only her lips moved. When the old priest, Eli, saw her lips moving without a sound, he thought she was drunk. He called out to her, "How long are you going to be drunk? Put away your wine."

Hannah was very much surprised to have Eli speak to her that way. "Oh, no, my lord, I am not drunk," she said. "I am a sorrowful woman, and I have been praying to the Lord to help me. Please do not think that I am a bad woman. I have been speaking out my soul to God." Then Eli said, "Go in peace. And the God of Israel give what you have asked."

After she had prayed to God about her trouble, Hannah felt comforted. She went back to her husband, and her face was happy and peaceful.

The next morning the family went home. Before long the Lord answered Hannah's prayer. He sent her the son she had asked for. She named him Samuel, which means "asked of God."

The next year, when Elkanah took his family to Shiloh to worship the Lord, Hannah did not go along, for the baby was too young to travel. She said to her husband, "I shall not go to Shiloh with you till the baby is older. Then I will bring him to the Lord, so that he may serve Him forever."

When little Samuel was about four or five years old, Hannah went along with the rest of the family to worship God at Shiloh. She and her husband took the little boy to Eli, the old priest. Hannah said to him, "I am the woman who was praying here in the tabernacle. It was for this child I prayed, and God has given me what I asked for. Now I am giving him back to the Lord. As long as he lives, he shall serve the Lord."

Hannah left her little boy with Eli, to be brought up in God's house. He helped the old priest.

Every year, when Elkanah brought his family to Shiloh to worship the Lord, Hannah came to see her little boy. Each year she brought him a little coat that she had made for him. Oh, how eagerly she looked forward to the days when she could see her precious son again! How proud she was of him when she saw how tall he had grown! She was still prouder when she saw how nicely he was learning to wait on Eli, whose eyes were dim with age.

Eli blessed Elkanah and his wife, saying, "May the Lord give you more children, to reward you for giving this child back to Him." God did give Hannah three more little boys and two little girls.

THE VOICE OF GOD Eli was a very old man. He had two grown-up sons, named Hophni and Phinehas. I am sorry to say that though the old priest Eli was a good man, his two sons were just the opposite. They behaved in such a shameful way that all the people of Israel were shocked at their wickedness. Eli could not live much longer, and the people dreaded what would happen when his wicked sons would become priests in his place.

Even as little boys Hophni and Phinehas had been very naughty. Their father had been much too gentle with them, and had not made them behave as they should. Since they were not corrected when they were children, they grew up to be very bad men. Their father talked to them about this, but it was too late to do anything with them. They would not listen to him now.

But God holds parents responsible for the way in which they bring up their children. When your father and your mother correct you for some fault, remember that they have to answer to God for the way they train you.

One evening little Samuel went to bed as usual. After a while, he woke up, thinking he had heard Eli call him. He ran to the old priest and said, "Here I am, for you called me." Eli thought Samuel had been dreaming. He said, "I did not call you. Lie down again and go back to sleep."

Samuel went back to bed. Soon he heard someone calling him again.

131

"Samuel! Samuel!" He jumped up again, and ran to Eli saying, "Here I am, for you called me." Again Eli said, "No, my boy, I did not call you. Lie down again and go to sleep."

Samuel went back to bed once more. Before long he heard the same voice calling, "Samuel!" Again he got up and went to Eli and said, "Here I am, for you *did* call me." Then Eli realized that it was the Lord who had called the child. He said to Samuel, "Go and lie down again. And if He calls you again, say, 'Speak Lord, for Your servant hears.'"

So Samuel went and lay down on his bed. And the Lord came and stood and called as He had before, "Samuel! Samuel!" Then Samuel answered, "Speak Lord, for Your servant hears."

Then God said to Samuel, "I am going to do a thing in Israel at which the ears of everyone who hears about it shall tingle. For those that honor Me, I will honor; and those that despise Me, I will despise. Because of the wickedness of Eli's sons, and because their father did not stop their wicked deeds, Eli's two sons shall die in one day, both of them. And I will raise Myself up a faithful priest, instead of the evil sons of Eli."

Samuel lay still until the morning. Then he got up and opened the doors of the house of God, as usual. He did not dare to tell Eli what God had said to him.

But Eli called him. "What did the Lord say to you?" he asked. "Tell me the whole truth. Do not hide anything from me."

Then Samuel told him everything that God had said. Eli himself was a man who loved and trusted God. His worst fault was that he had not controlled his wicked sons. He said, "It is the Lord. Let Him do what seems good to Him."

Samuel stayed with Eli. As he grew older, it became plainer and plainer that God was with him. All Israel, from the far north to the south, knew that God was making Samuel His prophet.

Chapter 66
WAR WITH THE PHILISTINES
I SAMUEL 4-8

BAD NEWS   As you remember, Samson killed many of the Philistines. After he died, the Philistines did not trouble the Israelites for a long time. But now Samson had been dead for many years, and the Philistines had increased and become strong again.

The Israelites fought against them and were badly beaten. About four thousand Israelite soldiers were killed. The elders said to each other, "Why has God allowed the Philistines to defeat us? Let us take the ark out of the tabernacle into the battle with us, so that it may save us from our enemies."

What was wrong with this plan? Do you remember that the golden ark was very sacred? It was kept in the Holy of Holies, where no one except the high priest might enter, and he only once a year. Even when the Israelites traveled, the ark was covered so that no one was able to see it.

The ark was the place where God lived among His people. When the Israelites carried the ark with them into battle they were trying to compel God to go along with them and give them the victory. If they had obeyed God, and trusted Him, He would have given them victory over their enemies. But they had put their trust in idols, not in the true God. It would not help them to carry God's ark into battle if the blessing of God did not go with it.

Eli's two wicked sons carried the ark into the battle. When it was brought into the camp, the people raised a great shout, so that the earth echoed with the sound. When the Philistines heard the shouting, they asked, "What is this great noise in the camp of the Hebrews?" And someone said, "The ark of God has been brought into the camp."

Then the Philistines were filled with terror, for they said, "God has come into the camp! Such a thing has never happened before! Woe is us! Who will deliver us out of the hand of these mighty gods? These are the very gods that brought all those plagues on the Egyptians!"

You see, the Philistines did not even know that the Israelites worshiped only one God, the true God. They thought they had many gods, like themselves. They expected to lose the battle, but they were too brave to run away. "Be strong now," they said to each other, "and fight as a man should fight. Otherwise you will become slaves of the Hebrews, just as they have been our slaves." And the Philistines fought bravely. They defeated the Israelites.

Eli's two sons, Hophni and Phinehas, were killed. And the ark of God was captured by the Philistines.

A messenger ran from the battlefield to Shiloh to carry the news to the people there. He tore his clothes and put earth on his head to show his grief. When he came to the city and told what had happened, all the people in the city cried out.

Blind old Eli was sitting by the side of the road, waiting for news. He was so worried about God's holy ark that he trembled all over. When he heard the sound of the people crying, he said, "What does all this noise mean?" The messenger said to him, "I am he that fled out of the army." Eli asked, "What happened there, my son?"

Then the messenger said, "Israel has fled before the Philistines. Many of them have been killed. Your two sons, Hophni and Phinehas, also are dead. And the ark of God is captured!"

When the messenger said that the ark of God had been captured by the Philistines, Eli fell over backward from his seat, and his neck was broken, and he died.

THE STORY OF THE ARK   The Philistines took the ark to one of their cities, called Ashdod. They brought the ark to the temple of their god, Dagon, and set it beside the idol.

In the morning, when they went into the temple, they found that Dagon had fallen down upon his face in front of the ark of God. They picked up the image and set it in its place. But the next morning they found that Dagon had fallen down again. This time his hands and his head were broken off, and there was nothing left but a stump.

The hand of the Lord was heavy on the city of Ashdod. The people became sick, and many of them died. They said, "The ark of the God of Israel must not stay here, for His hand is heavy on us and on our god Dagon."

They called a meeting of all the lords of the Philistines to decide what to do with the ark. They sent it to Gath, another of the Philistine cities. But God sent sickness to the people of Gath too. Many of them died.

Then they sent the ark to Ekron. When the Ekronites saw it coming, they cried out, "They have brought the ark of the God of Israel to us, to kill us all."

The Philistines were afraid to have the ark of God in their country any longer, but they did not know what to do with it. They called in their heathen priests and magicians to settle the problem.

The magicians said, "Make a new cart, and take two cows and hitch them to the cart. Take their calves away from them, and bring the calves home. Put the ark of the Lord on the cart, and set it on the road to Beth-shemesh. Put beside the ark offerings of gold, as a sin offering, so that the God of the Israelites may heal you from your plagues. If the cows go right along the road to Beth-shemesh, then you will know that it was the God of the Israelites who brought these plagues upon you. But if they turn back to their calves, you will know that this sickness came upon you just by chance."

The Philistines did just as the magicians had advised. And when the cart was set on the road to Beth-shemesh, the cows went straight along the road, lowing as they went. The lords of the Philistines followed them till they came to Beth-shemesh.

It was just the time of wheat harvest. All the people of the town were out in the fields. They saw the ark of God coming down the road and all the lords of the Philistines following it. How glad they were to see the ark!

Some Levites, the only ones who had the right to touch the ark, lifted it from the cart. They put the ark, and the box of presents the Philistines had sent, on a great rock that was standing there. Then they offered sacrifices to the Lord.

But the men of Beth-shemesh did something very wrong. Many of them came to see the ark of God. They forgot that the ark was holy. They forgot that no sinful man can touch the place where God Himself dwells, or he will die. They opened the lid with the golden cherubim on it and looked inside the ark. Instantly God punished them; many of them died.

Then the people of Beth-shemesh were afraid. They said, "Who is able to stand before this holy Lord God?" They sent a messenger to the people of another town, Kiriath-jearim, and said, "The Philistines have brought back the ark of the Lord. Come down and take it to your city."

The men of Kiriath-jearim carried the ark to their city. It remained there for twenty years.

SAMUEL AS JUDGE   Eli had judged Israel for forty years. After his death Samuel became the judge. God was with Samuel, and He spoke to Samuel as He had spoken to Moses and Aaron.

The Israelites were happy to know that God was again speaking to His people through a prophet. Many of the Israelites had begun to worship idols, but now they remembered that they were God's people. They longed to come back to the Lord and worship Him alone.

Samuel said to the Israelites, "If you return to the Lord with all your hearts, and put away your idols, and serve the Lord only, then He will deliver you from the Philistines. I will pray to the Lord for you."

So all the people came together at Mizpeh. The children of Israel fasted all day, not eating anything. They confessed, "We have sinned against the Lord."

When the Philistines heard of this great meeting, they thought it was a wonderful chance to attack the Israelites. They collected all their soldiers together and marched toward Mizpeh.

The children of Israel were very much frightened. They begged Samuel, "Don't stop praying for us." Samuel offered a lamb as a sacrifice to God, and he cried to God for Israel.

God heard Samuel's prayer. He sent a terrible storm to confuse the Philistines. The heavens grew black, the winds blew, the rain came pouring down. Peal after peal of the most fearful thunder shook the ground. Great streaks of lightning flashed across the heavens. The Philistines could not fight in such a storm. They broke their ranks and fled in terror. The Israelites pursued them, and won a great victory.

Samuel took a great stone and set it up where the battle had taken place. He named the stone Ebenezer, which means "Hitherto hath the Lord helped us."

The Philistines were so badly beaten that as long as Samuel lived they never again troubled the Israelites. They even gave up the cities which they had taken from Israel. Ekron and Gath and the other cities on the seacoast belonged to Israel again.

Every year Samuel went from Bethel to Gilgal, to Mizpeh, and back again to his own city of Ramah. He judged the people of Israel in all these places. The people no longer worshiped idols. They served the Lord and were very peaceful and happy while Samuel was their judge.

After many years Samuel became an old man. He made his two sons judges over Israel. These sons were not as God-fearing as Samuel had been; they did not judge the people justly. They took bribes, and gave corrupt judgments.

The elders of Israel came to Samuel. They said to him, "You are getting old, and your sons do not walk in your ways. Make us a king to judge us like all the other nations."

Samuel was troubled by this request. He did not know what to answer. He did what all men ought to do when they are in doubt — he prayed to God.

God told him to listen to the people. "The people have not rejected you, Samuel," God said; "they have rejected Me. They do not want Me to be their King any longer."

Samuel tried to reason with the people. He told them they would be sorry that they had ever asked for a king. For their king would take their sons and their daughters as his servants. He would take away their fields and give them to his friends. They would have to pay heavy taxes.

But the people refused to listen to Samuel's warning. They said, "We *will* have a king, like other nations, so that he may go out before us and fight our battles." Then the Lord said to Samuel, "Do as they ask, and make them a king."

135

Chapter 67
SAUL, THE FIRST KING
I SAMUEL 9-11, 15

CHOSEN BY GOD In the tribe of Benjamin there was a rich man named Kish, who had a son named Saul. In the whole land of Israel there was not a finer, more handsome young man than Saul. He was a head taller than any other young man in the entire kingdom.

Saul's father had a great many donkeys. One day some of them, which had been turned loose in a field to graze, had wandered away and were lost. Saul's father said to his son, "Take one of the servants with you, and go and look for the donkeys."

Saul and his servant started out. They hunted far and near but they could not find the lost donkeys. They went all through the land of Benjamin without finding any trace of the missing animals.

At last Saul said to his servant, "We had better go back, or my father will stop worrying about his animals, and begin to worry about us." This was easier to say than to do. They had wandered so far from home that they could not find their way back. Then the servant remembered that the prophet Samuel lived somewhere near the place where they were now. He would surely be able to tell them the way home.

The two men set out to find the house of the prophet. They met some young girls who were on their way to draw water. Saul asked them, "Does the prophet live near here?" "Yes," the girls answered. "If you hurry, you can find him easily, for there is a sacrifice in the city today. The people are waiting for him to come and bless the sacrifice before they sit down to eat."

Saul and his servant hurried into the city. Soon they met Samuel himself, going up to the sacrifice.

Now the very day before, God had spoken to Samuel. "Tomorrow about this time," He said, "I will send you a man out of the land of Benjamin. You are to anoint him king over My people Israel. He shall save them from the Philistines."

As Saul and his servant walked through the city looking for the prophet, God spoke to Samuel again and said, "This is the man I told you about yesterday. He is the one who is to be king over My people."

Saul came up to Samuel and asked very politely, "Tell me, I pray you, where the prophet lives." Samuel answered, "I am the prophet." Then he invited Saul to spend the day with him. He said, "Tomorrow I will let you go home, and will tell you everything that you want to know."

Saul had not said anything to Samuel about the lost animals, but Samuel added, "Do not be worried about the donkeys, for they have been found." Then he said something which surprised Saul still more. "Are you not the man for whom all Israel is looking?" Saul did not understand what Samuel meant. He said, "Why do you speak this way? I am no one of any importance."

Samuel did not explain to Saul. He took him along to the sacrifice. He made him sit in the highest seat of honor, and gave him the best of the food. Saul was very glad to get that fine dinner, for he and his servant had been wandering for three days in the hills, and all the food they had brought with them had long since been eaten.

Saul stayed with Samuel that day. The next morning he and his servant set out for home. Samuel went with them as far as the outskirts of the city. There he said to Saul, "Tell your servant to go ahead. You yourself must stay here a little while, until I can show you what God has said."

When the servant had gone on, Samuel took a bottle of holy oil and poured it over Saul's head. He kissed the young man and said, "I have anointed you king over Israel, because God has chosen you to be captain of His people. When you are on your way home, three signs will happen to you. First of all, you will meet two men who will say to you, 'The donkeys you were looking for have been found, and now your father has stopped worrying about the animals, and is instead worried about you.'

"Then, as you go on from there, three men will meet you and give you two loaves of bread. And last of all, you will meet a company of prophets. Then the Spirit of the Lord will come upon you, and you will be turned into another man!"

All these signs came true, just as the prophet Samuel had said. Then Saul knew that he had been chosen by God, and he loved the Lord, because God had changed his heart.

A week later Samuel called all the tribes of Israel together, to announce the new king publicly. "Present yourselves before the Lord," he said, "by your tribes." So the tribes passed by, by their thousands, and the tribe of Benjamin was taken. Then the families of Benjamin came past, and one family of Benjamin was taken. Last the men of that family came past, and Saul, the son of Kish, was taken. But Saul could not be found.

Saul was so shy and modest that he was afraid to face the people. The people asked God what they should do. God answered, "He has hidden himself among the baggage."

There the people found Saul. In triumph they brought him to Samuel. The prophet said, "See the man whom the Lord has chosen to be your king! There is no one like him among all the people."

Saul stood there, his head and shoulders above the crowd. When the Israelites saw the handsome young man who was to be their king, they went wild with joy. "Long live the king! Long live the king!" they shouted.

SAUL SAVES THE EYES OF HIS PEOPLE
Perhaps you remember there were three tribes of Israelites who stayed on the eastern side of the Jordan River — Gad, Reuben, and half of the tribe of Manasseh.

Near them lived the Ammonites. When the Israelites first came to Canaan, after their forty years of wandering in the desert, God had forbidden them to fight against the Ammonites, or to take their land, because these people were the descendants of Lot, the nephew of Abraham.

The Ammonites were now ruled by King Nahash, a very cruel and wicked man. He gathered an army together and came up to fight against the peaceful town of Jabesh-Gilead, one of the Israelite cities on the eastern side of the Jordan.

The people of Jabesh-Gilead were frightened to see an army approaching. They tried to make peace with King Nahash, promising that if he did not kill them, they would willingly be his servants. But even this did not satisfy the heathen king. "I will promise not to fight you," he said, "if you will let me put out all your right eyes!"

The men of Jabesh-Gilead heard these words with terror. They said to King Nahash, "Give us seven days to see if we can get some of our countrymen to help us. If there is no man who is willing to save us, then we will come out to you, and let you put out our right eyes!"

Messengers were sent out in great haste to try to get help. They came to the city where Saul lived, but the people of the city were afraid to fight such a powerful king without a leader. They lamented loudly about the horrible thing that had happened to their brothers in Jabesh-Gilead.

Just then Saul came home from his father's fields. He asked, "What is the matter? Why are the people crying so hard?" When he heard what had happened, he became very angry. "Those wicked Ammonites!" he said. "I will show them that they cannot put out the eyes of God's people!"

Then the Spirit of the Lord came upon Saul and made him very brave. He took a yoke of oxen and cut them in pieces. He sent the pieces over all the land of Israel, with this message: "Whoever does not come with Saul and Samuel to fight against the Ammonites, his oxen shall be cut in pieces, as these have been."

Then the fear of the Lord fell on the people, and they all came out quickly. Now that they had a leader, they were eager to help the men of Jabesh-Gilead. Soon Saul had an army of three hundred and thirty thousand men.

They sent the messengers back to Jabesh-Gilead and said, "Tomorrow, by the time the sun is hot, you will have help." How glad the people of the little town were when they heard this joyful news!

The next day Saul hurried with his army across the Jordan River. The Israelites met the host of the Am-monites early in the morning. The army of Nahash was so badly beaten that there were not two men left together.

This great victory made Saul the hero of the people. They were ready to do anything for this handsome soldier who had led them so well.

Not all the people had welcomed Saul when he was chosen. Some of them had said openly that they did not want him to be king. When all the others had shouted, "Long live the the king!" these men had been silent. When everyone else had brought presents to the new king, these men had said, "Saul will not be a good king."

Now, after Saul's great victory over the Ammonites, the rejoicing people said, "Where are those men who did not want Saul to be their king? Bring them here, so that we can kill them." But Saul said, "Nobody shall be killed today, for today God has given us a great victory." Then all the people offered sacrifices of thanksgiving to God. And all the men of Israel rejoiced greatly.

SAUL LOSES THE KINGDOM You probably remember that when Moses led the Israelites out of Egypt through the desert, the cruel Amalekites followed after them and shot at the people who were too weak or too old to keep up with the others. Because of this the Lord was angry with the Amalekites, and promised to fight against them forever.

After Saul had been king for a number of years, Samuel brought him a message from God. "The Lord once sent me to anoint you king over His people," Samuel said. "Now God commands you to go and fight against the Amalekites, and destroy everything that they have. Do not save anything alive."

Saul called his soldiers together

and marched south into the desert where the Amalekites lived. There was a great battle which the Israelites won. Saul captured Agag, the king of the Amalekites, and destroyed all the people as God had commanded. But he did not obey God's command to kill all the animals. He and his soldiers kept all the best of the Amalekite animals, destroying only those that were not worth saving.

That night God spoke to Samuel, "I am sorry that I ever made Saul king, for he has not obeyed Me."

Samuel rose up early to meet Saul the next morning. The king met him with the words, "Blessed are you in the Lord. I have done all that God commanded me."

"What, then," Samuel asked, "is this bleating of sheep and lowing of oxen that I hear?"

Saul answered, "The people saved the best of the sheep and the oxen to sacrifice them to the Lord. We have utterly destroyed all the rest."

Then the old prophet said, "I will tell you what the Lord said to me last night."

"I am listening," Saul answered.

Samuel said, "When you were little in your own sight, God made you king over Israel. Then the Lord said to you, 'Go and destroy the Amalekites.' Why did you not obey the Lord's command?"

Saul defended himself. "I have obeyed God," he said. "I have utterly destroyed the nation. It is true, my soldiers saved the best of the sheep and the oxen, but only to sacrifice them to the Lord."

Then Samuel asked, "Does the Lord have as great delight in sacrifices as in obedience? Behold, to obey is better than sacrifice. Because you have rejected the word of the Lord, He has also rejected you from being king."

Even now Saul did not realize what he had done. "I have done wrong," he said, "but now go with me to worship the Lord." He seemed to think that God would overlook his disobedience as a thing of no importance. But Samuel said, "I will not go to worship the Lord with you, for you have disobeyed God. Therefore the Lord has rejected you as king of Israel."

As the prophet turned to go, Saul caught hold of Samuel's robe, and it tore. Samuel said, "As you have torn this cloth, so the Lord has torn the kingdom from you, and has given it to a neighbor of yours who is better than you are."

Samuel went home to his house in Ramah. He never came again to see Saul, as long as he lived. He grieved because Saul had proved himself so bad a leader for God's people.

Chapter 68
DAVID, THE SHEPHERD BOY
I SAMUEL 16, 17

A SHEPHERD BECOMES KING For a while we shall leave Saul and his wars. Let us take a walk over the hills of Judah. Let us start at the little town of Bethlehem, where Ruth lived with her husband many years ago.

Do you see that fine house upon the hill? That is the house of Ruth and Boaz, which they built nearly a hundred years ago. They are dead now. Their son Obed is dead, too. Obed's son Jesse is living there with his family of eight sons, in the place where his grandfather Boaz and his grandmother Ruth once lived.

It is springtime. There are flowers on every side. The brook which flows through the meadows murmurs softly over the stones.

Oh, see those little snow-white lambs! How many there are! The sheep are nibbling the soft grass. Let us sit a while on this green hillside and watch them.

Listen! Did you hear that sweet sound? There it comes again. What is it? It must be a shepherd boy singing.

There he is, sitting down under that oak tree. He cannot see us, because we are behind some bushes. Listen!

The Lord is my shepherd;
I shall not want.
He maketh me to lie down in
green pastures.
He leadeth me beside still wa-
ters.

How sweet that song sounds! The boy has a harp in his hands. Perhaps he is going to play it. Be sure to keep behind the bushes. Do not let him see you!

Listen! He is singing again, and playing on his harp. He looks up at the sky as he sings.

The heavens declare the glory of
God;
And the firmament showeth His
handiwork.
Day unto day uttereth speech,
And night unto night showeth
knowledge.

What beautiful songs, and how sweetly sung! Who is this boy? How did he learn to play and sing so well?

He has taken up his shepherd's staff. He is going over the hill, calling the sheep. He has a name for each one. The sheep leave their nibbling and run at his call. He is leading them over the hill.

The shepherd has disappeared. We shall often meet him again, however. God has chosen him to play a very important part in the story of His people. This shepherd boy is to become Israel's king.

God had honored Saul by choosing him to be Israel's first king, but Saul had grown proud. He did not care to do what God wanted. He had not obeyed God's commands.

So after a time God told Samuel to fill his bottle with oil and to go to Jesse in Bethlehem, for the Lord had chosen one of Jesse's sons to be king instead of Saul.

Samuel went to Bethlehem, calling all the people of the village to a sacrifice. Jesse and his sons came with the others. Only Jesse's youngest son David was not called. He stayed in the field, watching the sheep.

Samuel looked at Jesse's oldest son, Eliab, who was very tall and fine looking. He said to himself, "Surely this is the man whom God has chosen to be king."

But God said to Samuel, "Do not judge by his handsome face and his tallness. Man looks on the outward appearance, but God looks into the heart. I have not chosen this one."

Jesse called his next son, Abinadab. Samuel said, "Neither has God chosen this one."

In turn, seven of Jesse's sons came before Samuel. The old prophet said, "God has not chosen any of these. Are these all the sons you have?"

"I have one more, the youngest," Jesse answered. "He is out in the field, keeping the sheep."

"Bring him here," Samuel commanded. "We will not sit down to supper till he comes."

David came in from the fields. He was a young boy of sixteen or seventeen. He was tall and fine looking; he had a well-formed body and a fresh, healthy color from being out of doors day after day with the sheep. He was so handsome that people loved to look at him.

When David appeared, God said to Samuel, "Arise and anoint him, for he is the one whom I have chosen to be king."

The prophet called the young boy to him and told him to kneel down. David came, blushing a rosy red, and kneeled before Samuel. The old man took the oil and poured it on David's head.

All David's brothers and the people of Bethlehem saw Samuel do this. From that time on, the Spirit of the Lord came into David's heart. Of course, he did not begin to rule at the moment when he was anointed, for Saul was still living. Saul did not even know that David had been chosen to be king after him. Only at the death of Saul did the kingdom come to David.

Although Saul continued to rule, God was no longer with him. His disobedience had showed that his heart was not good. When God's Spirit left Saul, an evil spirit came to trouble him. At times he was very sad.

Some of Saul's servants said to the king, "Why does not my lord command us to seek out a man who plays well on the harp? When the king feels sad, sweet music will soothe him and make him well again."

"Find me such a man," Saul commanded.

One of the servants said, "I know a man who plays well. He is the son of Jesse, who lives in Bethlehem. He is a brave young man and a good one. He is handsome, too."

David came to the palace to live for a time. When the king had his spells of sickness, David played on his harp. Saul felt better when he heard the lovely songs David played.

DAVID AND THE GIANT During all of Saul's reign, there was war with the Philistines. These people lived on the seacoast to the southwest of Judah, in the country where the giants had once lived. They had five big, walled cities and many small ones.

Over and over again the Philistines came up to fight with the Israelites. A short time after David had been anointed by Samuel, they again gathered their armies for war. Saul and his soldiers came to meet them. Each army was camped on a mountain, with the valley separating the camps.

With the Philistine army was a man who was more than nine feet tall. His name was Goliath of Gath, and he was one of the few giants left in the land. He could not come into an ordinary house, for he was too tall. He could not squeeze through an ordinary door, for he was too broad. If he could have managed to get in, his head would have hit the ceiling.

This giant was dressed in metal from head to foot. In his hand he held an enormous spear that was so heavy that an ordinary man could not even lift it.

Goliath came out every day and roared a challenge across the valley to the other mountain, where the Israelites stood. He shouted in his fearful voice, "I defy the armies of Israel! Choose a man to fight with me. If he kills me, then we will be your servants. But if I kill him, then you must be our servants."

It was no wonder that the men of Israel were frightened when they saw this giant and heard his boastful words. No one would ever dare to fight with a man so huge. Why, he could kill a hundred men just as easily as he could kill one! No Israelite dared to answer the giant when he roared his challenge, not even King Saul.

Since Saul was away at war, David had gone home to take care of his father's sheep in the fields of Bethlehem. His older brothers had joined the Israelite army.

One day Jesse, David's father, said to him, "Here are ten loaves of bread and a bushel of parched grain. Take them to your brothers at the camp. Take also these ten cheeses as a present to their captain. Find out how your brothers are getting along."

David left the sheep with one of his father's servants. He got up before daylight, to get an early start. The soldiers were getting ready to go out to fight as David came to the battlefield. Leaving his presents with the man in charge of the baggage, he ran quickly into the army to speak to his brothers.

Just as he was talking to them, the terrible giant Goliath came out. He stood on the mountainside and shouted again in his fearful voice, "I defy the armies of Israel! Send a man to fight with me!"

The Israelite soldiers were so afraid that they ran in every direction and hid. Some of the soldiers standing near David said, "Did you see that terrible giant? He comes like that every day. King Saul has promised to give a lot of money to anyone who will go and kill the giant. He has even promised to give his daughter to that man, as his wife. But no one dares to try. Who would have a chance against such a monster?"

David said, "I will go and fight the giant. He is only a heathen Philistine. How dare he defy the armies of the living God? God will help us to overcome him."

Some of the soldiers told King Saul what David had said. Saul was glad to find anyone who dared to fight against the giant. He sent for David. David said to Saul, "Nobody needs to be afraid of this giant. I will go and fight him." But Saul answered, "You are not able to fight this Philistine. You are only a boy. He has been a great fighter all his life."

David said, "While I was keeping my father's sheep, a lion came and stole one of my lambs. I ran after the lion, and pulled the lamb away from him. When the lion turned on me, I caught him by his beard and killed him. Another time a bear took one of the lambs. I killed the bear too. It was the Lord who kept me safe from the paw of the lion and the paw of the bear; He will also deliver me from this heathen Philistine."

"Go then," King Saul said, "and the Lord be with you!" At the same time Saul thought it would be safer for David to wear armor. He put his own helmet of brass on David's head, and a shirt made of little rings of brass on David's body. And he gave David his own sword. But David could hardly walk in this heavy armor. He said to the king, "I cannot wear these things because I am not used to them."

He took them off again. With his shepherd's stick and sling in his hand he ran down the mountainside to meet the giant on the other mountain. In the valley between the two mountains ran a little brook. David stooped down a moment and picked up five smooth stones out of the brook. He put them in the shepherd's

142

bag he had with him. Holding the sling in his hand, he ran toward the giant.

Goliath shouted his defiance again. He looked around to see if anyone dared to come out to fight him. When he saw David, he felt only scorn for this young boy.

David came nearer and nearer. The giant called out, "Am I a dog, that you come out to fight me with sticks?" He began to curse David by his gods, shouting, "Come on! Come on! I will give your flesh to the birds of the air and the beasts of the field to eat."

David shouted back, "You come to me with a sword and a spear and a shield. But I come to you in the name of the Lord of hosts, the God of the armies of Israel, the God you have defied. Today the Lord will deliver you into my power, so that all the people on the earth shall know that there is a God in Israel. Everyone shall see that the Lord can conquer without sword or spear. For the battle is the Lord's, and He will give you into our hands."

When Goliath heard this, he ran forward to kill David. And David ran toward the Philistine. He put his hand into his bag and took out a stone, which he put into his sling. He slung the stone right at the giant. The stone sank down deep into Goliath's forehead. He fell face downward on the ground.

David ran up to the giant. He pulled Goliath's big sword out of its sheath and cut off the giant's enormous head with it.

All the Israelites and the Philistines were watching the fight. When the Philistines saw that their giant was dead, they ran away as fast as they could go. The men of Israel raised a loud shout and ran after them till they came to the gates of Ekron and Gath.

Many Philistines were killed on this memorable day, and King Saul began to take notice of this young man who had done so brave a deed.

Chapter 69
DAVID BECOMES AN OUTLAW
I SAMUEL 18-20

THE CAUSE OF THE TROUBLE Saul was so much pleased with David for killing the giant that he kept the young man at the royal palace all the time, and would not let him go home again to his father's house and his flocks.

Saul had a son, named Jonathan, who was just about David's age. The two young men became great friends. Jonathan loved David as much as he loved himself, and David loved Jonathan deeply, too. They made a promise always to help each other in time of need.

Since Jonathan was Saul's oldest son, he would become king when his father died. He was always very handsomely dressed, because he was the crown prince. Jonathan loved David so much that he gave some of his princely clothes to David. He gave David even his sword and his bow and arrows.

David continued to live at the king's court. He went wherever King Saul sent him, behaving himself so wisely that Saul made him a captain in the army. Wherever David went, in Saul's house or in the army, people liked him.

But something happened that

caused trouble. When Saul and David came back from war with the Philistines, the women of the cities they passed through came out in a procession to meet King Saul. They wanted to show their pleasure in the victories over the Philistines. As they danced joyfully back and forth, shaking their timbrels, some of the women sang, "Saul has slain his thousands." Other women answered in song, "And David his ten thousands."

When Saul heard this, he was very angry, and jealous of David. He grumbled, "They sing that David has slain ten thousands, and that I have slain only thousands. If they think that David is so much better than I am, they will want him to be king instead of me."

The next day, the evil spirit visited Saul. David played on his harp, as he had done before, to make Saul feel better after an attack of this sort. Saul had a spear in his hand. His evil thoughts made him hate David. He threw the spear suddenly at David in an attempt to kill him. But David darted out of the way.

The same thing happened a second time.

After this, Saul would no longer have David in his house. He sent him into the army, making him a captain over a thousand soldiers. By this time David had grown to be a man, and the Lord was with him.

When Saul saw how wisely David behaved, he was afraid of him. But all the people of Israel loved him. So Saul thought of another way of killing David. He made up his mind to send David out to war against the Philistines, so that he would be killed in battle. "That will be much better," thought King Saul, "than for me to kill him."

He called David and promised that if he would kill a hundred Philistines, he might have Saul's daughter as his wife.

Jonathan was not the only one of Saul's family who loved David. His sister Michal was in love with the handsome, brave soldier-musician. David loved Michal in return. To win her he went out very willingly with his thousand soldiers, for he knew that the Lord wanted the Philistines killed.

So David went to war against the Philistines. And they did not kill him, as Saul had hoped. When he returned, Saul gave him the princess Michal as wife. But when Saul saw that his own daughter and all the people loved David, and that the Lord was taking care of him, Saul was more jealous than ever. He became David's deadly enemy.

Now that this attempt to kill David by sending him against the Philistines had not succeeded, Saul tried another way. He commanded his son Jonathan and his servants to kill David.

Jonathan loved David. Instead of killing him, Jonathan did everything he could to help David and to keep him safe. He told David to hide for a little while until he had a chance to talk to the king. "After that," he said, "I will come and tell you what my father says."

So David did. Jonathan approached Saul, speaking well about David. He said, "Do not hurt David, because he has been very good to you. Do not forget that he risked his life for you when he went and fought against Goliath. You were very glad when he did that. Why should you kill a man who has done nothing but good toward you?"

Saul felt ashamed of himself, and he promised that David would not be killed. Jonathan brought David to his father. Once more David lived in Saul's court.

Again the Philistines made war upon the Israelites. David and his thousand soldiers won another splendid victory over the Philistines. But again Saul became jealous of his handsome young captain. The evil spirit troubled him. One day, as he sat in his house listening to David play on his harp, he fell into an ugly temper and again threw his spear at David to kill him. David slipped away, and the spear went into the wall.

This time Saul's fury lasted. He sent messengers to watch David's house and kill him in the morning. Saul's daughter Michal defeated her father's plans, for she loved David. She let him down through a window where the messengers could not see him. He escaped to Samuel, who lived in Ramah, and there he stayed for a while.

DAVID AND JONATHAN David knew he could not keep on hiding from the king forever. Soon he came back secretly to see his friend Jonathan. He asked him, "What have I done to make your father want to kill me?"

Jonathan said, "You shall not die. I will talk to my father and find out why he is angry with you. He tells me everything, and he will tell me this, too."

"Your father knows that you love me," David replied. "He thinks, 'I will not let Jonathan know that I am going to kill David, because it will make him feel sad.' But truly, Jonathan, there is only a step between me and death."

"What do you want me to do?" Jonathan asked.

"Tomorrow is the time of the new moon," said David. "Your father has always had me eat at his table at the time of the new moon. I shall not come tomorrow.

"If your father asks why I am not there, say, 'David asked me if he might go to Bethlehem for a few days, because his family has a sacrifice there every year at this time.'

"If your father says, 'That is all right,' then I shall know that it is safe for me to come back. But if he is very angry, I shall know that he surely wants to kill me."

Jonathan said, "If I find out that my father intends to harm you, I will certainly let you know."

"But how will you tell me?" David asked.

"Let us go out to the field," Jonathan said, "where we can talk more freely."

When they were entirely alone in the field, Jonathan said, "Tomorrow I will find out how my father feels toward you. If he really intends to kill you, I will surely tell you, so you can hide from him. I know that God will take care of you. The Lord always takes care of those who put their trust in Him."

Jonathan was the crown prince, and he should have been king after his father. But he knew that God was going to take the kingdom away from Saul's family, and give it to David. Jonathan loved David so much that he was not jealous. All he wanted was for David to promise that when that time came, he would be kind to Jonathan's children.

"Hide down here in the field for three days," Jonathan said to David. "Tomorrow at dinner I will find out what my father intends to do to you. When I come back, I will bring my bow and arrows, as if I were going to practice shooting. I will bring along a boy to run after the arrows. If I say to him, 'The arrows are on this side,' then come out of your hiding place, for there is peace to you, and no danger.

"But if I say to the boy, 'The arrows are beyond you,' then you may know that my father is not friendly."

The next day was the time of the new moon. Always before, David had sat at the king's table for dinner on that day. This time he did not come.

The first day King Saul said nothing, but the next day he asked, "Where is David? Why hasn't he come for dinner yesterday and today?"

Jonathan said, "David begged me to let him go home for a few days, because his family has a sacrifice every year at this time."

Saul flew into a rage. Before all the people at the table he shouted at Jonathan, "You foolish fellow! You are friends with this David to your own hurt. Don't you know that as long as David lives, you will never be king? Go and get him at once, for he shall surely die." Jonathan protested, "Why do you want to kill him? What harm has he done?"

Saul was in such a temper that he hardly knew what he was doing. He could not speak; he rose from his chair and hurled his spear at Jonathan, his own son. Jonathan became angry, too. To think that his father

should treat David so shamefully! He left the table and would not eat anything. The next morning he went out into the field, taking a boy with him.

As the boy ran, Jonathan shot an arrow beyond him. He called, "Look, the arrow is further on, beyond you." As soon as the boy found the arrow, Jonathan called to him, "Hurry! Hurry!"

Before long, he gave his bow and arrow to the boy, telling him to take them back to the city. When the boy was out of sight, David came out of the place where he had been hiding. Even in this lonely place he had to be very careful not to let anyone see him, for Saul must not discover his hiding place.

David realized now that he would have to go far away, or he would surely be killed. Jonathan knew that he would have to say good-bye to his beloved friend. This was a sad parting. They put their arms around each other and kissed, tears rolling down their cheeks.

Jonathan said, "We will always remember the promise that we have made to each other, for we have sworn in the name of the Lord that we will always be kind to each other's children." Then with a final "Peace be with you," the two friends went their ways, David into the desert and Jonathan to the palace.

Chapter 70
STORIES ABOUT THE OUTLAWED DAVID
I SAMUEL 21-25

A SERIOUS GAME OF HIDE-AND-SEEK David knew that he would have to leave the country to escape from Saul. He went down to Gath in the land of the Philistines.

Even there he was not safe, for some men came to their king and

said, "Is not this David the king of the Israelites? The women sang of him, 'Saul has slain his thousands, and David his ten thousands.'"

They brought David before the king. But to avoid being captured David pretended to be crazy. He scratched on the doors of the gate and let his spit fall down on his beard. Seeing this, the king said to his servants, "Don't you see that this man is insane? Why do you bring such men here?"

Although David had saved himself this time, he could not stay in that city. Praying to God to help him, he took refuge in a big cave called the cave of Adullam, in the country of Judah. When David's father and brothers heard where he was, they came down there too. It was not safe for them to stay in their own home, for in those times if a king were angry with one man, he tried to kill all his family, too.

A great many Israelites who did not like Saul joined David in the cave. Before long David had four hundred men to follow him.

They could not stay in the cave of Adullam long, for fear Saul would find them. David led his men far away from the land of Israel to a city in the land of Moab, on the other side of the Jordan River. He arranged a safe place in the land of Moab for his father and mother who were too old for the dangers and hardships of his own life. They stayed there during all the time David was hiding from Saul.

Before long, God sent a prophet to David to tell him to return to Judah. David and his four hundred men did as the prophet told them. They found a thick woods where they felt they might be safe from Saul.

As soon as Saul heard where David was, he went after him with a large army. David and his men had to flee from one place to another to save themselves from Saul. For many days they hid in caves in the rough mountain country. But God took care of them. He did not let Saul find David.

Near where David was hiding there was a town whose people were not friendly to David. They offered to help Saul catch him. Saul was very pleased to hear these people were on his side. He told them to find out just where David was.

In a few days the king and his soldiers went down there. Just in time, David heard of Saul's coming. He hurried away as fast as he could, with Saul's army after him.

There seemed to be no chance for David to escape, for he and his men were almost surrounded by the king's army. When the end seemed very near, a messenger came to Saul and cried, "Hurry, for the Philistines have come into our land!" So Saul had to give up hunting for David in order to protect his country from the Philistine invaders.

David saw it would not be safe for him to stay where he was. He went over to a very wild and rough country near the Dead Sea. This place was called En-gedi, which means "the rocks of the wild goats." Here David and his men hid in a big cave.

After Saul had driven the Philistines out of his country, he took three thousand of his best soldiers and went to hunt for David. After hunting a long time, he became very tired, and went into a cave to sleep.

Saul had chosen the very cave in which David was hiding, but he did not notice David and his men, who were in the darkness at the back of the cave. Without bothering to look around at all, Saul lay down and went to sleep.

David's men whispered softly to him, "At last God has delivered your enemy into your hand. You can easily kill him." Without answering a word, David walked quietly to the place where Saul lay. With his sword he cut off a part of the king's loose, flowing robe. But he would not let his soldiers harm the king.

After a while Saul woke up and went out of the cave. David came to the opening of the cave and called out after him, "My lord the king!"

Saul turned around to see who was calling him. There stood David, the very man he was hunting!

David bowed himself down to the earth and said, "Why do you believe those who say I am your enemy? This very day I could have killed you, for the Lord delivered you into my hands. But I said, 'I will not harm him, for God has anointed him to be king.' See, my father, I could easily have killed you, but I only cut off a piece of your robe. The Lord judge between me and you; the Lord will look out for my cause. But I will never raise my hand against you."

Saul was startled to see David. When he heard David's friendly words, and saw that David had saved his life, he felt very much ashamed of himself.

"Is that your voice, my son David?" he asked. Saul was so sorry that he had been so cruel to David that the tears ran down his face. "You are a better man than I am," he said. "You have rewarded me good, and I have rewarded you evil. I wanted to kill you, but you saved my life. God will reward you for what you have done today. And now, I know well that someday you will be king. Promise now that when that day comes you will not kill all my children."

David promised, and King Saul went home. David and his men went back to the cave, for Saul could not be trusted. At any moment his ugly temper might come upon him, and then he would again try to kill David.

A WISE WIFE AND A FOOLISH HUSBAND At this time the good old prophet Samuel died. All the people of Israel went to Ramah for his funeral. David could not go, for Saul could not be trusted. Neither did David dare to stay any longer in his cave since Saul had discovered that hiding place.

With his men David went south of the Dead Sea to the wilderness of Paran, another rough country. On his way he passed by the farm of a very rich man named Nabal. This man was rude and stingy, but he had a very charming wife who was as sensible and generous as she was beautiful.

It was the time of the year when the sheep were being sheared. Since Nabal had many sheep and goats, he hired some men to come and shear his animals. He made a feast for these men, preparing a great deal of food.

David often had a hard time to get enough food for himself and his followers, for he now had over six hundred men with him in the wilderness. When he heard that the sheep shearers were Nabal's servants, he sent ten young men to Nabal with this message: "Peace be to you, and to your house, and all you have. All the time your shepherds were in the fields with us, we protected them. We never took away any of their sheep. Ask your young men, and they will tell you this is so. Now I beg you, be generous, and give us a little of the food you have prepared for your servants."

In those days it was considered very rude to turn away anyone who asked for hospitality. But the stingy Nabal answered, "And who is this David? Nowadays there are many servants who run away from their masters. Shall I take the food I have prepared for my shearers, and give it to men who may come from I don't

148

know where? I shall do no such thing."

The young men went back to David and told him how rudely Nabal had answered them. David was angry. He said to his men, "Put on, every one of you, his sword, and we will go and see about this."

In the meantime one of Nabal's servants ran quickly to Nabal's wife Abigail and said to her, "David sent messengers to our master, but our master flew into a rage at them. David's men were very good to us when we were in the fields taking care of the sheep. They protected us from thieves and wild beasts. But now David is angry at our master. You must decide quickly what to do to stop him, for we cannot even speak to our master about this."

Abigail was a wise woman. She acted quickly. She took two hundred loaves of bread, two big wineskins full of wine, five sheep already cooked, five measures of parched wheat, a hundred clusters of raisins, and two hundred cakes of figs. She loaded all these provisions on the backs of donkeys, and sent her servants to David with them. She herself rode on another donkey and followed them. She did not tell her husband Nabal of her intentions.

As soon as Abigail saw David, she slipped from the back of the donkey. Bowing down to the ground very politely, she apologized for the way her husband had acted. "Listen, I pray you;" she said, "to the words of your handmaid. I didn't see the young men you sent. I pray you, forgive our rudeness. For the Lord will surely make you victorious. And when the Lord has made you king over all Israel, then you will be glad that you have not shed blood without cause."

David was very much pleased with this beautiful and gracious woman. "Blessed be the Lord God," he said, "who sent you to meet me today. And blessed be your good advice which has kept me from killing Nabal. If you had not come, I would surely have punished him and all his family tonight."

Abigail went home. Nabal was having a feast in his house, a feast rich enough for a king. He was very drunk. That night Abigail did not tell him what she had done. But the next morning, when he was no longer drunk, she told him what danger he had been in, and how David and his men had planned to kill him. Nabal was so frightened that his heart almost stopped beating. About ten days after that, God sent a sickness to him, and he died.

When David heard of Nabal's death, he sent some messengers to Abigail to ask her to become his wife. So Abigail mounted her donkey again, and went to live with David.

Chapter 71
MORE STORIES ABOUT DAVID AND SAUL
I SAMUEL 26, 29-31; II SAMUEL 1

DAVID SAVES HIS ENEMY Saul did not keep his promise not to harm David. He might have done so, if it had not been for the people who lived near where David was hiding. These people were not friendly to David, so they told the king where he was.

Now Saul went to hunt for David with an army of three thousand soldiers. David had spies watching, and they soon brought him news about where King Saul was.

One night David and Abishai, one of his soldiers, went to the camp where Saul and his men were sleeping. God sent a sound sleep upon the army, so that none of the sentries awakened when David and Abishai stole softly into the camp. King Saul, too, was fast asleep. His spear was stuck in the ground at his head, with a pitcher of water close by. His general, Abner, was sleeping close to the king.

Abishai said softly to David, "God has given you this chance to kill your enemy. Let me kill him with one stroke of my spear. I won't have to strike him a second time."

"No," David said, "God has anointed Saul to be king. I will not kill the man God has anointed. Someday he will fall in battle, or his time will come to die peacefully, but I will not kill him."

So David took Saul's spear and the pitcher of water, and he and Abishai made their way to the top of a nearby hill. Then David called out to Saul's general, "Abner, Abner, do you hear me? I thought you were the bravest of the king's soldiers. Why haven't you taken care of your master, the king? Someone came to kill the king while you were sleeping. And now look! Where is the king's spear, and his pitcher of water?"

Saul recognized David's voice and said, "Is this your voice, my son David?"

David said, "It is my voice, O king. Why do you pursue after me? You have driven me out of the Lord's country into a heathen land. What have I done to deserve this? The king is hunting for someone no more important than a flea."

Saul realized he was guilty. "I have done wrong," he said. "Come back, my son David, for I will not try to harm you, because you have not killed me tonight when you had a chance. I have played the fool, and sinned badly."

"Here is your spear," David answered. "Let one of your young men come over and get it. And as I have saved your life today, so may the Lord save my life, and deliver me from my enemies."

Then Saul said, "Blessed are you, my son David! You will do great things."

Saul went home again, but he could not be trusted. He had already broken his promise once. David said to himself, "Saul will surely kill me someday if I stay here. The best thing for me to do is to escape to the country of the Philistines. When Saul hears I have left the country, he will stop hunting for me." So David took his six hundred men, with their wives and their children and all that they had, and crossed the boundary into the land of the Philistines.

The king of this country was very friendly to David. He gave David the town of Ziklag in the desert. Many more Israelites came to join David here. For many of the people sympathized with him in his struggle with Saul. They knew he had done nothing against Saul. Perhaps some of them had even heard that Samuel had anointed David to be king in the presence of the people of Bethlehem.

Some of the best Israelite soldiers joined David. These were brave men. They were so skillful with bow and arrow that they could shoot as well with the left hand as with the right. They handled a shield nimbly. They could run as fast as a wild deer.

David made these men captains of

his band. For a year and four months they all lived in Ziklag.

THE DEATH OF SAUL   After some time the Philistines made ready for another big battle with the Israelites. David was still living among the Philistines; so he and his men went to Gath, the royal city of the Philistines, to go with them to fight against the Israelites.

But the lords of the Philistines refused to take David and his men with them. They were afraid David would turn against them in the battle. They remembered that the women had sung, "Saul killed his thousands, and David his ten thousands."

It was a good thing the Philistines did not let David join them, for two reasons. The first reason is that a sad thing happened in that battle, and David would never have forgiven himself if he had had a part in it. The second reason is that when David returned to Ziklag he found the city burned. Wandering Amalekites had set fire to the city, and run off with all the women and children.

When David and his men discovered their homes had been burned, and their wives and children stolen, they wept till they had no tears left. David asked God if he should pursue the Amalekites. God told him to go, and promised he would recover all that had been stolen.

So David and his four hundred men started out. They did not know which way the thieves had gone, for there was no one living in that wild, lonely country to direct them. But in the field they found a poor, sick man who had been left behind by the Amalekites. He was almost dead, for he had had nothing to eat or drink for three days and nights. Lifting him up, the Israelites gave him some bread and water and some dried figs and raisins.

After the man had eaten, he revived enough to speak. They asked him if he knew where the Amalekites had gone. "Yes," he said, "I will show you the way if you promise not to kill me."

In their camp the Amalekites were eating and drinking and dancing because they had captured so much treasure. David attacked them at once. They fought all night and the next day. All the Amalekites were killed, except four hundred young men who galloped swiftly away on camels.

David's men got back everything that had been stolen — all their wives and sons and daughters, and all their flocks and herds. Besides that, they captured all the cattle belonging to the Amalekites.

Meanwhile the Philistines had prepared for war, and marched into the country of the Israelites. There was a great battle on the mountain of Gilboa. The Philistines fought hard. They gained the victory over the Israelites. Many of the Israelites were killed or very severely wounded.

Jonathan and two other sons of Saul were killed. And the Philistine soldiers followed hard after Saul. Saul was afraid that if the Philistines captured him, they would torture him. He said to the man who carried his armor, "Draw your sword, and thrust it through me, so that I may die, and not become a captive of the Philistines."

But the armor bearer was afraid to kill the king. So Saul took his own sword and stuck it in the ground with the point up. Then he fell upon the sword, to kill himself. He did not die at once. While he was in great pain he saw a young man, an Amalekite.

151

The wounded king managed to say, "Kill me, I pray you, for I am in great pain."

The young man saw that Saul was so badly wounded that he could not live. He did as Saul asked. When Saul was dead, the young man took the crown from his head and the bracelet from his arm, and carried them away.

The day after the battle the Philistines came to the battlefield to strip the dead and steal any treasures they might find. They found the bodies of Saul's three sons. When they found Saul's body, they were very glad. They sent the news of Saul's death into all parts of their land. They put his armor in one of their temples.

All this time, David knew nothing of what had been going on. He and his men were far away in the desert, fighting the Amalekites. Two days after David and his soldiers had conquered the Amalekites, and had brought back their wives and children to Ziklag, a messenger arrived from the battle at Gilboa. His clothes were torn, and he had earth upon his head.

The people all gathered around him. "Where do you come from?" David asked.

"I have escaped out of the camp of Israel," the young man answered.

"Tell me how the battle went," David said.

The young man answered, "The Philistines have won a great victory, and many Israelites have been killed. Saul and his son Jonathan are dead also."

"How do you know Saul is dead?" David asked. The young man showed David Saul's crown and bracelet. He told him how he had helped Saul out of his suffering.

When David and his soldiers heard this, they all tore their clothes. They mourned and fasted till evening, in memory of Saul and Jonathan and all the Israelite soldiers who had died.

David sang a beautiful song of mourning for Saul:

The beauty of Israel is slain upon the high places.
How are the mighty fallen!
Saul and Jonathan were lovely and pleasant in their lives,
And in their death they were not divided.
I am distressed for thee, my brother Jonathan.
Very pleasant hast thou been unto me.
Thy love for me was wonderful, Passing the love of women.

Chapter 72
DAVID, THE KING WHOM GOD LOVED
II SAMUEL 2, 5-9

THE ARK IS BROUGHT BACK Now that Saul and his sons were dead, the children of Israel were without a king. David knew that he was to rule after Saul's death, because Samuel had anointed him. He asked the Lord where he should go to be proclaimed king. God told him to go to Hebron. So David and his men left the burned city of Ziklag and went to live in the country around Hebron.

The death of Saul and his sons did not make the Israelites sad for long. The people knew that David would become their king, and they loved him. Great numbers of soldiers came to Hebron to crown their new king. Day after day they poured into the city, until there were nearly three hundred thousand men who had come to show their loyalty to David.

And so amid great joy and rejoicing David was crowned. He was thirty years old when he became king, and he reigned for forty years. The first seven happy years were spent in Hebron, where he had been crowned. Afterward Jerusalem became the royal city. It was built on a high hill, with deep valleys on three sides. It would be easy to defend in case of war.

After David and his leaders went to live in Jerusalem, the city was often called "The City of David." The king built a beautiful palace with fine cedar wood sent by Hiram, king of Tyre. He built other fine houses in Jerusalem, making it a beautiful city.

David loved and trusted the Lord, and tried always to serve Him. He became a great king, for God was with him.

Sometime after David had been living in Jerusalem, he remembered that the golden ark of the Lord was still in Kiriath-jearim. It had been there for twenty years, ever since it had been captured, and then returned, by the Philistines.

David talked to the important men of the country, suggesting that they bring the ark to Jerusalem. The people were very much pleased at this suggestion.

David planned to make the bringing of the ark a great celebration. He collected a whole orchestra of musicians, harp players, cornet players, trumpet players; and he himself wrote songs of praise to God, and trained choirs of singers to take part in the triumphant procession.

But David forgot, in the excitement of all his big plans, the most important part of moving the ark. He forgot that God had given careful directions about how the ark must be moved. Only the Levites were allowed to carry it, and even they could not touch the ark itself. They could only touch the poles which were threaded through the rings on the side of the ark. They were to carry these poles on their shoulders.

Why were these rules so important? They were important because they reminded God's people that God is a holy God, and that all men are sinners. There is only one way in which a sinful man can come into God's presence. He must put all his trust in the death of Jesus on the cross in his place.

Do you remember what happened to the men of Beth-shemesh, who looked into God's holy ark after the Philistines had brought it back? These men, who had forgotten that they were sinners and God is holy, had died. David knew all this, but he was so busy about his own big plans for the great celebration that he forgot all about God's holiness and his own sin.

David brought a new cart, and his men attached two oxen to it and set the ark on the cart. The people walked beside the cart, singing, and David himself played on his harp. In one place the road was very rough, and the oxen stumbled. Uzza, one of the men driving the oxen, put out his hand to steady the ark. Instantly Uzza fell down dead, without time to cry out.

David and the people were very much frightened. They did not dare to go any further. They carried the ark hastily into the nearest house. For David was afraid of God. He said, "How shall the ark of such a holy God come unto me?" There is a way, David. You would know the way back to God yourself if you only stopped to think. It is the way of forgiveness, the way God Himself has opened.

The ark stayed where it was for three months. Then, because God greatly blessed the family in whose house it was, David finally gathered up the courage to bring the ark to Jerusalem.

This time the Levites carefully carried the ark on their shoulders, as God had commanded. Once more David and all the people danced and sang as they went along. And, even more important, they offered sacrifices to God along the road, because they remembered that they were sinners and God is holy.

So they brought the ark to Jerusalem, where a tent had been made ready to shelter it. David appointed some of the Levites to take care of the ark. He wrote a song to be sung before the ark. This song ended with the words:

Blessed be the Lord God of
Israel
From everlasting to everlasting.
And all the people said "Amen," and praised the Lord. Once more worship was centered around the ark.

One day David realized that while he was living in a beautiful palace, God's holy ark was sheltered only by a tent. A wonderful thought came into his mind. He would build a beautiful temple for God's house, covered with gold and beautifully decorated. The prophet Nathan was pleased with David's plan.

That night God spoke to Nathan and gave him a message for David.

"Since the day that I brought the children of Israel out of Egypt," God said, "I have never commanded that a house be built for Me to live in. I took you, David, from being just a shepherd boy, and made you king over My people Israel. I have been with you wherever you went. And after you sleep with your fathers, your children shall reign after you in a kingdom that shall never end. And your son, whom I shall set upon your throne, he shall build a house for Me."

David felt very thankful and unworthy when he heard God's promise that his children should be kings over Israel forever. He gave up his plan of building a temple, but he made everything ready for his son to build it.

DAVID REMEMBERS A PROMISE King David fought many wars. God gave him victory over his enemies, the Philistines. He conquered the northern land as far as the Euphrates River on the east. He conquered the Ammonites to the east of the Jordan, the Syrians to the north, and the Edomites to the south in Mount Seir. All these nations became David's servants. David was now a very great king. He captured great quantities of silver and gold from all the countries where he had been fighting. He brought all this silver and gold and brass to Jerusalem, saving it up for the beautiful temple which God had said his son should make.

Now that his kingdom was safely established, David tried to find out if there were any of Saul's children or grandchildren to whom he could show kindness. He heard that one of Saul's old servants, Ziba, was still living. King David sent for Ziba and asked him, "Are there any of Saul's family left? I should like to be kind to them."

Ziba answered, "There is a son of Jonathan, named Mephibosheth. He is lame. He was five years old when that terrible battle was fought between the Israelites and the Philistines in which his father Jonathan and his grandfather Saul were killed. When the news of the battle came, his nurse snatched him up in a hurry to hide him. In her haste, she dropped the little boy. He has been lame in both his feet ever since."

The king said, "Find him, and bring him here."

When Mephibosheth came to the king, David remembered his love for Jonathan, and the sacred promise he had made to him. He said tenderly, "Mephibosheth."

The man bowed down to the ground and answered rather tremblingly, "I am your servant," for he did not know what the king wanted of him.

David said, "Do not be afraid, Mephibosheth. I will surely be kind to you, for the sake of your father Jonathan. I will give back to you all the land which belonged to your grandfather Saul. You yourself shall daily eat at my table with my own sons."

King David gave back to Mephibosheth all the land that had belonged to Saul. Ziba farmed the land for him. And Jonathan's lame son lived in Jerusalem and ate at the king's table.

So David remembered his promise to his friend.

Chapter 73
HOW THE GOOD KING SINNED
II SAMUEL 11, 12

One evening when David could not sleep very well, he got up out of bed and went up to the roof of his house. Perhaps it was cooler there; or perhaps David enjoyed the bright moonlight. All the roofs in Canaan were flat, with a railing around them. People often sat on their roofs or slept there.

David could see down into the court of a nearby house where a woman was washing herself. She was very beautiful. David sent one of his servants to ask the woman to come to see him.

This woman was Bathsheba, the wife of a man called Uriah, who was fighting for David beyond the Jordan River. Bathsheba came to see David, and the king fell in love with her. He could not have her as his wife because she was already married. David gave himself over to wicked thoughts. "Oh, if only her husband should be killed in the war! Then I could marry her."

David wanted her so much that he sent a letter to his general, Joab, telling him to put Uriah in the front of the hottest battle, so that he would be killed. Joab did this. He put Uriah at a most dangerous position near the wall of the city. Some archers on the top of the city wall shot Uriah. He died, as David had hoped.

When Bathsheba, the wife of Uriah, heard that her husband was dead, she mourned for him. After a time David married her. Before long a little son was born to them.

155

What David had done displeased the Lord. He sent the prophet Nathan to David. Nathan told David this story:

"There were two men in one city. One was rich; the other was poor. The rich man had a great many flocks and herds, but the poor man had only one little lamb, which he had brought up as a pet. The lamb ate from his plate, and drank from his cup, and slept in his bed with him. He loved it as much as if it had been his daughter.

"A traveler happened to visit the rich man. Instead of taking one of his own sheep to make a nice dinner for the traveler, the rich man took the poor man's lamb, and killed it."

When David heard this story, he became very angry. "As the Lord lives," he exclaimed, "the man who has done this shall surely die! He shall give four lambs back to the poor man!"

"You are the man!" the prophet Nathan said. "The Lord says, 'I anointed you king over Israel. I saved you from Saul, giving the kingdom to you. You have many wives. Uriah had only one wife. Why have you done this wicked thing? You have murdered him with the sword, and have taken his wife to be your wife. I will raise up trouble in your own family against you, to teach you how sinful you have been.'"

David answered, "I have sinned against the Lord."

Nathan said, "If you are truly sorry for your sin, the Lord will forgive you, and you shall not die. But because you have done this wicked thing openly, so that others are mocking God's people, the baby you love shall be taken away."

With these words Nathan went away. As he had said, the baby soon became very sick. David loved the child very much. He knew the child was dying because he had sinned. He could not bear to look at its dear little face, hot with fever. He lay on the ground all night and prayed to God to save the child's life. The men of his house tried to make him get up from the ground, but he would not get up nor eat with them.

After seven days the baby died. David's servants were afraid to tell him that the child was dead. They whispered to one another, "While the child was still alive he would not listen to us. How much more will he grieve now that the child is dead!"

When David saw his servants whispering, he asked them, "Is the child dead?"

"He is dead," they said. David arose from the ground. He washed himself and put on clean clothes. He went first of all to the house of the Lord to worship. Then he went to his own house and ate some food.

His servants were surprised. "How is this?" they asked. "When the child was still alive, you fasted and wept; now that he is dead, you arise and eat."

David answered, "While the child was still alive I fasted and wept, for I said, 'Perhaps God will be gracious to me and will let the child live.' But now he is dead. Why should I fast? I cannot bring him back again. I shall go to him, but he will not return to me."

The next year God gave David and Bathsheba another baby. They named him Solomon. God loved Solomon.

In his sorrow for his sin, David wrote a beautiful song — the Fifty-first Psalm:

Have mercy upon me, O God,
    according to thy lovingkind-
    ness; . . .
For I acknowledge my transgres-
    sions:
And my sin is ever before me.
Hide thy face from my sins, and
    blot out all mine iniquities.
Wash me, and I shall be whiter

than snow.
For Thou desirest not sacrifice;
    else would I give it:
Thou delightest not in burnt of-
    fering.
The sacrifices of God are a bro-
    ken spirit:
A broken and a contrite heart, O
    God, Thou wilt not despise.

Chapter 74
THE PLAN OF A BAD SON
II SAMUEL 15, 16

THE PRINCE WHO WANTED TO BE KING   King David's oldest sons were already grown men when Solomon was still a child. David's third son, Absalom, was a very handsome man, and David loved him especially.

In all the land there was not another young man so handsome as Absalom. He had beautiful hair which hung long and heavy over his shoulders. It was so thick that at the end of each year the part that he had cut off weighed six pounds.

Naturally the people talked about the king's son. Absalom liked to be noticed. He was married and lived in a house of his own. He had a fine chariot to ride in, and fifty men to run before him. When the people saw this procession coming down the streets of Jerusalem, they would stop in admiration and say, "There comes the king's son. How handsome he is!" They did not know that he was not as good as he was handsome.

Absalom tried hard to make the people of Israel love him. He stood often in the gate of the city. If some man from the country came to Jerusalem to have some dispute settled which he had had with a neighbor, Absalom called to him, and asked him what was the trouble. The man would be glad to have the king's son listen to his story. Absalom would be very friendly to the man. Instead of expecting the man to bow to him, he would put his arm around the man and kiss him.

In itself, of course, this was all right. It was good to be kind and friendly. But Absalom did not do these things because he was really friendly to the people, but because he wanted to be king someday. He thought that if he could win the love of the people, they would later help him to become king, even though he was not the one chosen by his father, King David.

And so he would say to the man with whom he talked, "See, your matter is right, but the king has no time to hear you. If I were made judge in the land, I would do justice to every man." The man would go away thinking, "What a fine man the king's son Absalom is! What a fine king he would make!" So Absalom stole the hearts of the people of Israel.

Meanwhile King David was reigning in peace and comfort. He had a long and happy rule. Most important of all, David truly worshiped God. In his time the children of Israel served God and put away all their idols. David organized a choir of many singers to praise God at the tabernacle. He built up Jerusalem into a strong and beautiful city, of which the Israelites were very proud. The land was prosperous and happy in David's reign. All the people loved their good king.

But this peace did not last. When David was getting to be an old man, his son Absalom made trouble for him.

Ever since the birth of Solomon, David had intended him to be king. From the time he was a little child, Solomon showed the promise of a wise and beautiful character. Perhaps Absalom knew that David planned to have Solomon become king after he was dead. If so, he did not intend to pay any attention to his father's wishes. He made up his mind that he himself was going to become king.

KING DAVID RUNS AWAY Absalom's character was so mean and deceitful that he did not even have the grace to wait until his father was dead before he started trouble. One day he asked his father if he might go down to the city of Hebron to keep a vow.

Absalom had been planning for years to seize the kingdom. All his plans had been made beforehand. He had sent spies throughout the whole kingdom, telling them as soon as they heard the sound of trumpets to shout out to the people, "Absalom is king in Hebron!"

With him Absalom took two hundred men from Jerusalem. He also sent for David's wise man, Ahithophel, to come and counsel him. At that time there was, of course, no telephone, or radio, or television, to send news flying here and there. It might be two or three days before King David would hear of what Absalom was doing. Absalom would have plenty of time to collect a big army.

For many years Absalom had been stealing the hearts of the men of Israel by pretending to be friendly to them. So when they heard the spies proclaiming, "Absalom is king in Hebron," many flocked to his side.

Someone who was still loyal to David ran to Jerusalem with the news that all the people of Israel had gone over to his son. The news came as a great shock to David. He loved Absalom, but he knew his son was a dangerous man; for one day Absalom, in a fit of anger, had killed his oldest brother Amnon. But David had not dreamed that Absalom would fight against his own father. He was not prepared for war. He did not know how large an army his son might have.

He said to his servants, "Let us hurry to get away, for Absalom may come with a big army, and attack the city, and kill all the people." So King David and all his household left Jerusalem in a big hurry. He did not go alone, for the six hundred brave men, who had been with him while he hid from Saul, went with him. The Levites went too, carrying the ark of God.

David said to Zadok and Abiathar, the priests, "Do not come with me, but go back into the city with the ark of God. If God is pleased with me, He will bring me back to Jerusalem someday. Stay in the city with your sons, Ahimaaz and Jonathan. You are priests, and Absalom will not

158

hurt you. You must find out for me what is going on, and then send me word by your sons."

David and all the people with him went over the brook Kidron and up the side of Mount Olivet. David felt very sad to think that his own son, whom he loved so much, had conspired against him. His heart was almost broken. Perhaps he remembered his own sin against Uriah, and how God had said He would raise up trouble for David in his own family, to teach him what a dreadful thing he had done when he murdered Uriah. Barefoot, his head covered for very grief, David went up the Mount of Olives, weeping as he went. All those with him covered their heads and wept too.

Someone told David, "Ahithophel, your wise counselor, has gone over to Absalom." This was a dreadful blow to David. He prayed to God, "O Lord, I pray Thee, turn the counsel of Ahithophel into foolishness."

As David came to the top of Mount Olivet, David's other counselor, Hushai, came to meet him. He had torn his coat with grief, and he had put earth upon his head. David was very glad to see that Hushai was friendly to him. He said, "Go back into the city, Hushai. Go back to Absalom, and say to him, 'I will be your servant, O King, as I have been your father's servant till now.' In that way you may fool Absalom, and work against Ahithophel. The priests are in Jerusalem, and they have their sons with them. As soon as you have any news, you can send it to me by those two young men."

So Hushai returned to Jerusalem. And King David ran away from the son whom he loved.

Chapter 75
THE FAILURE OF THE PLOT
II SAMUEL 17-19

GOOD ADVICE AND BAD While King David was fleeing from Jerusalem, Absalom and many of the people of Israel came to the city. David's wise counselor, Ahithophel, was with them.

The other wise man, Hushai, was still faithful to David. He came to Absalom and said, "Long live the king! Long live the king!" Absalom was surprised. "Is this your kindness to your friend David?" he asked. "Why didn't you go with him?"

Hushai said, "If the Lord and all the people of Israel choose you to be king, then I will stay with you. Why shouldn't I serve the son faithfully, just as I served the father?" Hushai seemed to be very much in earnest. Absalom was satisfied, accepting him as second counselor.

Then the new king asked Ahithophel, "Now what do you advise me to do?" Ahithophel was a very wise man. He said, "Let me choose out twelve thousand men and go after David. I will come upon him while he is tired and weak. The people who are with him will run away, and I will kill only the king. All the people I will bring back to you, and you shall be king in peace."

Absalom was greatly pleased with this wise advice. He did not want to follow it, however, until he had first heard what Hushai had to say. Hushai knew very well that Ahithophel's counsel was wise, and he did not want Absalom to follow it.

"The counsel that Ahithophel has given is not good at this time," he said. "Your father and the men with him are mighty men. They are angry now, like a bear robbed of her cubs. Your father will be too wise to stay with the people tonight. He will hide in some cave or some other secret place. If we go up there tonight, and some of our soldiers are killed, then our people will be frightened and will run away.

"Instead of going tonight, it will be better for you to wait until you can gather the whole nation of Israel and fight an open battle with your father. If you do this, we shall be so many that we can easily defeat him. Not one of his soldiers will be left. If he has hidden in a walled city, then we will pull down the walls till not one stone is left."

When Absalom and his friends heard this advice, they thought the counsel of Hushai better than the counsel of Ahithophel. It really was worse, but God made Absalom prefer Hushai's bad advice, to save David's kingdom from his rebellious son.

Hushai let no time pass before he went to Zadok and Abiathar, the priests. He told them the counsel which Ahithophel had given to Absalom, and then what his own advice had been. He said to them, "Send your sons quickly to David, and tell him it will not be safe for him to stay tonight on this side of the Jordan River. He must hurry and cross to the other side."

Jonathan and Ahimaaz, the sons of the priests, had not dared to come into Jerusalem, but were staying outside in the country. A young girl went out and gave them the message. A boy who saw them ran to tell Absalom that he had seen two men who seemed to be spies. Absalom sent some servants to arrest them.

In the meantime the priests' sons came to a house which had a well. They slid down into the well and hid. The woman of the house spread a cloth over the mouth of the well, and scattered ground wheat on the cloth. Soon Absalom's servants came past. They asked, "Where are Jonathan and Ahimaaz?"

The woman answered, "They have gone over the brook." The servants went on and looked for the young men. They returned to the city without having found any trace of them.

As soon as they were sure it was safe, Jonathan and Ahimaaz climbed out of the well and ran to David. They told him to cross the river at once. Absalom had decided to follow Hushai's advice, and gather a big army; but he might at any time change his mind and start out after David without waiting.

That night David and his men crossed the Jordan River. They went on toward a city that was far away from Jerusalem. Here David was given a fine present of food for his people. Besides this, he was given kettles to cook in, and dishes to eat from, and heavy rugs, such as the people in that country use to sleep on.

Many of the people of Israel still loved David and sympathized with him. As he passed through the country, the people came out of their houses. They wept to think that their good king should be so badly treated by his own son. Many of the men left their farms and joined David's

12: DAVID SPARING SAUL

13: DAVID KING OVER ISRAEL

company, to fight for their king if there should be a battle with Absalom's soldiers.

Soon David had a large army. There were thousands of soldiers with him, ready and eager to fight for their king. David divided his soldiers into three parts. He set his general, Joab, over one-third of the soldiers; and Joab's brother Abishai over another third; and a man called Ittai over the other third. David promised the soldiers, "I will go out with you to battle."

But the people said, "No, you must not go. If we run away, they will not care for us; and if half of us die, they will not care. But you are worth ten thousand of us. Stay in the city, ready to help."

ABSALOM'S DEATH   Absalom followed Hushai's advice. He came over the River Jordan with a big army, to fight against David in the forest near the city where David was. David's army went out of the city to meet Absalom's soldiers. David stood in the gate as his thousands of soldiers marched out. He spoke a special word to his three generals: "Deal gently for my sake with the young man Absalom." He loved Absalom so much that he did not want him harmed even though he was a traitor to his own father.

The two armies met in the wood. Absalom's army was beaten. Twenty thousand men were killed. To escape from David's soldiers, Absalom urged his mule into a gallop. As he sped forward under a thick oak tree, his long hair caught in the low branches of the tree. Absalom hung between heaven and earth, and the mule went on from under him.

A young man saw this happen, and ran to Joab, exclaiming, "I saw Absalom hanging in an oak tree!" Joab was a stern soldier, a man of iron. He did not intend to deal gently with the prince, for he thought Absalom deserved to die. "Why did you not kill him?" he asked. "I would have given you ten shekels of silver and a girdle."

But the young man answered, "If you had given me a thousand shekels of silver, I would not have put forth my hand to kill the king's son! I myself heard the king say to you and the others, 'Do not let anyone touch the young man Absalom.' If I had killed him, I would surely have lost my own life. The king would have heard of it, and you yourself would have been the first to blame me."

Joab did not stop to listen. He hurried to the place where Absalom was hanging from the branches of the big oak tree. Joab took three darts and thrust them into the prince. Ten young men, Joab's bodyguard, closed in and killed Absalom.

Then Joab blew the trumpet to stop the battle. Now that Absalom was dead there was no longer any cause for war. As the clear notes of the trumpet sounded through the woods, the soldiers stopped fighting and gathered around Joab.

Ahimaaz, the priest's son who had brought news to King David about Absalom's plans, begged Joab to let him run to tell the king that the battle was won. Joab refused, for he knew David would feel very sad when he heard his son was dead. Another messenger was sent. But Ahimaaz was young, and eager to be the first to break the news to the king that the battle was won. Finally Joab gave in. Ahimaaz ran after the first messenger, and soon overtook him.

King David was sitting in the gate of the city, waiting to hear news of the battle. A watchman stood on the roof over the gate. He called down to the king, "I see a man, all alone, running." The king said, "If he is alone, he has some news for us."

The watchman again called down to David, "I see another man running alone." The king replied, "He also brings news." The watchman called again, "I think the first one runs like Ahimaaz." The king answered, "He is a good man. He will bring good news."

As soon as Ahimaaz came near enough to be heard, he shouted, "All is well." Then he came nearer, bowed down before David, and said, "Blessed be the Lord thy God, who has delivered up the men who were fighting against the king."

David asked, "Is the young man Absalom safe?"

"When Joab sent me, I saw a great tumult, but I did not know what it meant," Ahimaaz answered. The king commanded, "Wait till this other messenger comes."

The other man came up, panting. "Tidings, my lord the king," he said. "The Lord has avenged you of all those who rose up against you."

The king asked, "Is the young man Absalom safe?"

"May all the enemies of my lord the king be as that young man is," said the messenger.

The king was grief-stricken. He went upstairs to the little room over the gate, put his head down on his arms, and cried, "O my son Absalom, my son, my son Absalom! Would I had died for you, O Absalom, my son, my son!" King David did not think of the victory, nor of his kingdom. He thought only of his dear son.

The soldiers were coming back from the battle with joy in their hearts because their beloved king was safe. When they heard that pitiful cry, "O Absalom, my son, my son!" their joy was turned into sadness.

Joab, that stern and strong soldier, was David's true friend in his own rough way. He said to David, "You have hurt all your soldiers, who have saved your life, and the lives of your sons and your daughters and your wives. I see that you love your enemies and hate your friends. If Absalom had lived, and all the rest of us had died, you would have been pleased.

"Get up, and go out to the soldiers to thank them. Speak kindly to them, or all your people will leave you, and you will not have any friends left. That will be worse than any trouble you have ever had in your whole life."

This advice was not gentle, but it was very wise. King David wiped his eyes, went downstairs, and sat in the gate to greet his soldiers as they came back from fighting for him.

DAVID'S TRIUMPHANT RETURN   After a few days, the people throughout the land of Israel began to say, "Our king, who saved us from the Philistines and from all our enemies, has fled out of the land on account of Absalom. But Absalom is dead now. Let us bring our king back to Jerusalem."

So David and all his household started to return to the royal city. The people of Judah were so delighted to have their beloved king back that the whole tribe came to meet him at the Jordan River. Ferryboats carried the king and his followers over the river. What shouts of joy rang through the air as David landed! What clapping of hands! The people ran along beside the king's procession, singing and dancing as they went.

The people of Judah went with the king all the way to Jerusalem, shouting, singing, and clapping their hands, overjoyed to get their beloved king back again.

David once more sat upon his throne in Jerusalem. He praised God for helping him in a beautiful song:

He sent from above, He took me,
He drew me out of many waters.
He delivered me from my strong
* enemy,*
And from them that hated me.
The Lord was my stay.

Chapter 76

THE WISEST MAN IN THE WORLD

I KINGS 1-3; I CHRONICLES 28, 29

THE ANOINTING OF SOLOMON   In his old age, when all was peaceful and his kingdom was easily governed by his helpers, King David spent his time getting everything ready for his son Solomon to build a temple for the Lord. He collected great quantities of gold, silver, brass, iron, and precious stones to be used in building the house of God.

There came a time when King David was too old to attend to the affairs of his kingdom. Now one of his sons, Adonijah, wanted to be king. Adonijah was a full brother of Absalom. He was very much like his brother, for he, too, was very handsome.

Adonijah did not try to kill David, as Absalom had done. He knew his father could not live much longer. Some distance away from Jerusalem Adonijah made a big feast, to which he invited all his brothers except Solomon. He invited Joab, David's general, too, and Abiathar the priest.

Nathan, the prophet, went to Solomon's mother Bathsheba. "Have you not heard," he said, "what Adonijah is doing? And David does not know about it. If you want to save your own life, and the life of your son Solomon, go and tell the king." Bathsheba went into the room where David was lying on a couch. As she

bowed low, the king asked her, "What do you wish?"

Bathsheba said, "My lord, you promised that Solomon should reign after you. And now Adonijah has made himself king, without letting you know. He has made a great feast, and invited all your sons, and also Joab and Abiathar. Now, O king, all the people of Israel are waiting for you to tell them who shall be king after you. Unless you do this, Solomon and I will be killed."

While she was still talking, Nathan came in. He repeated the news Bathsheba had given David. King David saw that Solomon must be made king at once, before he himself died. He said to Bathsheba, "Surely, Solomon your son shall reign after me, and shall sit upon my throne. I will crown him this very day."

Nathan the prophet and Zadok the priest took Solomon out of the city. Zadok anointed Solomon with oil. The soldiers blew a trumpet. All the people came running to see what was going on.

When they heard the shout, "Long live King Solomon!" all the people shouted too, "Long live King Solomon!" They joined the procession. Some of the soldiers marched ahead with trumpets. Then came Solomon,

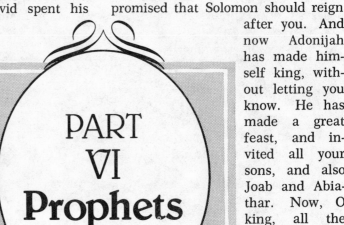

PART VI

Prophets

riding on the king's mule, with soldiers marching on each side of him. Next came more soldiers, and then the people, shouting, "Long live King Solomon!" The people were singing, dancing, piping on their flutes, and shouting so loudly that the earth echoed with the noise.

Adonijah and all his guests at the feast heard the great noise as the procession moved into Jerusalem. Joab asked in alarm, "What is this noise of the city in an uproar?"

The son of Abiathar, the priest, who had so often brought messages to David during Absalom's rebellion, came to bring news to Adonijah. "Truly, our lord, King David, has made Solomon king. He has sent his own bodyguard of soldiers with him, and they have made him ride on the king's own mule. Zadok the priest and Nathan the prophet have anointed him. A great company of people are with him, shouting and singing and rejoicing, so that the city rings with the noise. This is what you have heard."

When Adonijah's guests heard this, they were afraid to stay. Every one of them quickly slipped away and went home.

HOW SOLOMON GOT WISDOM Before David died, he called a great meeting of all the chief men of Israel. He stood up and told them that God had chosen Solomon to be king, and to build His temple. He urged them to remember to keep all the commandments of the Lord.

Then David turned to Solomon, and in the presence of all that great company he said to him, "And you, Solomon, my son, know the God of your father, and serve Him with a perfect heart and with a willing mind. For the Lord can read all your thoughts; if you seek Him, He will be found of you; but if you forsake Him, He will cast you off forever."

Then David gave Solomon the plan of the temple which God would help him build. He said to the people, "Solomon, my son, whom God has chosen, is still young, and the work is great, for the house is not for man, but for the Lord God. I have prepared gold and silver and brass and iron and wood and marble and precious stones. Who of you, now, is willing to help? Who will give a gift to God?" All the people offered to help Solomon. They gave a great deal of gold and silver and iron. And all the people blessed the Lord God of their fathers, and bowed their heads, and worshiped the Lord.

Solomon made a great sacrifice, offering a thousand burnt offerings to God. That night God appeared to Solomon in a dream, saying, "Ask what you would like to have Me give you."

Solomon said, "O Lord God, Thou hast made me king instead of my father David. And I am only a little child. I do not know how to go out or come in. And here I am in the middle of Thy people, a people so great they cannot be counted. Give me therefore an understanding heart, so that I may be able to rule Thy people, and to tell what is right and what is wrong."

God was pleased that Solomon had asked for this. He said, "Because you have asked for this, and have not asked for long life, or riches, or the life of your enemies, but instead for wisdom and understanding, behold, I have given you a wise and understanding heart, so that there shall never be any other man as wise as you. And I have also given you what you did not ask for, both riches and

165

honor. And if you walk in My ways, as your father David did, I will give you a long life too."

Then Solomon awoke, and it was a dream. But the dream was sent by God, and it came true. For Solomon became the wisest man who has ever lived. He was also very rich and highly honored, and he lived a long life.

Solomon spoke three thousand wise sayings, and he made a thousand songs. He knew all about trees, from the magnificent cedars of Lebanon to the tiny hyssop plant which springs out of a crack in the wall. He knew a great deal about animals, birds, creeping things, and fish. People came from all over the world to listen to the wisdom of Solomon.

One day two women came to Solomon with a dispute to be settled. One carried a living baby, and the other a dead one.

One of them said to the king, "O my lord, I live in the same house with this woman. I had a baby born to me; and after three days this other woman had a baby too. During the night her child died, because she lay on it while she was asleep. In the middle of the night she came and took my son out of my bed while I was sleeping, and put her dead child in the bed with me. In the morning when I woke up and took up my baby, it was dead! When I looked closely, I saw it wasn't mine at all, but hers. She had my baby in bed with her."

The second woman cried loudly, "O king, she is not telling the truth! The living baby is mine, and the dead baby is hers!" The first woman broke in again, "That isn't true! The dead baby is hers, and the living one is mine!"

Who could tell which one was right? Both of them wanted the living child; each of them refused the dead child.

The king said to one of his soldiers, "Bring me a sword." The soldier brought a sword. Then the king said, "Divide the living child in two, and give half to the one, and half to the other." The soldier picked up the baby, and raised his sword.

The true mother of the child raised a shriek: "O, my lord, give her the living child! Do not kill it!" But the second woman said, "What the king has decided is only fair. Divide the baby, and give us each half."

King Solomon said, "Give the living child to the first woman. She is the baby's mother!" So the child was given to his own mother, who loved him. When the people of Israel heard how wisely the king had judged, they understood that the wisdom of God was in him.

In the days of Solomon, the children of Israel increased in numbers until they were as many as the sands of the seashore, just as God had promised long before to Abraham. There was no war while Solomon was king. All the people of Israel and Judah dwelt safely, every man in his own home.

Solomon ruled over all the kingdoms that David had conquered, from the Euphrates River in the north to the border of Egypt in the south. And all the kings of these countries brought presents to him and served him.

Chapter 77

THE GOLDEN KINGDOM OF SOLOMON
I KINGS 5, 6, 8-10; II CHRONICLES 2-7, 9

THE SPLENDID HOUSE OF GOD In the fourth year of his reign Solomon began to build a temple for the Lord.

On the northern seacoast, near the Lebanon mountains, was the great and important city of Tyre. King Hiram of Tyre had always been a friend to David. Solomon sent him a letter in which he said, "You know that David, my father, could not build a house for the Lord because of his many wars. But now the Lord has given me peace with all my neighbors. I am going to build a temple for God. It must be a great one, for our God is a great God. I beg you to send me cedar trees out of the mountains of Lebanon."

King Hiram answered, "Blessed be the Lord God of Israel, who has given David a wise son. We will cut down as much wood as you need, and send it to whatever place you choose, on rafts." Solomon counted all the people who were left of the heathen nations who had once lived in Canaan. There were more than one hundred and fifty thousand of them. He sent these people to King Hiram, to be workmen for the building of the house of God.

The building was covered with pure gold, both inside and out. The walls and the doors were ornamented with cherubim and palm trees and open flowers. Inside there was a Holy Place, and a Holy of Holies, as in the tabernacle, but larger. There were two cherubim for the Holy of Holies that were fifteen feet high. Their wings were spread out so that each cherub touched a wall with one of his wings while their other wings met in the middle of the room. These cherubim were overlaid with pure gold.

A beautiful curtain of fine blue, purple, and crimson linen was hung in front of the Holy of Holies. It was embroidered with cherubim.

There was a laver of brass for the priests to wash in, fifteen feet across the top, supported by twelve figures of oxen made of brass. There were ten smaller lavers for washing the animals to be used for burnt offerings. Ten golden candlesticks furnished light for the Holy Place. A hundred golden basins were made, as well as spoons, snuffers, censers, and other things.

Solomon made two great pillars of brass to stand in front of the temple, each thirty-five feet high, and beautifully decorated with wreaths of chains, brass lilies, and pomegranates.

The people worked for seven years to build the temple. It was the most beautiful building in the land.

THE DEDICATION OF THE TEMPLE When everything was finished, Solomon gathered all the important Israelites to Jerusalem. They went to the tent where the ark had been placed in David's time. The Levites took the holy ark and all the holy dishes from the tent and brought them into the beautiful temple.

All the priests and the Levites were dressed in pure white linen. After they had placed the ark in the Holy of Holies, they arranged themselves in a big choir. A band of cymbals, psalteries, and harps played, as the choir sang to the Lord:

For He is good;
For His mercy endureth forever.

Even as they sang, the temple was filled with the cloud of the glory of the Lord.

Solomon stood upon a platform, where all the people could see him. After the singing, he knelt down and spread his arms toward heaven, praying aloud so that all the people could hear him:

"Lord God of Israel, there is no God like Thee in heaven above or on the earth beneath, who keepest covenant and mercy with Thy servants that walk before Thee with all their heart. But will God indeed dwell on earth? Behold, heaven and the heaven of heavens cannot contain Thee; how much less this house that I have built! When Thy people Israel shall pray toward this place, hear Thou in heaven, Thy dwelling place; and when Thou hearest, forgive. If they sin against Thee (for there is no man that sinneth not), and Thou be angry with them, yet if they return to Thee with their whole heart, saying, 'We have sinned,' then hear Thou their prayer in heaven, Thy dwelling place, and forgive Thy people. And if a stranger from a far country prays toward this house, then hear Thou in heaven, Thy dwelling place, so that all the people of the earth may know Thee."

When Solomon had finished his long prayer, he stood up and blessed all the people, saying, "Blessed be the Lord who has given rest to His people Israel. There has not failed one word of all His good promises. The God of our fathers be with us, as He was with them."

That night the Lord appeared to Solomon and said, "I have heard your prayer, and I will do what you ask. I have chosen and sanctified this house. And if you walk before Me, as your father David did, I will do as I promised your father. One of your children shall always be king. But if My people forsake Me, and put their trust in other gods, then I will drive them out of this land which I have given them, and away from this temple. And everyone seeing what is left of this house shall be astonished, and shall say, 'Why has the Lord done this?' And men shall answer, 'Because they forsook the Lord their God who brought them out of the land of Egypt, and served other gods; therefore the Lord has forsaken them.'"

THE VISIT OF A QUEEN Besides being very wise, Solomon was also very rich. He lived in great magnificence. After the temple had been built, Solomon made a beautiful palace for himself, and another for his wife, the daughter of the king of Egypt.

It took Solomon about twenty years to build the temple, his own palace, and the palace for his wife. Then he built some beautiful cities in the mountains of Lebanon to the north. These cities were so well built that even today, almost three thousand years later, they are still not entirely destroyed. When you are grown up, perhaps you will be able to go to that country and see their ruins.

Solomon had a large army of chariots and horses to defend his kingdom. He also built a navy in a city to the south on the Red Sea. These ships sailed around the country of Arabia to the land of Ophir. They brought back great quantities of gold to King Solomon, rare wood for the musical instruments used in the temple, precious stones, silver, ivory, peacocks, and monkeys.

Jerusalem became a very beautiful and rich city. Besides the temple and the king's palace, there were many streets with beautiful houses. In the gardens around the palace peacocks strutted, while chattering monkeys swung from the palm trees.

Inside the palace King Solomon made a magnificent throne of ivory, covered with pure gold. There were six wide steps leading up to the throne. On each step there were two carved lions, one on each side, twelve lions in all.

From far countries men came to see King Solomon, and to hear the wisdom that God had put into his heart. All these kings brought presents to King Solomon — gold and silver dishes, beautiful clothes, armor, delicious spices, horses, and mules. All the cups and dishes used in the palace were pure gold; none was silver. Solomon made silver to be as common as stones in Jerusalem.

Among the guests who came to hear the wisdom of King Solomon was the Queen of Sheba. Sheba was a rich country in faraway Arabia, on the shore of the Red Sea. The Queen of Sheba traveled in great splendor. She had a very great train of camels, for she had to cross about three hundred miles of hot, sandy desert. She wanted to talk to King Solomon especially about his God. In her faraway country she had heard of Solomon's wisdom, and of the mighty God of the Israelites.

When she came to Solomon she asked him many questions. She tested his wisdom. Solomon told her all that she wanted to know. She saw the houses he had built, tasted the delicious food on his table, and marveled at the great number of his servants and especially at the beauty of the temple.

She said to King Solomon, "It was a true report that I heard in my own country of your wisdom and your acts. I did not believe it until I saw it with my own eyes. The half of it was not told to me. Your wisdom and your riches are far greater even than I heard!

"Happy are your servants, who hear your wisdom all the time! Blessed be the Lord your God, who delighted to set you on the throne of Israel. It is because the Lord loved Israel that He has made you king."

The Queen of Sheba gave Solomon rich gifts of gold and precious stones, and a great abundance of the delicious spices that grew in her country. King Solomon in return gave the queen every beautiful thing which she admired in his palace. Loaded down with presents, the queen and her servants went back to their own country.

Chapter 78
THE BEGINNING OF BAD TIMES
I KINGS 11, 12; II CHRONICLES 10, 13

THE SPLIT IN THE KINGDOM   In spite of all Solomon's wisdom, he did some very foolish and bad things. That brought about his downfall.

Solomon married many heathen women. He had seven hundred wives, many of whom were the daughters of heathen kings. His first wife, you remember, had been the daughter of the Egyptian Pharaoh. Solomon also married some of the women of the heathen Canaanites.

You will remember that God had strictly commanded the children of

Israel not to marry heathen wives. Solomon was disobeying God when he did this.

In Solomon's old age his heathen wives turned away his heart from the true God and made him serve idols. He built a place for his Moabite wives to worship their abominable god Chemosh, and right near Jerusalem he let his Ammonite wives worship their cruel god Moloch. He built other places for all the idols of his heathen wives.

God was very angry with Solomon for doing this. The Lord had spoken twice directly to Solomon, and in spite of this the king had shamefully deserted his God.

The Lord said to Solomon, "Because you have not kept My covenant, I will take the kingdom away from you, and give it to your servant. For David's sake I will not do this in your lifetime, but I will do it when your son is king. But I will leave one tribe to your son, for David's sake, and for the sake of Jerusalem, which I have chosen."

One of Solomon's servants was a very able man named Jeroboam. One day God sent the prophet Ahijah to Jeroboam as he was walking in a field. The prophet came up to Jeroboam. Then he took hold of the new garment he was wearing, and tore it into twelve pieces.

Then he said to Jeroboam, "Take ten pieces, for thus saith the Lord God of Israel, 'I will tear the kingdom out of the hand of Solomon, and give ten tribes to you.'" Jeroboam was very much surprised to see the prophet do this strange thing. And when Solomon heard that God was going to give the kingdom to Jeroboam, Jeroboam had to escape to Egypt to save his life. He stayed there till Solomon was dead.

Solomon reigned forty years in Jerusalem. When at last he died, and was buried with his fathers, his son Rehoboam reigned in his place.

As soon as Jeroboam heard that Solomon was dead, he came back from Egypt. The people of Israel sent him with some of their chief men to ask a favor of Rehoboam. The prophet Samuel had warned the Israelites when they first asked for a king, that they would be sorry someday. For their king would make them work hard and pay high taxes. That warning came true in the time of Solomon.

Now the people asked Rehoboam to make things a little easier for them. The new king said, "Come back in three days, and I will give you my answer."

After the people's messengers were gone, King Rehoboam asked the old men, who had been counselors to his father Solomon, what he should answer. They said, "Speak kindly to them, and they will be your servants forever."

Then the king asked the young men, who were his own companions and friends, what answer he should give. These foolish young men had never had any experience in ruling a country. They said, "Tell the people, 'My father made your yoke heavy; I will make it heavier. My father beat you with whips; I will beat you with scorpions.'"

After three days the people came back, with Jeroboam at their head. The king answered them roughly, "My father made your burdens heavy; I will make them heavier." When the people heard these proud words, they said, "What do we care for David? Or David's family? We won't have such a king!" They left King Rehoboam and went home. They crowned Jeroboam as their king.

Two of the tribes, Judah and Benjamin, stayed faithful to Rehoboam. Judah was a very large tribe, but Benjamin was so small it was counted with Judah as one.

There were now two kingdoms — Israel and Judah. They were never joined together again. The family of David ruled over Judah, but many different families of kings ruled Israel.

HOW JEROBOAM MADE ISRAEL SIN
Jeroboam, the first king of Israel, was not a good king. The very first thing he did was wrong. He was afraid that many of the Israelites would become dissatisfied with him, and would go back to Rehoboam, who was their rightful king, since he was a descendant of David. Jeroboam was especially afraid to allow them to go to Jerusalem to worship there in the beautiful temple of God.

To keep the people from going to Jerusalem, Jeroboam made two golden calves. He set one of them up in Bethel in the south of his kingdom, and one in Dan in the north. Then he said to his people, "It is too far for you to go to Jerusalem to worship. Behold your gods, O Israel, which brought you up out of the land of Egypt!"

Jeroboam made new priests. Anyone who wanted to could become a priest. He had only to bring a bullock and seven rams for a sacrifice, and then he became a priest. Jeroboam made some feast days too, so that the worship of the golden calves would be as much like the worship of the Lord as possible.

When the God-fearing people saw that Jeroboam was trying to lead them to worship idols, they left the country of Israel and moved down to Judah, where the true God was

worshiped. Of course it was not easy for all of them to do this. They first had to sell their farms, to get the money to travel. Perhaps some of them could not afford to leave their homes and had to stay in the wicked kingdom of Israel, whether they wanted to or not.

On the other hand, there were also some of the people of Judah and Benjamin who were idol worshipers in secret. These people chose to live in Israel rather than in Judah. Israel was weakened by having these idol worshipers move in, while those who trusted God moved out. The priests and Levites had gone to Judah to live too. They could not stay in Israel where the king and the people were worshiping golden calves. So Israel was weakened, but Judah was strengthened.

I am sorry to say that although King Rehoboam of Judah was King David's grandson, he was not a very good man. His mother had been an Ammonite princess, one of King Solomon's heathen wives. She probably worshiped idols, and taught her son to worship them too.

King Rehoboam reigned for seventeen years. When he died, his son Abijah came to the throne of Judah.

Abijah was not pleased that Jeroboam had taken away all Israel. He was the great-grandson of David on both sides, for his mother was Absalom's daughter, and his father Rehoboam was Solomon's son. Abijah considered himself the rightful ruler of all twelve tribes.

To recapture the ten northern tribes Abijah went to war with Jeroboam. He was able to gather only four hundred thousand soldiers to fight against Jeroboam's army of eight hundred thousand men.

Before the battle started, King

Abijah went to a high place where Jeroboam and all his soldiers could hear him. He shouted across to them that God had given the kingdom to David and his sons forever. He reminded them that the true God was worshiped in His temple in Jerusalem every morning and evening. How could they hope to succeed, when they worshiped golden calves?

Jeroboam, instead of listening to this warning, took some of his soldiers and crept around behind the armies of Judah while King Abijah was talking. He did not care anything about the true God. He had twice as many soldiers as Abijah had, and he thought that was all that counted.

After King Abijah had finished talking, he turned around. What should he see but the Israelite soldiers both in front of him and behind him! But the soldiers of Judah trusted in God. They cried to Him for help. While the soldiers shouted, the priests sounded the trumpets. As they shouted, God Himself smote Jeroboam and all Israel. The soldiers of Israel ran away from the soldiers of Judah. God gave the men of Judah a great victory. Five hundred thousand of the Israelite soldiers died in that battle, and several cities — Bethel, and the southern part of Ephraim — were recaptured. So Abijah proved that it is better to trust in God than in great armies of soldiers.

Abijah died when he had reigned only three years. His son Asa was made king after him, while Jeroboam was still ruling in Israel.

Chapter 79
THE DIVIDED KINGDOM
I KINGS 13-16; II CHRONICLES 14, 15

KINGS OF ISRAEL		KINGS OF JUDAH	
Jeroboam	Zimri	Rehoboam	Asa
Nadab	Omri	Abijah	
Baasha	Ahab		
Elah			

THE BAD KINGS OF ISRAEL Jeroboam, who led Israel to worship idols, reigned for a long time. One day as he stood by the heathen altar which he had made for the worship of the golden calf, there came a prophet sent by the Lord from the country of Judah.

The prophet declared that one day there would be born a king of David's family whose name would be Josiah. This king would kill the priests of the altar Jeroboam had built, and would destroy the altar. Three hundred years later this prophecy came true. A king of David's line, named Josiah, did indeed go through all the land to destroy the heathen altars.

Perhaps this prophecy frightened Jeroboam. A short time later his son became very sick, and seemed about to die. Jeroboam did not pray to the golden calves to make his child better. He had made these calves for the Israelites to worship, but he did not believe in them himself.

Jeroboam told his wife to dress herself like an ordinary woman, so that no one would recognize that she was the king's wife, and to go to the prophet Ahijah to ask him whether the child would die. Ahijah, you remember, was the prophet of God who had foretold that Jeroboam was to be king of Israel by tearing his new garment into twelve pieces and giving Jeroboam ten of them. Ahijah was now very old, and almost blind.

God said to Ahijah, "Behold, the wife of Jeroboam is coming to ask you about her sick son; this is what you must say to her, for she will pretend to be another person."

When Ahijah heard the sound of her feet as she came in at the door, he said, "Come in, wife of Jeroboam! Why do you pretend to be someone else? I have heavy news for you. Go, tell Jeroboam, 'Thus says the Lord God of Israel, "I made you king over My people. I took the kingdom away from the family of David. But you have done more wickedness than all those before you. Therefore I will cut off your family. All of your sons shall die a violent death." Go home, now, and when your feet enter the city, your little son shall die. He alone of all your family will come to a peaceful grave, because he is the only one in all your family who loves and trusts God.'"

Jeroboam's wife went home to carry this terrible news to her guilty husband. As she entered the city, the child died, and went to be with God in heaven. All Israel mourned for the little prince. Soon after this, sinful Jeroboam died. His son Nadab, who was just as bad as his father, became king.

Nadab was king for only two years. Then a man named Baasha killed Nadab and made himself king over Israel. Baasha killed every man in the family of Jeroboam. The judgment of God, foretold by the prophet, came true.

Baasha was not a good king. He began his reign by murdering the whole family of Jeroboam. He wor-shiped the golden calves, and made the Israelites worship them too, just as Jeroboam had done.

God was angered by the wickedness of this king. He sent a prophet to tell him that because Baasha had made Israel sin, as Jeroboam had done, God would punish him as He had punished Jeroboam. Soon after this, Baasha died, and his son Elah became king.

A HAPPY LAND AND AN UNHAPPY ONE
All this time good king Asa was reigning in Judah. He destroyed all the idols that he could find, and commanded the people of Judah to worship the Lord.

For ten years there was no war in Judah. King Asa built high stone walls around many of his cities, to make them strong against any enemy. He trained a big army of soldiers for defense.

After Asa had reigned in peace for ten years, a great army came up out of Ethiopia, which was a country in Africa south of Egypt. Did King Asa put his trust in his trained soldiers? No, he did not. He prayed to God: "O God, our Lord, Thou art able to conquer just as well with those who have no power as with those who have a big army. Help us, O Lord our God, for it is in Thy name that we go out against this great multitude."

God listened to Asa's prayer. He gave the king and his men a great victory. The fleeing Ethiopians left behind many fine things in their tents, and also cattle, sheep, and camels. All of this the men of Judah took for themselves. They were richer after the war than they had been before. Again they had peace, for the enemies around them had learned to leave God's people alone.

God sent a prophet to good King Asa with this message: "The Lord is with you as long as you are with Him. If you seek the Lord, He will be found of you; but if you forsake Him, He will also forsake you."

Then Asa called all the people of Judah and Benjamin together for an outdoor meeting under the blue sky. A great many people from the tribes of Ephraim, Manasseh, and Simeon came also. For they saw that the king was trying to serve God, and that God was with him.

At this big meeting the people made a sacrifice to God of the plunder that they had captured from the Ethiopians. They promised to trust and serve the God of their fathers with all their heart and with all their soul. They determined to root out idol worship in Judah, and to put to death those who refused to serve God.

All together they shouted their pledge to serve God. The trumpets and the cornets rang out at the same time. The people all clapped their hands, because they were as happy as they could be. They were serving the true God, and nothing makes people so happy as to know that they are doing what God wants them to do.

God gave the people of Judah peace, and no nation came to make war against them. But meantime very bad things were going on in Israel. It was no wonder that God-fearing people did not wish to live there.

Baasha had killed all of Jeroboam's wicked family. But he, and his son Elah, who reigned after him, were both wicked kings themselves. Elah did not live very long. One day, when he was drunk, his servant Zimri came in and murdered Elah, and made himself king. Zimri killed all of Baasha's family, just as Baasha had murdered all the family of Jeroboam.

All these murders, committed in order to make Zimri king, did Zimri very little good. He was king only one week. The people did not want him to be their king. They chose Omri instead, who was captain of the army. With his soldiers Omri attacked the city where Zimri was. When Zimri heard that the city had been captured, he went into his palace and set it on fire. He was burned to death in the ruins.

Omri now became king of Israel. He was more wicked than any of the other kings who had ruled before him. After he had reigned for twelve years, he died, and his son Ahab became king.

Ahab was even worse than his father had been. He was the most wicked king that Israel ever had. His wife Jezebel was just as bad as he. She was the daughter of the heathen king of Sidon, who was also a priest of the idol Baal.

To please his wife, Ahab built a temple for Baal in the royal city, Samaria; and he set up the heathen Asherah idols. Queen Jezebel had four hundred priests to serve the Asherah, and Ahab had four hundred and fifty priests for the worship of the idol Baal.

There were still a few priests of God in Israel who tried to keep the people from worshiping idols. Jezebel tried to kill these priests. She hated the Lord, and did everything she could to root out His worship, so that Israel would become a heathen country.

Jezebel had a servant in her household, a very remarkable man named Obadiah. He was ruler over the royal house. Obadiah trusted the true God. He tried to serve Him, and to keep the Israelites from worshiping idols. When Jezebel tried to kill the priests of the Lord, Obadiah hid one hundred priests in caves, and fed them at his own expense.

With this wicked king and queen on the throne, the country of Israel became almost completely heathen.

Chapter 80

ELIJAH, THE STERN PROPHET
I KINGS 17-19

KING OF ISRAEL	KING OF JUDAH
Ahab	Asa

WHY THE KING BECAME ANGRY After so many murders, after so many idolatries, after so many wicked kings, God might well have destroyed the whole land of Israel, as, long before, He had destroyed the wicked cities of Sodom and Gomorrah. But God is a patient God, long-suffering and slow to anger. Over and over and over again God warned His people. Over and over again He sent them trouble to remind them how desperately they needed His help. Over and over again, when they repented and cried to Him, He had mercy on them and came to their rescue.

When Ahab was king, God raised up a prophet. His name was Elijah, and he was one of the greatest prophets that ever lived. God sent Elijah to warn Ahab that such sin as his would surely call down the terrible judgment of God.

Elijah lived on the east side of the Jordan River. When God gave him the message for Ahab, the stern and angry prophet crossed the river and came to Samaria. Up the marble steps of the magnificent palace he strode, into the very presence of the king. Lifting up his hands to the sky, he said in a solemn and ringing voice, "As the Lord God of Israel lives, before whom I stand, there shall be no rain or dew these years until I say so."

Then Elijah turned away from the wicked king and marched out of the palace. God said to Elijah, "Go away from here. Hide yourself near the brook Cherith. You can drink the water of the brook, and I have commanded the ravens to feed you there." So Elijah lived hidden near the brook. The ravens brought him bread and meat morning and evening; and he drank the water of the brook.

After a time the brook dried up because there was no rain. The Lord said to Elijah, "Arise, go to Zarephath. I have commanded a widow there to look after you."

Elijah immediately left the dried-up brook, and started on the long journey to Zarephath, more than one hundred miles to the north. It must have been a hard journey. Elijah had to go all that distance on foot. He had to travel secretly, for the king was hunting all over the country to find him. Ahab was going to kill that prophet who had dared to prophesy this terrible drought.

As he traveled across the land, Elijah could see the bare, brown fields where everything had shriveled up. Every day the sun rose blazing hot and traveled across the sky, scorching everything; and every day the sky was like copper, with never a sign of mist or a cloud. At last, after traveling a long, weary way, Elijah left the country of the Israelites and came to the town of Zarephath in the country of Sidon.

When he came to the gate of the city, he saw a widow gathering a few sticks to make a fire. "Give me," he said to her, "I pray you, a drink of water." When she started to get it, he called to her, "Please bring me a little piece of bread too."

The woman answered, "As the Lord your God lives, I do not have a single loaf of bread in the house. I have only a little flour left in the barrel, and a little olive oil in the jug. I have come out here to gather a few sticks to make a fire, so that I can bake one last little cake of the flour and oil I have left, for my son and me. After that is eaten, we have nothing more; we will have to die of hunger."

Elijah said to her, "Do not be afraid, for the God of Israel says that the flour in your barrel and the oil in your jug will not fail until the day that I send rain upon the earth."

So the woman made Elijah a little cake first. Then she made one for herself and her son. It turned out just as the prophet had said. No matter how often she baked, the flour in the barrel did not give out, and neither did the jug of oil. There was always plenty left. This was a miracle, something that only the mighty power of God can bring about. God gave his prophet Elijah power to work miracles.

Sometime after this, the woman's young son became very sick. Finally he died. The woman thought she must have committed some terrible sin, and that her son's death was the punishment for that sin. She came to Elijah in sorrow, saying, "O man of God, did you come here to punish me for my sin by killing my son?"

"Give the boy to me," Elijah commanded. Taking the boy out of his mother's arms, he carried him upstairs into his own bedroom. He laid him upon the bed. Then Elijah called to God, "O Lord, my God, let this child's soul come back into him again!"

What a strange thing to ask! Never had anyone who was dead come back to life again! Yet Elijah had faith that God could do even this. He lay down on the boy's body, and stretched himself out over it. He did this three times.

God answered Elijah's prayer. The child's soul came back into him again. He started to breathe. Elijah carried him to his mother and said to her, "See, your boy is living again!"

The happy mother flung her arms around her dear boy and kissed and hugged him. She exclaimed to Elijah, "Now I know that you are truly a man sent from God!"

WHO IS GOD? Three years passed without rain. Month after month slipped by, and not a drop of rain fell out of the sky. Day after day the sun rose and sent its scorching beams down on the parched earth. Day after day the people scanned the copper sky for the least sign of a cloud, but none appeared.

The rivers ran low and then dried up. The fields lay baked and brown under the blazing sun. The animals could not find a blade of grass. They were starving for something to eat. The people, too, were suffering from hunger. The little food they had was almost gone.

King Ahab said to Obadiah, the ruler of his house, "Let us go out into the country where the brooks and springs are, and see if we cannot find just a little grass for the horses and mules, so that they will not all die." In order to cover the whole country, Ahab and Obadiah went in different directions.

At this time Elijah was still living with the widow in Zarephath. God said to him, "Go, show yourself to Ahab. I will send rain upon the earth." So Elijah went down to the land of Israel. Out in the country he met Obadiah, who was looking for grass.

Bowing down to the ground, Obadiah asked, "Is it possible that you are my lord Elijah?" Elijah answered, "I am Elijah. Go, tell the king that I am here."

Obadiah said, "I don't dare to tell him, for he has hunted for you everywhere. He has made the people swear that you were not hidden in their homes. And now you say, 'Go, tell King Ahab that Elijah is here.' As soon as I go to tell him, the Spirit of the Lord may carry you away somewhere else. When Ahab cannot find you, he will kill me.

"I have been a worshiper of God since my youth. Did no one tell you what I did when Jezebel killed the prophets of the Lord? I hid one hundred of them in two caves, and fed them myself with bread and water."

But Elijah promised, "As truly as the Lord God of Israel lives, today I will show myself to Ahab." Then Obadiah went to meet King Ahab and told him that Elijah had been found. When Ahab saw Elijah, he said, "Are you the one who is troubling Israel?"

Elijah answered sternly, "I have not troubled Israel. You and your wicked father have troubled Israel, because you have forsaken the commandments of the Lord and have worshiped Baal. Now gather all the people of Israel to Mount Carmel. Bring the four hundred and fifty prophets of Baal, and the four hundred prophets of the Asherah."

Ahab sent messengers throughout the land of Israel for all the people to come to Mount Carmel to meet the prophet Elijah. The people gathered at the mountain. Ahab brought the prophets of Baal and of the Asherah.

Elijah stood up boldly before the people. In a ringing voice he cried out to them, "How long are you going to be undecided? If the Lord is God, follow Him; but if Baal, then follow him."

The people did not answer a word. They knew that they had left their God to worship Baal. Shame covered their faces. Perhaps some of them wished to say, "We will follow the Lord," but they were afraid to say this right in the presence of the king and the eight hundred and fifty heathen prophets.

There stood the brave prophet all alone on one side, with the great crowd of people and the eight hundred and fifty prophets of Baal and the Asherah on the other side. Again the prophet's voice rang out over the mountain.

"I am the only prophet of the Lord, but Baal's prophets are four hundred and fifty men. Let them give us two bullocks for sacrifices. Let Baal's prophets choose one bullock. Let them lay it on the wood, but put no fire under it. I shall prepare the other bullock, put it on the wood, but set no fire under it. Then let the prophets of Baal call on the name of your gods, and I shall call on the name of the Lord. The God that answers by fire, let him be God!"

The people raised a shout, "Yes, that is right. Let us do that!"

FIRE FROM HEAVEN Which prayer would be answered?

177

The heathen priests took the bullock which was brought to them. While the host of people watched in great excitement, the bullock was made ready. Then the priests of Baal ran around and around the altar in a frenzy, shouting and screaming and howling, "O Baal, hear us; O Baal, hear us!"

But there was no voice, nor anyone that answered.

After the priests had shouted to Baal all morning without getting any answer, Elijah began to make fun of them. He shouted mockingly, "Cry louder! He is a god. Perhaps he is talking, or he is on a journey, or perhaps he is asleep and must be waked up. Cry louder! Make him hear you!"

The frantic priests screamed and howled, "O Baal, hear us!" They ran around the altar, and cut themselves with their knives until the blood gushed out. They kept this up all day long. By evening there was no breath left in them.

But there was no voice, nor anyone that answered.

At last Elijah said to the people, "Come near to me." They all came as near as they could. Elijah found an old altar of the Lord that had been broken down. With twelve large stones he built up this altar in the name of the Lord.

He cut the bullock in pieces and laid it on the wood. He dug a little ditch around the altar, and then, so that the people could see he was perfectly honest, and was not playing any tricks, he said, "Fill four jars with water, and pour it on the sacrifice and on the wood on the altar." And they did it. Elijah said, "Do it a second time." And they did it a second time. Then he said, "Do it a third time." And they did it the third time.

The water ran down around the altar, soaking everything and filling the ditch.

When everything was ready, Elijah lifted up his face to heaven. He prayed very solemnly. More than sixty years had passed since the kingdom of Israel had separated from the kingdom of Judah, and since the people of Israel had been led into idol worship by their wicked kings. The old people could remember when Solomon was king, and when all the tribes of Israel went up to Jerusalem to worship God. Many of the younger people were hearing a public prayer to God for the very first time, although they had heard many prayers to the idol Baal. When they heard Elijah begin to pray so solemnly and earnestly, they were very much impressed.

Elijah prayed, "Lord God, the God of Abraham, of Isaac, and of Jacob, let it be known this day that Thou art God in Israel, and that I am Thy servant, and that I have done all these things at Thy word. Hear me, O Lord, hear me, that this people may know that Thou art the Lord God, and that Thou hast turned their hearts back again to Thee."

Even as Elijah prayed, suddenly the fire of God fell down from heaven upon the altar. It burned the bullock and the wood. In a minute the whole altar was ablaze. The fire was so hot that the water in the trenches boiled away, and even the stones of the altar and the ground around the altar burned.

The astonished people fell on their knees and cried out, "The Lord, He is God! The Lord, He is God!" When they saw the power of their own God, they were disgusted with the false heathen idols, and with the senseless screaming of the heathen prophets.

Then Elijah commanded them to

capture all the prophets of Baal. He brought them down to the brook Kishon, and killed them there. Then he said to Ahab, "Go, eat and drink, for there is a sound of abundance of rain."

Elijah himself went to the top of Mount Carmel and threw himself down on the ground and prayed. He said to his servant, "Go up and look toward the sea." The servant went and looked. He came back to Elijah and said, "There is nothing." Elijah said, "Go again, seven times." When the servant came back the seventh time, he said, "A little cloud, as big as a man's hand, is rising up out of the sea."

Elijah commanded him, "Go, tell Ahab, 'Get your chariot ready and hurry home, before the rain stops you.'" The heavens became black with stormy clouds. There was a great rain. Elijah tucked up his robe into his girdle and ran before Ahab's chariot all the way into Jezreel, through the heavy rain which had come in answer to his prayers.

GOD COMFORTS ELIJAH Queen Jezebel was not present when Elijah called down fire from heaven. When Ahab told her how Elijah had killed all the prophets of Baal and of the Asherah, she was furiously angry. She sent a messenger to Elijah, to tell him: "Let the gods do so to me and more also, if I make not your life like the life of one of these prophets you have killed, by tomorrow about this time!"

Elijah left Jezreel in a great hurry. He went south to the country of Judah. He was still afraid to stop. He left his servant there, and went a day's journey further into the wilderness.

Then he could go no further. He was tired and discouraged. He had hoped the people of Israel would turn back to God. Now he saw that as long as wicked Queen Jezebel was on the throne, there was very little chance the people would serve the Lord.

Poor Elijah sat down under a juniper tree. He thought that all that he had done was of no use. "It is enough, now, O Lord!" he said; "take away my life!" The tired prophet, who had been walking night and day without food or drink, was so exhausted that he fell asleep under the juniper tree.

But God was taking tender care of His tired servant. While Elijah was sleeping, an angel touched him and said, "Arise and eat." When Elijah awoke, he saw a cake baked on the coals, and a bottle of water. He ate and drank, for he was hungry and thirsty after his long journey.

After eating and drinking, he lay down once more and slept again. The angel again touched him and said, "Arise and eat, for the journey is too long for you." Elijah had slept so long that he was thoroughly rested. He sat up and ate again, till his hunger was entirely satisfied.

Strengthened by the food, the prophet traveled for forty days and nights. Further and further south he went, through the terrible desert over which the children of Israel had traveled during the forty years of their wanderings. At last he came to the mountain of Sinai, where God had given the Ten Commandments to Moses and the children of Israel.

Here Elijah was safe from Jezebel. He found a cave in which to live. After a time, God spoke to him and asked, "What are you doing here, Elijah?" Elijah answered, "I have worked hard for the Lord God of hosts, but the children of Israel have forsaken Thee, and have thrown down Thy altars, and have killed Thy prophets with the sword. I, even I only, am left, and they seek my life to take it away."

"Go out and stand upon the mountain before the Lord," came God's command. So Elijah went out upon the mountain. A terrible wind came up. It was so strong that it broke great pieces off the mountain, and cracked great rocks open. But the Lord was not in the wind. After the wind had gone down, there came a dreadful earthquake. The whole mountain shook and trembled. But the Lord was not in the earthquake. After the earthquake, there came a fire. But the Lord was not in the fire.

Elijah stood there and saw the terrible hurricane shrieking around the mountain, uprooting trees and breaking the great rocks; then the dreadful earthquake, making the solid mountain shake and tremble; and then the furious fire raging among the trees of the mountains. He understood something of the strength and power of God. God was much stronger than wicked Ahab and Jezebel, or all the wicked people of all the world.

After the wind and the earthquake and the fire, Elijah heard a still, small voice. He knew immediately that it was God speaking to him. God asked, "What are you doing here, Elijah?" Elijah answered as he had the first time: "I have worked hard for the Lord God of hosts: for the children of Israel have forsaken Thee, and thrown down Thy altars, and killed Thy prophets. And I, even I only, am left, and they seek my life to take it away."

The Lord commanded Elijah to return to the country of Israel. He must go to the city of Damascus, and anoint a new king over the country of Syria, instead of Ben-hadad who was ruling there. Then he had to anoint a new king over Israel, instead of Ahab. Last of all, he must anoint a new prophet to take his own place, and do his work after he died. Finally God said to Elijah, "I still have left in Israel seven thousand, even all the knees which have not bowed unto Baal and every mouth which has not kissed his image."

Seven thousand others who were true to God! That encouraged Elijah. And to think that wicked Ahab would not be king much longer — that made him glad. And then to know that his hard work as a prophet was almost finished — that made him happy too.

It was not easy to be a prophet in those wicked days, and to have to stand up for God all alone when nearly everybody else was worshiping idols. Elijah was very brave and courageous. He had dared to come before a wicked and idolatrous king, and to proclaim the true God, and then put all the prophets of Baal to death. Yes, he was very glad to know that he would not have to live much longer in this wicked world.

Elijah left the cave on Mount Sinai and started on his long journey back, as God had directed. When at last he reached the land of Israel, he saw a man named Elisha plowing a field with twelve yoke of oxen. Elijah did not stop to speak to him. As he passed by, he threw his coat over Elisha's shoulders without saying a word. Elisha knew what that meant. It meant that God had chosen him to follow Elijah, and to be prophet after him. He ran after Elijah and said, "Let me first go and tell my father and mother, and kiss them good-bye. Then I will come and follow you."

Elisha lived with Elijah from that time on. He waited on the old prophet and took care of him. It was pleasant for Elijah to have a friend and companion to talk to and to pray with. And Elisha had a wonderful teacher to show him how to become a prophet of the true God.

Chapter 81
STORIES ABOUT ISRAEL'S WICKED KING
I KINGS 20, 21

KING OF ISRAEL	KING OF JUDAH
Ahab	Jehoshaphat

GOD HELPS AHAB   North of the kingdom of Israel was the great kingdom of Syria. It was much larger than Israel. Its king, Ben-hadad, gathered his soldiers together and made war against Israel. With him went thirty-two other kings, who had horses and chariots. This great host surrounded Samaria, which was Ahab's capital city, and besieged it.

Ahab was terrified. The king of Judah had strengthened his country, and had trained a big army. But Ahab had done nothing to protect his country. He had only seven thousand soldiers.

King Ben-hadad was a proud, cruel king. He sent an insulting message to Ahab: "Thus says Ben-hadad, 'Your silver and your gold are mine; your wives also, and your children, are mine.'"

King Ahab shook with terror. What should he do? He had no army. And he had no God to go to for help. He and Queen Jezebel had torn down the altars of the Lord. Jezebel had killed the prophets of God wherever she could find them. Baal had taken the place of the Lord God of Israel. Could they get help from Baal? No, even Ahab knew better than to expect help from Baal.

Ahab sent a humble reply to Ben-hadad, saying, "My lord, O king, as you say, I am yours, with all that I have." Ben-hadad was not satisfied with this answer. He was a bully. He knew that Ahab had only a tiny army. He sent Ahab another insulting message: "Tomorrow I will send my servants to search through your house, and the houses of your servants, and whatever they find that is pleasant in their eyes, they will take it away."

Then the king of Israel called all the elders of the land and said, "See how this man seeks mischief." The elders advised the king, "Do not listen to him." So King Ahab finally mustered up a little courage. He sent a message back to Ben-hadad: "What you asked me in the first place I will do, but this last demand I will not submit to."

This was just what Ben-hadad wanted. Now he had a good excuse to pounce on Ahab. He and the thirty-two kings would go and crush Ahab and his seven thousand soldiers to powder. "The gods do so to me, and more also," he replied to Ahab, "if what is left of Samaria when I am through with it, is enough for a handful of dust." But Ahab answered, "Tell him not to boast before he has fought the battle." When this message arrived, Ben-hadad and the thirty-two kings were drinking in their tents. Ben-hadad said, "Get ready to fight against the city."

Ben-hadad and the other kings would probably have crushed Ahab and Samaria just as they had planned, if something had not happened to prevent it. God sent a prophet to Ahab, who said, "Have you seen this great army? I will deliver it into your hand, and you shall know that I am the Lord." Ahab said, "Who shall do the fighting?" The prophet answered, "The young princes."

Ahab sent word quickly for all the young princes to come to him. How many do you think there were? Only two hundred and thirty-two! By noon the Israelites were ready. The little army of seven thousand men, led by the two hundred and thirty-two princes, ventured out of the city, to fight against the hosts of the Syrians.

Ben-hadad and the thirty-two kings were still drinking in their tents. Someone brought the news that soldiers were coming out of Samaria. Ben-hadad, half-drunk as he was, did not trouble himself. He commanded, "Whether they have come for peace or for war, capture them alive."

The Israelites were not afraid, because they knew that the God of their fathers was helping them. Every one of the two hundred and thirty-two princes and the seven thousand soldiers picked out a Syrian and fought him. When the Syrian soldiers saw the courage of the Israelites, they soon gave way. The poor heathen soldiers had no God to help them; and their king, who should have been leading his soldiers, was drunk. That large army became a mere rabble of fleeing and terrified soldiers. Even King Ben-hadad got on a horse and galloped away. The Israelites chased after the Syrians, and killed many more of them.

Why had God helped the wicked King Ahab, who had forgotten the Lord, and torn down His altars, and worshiped the idol Baal? There were two reasons. Although the Israelites had forgotten God, He had not forgotten them. They were His people. He loved them. There were still seven thousand of the Israelites who had not worshiped Baal. Perhaps some of the others would turn back to God when they saw His power and His protecting care of His people.

The other reason was this. Although the Israelites were God's special people, yet all the earth belongs to God. The Lord wanted the Syrians, who lived right next to the Israelites, yes, and all the nations of the earth, to know His power, and His protecting care of all who put their trust in Him.

HOW AHAB TREATED GOD'S ENEMY With God's help the Israelites had crushed the Syrians. The Lord sent a prophet to King Ahab with this message: "Next year Ben-hadad will come back. Make your army and your kingdom strong, so as to be ready for him."

When King Ben-hadad got back to Syria with the remnant of his army, his servants said to him, "The God of the Israelites is a God of the hills. We made a mistake in fighting against them in the hill country. Let us go back next year and fight them in the open, on the plain. Then we shall be able to defeat them."

The following year Ben-hadad returned to make war against Israel. This time he did not go as far as Samaria, for that city was on a hill. He set up his camp on the lowlands, just east of the Sea of Galilee. The children of Israel were able to gather only a small army to meet the great host of the Syrians. But again a prophet came to King Ahab and said, "Because the Syrians have said, 'The Lord is God of the hills, but not God of the valleys,' therefore I will deliver all this great multitude into your hand, so that all people may know that I am the Lord of all the earth."

Again the Israelites were victorious in a great battle. One hundred thousand Syrian soldiers died in that battle.

What became of King Ben-hadad? The king fled into a house and hid himself in an inner room. He knew the Israelites would soon find him and kill him. But his servants said to him, "We have heard that the kings of Israel are merciful kings. Let us now dress ourselves in rough sackcloth, and put ropes on our heads, and go to the king of Israel. Perhaps he will spare our lives."

So the servants dressed themselves in sackcloth, and put ropes on their heads. They went to King Ahab and said, "Thy servant Ben-hadad says, 'I pray thee, let me live!'" Ahab said, "Is he still alive? He is my brother." He sent for Ben-hadad, and invited him to come up into the chariot with him. He made friends with him and let him go.

Twice God had delivered wicked Ben-hadad into Ahab's power. Instead of killing this enemy of God's people, Ahab made an alliance with him and let him go. God sent a prophet to Ahab to say, "Because you have let go this man whom I appointed to utter destruction, your life shall pay for his life."

Ahab went home to his palace in Samaria, displeased. Although he had put God out of his thoughts, and out of his kingdom, as much as he could, he could not get away from Him. God was still ruling him and the kingdom of Israel.

AHAB, THE THIEF A man named Naboth had a vineyard next to King Ahab's palace in Jezreel. This land had come down to Naboth from his fathers, for you remember that by the law of Moses no man could sell his land. Each man's farm must always remain in his own family.

King Ahab wanted Naboth's land for a vegetable garden, because it was right next to his palace. He tried to buy it, offering to give Naboth a better vineyard for it; or, if Naboth preferred, Ahab would pay for it in money. But Naboth would not sell it. He said, "The Lord forbids me to sell the land which has come down to me from my fathers."

Ahab was very much displeased. He went home, entered his bedroom, and lay down. He turned his face away, and would not come to dinner. The king of Israel sulked!

His wife Jezebel came to see what was the matter. She asked, "Why are you so sad? Why do you not come to dinner?" Ahab answered, "Because I asked Naboth to let me buy his vineyard, but he will not sell it to me."

Jezebel looked scornful. "Is that all that is the matter?" she asked. "Are you really king over Israel? Come and eat, and enjoy yourself. I will get Naboth's vineyard for you." Jezebel, having come from a heathen country, did not care about the law of Moses.

She wrote letters to the elders of the city. She signed them with Ahab's name, and sealed them with Ahab's seal. She wrote thus: "Proclaim a fast, and set Naboth in front of all the people. Bring in two rough men, and have them say, 'Naboth cursed God and the king.' Then carry him outside the city, and stone him to death."

The elders were afraid to disobey Jezebel. They proclaimed a fast and set Naboth in front of all the people. Two wicked men, whom they had bribed, came in and said, "We heard Naboth curse God and the king." As the law of Moses commanded, the people carried Naboth outside the city and stoned him to death. His blood stained the stones where he fell, and the dogs licked it up.

When Jezebel heard the news, she said to Ahab, "Arise, and take possession of Naboth's vineyard, which he would not sell you. He is not alive; he is dead."

Then the word of the Lord came to Elijah, saying, "Arise, go down to meet Ahab. He has gone to take over Naboth's vineyard. Say to him, 'Thus saith the Lord, "In the place where the dogs licked the blood of Naboth, there shall dogs lick your blood."'"

Elijah arose and strode sternly into the vineyard. Ahab was looking around at the vines, delighted that at last he owned this piece of land. Realizing that someone was behind him, he turned around. There stood the stern and frowning Elijah, whom Ahab had not seen for many years.

Ahab tremblingly gasped, "Have you found me, O my enemy?"

Elijah said, "I have found you because you have sold yourself to do wickedness. God will punish you for this murder. He will take away all your sons. None of your family will be left, because of the wicked thing that you have done. You have provoked God to anger and made Israel to sin. And Jezebel also shall die a violent death."

There was never a king so wicked as Ahab, who sold himself to do wickedness in the sight of the Lord; and Jezebel his wife stirred him up. Yet Ahab was an Israelite. He knew that God rules the world, and he had seen God's power. After hearing Elijah's terrible words, he was sorry for what he had done. He tore his clothes, and put rough sackcloth on his bare skin. He would not eat, nor would he see any visitors.

The Lord said to Elijah, "Do you see how Ahab has humbled himself before me? Because he has repented, I will not bring this trouble upon him and his family in his lifetime; but in his son's days, I will bring trouble upon his family."

Chapter 82
THE DEATH OF AHAB
I KINGS 22; II CHRONICLES 17, 18

KING OF ISRAEL
Ahab

KING OF JUDAH
Jehoshaphat

GOOD KING JEHOSHAPHAT What was happening in the kingdom of Judah while wicked King Ahab was ruling in Israel?

After reigning for forty-one years, God-fearing King Asa died. He had a splendid funeral, for he was much loved. Jehoshaphat, his son, was made king. He, too, was a good king. The country prospered, and the people were happy.

Jehoshaphat made his country strong, especially on the northern border, where it joined the country of Israel. He built high walls around the border cities. He put soldiers in these cities, and also in the towns of Ephraim which his father Asa had taken away from Israel.

Jehoshaphat trusted the Lord, as David had done. God helped Jehoshaphat in all that he did. He made him rich and prosperous.

When the nations around him saw how the king of Judah prospered because he trusted in God, they were so much impressed that they, too, were inclined to fear and honor God. None of these countries tried to make war on Jehoshaphat. They brought him presents instead.

To make his country strong, Jehoshaphat built up a large army of more than a million trained soldiers, commanded by five captains.

This good king did another wise thing, even more important. He appointed men to teach the law of Moses to all the people. These teachers traveled around the land, carrying the book of the law with them.

Before this time, the people had had very little chance to learn the law, for books were so rare that only kings or very rich men could afford to own them. The books they did have were not printed, but were written by hand with great care. Instead of paper, they were made of parchment, which is a fine white leather made from sheepskins.

If you could see one of these books you would hardly recognize what it was, for it would not look at all like the one you are reading. These books were not made of many separate sheets. They were simply long strips of parchment, with a stick at each end, so that the strips could be rolled up, much as our window shades are rolled.

Although good King Jehoshaphat took care that the people should learn the law of God, he made one great mistake. He became friends with wicked King Ahab, who had forgotten God. With a great many servants and soldiers, Jehoshaphat made a visit to King Ahab. A great feast was given in his honor, to which all the nobles of the land were invited.

During the feast Ahab said to Jehoshaphat, "Do you not remember that the city of Ramoth in Gilead belongs to us, although the king of Syria has taken it away from us? We ought to go to war against the king of Syria, to get our city back again. Will you go with me?" Jehoshaphat agreed with Ahab, but he said, "Let us first ask God about it."

THE PROPHET WHO WOULD NOT LIE
Ahab probably did not want Jehoshaphat to know that he did not worship God any longer; or perhaps he had gained a little faith since God had helped him in his last two wars. At any rate, he gathered together four hundred false prophets. These men were not prophets of Baal, nor were they true prophets of God. They were not prophets at all. They pretended that God spoke to them, but they made up their own prophecies.

King Ahab said to these men, "Shall I go up to Ramoth-gilead to battle, or not?" The false prophets had received no word from God to give to the king, but they wanted to say what would please Ahab. So they said, "Go up, for the Lord will give you the city!"

185

Jehoshaphat saw that they were not true prophets of God. "Don't you have a true prophet of God in your country?" he asked. Ahab answered, "There is one prophet of God in my country, named Micaiah; but I hate him, for he never prophesies any good unto me, but always evil."

King Jehoshaphat answered, "Do not say that!" He wanted a true message from God before he went to war. So Ahab sent a messenger to tell Micaiah to come to him. The messenger said to Micaiah, "All the four hundred prophets say nothing but good to the king. You must do the same, and speak favorably."

Micaiah was a true prophet of God. He did not make up his prophecies just to please the wicked king. He was angry with the messenger. "As the Lord lives," he said, "whatever the Lord tells me to say, that is what I will say."

The two kings sat on two thrones near the gate of Samaria. Before them stood the four hundred prophets, who kept saying, "Go up to Ramoth-gilead, for God will give it into your hands." One of the false prophets made two horns of iron. He said, "Thus saith the Lord, 'With these horns you will push the Syrians till they are consumed.'" These words, like all their other prophecies, were lies. God had not spoken to the false prophets at all.

King Ahab said to Micaiah, "Shall I go and fight against Ramoth-gilead, or not?" Micaiah answered, very sarcastically, "Go, and prosper, for the Lord will deliver the city into your hand."

Ahab could tell from the tone of the prophet's voice that he was being mocked. He cried angrily, "How many times must I warn you to speak

nothing but the truth, which God says to you."

Then Micaiah threw up his arms, raised his face toward heaven as if he saw a vision, and said, "I saw all Israel scattered upon the hills, as sheep that have no shepherd, and the Lord said, 'These have no master. Let them go back to their homes.'"

This vision meant that Ahab would be killed if he went into the battle, and the Israelites would be scattered, without a king. Ahab turnd to Jehoshaphat and said, "Did I not tell you that he would prophesy no good for me, but only evil?"

But Micaiah was not yet through. Again he held up his arms, raising his eyes as if he saw a vision. In a commanding voice he went on, "I saw the Lord sitting on his throne, surrounded by all the host of heaven. The Lord said, 'Who will persuade Ahab to go up to Ramoth-gilead and be killed?'

"One spirit said one thing, and another spirit said something else. At last a spirit came and stood before the Lord and said, 'I will go and persuade Ahab.' The Lord asked, 'How will you persuade him?' The spirit answered, 'I will be a lying spirit in the mouths of all King Ahab's prophets.'

"Now listen, King Ahab. God has put a lying spirit into the mouths of all your prophets. What they have said is not true. The Lord has told me that if you go up to Ramoth-gilead, you will die there."

AHAB'S PLAN TO CHEAT DEATH For many years Ahab had lived like a heathen, never thinking of God nor trying to obey Him. Now, when God sent him this message by Micaiah, it did not mean much to him. Four hundred prophets told him to go to

Ramoth-gilead; only this one told him not to go. He wanted to do what the four hundred advised.

Ahab called his soldiers and said, "Put Micaiah in prison, and feed him with prison bread and bad prison water, till I come back from this war. I shall soon come back in peace." Micaiah said, "If you come back in peace, then the Lord has not spoken by me!"

The two kings went to Ramoth-gilead. Ahab said to Jehoshaphat, "I will disguise myself as a common soldier, but you wear your royal robes." Ahab thought that if no one knew who he was, he would not be killed. He forgot that God sees through our clothes to our very hearts.

The king of Syria had thirty-two captains. He commanded them, "Fight neither with small nor with great, but only with the king of Israel." When these men saw Jehoshaphat, dressed in his kingly robes, they thought he was the man they were looking for. They surrounded him, but Jehoshaphat cried out in terror, "I am not the king of Israel." And God helped him, for God moved the hearts of the captains to go away from him.

It so happened that a soldier in the Syrian army drew his bow and shot into the air aimlessly. That arrow flew straight to King Ahab and pierced the tiny hole where his armor was fastened together. Ahab said faintly to the driver of his chariot, "Turn around and drive me out of the battle, for I am wounded." The fierce battle went on, while Ahab was held up in his chariot by his men. At evening he died. His men took his body to Samaria, where it was buried.

Ahab's servants took the chariot to the pool outside Samaria to wash it. There the wild dogs of the city licked up the blood of wicked King Ahab in the very place where Naboth had been stoned. So the prophecy Elijah had spoken came true.

Chapter 83
GOD PROTECTS HIS PEOPLE
II KINGS 1; II CHRONICLES 19-21

KING OF ISRAEL	KINGS OF JUDAH	
Ahaziah	Jehoshaphat	Jehoram

FIRE FROM HEAVEN SAVES ELIJAH Ahab was now dead, but his wicked wife Jezebel was still living. Their son Ahaziah was now king in Israel. Like his father and his mother, this king was wicked. He did not worship God but the heathen idol Baal.

Ahaziah was king for only two years. He fell out of an upstairs window in his palace, and was hurt very badly. He wanted to know whether he would get better, or would die. He sent a messenger to one of the cities of the Philistines, where there was an idol named Baal-zebub, to ask whether he would get well or not.

God was angry with Ahaziah. Before his messenger had gone far, he was met by an austere old man. It was the prophet Elijah, sent by God with a message. He strode up to the man and demanded, "Is it because there is no God in Israel, that you send to inquire of Baal-zebub? Therefore, thus says the Lord, 'Because you have done this, you will not get up from your bed, but will surely die.' "

The messenger came back to the sick king. "Why have you come back?" Ahaziah asked. He replied, "There came a man to meet me. He commanded me to come back to the king and say, 'Is it because there is no God in Israel that you send to inquire of Baal-zebub? Because you have done this, you will not get well, but will surely die.' "

When the sick king heard these dreadful words, he had a suspicion that the prophet might be the terrible Elijah who had come so many times to his father Ahab with warnings of judgment. If it were Elijah, he knew he would surely die, for Elijah's prophecies always came true.

"What kind of man was he?" he asked. "He was a hairy man, wearing a leather belt," was the answer. Then King Ahaziah knew it was Elijah. As his mother Jezebel had done, he tried to kill the prophet. He sent a captain with fifty soldiers to find Elijah and bring him to the palace, so that Ahaziah could punish him for his bad news. The captain of the fifty soldiers found Elijah sitting on the top of a hill.

"O man of God," the captain called out, "the king has said, 'Come down!' " Elijah knew very well that the king meant to kill him. He answered, "If I am a man of God, God will take care of me by sending fire down from heaven to consume you and your soldiers." Before the terrified man could do anything, the fire of God came down from heaven and consumed him and his fifty soldiers.

Did Ahaziah bow before the mighty God when he heard this news? No, he sent another captain with another fifty soldiers. The second captain came to Elijah and said, "O man of God, the king says, 'Come down quickly.' " Elijah answered, "If I am a man of God, let fire come down from heaven, and consume you and your fifty soldiers." And the fire of God came down from heaven again and consumed him and his fifty soldiers. God protected His faithful prophet who dared to stand up for the Lord and reprove a sinful king, even at the very risk of his own life.

Ahaziah sent a third captain with fifty more soldiers. This captain feared the God of the Israelites, even though King Ahaziah did not. When he approached the prophet, he fell down upon his knees and begged, "O man of God, I pray you, let my life, and the lives of these fifty soldiers, be precious in your sight."

God told Elijah to go with this man. So Elijah went to see the sick king. He entered the bedroom and said boldly, "Because you have sent to ask the idol whether you will get well, instead of asking the God of Israel, therefore you will never be able to leave your bed again. You will soon die."

In a short time this prophecy of Elijah was fulfilled. King Ahaziah died. As he had no son, his brother Joram, who is sometimes called Jehoram in the Bible, became king.

A VICTORY WITHOUT A BATTLE After the death of Ahab, King Jehoshaphat returned to his own country. He went throughout the land, urging his people to worship the Lord. He appointed judges in all the important cities, warning them to be just, since they must answer to God, not to man.

After a time some messengers

came to Jehoshaphat, who said, "A great army of Moabites and Ammonites and Edomites is coming to fight against you. They have already come as far as En-gedi." This was the wild, rocky country west of the Dead Sea, called the Rocks of the Wild Goats, where David once hid from Saul.

Jehoshaphat proclaimed a day of fasting throughout all the cities of Judah. The people of the land came to Jerusalem and stood before the temple — the women and children as well as the men. The king stood in the court of the temple. He raised his arms and his face to heaven and prayed: "O Lord God of our fathers, art not Thou God in heaven? And rulest Thou not over all the heathen? And in Thy hand is there not power and might, so that none is able to withstand Thee? O our God, we have no might against this great company that is come against us, neither know we what to do: but our eyes are upon Thee."

While the people were praying, the Spirit of the Lord came upon a Levite and told him to say, "Thus saith the Lord unto you, 'Be not afraid of this great multitude, for the battle is not yours, but God's. You shall not need to fight. Stand still, and see the salvation of the Lord. Fear not. Tomorrow go out against them, for the Lord will be with you.'"

King Jehoshaphat dropped down on his knees and bowed his head. The host of people worshiped the Lord, while some of the priests rose up to sing the praises of the God who protects all those who trust in Him, and who answers the prayers of His children.

The next morning the people rose early and went into the wilderness to meet the enemy army. In front of them marched a large choir, singing to God as they went. As the children of Israel sang, the Lord made the Moabites and the Ammonites fight against the Edomites. After they had destroyed the Edomites, they began to fight each other.

There was a watchtower in the wilderness. As soon as the Israelites reached it, they climbed up to see where the enemy was. To their unspeakable surprise, the whole country was covered with dead bodies. Not a living man could be seen!

On the battlefield the children of Israel found a great abundance of gold and precious jewels. It took them three days to carry away all the treasures they found.

On the fourth day they came together and thanked God for the wonderful things He had done for them. Not only had their enemies been destroyed, but they themselves were going back much richer than they had come out. With King Jehoshaphat at their head, the Israelites marched back to Jerusalem in a joyful procession, accompanied by the triumphant notes of trumpets, and the sweet sound of harps and psalteries.

Of course, the news of this wonderful victory was heard in all the countries round about. All the heathen nations were afraid when they heard how the Lord fought the enemies of His people.

God gave the land peace. Jehoshaphat reigned over the land twenty-five years. He was like his father Asa, doing what was right in the eyes of the Lord. At last his time came to die. He slept with his fathers, and was buried with them in the city of David. His son Jehoram reigned in his place.

Jehoram was a very bad man, and

a very bad king. As soon as he became king, he killed his six brothers and some of the princes of Judah, so that they would not try to take the kingdom away from him.

Why did Jehoram copy wicked King Ahab instead of his father, good King Jehoshaphat? It was because he had Ahab's daughter for his wife. You remember that Jehoshaphat once paid a visit to King Ahab. He had taken his young son with him on that visit. Jehoram had fallen in love with Ahab's pretty daughter Athaliah. He did not know that she was just as bad a woman as her mother. He married her and brought her back to Jerusalem.

Just as wicked Queen Jezebel had influenced King Ahab, so Athaliah influenced Jehoram. He became an idolater. What was worse, he forced his people to worship idols, too. The old prophet Elijah, who had so many times warned King Ahab, sent a letter to Jehoram, saying: "Thus saith the Lord God of David, your father, 'Because you have walked in the ways of the kings of Israel, not in the way of your father Jehoshaphat, and have made My people worship idols, and have murdered your brothers, who were better men than you are, therefore you shall have trouble in your family, and you yourself shall suffer great sickness.' "

God permitted the surrounding nations to make trouble for Jehoram. The Philistines and the Arabians forced their way into the land. They came to Jerusalem and even invaded the king's palace. They stole all the fine things they found. They took away all Jehoram's wives and sons, except one. Only his youngest son was left.

Then Jehoram himself became very sick. After two years he died. No one was sorry at his death, for he had been a bad ruler. He was buried in Jerusalem, but not in the graves of the kings.

Chapter 84
THE CHARIOT OF FIRE
II KINGS 2

KING OF ISRAEL
Joram

KING OF JUDAH
Jehoram

We must leave the kings of Israel and of Judah for a while. The time has come for us to say good-bye to the great prophet Elijah.

Elijah lived in evil days. In his lifetime King Ahab had been on the throne of Israel, and after him his wicked son Ahaziah. Still more wicked than either was the idolatrous Queen Jezebel. Ahab and Jezebel had turned the hearts of the people of Israel away, so that the Lord was forgotten except by a faithful few.

It had been Elijah's mission to tell these idolatrous kings that God would surely judge their sin. He always came to announce some dire punishment for their wickedness. Instead of changing their ways, and listening to the warnings from God, the kings tried over and over to kill Elijah. Only God's tender care had saved his life.

At last Elijah's work was done. God was going to take him to heaven. Elijah and Elisha were living at Gilgal when the word of the Lord came to tell Elijah to depart. "You stay here," the old prophet said to Elisha, "for the Lord has sent me to Bethel."

But Elisha could not bear to part from Elijah. "As the Lord lives," he said, "I will not leave you."

Together they went to Bethel, where there was a school of the prophets. The prophets came out to meet Elisha, asking, "Do you know that God is going to take your master away today?" Elisha answered, "Yes, I know it. Hold your peace."

Again Elijah said to Elisha, "Stay here, for the Lord has sent me to Jericho." But Elisha answered, as before, "As the Lord lives, and as your soul lives, I will not leave you." At Jericho there was another school of the prophets. These prophets, too, came to Elisha and asked him, "Do you know that God is going to take away your master today?" And Elisha answered, "Yes, I know it. Hold your peace."

Elijah said to Elisha, "You had better stay here. The Lord has sent me to the Jordan." But Elisha said again, "As surely as the Lord lives, and as your soul lives, I will not leave you."

The prophets from Jericho knew something wonderful was going to happen. They went up to a high place, where they could watch.

When Elijah and Elisha came to the Jordan River, Elijah took his coat and wrapped it together. He struck the waters with it, and the waters were divided, so that Elijah and Elisha walked through the river on dry ground.

On the other side of the Jordan Elijah said to Elisha, "Is there anything you would like to have me do for you, before I am taken away from you?" Elisha said, "I would like to ask for a double portion of your spirit." Elijah answered, "You have asked a hard thing, but if you see me when I am taken away, you shall have it."

The two men walked on together. As they were walking and talking, a most marvelous thing happened. There appeared out of the sky a chariot of fire and horses of fire, come down from heaven to carry Elijah up to God.

Elijah climbed into the chariot. His coat fell off, and dropped at Elisha's feet. The horses and the chariot flew in a whirlwind up into heaven. As Elisha saw them go, he cried out, "My father, my father, the chariots of Israel, and the horsemen thereof!" He watched and watched till the chariot disappeared in the blue of the sky.

Then he picked up Elijah's coat and went back to the bank of the Jordan. He wrapped the coat together, struck the water with it, and said, "Where is the God of Elijah?"

The waters divided, just as they had done for his teacher, showing that God had chosen him to take Elijah's place. The young men from the school of the prophets, who had been watching everything from a distance, came to meet Elisha. They bowed before him, for they saw that the spirit of Elijah was resting on him.

Chapter 85

ELISHA, THE GENTLE PROPHET

II KINGS 4, 5

TWO BOYS SAVED FROM SLAVERY

Like Elijah, Elisha was a prophet of God. But he was a very different sort of man, and he had a very different sort of work to do. He was not like the stern Elijah, nor was he sent to warn kings.

Let us go back a little over the story of Judah and Israel. King Ahaziah of Israel, you remember, fell out of a window, and sent to an idol to find out whether he would get well. God was angry with him, and gave him only two years as king.

Since Ahaziah had no son to rule after him, his brother Joram became king of Israel. Joram was not a good man, but he was not as wicked as his father Ahab or his brother Ahaziah.

Good King Jehoshaphat was still reigning in Judah when Joram became king of Israel. His son Jehoram, who became the next king, was not God-fearing. He worshiped idols, as Ahab had done, because he had married Ahab's daughter. God punished him with sickness and war.

It was in the days of these kings that Elisha lived. He worked among the ordinary people, teaching them and helping them.

One day a woman came to him for help. Her husband had been one of the sons of the prophets. He was now dead, and the woman was so poor that she could hardly get enough to eat.

This poor widow had a debt which she could not pay. One day the man to whom she owed the money came to her house to take away her two sons, to make them slaves. In those hard times, if a person could not pay his debts, his children were sold as slaves, although this was against the law God had given to Moses.

The poor woman did not know what to do. In her trouble she came to Elisha. The prophet asked, "What do you have in your house?" She answered, "All I have left is a little pot of olive oil." Elisha said, "Go and borrow from your neighbors all the jars that you can find. Then shut the door, so that no one can come in. Pour oil from your pot into all those jars."

The woman sent her sons to all the neighbors to borrow pots and containers. Then she shut her door. She poured olive oil into the jars as the boys brought them to her. God made her oil increase so much that there was enough to fill all the borrowed jars.

Then she came and told Elisha what had happened. He said, "Go, sell the oil, and pay your debt. You and your children can live on what is left over."

So Elisha helped one poor woman.

HOW A DEAD CHILD BECAME ALIVE

There was a rich woman living in Shunem, a town which Elisha often visited. As often as the prophet came to Shunem, this woman invited him to come to her house for supper. She became well acquainted with him.

One day she said to her husband, "Let us build a little room upstairs for this holy man who comes this way so often. Let us put a bed in it,

14: ELIJAH AND AHAB IN NABOTH'S VINEYARD

15: ELISHA AND THE SHUNAMMITE

and a table, and a chair, and a light, so that he can stay all night whenever he pleases." So they built a room for the prophet.

Elisha was very much pleased with the kindness of this good woman. One day, while he was at her home, he said to his servant Gehazi, "Ask her to come here."

When the woman came in, Elisha said, "It was very good of you to do all this for me. Now I would like to return your kindness, and do something for you. What shall I do for you? Shall I speak to the king for you, or to the captain of the army?"

She said, "No, thank you. I do not want anything." After she had gone, Elisha said to Gehazi, "What can I do for her?" Gehazi knew by this time that Elisha could do wonderful things, by the power of God. So he said to Elisha, "She has no child, and her husband is an old man."

Elisha called the woman back again, and said to her, "Next year you shall have a baby boy."

Oh, how delighted the woman was! She had never had a baby, although she had wanted one more than anything else in the world. She could hardly believe Elisha. All that year she began to get ready for the darling baby that Elisha said was coming to her. How happy she was as she sat sewing the tiny baby clothes she was making for him!

The next year the baby came. Oh, how she loved him. How happy she was when she rocked him to sleep in her arms!

By and by he grew up to be a sturdy little boy. When he was five or six years old, he went out one day to his father's farm to see the reapers gather in the wheat. It was a hot summer day. The sun poured down on the harvest field. In the heat, the little boy got a sunstroke. He cried to his father, "My head! My head!"

"Carry him to his mother," his father commanded one of the servants. The little boy was carried back to the house. His mother did all she could for him. She held him on her lap, and put cool water on his head, but he got worse and worse. About noon he died.

His mother carried him upstairs to Elisha's room and laid him on the bed. Then she called to her husband and said, "Send me, I pray you, one of the servants, and one of the donkeys, that I may run to the man of God." Then she saddled the donkey and said to the servant, "Drive as fast as you can!"

Elisha saw the woman coming along the road, far off. He said to Gehazi, "Run, and meet her, and ask her, 'Is it well with you? Is it well with your husband? Is it well with the child?'"

Gehazi ran to meet her, but she did not want to tell her trouble to Gehazi, so she just answered, "It is well," and hurried on. When she came to Elisha, and saw the good man who had been her friend, she threw herself on the ground and burst into tears, catching hold of the prophet's feet.

Gehazi was going to push her away, but Elisha said, "Let her alone. She is in trouble." Between her sobs the unhappy mother managed to say, "Did I ask for a son?"

Elisha said to Gehazi, "Run quickly to her house. Do not stop to talk to anyone on the way. Lay my staff on the face of the child." Gehazi tucked his long robe into his belt, so it would not get in his way, and ran as fast as he could run. Elisha and the child's mother followed.

Gehazi laid Elisha's staff on the

dead child's face, but it did no good. He ran back to meet Elisha and said, "The child did not awaken."

When Elisha reached the woman's house, he went up into his own little room, where the child lay on the bed. Elisha lay down upon the bed over the child, and put his mouth on the little boy's mouth, his eyes over the boy's eyes, and his hands upon the child's hands. The dead body of the little boy became warm.

Then Elisha got up and walked about a little. Again he stretched himself upon the child. The boy sneezed seven times, and opened his eyes. Elisha called his servant and told him to bring the child's mother.

The dear little boy lay on the bed with the rosy color of health on his cheeks. When he looked up at his mother, and stretched out his arms to her, she was overcome with joy. She first fell down at Elisha's feet, but she could not find any words to thank him. Then she took up her little son and carried him down to his own room.

THE GENERAL WHO OBEYED ORDERS
To the north of Israel lay the land of Syria, where Ben-hadad ruled. This man had been king for many, many years, and had often made war against Israel. Twice he and the Syrian army had been defeated by the Israelites under Ahab. In another war between the two countries Ahab had been killed. But when Joram became king of Israel there was peace with Ben-hadad, although at times the Syrians came in bands and stole the property of the Israelites.

The captain of the armies of Ben-hadad was a man named Naaman. He was a great favorite with his master, partly because he was so successful in battle. God had helped Naaman to conquer many of Syria's enemies. But now Naaman had become very sick. He had that most terrible of all diseases, leprosy.

Sometime before our story begins, a band of Syrians had gone down into the northern part of the land of Israel, and had stolen a little girl. She became a servant in Naaman's house, and waited on the general's wife.

One day the little girl said to her mistress, "Oh, how I wish that my lord Naaman were in Samaria, for there is a prophet there who can cure him of his leprosy."

The words of the little girl were repeated to the king. They caused a great sensation in the court, for no one had ever heard of anyone who could cure leprosy. Ben-hadad said to Naaman, "If it is true that there is a prophet in Samaria who can cure you, you must go and see him. I will give you a letter of introduction to King Joram."

So Naaman went to Samaria. He took a fine present with him — a great treasure of gold and silver, and ten beautiful silk robes.

When he arrived in Samaria, he went to the palace and delivered his letter to the king. The letter read: "I am sending my general Naaman to you, so you can cure him of his leprosy."

King Joram was frightened when he read this message. He tore his clothes in dismay. He thought the letter was no more than an excuse to get him in trouble. "Am I God," he said, "to kill and to make alive, that he sends this man to me to be cured of leprosy? See how Ben-hadad tries to pick a quarrel with me!"

Elisha sent a messenger to Joram, saying, "Why do you tear your clothes? Let the general come to me, and he will see that there is a prophet in Israel."

In great style, with his fine horses, his beautiful chariot, and his long train of servants, Naaman drove to Elisha's house. Elisha did not even come out to meet him. He sent his servant to say, "Go and wash in the Jordan River seven times, and you will be cured."

Naaman was an important man. He was rich and honored. No one had ever dared to treat him in this careless fashion. He said angrily, "I expected he would surely come out, and call on the name of his God, and wave his hand over the sore places! The idea of just sending out his servant to me! And telling me to wash in the Jordan River! Are not the rivers of Damascus much better than the Jordan? If that is what the cure requires, I will wash myself in them!" And, in a great rage, he started out for home.

Naaman was a kind master. His servants loved him, and wanted him to get well. After they had gone some distance along the road, they dared to say to him, "My father, if the prophet had told you to do something very hard, wouldn't you have done it? Then why not try this easy thing that he told you? He only said, 'Wash, and you will be well.'"

Naaman was proud. He had been insulted. He was angry. But pride and anger will not cure leprosy. A man who has a hopeless disease can hardly afford to be insulted by the treatment his doctor suggests. And so at last the unhappy general said to himself, "Why not try it? What have I to lose?"

He rode to the Jordan River. He took off his clothes and waded into the water. He ducked under seven times. When he came out of the

river, the dreadful disease had disappeared. His body was no longer deadly white. It was pink and rosy as a little child's.

It was not the Jordan River that had healed Naaman. The general understood this quite well. It was Elisha's God, the God of heaven and earth, the One who does indeed decide who shall live and who shall die. For when Naaman took Elisha at his word, when he swallowed his pride and put his trust in Elisha's God, then he found something even more precious than life and health. That day Naaman found God.

Naaman and all his servants turned around and rode back to Elisha's house. This time the prophet came out to meet them. "Now I know," Naaman said to Elisha, "that there is no God in all the earth but the Lord. I beg you, take a little present, as an expression of my gratitude to your God."

But Elisha would not take a present. "As the Lord lives," he said, "before whom I stand, I will not take anything." It was not Elisha, but God, who had worked this miracle. He wanted Naaman to understand this clearly.

Then Naaman said, "I pray you, let me take home with me to Damascus two mules' loads of earth. From now on I will worship and offer sacrifices only to the Lord. And may God forgive me this one thing, that when I have to go with my master King Ben-hadad into the temple of the idol Rimmon, and the king worships the idol, may God forgive me that I bow too." Elisha said to him, "Go home in peace!" So Naaman and his great train of servants set out for Damascus, carrying with them two loads of earth from the land of the true God.

THE SERVANT WHO WAS GREEDY Gehazi, Elisha's servant, said to himself, "What a shame that my master did not take some of the fine presents Naaman offered him! I will run after him, and get some of them for myself."

Gehazi ran after the Syrian. When Naaman saw him coming, he stopped his chariot, thinking that Elisha had sent Gehazi. He asked, "Is all well?"

Gehazi said, "Yes, all is well. But just now there came to see us two young men who are sons of the prophets. My master sent me after you to ask you to give them a talent of silver and two robes."

Naaman was only too glad to do this. He urged, "One talent is not enough. Take two talents." He gave Gehazi two bags filled with silver, and two suits of beautiful silk clothes. He sent two of his servants along with Gehazi to carry the money.

But Gehazi did not want them to carry those bags back to Elisha's house. No indeed! He stopped them when they came to a secret place. There he hid the money. He sent Naaman's servants back to their master. He himself went on to Elisha's house, as though nothing had happened.

"Where have you been, Gehazi?" Elisha asked.

"Your servant went nowhere," answered Gehazi.

Elisha said, "Did not my heart go with you, when the man turned again to meet you? Is this a proper time to be taking money, or trying to become rich? The leprosy of Naaman, therefore, will stick to you and to your children forever."

And Gehazi went out of the room a leper, as white as snow.

Chapter 86
TROUBLE WITH SYRIA
II KINGS 6-8

KING OF ISRAEL	KINGS OF JUDAH	
Joram	Jehoram	Ahaziah

ELISHA FOOLS THE SYRIANS Since the death of Ahab there had been peace with Syria. But now Ben-hadad, the king of Syria, again planned to go to war against Israel.

The Syrians chose carefully the place where they wanted to fight. There they set up their camp secretly, hoping to surprise King Joram. But Elisha sent a message to Joram, "Do not go near such and such a place, because the Syrians are camped there." So Joram saved himself from the Syrians.

This happened two or three times. Ben-hadad could not understand why the king of Israel never came near his hidden camp. He thought there must be a traitor in his army who told the king of Israel where the camp was, so that Joram could avoid it. He said to his soldiers, "Will you not show me which one of you is a traitor, and gives away our secret plans to the king of Israel?"

One of his servants answered, "None of us is a traitor, my lord, O king. But Elisha, the prophet in Israel, tells the king of Israel the very words you speak in your bedroom." King Ben-hadad commanded, "Go and find out where he is, so that I can capture him." Some men went to search for Elisha. When they returned they said, "He is in Dothan."

Early one morning soon after this, Elisha's servant went outdoors. He was terrified to see the whole city surrounded by Syrian horses and chariots. He ran into the house to tell Elisha and cried, "Alas, my master, what shall we do?"

Elisha answered, "Do not be afraid, for those that are with us are more than those that are with them." Then Elisha prayed and said, "Lord, I pray Thee, open his eyes, that he may see." God opened the servant's eyes, and he saw what few men have ever seen, what cannot be seen with the eyes of our body, but only with the eyes of faith: the whole mountain was filled with horses and chariots of fire sent from God to protect Elisha.

When Ben-hadad's soldiers came into the city, Elisha prayed to the Lord, "I pray Thee, smite this people with blindness." And the Lord smote them with blindness, so that they did not recognize where they were, or to whom they were talking. Elisha said to them, "You have made a mistake. This is not the way, nor is this the right city. Follow me, and I will bring you to the man you are looking for."

He led them straight to the capital city of Samaria. When they were in the middle of the city, Elisha said, "Lord, open the eyes of these men, so that they may see where they are." When God opened their eyes, they saw that they were in the middle of Samaria, surrounded by their enemies!

King Joram was very excited. Here were his enemies trapped in his biggest city, where he could easily kill them! He called out to Elisha, "My

father, shall I kill them? Shall I kill them?"

Elisha said, "No, that would not be right. Give them bread and water, so that they may eat and drink, and send them back to their master."

So Joram set food and drink before them. Afterward he sent them back to King Ben-hadad.

A CITY ESCAPES STARVATION For a time the Syrians were ashamed to come again to the land of Israel. But peace did not last. Ben-hadad came again in earnest to fight against Samaria.

With him he brought a great host of soldiers. They surrounded the city of Samaria, so that none of the people of the city could go out or come in. There is nothing more dreadful than such a siege. It means slow starvation for the people inside the city walls.

Before long all the food in the city of Samaria was eaten up. The starving people could not get any more food from the farmers outside, because the Syrian soldiers would let no one into Samaria. The little food that was left was so expensive that poor people could not buy it. The people killed every animal that was in the city and ate it — even animals that were not fit to eat. Even those were very, very expensive. The head of a donkey cost eighty pieces of silver.

King Joram took a walk on the wall of the city. On every side he could see people in distress, suffering from starvation. He blamed Elisha for this siege, and he determined to kill the prophet that very day.

Elisha was in his house, sitting with the elders of Israel. When the king arrived, he said to Joram, "Hear the word of the Lord. Tomorrow about this time a measure of fine

197

flour shall be sold in the gate of Samaria for a shekel, and two measures of barley for a shekel." The captain on whose arm the king leaned said scornfully, "Even if the Lord made windows in heaven, how could this ever happen?"

"You shall see it with your own eyes," Elisha answered, "but you shall not eat any of it."

On the same day four poor lepers sat by the gate of the city. They said to each other, "Why should we sit here until we die? If we go into the city, we shall surely die of the famine. If we stay here, we shall die too. Let us go down to the camp of the Syrians. If they save us alive, we shall live. If they kill us, we can meet nothing worse than death."

The lepers rose up in the evening to go to the camp of the Syrians. When they came to the edge of the camp, there was no man there. What had happened? The Lord had made the Syrians hear a noise of chariots and a noise of horses, even the noise of a great army. The Syrian soldiers had said one to another, "Lo, the king of Israel has hired the kings of the Hittites and of the Egyptians against us. Oh, hurry, let us run, or we shall all be killed!" In their terror they had left their tents and their horses and everything else just as it was, and had run for their lives.

The lepers went from one tent to another. There was no one in any of the tents. The lepers ate and drank till they were satisfied. Then they carried away gold and silver and fine clothes, and hid them. At last they said to each other, "We are not doing right. This is a day of good news. We ought to go and tell the king. We will surely get in trouble if we selfishly keep this to ourselves."

They returned to the city. It was late at night. The city gate was shut tight, locked and barred against the Syrians. The lepers stood outside the gate and shouted to the guard, "We went to the camp of the Syrians, and there was no one there. All was as still as death. The horses and donkeys were tied, and the tents not taken down."

The guard sent this message to the king. The king got up in the middle of the night. He did not believe this news was true. He said, "I will tell you what the Syrians have done. They know that we are hungry. They have only pretended to go away. They have hid themselves in the field, saying, 'When they come out of the city, we shall catch them alive, and get into the city.'"

But some of King Joram's servants said, "Let us take five of the horses that are left, and go and see if this good news can possibly be true."

These men went out to the camp of the Syrians. There was no one in the camp. They went on till they came to the Jordan River. All the road was littered with garments and kettles and other things which the Syrians had thrown away in their panic. There was no sign of a Syrian soldier anywhere. The messengers went back and told the king.

Then the people streamed out of the city to the camp of the Syrians. They were frantic to get food. They came in such a rush that many people were knocked down and hurt. The king appointed the captain on whose arm he had leaned to take charge of the gate.

The people who got to the camp first satisfied their hunger. Then they took bags of flour and meal back to the gate. There they sold this to latecomers who had just reached the gate. As Elisha had said, the captain who doubted God's promise saw two measures of barley sold for a shekel, but he himself did not eat any of it. For the people trampled him underfoot, and he died.

A THOUGHT THAT BECAME A MURDER Do you remember that when the Lord appeared to Elijah in the still small voice on Mount Sinai, He told the prophet to go back and anoint a new king over Syria and a new king over Israel? Elijah did not accomplish this work in his lifetime. He left it for Elisha to finish.

Elisha went to Damascus in Syria. King Ben-hadad was sick. He was now an old man, for he had reigned for a long time. Ben-hadad was a heathen who worshiped the idol Rimmon. Even after God had cured his great general Naaman of leprosy, Ben-hadad did not worship the Lord. He must have learned something about the greatness of the God of Israel, however. When his servant Hazael told him that Elisha, the man of God, had come to Damascus, Ben-hadad said to him, "Take a present, and go meet the man of God. Ask him to inquire of the Lord whether I will get over this disease or not."

Hazael went to meet Elisha. He spoke very respectfully. "Your son Ben-hadad, king of Syria, has sent me to ask you whether he will get over his sickness."

Elisha answered, "Go, tell him that he will get well." Then, looking very seriously at Hazael, Elisha continued, "But the Lord has showed me that he will surely die."

Hazael was very much puzzled by this strange message. He was still more perplexed when he saw how earnestly and solemnly Elisha was looking at him. Big tears rolled down Elisha's cheeks.

Hazael asked, "Why do you weep, my lord?"

Elisha answered, "Because I know all the dreadful things that you are going to do to the children of Israel. You will burn their cities. You will kill their young men with the sword. You will dash their little children to death on the rocks."

Hazael was horrified. Why did Elisha say such things about him? He would never do anything so terrible. He protested, "Is your servant a dog that he should do such horrible things?"

Elisha gave an answer that astonished Hazael. He said, "The Lord has shown me that you are to be king of Syria."

Can you imagine Hazael's feelings? What! Was he to be king of Syria when Ben-hadad died? He kept thinking about this all the way home to the palace.

Ben-hadad asked him, "What did Elisha say?" Hazael answered, "He said you would surely get well again." But he did not tell the king the rest of what Elisha had said.

That night Hazael could not sleep. He kept thinking of what Elisha had said — that he should be king after Ben-hadad. How wonderful that would be! But he would have to wait a long time, for Elisha had said Ben-hadad would get well again. Hazael almost wished Elisha had said Ben-hadad would die of this sickness. Then he could be king immediately. The more he thought about it, the more Hazael wished that the king would die. At last the sinful thought came into his heart that it would be very easy to make him die. He was old and sick.

The next morning he took a thick cloth and dipped it in water. He spread it over Ben-hadad's face, holding it down tight so that Ben-hadad could not breathe.

The weak, sick old man struggled a little, but his struggles soon stopped. He was dead. Probably the Syrians never knew that Hazael had murdered their king. They thought he had died naturally of his sickness.

But Elisha knew the truth, and Hazael knew.

The new king, who had begun his reign by murdering his master, became a cruel and bloody king. In the course of time he did all the wicked things that Elisha had foretold of him.

Chapter 87

THE SOLDIER-KING, JEHU

II CHRONICLES 22; II KINGS 9, 10

A SECRET ANOINTING We have not heard about the kingdom of Judah for a long time. The last thing we learned about it was that King Jehoram, the wicked son of good King Jehoshaphat, became sick and died. Then Jehoram's son Ahaziah became king. He was bad like his father, for his mother Athaliah, who was the daughter of Ahab and Jezebel, persuaded him to act wickedly.

Soon after he became king, he went down to see his uncle, King Joram of Israel. The two kings decided to make war on Ramoth-gilead, a city which the Syrians had taken away from the Israelites. You remember that once before the kings of Israel and of Judah had tried to recapture this city. It was in that battle that Ahab was killed.

In this second battle the Israelites were successful in taking the city, but King Joram was wounded in the fight. He and Ahaziah went back to the city of Jezreel, leaving the army at Ramoth-gilead.

Both of these kings belonged to the family of Ahab. God had punished Ahab for his wickedness, and He had said that every man of Ahab's family would die a violent death. Part of this prophecy had already been fulfilled in the death of Ahab. God was going to send a rough and violent man to carry out the rest of the judgment upon Ahab's family, and upon Jezebel.

This man was Jehu, one of the captains of the Israelite army. Jehu was a very energetic man, quick to act. Whatever he did, he did with force and decision.

The prophet Elisha was still living in Israel. One day he summoned one of the young prophets, gave him a jar of oil, and sent him to Ramoth-gilead, where the Israelite army was camped.

The young prophet took the oil and went to Ramoth-gilead. There he found Jehu sitting with the other captains of the army. The messenger from Elisha said, "I have a message for you, O captain."

"For which one of us?" Jehu asked.

"For you, captain," replied the young prophet.

Jehu got up and went into the house with the young man. The prophet poured the oil on Jehu's head,

200

saying, "Thus says the Lord God of Israel, 'I have anointed you king over the people of the Lord, even over Israel. You shall destroy the whole family of Ahab, because King Ahab and Queen Jezebel have killed My servants the prophets.' "

When the prophet had said this, he opened the door and ran away as fast as he could. Jehu went back outside to where all the other officers were sitting. "What did that crazy fellow say to you?" they asked.

At first Jehu would not tell them. "Oh, you know what kind of man he is," he said. But the officers were not satisfied with this answer. "That is not the truth!" they cried. "Tell us truly what he said to you."

Finally Jehu told them. "This is what he said to me: 'Thus saith the Lord, "I have anointed you to be king over Israel." ' "

The officers were glad, for they hated the wicked family of Ahab. Each of them took off his coat and laid it on the stairs to make a carpet for Jehu to walk on. They blew the trumpets loudly, and shouted, "Jehu· is king!"

All this happened in Ramoth-gilead, where the whole army was still camped, although King Joram and King Ahaziah had gone back to the city of Jezreel after the battle. Being a man of action, Jehu commanded that the gates of the city be closed, so that no one might go to warn Joram that Jehu had been made king.

Then all the captains got into their chariots and drove furiously to Jezreel.

GOD'S TERRIBLE JUDGMENT ON A WICKED FAMILY   There was a tower in Jezreel where a guard kept watch night and day to make sure no enemy was approaching. As the watchman was gazing this way and that over the country, he spied a cloud of dust in the distance. Soon he saw it was a company of horsemen. He sent word to the king.

King Joram sent a man on horseback to meet the men who were approaching, and to ask if they came in peace. The messenger galloped out of the gates. When he came to Jehu he asked, "Is it peace?"

"What have you to do with peace?" said Jehu. "Stay here behind me. Do not return to the king."

The watchman on the tower sent word to King Joram that he had seen the messenger gallop away and speak to the horsemen, but that he did not come back.

The king sent a second man with the same message. Again Jehu answered, "What have you to do with peace? Stay here with me."

The watchman on the tower sent word again to the king. "The second man went, but he does not come back either. I think it must be Jehu who is coming, because he drives furiously."

Since Jehu was the leader of the army, Joram thought that he might be coming to tell him that the Syrians, or some other enemy, had attacked some of the Israelite cities. He sent for his chariot and for the chariot of King Ahaziah. Together the two kings drove out to meet Jehu. As soon as he was near enough, Joram called out anxiously, "Is it peace, Jehu?"

Jehu shouted back, "How can there be any peace, as long as your wicked mother Jezebel has done all this evil?"

King Joram saw at once that something was wrong. He turned his chariot around to escape. As he went, he called out to King Ahaziah, "There is treachery, O Ahaziah!"

Jehu was a very quick and strong man. In an instant he drew his bow with all his strength and shot King Joram through the heart. The king sank down dead in his chariot.

When King Ahaziah saw this, he turned his chariot and fled. Jehu hurried after him, calling to his captains, "Shoot him, too!" The captains killed Ahaziah, for he was also a wicked member of the family of Ahab. His servants carried their dead king back to the kingdom of Judah, where he was buried with the kings in the city of David.

Jehu and his company drove on till they reached the city of Jezreel. When Queen Jezebel heard what Jehu had done, she painted her face and carefully arranged her hair. As Jehu entered the palace gate, she leaned out of an upstairs window and called to him, "Is it peace, you murderer of your master?"

Jehu did not answer her taunt. He shouted, "Who is on my side?" Two or three servants looked out of the window at him. "Throw her down!" he called. The servants pitched Jezebel out of the window. She struck the stones below and was killed instantly. Her blood spattered on the wall and on Jehu's horses. He drove his chariot over her body.

Jehu did not spare a single man of Ahab's family. He killed them all, obeying God's command to rid the land of that wicked family.

BAAL IS DEAD After Jehu had killed all the wicked family of Ahab, he had another important task. He had to drive idolatry out of the land. In Samaria almost all the people were idolaters, for King Ahab and Queen Jezebel had made them worship idols.

Jehu wanted to gather all the prophets and priests of Baal together, so that he could kill every one of them, and thus wipe out idolatry in the Lord's country.

In order to catch all of them together, Jehu played a trick. He gathered all the people together and said, "Ahab served Baal a little, but Jehu will serve him much! I am going to make a great sacrifice to Baal. Every priest and prophet of Baal, and everyone who wishes to serve him, must be present for this grand occasion."

From all over the country the worshipers of Baal came to the sacrifice. They were afraid to disobey a man so harsh as Jehu had shown himself to be. The temple was filled from one end to the other with the worshipers. They stood so crowded together that they were barely able to breathe.

Jehu said to the man who kept the robes the Baal worshipers wore in the temple, "See to it that every man in the temple has the proper robe." Then he shouted to the people in the temple, "Be sure there are no worshipers of the Lord there with you, but only the worshipers of Baal!"

Then Jehu posted eighty men all around the outside of the temple. "If you let any of these men escape," he said to them, "you will pay for it with your own lives." Turning to his soldiers, he said, "Go into the temple of Baal, and kill everyone there. Do not let one of them escape."

The soldiers obeyed Jehu. Not one of the worshipers of Baal escaped. Then Jehu sent soldiers into the temple to bring out all the images that were there and burn them. The image of Baal was broken down. Jehu's soldiers made a rubbish heap of the temple itself.

All these terrible things were

necessary because the wicked family of Ahab had turned the people away from the true God to the worship of Baal. God had been almost forgotten in the land.

God had sent the rough-and-ready Jehu to rid the land of Ahab's family. A gentler man than Jehu could not have done it. Jehu was rewarded for his work. God promised that his sons would be kings after him for four generations.

Now the people of Israel might have turned back to the Lord, if they had had anyone to teach them the ways of God. But Jehu, although he was a great soldier, was no teacher. He destroyed the worship of Baal, but he did not try to teach the people to worship and trust God.

When the first king of the divided kingdom, Jeroboam, had ruled, he had set up two golden calves for the people to worship, so that the children of Israel would not have to go to Jerusalem to worship. These golden calves were still worshiped.

The people had become so idolatrous that they could not understand how they could worship a God whom they could not see. How foolish and wrong this seems to us now! We know that we can worship God, and pray to Him, even if we cannot see Him.

But even in Israel not all the people worshiped the golden calves. God sent many prophets to teach the people about the Lord. Some of the people listened to the prophets and worshiped their own God in the right way.

Because most of the Israelites forgot God, He let Hazael, the king of Syria, come to fight against the Israelites. Hazael destroyed many of their towns.

King Hazael was very cruel in his victories. You remember how Elisha wept when he saw how Hazael would burn the Israelite cities, and kill their young men with the sword, and dash their babies to death on the stones. All these terrible things happened in the reign of Jehu.

Chapter 88
THE LITTLE BOY WHO BECAME KING
II KINGS 11-13; II CHRONICLES 22-24

KINGS OF ISRAEL		KING OF JUDAH
Jehu	Jehoahaz	Joash

HOW JOASH WAS KEPT SAFE While Jehu was king in Israel, what was happening in the kingdom of Judah?

Jehu killed King Ahaziah, who was the grandson of Ahab. Ahaziah had ruled only one year. Even in that short time he did evil in the sight of the Lord, for his wicked mother Athaliah persuaded him to do as Ahab had done.

After Ahaziah was dead, Athaliah became a monster of wickedness. She killed Ahaziah's children, her own grandchildren! She did not want any of them to become king, for she wanted to reign herself.

But one little baby was saved. When Ahaziah's sister Jehosheba saw that their grandmother was killing all the little princes, she stole the littlest one, a tiny baby, and hid him with his nurse. She kept him close by her, and never let his grandmother see him. His name was Joash. For six years Jehosheba kept the little boy hidden away from his bloodthirsty grandmother who had made herself queen.

Jehosheba was married to a very good man named Jehoiada, who was the high priest of God. Little Joash was hidden in the temple of the Lord. He was safe there, for Athaliah never went near God's temple. No one knew that one of King Ahaziah's sons was still alive. His aunt and his uncle kept the secret.

At this time things seemed very dark to the people of Judah. They hated Queen Athaliah because she was so wicked. Besides, she was a foreigner, not of the royal line of David. The people wanted a king of David's line.

God had promised that David's children should rule forever. How could this be, when all the family of David had been killed? The people could not understand why God had let the whole royal line of David be wiped out.

When little Prince Joash was seven years old, the priest Jehoiada sent for all the captains of the army to come to Jerusalem. He told them that when wicked Queen Athaliah had killed the princes, one little baby had been saved. He made them all swear an oath of allegiance to little Joash.

You can imagine with what joy the people heard that one prince of the royal line had been saved. Jehoiada brought Joash out, and showed him to the captains of the army. He ordered all the soldiers to stand close around the little prince to protect him from harm.

After he had placed this armed guard around the prince, Jehoiada invited all the people of Judah to come to the crowning of their new king. He put the crown upon the little boy's head and anointed him with oil. Joash was king! The sound of the trumpets burst forth, and the people all shouted, "Long live the king! Long live the king!"

Queen Athaliah heard the blaring of the trumpets and the shouting. She came to the temple to see what this uproar was all about. There she saw the little king standing by the pillar in the temple, and all the soldiers around him with spears and shields. The people were clapping their hands and rejoicing. The queen tore her clothes and threw up her hands, screaming, "Treason! Treason!"

Jehoiada said to the soldiers, "Kill her, but outside. Do not kill her in God's holy temple." Athaliah ran out to the driveway where the horses came up to the palace. There the soldiers killed the wicked woman who had herself caused so many murders.

Jehoiada made all the people promise that they would be the Lord's people. The little king had to promise that he, too, would serve the Lord.

Then the people went to the temple of Baal and broke it down. For the grandchildren of Ahab had dared to build a temple to Baal even in the holy city of Jerusalem.

Forming a great procession, the people brought the little king into the royal palace. They lifted him up to the king's throne. There he sat, with the king's golden crown on his head and the king's golden scepter in his hand. How small he must have looked on that beautiful throne!

Joash was only seven years old when he was made king, but he served the Lord, for the good priest Jehoiada had brought him up, and had taught him about God.

It was not so long ago that the whole nation of Judah had been God-fearing. Joash's great-grandfather

Jehoshaphat had been a good king, and had reigned twenty-five years. His son Jehoram had married the wicked Athaliah, and had worshiped idols. He had reigned only eight years, and his son Ahaziah had been on the throne only one year. Even though wicked Queen Athaliah had seized the throne for six years, only fifteen years had passed since the days of good King Jehoshaphat.

Most of the people could remember those days. They were very happy when they saw that little Joash was growing up to be a God-fearing man. God let King Joash reign for forty years.

JOASH FORGETS GOD   When the boy Joash grew up, it came into his heart to repair God's holy temple. Almost one hundred and fifty years had passed since Solomon had built the temple. Some parts had become worn out and needed to be repaired. The sons of Athaliah had taken many of the golden dishes and had put them in the temple of Baal.

Long ago Moses had commanded that every man twenty years old should bring half a shekel to the Lord every year. This command had been sadly neglected while Athaliah was queen in Jerusalem.

Joash had the carpenters make a strong chest and bore a hole in the top of it. They set the chest by the gate of the temple. When the worshipers brought their half shekel, or when they wished to give some special offering to the Lord to show their thankfulness for His blessings, they dropped the money into this chest. When the chest was full, the high priest and the king's secretary took the money out and put it into bags.

The people were so pleased to have their beautiful temple built up again

that they kept bringing a great deal of money. Every day the chest became full and was emptied. The money was used to pay the men who worked on the temple, and to buy wood and stone to repair its walls. The money that was left was used to buy gold and silver dishes for the service of the Lord. At last the temple was finished. Once again it was stately and beautiful.

As long as the good old priest Jehoiada lived, King Joash was a good ruler. But Jehoiada was already ninety years old when Joash was crowned. At last the old priest died, at the age of one hundred and thirty years. The people loved him so much for all the good he had done that they buried him with the kings in the city of David.

After Jehoiada's death, some very sad things happened. I wish I could leave them out, but nothing can be left out of a Bible story.

The princes of Judah came to King Joash and said that they were tired of worshiping the Lord. They wanted to go back to their idol worship. Joash himself felt the same way! So the people left the Lord and returned to worshiping Baal and the Asherim.

God sent prophets to warn them to turn back to the only true God, but they would not listen. The Spirit of the Lord came upon Zechariah, the son of the good old priest Jehoiada. He said to the people, "Why do you break the commandments of God? Because you have forsaken the Lord, He has also forsaken you."

But the king and the people would not listen to Zechariah. Joash forgot that it was Zechariah's father who had saved him, when he was just a baby, from his bloodthirsty grandmother Athaliah, and who had crowned him king. He ordered the people to throw stones at Zechariah to kill him. What made it still worse was that they did this in the court of the holy temple. Just before Zechariah died, he said, "May the Lord remember what they have done, and punish them for it."

God did punish Joash and his people for these sins. I am sure you remember Hazael, the king of Syria, who murdered Ben-hadad by smothering him with a wet cloth held tight over his face. God used this merciless man to punish the kingdom of Israel and the kingdom of Judah for trusting in idols instead of in the one true God.

Hazael came first against Israel, which was nearer to Syria than Judah was. Although the son of Jehu, who was now on the throne, had not followed the Lord, when danger threatened him he prayed to God for help. And the Lord heard his prayer and turned away the army of the Syrians.

Then Hazael marched on to Judah and to Jerusalem. He did not have a large army, but God allowed him to kill all the princes of Judah, because they had forgotten the God of their fathers. Joash took all the sacred golden things out of the temple of the Lord and sent them to Hazael, to bribe him to go away from Jerusalem.

Many of the people of Judah became very angry with their king. He had begun his reign so well by repairing the temple of the Lord, but he ended it so badly by forsaking the God of his fathers.

Two of his servants conspired against Joash, because he had murdered Zechariah, the son of the good old priest Jehoiada. They slipped into the bedroom where he lay sick, and killed him.

When the people of Judah found out their king was dead, they buried him, but not in the graves of the kings. They did not think he deserved that honor, for he had turned away from the Lord.

King Joash began to reign when he was seven years old. He was king for forty years. If he had obeyed God, he might have reigned for many years longer.

Chapter 89
ELISHA'S LAST PROPHECY
II KINGS 13

KINGS OF ISRAEL		KINGS OF JUDAH	
Jehu	Jehoash	Joash	Amaziah
Jehoahaz			

During the forty years that Joash reigned in Judah, three kings reigned in Israel. They were all of Jehu's line, for God had promised Jehu that, because he had destroyed the whole wicked family of Ahab, his sons should be kings of Israel for four generations.

Jehu reigned in Israel for twenty-eight years. Although he destroyed the idols of Baal and all the priests of Baal, he did not destroy the golden calves that were in Bethel and in Dan. The people still worshiped these calves. Jehu's son Jehoahaz became king after him. He also worshiped the golden calves, even though God had strictly forbidden this in the Ten Commandments. God punished the Israelites for trusting in the golden calves instead of in the only true God by letting Hazael, the cruel king of the Syrians, attack them. But when the Israelites in their trouble turned back to God, and asked Him to help them, He heard their prayers. He made the Syrians go back to their own country. How patient God was with these sinful people of His!

Jehoahaz reigned only seventeen years. When he died, his son Jehoash became king. He, too, worshiped the golden calves, as his fathers had done; yet he was not as wicked as King Ahab had been.

In the days of Jehoash, the kind old prophet Elisha, who had lived in the kingdom of Israel all these years, became very sick. The king was very sad when he heard that he might soon lose his friend the prophet. Elisha had helped him to govern his kingdom. He had often given him good advice. Who would help him govern and fight when Elisha was gone? Who would pray to the Lord for him?

With these sad thoughts turning over in his mind, Jehoash went to see Elisha, who lay on his bed, pale and weak. Big tears rolled down the king's cheeks as he sobbed, "My father, my father!"

Elisha, sick and weak, said to the king in a feeble voice, "Take a bow and arrows."

The king went into the next room and found a bow and arrows. He came back to Elisha's bedside with them. The prophet said weakly, "Put your hand upon the bow."

The king stretched the bow with his strong young arms. With a great effort the sick prophet raised himself to a sitting position, leaned over, and laid his thin white hands over the king's strong brown ones. "Open the window," he said. When the window was open, he said, "Shoot!"

As the king shot an arrow, Elisha said, "That is the Lord's arrow of victory over Syria. You shall fight the Syrians till you have conquered them."

Then he said, "Take the arrows, and strike the ground." The king struck the ground three times with the arrows. Elisha said, "Why didn't you strike the ground five or six times? Then God would have helped you to conquer the Syrians utterly. Now He will give you the victory only three times."

The old prophet fell back upon the bed, exhausted. Soon afterward he died and was buried.

Not long after Elisha's death, another man died. While his friends were burying him, they saw a band of robbers approaching. In their fear and their hurry to get away, they dropped the body of their friend into the first grave they saw. This happened to be Elisha's. As soon as the body of the dead man touched the bones of Elisha, he revived, and stood up on his feet.

Elisha's prophecy about Jehoash's victory over the Syrians came true. Hazael, that cruel Syrian king who had murdered his master, died. His son, who was also named Ben-hadad, became king. Jehoash went to fight with this second Ben-hadad three times. Just as Elisha had said, he was victorious. He won back the Israelite cities which Hazael had taken away.

Chapter 90

A PROUD KING DEFEATED
II KINGS 14; II CHRONICLES 25

KING OF ISRAEL	KING OF JUDAH
Jehoash	Amaziah

While Jehu and Jehoahaz and Jehoash were reigning in Israel, the boy-king Joash ruled in Judah. As I have told you, he was murdered by his servants when he was forty-seven years old.

His son Amaziah was king of Judah at the time when Jehoash was king of Israel. Like his father Joash, he was a good king in the early years of his life; and, like his father, he did wrong later.

Amaziah tried to build up a strong army to defend his kingdom. He numbered all the men able to fight. There were three hundred thousand of them. For one hundred talents of silver Amaziah hired one hundred thousand brave men from Israel to fight for him also. He thought that with such a big army he could conquer any of the heathen nations around him.

Then a prophet came to him with a warning from God. "O king," the prophet said, "do not let the Israelite soldiers go with you to fight, for God will not help the Israelites in battle. He is angry with them for worshiping the golden calves."

Amaziah objected, "But I have already paid them a hundred talents of silver. If I let them go home now, I shall lose all that money."

"Never mind about the money," the prophet replied. "God is able to give you much more money than that."

Amaziah obeyed the prophet. He sent the Israelite soldiers home. You would think, would you not, that those soldiers would have been satisfied. They got their pay, and they did not have to fight. Strangely enough, they were angry instead. They went to some of the cities of Judah and killed three thousand people in revenge.

Even after the Israelite soldiers had gone home, Amaziah still had a big army of his own. With his three hundred thousand soldiers he marched to the Valley of Salt, south of the Dead Sea, where the Edomites lived. He fought against them and won the battle.

In Edom, King Amaziah saw some heathen idols. He brought the images home with him, and set them up in his house. God was angry with Amaziah for worshiping the idols of Edom. He sent a prophet to King Amaziah with a warning message: "Why have you trusted in the gods of Edom when you saw that they were not even able to deliver their own people from you?"

But Amaziah did not listen. He was so overconfident because of his victory against the Edomites that he sent a threatening message to King Jehoash of Israel.

King Jehoash had just come home from fighting against the Syrians. He had won some splendid victories over the Syrian king, winning back the cities his father had lost. He did not want to fight against the people in Judah. He sent a message back to King Amaziah.

"You have conquered the Edomites," he said, "and now you are boastful. Stay at home. Why should you meddle in our affairs, to your own hurt? I warn you that you will be beaten if you attack us, and many of your soldiers will be killed."

Amaziah would not listen. God was going to let him be beaten because he no longer trusted in the true God, but instead in the idols he had brought from Edom.

So the armies met. King Amaziah suffered a dreadful defeat. Worse than that, King Jehoash marched on to Jerusalem, and broke down a large part of the high stone wall which protected the city. He went on to the temple, and took all the gold and silver that he could find. He also stole all the treasures from the king's palace.

Soon after this battle Jehoash, king of Israel, died. His son Jeroboam became king. Amaziah lived fifteen years longer. They were not happy years, for his people were angry with him. They blamed him for the defeat which had spoiled their city and the

temple, and had cost so many lives.

The people of Judah began to wish that they had no king to lead them into foolish and unnecessary wars, and to turn them away from God to the worship of idols. They began to talk about punishing the king for what he had done.

A rumor of all this talk came to the king's ears. He thought he had better escape before these plans could be put into action. He fled down to Lachish, in the country of the Philistines. Some of the soldiers in the army chased after him. They killed him in Lachish, and brought his body back to Jerusalem.

Amaziah, like his father Joash, began his reign in the fear of God, but ended it by turning away to worship idols. Like his father, too, he was killed by his own people. In spite of these sad experiences, the people made Uzziah, Amaziah's son, king. He was only sixteen years old.

Chapter 91

JONAH, THE UNWILLING PROPHET

JONAH

KING OF ISRAEL
Jeroboam II

KING OF JUDAH
Uzziah

RUNNING AWAY FROM GOD During the long reigns of Uzziah and Jeroboam II, we shall leave the two kingdoms for a while, and take a journey to the faraway city of Nineveh. Nineveh was five hundred miles from Judah. It was the capital of Assyria, which at that time was the greatest country in the world. Nineveh was a very big city of almost a million people. It was very rich and beautiful, full of wonderful palaces and temples. But it was also a very wicked city.

It happened that in the days of King Jeroboam II there was a prophet in Israel named Jonah. The Lord spoke to Jonah, saying, "Arise, go to Nineveh, that great city, and cry out against it, for their wickedness is come up before Me."

But Jonah did not want to go to Nineveh. He did not want to obey God. Instead of starting out on the long journey to Nineveh, across the sandy desert, he set out in exactly the opposite direction, in order to run away from God.

He went down to Joppa on the sea-coast. There he found a ship that was going to Tarshish in Spain. He paid his fare and boarded the ship. He was going to escape from God! But Jonah could not escape from God, for God is everywhere!

Deep down into the hold of the ship Jonah went. He lay down and fell fast asleep. The sailors loosened the ropes and hoisted the sails. The wind filled the sails, and the ship glided gracefully away from the harbor and out into the open sea.

God saw Jonah disobeying Him. He sent out a great wind on the sea. The blue sky became overcast with black clouds. The winds began to howl and roar. Great waves tossed the ship hither and thither. One moment the ship rose to a fearful height on the top of a mounting wave, and then it fell to a dizzying depth. Great waves swept over the deck.

The sailors were in terror for their lives. They threw all the freight on the ship out into the sea, to make the ship lighter. Every one of them cried out to his own god, beseeching him to save them.

Jonah lay fast asleep in the hold while all this was happening. There the shipmaster found him lying stupidly asleep and paying no attention to the danger they were in. The shipmaster shook him awake and said sharply to him, "What do you mean by sleeping at such a time as this? Get up, and pray to your God to save us!"

"Someone must have done some dreadful wrong," the sailors began to say to each other. "God is sending this storm to punish him. Come, let us cast lots, and find out who is the guilty one."

When the sailors cast lots, the lot fell on Jonah. The frightened men gathered around him and said, "Tell us who you are, and what you have done to make your God so angry with you and bring this fearful storm upon us."

Jonah did not lie. He said, "I am an Israelite. I serve the Lord God of heaven, who made both the sea and the dry land. It is because I am running away from the presence of my God that this storm has come up."

"What must we do," the sailors asked him, "so that the sea may become calm again?"

Jonah said, "Take me up and throw me into the sea; then the sea will become calm again. For this terrible storm has come upon you because of my sin."

The sailors hated to do this. They rowed with all their might, trying to bring their ship back to shore. But it was no use. The storm became even worse. The waves rose higher and higher, threatening to sweep all of them into the sea.

These sailors were honest, upright people. They cried to the Lord, saying, "We beseech Thee, O Lord, do not let us die for this man's sin, and do not blame us for his drowning, for it is Thou, Lord, who hast sent this storm."

Then they threw Jonah overboard into the wild, raging sea. At once the water became calm. When they saw this happen, the sailors feared God exceedingly. They offered a sacrifice to Him, and promised to serve Him from then on.

But Jonah—what became of him? Down, down, down Jonah sank. The waves and the billows passed over him. The weeds tangled about his head. But God had not forgotten Jonah, even though Jonah had disobeyed God. God sent a great fish.

The fish opened his mouth and swallowed Jonah, just in time to save him from drowning.

Jonah remained in the fish for three days and three nights. God kept him alive even inside the fish. Now Jonah had time to think of many things, and time also to pray. Jonah cried desperately to God to help him out of this watery grave. And God heard him, and had mercy on him — though he did not deserve God's mercy — and saved him. God spoke to the fish, and the fish vomited Jonah out again upon the dry land.

A PROPHECY THAT DID NOT COME TRUE   The word of the Lord came to Jonah a second time: "Arise, go to Nineveh, that great city, and bring it the warning I have sent."

This time Jonah obeyed God at once. He started on the long, long journey. He must have traveled either on a donkey or on a camel. He had many miles to go over sandy deserts. It took him many days to make the journey.

At last he reached the great city of Nineveh, in the far eastern land of Assyria. He began to walk through the streets of the city, and as he went, he cried out in a loud voice, "Yet forty days and Nineveh shall be destroyed! Yet forty days and Nineveh shall be destroyed!"

All the people stopped to listen to this strange message, asking, "Who is this man?" and "What is he saying?" Someone answered, "He says he is a prophet of the great God who made the whole world. His God has sent him to warn us that our city is going to be destroyed in forty days because of our wickedness." When the people heard this, they were filled with fear. "What shall we do?" they cried. "What shall we do?"

The people of Nineveh believed God. They proclaimed a fast. To show that they were truly sorry for their sins, nobody in the city ate anything. They took off their fine silk clothes and dressed instead in rough sackcloth — all of them, the rich people and the poor, the great and the humble.

When the king of Nineveh heard Jonah's warning, he arose from his throne, took off his royal robes, and covered himself with rough sackcloth. He sat in the ashes instead of on his golden throne.

The king sent criers throughout the streets of Nineveh, and had posters put up on all the street corners with this message:

BY ORDER OF THE KING AND
OF HIS NOBLES

Let neither man nor beast taste any food. Let them not eat, nor drink. But let them be covered with sackcloth, both man and beast, and let them cry mightily unto God. Let them turn every one from his evil ways, and from the violence that is in his hands.

Who can tell whether God will not turn away His fierce anger, so that we do not die.

When God saw that the people of Nineveh turned from their wicked ways, He did not destroy the city. Repentance and prayer saved Nineveh from destruction.

But Jonah was displeased that God was merciful to the people of Nineveh. He wanted God to punish the city. He even dared to say to God, "O Lord, this is just what I said would happen when I was still in my own country. This is the reason I ran away to Tarshish. For I know that Thou art a gracious and merciful God, slow to anger, and of great lovingkindness. I was afraid that if

211

I preached to the people of Nineveh, they would turn from their sins and be forgiven. Now, therefore, O Lord, take away my life. I would rather die than live if Nineveh is not to be destroyed."

Then Jonah went outside the city, and made himself a little arbor of leaves and branches to shield him from the hot sun. He sat down under it to watch and see whether God would answer his prayer and destroy the city of Nineveh.

God made a fast-growing plant come up out of the ground to shade Jonah's arbor. Jonah was very glad to have the shade, for the sun was very hot.

The next day the Lord sent a worm which ate the stem of the plant so that it withered and no longer shaded Jonah's arbor. The sun beat down so hot upon his head that the prophet almost fainted, and wished that he was dead.

Then the Lord said to Jonah, "You are sorry about the plant which came up in one night, and withered the next night. Should I not have pity on that great city of Nineveh where there are a hundred and twenty thousand children so young they cannot yet tell their right hand from their left hand?"

So God taught Jonah the lesson of mercy.

Chapter 92
STORIES ABOUT THE TWO KINGDOMS
II KINGS 14, 15; II CHRONICLES 26, 27

KINGS OF ISRAEL		KINGS OF JUDAH	
Jeroboam II	Menahem	Uzziah	Jotham
Zachariah	Pekahiah		
Shallum	Pekah		

SIX WICKED KINGS Jeroboam II had a long reign as king of Israel, for he ruled forty-one years. He was not a good man. He was the fourth king of Jehu's line. Like all the others of Jehu's family, he worshiped the golden calves.

Although Jeroboam was not a good king, he waged some very successful wars against the neighboring country of Syria, which had oppressed the Israelites for many years. The children of Israel suffered so much from the cruelty of the Syrians that God had pity on them. He saved them through Jeroboam. God gave King Jeroboam great victories over the enemy. The Israelites recovered some of the cities which the Syrians had taken away.

Israel became a large country again, as it had been in Solomon's time.

But in spite of God's mercy and His help against their enemies, the people continued to worship the golden calves. The people of Israel lived lives of great luxury and drunkenness. The rich people cruelly oppressed the poor. God was forgotten in the land.

God sent the prophets Amos and Hosea to warn the people that if they did not turn from their wicked ways, God would surely punish them. "There is neither truth, nor mercy, nor knowledge of God in the land," Hosea said, "but only swearing and lying and killing and stealing. Therefore everyone in the land shall be de-

212

stroyed, if they do not repent." And Amos added, "The eyes of the Lord God are upon the sinful kingdom, and 'I will utterly destroy it from off the face of the earth,' says the Lord. 'All the sinners of My people shall die by the sword.'"

Amos prophesied during the reign of Jeroboam II. That king was wicked, but the kings who came after him were still worse.

At the death of Jeroboam, his son Zachariah became king. He reigned a very short time. He had been on the throne for only half a year when Shallum, one of his servants, killed him. Thus the family of Jehu came to an end. As God had promised Jehu, his family had been kings of Israel for four generations.

Shallum, who had killed Zachariah, ruled for just one month, and then he was killed by a man named Menahem, who ruled for ten years. Menahem was a savagely cruel man. He made a raid into Syria, and killed all his captives with cruel torture.

This was the time when the great country of Assyria had become the strongest country in the world, very much larger than either Israel or Syria. The king of Assyria came to fight against the little kingdom of Israel. If Menahem had been a good king, he would have prayed to God to help him. But he gave no thought to God. He bribed the king of Assyria to go away and not fight against Israel, with a thousand talents of silver.

God was almost forgotten in Israel. The land was full of drunkenness and sin of every kind. The people worshiped the golden calves and other idols. They even burned their little children alive on the altars of Moloch. They thought the idol was pleased to have little children sacrificed to him. There was no goodness

or peace in the land. The people had become as wicked as the Canaanites whom God had driven out of the land because of their great sin.

After ruling ten years, King Menahem died. His son Pekahiah became king. Pekahiah was no better than his father. He reigned only two years. Then one of his generals named Pekah killed him. Pekah reigned for twenty years.

During all this time, while Israel had six bad kings, there was only one king in the land of Judah. Good King Uzziah reigned there for many years.

A GOOD KING WHO BECAME A LEPER Uzziah was only sixteen years old when he began to reign. He was king for fifty-two years in Jerusalem.

Uzziah feared and trusted God, and God made him prosperous. During his reign the kingdom of Judah lived in the fear of God and was happy and prosperous.

King Uzziah went to fight against the Philistines. The Lord helped him to conquer the Philistine cities and to break down their walls. He also subdued the Arabians, and the Ammonites had to bring tribute to him.

He repaired the city wall of Jerusalem where it had been broken down. He built strong, fortified towers at the city gates. And he built fortified towers in the desert, so that if any army should attack him, his soldiers in these towers could defend the country.

Uzziah had engines placed on the towers of Jerusalem, to be used for shooting arrows and big stones. These engines were invented by clever men in his kingdom. The people had never had anything like them before.

This wise king trained a big army of more than three hundred thousand

213

soldiers, equipped with shields and spears and helmets. The army also had bows, and slings to shoot stones.

King Uzziah loved farming. He had vineyards and large flocks of sheep and cattle for which he ordered a great many wells dug.

All these things were considered so wonderful in those days that the fame of Uzziah spread far abroad, even to Egypt. He was marvelously helped by God. His kingdom became very strong.

But Uzziah's strength made him proud. He thought that he could go into the temple to burn incense upon the golden altar of incense, just as the priests did. The priests warned him. "You have no right," they said, "to burn incense. Only the priests of Aaron's family, who have been specially consecrated, are allowed to go into the holy place to burn incense. God will be angry with you if you do this."

Uzziah would not listen. He picked up the censer with the hot coals in it, and the incense, and went into the Holy Place. As he stood there, God punished him. The dreaded white spots of leprosy suddenly appeared on his forehead. The priests looked in horror and astonishment at the deadly spots. They pushed him out of the temple. Uzziah himself hurried to leave, because God had smitten him with leprosy.

All the rest of his life Uzziah had to live in a house alone. He could never go into the temple again. Although he was still king, his son Jotham had to do the ruling. At last Uzziah died, after a very long reign of fifty-two years. He was buried with his fathers in Jerusalem, and Jotham became king.

Like his father, Jotham trusted God and tried to do what was right. Because of this, God helped him, and gave him success in his battles. Jotham became a mighty king.

He, too, built castles and towers to make his kingdom strong, as his father Uzziah had done. And, like Uzziah, he defeated his enemies, among whom were the Ammonites.

The people of Judah were happy and prosperous when their kings trusted and feared the Lord.

After reigning sixteen years, King Jotham died, and his son Ahaz became king.

Chapter 93
"HERE AM I — SEND ME"
ISAIAH 6, 7, 9, 53

KINGS OF ISRAEL		KINGS OF JUDAH	
Jeroboam II	Pekahiah	Uzziah	Ahaz
Zachariah	Pekah	Jotham	Hezekiah
Shallum	Hoshea		
Menahem			

In these days there lived in the kingdom of Judah one of the greatest prophets the world has ever known. His name was Isaiah.

Isaiah was born in the last part of Uzziah's reign. He prophesied after Uzziah's death, during the reigns of the three succeeding kings. These prophecies were gathered together into a book. You may read them in the Bible.

In the year of King Uzziah's death, Isaiah had a wonderful vision. He saw God Almighty, high and lifted up, sitting upon a throne. All around Him were the seraphim, angelic beings who had six wings. With two wings each one covered his face, with two he covered his feet, and with two he flew.

The seraphim cried, "Holy, holy, holy is the Lord of hosts! The whole earth is full of His glory!" When the seraphim cried these words, the foundations of the temple shook, and all the place was filled with smoke.

Isaiah was terrified at the voice of the seraphim, and the shaking of the temple, and the smoke. He cried out, "Woe is me! For I am a man of unclean lips, and I live among people of unclean lips! I will die, because my eyes have seen the King, the Lord of hosts!"

Then one of the seraphim took a hot coal from the altar, and touched Isaiah's mouth with it. He said, "This has touched your lips, and your sin is taken away."

Then Isaiah heard the voice of the Lord saying, "Whom shall I send, and who will go for us?"

Isaiah answered, "Here am I; send me!"

The Lord gave Isaiah many messages for the children of Israel. Some of these were warnings that if they did not turn away from idols, and trust only in the one true God, they would surely be punished. Others were wonderful promises of forgiveness for all who put their trust in God's salvation. Still other messages told what was going to happen in the future.

But the most wonderful of all these prophecies are those that tell of the coming of Jesus, which Isaiah wrote more than seven hundred years before Jesus was born.

As you remember, God had promised Eve that through one of her children He would bring back goodness and everlasting life to man. God had promised Abraham that in one of his descendants all the world would be blessed. And God gave promises to others that someday a child would be born who would be the Saviour of the world.

Some of the most glorious of these promises were given to Isaiah. Listen to the things he spoke about, hundreds of years before they actually happened:

> *A virgin shall conceive and bear a son,*
> *And shall call His name Immanuel.*

This promise was repeated in other words:

> *Unto us a child is born, unto us a son is given.*
> *And the government shall be upon His shoulder:*
> *And His name shall be called*
> *Wonderful, Counsellor, Mighty God,*
> *Everlasting Father, Prince of Peace.*

Isaiah foretold Jesus' suffering as well as His birth:

> *He is despised and rejected of men,*
> *A man of sorrows, and acquainted with grief.*

Isaiah said that it was for our sins that Jesus would suffer:

> *He was wounded for our transgressions;*
> *He was bruised for our iniquities.*

How well did the Israelites understand these prophecies? They could not know, as we do, that God was going to send His own Son to die for our sins. But they did know that God had promised to send them a Saviour. Isaiah's prophecies made them look forward all the more eagerly to the time when the promised Saviour would come. During the seven hundred years before the birth of Jesus, they waited and hoped and prayed for His coming.

Chapter 94
THE END OF THE KINGDOM OF ISRAEL
II KINGS 16, 17; II CHRONICLES 28

KINGS OF ISRAEL
Pekah   Hoshea

KING OF JUDAH
Ahaz

HOW ISRAEL FOUGHT AGAINST JUDAH
Now I have a very sad story to tell. It is about the son of Jotham, King Ahaz of Judah. Although he was the son of good King Jotham, and the grandson of good King Uzziah, Ahaz was one of the very worst kings that Judah ever had. He undid all the good that his father and his grandfather had done.

Ahaz made images of Baal. He burned his children to death in the fires of Moloch, as the wicked heathen did. He sacrificed to heathen gods on the hilltops and under every green tree.

When King Ahaz turned to idols, a great many of his people forsook the Lord also. All the nations around them worshiped idols, and the people of Judah wanted to be like their neighbors.

God sent an army of Syrian soldiers against the men of Judah. He did this to warn them to return to the true God. The king of the Syrians fought with King Ahaz, and God allowed the Syrians to conquer. They carried away to Damascus very many of the people of Judah as captives.

Pekah, the king of Israel, also had a great battle with Ahaz. In one day Pekah's soldiers killed one hundred and twenty thousand of the men of Judah. The Israelites carried away to Samaria two hundred thousand women and children of Judah, to make slaves of them.

In Samaria there was a prophet of the Lord. He was horrified to think the Israelites would enslave all those women and children of their own race. He went out to meet the soldiers as they returned from the war and said to them, "God delivered the men of Judah into your hands as a punishment for their sins. You have killed them. Now you intend to make slaves of their wives and children. But God is angry with you for your sins also. You must give up these captured women and children."

Some of the leaders of the tribes of Israel stopped their victorious soldiers at the city gates. "You shall not bring these captives into the city," they said. "They are our brothers. The anger of God is already fierce against us."

So the soldiers had to release their captives, and give up the treasures they had stolen from Judah. The leaders of the tribes used the stolen clothing to dress the captured women and children. They gave them food and drink. Those who were too weak to walk they put on donkeys, and sent them all back to their own country.

What a sad homecoming that was!

216

16: THE FALL AND CAPTIVITY OF ISRAEL

17: JOSIAH HEARING THE WORDS OF THE LAW

In thousands of homes the husband and father was dead. In thousands of homes the sons and daughters had been carried away as slaves to Damascus.

This was indeed a hard lesson about what happens to those who trust in idols. But the people of Judah had not learned the lesson yet. Instead of praying to God to save him from the Israelites and the Syrians, King Ahaz sent a message to the king of Assyria, begging him to come and help.

King Ahaz took all the gold and silver out of the temple and sent it to the king of Assyria to pay for his help. The king of Assyria came as far as Damascus. He fought against Damascus and killed the Syrian king.

Ahaz also went to Damascus, to help in the battle. There he offered sacrifices to the heathen gods of Syria. He thought these gods had helped the Syrians defeat Judah, and that if he sacrificed to them, they might help him too. He never thought of asking the only true God to help him.

Ahaz took a great fancy to the heathen altar in Damascus. He sent a pattern of it back to the priest in Jerusalem, and that bad priest made a copy of the heathen altar in Jerusalem, ready for use. When Ahaz came back from Damascus, he worshiped the heathen idols of the Syrians on the altar which the priest had built. Worse than that, he closed the doors of the temple of the Lord in Jerusalem. He cut up the gold and silver dishes in the temple. He built heathen altars on every street corner in Jerusalem, and in every city of Judah.

Ahaz made a great mistake in asking the king of Assyria to help him, for at that time the kingdom of Assyria was trying to conquer the whole world. As long as Damascus was not conquered, the kings of Assyria were kept from attacking Israel and Judah, for Damascus was between Assyria and Israel. Now that Damascus had fallen into the hands of the Assyrians, nothing stood in their way. They would attack Israel next. And after that, Judah.

THE TEN LOST TRIBES We have reached a chapter which is very sad indeed.

At last dreadful judgment came upon the children of Israel. God could bear with them no longer. They had become as sinful as the heathen who lived in the land before them, whom God had driven out.

Again and again the Lord had sent prophets to say, "Turn back from your wicked ways, and trust only in Me." But the people would not listen. They refused to obey God, and trusted instead in the heathen idols.

They made images, and bowed down before the golden calves, and before the Asherah. They worshiped the sun and the moon and the stars. They sacrificed their sons and daughters on the fiery altars of Moloch. They used all kinds of magical enchantments to make their wishes come true. The Lord had been patient for hundreds of years. He had taught them, He had warned them, He had even helped them in trouble. But they would not learn. Now, at last, the day of repentance was past. The terrible day of God's judgment had come.

After reigning twenty years, King Pekah was killed by Hoshea, who became king and ruled for nine years. He also was a wicked king.

During Hoshea's reign the king of Assyria attacked Israel. Since the city of Damascus had been conquered, there was nothing to prevent him from capturing Samaria, the capital of Israel. He made Hoshea a puppet king, and forced him to pay tribute to Assyria.

After a while Hoshea rebelled. He did not send the tribute money, and he begged the king of Egypt to help him fight against Assyria.

Then the great king of Assyria surrounded Samaria with his army and besieged it for three years. Finally the city fell. Hoshea was made a prisoner. Most of the people of Israel were carried off to the land of Assyria. God no longer allowed them to live in their own land because of their unfaithfulness to Him.

Oh, what a weeping and wailing as the Israelites looked for the very last time at the dear homes which had come down to them from their grandfathers! How could they ever say good-bye to all they loved? How could they ever leave it all, and never come back?

The Israelites were driven far away to the distant land of Assyria. There they were scattered among the heathen nations. Nobody knows what became of them in the end. They are the ten "lost tribes" of the children of Israel.

These tribes were no longer God's people, because they had refused to trust in Him. There is no further record of them in the Bible. They were lost and forgotten forever. The rest of our Bible story is about the people of Judah.

Only a few of the very poorest of the Israelite people were left behind. Foreigners from Babylon were brought in to live in the land of Israel. These people brought their heathen idols with them. The few Israelites who were left soon mingled with the Assyrian foreigners, who worshiped their own idols and also the God of the Israelites.

Their children and their grandchildren followed their example, and sacrificed both to the true God and to heathen idols. In later years these people were known as Samaritans. The people of Judah despised them, because they were not true Israelites.

Chapter 95
HEZEKIAH, THE GOOD KING
II KINGS 18-20; II CHRONICLES 29-32

KING OF JUDAH
Hezekiah

A SERVANT OF GOD How sad and pitiable was the condition of the children of Israel! The ten tribes were far away from the land that had been promised to their fathers. They were captives in a strange land, with no hope of ever going back to their own country. God had judged them because of their sins.

The condition of Judah was almost as sad. There were few people left in the land. These few were very unhappy, for in almost every family someone had been killed in battle or had been taken captive in the wars against Syria and Israel.

At least one good thing had happened. The wicked King Ahaz, who had led the people into sin, was dead. His son Hezekiah was king now. Although Hezekiah's father had been a bad man, his mother had been a good woman, the daughter of a prophet. She had brought up her son to fear and trust in God.

Hezekiah was one of the best kings that ever ruled over Judah. From the beginning of his reign he sought the Lord, as David had done, trying to undo the wicked deeds of his father. God was with Hezekiah, and prospered him in whatever he did.

During the reign of Ahaz, the Levites had been scattered abroad, because God's temple was shut up, and no sacrifices were offered. The temple was dirty and full of rubbish. In the very first year of his reign Hezekiah opened the doors of the temple of the Lord, which his father had closed. He gathered together all the Levites and the priests and told them to clean the temple. He knew that it was because their fathers had forgotten God that God had forsaken them.

The Levites cleaned away all the dirt and filth in the temple. This took them eight days. When they had finished, they said to King Hezekiah, "We have cleaned the whole temple, and the altar of burnt offering, and the table of showbread, and all the dishes. We have replaced all the dishes that King Ahaz took away."

It was hard for anyone to know just how to worship God in the right way, because the service of God had been forgotten for so many years. This earnest young king did his very best to bring the people back to the true worship.

He gathered the rulers of the city. Together they went up to the house of the Lord. There they offered a sin offering for the great sin of Judah and Israel in turning away from God. The king invited anyone who wanted to bring a thank offering to the Lord

to come to the temple and give it. Many people responded generously.

The prophet Isaiah must have helped and advised Hezekiah in all this. He must have rejoiced to see the regular worship of God established again in Judah.

Now that King Hezekiah knew that his people wanted to turn back to the worship of God, he made up his mind to go still further and to revive the feast of the Passover. He sent letters of invitation to the people to come to Jerusalem to celebrate this feast. These letters passed from city to city, not only through the country of Judah, but also through the land which had once been the kingdom of Israel. Hezekiah invited any poor Israelites who might have been left in the land to come to Jerusalem to join in the feast.

In Judah all the people obeyed the message which the king had sent out. Among the few Israelites who were left, however, most of the people had been worshiping idols for many years. They had forgotten all about the Passover.

"Come to the Passover? No, indeed! We are not going to Jerusalem for such foolishness as that!" most of them said mockingly. Yet even in Israel some people obeyed the letter of Hezekiah, for even in wicked Israel there always remained some families who still worshiped their own God.

A great number of people came to Jerusalem for the Passover. They were so happy to celebrate the feast again that when the first seven days were up they decided to continue it for another week. There was great joy in Jerusalem, for there had not been such a feast since the time of King Solomon.

King Hezekiah did another important thing. He commanded the people to bring to the temple a tenth of their corn and wine and oil and whatever else they raised, as God had commanded long ago in the days of Moses. The priests and the Levites did not have any farms of their own. They must spend all their time serving God in His holy temple. When the people neglected to bring gifts to the Lord, the priests had to go hungry.

For many years the priests had had a hard time, but now these times were over. Once again the people brought one-tenth of their corn and wine, their oil and honey, to the house of the Lord for His servants.

JERUSALEM IN DANGER Ever since the people of Israel had been carried away captive to Assyria, the people of Judah had been afraid that the same thing might happen to them. They knew they would never be strong enough to resist the Assyrian king if he attacked their little kingdom.

After Hezekiah had been king for fourteen years, the very thing the people dreaded happened. King Sennacherib of Assyria attacked Judah. Terror filled the hearts of the people when they heard of the coming of this mighty king with his great army.

Sennacherib was great, and had a large army, but King Hezekiah did not give up. He trusted in God to help him. He consulted with all his princes, and they decided to stop up all the brooks outside the city, so that the armies of Sennacherib would not have any water to drink.

Hezekiah did more than that. He built up the wall around Jerusalem where it had been broken down. He made it much higher, and he placed a second wall outside the first one.

How fast and how eagerly the people worked!

Hezekiah spoke encouragingly to his soldiers. "Be strong and courageous," he said. "Do not be afraid of the king of Assyria, nor of all his soldiers. We have more to help us than they have. They have only human help, but we have the Lord our God to help us and to fight our battles."

It took great faith to trust in God when the great king of Assyria came. Sennacherib was conquering all the world at that time, and carrying away captive the peoples of the lands he conquered to Assyria. Onward he marched with his victorious armies, defeating every nation in his way.

The Assyrians were cruel to the nations they conquered. Wherever their armies went, they left ruin. Towns became smoking heaps of ashes. Princes were tortured, and those who resisted were killed without mercy. The main roads were choked with great trains of captive slaves and animals carrying plunder of all sorts to Nineveh. It was not surprising that the people of Judah were terrified when they heard that this army was coming against them.

King Sennacherib did not come straight to Jerusalem. He wanted to conquer a city of the Philistines first. He sent some of his generals and a great army of his soldiers to Jerusalem with a message to the Jews and to King Hezekiah. These men came as near to the city walls as they could and they shouted loudly, so all the people on the walls could hear.

"Do not let Hezekiah deceive you," they shouted, "for he will not be able to deliver you out of the hand of the king of Assyria. Do not listen to him when he says, 'The Lord will deliver us!' Have any of the gods of the nations been able to deliver their lands from the king of Assyria?"

The officers of Hezekiah said, "Do not speak in the Jewish language for all the common people to hear. Speak to us in the Syrian language, for we officers understand Syrian."

But Sennacherib's general said, "No, indeed! Our master sent us to speak to the common people in their own language, not to the officers." And he shouted again, "Do not let Hezekiah make you trust in the Lord, saying, 'Surely the Lord will deliver us,' for this city will be delivered into the hand of the king of Assyria!"

The people on the wall heard what he said. They trembled with fear, but they did not say a word, for King Hezekiah had commanded them not to answer.

THE ANGEL OF DEATH   The Assyrian general had also brought a letter to King Hezekiah, which repeated the boast he had made to the people on the wall — that no god had ever been able to save his people from the king of Assyria, and that no god ever would.

When Hezekiah received the letter, and read it, he went into the house of the Lord, and spread the letter out before the Lord. Then Hezekiah prayed, "O Lord God of Israel, who dwellest between the cherubim, Thou art God, even Thou alone, of all the kingdoms on the earth. Thou hast made heaven and earth. Lord, bow down Thine ear, and hear; open, Lord, Thine eyes, and see; and hear the words of Sennacherib which he has sent as a charge against the living God. Now, therefore, O Lord our God, save us, I pray Thee, out of his hand, that all the kingdoms of the earth may know that Thou art God, even Thou alone."

Then Isaiah sent a message to Hezekiah, saying, "Thus saith the Lord God of Israel, 'I have heard what you have prayed to Me against Sennacherib. Because the king of Assyria rages against Me, I will put My hook in his nose, and My bridle in his lips, and I will turn him back by the way he came. He shall not come into this city, for I will defend this city, to save it, for My own sake, and for My servant David's.'"

That night the angel of the Lord went out and struck down a hundred and eighty-five thousand soldiers in the camp of the Assyrians. In the morning they were found lying dead on the ground in the camp. The great Assyrian army was shattered.

Where was Sennacherib's power now? Gone, all gone, in a single night. Shamed and humbled, the proud king turned his face homeward — a weak and powerless man, a king without an army. Sometime afterward, as he came into the house of his god, his own sons stabbed him to death.

Do you think that the nations around Judah heard of this miraculous way in which God had saved His people from the great king of Assyria? Of course they did. Many of them brought presents to the temple of that wonderful God in Jerusalem, and to King Hezekiah.

Sometime after this King Hezekiah became very sick. The prophet Isaiah came to him and said, "Get ready to die, for your time has come." When Hezekiah heard this, he felt very sad. Must he die so soon, while he was still young? He was only forty years old. He had hoped to have a long and prosperous reign.

Hezekiah turned his face to the wall. He began to weep. Bitter tears rolled down his cheeks. He prayed to the Lord to let him live. "Remember,

221

I pray Thee, Lord, how I have walked before Thee, and tried to please Thee."

The Lord answered Hezekiah's prayer before Isaiah had left the city. He told the prophet to go back and say, "Thus says the Lord, 'I have heard your prayer, I have seen your tears. I will heal you. In three days you will be well enough to go to My holy temple. I shall add fifteen years to your life.' "

I think that of all the men who have ever lived Hezekiah was the only one who knew exactly when he would die. He lived just fifteen years longer.

They were very happy years. Hezekiah trusted God. His people loved him, and even the heathen honored him.

He enjoyed great riches and honor. He built treasuries to hold his silver and his gold, and all his precious stones and jewels. He also built storehouses for corn and oil, and barns for all his flocks and herds.

At last the promised fifteen years were over. Hezekiah slept with his fathers. He was buried in the finest of the tombs of the sons of David. All Jerusalem and Judah mourned for this good king.

Chapter 96
A WICKED KING WHO REPENTED
II KINGS 21; II CHRONICLES 33

KINGS OF JUDAH
Manasseh   Amon

After Hezekiah's death, his son Manasseh reigned in his place. Manasseh ruled longer than any other king of either Israel or Judah. He was twelve years old when he became king, and he reigned fifty-five years.

You will expect me to say that he was a good king, like his father Hezekiah. How I wish I could say that! But Manasseh was probably the worst king Judah ever had. He was more like Ahab, the wicked king of Israel, than like his godly father Hezekiah.

Manasseh undid all the good that his father had done. He rebuilt the heathen altars his father had broken down. He made altars for Baal, and worshiped the Asherah. He bowed down to the sun and the moon and the stars, building altars for them in the very courts of God's holy temple.

Though it is hard to believe, this wicked king burned his own children to death in the arms of the dreadful heathen idol Moloch! He was a savage man, who killed so many innocent people in Jerusalem that the streets of the city ran with blood. Under Manasseh the people of Judah became even more wicked than those nations which God had destroyed when the Israelites came to Canaan.

How could the same people who so earnestly sought and trusted God in Hezekiah's time turn so soon to idolatry? The answer is that these were not the same people. The older generation had died, and these were their children. When they had a God-fearing king, the people of Judah worshiped God for a little while, but at heart they were still a nation that served Baal, and the Asherah, and the sun and moon and stars, not the living God. Just as soon as their good king died, the people and their children turned away from God.

Though God is very loving and merciful, He is also just. He cannot let wickedness go unpunished. He sent prophets to Manasseh and the people of Judah to warn them that they must turn from their sins, but the people would not listen. "Because Manasseh has done these abominations," God said, "I will bring such evil upon Jerusalem that whoever hears about it, his ears shall tingle. I will wipe Jerusalem as a man wipes a dish and turns it upside down. I will deliver them into the hands of their enemies, because they have done that which is evil in My sight."

Nothing is surer than that God's judgment will at last fall on those who do not repent of their sins. And it fell on Manasseh. God sent the Assyrian armies against Judah. They captured Manasseh, chained him, and carried him away to Babylon.

During his imprisonment Manasseh became a changed man. He did not cry out for help to Baal or the Asherah or Moloch. No, he remembered the God of his father Hezekiah. He began to pray very earnestly to God. The Lord heard his prayer and mercifully brought him back to Jerusalem to be king again.

So Manasseh learned that the Lord is the only true God and that only those who trust in Him will be saved. He was truly a changed man. The rest of his life he tried to undo the wickedness that he had done before. He took away the idols he had put into God's temple. He sacrificed peace offerings and thank offerings to God. He commanded the people of Judah to serve the Lord. He was the only king who began his reign in wickedness and ended it in goodness.

Manasseh's son Amon reigned only two years. In that short time he did much evil. He sacrificed to all the images which his father had made and which he had not had time to destroy before he died. Amon did not change for the better as his father had. Instead he became worse and worse. After two years, his servants killed him in his own house.

The people of Judah took Amon's little son Josiah, who was only eight years old, and made him king.

Chapter 97
STORIES ABOUT KING JOSIAH
II KINGS 22, 23; II CHRONICLES 34, 35

KING OF JUDAH

Josiah

GOD'S BOOK IS FOUND Eight-year-old Josiah was a little boy-king, as Joash had been. Unlike little Joash, Josiah did not have to be kept hidden and guarded. Nobody wanted to kill little Josiah. Everyone wanted him to be king. He was of David's line, the direct heir to the throne. The whole nation of Judah crowned Josiah king. They all watched over the safety of their little boy-king.

Although Josiah was just a young child, he proved that even a child can trust and serve God. He tried to do what was right, even at the very beginning of his reign. As he grew up, he began to clear out of Jerusalem all the idol images and the altars of heathen gods.

Josiah stood and watched his men, directing them as they worked. He had them break down the metal and carved images of Baal, and grind them into little pieces, scattering the dust on the graves of those who had worshiped them.

Josiah even went through the cities of Israel to destroy their idols. There had been no king in Israel since the people had been carried away. When Josiah visited the Israelite cities, he took workmen along with heavy axes and hammers. Wherever they found any idols or heathen altars, the men smashed them to pieces and ground them to powder.

After all the idols had been destroyed, Josiah sent skilled workmen to repair the temple. It needed a lot of repair, for it had been neglected for many years. While the men were working in the temple, Hilkiah, the high priest, found an old book hidden away in a corner. He was very much interested in what this book could be. He showed it to one of the other priests. When they read the book, they found that it was the law of Moses.

They showed this book to the king. The priest read to Josiah the words which Moses had written long ago. If this was not the same book that Moses had written, it was an exact copy. Six hundred years had passed since Moses wrote his book and put it in the Holy of Holies beside the ark. That first book may have become worn out, for Moses had commanded the priests to take the book out of the Holy of Holies every seven years, and read it to the people.

Good King Jehoshaphat had sent teachers throughout his kingdom to teach the people the law of the Lord. Each of these teachers had carried with him a copy of the book of the law, which some careful priest had copied from the original book in the Holy of Holies.

More than two hundred years had passed since that day. The custom of reading the law aloud to the people every seven years had been neglected. The people had broken God's law continually, partly because they had wicked hearts and did not wish to obey, but also partly because they were ignorant of what God had commanded.

Josiah himself had never heard the law read. For the first time now he heard those terrible judgments that would come upon the children of Israel if they turned away from God, and trusted idols instead:

The Lord will send upon you trouble in everything you set your hand to do, until you are destroyed, and perish quickly, because of the wickedness of your doings. A nation which you do not know shall eat up the fruit of your land and of all your labors. You will carry much seed into the field, and gather little in. You will have sons and daughters, but not enjoy them; for they will go into captivity. You will be an astonishment, and a proverb, and a byword among all nations, because you did not serve the Lord.

When Josiah heard these words, and realized that his people had broken all God's commandments, he tore his clothes in sorrow and in fear. He sent the priests to ask God about these judgments.

Isaiah, the prophet, had been dead for a long time. His place had been taken by a prophetess, a woman named Huldah. Josiah's messengers went to her. When they told her what they had come for, she said to them, "Thus saith the Lord, 'Tell the man that sent you to me, "Behold, I will bring upon this place and the people living in it all these things which are written in the book which you have read to the king of Judah, because they have forsaken Me and worshiped other gods." As for the king of Judah who sent you to Me, say to him, "Because you humbled yourself before Me when you heard these words, and wept in sorrow before Me, behold, I have heard you. You shall come to your grave in peace, and shall not see the evil which I will bring upon this place, and upon the people that live here." ' "

So the messengers brought this word back to the king. Then Josiah called a great meeting of all the people, both young and old. He read to them the words of the book which had been found in the temple. Then King Josiah stood up before his people and made a solemn promise to serve the Lord. He made the people promise that they, too, would serve God.

JOSIAH PICKS A FIGHT King Josiah determined to destroy thoroughly all the idols in the land, even more completely than he had done before. He made the priests bring out of God's holy temple all the dishes that had been made for the idol Baal, and for the worship of the sun and the moon and the stars. Josiah had these dishes burned and their ashes carried away.

He had the houses of the witches pulled down, so that nobody could go to consult these people. It was one of God's commands that there should be no witches or fortune-tellers among His people.

Then King Josiah went to a terrible place called Tophet. This was the valley where the people sacrificed their little children to the idol Moloch. By filling this valley with filth, King Josiah made it such a vile place that no one would ever go there again to worship Moloch. Near God's temple in Jerusalem were some fine horses which had been given to the sun god when Judah worshiped idols. King Josiah drove the horses away and burned the sun god's chariots with fire.

On the Mount of Olives, across from Jerusalem, there were still standing some of the altars King Solomon had built for his heathen wives. These altars had been there for three hundred years. King Josiah broke them all down. He burned dead men's bones on the altars, so that nobody would ever sacrifice there again.

He went to Bethel, where there was still left one of the golden calves King Jeroboam had set up. As King Josiah was standing in the graveyard at Bethel, directing his men to dig up men's bones to burn on the heathen altars, he saw a grave on the hillside with some writing on it. "What writing is this that I see on that stone?" he asked.

The men answered, "That is the grave of a prophet who lived three hundred years ago, and who foretold these things which you have done to these heathen altars." This was true. Three hundred years before, when wicked King Jeroboam first made this altar for the worship of the golden calf, a prophet had told him that a king named Josiah, of David's family, would someday burn men's bones on that altar.

Josiah killed all the heathen priests that were in his kingdom and burned their bones on the heathen altars, to make these altars unclean, so that no one would ever offer sacrifices on them again. For the Israelites believed that any contact with a dead body made a person unclean, and no longer fit to worship God.

If all the kings of Judah had been like Josiah, there would have been no idolatry in the land. He turned to the Lord with all his heart and with all his soul and with all his might. He tried to live in every way according to the law of God. Because Josiah trusted God, God postponed the punishment that was coming to Judah for its wickedness. That punishment was surely coming, though. Josiah was the last actual king of Judah.

At the end of Josiah's life, Necho, king of Egypt, passed through Judah on his way to fight against the king of Assyria. At that time Assyria and Egypt were the two greatest countries of the world. They were always fighting each other, and their armies always passed through Palestine, because the land of the Israelites lay between them.

King Josiah wanted to fight against the Egyptian king. He called his army together and got ready for battle. But Necho sent word to Josiah, "I did not come to fight with you. I only want to pass through your country, to fight against my enemy, the king of Assyria. God has commanded me to fight against the Assyrians, and to do it quickly. Let me alone, to do what God has commanded."

But Josiah was determined to fight the king of Egypt. He disguised himself in the clothes of an ordinary soldier and went out to fight against the Egyptian army. In the battle he was wounded. Sorrowfully his servants carried the wounded king back to Jerusalem, where he died.

All Judah and Jerusalem mourned for good King Josiah. The men and women sang sad songs of affection for their beloved king. Jeremiah, the prophet, mourned him too.

The people wanted Josiah's second son, Jehoahaz, to be king. The priests anointed him with oil to be ruler in his father's place.

Chapter 98
THE MAN WHO HAD TO PROPHESY
JEREMIAH 1, 20, 36; II KINGS 24; II CHRONICLES 36

KINGS OF JUDAH
Josiah
Jehoahaz   Jehoiakim

PEOPLE WHO HATED THE TRUTH During the reign of Josiah, a child was born who was to become a great and important man. His name was Jeremiah. He was the son of a priest.

When he was scarcely more than a boy, God spoke to Jeremiah, saying, "Before you were born I knew you, and chose you to be a prophet to the nations." But Jeremiah was afraid to be a prophet. He said, "O Lord God, behold, I cannot speak, for I am only a child."

But the Lord said, "Do not say, 'I am only a child,' for you shall go wherever I send you, and shall speak whatever I tell you. Do not be afraid of anyone, for I am with you, to care for you." Then the Lord put out His hand and touched Jeremiah's mouth. And He said, "See, I have put My words in your mouth."

In the time of Josiah, the people of Jerusalem turned back to the Lord. But after his death, when his son became king, they turned again to their idolatry and wickedness. God sent Jeremiah to warn them that such wickedness would surely bring dreadful judgments upon them. He told Jeremiah to plead with them to turn back to their God, and He promised that all their sins would be forgiven if only they repented and trusted in Him.

"The children of Israel have forgotten the Lord their God," Jeremiah prophesied. "Run to and fro through the streets of Jerusalem, and see if you can find one man who executes justice and speaks truth. They oppress the stranger and the fatherless and the widow. They shed innocent blood. They seek after strange gods.

"O Jerusalem, wash your heart from wickedness, that you may still be saved. For thus says the Lord, 'Return, you backsliding children, and I will heal you. And I will not then cause my anger to fall on you, for I am merciful.'

"To whom shall I speak, and give warning, that they may hear? Just as you have forsaken the Lord, and served strange gods, so you yourselves shall serve strangers in a land that is not yours. The whole land shall be desolate. For this is a nation that does not obey the voice of God, and will not receive correction."

The rulers of Judah were angry that Jeremiah prophesied so much evil. They put the prophet in the stocks, a wooden frame which held Jeremiah's feet so that he could not move. For a whole day Jeremiah was left there. The stocks hurt his feet. Rude people came and laughed at him.

When he was set free, the prophet said to himself, "I will not mention God any more, nor speak in His name." But Jeremiah found he could not help prophesying. For God's word was in his heart like a burning fire shut up in his bones.

Jehoahaz was not a God-fearing king, as his father Josiah had been. He built himself a beautiful palace of cedar wood, painted bright red. He made the builders work without any pay. He was not interested in his people, and he did not take care of the poor.

The Egyptian king Necho, whose soldiers had killed Josiah, marched into Judah. He captured Jehoahaz and carried him off to Egypt. There he was kept in prison the rest of his life. Necho made Jehoahaz' brother Jehoiakim king. He forced the Israelites to pay him a big sum of money as tribute every year. The terrible judgments Jeremiah had prophesied began to come true.

THE BOOK THAT WAS BURNED Jehoiakim reigned eleven years. Although he was a son of good King Josiah, he did all the wicked things that the kings before him had done. He murdered people without cause and without pity.

God sent Jeremiah with another warning to this king. God said, "I will raise up the Chaldeans, a bitter and quick nation. They will march through the land of Israel, and possess it. Their horses are swifter than leopards, and more fierce than wolves. Their horsemen shall come from far."

When Jeremiah brought this message, King Jehoiakim shut him up in prison, so that he could not prophesy to the people.

The Lord commanded Jeremiah to take a roll or book, and to write down all the prophecies God had spoken to him from the beginning of his work as prophet. Jeremiah sent for Baruch, who was a scribe or public writer. He told him all the prophecies God had given him, and Baruch wrote them down.

Jeremiah said to Baruch, "I am shut up here in prison. I cannot go to the house of the Lord. You go to the temple, and read all the words written in this roll to the people who come to the temple. It may be they will turn from their evil ways, and pray to the Lord."

Baruch took the roll which he had written at Jeremiah's dictation to the temple, and read it to all the people. A man named Michaiah was very much interested. He went to the king's house and told the princes who were sitting there what he had heard.

The princes were alarmed at what they heard. They sent for Baruch and asked him to read the roll to them. When they had heard of the dreadful judgments which would surely happen to them if they did not turn from their wicked ways, they said, "The king ought to know what this book says. We shall tell him about it. But you and Jeremiah must first hide yourselves, or the king may kill you."

Then the princes went to the king and told him about Jeremiah's dreadful warnings. The king sent a scribe to get the roll. The scribe read the prophecies aloud as the king sat in his beautiful winter palace before an open fire.

The king's father Josiah had torn his clothes in sorrow and in fear when the book of God's law, which had been found in the temple, was read to him. But this king was not God-fearing. When the scribe had read three or four pages, King Jehoiakim scornfully took the book, cut out with his knife the pages which had been read, and threw them into the fire. So he did with all the pages, until the whole roll had been burned. Then he sent his soldiers to arrest Jeremiah and Baruch. But God had hidden Jeremiah and Baruch so that they could not be found.

God said to Jeremiah, "Take another roll, and write in it the same words that were in the first roll. Say to Jehoiakim, 'You have burned this roll, and refused its warning. Therefore you shall have no son to rule after you. Your dead body shall be thrown out into the heat of the day and the frost of the night.' For I will bring upon the people of Jerusalem all the evil that I have spoken in this roll, because they refused to listen to My warnings."

Chapter 99

THE CAPTIVITY OF JUDAH

II KINGS 24, 25; II CHRONICLES 36; JEREMIAH 37-40; LAMENTATIONS 1; PSALM 137

KINGS OF JUDAH	
Jehoiakim	
Jehoiachin	Zedekiah

THE KING OF BABYLON COMES The day of salvation was over for the people of Judah. The time of judgment had come.

Meanwhile another nation had grown into power, the nation of Babylon, sometimes called Chaldea. Nebuchadnezzar, the king of Babylon, was a mighty man. He conquered Egypt and Assyria. He fought against all the surrounding countries, and ruled all the land from the Euphrates River to the Nile.

At last he came with his mighty army against Judah. He captured King Jehoiakim and put him in chains. He made Jehoiakim's son Jehoiachin king over the people of Judah. He carried away into captivity the highest princes of Judah. He took many of the golden dishes from the temple Solomon had built, and carried them to the temple of his idol in Babylon.

This was the first time King Nebuchadnezzar came to Jerusalem, but it was not the last. In three months he came again. This time he took the young king Jehoiachin, his mother, his wives, and his servants, and carried them all away to Babylon. He took captive the princes and the soldiers and all the workmen who were clever at making things. Ten thousand captives were carried away to Babylon.

Nebuchadnezzar also carried away the rest of the treasures from the temple and the royal palace. The beautiful golden dishes which were too large to be carried easily he broke in pieces.

The awful prophecies of Jeremiah came true. Mothers and fathers, old men and babies, were torn from their homes, and sent to faraway Babylon. It was a long, long journey, over burning sands. The soldiers drove them on, and treated them cruelly, so that many died on the way. The poor people plodded the seven hundred weary miles, weeping as they went.

Nebuchadnezzar left a few of the poorest of the poor in Jerusalem. They were not worth taking. He made Zedekiah, the third son of good King Josiah, king of these people at Jerusalem. He made Zedekiah promise before God that he would not rebel against Babylon.

But Zedekiah also was a wicked man. He did not turn to God, even in these awful troubles. Neither he nor the people who were left would listen to Jeremiah. They went on doing evil in God's sight. Jeremiah warned Zedekiah to keep his promise to Nebuchadnezzar, but he would not listen. He rebelled against the king of Babylon.

Then Nebuchadnezzar came against Jerusalem again. He made forts outside the walls of Jerusalem, and besieged the city. The angry princes accused Jeremiah of being a friend of the enemy, and they put him in prison.

For two years the city held out. There was no food left, and the people were starving. King Zedekiah sent secretly for Jeremiah and asked, "Is there any word from the Lord?" for he was greatly worried about the large army which surrounded the city.

Jeremiah answered, "There is a message. God says that you shall be delivered into the hands of the king of Babylon." Then Jeremiah begged the king not to send him back to prison. The king commanded that he should be kept in the prison yard instead of in the dungeon, and that a piece of bread should be given him each day as long as there was any bread in the city.

Jeremiah spoke to the people, telling them not to fight against Nebuchadnezzar. He told them that God said they would surely die by the sword, by famine, and by disease if they stayed in the city; but if they went out and surrendered, their lives would be saved.

The princes were angry. They said

to Zedekiah, "Jeremiah should be put to death. He weakens the people. He tells them to give up, and he takes all their courage away."

Zedekiah was a weak king. He said, "Do what you wish with him. I cannot stop you."

So the princes took Jeremiah and put him in the king's prison. There was a deep dungeon in the center of the prison. They put ropes under his arms and let him down into the dungeon. There was no water there, but the bottom was all slimy mud. Jeremiah sank deep into the mud.

In the king's household there was a kindhearted Negro. He heard what had happened to Jeremiah, and he went and told the king, "The princes have treated Jeremiah shamefully. They have thrown him into that awful dungeon where he is surely going to die."

King Zedekiah said, "Take thirty men, and get him out of the dungeon." The Negro quickly called thirty men and went into the dark prison. He took some old rags and clothes with him, which he threw down to Jeremiah. Then he called to him, "Put these under your arms, so that the cords will not hurt you."

So they pulled Jeremiah out of the dungeon. The king did not set him free, but kept him in the prison yard. There he could have air and sunshine. For God had promised to take care of him.

THE FALL OF JERUSALEM While Jeremiah was in the dungeon, the long siege went on. The Babylonian soldiers still surrounded the city. Almost all the food in Jerusalem was gone, and the people were starving.

After a siege of two years, the Babylonian soldiers at last broke the walls of Jerusalem with their war machines. They poured into the city. When Zedekiah and his princes saw that the soldiers had at last succeeded in battering down the strong walls, they tried to escape secretly by the gate of the king's garden. It was too late. The Babylonian soldiers saw them go. They chased after Zedekiah and his princes and soon caught them. They brought the king and his princes and his children to King Nebuchadnezzar.

The victorious king did a most cruel thing. He had all the princes and all Zedekiah's children killed before his eyes. That dreadful sight was the last Zedekiah ever saw on earth, for right after that Nebuchadnezzar had his soldiers put out Zedekiah's eyes. The blind king was taken to Babylon and put in prison for the rest of his life.

Then the soldiers destroyed the city. They burned Solomon's beautiful temple, the pride of the Jews, after first taking out of it everything that could be carried away. All the golden spoons and dishes and candlesticks were taken away. The magnificent brass pillars which stood before the temple were broken in pieces and carried to Babylon.

The soldiers burned all the fine houses of Jerusalem, and broke down the walls that had surrounded the city. As a final measure, King Nebuchadnezzar carried away most of the people who were still left in the land, leaving only the poorest.

At last God's terrible judgment had come. The once splendid city lay in ruins. The walls were broken down, the houses were burned, and the temple was a heap of ashes. The city lay desolate and deserted.

The soldiers put chains on Jeremiah to take him away with the other captives, but Nebuchadnezzar commanded that the prophet be set free, unhurt. He could go to Babylon with the captives if he wished, or he could stay behind with the few poor people who were left.

Jeremiah chose to stay in his own land. He sang sad lamentations about the fall of Jerusalem:

> How doth the city sit solitary,
> that was full of people!
> She weepeth sore in the night,
> and her tears are on her
> cheeks.
> Judah is gone into captivity.
> She dwelleth among the nations,
> she findeth no rest.

The poor captives in Babylon also sang songs:

> By the waters of Babylon,
> There we sat down, yea, we
> wept,
> When we remembered Zion.
> How shall we sing the Lord's
> song
> In a foreign land?

While Judah was in captivity, Jeremiah continued to bring God's messages. He told the captive Israelites not to be discouraged. They were not to be forsaken forever, as the ten tribes had been. After seventy years God would bring them back to their own country.

Although the people had forgotten God, God still loved them. He had said, "They will be My people, and I shall be their God." He loved Israel with an everlasting love, and He promised, "I will gather you out of all the countries where I have driven you in My anger."

It was comforting to the poor captives in Babylon to know that after seventy years God would bring their children back to their own land.

Jeremiah brought a still more comforting message. He began to prophesy about the coming of Jesus, who was to be a blessing to the whole world.

Jeremiah also prophesied about the downfall of Babylon, which would come as a punishment for its cruelty and wickedness. These prophecies about Babylon were written in a book and given to one of the princes who went into captivity. When he reached Babylon he was to read the whole book to the Jews there. Then he must tie a stone to the book, and throw it into the Euphrates River, saying, as he did so, "So shall Babylon sink and shall not rise."

These prophecies about Babylon have come true, for that city is so completely destroyed that it is difficult today to find even the place where it once was. Its magnificent palaces are nothing but heaps of ruins covered by drifting sands. Wild animals howl above the places where once were the proud streets leading to Nebuchadnezzar's court. Babylon became indeed utterly desolate.

Chapter 100
DANIEL
DANIEL 1, 2

THE BOY WHO REFUSED THE KING'S FOOD When Nebuchadnezzar came to Jerusalem the first time, in the reign of Jehoiakim, he ordered one of his officials to bring back to Babylon some of the young Jewish princes, to be attendants in Nebuchad-nezzar's palace. He was to choose young boys who were handsome and intelligent and well mannered. They were to be taught the Baby-lonian language and trained in all the manners and wisdom of the land.

In due time the Jewish princes arrived at the king's court. Among them were four who were of royal blood. Very likely they were nephews of good King Josiah. Their names were Daniel, Shadrach, Meshach, and Abed-nego.

Nebuchadnezzar wanted the princes not only to be healthy but also well educated. He commanded that they be given the same food as was served at the king's own table, and they must drink the same kind of wine the king himself drank.

This command worried the four young princes from Jerusalem. Long ago Moses had given the Jews very strict rules about what kinds of food they might eat. They were allowed to eat only meat from animals that were called clean. Even these ani-

PART VII Exile

mals must be killed in a special way, so that no blood would be left in them. If the boys would eat the meat that the king sent them, they would surely break the Jewish law. Besides this, the food and wine on the king's table would first of all have been offered to the Babylonian idols, so that it was not proper for a believer in the true God to eat it.

Although Daniel had been taken away from home while he was still young, he loved and trusted the Lord. He made up his mind that he would not eat the king's meat, nor drink the king's wine, no matter what happened.

Daniel asked the servant in charge of the young princes if he might be excused from eating the king's meat and drinking the king's wine. God was taking care of Daniel, even though he was so far from home and in a heathen land. God made the master of the young princes friendly to Daniel. He said to Daniel, "I would gladly let you eat whatever you like, but I am afraid of the king. If he sees that you look thinner and paler than the other boys, he will cut off my head!"

Daniel did not give up. "Will you let us try it for ten days?" he asked. "Give us vegetables to eat, and water to drink, and then compare our faces

232

with the faces of the other boys who eat the king's food, and decide from this."

So the man let them try it for ten days. At the end of ten days Daniel and his three friends were healthier and handsomer than any of the others who had been eating the king's food and drinking the king's wine.

God gave these four boys knowledge and skill in all learning and wisdom, and to Daniel He gave understanding of visions and dreams.

At the end of three years, the man in charge of the young princes took them in to see King Nebuchadnezzar. By this time the boys had learned to speak the Babylonian language very well, and they had also learned the correct manners for the court, so that they would know how to answer the king politely when he spoke to them.

After all the young princes had been brought in to see the king, and he had talked to them all, he chose Daniel, Shadrach, Meshach, and Abed-nego to stand before him and to serve in his court. For in matters of wisdom and understanding the king found these four boys ten times better than all the magicians and astrologers in his kingdom.

THE FORGOTTEN DREAM One night Nebuchadnezzar had a strange dream. Like all heathen people, the king was superstitious. He was afraid of dreams and signs.

In Babylon there were a great many magicians and astrologers who made a business of explaining dreams. King Nebuchadnezzar called all these wise men together and said to them, "I have had a dream, and I am troubled about what the dream means."

All the magicians answered, "O king, live forever! Tell us the dream, and we will tell you the meaning."

Nebuchadnezzar said, "I have forgotten the dream. If you are really magicians, you will be able to tell me what I dreamed. Unless you can tell me the dream, and its meaning, you will be cut in pieces, and your houses will be destroyed. But if you can tell me the dream and its meaning, you will receive gifts and rewards and great honor. Now, therefore, show me the dream, and tell me what it means."

The magicians were terribly frightened at this unreasonable demand. They knew that Nebuchadnezzar, who had conquered the whole world, could do to them whatever he liked. He could kill them if he wished, and no one could lift a hand to help them. Every time the king became angry, his servants were in terror for their lives. So they answered tremblingly, "The king is asking us to do an impossible thing. No one can tell the king what he has dreamed except the gods, who do not live on earth."

At this the king flew into a rage. "You could tell me what I dreamed if you were real magicians. Now I know that you are not wise men at all. You are just pretenders. If you cannot tell me what I dreamed, how can I know that you can tell me the real meaning? Perhaps you just make that up as well." Then he turned to his soldiers. "Kill them all!" he commanded.

Throughout the city the captain of the king's guard hunted for all the wise men, the magicians, the astrologers, and the sorcerers. Daniel and his three friends were to be killed, too, for they also were considered wise men.

Daniel asked the captain, "Why is the king in such a hurry to kill all the wise men?" When he heard what had happened, Daniel went in to see the king. This was a very brave thing to do, for he knew that the king was in a terrible temper, and that he might order Daniel killed on the spot. But Daniel trusted in God to keep him safe.

Daniel came forward, bowing low to the ground. He said, "O king, live forever! If the king will give me time, I think I shall be able to tell him what he dreamed." When the king agreed to wait, Daniel went home. He and his three friends all prayed to God that He would show Daniel the king's dream, so that they would not be killed with the other wise men.

That night God revealed the secret to Daniel when he was asleep. Daniel thanked God for His goodness in telling him the king's dream. He said, "Blessed is the name of God. He removes kings, and sets up kings. He reveals the deep and secret things, for He knows what is in the darkness."

Then Daniel went to the captain of the king's guard and said to him, "Do not kill the wise men. Bring me to the king, and I will tell him his dream and its meaning."

The captain rushed Daniel to Nebuchadnezzar and said to the king, "O king, live forever! I have found a man of the captives of Judah who can tell the king his dream and its meaning."

Nebuchadnezzar said to Daniel, "Are you able to tell me what I dreamed and what it means?"

Daniel answered, "It is impossible for the wise men and the magicians to tell the king a dream which he himself has forgotten. But there is a God in heaven. He it is who sent this dream to the king, to show him what is going to happen in times to come.

"God has revealed this secret to me, not because I am wiser than any other man, but so that I should explain the dream to the king, for God wishes you to know the meaning.

"Your dream, O king, is this: You saw an image of great brightness and terrible appearance. The head of the image was of fine gold; his breast and arms were of silver; his belly and his legs were iron; and his feet were partly iron and partly clay.

"In your dream you saw a stone cut out of the mountain without human hands. This stone came rolling down the mountain. It bumped against the feet of the image that were made of iron and clay, and it broke the feet to pieces. The iron and the brass and the silver and the gold were broken into small pieces like fine dust. The wind blew them away. After that, the stone that broke the image began to grow until it became a great mountain which filled all the earth.

"This is what you dreamed, O king. Now I shall tell you the meaning of it.

"You, O king, are king of kings, for the God of heaven has given you a kingdom, and power, and strength, and glory. And wherever men live, and even the animals in the field and the birds in the sky, God has given them all into your hand, and made you ruler over all of them. You, O king, are the head of gold.

"After you there will come another kingdom, a kingdom of silver, not as powerful as yours. And after that shall come a kingdom of brass which also shall rule over all the world. And the fourth kingdom shall be as strong as iron. And the feet you saw, which were partly clay and partly iron, are a kingdom that shall be partly strong and partly weak.

"And the stone which you saw cut out of the mountain without human hands, which broke in pieces the iron and the clay and the brass and the silver and the gold, that stone is the kingdom which the God of heaven shall set up, a kingdom which shall overcome all the others. That kingdom shall stand forever.

"The great God has made known to the king what shall come to pass hereafter. For the dream is certain and its meaning sure!"

Nebuchadnezzar was very much astonished when he heard Daniel tell his dream and what it meant. He realized that there is a great God, much greater than his heathen idols, and that this God brings whatever happens to pass. The king fell down on his face before Daniel and said, "Truly, your God is a God of gods, and a Lord of kings, and a revealer of secrets!"

Then the king made Daniel a great man in the kingdom and gave him many rich presents. He made him ruler over the whole province of Babylon, and the chief governor over all the wise men of Babylon.

Daniel did not forget his friends. He asked the king to make *them* rulers over the province. Daniel himself remained close to the king.

This wonderful dream which God sent to Nebuchadnezzar came true in later days. After the Babylonian kingdom came the Persian kingdom; and after that, the kingdom of Greece; and still later the Roman empire. In the days of the Roman empire, Jesus Christ, the long-promised Saviour of the world, was born. With Him began the kingdom of God which has spread over the whole world.

Chapter 101
THE FIERY FURNACE
DANIEL 3

"BOW DOWN TO THE IMAGE!" We may be thankful that we live today, and not long ago, in the days of the Babylonian empire. Today, in this country and in most of the countries of Europe, everyone can have whatever religion he thinks is right. But in the time of Nebuchadnezzar, the king could force his subjects to pray to the god the king believed in.

Although Nebuchadnezzar had learned something about the God of the Israelites at the time of his strange dream, he was still a heathen. He had learned something of the greatness of the God of the Israelites, but he did not understand that the Lord is the *only* true God. He thought that the Jewish God was only one of the more powerful gods that were worshiped by the different nations. He himself worshiped an idol which, he believed, had made him the greatest king in the world.

You would naturally expect that the Jews, who had been carried into captivity because they had forgotten God, would now be happy to go on worshiping idols like the people around them. Strange to say, now that they were in a foreign country, they began to realize how foolish idolatry was. Their own religion seemed much more precious to them. Thus God taught them in captivity the lesson they had refused to learn in their own land.

The prophet Jeremiah had promised that they would return to their own land after seventy years of captivity. This prophecy was very comforting to the Jews. It made them more careful to keep their own religion, so that they and their children would not forget God.

Then something happened which made it hard for the Jews to worship their own God. The Jews were not the only people who had been carried away captive to Babylon. Nebuchadnezzar had taken people captive in many lands and brought them to his capital. All these people had their own gods in whom they trusted.

Nebuchadnezzar believed that it was the idol he worshiped that had helped him to conquer the world. To show his gratitude, the king had his workmen make a wonderful golden image of this god. The image was ninety feet high and nine feet wide. The king had it set up in the plain outside the city, so that everybody could see it for miles around. When the sun shone on it, the image glistened and glittered with a great brilliance.

Then Nebuchadnezzar gathered together all the princes and governors and captains and judges and counselors of the kingdom for the dedication of the image he had set up.

A herald was sent out with a trumpet. He cried aloud, "To you it is commanded, O people, nations, and languages, that when you hear the sound of the cornet, flute, harp, sackbut, psaltery, dulcimer, and all kinds of music, you fall down and worship the golden image that Nebuchadnezzar the king has set up. Whoever does not fall down and worship, shall in the same hour be thrown into the burning, fiery furnace."

The people knew that the king would do what he threatened. Therefore, when they heard the sound of all kinds of music, they all fell down and worshiped the golden image.

THREE MEN WHO REFUSED TO BOW DOWN The people all bowed down to worship the golden image, except for three men. Some men told the king about this. "O king, live forever!" the talebearers said. "You made a decree that everyone should fall down and worship the golden image when he heard the sound of all kinds of music, and that whoever did not do this should be thrown into the burning, fiery furnace.

"Now, O king, there are certain Jews whom you have set over the province of Babylon, Shadrach, Meshach, and Abed-nego. These men, O king, have not obeyed you. They do not serve your gods, nor worship the golden image which you set up."

No one before had ever disobeyed the king. All his subjects performed his slightest wish, because they were afraid for their lives. Nebuchadnezzar was astonished at the daring of these three Jews. In a furious rage he commanded that they be brought before him. Then the three men appeared before the king.

Nebuchadnezzar said to them, "Is it true, Shadrach, Meshach, and Abed-nego, that you do not serve my gods, nor worship the golden image I have set up? I will give you one more chance. If you are now ready when you hear the sound of all kinds of music to fall down and worship the image I have set up, well. But if you do not worship, you shall be thrown in the very same hour into the middle of the burning, fiery furnace. And who is that God who will be able to deliver you out of my hands?"

The three men bravely answered the king, "O Nebuchadnezzar, we are not afraid to answer you. Our God is able to save us from the burning, fiery furnace, and He will deliver us out of your hand, O king. But even if He does not save us from the fire, still we will not serve your gods, nor will we worship the golden image which you have set up!"

This defiant answer made the king so furious that he commanded that the furnace be heated seven times hotter than usual.

The strongest and biggest soldiers in the army bound the three men and threw them into the burning, fiery furnace. Because the king had ordered the furnace to be made seven times hotter than before, the roaring flames leaped out at the soldiers. Their clothes caught fire, and they burned to death.

Nebuchadnezzar watched as Shadrach, Meshach, and Abed-nego were thrown into the furnace. Soon he saw something in the fiery flames that astonished him. He called out to his wise men, "Did we not throw three men, bound, into the middle of the fire?" They answered, "True, O king. There were three men."

Nebuchadnezzar cried out in surprise, "I see four men, not bound, but free, walking in the middle of the flames! They are not burned nor hurt in the least. And the fourth one looks like a son of the gods!"

The king went a little nearer to the furnace and shouted, "Shadrach, Meshach, and Abed-nego, you servants of the Most High God, come out, and come here!" Then Shadrach, Meshach, and Abed-nego came out from the middle of the fire.

The princes and wise men gathered around them and stared at these men upon whose bodies the fire had no power. Not a hair of their head was singed, nor were their clothes burned. There was not even any smell of burning on them.

The king exclaimed, "Blessed be the God of Shadrach, Meshach, and Abed-nego, who has sent His angel, and delivered His servants who trusted in Him, and who dared to risk their lives rather than worship any god except their own God!

"Now, therefore, I make a decree that any people, or nation, or language who says anything against the God of Shadrach, Meshach, and Abed-nego shall be cut in pieces, and their houses shall be torn down and made into a rubbish heap; because there is no other God that can deliver His servants like this."

How do you think the captive Jews felt when they saw that their God was able to protect His servants even in the fiery, burning furnace? It made them see that the idols of the heathen were useless and that their own God was all-powerful. And many of the heathen people, too, began to look with great respect upon the God of the Hebrews.

Chapter 102
THE KING WHO LIVED IN THE FIELDS
DANIEL 4

We have now come to a very remarkable chapter in our Bible. It is strange because it was written by a Babylonian king. Yes, it was truly written by that great king Nebuchadnezzar.

God put into the heart of the king the words he wrote, for God inspired all the authors of the Bible and told them what to write. God made such a wonderful thing happen that Nebuchadnezzar wanted to tell the world about it.

One day, as Nebuchadnezzar was resting in the palace, he had a dream or vision which troubled him. He sent for all the wise men of Babylon to explain the dream to him. Not one of the wise men could tell the king what his dream meant. At last Daniel came in, and the king told him the dream:

"I saw a very tall tree in the middle of the earth. It grew tall and strong, and the top of it reached the sky, and it could be seen from every corner of the earth. Its leaves were green, and its fruit was so plentiful that there was food enough for all. The beasts of the field rested in its shadow, and the birds of the heaven lived in its branches.

"Then I saw a watcher, a holy one, come down from heaven. He cried aloud and said, 'Chop down the tree, cut off its branches, shake off the leaves, scatter the fruit. But leave the stump in the ground, with a band of iron and brass around it. Leave it in the tender grass of the field. and let it be wet with the dew of heaven. Let his heart be changed from a man's, and let a beast's heart be given him. Let seven years pass over him.

" 'This is to come to pass by the command of the holy ones, so that all people may know that the Most High God is the ruler of men, and that He gives the kingdom unto whomsoever He will.' "

When Nebuchadnezzar told this strange dream, Daniel was astonished and shocked. He understood the dream. It told what was going to happen to the great king, but the prophecy was so distressing that Daniel did not dare to tell the king. He stood silent before Nebuchadnezzar, not saying a word.

At last the king, who was watching Daniel's face, saw that he knew the meaning. He said to him gently, "Daniel, do not be afraid to tell me what the dream means."

Daniel said, "My lord, the dream is so terrible, and its meaning so bitter, that I wish it were going to happen to your enemies instead of to you.

"The tree that you saw, which grew so strong and tall that it reached up to the sky and could be seen over the whole earth, which had beautiful leaves and plenty of fruit, which gave shade to all the animals — this wonderful tree is you, O king! You have grown and become strong, for your kingdoms reach to the end of the earth.

"You saw a holy watcher coming down from heaven, saying, 'Chop down the tree, but leave the stump of the tree in the earth, in the tender grass, and let it be wet with the dew of heaven. Let him live with the beasts of the field till seven years have passed by.'

"This is the meaning, O king! You will be driven away from men. You will have to live with the beasts of the field. For seven years you will have to eat grass like an ox, and be wet with the dew of heaven, until you know that the Most High God is the ruler in the kingdom of men, and that He gives power to whomsoever He will."

It was no wonder that Daniel had hesitated to tell the king this heavy news! There was one thing Daniel could say to the king that had some comfort for him. It was this: "In your dream you saw that the holy one commanded that the root of the tree be left in the ground. That means that you shall not lose your kingdom. After you have learned that God is the ruler over men, your kingdom shall be given back to you again."

A whole year passed before the dream came true. One day, as the king was walking in the palace and looking at the magnificent city of Babylon, he said to himself, "Is not this great Babylon that I have built by the might of my power, and for the honor of my majesty?" As he spoke these boastful words, there came a voice from heaven, saying, "O King Nebuchadnezzar, the kingdom is departed from you!"

In that same hour punishment for his pride came upon the king. He suddenly became insane, so that the nobles of his palace had to drive him away into the fields, far away from men. He ate grass like an ox, and his body was wet with the dew of heaven. His hair grew long like eagles' feathers, and his nails like birds' claws.

Nebuchadnezzar stayed in this pitiable condition for seven long years.

"And at the end of seven years," he wrote later, "I lifted up my eyes to heaven, and my understanding came back to me. I blessed the Most High God, and I praised and honored Him who lives forever, whose reign is everlasting, and whose kingdom is from generation to generation. He alone rules, and no one can stay His hand, or say to Him, 'What doest Thou?' "

Nebuchadnezzar lived about a year after this. Once more he ruled his splendid kingdom, but no longer did he say, "Is not this great Babylon which I have built?" Instead he praised God, for his heart was so wonderfully changed that he became a worshiper of the Lord.

Nebuchadnezzar wrote his letter to all the people of the earth. His words, proclaiming the greatness of God, have come down to us, for they have become part of our Bible.

Chapter 103
THE FALL OF BABYLON
DANIEL 5

THE WRITING ON THE WALL Not long after Nebuchadnezzar died, his grandson Belshazzar came to the throne. This new king did not serve God. He took away from Daniel the important positions which Nebuchadnezzar had given him.

After this king had reigned for several years, he gave a feast for a thousand of his lords in his magnificent palace. The banquet hall was so large that it could easily hold the party of a thousand men at the tables.

To make the feast even more splendid, Belshazzar sent for the golden and silver dishes which had been stolen from the temple of the Lord in Jerusalem. These sacred dishes had been stored all these years in the temple of the Babylonian idols.

The dishes were brought, and the king and his nobles and his princes and his wives drank wine out of the golden dishes which had been dedicated to the service of God. And as they drank they praised their own gods of gold and silver and brass and wood and stone.

Suddenly on the wall, in the brightest spot just opposite the great lampstand, there appeared the fingers of a man's hand. The hand showed plainly in the brilliant light. Everyone in the banquet hall saw it. They stopped drinking and stared in amazement. "What is it? What is it?" they asked each other. "How did it get there?"

While they watched, the fingers began to write some words in an unknown language on the wall. No one knew what the words meant, but everyone felt that the message must be a dreadful one.

The king was panic-stricken. He knew that he had done wrong to use the treasures of the temple of God for his drunken feast. His legs grew weak and trembled. His knees knocked together. Finally he managed to pull himself together, and he commanded loudly, "Quickly, bring the astrologers and the magicians to read this writing!"

To spur them on, he shouted, "Whoever can read this writing, and tell me what it means, shall be clothed in scarlet, with a gold chain around his neck, and he shall be made third ruler in the kingdom!"

All the wise men hurried into the banquet room. They looked for a long time at the writing on the wall, shaking their heads. None of them could read it. King Belshazzar was more frightened than ever. His face turned white, and he shuddered with dread. Perhaps he remembered how God had punished his grandfather Nebuchadnezzar for his pride.

There was one person who was not present at the great banquet. This was Belshazzar's grandmother, the old queen who was Nebuchadnezzar's widow. When she heard what had happened, she hurried to the banquet hall.

"O king, live forever!" she said. "Do not let your thoughts trouble you so. There is a man in your kingdom in whom is the spirit of the holy gods. In the days of Nebuchadnezzar wisdom like the wisdom of the gods was found in this man. He was made master of the magicians because he could explain dreams. Let Daniel be called, and he will show you the meaning of this writing."

The king sent for Daniel. "Are you that Daniel," the king asked him, "whom my grandfather brought out of Judah with the captives? I have heard that the spirit of the gods is in you, and that you have understanding in dreams. My wise men and astrologers cannot read this writing. If you can read it, and tell me what it means, you shall be clothed in scarlet. You shall have a gold chain around your neck, and be the third ruler in the kingdom."

"Keep your gifts," Daniel said, "or give them to someone else. I will read the writing to the king and tell him its meaning.

"O king, the Most High God gave your grandfather a kingdom and majesty and glory and honor. All peoples and nations and languages trembled and feared before him. Whom he would he killed, and whom he would he kept alive. But when he became proud, he was taken from his throne. He was driven from the sons of men and made like the beasts. He was fed with grass like oxen, and his body was wet with the dew of heaven, until he learned that the Most High God rules among men, and that He gives power to whomsoever He chooses.

"And you, O Belshazzar, knew all this, and yet you have not humbled your heart. You and your princes have drunk wine out of the dishes from the temple of God, and have praised the gods of silver and gold

18: NEBUCHADNESSAR CALLS THE THREE MEN FROM THE FIERY FURNACE

19: LAYING THE FOUNDATION OF THE SECOND TEMPLE

and brass and iron and wood and stone, who cannot see, or hear, or know anything. And you have not glorified the God who gives you life and everything that you have."

Then Daniel read the message on the wall. "This," he said, "is the writing on the wall. MENE, MENE: God has numbered your kingdom and finished it. TEKEL: You are weighed in the balances and found lacking. UPHARSIN: Your kingdom is divided, and given to the Medes and Persians."

Though this was a frightening message, the king kept his promise. He commanded his servants to bring a royal robe of scarlet for Daniel, and a heavy gold chain. The king stood up among his princes and proclaimed that Daniel was to be the third ruler in the kingdom.

THE PERSIANS ENTER THE CITY The feast went on again, but no one felt like eating or drinking. The guests were talking about the writing on the wall. For they knew that danger was near.

A king named Cyrus had arisen in the kingdom of Persia, far to the east of Babylon. This new and powerful king was conquering many countries. First he attacked his neighbor, the country of Media. Then he marched against Babylon, Belshazzar's country, and conquered that. Only the city of Babylon had not yet fallen into his power, for its walls were high and strong.

Cyrus gathered his soldiers around Babylon to besiege it. His men could not break down the high, strong walls, nor could they climb over them. He had no hope that the people of the city would starve, for he knew that they had enough food stored away to last for twenty years. They would never suffer from thirst, for the great river Euphrates ran under the wide walls right through the city.

Behind their high walls the people of Babylon felt perfectly safe. They were so sure that Cyrus could never get into the city that they had come to Belshazzar's feast without hesitation.

But listen! What was the sound they heard? Could it be trumpets? And marching feet? Had Cyrus done the impossible, and found a way into the city?

The sound of marching feet came nearer and nearer. The terrified nobles tried to escape from the banquet hall. But it was too late. The palace was surrounded by Persian soldiers. There was no escape. All the guests were killed right there in the banquet hall. Belshazzar, the king, died with them.

How did Cyrus get into the city? We do not know. There is an old story that his soldiers dug a new channel for the river and turned the water into this new riverbed. Along the empty channel, under the high walls, the soldiers crept quietly into the city.

Perhaps this is just what happened. Or perhaps some traitor in the city of Babylon opened the gates while the king and all his lords sat drinking in the banquet hall.

But however Cyrus got into the city, we do know that the warning which had so mysteriously appeared on the wall was God's announcement of judgment. God had finished Belshazzar's kingdom and given it to the Medes and Persians.

An even older prophecy of judgment came true at the same time.

Many years before, Jeremiah had foretold the fall of Babylon. In this night the kingdom of Babylon was destroyed forever. It became part of a far greater kingdom, ruled over by Cyrus the Persian, one of the greatest conquerors the world has ever seen.

Chapter 104
DANIEL IN THE LIONS' DEN
DANIEL 6

THE JEALOUS RULERS It was a happy day for the captive Israelites when the Persians conquered Babylon. These people were much kinder than the Babylonians had been. They followed a religion quite different from the idol worship of the other heathen nations.

The founder of this religion was a man called Zoroaster. He lived alone in the mountains for twenty years, trying to find out what the truth is, by thinking.

He believed in only one great god, not in many gods. He thought that this god had angels to help him. He also believed that there was a wicked spirit, who had bad spirits to help him.

Zoroaster taught his followers to live well, for he was sure that there would come a judgment day when people would be either punished or rewarded for the way in which they had lived.

Some people think that perhaps this man got his ideas from the first Israelites who went into captivity. Even among the ten tribes who were taken captive because they worshiped idols there were some people who were true to God. Perhaps Zoroaster had heard some of the captive Jews talking about the one great and good God, and about angels, and about the devil, and about a great judgment day. At any rate, these beliefs made the Persians better and kinder people.

The mighty Persian empire was too large to be ruled by one man alone. Cyrus put Darius, a man sixty-two years old, on the throne of Babylon to rule that part of his empire for him. Darius was an old man when he came to the throne. Only three years later he died. In that short time something of great importance happened to Daniel.

Darius divided his kingdom into many smaller parts, and over these parts he placed princes. Over the princes there were three presidents, and Daniel, the captive Jew, was chief of the presidents.

It was only natural that Daniel should be chosen for an important office. His wisdom was well known, and so was his goodness. Even the scarlet robe which Belshazzar had placed on him showed that he was a person of rank.

But when Darius set Daniel, a Jew, over all the other rulers, these princes became jealous. They tried to think of some way in which they could make trouble for him. They watched him carefully, to see if they could find anything wrong with his work. But Daniel was so faithful that they soon saw that this was useless.

Finally they thought of another way in which to make trouble for him. They knew that he was a faithful worshiper of God. They said to each other, "The only way in which we can get the better of him is through his religion."

And so they planned a trick. They

went to King Darius. They said, "King Darius, live forever! All the rulers of the kingdom have agreed to ask you to make a royal command that whoever prays to any man or god for thirty days, except to you, O king, shall be thrown into the den of lions. Now, O king, make the decree and sign the writing, so that it may become one of the laws of the Medes and Persians, which cannot be changed."

The king was pleased with this idea. He thought the princes were trying to make his power known to the people. He never dreamed what was behind their request. All unsuspecting, he signed the decree.

THE GENTLE LIONS   All through his captivity Daniel remembered the prayer which Solomon had prayed at the dedication of the temple in Jerusalem: "And if Thy people sin against Thee, and Thou deliver them over to their enemies, and they carry them away captives into a land far off; yet if they return to Thee with all their heart, and pray toward the city which Thou hast chosen, and this house which I have built for Thy name, then hear Thou from heaven, Thy dwelling place."

Three times a day Daniel opened the windows of his room toward Jerusalem, kneeled down, and prayed to the Lord. When he heard what the princes had done, and knew that the king had signed the decree so that it could not be changed, he did not give up his daily prayers, even though to pray meant certain death. He went into his bedroom, as he had always done, where his windows were open toward Jerusalem, and he kneeled down and prayed to God.

The men who had persuaded the king to sign the decree were elated. "We've got him now!" they cried.

They hurried to the king and said, "O king, live forever! Did you not sign a decree that any man who prayed to any god or man except to you, for thirty days, would be thrown into the den of lions?"

The king replied, "That is true. It is part of the law of the Medes and Persians, which cannot be changed."

"O king, live forever!" the rulers answered triumphantly. "That Daniel, one of the captives of Judah, does not obey your decree. He prays to his own God three times every day!"

When Darius heard this, he was very, very sorry that he had ever signed that decree. He knew that Daniel was a good man. He spent that whole day trying to think of some way to save Daniel.

That evening the rulers came to the king again and said, "You know, O king, that it is the law of the Medes and Persians that no decree signed by the king may be changed."

The king knew that. He knew he could do nothing to help Daniel. The law had been signed, and could not be changed. He commanded that Daniel be brought in. He spoke very sorrowfully to him, "Your God, whom you serve so faithfully, He will deliver you."

The king's soldiers opened the lions' den, and threw Daniel down into it. A great stone was laid upon the opening. The king unwillingly put his own seal upon the stone so that no one might move it.

Sadly the king went back to the palace. He could not eat any of the fine food which had been prepared for him. When the musicians came in to play for him as usual, he sent them away. At last he went to bed, but he could not sleep. All night long he tossed from side to side. There was no sleep for Darius that night!

Meanwhile the men who had plotted against Daniel went home, elated. "That's the end of Daniel," they said to each other. "He will never trouble us again!"

And how did Daniel spend the night? Did the hungry lions tear him apart and devour him? No, Daniel was safe, as safe as if he had been home in his own room. God did not let the lions hurt His servant, or even frighten him. An angel came down from heaven to shut the lions' mouths.

Very likely the lions came and rubbed themselves against Daniel; and when he petted them, they purred like great pussycats. Perhaps they lay down and let Daniel rest against their soft bodies. Perhaps Daniel spent the night in sleep, for he knew that he was perfectly safe.

As soon as the gray dawn came peering through the windows of the palace, the tired king, who had not slept a wink all night, got up and dressed, and hurried to the lions' den. He was pale with weariness and anxiety. Had Daniel's God been able to save him from the hungry lions?

As soon as he reached the den the king called out, "Daniel, O Daniel, servant of the living God, has your God, whom you serve continually, been able to deliver you from the lions?" He waited anxiously. Would he hear only the savage roar of the lions in answer?

Clear and strong came back the voice of Daniel, "O king, live forever! My God sent His angel to shut the lions' mouths, so that they did not hurt me!"

The king was very glad. He commanded that his servants should take Daniel out of the den. He had not been hurt in any way, because he trusted in God.

Then Darius commanded his servants to bring those men who had plotted against Daniel, and to throw them into the den. The hungry lions sprang on them before they had even fallen to the bottom.

King Darius became convinced that the God of Daniel must be the one about whom Zoroaster had taught. No one else could do such marvelous things.

He made another decree, far better than the first. He commanded all people everywhere to worship the God of Daniel, who had saved His servant from the lions: "I make a decree that in every dominion of my kingdom men tremble and fear before the God of Daniel: for He is the living God, steadfast forever, and His kingdom shall never be destroyed. He delivereth and rescueth, and He worketh signs and wonders in heaven and on earth, and He hath delivered Daniel from the power of the lions."

Daniel became an important man in the kingdom, for God was with him. When Darius died three years later, the great Cyrus came to the throne, but Daniel still prospered.

God sent Daniel some visions of things that were going to happen in the future. He sent an angel to tell Daniel that God loved him, and that God would always be with him because he trusted in God.

BACK TO THE PROMISED LAND
EZRA 1-3; ISAIAH 44, 45

THE PERSIAN KING WHO DID GOD'S BIDDING   Daniel was just a boy when he first came as a captive to Babylon. He lived at the court during the reign of Nebuchadnezzar. After this king came one or two others, then Belshazzar, and then Darius.

When Cyrus came to the throne after the death of Darius, Daniel was a very old man. He had held many high positions in the kingdom. He had been in great danger many times, but God had always wonderfully saved his life.

At the beginning of the captivity, the prophet Jeremiah wrote a letter to the captive Jews, telling them that after seventy years God would bring them back to their own country. The seventy years had now passed. God had not forgotten His people. He had already planned their return, which He brought about in a most unexpected way.

No sooner had Cyrus become king than God put it into his heart to allow the Jews to return to Jerusalem. Even more surprising, King Cyrus offered to help them rebuild the temple which had been destroyed. This is what the king announced:

PROCLAMATION OF CYRUS TO THE JEWS
The Lord God has given all the kingdoms of the earth to me. He has commanded me to build Him a house in Jerusalem, which is in Judah.

Now, let all His people go up to Jerusalem, and build the house of the Lord God of Israel, for He is the true God.

If there are any who do not go up, let them help those who do go, *with silver and gold, with food, and with beasts to travel on.*

How astounded the Jews must have been when they read this proclamation posted on the street corners! Was it really true that they were going back to Jerusalem to rebuild the temple? They could hardly believe it.

Excited meetings were held on the streets and in the houses. The people were so happy that they danced and sang, shouting and clapping their hands. One of their poets wrote a song about it, which is our Psalm 126.

One hundred and fifty years before Cyrus was even born, Isaiah had prophesied about him. Isaiah had mentioned Cyrus by name, and had told just what he would do. Isaiah had known all this because God told him what to say. God knows everything that will happen even to the end of the world, because God is the one who makes it happen. He is the ruler of all the world.

Listen to what Isaiah said:

Thus saith the Lord to Cyrus, whose right hand I have held, to subdue nations before him. He is My shepherd, and shall perform all My pleasure, even saying to Jerusalem, Thou shalt be built, and to the temple, Thy foundation shall be laid. Say to Cyrus, I have called you by your name, though you have not known Me. I will direct all your ways. You shall build My city, and shall let My captives go, saith the Lord of hosts.

Did Cyrus know about these prophecies? It is not likely, although it is just possible that Daniel told him about them. But whether Cyrus ever heard what Isaiah said, he was obeying God's command when he sent the Jews back to Jerusalem. It was by God's power that Cyrus had become so great a conqueror, for God had work for Cyrus to do, even though Cyrus probably never really knew the one true God.

THE WORK ON THE TEMPLE With glad hearts the Jews began to get ready for the long journey back to their own country. It was more than five hundred miles to Jerusalem. Even today that is a great distance. At that time it was a much longer and harder journey.

When they would arrive, the people would find the temple destroyed and their houses in ashes. Jerusalem had been in ruins ever since it was burned by Nebuchadnezzar. Not a single house had been left standing. Clearing away all the rubbish and building new houses to live in would take at least a year. During the time of rebuilding the Jews would have to live in tents.

For this reason not all the Jews were able to go back to Jerusalem. Some families had a grandfather or grandmother who was too old to stand hard travel and rough living conditions. Some had little babies who could not live through such a long journey.

Daniel was one of the many Jews who did not go. He was now at least eighty-five years old. He could not have endured the long journey, nor the rough life the Jews would have to live while they were rebuilding the city.

Only the youngest and strongest men and women went back. The people who had to stay behind in Babylon helped the others with money, with goods of all kinds, and with animals to ride on.

King Cyrus helped them too. He gave back to them all the gold and silver dishes which Nebuchadnezzar had taken out of the temple in Jerusalem. These things had been carefully kept in a heathen temple, for they were very valuable. King Cyrus had his treasurer count them, and give back every single dish — five thousand four hundred of them.

The travelers were heavily loaded for their long journey. Besides the rich treasure of the temple, they had to take along household goods with which to begin housekeeping.

Fifty thousand people made the journey back to Jerusalem. Most of them had to walk, for the camels and donkeys were needed to carry the dishes for the temple and the household goods.

As they went, the men and women sang. This made the long journey pleasant and cheerful. In the evenings they took the tents from the backs of the camels and set them up on the warm sand. They made little bonfires and cooked their suppers. As they lay down to sleep, they said happily, "We are one day nearer home."

At last they reached their own country. They found the ruins of the temple — nothing but a heap of rubbish. After clearing the rubbish away, they built an altar in the court on which they offered sacrifices to God every morning and every evening.

Each family began to look for the plot of land which Joshua had given to their fathers. While they were in Babylon they had been very careful to keep family records, so that they would know when they went back to Judah where they were to live. Each man settled down on the land which had belonged to his fathers.

After they had been in Jerusalem for a year, and had built houses to live in, they began to build the temple. On the day when the foundation was laid, they had a joyful meeting. They praised God, singing together the song of David, "Because He is good, and His mercy endureth forever toward Israel."

Many of the old priests and Levites, who remembered the first temple before it had been burned, wept; for they knew that the new temple could never be as glorious as the first one had been. It was impossibie to tell the noise of the shouts of joy from the noise of the weeping of the old men. There was a shouting and weeping which could be heard a long way off.

Chapter 106
THE REBUILDING OF THE TEMPLE
EZRA 4-6; ZECHARIAH 2, 4, 9

QUARRELSOME PEOPLE WHO STOPPED THE WORK As you remember, the ten tribes of Israel were taken into captivity by the king of Assyria. Foreign nations were then brought into Samaria to fill up the land.

These foreigners lived in Samaria all the seventy years while the Jews were in captivity in Babylon. Now when they saw that some of the Jews had come back from captivity, and were building up the temple, they came to the high priest. "Let us help you build the temple," they offered. "We have worshiped your God ever since we came to this country."

But the elders of Israel refused. They knew that the Samaritans worshiped idols at the same time as they worshiped the Lord. They said, "You have nothing to do with building a house to our God. King Cyrus has commanded us to build it."

This answer made the Samaritans very angry. Instead of helping the Jews, they did everything they could to hinder them.

Meanwhile King Cyrus had died after a short reign. Another king ruled for a little while, and after him, another king named Artaxerxes.

Knowing that the Jews no longer had King Cyrus to protect them, the Samaritans wrote a letter to this new ruler. The letter said: "Let it be known to the king that the Jews who have come here to Jerusalem are rebuilding that rebellious city. They have already finished the walls and joined the foundations.

"If this city is built up again, the people will not pay tribute to the king. Let the records of earlier kings be searched. It will be found that this city has always been a rebellious city. That is the reason it was destroyed."

Artaxerxes sent an answer to the Samaritans. "Your letter has been read to me," he wrote. "I commanded that search be made in the old records. It has been found that Jerusalem was always a city which rebelled against its rulers. I command that these Jews stop building their city until I tell them that they may continue."

When the Samaritans received this letter, they hurried as fast as they could to Jerusalem. There was nothing for the Jews to do but to lay down their tools and stop the work. Their dreams were not yet to come true.

As long as Artaxerxes ruled, the Jews did nothing to finish the temple. They were so discouraged that they did not even think of protesting.

Not long after this, Artaxerxes died. After him there came a king named Darius. This second Darius was a very great ruler, even greater than Cyrus had been. His kingdom reached from India to Egypt. He ruled his kingdom wisely and well. He is called Darius the Great.

God sent two prophets with a message to the Jews. He wanted them to go on building the temple. He reminded them that they did not work in their own strength, but in His. They were poor and weak, but God is all-powerful. The messages were addressed to Zerubbabel, who was their leader:

This is the word of the Lord unto Zerubbabel, saying, Not by might, nor by power, but by My spirit, saith the Lord of hosts. . . . The hands of Zerubbabel have laid the foundation of this house; his hands shall also finish it. . . . Sing and rejoice, O daughter of Zion: for lo, I come, and I will dwell in the midst of thee, saith the Lord.

Then God reminded them of the promise He had given so long ago, and had repeated over and over, to Abraham, and to David, and to Isaiah. This was the promise that someday He was going to send a Saviour who would be a blessing to all the world. This Saviour would be their true and everlasting king:

Rejoice greatly, O daughter of Zion; shout, O daughter of Jerusalem: behold, thy King cometh unto thee: he is just, and having salvation; lowly, and riding upon an ass, and upon a colt the foal of an ass.

These promises encouraged the Jews. They went back to their work on the temple with new determination. They began to look forward to the coming of the promised Saviour more than ever before.

A DECREE FROM PERSIA As soon as the Jews again started work on the temple, the same quarrelsome Samaritans came to make trouble once more. "Who told you to go on building this temple?" they asked. "We will tell the king what you are doing if you do not stop." But this time the Jews would not stop, for God had commanded them to go on building.

When the Samaritans saw that they could not make the Jews stop, they wrote another letter. This one was addressed to Darius the Great, who was king now.

Long before this, writing had become quite common. Many people knew how to write. All the kings had scribes who kept a record of the events of the king's reign. These records were stored in the king's library, so that later rulers could read what had been done.

This is the letter the troublesome Samaritans wrote:

"Unto Darius the king, all peace!

"Be it known unto the king that we went to Jerusalem, to the temple which the Jews are rapidly rebuilding. We asked them who commanded them to go on building the temple, and they answered, 'We are servants of the God of heaven and earth, and we are building the house which was built many years ago by a great king of Israel. Our fathers made God angry, and He let King Nebuchadnezzar carry them away captive, and destroy this temple. But King Cyrus, in the first years of his reign, made a decree that this temple should be rebuilt. He sent us back here, and told us to build it.'

"Now, therefore, if it seem good to the king, let a search be made in the king's library, to see whether it is true that Cyrus made a decree that this temple should be rebuilt. And let King Darius notify us what his pleasure is about this matter."

When Darius received this letter, he commanded his servants to search in the library where the rolls were stored, to see if such a record could be found. And in the library they found a roll which said, "In the first year of Cyrus he made a decree about the temple of God in Jerusalem. This was the decree: 'Let the house be built, and let the foundations be strongly laid, with three rows of great stones, and a row of new timber. Let the cost be taken out of the king's treasury.' "

When King Darius found this record, he wrote to the Samaritans:

"I, King Darius, command that you let these Jews alone. Let them go on building the house of their God. Help them with money, and with goods, and with everything they need. Take the cost out of the king's treasury. Give them also young bullocks, rams,

lambs, wheat, salt, wine, and oil, and whatever they need for offerings to their God. Let all of these be given to them day by day without fail, so that they may pray to the God of heaven for the life of the king and his sons.

"And I also make a decree that if anyone changes this law, timbers shall be pulled down from his house, and a gallows shall be built from these timbers, and he shall be hanged thereon."

This dreadful threat frightened the Samaritans. Instead of hindering the Jews, they helped them as the king had commanded.

So the children of Israel built the temple and finished it. In all, the work took about twenty years. After it was finished, they had a dedication service. They offered hundreds of bullocks, rams, and lambs. They set up again the service of the priests and Levites, as Moses had commanded.

Last of all they celebrated the Passover with great joy. For the Lord had made them glad by bringing them back from Babylon, and by inclining both King Cyrus and King Darius to help them build a house for their God.

Chapter 107
ESTHER, THE BEAUTIFUL QUEEN
ESTHER 1, 2

THE FEAST THAT LASTED A WEEK We have come now to a very interesting story of what happened to some of the Jews who did not go back to Palestine. Although fifty thousand Jews had returned, there were many who stayed behind for one reason or another. These people were scattered throughout the great kingdom

of Persia. Wherever they went, they carried the knowledge of their great God with them.

At the time of our story, Darius the Great was dead. Ahasuerus now ruled the empire. King Ahasuerus was not a wise and God-fearing man, as Darius had been. He was foolish and weak.

The capital of the empire had been removed to another city. The splendor of Babylon had been destroyed. Its wonderful walls, three hundred feet high, had been broken down. The hundred gates had been carried away. The whole city was in ruins.

Shushan, the new capital, was even more magnificent than Babylon had been. King Ahasuerus lived there in great splendor. He ruled an empire which stretched from India in the far east to Ethiopia, south of Egypt, in the west — a country as big as the United States.

In the third year of his reign, Ahasuerus invited the princes and nobles of all the provinces of his kingdom to a feast in Shushan. What a wonderful gathering that was! There were princes from India, magnificently dressed in rich embroidered silks ablaze with glittering diamonds, rubies, and pearls. They rode in state in curtained chairs perched high on the backs of elephants.

There were wild-looking Arab tribesmen from Arabia who seemed to fly along on their swift horses, heavy silver chains dangling from their necks as they rode.

From Ethiopia came black princes, wearing enormous turbans on their heads, and bearing rich gifts for the king. Many more princes, from all parts of the empire, came at the king's command.

For six months King Ahasuerus entertained all these royal guests in Shushan, showing them all the splendor of his kingdom. At the end of their visit he gave a feast to all the people of the capital city. Young and old, rich and poor, great and humble — all were invited.

The garden of the palace was beautifully decorated for the party with violet and white and green curtains, fastened with purple and white ribbons to silver rings in the marble pillars. There were couches made of gold and silver for the guests to rest on. The ground was paved with red, blue, white, and black marble. An abundance of wine was served in gold and silver cups.

While the king was entertaining the men of the city in the garden, his wife, Queen Vashti, was giving a feast for the women inside the palace. For a whole week this celebration lasted, and everyone was very gay. Yet serious trouble was soon to come.

A JEWISH GIRL BECOMES QUEEN   On the seventh day of the feast, King Ahasuerus, who had drunk far too much wine, sent his servants into the hall where the queen was entertaining the women. He ordered the servants to bring the queen out to the garden, wearing the royal crown on her head, so that all the people and the princes could see how beautiful she was.

If the king had not been drunk, he would never have made this demand. He would have known that the queen was too modest to come out into the garden to be stared at by a crowd of men.

The servants came back without the queen. She refused to come at the king's command. The king was furiously angry. He consulted his counselors and asked, "What shall we do unto Queen Vashti, because she has refused to obey my command?"

The counselors answered, "The queen has done wrong not only to the king, but to all the princes and the people as well. When the women of the kingdom hear what Vashti has done, they, too, will refuse to obey their husbands.

"If it please the king, let him make a royal decree that Vashti shall be queen no longer, because she has disobeyed the king. Let her crown be given to someone else who is more obedient than she is. When all the people in your empire hear about this, then all the wives everywhere will obey and honor their husbands."

King Ahasuerus was pleased with this advice. To all parts of his empire he sent letters written in the various languages of the peoples of the empire, saying, "Every man shall be ruler in his own house by order of the king."

Later, after the king had gotten over his anger at Queen Vashti, his servants said to him, "Let officers be appointed in all the provinces of the kingdom. Let them gather together the most beautiful young girls of the empire. Let these girls be brought to the palace, and the one who pleases the king shall be queen instead of Vashti."

The king thought this was a good idea. He commanded his servants to begin to hunt everywhere for lovely young girls. Many beautiful girls from all parts of the empire were brought to Shushan. Each one, after living in the palace for a while, appeared before the king.

Now it so happened that in the city of Shushan there lived a Jew named Mordecai, who had a beautiful young cousin, Esther. Since her father and mother were dead, Mordecai had brought her up as his own daughter. Esther was chosen as one of the young girls who were to be brought to the palace so that the king might pick a new queen from among them. She did not tell anyone that she was Jewish.

When Esther finally came before Ahasuerus, he loved her more than all the others. He set the royal crown on her head, and made her queen instead of Vashti.

Every day Mordecai walked outside the court of the women's house and sat in the palace gate, to find out how Esther was. While he lingered about the palace, he discovered a plot which two servants had made to kill the king.

Mordecai sent a message to Esther about what he had discovered, and she told Ahasuerus about the message. The king ordered an investigation made, and the two traitors were hanged. What Mordecai had done was written down in the records of the kings of Media and Persia, but the king forgot to reward the man who had saved his life.

Chapter 108
QUEEN ESTHER SAVES HER PEOPLE
ESTHER 3-10

A PRINCE WHO HATED THE JEWS There was a man named Haman whom the king liked better than all his other princes. Haman was given many honors which the other nobles did not receive.

Wherever Haman walked or rode, all the other princes and the king's servants bowed low, with their faces to the ground. Haman walked proudly between these rows of men. He thought he was more important than anyone else on earth.

The only person who did not bow down when Haman passed was Mordecai. The servants in the king's gate said to Mordecai, "Why do you disobey the king's command, to bow down to Haman?" And when they could not get him to bow down, they told Haman.

Haman was furiously angry. He began to think of some way to punish Mordecai. He was so angry that he was not satisfied just to kill Mordecai alone. When he found out that Mordecai was a Jew, he resolved to kill all the Jews in the empire.

He did not dare to do this without the king's permission. There were thousands of Jews in the kingdom. Every year they paid the king a great amount of money in taxes. If the Jews were all killed, the king would lose this money. And if the king did not happen to be pleased to have all the Jews murdered, he might turn on Haman and have his head cut off for doing such a thing. Kings in those days might be very fond of a man one minute, and the next minute order him beheaded.

Like all heathen, Haman was very superstitious. He did not dare to ask the king for this favor until he had first cast lots to find out what day was a lucky one for this request. In that country, where everybody believed in luck and signs and dreams, there were men whose work it was to cast lots. Haman ordered these men to cast lots for him daily, until they found a lucky day for him to get the king's permission to kill all the Jews.

Day by day, and month by month, the magicians cast lots, but every day turned out unlucky for Haman. At last, after a whole year, the lot turned out favorable.

When Haman went to the king, he did not say that he was angry with Mordecai because Mordecai refused to bow down to him and do him honor. He knew well enough that King Ahasuerus would never let him kill thousands of people for such a reason. He said instead, "O king, live forever! There is a certain people scattered abroad among the people in all the provinces of your kingdom. Their laws are different from the laws of all other peoples. They do not keep the king's laws; therefore it is not for the king's profit to let them live. If it pleases the king, let it be written that they are to be destroyed. I will pay ten thousand talents of silver into the king's treasury, so that the king will not lose any taxes by having them killed."

Haman was an extremely rich man. Ten thousand talents of silver was a very large sum of money. But although Haman was very rich, King Ahasuerus was even richer. For all the provinces of his empire paid him huge sums in taxes. So he said to Haman, "Keep your money! You may have the people too. Do whatever you like with them."

The king gave Haman his royal ring with his seal carved in it. Now Haman could write anything he pleased and sign it with the king's seal. Then it would become a law of the Medes and Persians which could not be altered.

Oh, how happy Haman was! The lot had spoken truly. It was certainly a lucky day for him!

Haman called in all the king's scribes or secretaries. He had them write out a proclamation for all the governors of all the king's provinces. This is what the proclamation said:

THE KING'S DECREE
On the thirteenth day of the twelfth month, you are to kill all the Jews, both young and old, little children and women.

Riders on swift camels went out in every direction to carry the news to the furthest corners of the king's great dominions. And Haman sat down to drink with the king.

In every land where the king's message came, there was weeping and wailing and mourning. This terrible message meant that all the Jews in the world were to be killed at the end of the year. Even those in Judah, who had just finished rebuilding the temple, were included.

Since they first began to be a nation, the Jews had never been in such great danger. If Haman's plot would succeed, there would not be one Jew left in the whole world. Could anything save them?

THE BRAVE QUEEN When Mordecai heard that all the Jews were to be killed, he tore his clothes, put on sackcloth and ashes, and went out into the city, raising a loud and bitter cry. He came in front of the king's palace and wept at the gate. He could not go in, for no one clothed in sackcloth was allowed in the palace.

Queen Esther did not know about Haman's wicked plot. But some of her maid-servants told her that Mordecai was lying outside the gate in sackcloth and ashes. Esther sent Mordecai some good clothes to wear instead of those that were torn and covered with ashes. But Mordecai sent them back again.

Now Esther was really alarmed. What was the matter with Mordecai? Was someone in the family dead? She sent one of her servants to find out. Why was Mordecai dressed in mourning clothes?

Mordecai told the servant the whole story of Haman's plot. He gave the servant a copy of the decree to show to the queen. He wanted her to go in to the king, and beg him not to let all her people be killed.

Esther was frightened when she heard this message. She told the servant to say to Mordecai, "All the king's servants and the people of the court know that any man or woman who comes into the inner court without being sent for is sure to die unless the king holds out the golden scepter as a sign that he may live. I have not been called to the king for thirty days. How could I go to see him?"

Mordecai knew that this was true. But he knew, too, that the Jews were in dreadful danger. He sent Esther another message, saying, "Do not think that you will be saved when all the Jews are killed, just because you are the queen. If you don't speak to the king, the Jews will be saved in some other way, but you and your family will be killed. Who knows whether you were not made queen for just such a time as this, so that you can save your people?"

Esther was panic-stricken when she thought of going to the king without being called. But she bravely decided that she would try to save her people, even if she lost her own life in the attempt.

She answered Mordecai: "Gather all the Jews in the city together. Fast for me, neither eating nor drinking for three days. I and my maidens will do the same. Then I will go in to the king. And if I die, I die!"

After three days Esther put on her royal dress and stood in the inner court of the palace. Her heart almost stopped beating as she waited. But when the king saw his beautiful young queen, he smiled and held out the golden scepter that was in his hand.

Esther came in and touched the tip of the scepter. The king spoke kindly to her. "What do you wish, Queen Esther? What is your request? It shall be given to you, even to the half of the kingdom."

Esther was far too frightened to tell the king at once what she wanted. She answered, "If it seem good to the king, let the king and Haman come to the banquet which I have prepared today."

The king was very much pleased. He said to one of his servants, "Tell Haman to make haste and to come to the queen's banquet."

So the king and Haman came to the banquet which Esther had prepared. And the king said again to Esther, "What is your request? It will be granted to you, even to the half of the kingdom."

Esther was still afraid to tell him. She said, "My request is this: If I have found favor in the sight of the king, and if it please the king to grant my request, let the king and Haman come again to another banquet which I shall prepare for them. I shall tell the king tomorrow what I desire."

When Esther postponed telling the king what she wanted, he became very curious and eager to know what it was, of course.

Haman went home delighted. He was proud to think that he, and he alone, had been invited with the king to the queen's banquet. But as he went out of the gate, all his joy left him, for he saw that the Jew, Mordecai, did not bow down to him.

Haman called his family and his friends together. He boasted of how rich he was, of how many children he had, and of how the king had promoted him above all the other princes. Last of all he said, "Esther the queen asked no man to come with the king to the banquet which she had prepared except myself, and tomorrow I am again invited with the king to the queen's banquet. Yet all these honors that I have received amount to nothing so long as I see Mordecai the Jew sitting at the king's gate!"

Seeing that Haman was so disturbed, his wife and his friends said to him, "Let a gallows be made seventy-five feet high. Tomorrow ask the king's permission to hang Mordecai on the gallows. Then you can go merrily to the banquet with the king."

This idea pleased Haman. He had the gallows built that very afternoon. He watched it going up higher and higher. He thought how greatly he would enjoy seeing his enemy hanging up there!

HAMAN'S REWARD That night the king could not sleep. He commanded one of his servants to bring the book of the records of his reign. The book was brought and read to the king.

In the book it was written that Mordecai had once discovered a plot of the king's servants to murder King Ahasuerus. As the servant read this, Ahasuerus asked, "What reward has been given to Mordecai for this?"

"Nothing has been done for him," the servant replied. The king asked, "Who is outside in the court?"

"Haman is waiting there," the servants told him. Early as it was, Haman had just come into the outer court to ask the king's permission to hang Mordecai on the gallows which had been built the afternoon before.

"Let Haman come in," the king ordered. After his favorite had entered, the king asked him, "What shall be done to the man whom the king delights to honor?" Haman thought in his heart, "To whom would the king delight to show honor more than to myself?"

So he immediately thought of the thing that he would like most of all, and he said, "Let the servants bring the royal robes which the king wears, and also the horse that the king rides on, and the royal crown. Let all this be given to one of the king's most noble princes, that with these things he may dress the man whom the king delights to honor. Let that man be led on horseback through the city, and let the prince proclaim before him, 'Thus shall it be done to the man whom the king delights to honor!' "

Then the king said to Haman, "Hurry, and take the horse, and the royal clothes, and do just what you have said to Mordecai the Jew, who sits at the palace gate. Let nothing fail of all that you have said."

Haman's bitter disappointment knew no bounds! He had supposed that he was the one who was to wear the fine clothes and the crown, and to ride on the king's horse. Now he found instead that he was to lead the horse, and that his hated enemy Mordecai was the one to ride in state!

But he had to obey the king. He dressed Mordecai in the king's royal robes. He put him on the king's finest horse with its gold and silver harness, and led him through the streets of the city. As he went, he shouted, "Thus shall it be done to the man whom the king delights to honor!"

Everybody in the street bowed low to Mordecai as he rode along. Oh, how it pained Haman to see that! He was the one to whom the people had always bowed — and now they were bowing to his hated enemy! And *he* was the servant who had to lead the horse through the streets!

After the procession was over, Haman was so embarrassed that he hurried home, mourning and with his head covered. He told his wife and his friends everything that had happened. While he was still talking to them, the king's servant came to take him to the banquet that Queen Esther had prepared. Haman had forgotten all about it in his embarrassment.

During the banquet, the king again asked, "What is your petition, Queen Esther? It shall be given to you, even to the half of the kingdom."

Esther clasped her hands. With a beseeching look in her eyes she fell on her knees and said, "If I have found favor in your sight, O king, and if it pleases the king, let my life be given me, and the life of my people. For we are sold, I and my people, to be destroyed."

The king sprang up, furious with anger. "Who has dared to do such a thing?" he demanded.

Esther, turning, pointed to Haman. "The enemy is this wicked Haman," she said. Choking with anger, the king went out into the palace garden.

When Haman saw how angry the king was, he realized that he was in very great danger. He walked up to Queen Esther to beg her to save his life. In his excitement he fell down on the couch where Esther was. Just then the king returned. Seeing Haman on Esther's couch, he became even more enraged. He burst out, "How dare he touch the queen!"

One of the servants, who saw how angry the king was, volunteered, "There is a gallows, seventy-five feet high, which Haman built for hanging Mordecai, who is the king's friend. It is standing in the garden of Haman's house."

Then the king said, "Hang him on it!" Haman was immediately taken out and hanged on the gallows which he had made for Mordecai.

Esther told the king all about the cruel plot that Haman had made. She also told him that Mordecai was her cousin, who had brought her up like a father. The king sent for Mordecai, and gave him the ring which he had once given to Haman. He made Mordecai the highest officer in the whole kingdom of Persia.

A TIME OF REJOICING   Haman was gone, but the decree he had sent out was still in effect. The decree had gone out to all parts of the kingdom that on the thirteenth day of the twelfth month all the Jews were to be killed. This was a law of the Medes and Persians which even the king could not change.

Esther came to see the king once more. She fell down at his feet, begging him with tears to undo the mischief that Haman had done. Again the king held out his golden scepter to Esther. She stood up and said, "If it please the king, and if I have found favor in his sight, let there be made a law to change the letters which Haman wrote to destroy all the Jews in the king's provinces. For how can I endure to see this evil happen to my people?"

The king answered, "Haman has been hanged upon the gallows, but the writing cannot be changed, because it is a law of the Medes and Persians. But I will have Mordecai send another message to all the Jews."

So the writers were called in. Mordecai had them write letters to all the provinces. These letters were written in the king's name, and sealed with the king's ring. They were sent hastily by the king's swift messengers. This is what the letters said:

PROCLAMATION

On the thirteenth day of the twelfth month, according to the first proclamation, all the Jews were to be destroyed. The king hereby gives the Jews permis-sion to gather themselves together, and to fight against all those who attack them. They may defend themselves, and kill all who try to kill them.

In every town in the great empire, little and big, a copy of this proclamation was posted in the marketplace. In those days there were no newspapers or telephones or radios or television. But I suppose that there was not one person in all that vast empire who did not know about those two proclamations posted up side by side in the marketplaces. The first was Haman's proclamation sent in the king's name that all the Jews were to be killed. Next to Haman's proclamation was posted Mordecai's letter, also sent in the king's name, that the Jews in every city should gather themselves together and fight for their lives, and that they should destroy all those who tried to kill them.

The Jews in all the king's dominions had nine months to prepare for the fateful day. When at last it came, they gathered in all their cities. All the rulers of the provinces helped them. The Jews got the better of all their enemies, and they hanged the the sons of Haman on the gallows their father had built.

The Jews rested the next day. They made it a holiday, a time of feasting and gladness.

Meanwhile Mordecai had become a great man. He was clothed in royal robes of violet and white, and he wore a golden crown on his head. As time passed, he advanced to even greater power, becoming the king's right-hand man.

He wrote to all the Jews, telling them that the fourteenth and fifteenth days of the twelfth month should be celebrated every year in memory of the terrible days when the whole race of the Jews had been in danger of being destroyed.

These two days are called the Feast of Purim. Even to this day the Jews keep this feast every year, in remembrance of the time when the Jewish race was saved from destruction.

Chapter 109
EZRA, THE TEACHER OF THE LAW
EZRA 7-10

THE SECOND COMPANY OF PILGRIMS There was a Jew living in Persia who had spent all his life studying the Word of God. His name was Ezra. Besides studying the Bible himself, Ezra taught it to other Jewish people. All Persia knew about him, even the king.

God gave this learned man the desire to go back to Judah to teach the people who had gone back there about God, about how He wanted people to live, and how He wished to be worshiped.

Ezra asked the king to let him go to Judah for this purpose. The king was very kind. He not only let Ezra go, but he allowed any other Jews who wished to go with him to do so. Besides this, the king and the nobles of Persia gave Ezra a splendid present of gold and silver, and of costly dishes for the temple of God. This treasure was an offering to the great God.

King Artaxerxes promised to pay all Ezra's expenses for the temple out of the king's treasury. Like Cyrus and Darius, this king believed in the great God of heaven, and thought he ought to honor Him.

When the Israelites were carried away to Babylon by Nebuchadnezzar, it was a bitter lesson for them, but it was a blessing to those heathen people among whom they were captives. In their own land the Jews had worshiped idols; but when they found themselves in a heathen country, they gave up their idolatry and turned back to the one true God.

It was through the captivity of the Jews that Nebuchadnezzar saw something of the power of God. When Daniel was able to tell the king the dream he had forgotten, Nebuchadnezzar was deeply moved. All the people in Babylon were filled with wonder when they saw how God kept Shadrach, Meshach, and Abed-nego safe in the fiery furnace where they had been thrown for refusing to worship the golden image.

Afterward when God humbled the great Nebuchadnezzar by driving him out to live among the cattle for seven years, the king said when he recovered, "Now I, Nebuchadnezzar, praise and honor the King of heaven." Nebuchadnezzar did not give up his heathen gods altogether, but he did learn about the power of the one true God.

In Belshazzar's time God showed His power in the handwriting on the wall, and in the time of Darius by saving Daniel from the lions.

Later Cyrus the Persian and Darius the Great sent the Jews back to Jerusalem with gifts for their temple, and animals to sacrifice, so that they would pray to the God of heaven for the lives of the king and his sons.

Now when Ezra went back to Jerusalem with his band of Israelites, the king gave him all kinds of provisions for the service in the temple. The king also gave Ezra authority to set up judges over the people, and to teach the Jews the law of their God.

So the captivity of the Jews, which had been such a painful lesson for them, was a blessing to the heathen peoples. Many who had never before heard of the true God learned about Him. And the knowledge of God was never again completely forgotten in those countries, for we know that the wise men who came to see the baby Jesus came from these lands.

EZRA IN JERUSALEM About six or seven thousand people returned to Judah with Ezra. Before they actually started, they camped for three days on the banks of a river, and here Ezra proclaimed a fast. They spent these three days in prayer, asking God to guide them and to take care of them and their little children on this long and dangerous journey.

Before them lay several hundred miles of hot desert country where they were almost certain to meet with wild robber bands. Ezra said, "I was ashamed to ask the king for a band of soldiers and horsemen to protect us, because we had said to the king, 'Our God will take care of us.' So we fasted, and prayed God to take care of us, and He answered our prayer.

"And I found that there were no priests with us; so I sent back to ask some priests to come with us, so that we could have ministers for the house of our God. Two hundred and fifty priests and Levites joined our band. I chose twenty-two of the priests, and I gave them charge of the silver and the gold and the dishes that the king and his lords had offered."

So the pilgrims started on their long journey. Four months later they reached Jerusalem. It was now eighty years since the first group of Israelites had returned from Persia. Most of those who had made the first journey were dead. And not one of those in Ezra's band had ever seen their own country before.

As soon as Ezra reached Jerusalem, the priests with him delivered the treasures they had brought to the temple, and offered sacrifices to the Lord.

Not long after they arrived, some of the leaders of the first group to return came to see Ezra. They had heavy news for him. Many of the returned Israelites had married heathen wives. They had forgotten God's strict command not to mingle with the heathen. Even some of the leaders were guilty.

Ezra was horrified when he heard this. He tore his clothes and mourned all day. It was no wonder that Ezra was horrified, for the people had suffered seventy years of captivity because of their idolatry. If they married heathen wives, they would soon drift back into idolatry again. Then they would again have to suffer God's judgments because they had forsaken Him.

In the evening, after mourning all day, Ezra fell down upon his knees, spread out his hands, and prayed to the Lord. He said, "O my God, I am ashamed, and blush to lift up my face. We have sinned — our sin is so great that it has reached up to the heavens. What shall we say? We have forsaken Thee. If we again break Thy commandments, wilt Thou not be angry with us, and consume us?"

While Ezra was praying and weeping, a very great company of men and women and children joined him, all of them weeping because of their sins. One of the men said to Ezra,

"Come, let us make a promise to God that we will send away all our heathen wives."

So they called a meeting. They agreed that all those who had married heathen wives must come at appointed times to Ezra and one or two other leaders. After due judgment, those who were guilty would have to send away their heathen wives. Thus the people honored God, and put away their idolatry.

Chapter 110
NEHEMIAH, THE GOVERNOR OF JERUSALEM
NEHEMIAH 1, 2, 4, 6, 8; MALACHI 3

WHY THE KING'S SERVANT WAS SAD In Persia there was a rich Jewish nobleman named Nehemiah, who held the high office of cupbearer to the king. This position was a very important one. It was given only to a very trustworthy person. The cupbearer had to taste every cup of wine that he handed to the king so that no one would have a chance to poison the king.

One day a man who had been in Judah came back to the capital city of Persia. He brought bad news. "The people who have returned to Jerusalem," he said, "are not making any progress. The walls of the city are still broken down, and the gates which were burned have not been replaced."

When Nehemiah heard this, he felt very sad. As he went about his work he kept praying to God to help Jerusalem. His grief showed in his face.

The king noticed that his cupbearer looked unhappy. "Why do you look so sad today?" he asked. "You are not sick, so this must be sorrow of heart."

Nehemiah was frightened, for servants should never look sad in the presence of the king. Yet he dared to say, "Let the king live forever! Why should I not be sad when the city where my fathers are buried still lies waste, and its gates are burned with fire?"

The king asked graciously, "What can I do to help you?"

"If it pleases the king," Nehemiah answered, "and if I have found favor in his sight, I would ask that you send me to Judah to the city where my fathers are buried, so that I may build it up again."

It did please the king to send Nehemiah, and he appointed him governor of Judah. The king gave him letters to the governors of the countries through which he would have to travel, to let him pass through in safety. The king also gave Nehemiah a letter to the keeper of the king's forest, directing him to give the Jews timber to build up the walls of the city, and a palace for the governor. The king also sent with Nehemiah a company of soldiers and horsemen, to protect him as he passed through wild places.

Nehemiah reached Jerusalem safely. After a day or two of rest, he and a few other men mounted horses and rode all around the city of Jerusalem at night, to see in what condition the walls were. The city was in very bad shape. The walls were still all broken down, and the gates had been burned. There were great empty spaces in the city where heaps of rubbish had lain ever since Nebuchadnezzar burned the city.

The desolate condition of Jerusalem distressed Nehemiah very much. The next day he talked to the rulers of the city and said to them, "You see how bad the condition of Jerusalem is! The city lies waste, and the gates have been burned. Let us build up the walls of our city again!"

The rulers were only too eager to begin. Nehemiah divided up the wall around the city. Each family was given a part of the wall nearest its own house to rebuild.

Soon some of the Samaritans living nearby made trouble for Nehemiah. They laughed at Nehemiah for trying to build up the walls. One of them said mockingly, "What are these feeble Jews doing? Where will they get stones to build the wall? Are they going to dig them out of the heaps of rubbish?"

Another said disdainfully, "Such a wall as they are building! Why, if even a fox should go up, he would break it down!"

Nehemiah did not answer their mocking words. Instead he cried to God, saying, "Hear, O our God, for we are despised!"

The Jews went on building the wall. They worked hard, and soon the wall was almost finished. When the Samaritans saw that the walls were really being rebuilt, they were very angry. They decided to attack Jerusalem and stop the work.

The Israelites did not stop building. Instead they prayed to God even while they went on with the work. Nehemiah placed people behind the wall, with swords and spears and bows. He said to them, "Do not be afraid of them. Remember that our God is great and strong. Fight for your sons and your daughters, your wives and your houses!"

When the Samaritans discovered that their plot was known, they realized that they were beaten.

Nehemiah wrote, "From that time on, I divided my people. Half of them went on building the wall, and the other half held weapons, so as to be ready to fight in case of attack.

"Those who built on top of the wall, and those who carried up the building materials, worked with one hand, carrying a weapon in the other hand. Each of the builders had a sword by his side. Close by me was the man who sounded the alarm trumpet.

"I said to the people, 'The work is great, and we are separated one from another on the wall. In whatever place you hear the trumpet sounding, gather quickly to that place. Our God will fight for us.'

"At the same time I said to the people, 'Let everyone with his servant remain in Jerusalem all night, to be a guard to us at night.' For there were many men working on the wall who did not live in Jerusalem, but in some of the nearby towns. Neither I, nor my brothers, nor my servants, nor the men of the guard which followed me — none of us put off our clothes at night, for we were always prepared to fight."

At this time the work was again interrupted by the bitter complaints of the poor people among the Jews. For some of those who had returned from Babylon had grown rich by oppressing their poorer brethren, so that some of the people were too weak from hunger to work on the walls.

Food was so expensive that many had had to sell the land which they had inherited from their fathers, and had even sold their children as slaves to buy enough corn to keep body and soul together.

When Nehemiah heard this, he was very angry. He called the princes and rulers together and said to them, "We have been saved from captivity among the heathen, and will you now sell your own brothers as slaves?" The rich nobles and princes did not answer Nehemiah, for they could not think of any excuse for what they had done.

Then Nehemiah said to them, "Give the people back their lands and their houses, and the money, and the corn and oil and wine which you have taken from them." The nobles said, "We will give back to them everything we have taken away." Nehemiah called the priests, and had them take a solemn oath from the princes that they would surely do as they had promised.

Nehemiah wrote, "Also I shook my lap, and said, 'So may God shake out every man from his house and his profits, if he does not keep this promise!'

"The king had appointed me to be governor. For the twelve years that I ruled I did not accept any salary, because the people were poor. Moreover, I fed many of the people at my own expense."

JERUSALEM REBUILT AT LAST "Now it came to pass," wrote Nehemiah, "that when the Samaritans heard that I had almost finished the wall, they tried another way to hinder me. They said to me, 'Come, let us meet together in one of the villages,' for they planned to do away with me secretly.

"But I sent messengers to them, saying, 'I am too busy. I am doing a great work, and cannot take time to come to talk to you. Why should the work stop, while I come down to you?'

"They asked me four times, but I did not go. The fifth time they sent a man with a letter which said, 'It is reported among us that you are re-building the wall so that you can make yourself king in Jerusalem. If you do not meet with us, we will tell the king of Persia what you are doing.'

"I sent word to them, 'We are doing no such thing. You are making this up in your own heads.' And I prayed to God to strengthen us in the work."

Then one of the leaders of the Jews said to Nehemiah, "They will come at night and kill you. You should lock yourself inside the temple to escape from them."

For there were as yet no gates to the city. But Nehemiah said, "It is not fitting that I should hide in the temple when others are exposed to danger. I will not do it."

At last the wall was finished. It had taken fifty-two days to complete it. Nehemiah had done a remarkable thing in getting the wall finished in less than two months. He had worked very hard, and all the other people, too, had worked with all their might.

Then all the people gathered together as one man into the street before the Water Gate. They asked Ezra to bring the books of Moses, which the Lord had given unto His people. Ezra stood high up on a platform that they had made, and he opened the book in the sight of all the people, and all the people, both men and women, stood up. Then Ezra blessed the Lord, the great God. And all the people answered, "Amen, Amen!" and they lifted up their hands, and bowed their heads, and worshiped the Lord.

Ezra read from the Word of God carefully and distinctly, and as he read, he explained it, so that everyone could understand. The people listened attentively. It was a long time since they had heard the Word of God read. Perhaps some of them had never heard it before. Ezra read how God had led their fathers out of Egypt, how He had cared for them in the desert, how He had given them His law telling them how He wanted them to live and how to worship Him, how they had sinned, and how God had forgiven them over and over.

The people wept as they listened. But Ezra and Nehemiah said to them, "You must not weep today, for the joy of the Lord is your strength. This day is holy to your God. Go home and have a feast. Eat and drink, and give food to those who are poor."

So the people went home to eat and drink and have a happy holiday. The next morning they came again to listen to the Word of God, to His laws, to the story of His love and mercy, and to the precious promises He had made.

While Nehemiah was governor, there lived a prophet named Malachi. He wrote the last book of the Old Testament.

Malachi reminded the people of God's promise to send a Saviour. "The Lord, whom ye seek," he said, "shall suddenly come to His temple, even the messenger of the covenant, whom ye delight in: behold, He shall come, saith the Lord of hosts."

Malachi also foretold the coming of John the Baptist: "Behold, I will send My messenger, and he shall prepare the way before Me."

To comfort the people, Malachi said, "Then they that feared the Lord spoke often one to another; and the Lord hearkened, and heard it, and a book of remembrance was written before Him for them that feared the Lord, and that thought upon His name. 'And they shall be Mine,' saith the Lord of hosts, 'in that day when I make up My jewels.'"

These are almost the last words in the Old Testament, and they are words that strengthen and comfort us even today. God remembers those who love Him and trust in Him. If you put all your trust in the death of our Saviour, Jesus, you can know that you are one of those God has chosen for His own. Whatever happens, you can always be certain of His love, His care, and His abiding presence in your life.

New Testament

20: THE WISE MEN OF THE EAST

21: THE WONDERFUL HEALER AT CAPERNAUM

THE PRIEST WHO COULD NOT TALK
LUKE 1

After the Old Testament was finished, about four hundred years passed before the New Testament was begun.

What happened to the Jewish people in those four hundred years? The Bible does not tell us, but we can find out by reading books of history written in that time.

During all these years most of the Jews were living in the land of Palestine — waiting. They had been waiting since the time of the great prophet Isaiah. They had been waiting and longing since the time of their great father Abraham.

For what were the Jewish people waiting, and longing, and praying?

They were waiting for a child, the child God had promised to send to some Jewish mother. God first gave this promise to Eve, when He said that someday one of her children would defeat Satan, who had brought sin and death into the world by tempting Eve to disobey God. This wonderful child who was going to come would again bring goodness and everlasting life to man.

Many years afterward, God promised Abraham that this child would be one of his descendants, and that all the nations of the earth would be blessed in Him. Nineteen hundred years had passed since that time, but during all those centuries the Jewish people had been looking for the promised child.

The great prophet Isaiah, who lived about seven hundred years before the child was born, foretold His coming in these words: "Unto us a child is born, unto us a son is given: and the government shall be upon His shoulder: and His name shall be called Wonderful, Counsellor, The mighty God, The everlasting Father, the Prince of Peace."

The prophet Micah had even foretold where this wonderful child would be born — in the town of Bethlehem. God had sent many other wonderful promises about the child He would send. No wonder every Jewish mother wished to have a little son! No wonder she hoped, deep in her heart, that the long-promised child would come to her!

When at last the time came for the child to be born, God sent a messenger to announce His coming.

In the hill country, not far from Jerusalem, there lived an aged priest and his wife, Zacharias and Elisabeth. This elderly couple had one great grief — they had no child. For many years they had prayed for a child, but God had not granted their prayer.

Twice a year Zacharias went to

PART VIII Saviour

Jerusalem to take his turn at serving in God's temple. One day, while he was burning sweet-smelling incense on the altar in the Holy Place, and all the people were outside praying and worshiping God, Zacharias saw a bright and glorious angel standing beside the altar.

Zacharias was very much frightened. The angel said to him, "Do not be afraid, Zacharias. Your prayer has been heard. You and Elisabeth are going to have a son, whom you must call John. He will bring joy to many people, for he is to make the people ready for the blessed child promised to God's people long ago."

Zacharias was amazed. He asked, "How can I be sure that this is true? I am an old man, and my wife is old too."

The angel answered, "I am the great angel Gabriel, who stand in God's holy presence. God sent me to tell you this glad news. But because you have not believed my message, you shall be dumb and unable to speak until the child is born."

While the angel was talking to Zacharias, the people outside wondered why he stayed so long in the Holy Place. When at last he came out, he could not speak to them and had to motion to them with his hand. They realized that he must have seen a vision in the temple.

After a few days, when Zacharias was through with his work in the temple, he returned home. When Elisabeth knew that God was going to give her a son in her old age, she was very happy.

Chapter 2
THE MESSAGE OF THE ANGEL
LUKE 1; MATTHEW 1

In the city of Nazareth there lived a young girl named Mary, who was a cousin of Elisabeth. She was not yet married, but she soon would be, for she had promised a man named Joseph that she would become his wife.

One day, when Mary was alone, the angel Gabriel appeared to her with a joyful message. The angel said to Mary, "God is with you; you are blessed among women!" Mary was puzzled. No one had ever spoken to her like this. She did not know what to make of it.

The angel said, "Do not be afraid, Mary. You are going to have a son whom you shall call Jesus. He will be great, and the Lord God will give Him the throne of His father David. His kingdom will last forever!"

Mary asked, "How can I have a son when I am not married?" The angel told Mary that her son would not have any earthly father. He would be the son of God Himself. And since He was to be the son of God and of Mary, He would Himself be both God and man. The angel added, "Your cousin Elisabeth also is going to have a son in her old age."

Mary said, "Behold, I am the handmaid of the Lord; let it happen to me as you have said."

Mary was so filled with joy and wonder that she could hardly contain it. She could not keep this news to herself! She felt she must tell someone. So she packed up a few things, and went to visit her cousin Elisabeth.

As soon as Mary came into the house, Elisabeth called out in a loud voice, "Oh, you are a blessed woman! And you will have a blessed child! It is a great honor that the mother of my Lord should come to visit me!"

Mary answered, "I am filled with love and praise for God. He has done great things for me. Although I am only a poor girl, the whole world will call me blessed. For our God has remembered the promise He made to Abraham and to his children forever."

Mary and Elisabeth were so happy talking to each other about the wonderful things God had done for them that Mary stayed three months. Then she went back home. She had to start making clothes for the little baby that was coming. And she still had to tell Joseph about the wonderful thing that had happened to her.

Joseph had not seen the angel who had told Mary that she was to be the mother of the long-promised Saviour. He did not understand how such a thing was possible. He began to think it might be better if he did not marry Mary.

While Joseph was wondering what to do, he had a remarkable dream one night. An angel appeared to him, saying that he should not be afraid to marry Mary. Her child would be the son of God. They were to call Him Jesus, which means "Saviour," because He would save His people from their sins. When Joseph woke up, he did not forget his dream. He married Mary, as the angel had commanded.

Not long after this, Elisabeth's baby was born. When the child was eight days old, the friends and relatives of the family came to Elisabeth's house to give the baby a name, as was the custom among the Jews. They were going to call the child Zacharias, after his father, but Elisabeth said firmly, "No, we are not going to call him Zacharias. His name is John."

The friends and relatives thought this was very strange. "No one in your family is named John," they said. Zacharias was still unable to talk, but they made signs to him as to what name he wanted the baby to have. Zacharias asked for a writing tablet. On it he wrote, "His name is John."

While the friends were wondering about this, all at once Zacharias was able to speak again. First of all he praised God for His goodness, because God had remembered His promise to send the long-awaited Saviour into the world. Then Zacharias turned to his little son and said, "And you, child, shall be called prophet of the Most High, for you shall go before the face of the Lord to prepare His ways."

John grew up big and strong. He loved to be alone so that he could think about God. When he became a young man, he went to live all by himself in the desert to prepare himself for his work of announcing the coming of God's son and God's kingdom into this world.

Chapter 3
THE HOLY NIGHT
LUKE 2

It happened in those days that the Roman emperor, Caesar Augustus, who ruled over most of the world, ordered every citizen of the empire to return to his birthplace to be registered. This census was to provide a record of all who must pay taxes or serve in the emperor's armies.

Joseph and Mary lived in Nazareth, but Joseph had been born in Bethlehem, and was a member of the family of King David, whose birthplace was Bethlehem. So Joseph and Mary traveled to Bethlehem.

Bethlehem was only a little town. It was crowded at this time, for many people whose ancestors had lived in Bethlehem had come to be registered. By the time Joseph and Mary arrived, every house was full of visitors. No one had room for them. What were they to do? They surely could not spend the night in the street!

There was only one place where they found a welcome. That was a stable where animals were sheltered. Here Mary and Joseph found a bed of soft, sweet hay.

That night was a blessed night, and that lowly stable became a holy place. For on that night the Saviour of the world was born. God sent His own son into the world to be Mary's baby.

How happy Mary was, now that she held the promised child in her arms! Her heart was filled with love and adoration. This tiny child was her own baby, but He was also the son of the great and mighty God. Mary looked at Him tenderly and adoringly, for she knew that this tiny child was to be the Saviour of the world. She put some clean hay in the manger out of which the cattle ate, and laid the baby on this soft bed.

When a prince is born, all the bells throughout the kingdom are rung for joy. Heralds and trumpeters ride in every direction to proclaim the birth of the king's son. So, too, when God's son was born, heralds announced His coming. They were not men riding on horses, blowing trumpets of brass. They were bright and shining angels.

On the night when Jesus was born, there were shepherds in the fields near Bethlehem, keeping watch over their sheep in the darkness. Suddenly the glory of the Lord shone round about them. A light from heaven more glorious than the light of the sun filled the sky. An angel of the Lord came near them, and they were very much afraid.

The angel said, "Do not be afraid, for I bring you good news of great joy which shall be to all the people. For unto you is born this day in the city of David a Saviour, who is Christ the Lord. And this will be a sign for you. You will find the baby wrapped in swaddling cloths and lying in a manger."

Suddenly the sky was filled with angels, praising God and saying, "Glory to God in the highest, and on earth peace among men in whom He is well pleased."

The glory of God was shining over all the earth, as if heaven itself were opened and the shepherds could see into it. They forgot their sheep as they looked at the dazzling glory and listened to the wonderful words. How radiant the light! How glorious the angels! How marvelous the music!

No king's son was ever announced with such splendor! The angels sang with joy that the Saviour was born, who would save His people from sin and death.

After the angels had gone back to heaven, the shepherds said to each other, "Let us now go to Bethlehem to see this strange thing which the Lord has told us about." As fast as they could, they hurried to Bethlehem. There in the stable they found Joseph and Mary, and the baby lying in a manger. The shepherds understood that this was the child who had been promised to their fathers for so many hundreds of years. They kneeled down in adoration before Him.

As they went back to their sheep,

they were so filled with the wonder of what they had seen and heard that they glorified and praised God. They stopped everyone they met to tell about the glorious angels and their message.

When the baby was eight days old, he was given the name Jesus, as the angel had commanded.

It was the custom among the Jews when a baby boy was forty days old to bring him to the temple and present him to the Lord. Therefore a little more than a month after the baby Jesus was born, Mary and Joseph brought Him to Jerusalem.

In the city there was an old man named Simeon. He was one of the people who had been longing and praying most earnestly for the promised child to be born. God had spoken to Simeon, and told him that before he would die he would see the Saviour.

Just as Joseph and Mary brought the child Jesus into the temple, the Holy Spirit led Simeon there. Simeon knew at once that this baby was the Saviour. He took Jesus in his arms and, looking up to heaven, he said, "Now, Lord, I am ready to die, for I have seen the promised child who is to be the Saviour of the world and the glory of Thy people Israel."

In the temple there was also a very old lady who spent most of her time there praying to God. When she saw the baby Jesus, she, too, knew that He was the long-awaited Saviour. She carried the glad news to all the people in Jerusalem who had been waiting and longing for His coming.

Chapter 4
A STAR IN THE EAST
MATTHEW 2

Although the baby Jesus was now more than a month old, Mary and Joseph had not yet gone back to their own town of Nazareth. Perhaps they thought the baby was still too young to travel. While they were still in Bethlehem, a very strange thing happened.

In those days there were wise men in some of the eastern countries who used to study the stars at night. They did not know as much about the stars as we do, because they did not have telescopes; but still they did learn many things about the sky. They knew where to find many of the bright stars, which they studied night after night. They came to know a great deal about the movement of the stars.

Some of these wise men lived far to the east of the land of the Jews. Perhaps the country in which they lived was Persia, for in that climate the stars are very bright and easy to watch

One night, while these wise men were gazing into the sky, they saw a new star, an unusually bright one. This discovery excited them. As they watched the star, they could see it move. They were still more surprised. What could this mean?

In those days men believed that a bright new star like this had special meaning. Perhaps it meant that a child was born who would become a great king or a wise general. So the wise men watched this strangely moving star, and they decided it must have been sent to announce the birth of a great king.

They were so sure of this that they started out to find the prince whose birth the new star celebrated. They took along rich gifts for the baby king. They made the journey on camels, for most of the way led through deserts. During the hot day the wise men slept. They traveled in the cool night when they could see the star.

At last the wise men rode into the streets of Jerusalem. The people of the city gazed curiously at these important-looking strangers. Who could they be? Where had they come from?

Soon the strangers stopped. They called out to some of the passers-by, "Where is the child that is born King of the Jews? We have seen His star in the east, and we have come to worship Him."

A crowd gathered around to hear what the travelers were asking. The word passed from mouth to mouth: "These men say that a king of the Jews has been born. Where is he? We have not heard about any king."

Someone hurried into King Herod's palace and said, "Some foreign-looking men rode into Jerusalem today on their camels. They are asking everybody, 'Where is the child who is born to be King of the Jews?' They say that they saw his star in the east, and that they have come to worship him!"

King Herod was troubled by this news. Was it possible that some child had been born who was going to be king instead of him and his sons? He called in the chief priests and scribes and asked, "Tell me, where do the scriptures say that the Saviour is to be born?"

The priests and scribes knew about the old prophecy, for they spent all their time studying the Old Testament scriptures. They answered the king, "He is to be born in Bethlehem, because it was written by the proph-

et, 'And thou, Bethlehem, in the land of Judah, out of thee shall come forth a governor who shall be the shepherd of my people Israel.'"

Then King Herod sent for the strangers. He asked them exactly when they had seen the star. "Go to Bethlehem," he said. "Look there for the child. When you have found him, come back and tell me, for I, too, would like to go and worship him."

Of course, Herod had not the slightest intention of worshiping the newborn king, for he was a wicked, cruel man. He meant to kill the baby as soon as he found out where He was, so that the child could not grow up and become a king.

The wise men left the palace and started out for Bethlehem, which was only a few miles away. It was night. To their joy they saw the star shining in the sky above them. The star was moving. The wise men were sure it had been sent to guide them to the place where the child was. They followed it till they came to Bethlehem. At the very place where the young child was, the star stood still.

The wise men went into the house. There they saw the little child whose star they had followed so far, and they kneeled down and worshiped Him. Opening their treasures, they took out the precious gifts which they had brought — gold, and rare perfumes called frankincense and myrrh.

The wise men had found the child they were looking for, but they did not go back and tell Herod about Him. God, who was taking care of His son all the time, sent a dream, warning the wise men not to go back to Herod. They went home to their own country by another way, and Herod waited for them in vain.

Chapter 5

WARNED BY A DREAM
MATTHEW 2

After the wise men had gone back to their own country, God sent an angel to Joseph in a dream, who said, "Get ready quickly. Take the baby and His mother, and go away from here at once. Hurry far away into the land of Egypt. Stay there till I tell you to come back again. Herod will try to find the baby to kill Him."

Then Joseph got up, and woke Mary up. "God has sent me a dream," he told her. "An angel spoke to me and told me that Herod is going to try to kill the baby. We must go to Egypt, and stay there till He tells us to come back. Hurry and get ready. We must go at once, and get as far away as possible before morning comes."

Mary dressed herself as fast as she could. She wrapped some clothes together in a bundle, while Joseph went to find a donkey for her to ride on. Soon they were ready to start.

Mary wrapped her precious baby up warmly, holding Him in her arms as she rode on the donkey. Without telling anybody, they slipped away in the darkness. They rode all night, and when the daylight came they were many miles away.

And it was a good thing they were. When Herod discovered the wise men had gone home without telling him where to find the baby, he was furiously angry. For he was determined to kill the baby who was to become king.

He sent his soldiers to Bethlehem with orders to kill every baby boy in the whole town, from little new-born babies to those that were two years old. "Now," thought the wicked king, "the baby whose star the wise men saw will surely be killed."

Herod could not kill God's son! Jesus was safe in Egypt. He was lying in His mother's arms under the shade of a waving palm tree, and the warm Egyptian sun was smiling down upon them.

But what a scene of terror in Bethlehem! The soldiers went into every house, killing every baby boy they found. In vain the mothers tried to save their children. In vain they cried. They could not be comforted.

Not long afterward wicked Herod died. When Herod was dead, an angel of the Lord appeared again in a dream to Joseph in Egypt and said to him, "Arise, take the young child and His mother, and go back to the land of Israel, for the people who wished to kill the child are dead."

So Joseph took Jesus and Mary back to the land of Israel. But when he heard that Herod's son was now king, he was afraid to go near the city of Jerusalem where the king lived. Instead he went to Nazareth, far to the north of Jerusalem.

Chapter 6

THE BOY IN THE TEMPLE
LUKE 2

Jesus grew up in the little town of Nazareth. As he grew older He became a fine, tall boy. Joseph was a carpenter, and Jesus often helped him in his shop.

Although Jesus was a boy like other

boys, in one way He was very different from any other person who has ever lived. He never did anything wrong. He never even thought anything wrong, or wanted to do anything wrong. He could not, for He was the blessed Son of God.

All other children, since the time when Adam and Eve sinned, have been born with sinful hearts. Jesus was one of Eve's children, but He was also the Son of God. He did not inherit the sinful nature of His mother. He was perfectly good throughout His whole life.

Even as a small child Jesus showed how much He loved God. When Jewish boys were twelve years old they went along with their parents to Jerusalem to celebrate the Passover feast which was held there every year. Jesus was very happy when He was old enough to go to Jerusalem to God's temple.

Nazareth was sixty miles from Jerusalem — a great distance in those days. At the time of the Passover many people traveled to Jerusalem together. As they passed through the cities and villages, all along the way others joined those who were traveling from Nazareth, till there was a great procession of people on their way to keep the feast.

Some of the people walked, while others rode on donkeys. At noon they all sat down by the roadside to eat their simple lunch. At night they wrapped themselves in their coats and lay down on the ground to sleep together under the open sky.

After several days of traveling, the people from Nazareth reached Jerusalem. The Passover celebration lasted seven days. At the end of the week they started home again.

There were so many friends and neighbors traveling together that Joseph and Mary did not notice at first that Jesus was not with them. When they did miss Him, they did not worry. They thought, "He is surely somewhere in the crowd. Probably He is walking along with some of His friends."

For a whole day Joseph and Mary went on without Jesus. As they went along, they asked here and there, "Have you seen our son Jesus?"

The answer was always, "No, we have not seen Him. He has not been with us at all." Joseph and Mary inquired of everyone, but they could not find anyone who had seen Jesus. At last they became alarmed. Was their precious boy lost? What could have happened to Him?

There was nothing to do but to go back to Jerusalem. They had a whole day's walk back to the city. They inquired of everyone they met along the way, "Have you seen anything of our son? He is twelve years old, a fine, tall, strong boy." Always the answer was the same. No one had seen Jesus.

When Joseph and Mary reached Jerusalem, they spent two days walking up and down the streets of the city looking for Jesus. At last they looked for Him in the temple, and there they found Him. He was sitting among the learned men, called doctors of the law. He was listening to their talk, and He was asking them questions.

All the teachers were amazed to think that a twelve-year-old boy could give such wise answers to the questions they asked Him, and that He was asking them questions they could not answer.

Joseph and Mary were very much surprised to see Jesus talking to the doctors of the law. Yet they could not forget how anxious they had been. His mother said to Him, "Son, why have You done this? Your father and I have been looking everywhere for You, and have been very worried because we could not find You."

Jesus answered, "Why did you look for Me? Didn't you know that I must begin to do My Father's business?"

Jesus meant that He must begin to do the work of His Father in heaven. But Joseph and Mary did not understand this answer. They did not know that He meant there was work He must do for God.

Jesus went back to Nazareth with His parents. But Mary kept all these sayings in her heart, and wondered about them.

Chapter 7

THE PREACHER IN THE DESERT
MATTHEW 3; MARK 1; LUKE 3; JOHN 1

While Jesus was growing up in Nazareth, His cousin John, the son of Zacharias and Elisabeth, had gone to live in the wilderness. It was lonely there, but John wanted to be away from people so that he would have time to think about God.

God took good care of John, for He had great work for John to do. John was to preach to the Jewish people, to make them ready to listen to Jesus, who would soon begin to teach.

John lived a rough life in the desert. He ate locusts, as the people of the desert still do. There was plenty of honey which wild bees stored away in holes in the rocks. John dressed in a loose, rough shirt made of camel's hair, with a leather girdle around his waist.

While John was living in the desert, both he and Jesus were about thirty years old. It was time for them to begin the work that they had been born to do. God spoke to John in the wilderness, telling him to go and preach to the people, to prepare them for the coming of Jesus.

Gradually the people of Jerusalem and throughout the land of Judaea learned that there was a man preaching in the desert near the Jordan River. He was strange and wild-looking, dressed in rough camel's hair, wearing a leather girdle around his waist.

"Who is he?" they asked. "Where did he come from?" Nobody knew. "For a long time he has lived in the desert," people said. "He is a holy man, a prophet."

Great crowds came out to hear John preach. And what was this strange man saying? He was telling the people that they were sinful, for before people *look* for a Saviour, they must know why they *need* a Saviour, and what they must be saved from. "Turn away from your sins," John said to them. "For even now the axe is laid at the root of the tree. Every tree that does not bring forth good fruit will be cut down and burned."

The people were struck to the heart by John's preaching. Great numbers of them came to John and said, "We are sorry for our wickedness. We want to live better lives. What must we do?"

"Turn away from your sins, and be baptized," John said. Many who had been leading sinful lives listened to John. John baptized them in the Jordan River.

People began to ask, "Is it possible that John is the long-expected Saviour? Or can he be the prophet Elijah come back to life?" So many people flocked to hear him and be baptized, and there were so many questions about who he was, that at last the Jewish leaders in Jerusalem sent several priests and Levites down to the Jordan River where John was baptizing, to find out the truth.

"Who are you?" these messengers asked John. "Are you the Christ whom God has anointed to be our Saviour?" For the Jewish people called the Saviour whom they expected *Christ,* which means "anointed," since God had promised to anoint the man He sent to save them with a special power from the Holy Spirit.

"No," John said, "I am not the Christ."

"Are you Elijah?"

"No," John said, "I am not Elijah."

"Then who are you?" asked the priests. "We have been sent to find out."

"I am just a voice in the wilderness," John said, "crying, 'Prepare the way of the Lord.' There is one who will come after me who is mightier than I. He is so much greater than I am that I am not worthy to stoop down and untie His shoes." With such words as these John tried to prepare the people for the coming of Jesus.

The next day, as John was preaching, he saw Jesus Himself coming among the people to be baptized.

After Jesus had been baptized, He came up out of the water, praying. Then the heavens were opened, and the Holy Spirit came down in the form of a dove and rested on Jesus. At the same moment a voice came out of heaven, saying, "Thou art My beloved Son, in whom I am well pleased."

How surprised the people must have been! They looked at Jesus in awe. Many of them had thought that John was the expected Saviour, even after he had said, "I am not the Christ, but I come to prepare the way for Him."

Seeing how surprised they were, John said, "See! This is the Lamb of God, who takes away the sin of the world. This is the person I told you about when I said, 'After me there comes someone who is greater than I am.' I myself did not know who it would be, but God said to me, 'I will send My Spirit upon Him in the form of a dove, and the Holy Spirit will remain with Him. That is the one who is My Son.' Now I have seen this, and I have told you that this Jesus is the Son of God."

When the people went home that night, they could talk only of the strange things which had happened that day. Those who had been longing and praying for the Saviour to come — how happy they must have been that night!

Chapter 8
SATAN TALKS TO GOD'S SON
MATTHEW 4; MARK 1; LUKE 4

After Jesus had been baptized, the Spirit of God led Him into the wild and lonely wilderness, where only wild beasts made their homes. For forty days and forty nights Jesus stayed there. During all that time He had nothing to eat. Then, when He was very hungry, and weak from lack of food, the devil came to Him and tried to make Him do something wrong.

Satan knew that Jesus was perfectly good, and that He was the Son of God as well as the son of Mary. Sin and death had come into the world when Adam and Eve listened to Satan's lies and disobeyed God. Jesus had come to save people from sin and death. Now Satan tried to persuade Jesus to do wrong, as he had persuaded Adam and Eve so long ago.

Knowing how hungry Jesus was after eating nothing for forty days, the devil whispered slyly, "If you are God's son, turn this stone into bread so you will have something to eat."

Jesus answered, "God says man needs more than bread to live. He needs every word God has spoken."

Satan tried again. This time he took Jesus into Jerusalem and set Him on the highest point of the temple. "If you are the son of God," he said, "throw yourself down to the ground, for it is written in the scripture, 'He shall give His angels charge over thee, and in their hands they shall bear thee up, lest thou dash thy foot against a stone.'"

But Jesus answered, "It is also written in the scriptures, 'Thou shalt not tempt the Lord thy God.'"

Still Satan did not give up. He took Jesus to the top of a very high mountain. In a moment of time he showed Jesus all the kingdoms of the world and their glory. Then he said to Jesus, "All this power and glory belongs to me, and I can give it to whomever I wish. If you fall down and worship me, I will give it to you."

But Jesus had come into the world to conquer the devil, not to worship him. So He said, "Get thee behind me, Satan, for it is written in the scriptures, 'Thou shalt worship the Lord thy God, and Him only shalt thou serve.'"

The devil saw that Jesus resisted all his temptations. For a time he left Jesus alone.

Jesus had defeated Satan, but He was tired and worn out and almost starved with hunger. God sent angels down from heaven to look after the weak and starving Jesus. They gave Him all that He needed, and soon He was rested and strong again.

Chapter 9
JESUS CHOOSES HIS DISCIPLES
JOHN 1

One day, as John and two of his followers were standing together, Jesus walked past them. John said, "Behold the Lamb of God!"

The two who were with John could not bear to lose sight of this stranger whom John called "the Lamb of God." They left John standing there and followed Jesus at a distance. Jesus turned and saw them. "What are you looking for?" He asked.

They said, "Master, where do You live?"

"Come and see," Jesus answered.

So the two men went along to the place where Jesus was staying. They spent several hours with Him. How happy they were to listen to His wonderful words! They became His followers, or disciples, as people in those days called men who followed a great teacher.

One of the two men who visited Jesus that day was Andrew. The first thing Andrew did after spending that afternoon with Jesus was to find his brother Simon. "Simon," he said, "I have a wonderful thing to tell you.

273

We have found the long-expected Saviour."

Simon went with Andrew to talk to Jesus, and he, too, became one of Jesus' closest friends. Jesus gave Simon a new name which fitted him very well — the name Peter, which means "a rock."

The next day Jesus found a man named Philip whom He wanted to be one of His disciples. He said to Philip, "Follow Me!" Philip followed Jesus gladly. He wanted his friend Nathanael to know this new teacher too. He said to Nathanael, "We have found the long-expected one, about whom Moses and the prophets wrote. His name is Jesus of Nazareth."

Nathanael could hardly believe this news. The Jews did not expect the Saviour to come from Nazareth. The prophets had said He would be born in Bethlehem. Nathanael had never heard the story of Jesus' birth in the stable in Bethlehem. "Can any good thing come out of Nazareth?" Nathanael asked doubtfully.

"Come and see," Philip urged.

So the two friends set out. When Jesus saw Nathanael coming toward Him, He said, "There is a truly good man."

"How do you know what kind of man I am?" asked Nathanael in surprise.

Jesus answered, "Before Philip called you, when you were sitting under the fig tree, I saw you, and I knew what kind of man you were."

Nathanael saw that Jesus knew things no man could possibly know. He opened his heart to Jesus. "Master," he said, "truly You are the Son of God, You are the King of Israel."

"Just because I said I saw you under the fig tree, you believe on Me?" Jesus said. "You shall see greater things than this. You shall see heaven opened, and the angels of God coming down on Me."

In this way Jesus gathered a little group of friends, or disciples. They followed Him wherever He went, listening to His teaching.

Chapter 10
JESUS AT THE WEDDING FEAST
JOHN 2

A few miles from Nazareth was a little town called Cana. The people of the two villages probably visited each other often, since they lived so near each other. Their children played together in the fields, and every year the people walked together down the road to Jerusalem to celebrate the Passover.

Mary, the mother of Jesus, had some friends in Cana. A few days after Jesus met His first disciples, these people invited Mary and Jesus and His friends to a wedding party. In those days it was the custom to celebrate a wedding by holding a great feast. Sometimes the party

lasted two or three days. The guests had a good time, talking and eating and drinking.

Many people besides Jesus and His friends went to the wedding in Cana — more people than had been expected. Before the feast was over, the servants discovered that there was not enough wine for all the guests. They were embarrassed.

Mary discovered the trouble. She knew that her son had great power. She did not ask Him to help, but she said to Him simply, "They have no wine." To the servants she said, "Do whatever He tells you." She believed that Jesus would help them.

Near at hand there were six stone jars, each one almost as large as a barrel. Water for the household was kept in these jars, for the Jews washed their hands and feet before eating. Jesus said to the servants, "Fill the jars with water." When they had done this, He said, "Pour some out and take it to the ruler of the feast."

The servants had filled the jars with water. What they drew out was not water, but fragrant, miraculous wine. Can you imagine how surprised they must have been when they discovered this?

The man who was chosen to be the ruler of the feast had to taste the food before it was served to the other guests. The servants brought him some of the new wine, but they did not tell him where it came from. When he had tasted it, the ruler of the feast said to the bridegroom, "Usually people serve the best wine first, and when people have drunk to their satisfaction, they set out poorer wine. You have kept the best till now."

This miracle was a sign of the wonderful power which Jesus had, and which He used to help others. It was the first time people realized that Jesus could do things no one else could do. His disciples remembered that He had said to Nathanael, "You shall see greater things than this." And they believed on Him.

Chapter 11
THE FATHER'S HOUSE
JOHN 2, 3

Soon after Jesus chose Peter and the others to be His disciples, they traveled together to the city of Jerusalem. It was the time of the year when the feast of the Passover was held, and from all parts of the land people set out for Jerusalem.

For many, many years the Jews had held this feast in memory of that terrible night when Israel fled out of Egypt. In that night every first-born child among the Egyptians died, but God passed over the houses of the Israelites which were sprinkled with the blood of a lamb. To show their gratitude, every Jew twelve years old or older celebrated the feast in Jerusalem for one week every year.

Jesus and His disciples went to the feast with all the rest of the people. Jesus was eager to visit the temple, which was His Father's house. But when He got there, He found only noisy confusion in the court of the temple. The place was crowded with men selling oxen and sheep and doves to be used as sacrifices. At other tables men were changing foreign money into the kind of coins the priests said had to be used to make a gift to the temple. The bellowing of the animals mingled with the bargaining of the merchants and the loud complaints of those who thought they were being cheated. The temple looked like a marketplace instead of a holy place where God was worshiped.

All this made Jesus very angry. He made a whip out of cords and with it drove the merchants and their animals out of the temple. He overturned the tables of the money changers, and told the men who sold doves to take them somewhere else. "Do not make My Father's house a marketplace," He said.

275

The Jews said to Him, "What right have You to do this?" Jesus answered, "Destroy this temple, and in three days I will raise it up again."

The Jews thought He meant that He could rebuild in three days their beautiful temple which had taken forty-six years to build. But when Jesus said "temple," He meant His body, which the Jews would crucify, and which would rise again from the grave in three days. Even His disciples did not understand what Jesus meant, but after His death and resurrection they remembered that He had said this.

Many others who saw Jesus and heard His teaching began to believe in Him. They saw Him heal sick people just by laying His hands on them, or by speaking to them. They knew that He said the truth when He said He was the Son of God.

Those who truly believed were baptized by the disciples.

Some of the people who now followed Jesus had been baptized earlier by John, who was still preaching and baptizing near the Jordan River. John's disciples came to him and said, "Teacher, the man whom you called the Lamb of God is now baptizing people. Many are leaving us and listening to Him."

John answered, "I told you that I am not the Saviour. I was sent to prepare the way before Him. I am very happy that He has come. I am from the earth, but He comes from heaven. God sent Him, and He speaks the words of God. God loves Him. Whoever believes on the Son of God has everlasting life. Whoever does not believe on Him shall not have everlasting life, but shall remain under God's anger with those who are sinful."

Chapter 12
A VISIT BY NIGHT
JOHN 3

Now I shall tell you something very hard to understand.

Before Jesus was born as a little baby in Bethlehem, He was with God in heaven. *He Himself was God.* Jesus always has been God. He was God long before God made the world and the first man and woman. He is God the Son.

We know that there is only one God. But that one God is three persons — three separate and equal persons — God the Father, God the Son, and God the Holy Spirit. Before Jesus came to earth as Mary's son, He already was God the Son. He lived in heaven with God the Father and God the Holy Spirit. The Father created the heavens and the

earth. The Holy Spirit lives in our hearts today, and makes us love what is right. The Son, Jesus, died for our sins. These three are one God, and have always lived. They never *began* to live, for they have no beginning and they have no end. They are eternally God. We know that this is true because Jesus told us.

This Jesus who walked about on earth was truly God. He went about healing the sick and preaching. And the people loved Him. They listened eagerly to His preaching.

Among those who listened to Jesus was a man named Nicodemus. Nicodemus was a ruler of the Jews, a Pharisee. The Pharisees were men who kept all the laws of Moses very strictly; and they kept many other rules besides, rules which they themselves had added to God's law. They were very proud of their strictness and thought they were better than other people, even better than Jesus. They would not listen to Jesus.

But Nicodemus was not like the other Pharisees. He heard Jesus teach and saw the miracles, and he wondered what kind of man Jesus was. He did not quite dare to visit Jesus openly, for fear the other Pharisees would make fun of him. But he did want to know more about this teacher who talked about God and His kingdom.

So Nicodemus visited Jesus at night. He said to Jesus, "Teacher, we know that God sent You, for no one could do these miracles You do unless God is with Him."

Jesus said to him, "No man can see the kingdom of God unless he is born again." That was a strange answer. Nicodemus did not understand. Surely he wished to see the kingdom of God. But he was a grown man. How could he be born again? Must he become a baby again?

Jesus said, "Truly, truly, unless a person is born of water and the Spirit, he cannot enter the kingdom of God." Then Jesus went on to explain. No one of us can be a child of God unless we first get a new heart. Jesus made that very emphatic when He said, "Truly, truly. . . ." But if we believe in Jesus, the Holy Spirit gives us a new heart. We are "born again." We become children of God.

You and I cannot understand how the Holy Spirit gives us a new heart, just as we cannot understand how the wind blows. But Jesus said to Nicodemus, "God so loved the world that He gave His only Son, that whosoever believeth on Him should not perish, but have everlasting life." To be born again, we must believe in Jesus.

Nicodemus was a "good" man. He kept the law of God carefully. But that was not enough to open the way into the kingdom of God. Keeping rules does not get us into the kingdom of God at all. Unless the Holy Spirit gives us a new heart, and we put our trust in Jesus who died to pay for our sins, we cannot see the kingdom of God.

Nicodemus listened carefully. He had never heard such strange words. He could not understand them. But when he went away, he thought and thought about it; and after a while he did believe in Jesus. He was born again, and he became a child of God.

Chapter 13
THE WOMAN AT JACOB'S WELL
JOHN 4

After a time Jesus left Judaea and started back to Nazareth, the town in Galilee where He had grown up. This was a distance of more than sixty miles.

As Jesus and His disciples walked along, they came to a city of Samaria where there was a very old well, dug long ago by Jacob.

In that hot country, water is very precious. There was usually only one well in a whole village. Every day the people brought their pitchers there and drew up as much water as they needed. The well of Jacob probably had a low stone railing around the top to keep people from falling in. This stone railing made a good seat. Very likely a few palm trees grew over it and made the spot shady.

Jesus was tired from His journey. He sat down by Jacob's well to rest. It was noon. The disciples went to the village to buy some food.

While Jesus was sitting there, a Samaritan woman came to the well to get water. Jesus was hot and thirsty, and He was tired. He asked the woman to give Him a drink of water.

The woman was very much surprised that Jesus, who was a Jew, should ask for a drink from a Samaritan. The Jews hated the Samaritans, and would have nothing to do with them, for many Samaritans had married heathen women, and though they worshiped the true God, their religion was a mixture of truth and idol worship.

The woman asked Jesus, "How is it that You are willing to ask me, a Samaritan woman, for a drink?"

Jesus said, "If you knew who I am, you would ask Me to give you living water."

The woman said, "Sir, the well is deep, and You have no pitcher to let down into it. How can You get that living water?"

"Whoever drinks this water will be thirsty again," Jesus answered. "Whoever drinks the water I give him will never be thirsty again, for the water I give him will be a well of water springing up inside him unto eternal life."

Jesus was not speaking of the kind of water we drink. He meant He would put His Spirit in her heart, and that her soul would be refreshed by His Spirit, just as her body was by water.

The woman did not understand this. She said, "Sir, give me this water, so that I will never be thirsty again, nor have to come here to get water."

To make the woman realize that He was not an ordinary man, Jesus told her many things about her past life. She was startled. How could this man know about these things she had done long ago? He had never seen her before! She said to Him, "Sir, I see You are a prophet."

Then she asked Jesus something which had often troubled her. "Our fathers," she said, "always have worshiped in this mountain. But you Jews say that Jerusalem is the place where men ought to worship. Which is right?"

Jesus was always teaching the people about His heavenly Father. When the Samaritan woman asked this question, Jesus answered it in such a way that He taught her more about God than she had ever known.

"God does not command us to worship Him in any special place," He said. "It is in our hearts that we must worship Him. God is a Spirit, and they that worship Him must worship Him in spirit and in truth. That is the kind of people God is looking for to worship Him."

More than ever the woman realized that she was talking to a remarkable person. She said, "I know that the Saviour is coming, and when He comes, He will tell us the truth about everything." Even the Samaritans knew about the promised Saviour, and longed for His coming.

Jesus said to her, "I am the Saviour!"

The woman was so excited by this news that she left her water pitcher by the well and hurried into the city. "Come with me and see a man who told me everything I did in my whole life," she said to everyone she met. "Don't you think this must be the Saviour?"

Many of the people went with her to see for themselves. Some of them believed in Jesus because of what the woman said. They begged Him to stay with them, so that they might hear His wonderful words.

Jesus stayed two days with the Samaritans. Many accepted Him as the Saviour. No longer did they believe just because of what the woman told them. After they had heard Him, they knew that this truly was the Christ, anointed by God to be the Saviour of the world.

Chapter 14
THE FATHER WHO BELIEVED
JOHN 4

Everywhere Jesus went the people were eager to hear His blessed words. The disciples had accepted Him gladly, without hesitation. So had many of the Jews in Jerusalem who saw His miracles. Even the Pharisee Nicodemus had said, "We know that You are a teacher come from God."

When Jesus passed through the land of the Samaritans, many more people believed on Him as they heard His words and saw His works of healing the sick. "The long-expected Saviour has come," the people said, and they were filled with joy.

After Jesus had stayed two days with the Samaritans, He continued His journey into Galilee. The people of Galilee were glad Jesus had come. They, too, had been in Jerusalem for the Passover, and had seen the miracles Jesus did there. They wanted to know more about this teacher. The sick and the lame and the blind hoped that He would heal them.

In Capernaum, which was a large city of Galilee, there lived a nobleman whose little son was very sick. The poor father had almost given up all hope that the boy would live. He was heartbroken.

This father had heard of the miracles Jesus did. He knew about the water being turned into wine at the wedding in Cana, which was only twenty miles from his home. He had heard of the people Jesus healed at the feast in Jerusalem. The news that Jesus had come to Galilee and was staying at Cana gave him hope. Could he possibly get this wonderful healer to come and see his son? Perhaps his boy, too, might be made well again!

The anxious father hurried to Cana. He found Jesus and told him about the sick boy. He begged Jesus to come and heal his son.

Jesus did not go down to Capernaum. He could cure the sick boy without going to see him. He said to the father, "Go back home, for your son is living."

The man believed what Jesus said. He went home, happy and confident. On the way his servants met him with the glad news that the boy was better, and his fever was gone.

"When did he begin to get better?" the father asked.

"Yesterday, at one o'clock, the fever left him," the servants answered. And the father remembered that this was the very moment when Jesus had said, "Your son will live."

What a happy house that was that

night! The thankful father knew that his dear son had been given back to him from the very door of death.

He and all his family believed in Jesus, because they had seen His great power.

Chapter 15
THE MOB THAT WANTED A MIRACLE
LUKE 4

At last Jesus came to His own city, Nazareth, where He had grown up. His mother and His brothers and His childhood friends still lived there. They must have been eager to see Him again, for since the Passover in Jerusalem everyone had been talking about the miracles Jesus did there.

It was Jesus' custom, wherever He happened to be on the Sabbath day, to go to the synagogue, as the Jews called their meeting place. He often read parts of the Old Testament to the people, and explained what it meant. And so, on that Sabbath day which Jesus spent in Nazareth, He went as usual to the synagogue, and stood up to read to the people.

In those days the Bible was not printed in one book of many pages, as it is today. It was written on long, wide strips, each book rolled up separately. One of these rolls — the roll of the prophet Isaiah — was given to Jesus to read.

Isaiah had lived hundreds of years before the birth of Jesus, but God had told him many things that would happen after his death. Many times Isaiah had prophesied about the Saviour whom God would send to save His people. These prophecies were often read in the synagogue on the Sabbath day. The people knew many of them by heart.

As Jesus stood up to read from Isaiah, the people listened very attentively. He opened the roll to the sixty-first chapter, the first verse.

These are the words He read: "The Spirit of the Lord is upon me, because He has anointed me to preach good tidings to the poor; He has sent me to proclaim release to the captives and recovering of sight to the blind; to set at liberty them that are bruised; to proclaim the acceptable year of the Lord."

When He had read this to the people, Jesus rolled up the book and gave it back to the attendant. Then He sat down — for it was the custom in those days for the speaker to sit. The people listened closely. They had heard such strange reports of His teachings and His miracles! They were eager to see for themselves.

"Today," Jesus said, "these words that I have read have come true in your sight." Jesus meant by this that He was the one whom God had sent to preach the gospel to the poor, to free the captives, to give sight to the blind, to deliver prisoners, and to preach the coming of the Lord.

How do you think the people felt when He said this? Did they say, "The Saviour has come at last! What a great honor that He should be one of us! How proud we are that we have known Him all His life!"

No, that is not what they said. Instead, they said, "How can this man be the Saviour? He is only a carpenter's son. We know His family — His mother Mary and His brothers. They are common people, just like us. What right has He to claim to be the Saviour? Why doesn't He perform some miracles for us to see?"

The people became angry. They got up and pushed Jesus out of the synagogue. The city of Nazareth was built on a high hill. Several of the streets ended just at the top of a steep cliff. The angry mob pushed Jesus along one of these streets, intending to throw Him over the cliff and kill Him.

But they had no power over the Son of God. Jesus passed right through the middle of the crowd and went on His way.

Chapter 16
THE CROWD AT JESUS' DOOR
MATTHEW 8; MARK 1; LUKE 4

After the people of Nazareth tried to kill Him, Jesus went to Capernaum. This town was built on the shore of a beautiful lake called the Sea of Galilee.

The people of Nazareth, who had been so curious to see some of Jesus' wonderful miracles, did not see them. Because they did not believe in Him, Jesus healed only a few sick people there. The people of Capernaum, however, were eager to listen to Jesus. He taught in their synagogue every Sabbath day, and because they were so anxious to listen to His wonderful words, Jesus spent a great deal of time with them.

The people were astonished at the words Jesus spoke, for He talked as if He had a right to tell them about God and to teach them how to live. And indeed He did have this right, for He was the very Son of God Himself. When the people heard His words, it seemed as if a great light had come into their souls.

One Sabbath, after teaching in the synagogue, Jesus went to Peter's house in Capernaum. Peter's mother-in-law was very sick with a fever. Jesus came to her bedside, and took hold of her hands. Lifting her up, He commanded the fever to go away. Immediately the fever left her, and she got up and helped prepare supper.

This same Sabbath, when the sun was setting, the people of Capernaum brought their sick friends to Jesus. They came at the end of the day because they did not want to break the Sabbath, which for the Jews lasted from sunset Friday till sunset Saturday. The Pharisees were very strict about the rules for keeping the Sabbath. It was against their rules to heal a sick person on the Sabbath, or to carry anyone or anything anywhere.

That evening it seemed as if the whole city was gathered at Jesus' door. When Jesus saw this great crowd, He laid His hands on the sick and healed them. Jesus came into this world to heal people from sin and its results. Sickness is one of the unhappy things sin has brought into the world. Jesus was glad to heal people and to help them.

The next day Jesus got up very early in the morning, long before it was light. He went by Himself to a quiet place where there was no danger of anyone disturbing Him, for He wanted to talk to His Father in heaven. He often went away alone so that He could talk to God. Jesus loved God perfectly, and it made Him very happy to be alone with God.

When morning came, Jesus' disciples and friends could not find Him. They became worried. Where could their wonderful teacher and healer be? Would they never see Him again?

At last they found Him in the desert, where He had gone to pray. They gathered close around Him and begged Him to stay with them. But Jesus said, "I must go to the other cities also. God has sent Me to teach all the people."

Jesus went through all the cities of that part of Galilee, preaching in the synagogues and healing the sick. The people who loved Him most said to themselves, "Well, if He cannot stay with us, we shall have to go with Him. We must be close to Him to hear what He says and to see the wonderful things He does." And so, as Jesus went from one city to another, great crowds of people began to follow Him.

Chapter 17
THROUGH THE ROOF TO JESUS
MATTHEW 9; MARK 2; LUKE 5

After teaching in many of the towns of Galilee, Jesus came back to Capernaum. As soon as the people there saw that their beloved teacher had come back to them, they hurried to see Him. There was such a crowd that the house could not hold one more person, and even outside the people crowded around the door to listen.

In Capernaum there was a poor, sick man who could not walk because his whole body trembled and shook. He had to lie in bed all the time, and his family had to feed and dress him. No doubt this poor man had heard of all the people whom Jesus had cured on His first visit to Capernaum, but he had not been able to go to Jesus because he could not walk.

As he lay on his bed this man heard a great noise outside. What was happening? Soon four of his friends rushed in. "Jesus has come again!" they cried. "We are going to carry you to Him, and He will make you well!"

Each of the friends took a corner of the mattress on which the sick man lay. They carried him out of the house and along the street till they reached the place where Jesus was. But when they reached the house, they discovered they could not get in. They could not even get near the door because of the great crowd that had come to see Jesus. It seemed as if all the sick and lame and blind people of the whole city were gathered in front of that door.

What a disappointment for the poor man and his friends! But now that they had come this far, they refused to give up. At last they thought of a plan.

Outside the house there was a stairway leading up to the roof. In that country such stairways were very common. The houses were only one story high, and the people often spent a lot of time on the flat roofs of their homes. Sometimes they slept there on hot nights.

Up this outside stairway the friends of the sick man carefully carried him. They laid him down on the roof and began to pull up the tiles of which the roof was made. When they had made a large hole, they tied a strong rope to each corner of the mattress. Then, with one man holding each corner, they very carefully lowered the bed right down into the room below, in front of Jesus.

Jesus was glad to see how eager

these people were to get their friend cured, and that they truly believed Jesus could heal him. But Jesus did not say to the sick man, "I will heal you." He said something much more startling: "Son, your sins are forgiven."

Among the great crowd of people in that house there were many learned scribes and Pharisees who had come to see Jesus and to listen to Him. They were horrified to hear Jesus say, "Your sins are forgiven." They said to each other, "What right has any man to say such things? No one can forgive sins except God."

Of course they were quite right that only God can forgive sins. But they were wrong because they refused to believe that Jesus was God. Jesus said to this man, "Your sins are forgiven," just to make the scribes and Pharisees understand that He was God.

Jesus could read the thoughts of the scribes and the Pharisees. He said to them, "Why do you think I have no right to forgive sins? I will prove to you that I am God, and that I have a right to forgive sins. I will do something only God can do." Turning to the sick man, He said, "Get up, pick up your mattress, and go home."

The sick man had been unable to walk for a long time. But when Jesus spoke to him like this, he stood up like a well man, rolled up his mattress under his arm, and walked away.

No doctor could have cured a man in this way. This cure showed that Jesus was not man, but God; and because He was God, He could also forgive sins. And just as He forgave this man's sin, so, if we pray to Him in heaven, He will forgive us our sins.

Chapter 18
MATTHEW AND HIS FEAST
MATTHEW 9; MARK 2; LUKE 5

Every day a man named Matthew sat by the side of one of the main roads near Capernaum. He collected taxes from the Jews for the Roman government, and the main road leading through the city was a convenient place for the people to pay the money.

One day, as Jesus walked along this road with His friends, He said to Matthew, "Follow Me!" for He wanted the tax collector to be one of His disciples. Matthew was glad to be chosen. He got up and followed Jesus at once.

From that time on Matthew was one of Jesus' faithful friends, and followed Him wherever He went. Many years later he wrote the first book of the New Testament, telling about the life of Jesus.

The first thing Matthew did after Jesus called him to be a disciple was to invite Jesus and the other disciples to a fine party in honor of his new master. Most of Matthew's guests were tax collectors, or publicans, as the Jews called those who collected taxes.

No people were more hated by the Jews than these publicans, because they worked for the Roman government. The Jews were a proud people who hated their Roman rulers. They wanted a king of their own. They hated to have to pay taxes to the Romans, and they especially despised the Jewish people who worked for the Romans to collect these taxes. Besides this, many of the publicans were dishonest and used their position to extort more tax money from the poor people than was actually due. The extra money they used to line their own pockets.

Most of the Jews would not associate in any way with the tax collectors, but the Pharisees hated them most of all. The Pharisees thought they were much better than ordinary men. They would not even talk to a publican, much less go into his house. They were shocked to see Jesus actually eating with Matthew and his friends. "Why does your teacher eat with publicans and sinners?" they asked the disciples.

Jesus heard the question. He did not wait for the disciples to answer. He said, "People that are well do not need a doctor. I did not come to help good people, but to call sinners to be sorry for their sins."

Jesus meant to say, "I am the great doctor. I have come to cure the worst sickness of all, which is sin. You Pharisees are sure you are so good that you do not need a doctor. These people know that they need Me. If they are great sinners, then they are just the ones I have come to help. That is why I eat with them!"

Chapter 19

THE WITHERED HAND MADE WELL

MATTHEW 12; MARK 3; LUKE 6

One of the laws which the scribes and Pharisees were most strict about was the Sabbath law. You and I also rest from our everyday work on the Lord's day, and go to church to worship Him and learn about Him. But the scribes and Pharisees were so strict about keeping the Sabbath that they would not even help a person who was in trouble or pain.

One Sabbath Jesus went to the synagogue as usual. There was a great crowd there to hear Him teach. Among them were some Pharisees. As Jesus stood up to teach, He saw a man whose right hand was withered and useless. The Pharisees knew this man was there among them, and they knew that Jesus sometimes healed the sick on the Sabbath. They watched to see if they could catch Him breaking the Sabbath again.

Jesus knew just what they were thinking. After the service was over, He called to the man to stand up where everyone could see him. Then Jesus said to the Pharisees, "Is it lawful on the Sabbath day to do good or to do harm, to save a life or to destroy it?"

No one answered a word. Jesus looked around at all of them with anger. He was grieved because they had such hard hearts. Then He turned to the man and said, "Stretch out your hand." The man lifted his lifeless hand, which he had not been able to use for many years. It was perfectly well!

The Pharisees were filled with fury. They plotted together what they could do to Jesus. But the people adored Jesus, because He was always ready to help them, just as He had healed this man with the withered hand. When Jesus talked to them about His Father in heaven, they listened eagerly, and many believed that He was the Son of God. Great crowds followed Him everywhere. Jesus' popularity made the scribes and Pharisees very jealous. They hated Him because He did not look up to them, and often spoke against their teachings.

Jesus went up the mountain to pray. He was so happy talking to His Father that He stayed there all night. When the morning came, He called His disciples to the mountain. He chose twelve of them to be His special followers, or apostles. After He had gone back to His Father in heaven, these men were to tell the whole world what they had seen and heard.

The twelve whom Jesus chose were Peter, his brother Andrew, James and his brother John (both of these were sons of Zebedee), Philip, Bartholomew who came to Jesus at the very beginning of His teaching, Thomas, Matthew the publican who had held a feast for Jesus, James and his brother Judas (the two sons of Alphaeus), Simon, and Judas Iscariot. These twelve men stayed close to Jesus and followed Him wherever He went for about two years more, until His work on earth was finished.

Chapter 20
THE SERMON ON THE MOUNT
MATTHEW 5-7; LUKE 6

Because there was such a great crowd of people following Him, Jesus went up the side of a mountain and sat down where all the people could see and hear Him. The disciples seated themselves beside Him and all the other people in a great half-circle below Him. For a long time He talked to them.

Don't you wish you could have been one of the people who sat on the hillside that day and listened to Jesus? We cannot see Him and hear Him talk, as they did that day. But even though we live long afterward, we, too, know what Jesus said as He talked to the people.

One of Jesus' disciples was Matthew, who had been a tax collector when Jesus called him. God told Matthew to write down Jesus' words, so that this wonderful sermon on the mountain would not be forgotten. God helped him to write it without a mistake. So, you see, Jesus talked that day not only to that great crowd of people who were sitting on the mountainside below Him, but also to us, and to all the people in the world.

These are some of the things Jesus said that day:

"Blessed are those who hunger and thirst after righteousness, for they shall be filled." Jesus meant that those people are blessed whose longing to be good is just as real as being hungry and thirsty. God gives good hearts to those who long for them.

"Blessed are the merciful, for they shall obtain mercy," Jesus told the people. If we are kind to those who are weak and sinful and suffering, God will remember it, and will be kind to us when we are weak and sinful.

Jesus said, "Blessed are the pure in heart, for they shall see God. Blessed are the peacemakers, for they shall be called sons of God." You have the blessing of Jesus when you try to do right because you love Him, even if your friends make fun of you and try to stop you. When people sneer at you, and say mean things about you because you are trying to do what pleases God, do not be discouraged. Be glad, for you will have a great reward in heaven. The prophets long ago were treated the very same way.

Jesus gave encouragement to His disciples and to all who trust in Him. "You are the light of the world," He said. "Let your light shine before men, that they may see your good works, and glorify your Father who is in heaven." When we love Jesus, and try to show our love in the way we live, we are shining for Him.

Jesus went on, "You have heard that it was said, 'Love your neighbor, and hate your enemy.' But I say to you, 'Love your enemies. Bless those who curse you. Pray for those who try to harm you.' For if you love only those who love you, you do not deserve a reward. Even sinners do that. You should try to be perfect, as your Father in heaven is perfect.

"If someone does something which hurts you, forgive him. For you yourself do many wrong things, and your heavenly Father forgives you. If you do not forgive those who treat you badly, neither will your heavenly Father forgive the bad things you do.

"Trust God to take care of you, for He knows everything you need. Remember how wonderfully God takes care of the birds, and the lilies of the field. They do not work hard, and yet God takes care of them. How much more will He take care of you!"

As Jesus was telling the people these things, they listened very quietly so that they would not miss a word. The things which Jesus spoke seemed very wonderful to them, for He talked as if He knew God, as if He had come down from heaven to bring them a special message from the heavenly Father. Many times He spoke as if He was God Himself, and the people listened in amazement.

When Jesus first began to teach, the people thought He was a wise prophet or teacher. But as they listened to Him and saw His miracles, many began to believe that He was truly the Christ, anointed by God to be their Saviour.

Chapter 21
JESUS GIVES BACK HEALTH AND LIFE
MATTHEW 8; MARK 1; LUKE 5, 7

After talking to the people on the mountainside, Jesus went down the mountain, and the great crowd of people followed Him. Some of them were sick, or lame, or blind, and hoped that Jesus would heal them. But all the people, the sick and the well, tried to keep away from one man who had listened to Jesus and was now following Him.

This man had the terrible disease called leprosy. His body was gradually wasting away. No cure for this disease was known at the time of Jesus. Lepers were not allowed to live with other people, or even to come near them.

Sick and lonely and unhappy, the man with leprosy came as near to Jesus as he dared. There he kneeled down and bowed his head to the ground, saying, "Lord, if You are willing, You can make me well."

Jesus was not afraid of this dreadful disease. He stretched out His hand and laid it tenderly on the leper's shoulder and said, "I am willing. Be made well!" Immediately the

22: JESUS STILLING THE STORM

23: THE FEEDING OF THE FIVE THOUSAND

man's sores disappeared and his flesh became clean and fresh and healthy.

"Don't tell anybody," Jesus said to the man, "but go to the priest, and offer the gift Moses commanded." But what had happened to him was so wonderful that the man could not keep quiet. He told everybody he met about it.

It was hard for people to believe that anyone having such a dreadful disease as leprosy could be cured. Soon, however, a much more wonderful thing happened, so that they could no longer doubt Jesus' power.

As Jesus went about the country teaching, He came to a city called Nain. His disciples were with Him as usual. Many others who were merely curious about His teaching and His miracles were walking along with them.

As Jesus and His companions approached the city, they met a funeral procession. A young man of the city had died, and the people were taking his body to be buried. His mother walked at the head of the procession, weeping as she went. She had lost her husband before this, and now her only son was dead too. Who would look after her now?

Jesus saw the weeping mother and said tenderly to her, "Do not cry." He motioned with His hand, and the men who were carrying the young man's body stood still. "Young man, get up!" Jesus said. At these words the dead man sat up and began to talk.

Everyone gasped in amazement. Since the world began, no doctor had ever been able to bring a dead man back to life. Only God can make the dead live again. The people began to praise God. They said, "A great prophet has appeared among us," and "God has visited His people!"

Chapter 22

STORIES WHICH JESUS TOLD
MATTHEW 13; MARK 4; LUKE 8

One day Jesus sat down by the shore of the beautiful Sea of Galilee. A great crowd gathered to listen to what He said. Jesus got into a boat, so that everyone could see and hear Him. As they listened, Jesus told them some stories which had a hidden meaning. These stories we call parables.

The first story Jesus told was the parable of the sower:

There was a man who went out to sow seed in his field. As he sowed, some seed fell by the wayside, and the birds came and ate it. Some fell in rocky places where there was not much earth. This seed grew quickly, but when the sun came up, it withered, because it did not have enough moisture.

Other seed fell among the thorns, and the thorns grew up with the grain, and choked the grain. Still other seed fell on good ground, and grew, and bore fruit, some a hundredfold, some sixtyfold, some thirtyfold.

After Jesus had told this little story, He explained the meaning of the parable to His disciples. The seed is the word of God. When people hear God's word, but do not understand it, immediately Satan comes and takes away the words which they have heard, and they forget them. These people are the seed sown by the wayside, which the birds pick up and eat.

The seed sown in rocky places means the people who hear the word of God with joy, but who have no root in themselves. When trouble comes, or when they are laughed at for being Christians, they give up. They believe only for a little while.

The seed sown among the thorns refers to the people who hear the word of God but who are so busy with the cares of this world or with attempting to get rich that the word they have heard is choked by other things.

The seed sown upon good ground stands for the people who hear God's word, and understand it, and let it grow in their lives in love and goodness.

Jesus told the people another little story or parable:

The kingdom of heaven is like a man who sowed good seed in his field. During the night his enemy came and sowed weeds among the wheat, and went away again.

When the wheat grew up, the weeds grew up too. The man's servants said to him, "Sir, did you not sow good seed in your field? Then why is it full of weeds?"

The man said, "An enemy has done this."

"Shall we go and pull up the weeds?" the servants asked.

"No," their master said, "for there would be too much danger of pulling up the wheat at the same time. Let both grow together till the harvest, and then I will have the reapers gather the weeds and burn them, and gather the wheat into my barn."

Afterward, when Jesus went into the house where He was staying, the disciples asked Him to explain the parable of the wheat and the weeds. He said to them, "I am the one who sows good seed. The field is the world. The good seed is the people who love God. The weeds are those who serve the devil. The enemy that sowed the weeds is the devil himself. The harvest is the end of the world; the reapers are the angels.

"Just as the weeds are gathered up and burned with fire, so it shall be at the end of the world. I will send My angels, and they will gather all the people who serve the devil instead of God, and will throw them into the fire. But the children of God will shine forth as the sun in the kingdom of their Father."

Is it any wonder that those who heard this teaching were surprised? If Jesus was just an ordinary man, as the Pharisees said He was, how could He say, "At the end of the world, I will send My angels"? No wonder the people were surprised. No wonder they said, "No man ever spoke like this!"

Chapter 23
THE WINDS AND THE WAVES OBEY
MATTHEW 8; MARK 4; LUKE 8

For several days Jesus continued to teach the people by the Sea of Galilee, telling them parables and healing their sick. After a time He became very tired, for the people were so eager to hear Him that they would not allow Him to rest, and hardly gave Him time to eat. One day He said to His disciples, "Let us row over to the other side of the lake."

So they all got into a boat. Jesus went to the end of the boat, to lie down and rest. The disciples took turns rowing. The rocking motion of the boat was soothing, and Jesus soon fell asleep.

There is no sweeter place to sleep than on the water, with the oars keeping time, the boat softly rocking, and the breezes gently blowing. Jesus' disciples, who loved Him dearly, were very glad to see their beloved teacher resting.

But soon there came a change in the weather. Dark clouds began to form. Puffs of wind began to blow, and the lake no longer was smooth. Big waves began to break against the boat, and the spray dashed over the disciples.

Jesus slept on. The disciples bent to the oars and rowed with all their might. The sky grew blacker, the wind howled, and the waves tossed and beat into the boat, so that soon the bottom was full of water. The disciples were experienced sailors — several of them had been fishermen before Jesus called them to follow Him — but they had never seen a storm as bad as this one. They were terrified. At last, in an agony of fear, they woke Jesus up. "Teacher! Don't You care that we are going to drown?"

Jesus looked out over the raging water and the stormy sky. Then He said quietly to the sea, "Peace! Be still!"

The wind stopped. The sea grew calm. The black clouds drifted away. In a few minutes, instead of the roaring storm and the raging waves and the black clouds and the howling wind, there was a blue sky, and a quiet sea, and a soft, still air, as the boat gently slipped over the rippling waves.

The disciples gazed in wonder at the marvelous change that had come over the water. Then they looked in amazement at Jesus. They said to each other, "Who is this, that even the wind and the sea obey Him?" They knew that only God can rule the wind and the waves, and raise the dead back to life. They were afraid as they realized more than ever before that the very Son of God was with them in that little boat.

When the boat reached the other side of the lake, Jesus stayed there for a while, teaching and healing the people. Then, after a few days, He went back again to Galilee across the lake. A great crowd of people had gathered on the seashore to meet Him, for they had heard that Jesus was coming back. As He stepped out of the boat, they gathered around Him to welcome back the great teacher whom they loved.

Chapter 24
THE LITTLE GIRL BROUGHT BACK TO LIFE
MATTHEW 9; MARK 5; LUKE 8

In the city where Jesus now was there lived a rich man named Jairus. He was the ruler of the synagogue and therefore a very important man. He had only one child, a daughter, twelve years old, whom he loved dearly.

One day the little girl became very sick. In spite of everything her parents did for her, she grew worse and worse. Her cheeks were hot with fever. As her father and mother sat in agony by the side of her bed, they realized that she was going to die.

While they sat helpless beside her bed, they heard someone shouting,

"The Master has come back!" Then they heard the sound of hurrying feet, as people passed by on their way to the seashore.

The mother said, "Go quickly! Beg Him to come! *He* can save her life." Jairus ran as fast as he could to the seashore. He fell down at the feet of Jesus and begged, "My little daughter is at the point of death. I pray You, come and lay Your hands on her, so that she may be healed. If You do, she will live!"

Jesus went with him, all the people following. There was such a crowd that Jesus could hardly walk, for the people pressed against Him on every side.

In that crowd there was a poor woman who had had a bleeding sickness for twelve years. She had been to see so many doctors that all her money was used up. The doctors had not been able to help her, and she was getting worse all the time.

This poor woman was very timid. She was afraid to ask Jesus to help her with so many people around. She said to herself, "I will steal quietly up behind Him, and touch His clothes. If only I can do that, I shall be made well."

With the strength of desperation the woman pushed her way through the crowd until she came up behind Jesus. She timidly put out her hand and just touched the hem of His garment. Immediately she could feel that her blood had stopped flowing and that she was healed.

Then Jesus turned around and said, "Who touched Me?"

All the people around Him said, "Not I!" Then Peter said, "Master, there is such a crowd around You that everyone is pressing against You. How can You ask, 'Who touched Me?'?"

"I know someone touched Me," Jesus said, "for I felt power go out from Me."

When the woman heard Him say this, she realized that Jesus knew she had been cured. She was frightened, but she came and fell down on her knees. The poor woman trembled all over as she confessed what she had done. Jesus was kind to her, as He always was to those who needed kindness. "Daughter," He said gently, "because you have believed in Me, you are made well. Go in peace."

How happy these tender words must have made the woman! She surely remembered to the end of her life that Jesus called her "Daughter."

While all of this was happening, there was bitter grief in the home of Jairus. The little girl had died. Someone brought the news to Jairus, saying, "Do not trouble the Master any more. Your little daughter is dead."

These people thought Jesus was a wonderful doctor, who could cure all kinds of diseases. They had seen Him give sight to the blind and hearing to the deaf. But that anyone could bring the dead back to life seemed so impossible that they did not even dream of asking Jesus to do it.

Before Jairus could grasp this terrible news, Jesus said quietly, "Do not be afraid. Only believe, and she shall be made well again." And so the company went on till they came to the home of Jairus.

The house was full of people, for the neighbors had come to sympathize with the poor mother. There was a great deal of loud crying and mourning. Flute players were playing sad tunes on their flutes. This was the custom among the Jews when someone died.

Jesus said to the mourners, "Why do you make such a tumult? The little girl is not dead. She is only sleeping." By this He meant that He would awaken her out of death, as a person wakes up out of sleep.

The mourners laughed at Him scornfully. Had they not themselves seen the dead child? They simply did not believe that Jesus' power could awaken the child from the sleep of death.

Jesus sent all the mourners away. He allowed only the father and the mother and His three disciples Peter, James, and John to stay. He went into the room where the dead child lay. He took her hand in His and said to her, "Little girl, get up!" At these words the child's soul came back into her body. She opened her eyes and looked at Jesus and at her father and mother. Then she sat up and walked around the room.

For several days the little girl had been too sick to eat anything. Jesus knew she must be hungry, so He said to her mother, "Give her something to eat."

It was a happy family that night, as the father and mother and little daughter sat and talked about the wonderful teacher who had done more for them than they would ever have dared to ask.

Chapter 25
THE WISH OF A YOUNG GIRL
MATTHEW 14; MARK 6; LUKE 9

Jesus called His twelve apostles to Him, and sent them out, two by two, to prepare the way before Him. He told them to go to all the cities of the Jews, telling the people to repent of their sins, to be sorry for all the wicked things they had done, because the kingdom of heaven was close at hand.

The disciples were to go without taking any food or money, and even without an extra pair of shoes and a coat. In every city they were to look for some hospitable people, and to stay with them as long as they were in that city. Jesus gave these men the power to heal all kinds of sickness.

Soon in every village and town the Jews began to hear about these wonderful new preachers. The disciples went through the land, healing the sick, telling the people to be sorry for their sins, and teaching about their wonderful Lord.

Finally even King Herod heard about Jesus. The stories of the wonders Jesus did worried Herod, because they reminded him of a wicked thing he had done.

The king had good reason to be troubled. Sometime before this, he had divorced his own wife and had married instead the wife of his brother Philip. This was a great sin, and John the Baptist had not hesitated to tell Herod that he had done wrong.

Herod knew that he had done wrong, but he was angry that John should dare to say so. He sent his soldiers to the Jordan River where John was preaching, to arrest John and throw him in prison.

Herod's wife was even angrier at John than her husband was. She was determined to kill him because of what he had said. Herod knew that John was really a good and holy man. He knew, too, that all the people believed that John was sent from God. If anything happened to John, the people might even attack Herod's palace. So Herod kept John safely locked up in prison. Sometimes, when he felt like it, he even had John brought to his own rooms and listened to his preaching.

While John was still in the dark prison, the king's birthday came around. Herod gave a big birthday party and invited all his lords and captains, as well as the chief men of Galilee. It was a splendid feast indeed. During the party the pretty daughter of Herod's wife came in and danced. All the guests were delighted. "What a beautiful girl!" they exclaimed, and, "How gracefully she dances!"

Herod himself was pleased with her dancing, and with the success of his party. With an oath he said to the girl, "Ask anything you want, even to half of my kingdom, and I will give it to you."

The girl went out and said to her mother, "Mother, the king was pleased with my dancing, and he promised to give me anything I want. What shall I ask for?"

The wicked queen had been waiting for just such a chance as this. She said, "Ask for the head of John the Baptist on a platter."

The girl went back to the room where the feast was being held and said to the king, "My wish is that you give me the head of John the Baptist on a platter."

The king was horrified. He had not dreamed she would ask for anything like this. He thought she would ask for a pearl necklace perhaps, or some other jewel. And yet he had promised he would give her whatever she asked for, even to the half of his kingdom. He had sworn an oath to do it, in the presence of all his guests.

Herod did not want to kill John the Baptist, for he knew that John was a good man. But he was ashamed to break the oath he had made before all his guests. He called a soldier. He told the man to go to the prison and cut off the head of John the Baptist, and to bring it to the banquet hall.

Soon the soldier came back, carrying John's head on a platter. The young girl, who had enchanted them all with her dancing, marched out of the room with the platter and gave it to her mother.

The disciples of John heard that their teacher was dead. They came to the prison and asked for John's body. Very lovingly they buried it.

But Herod's conscience troubled him. The reports he heard about Jesus made him uneasy. Who was this man who could raise the dead? Some people said, "John the Baptist has come back from the dead." Others said, "Elijah has come again." Still others said, "One of the old prophets has risen."

Herod was worried. He said, "John I beheaded. Who is this man about whom I hear such things? It must be John the Baptist come back from the dead!"

Chapter 26
FIVE LOAVES OF BREAD AND FIVE THOUSAND PEOPLE
MATTHEW 14; MARK 6; LUKE 9; JOHN 6

After a while the twelve apostles, whom Jesus had sent out to preach in the villages, came back. Each one told what he had done and what he had taught. The disciples were tired from their journeys, but so many people crowded around them they could not get a chance even to eat.

Jesus said to them, "Come apart, to a desert place, and rest a while." They all got into a boat and rowed to the other side of the lake.

The people guessed where they were going. They ran as fast as they could around the end of the lake. When Jesus and His disciples reached the other side, there was a great crowd of people waiting for them.

Jesus was sorry for the people, because they were like sheep who had no shepherd. They wanted to learn, but there was no one but Jesus to teach them. So He talked to them all afternoon.

By and by the sun began to sink, and evening came. The people had been listening to Jesus all afternoon. Now it was supper time, but they had nothing to eat. In their hurry to run after Jesus they had forgotten to bring any food with them.

Jesus knows everything. He knew that the people who had been listening to Him were now tired and hungry. He said to Philip, "Where can we buy enough bread for such a crowd of people?"

"Two hundred denarii would not be enough," Philip said, "to buy even one small piece for each one of them." Two hundred denarii would be about thirty-two dollars in our money, but it was a very big sum for the poor disciples. A man who worked hard all day earned one denarius; to earn two hundred would take a man more than half a year. Probably all the disciples together did not have that much money. Philip meant, "Even if we had such a big sum of money, it would not be enough to give them a good supper. We could give each one only a tiny piece of bread."

Although the disciples had been such a long time with Jesus, and had seen Him do so many wonderful miracles, they still did not understand that there was nothing He could not do. "Send them away," they said to Jesus, "so that they may go to the nearby towns and get something to eat."

But Jesus said, "You give them something to eat."

"There is a boy here who has five barley loaves and two fish," Andrew said, "but what would that be among so many people?"

"Tell the people to sit down in groups on the grass," Jesus said.

Soon all the people were seated on the soft green grass, wondering what new thing the Teacher was going to do. Most of them were men, but there were a great many women and children there too. The members of each family sat together. When everyone had sat down, it was easy to count them, for they were arranged in groups of fifty or a hundred. There were about five thousand people there, all eagerly watching to see what would happen.

Jesus took the five loaves and the two fish. Looking up to heaven, He thanked God for the food. Then He broke the five little loaves into pieces. He gave them to the disciples, and they gave them to the people. Jesus did the same with the fish.

The disciples put the pieces into baskets and passed them to the people, so that everyone could take just as much as he wanted. No matter how much was taken out of the baskets, there was always plenty left.

The people seated at the outside edges of the crowd were probably wondering if there would be any left when their turn came. But there was enough, and indeed more than enough!

After the meal Jesus told His disciples to gather up the pieces that were left over, so that nothing would be wasted. The disciples collected twelve baskets full of broken pieces left over from the five little barley loaves and the two fish. In the end there was more than there had been in the beginning, though five thousand people had had all they wanted to eat.

The people began to talk excitedly to each other. "This is certainly that prophet who has been promised for many hundreds of years," they said. "We have heard His great teachings, and seen many of His wonderful miracles! This must be the Saviour! He ought to be our king! There are five thousand of us here. Let us all march to Jerusalem and crown Him as our king!"

The Jewish people expected that the promised Saviour would come as a glorious king, who would lead the people to victory over all their enemies. Then they would get rid of the hated Roman rulers. Once again they would have a king of their own in Jerusalem, where David and Solomon had ruled.

But Jesus did not come to be an earthly king. He came to be king over the hearts of men. All the people who have ever loved and trusted Jesus are the subjects of His kingdom, the kingdom of heaven.

When Jesus found that the people were planning to make Him an earthly king, He slipped quietly away.

Chapter 27
WALKING ON TOP OF THE STORMY WATER
MATTHEW 14; MARK 6; JOHN 6

While the people were busy planning to make Jesus their king, He told His disciples to get back into the boat and row across the lake. He said that He would follow them later.

Jesus Himself slipped away quietly and went up the mountain to pray. Soon it became dark. Jesus was talking to His heavenly Father. He did not mind the darkness. But His disciples, who were rowing on the black water, were afraid.

The disciples had a long stretch of water ahead of them. It was about four or five miles to land. If there had been a bright moon shining in the sky, and if the wind had been calm and still, it would have been delightful to row in the cool evening, after the heat of the day.

But soon the wind began to rise, and the waves frothed with whitecaps. The disciples had a hard time to make the boat go against the wind and the waves. It kept swerving first to one side and then to the other, as the big waves dashed against it. If the disciples had not been experienced sailors, they could not have managed the boat at all in that rough sea.

While they were struggling to keep the boat safe, Jesus was on the mountain, praying all during the night. Just before dawn, while it was still dark, Jesus went to His disciples.

How could Jesus reach the disciples when they were out on the lake? They had been rowing all night, and were now far from the shore. How could Jesus cross the stormy water? He did what no man can do. He walked on top of the water.

When the disciples saw a white figure coming toward them out of the darkness, they were terrified.

They thought it was a ghost they saw, and they cried out in fear. Of course, there are no ghosts. But even the bravest person would be startled to see a figure in the darkness walking on the water.

Jesus did not want His disciples to be frightened. He called out to them, "Be of good cheer! It is I! Do not be afraid!" Peter was filled with the thought of the wonderful power of Jesus. He felt that Jesus ruled all the world, and that He could do all things. And if He could do all things, He could even make a poor, weak man like Peter able to walk on the water.

So Peter called to Jesus, "Lord, if it is You, tell me to come to You on the water!"

Jesus said to Peter, "Come!"

Peter got out of the boat. For a few minutes his heart was so filled with the thought of Jesus' almighty power that he, too, was able to walk on top of the waves. But soon Peter looked around at the howling storm, and as his trust in Jesus weakened, he began to fear the storm. When Peter stopped trusting Jesus, he began to sink. In a panic he cried out, "Lord, save me!"

Jesus stretched out His hand and took hold of Peter, saying, "Oh, you of little faith! Did you not know that I could keep you from sinking?" With Jesus holding his hand Peter was not afraid. He thought only of Jesus by his side; he did not notice the waves. So the two of them walked on the water till they reached the boat.

As soon as Jesus was in the boat, the wind stopped. The disciples were so filled with wonder that they came and kneeled down before Jesus, saying, "Truly, You are the Son of God."

After they had worshiped Jesus and looked around, they saw to their surprise that the boat was now close to the shore, and that they did not need to row any longer.

Chapter 28
FRIENDS AND ENEMIES
MARK 6, 7; JOHN 6

Jesus and His disciples were now near the city of Bethsaida. This was beautiful country, rich and green. Bushes with sweet-smelling flowers something like roses grew right down to the water's edge.

When the people there saw Jesus and His disciples landing on their shore, they wondered who these strangers were who had come to visit them. Someone, who perhaps had seen Jesus before in some other place, soon discovered that this was the wonderful teacher and healer of whom everybody had heard.

As soon as the people discovered who their visitor was, they sent messengers into the country all around to tell the sick people that the healer had come to their city.

Oh, what excitement there was! All the people who had sick relatives or friends brought them on mattresses and laid them on the ground near Jesus. The sick people begged to be allowed just to touch the border of His robe. As many as touched Him were made perfectly well.

This city where Jesus was healing the sick was a long way from Jerusalem, at least sixty miles. But even that distance did not keep some of the people from Jerusalem from following Jesus. His enemies, as well as His friends, followed Him to hear His teaching.

In Jerusalem there were many proud scribes and Pharisees who would not have anything to do with ordinary people. These men had made up many rules about serving God. They thought that anyone who did not keep all their rules, in addition to God's law, was a great sinner. These scribes and Pharisees were too proud to mingle with the common people who followed Jesus and listened so eagerly to His teaching. They looked down on Jesus Himself because He had not gone to their schools, and because He ate and talked with the common folk.

But the Pharisees kept hearing things about this new teacher. Every day they met someone who talked about the great crowds that were following Jesus. "There is no doubt about it," the Pharisees said to each other, "that this teacher does wonderful things. He cures blind and deaf people, and heals all kinds of diseases. Some say He can even raise people from the dead. All the people are leaving us to follow Him."

Others said, "His teaching cannot be true, because He does not teach as we do. He even heals on the Sabbath day, so He cannot be a good man. We must do something to stop

His deceiving the people like this."

And so some of the Pharisees and scribes traveled the sixty miles from Jerusalem to the place where Jesus was teaching. They did not come to learn, but to find fault.

"Why do you eat bread with unwashed hands?" the scribes asked the disciples. For the Pharisees often washed not only their hands but their cups and their pots and their tables and many other things. Jesus said, "Eating with unwashed hands does not make men wicked. It is not what goes into a man's mouth, but what comes out of his heart that is sinful. For out of the heart come lying, and killing, and stealing."

The Pharisees became very angry when Jesus told the people that there were more important things than keeping the rules of the Pharisees.

Even some of Jesus' followers began to leave Him, because they did not understand some of the things He said. One day He told them, "I am the bread of life: he that comes to Me shall not hunger, and he that trusts in Me shall never thirst. For I have come down out of heaven." The Jews said, "This is the carpenter's son. How can He say that He has come down out of heaven?" So many of them left Him, and followed Him no more.

Chapter 29
AN ANSWERED PRAYER
MATTHEW 15; MARK 7

North of the land of the Jews, on the shores of the Mediterranean Sea, lay a country which was small but famous. Its ships sailed far and wide over the seas, and its cities, Tyre and Sidon, were known throughout the whole world.

The people of this land did not

worship the true God. Most of them worshiped idols and knew very little about the God the Jews worshiped. Recently some of those who had visited Jerusalem had come home with very strange stories. They said that a prophet named Jesus had begun to travel through the land of the Jews, teaching the people about God and healing all sort of diseases. Why, some people even claimed He could make the blind see, and the deaf hear, and the lame walk! There had never been such a wonderful teacher. Crowds of people were following Him wherever He went, hoping He would heal them.

Jesus wanted to have some time alone with His disciples. There were many things He wanted to teach them about God before He went back to His Father in heaven. But the people would not give Him any rest. From morning till night they crowded around Him.

So Jesus led His disciples away from the Sea of Galilee to the northwest, to the land of Tyre and Sidon. In one of the villages they found a house to stay in. Jesus did not want anyone to know where He was, so that He would have time to talk quietly to His disciples. But even here He could not keep His presence hidden. Before He had been there long, a woman came and fell down at His feet in tears.

This woman was not a Jew, but one of the people of the land. Somehow she had heard of Jesus, and believed that He was able to help her. "Have mercy on me, Lord, Thou Son of David!" she said. "An evil spirit torments my little daughter."

Jesus did not answer a word. It seemed as if He was not even listening. She was desperate. She cried again, "Lord, help me!" The disciples said to Jesus, "Send her away. She is making such a noise!"

Jesus wanted His disciples to see how great the woman's faith was. He said to her, "I was sent to the lost children of Israel."

The woman knew that the Jews were proud of being God's chosen people. She knew she was not one of the chosen people. But she kept on begging, "Lord, help me!"

Jesus answered, "It is not right to take the children's bread and throw it to the dogs." The Jews called people of other nations "dogs," because they were certain God did not care what happened to these foreigners. But the woman would not give up. She was so sure Jesus was able to help her that she kept on asking. She said, "Yes, Lord, but even the dogs eat the crumbs that fall from their master's table." All she wanted was a little crumb — that her daughter should be made well.

He said, "O woman, you have great faith in Me. You shall have what you ask. The evil spirit has left your daughter."

The woman believed Jesus. Joyfully she ran home. The little girl was lying on her bed, perfectly well. The mother's prayer had been answered because she trusted in Jesus.

Chapter 30
HUNGRY PEOPLE FED
MATTHEW 15; MARK 8

Day by day more people came to see Jesus, bringing with them members of their family or friends who were sick. Some were lame, limping painfully along on crutches, hardly able to walk. Others who had never walked in all their lives had to be carried by their friends. There were blind people who had to be led by the hand. There were deaf people who had never heard a sound, and dumb people who had never been able to speak. There were people suffering from all kinds of diseases.

One by one Jesus healed them all. He made the blind see, the lame walk, and the deaf hear. Those who had been injured were now well again. Crowds of people watched with joy as they saw their sick friends made strong and healthy. They were glad, and they praised God.

The crowd was so large that it took Jesus three days to heal all of them. Of course you will ask, "What did all those people do at night?" Galilee is a warm country. At night the people just lay down on the warm ground, wrapping their coats around them, hoping that tomorrow their turn would come to be cured.

Some of them had brought a little food with them, but this was soon gone. After the first day the people had nothing to eat. By the third day they were very hungry.

If you were blind and had never seen the light of day in all your life, and if you had come to Jesus to be healed, but your turn had not come yet, do you think you would go home to get something to eat, and lose the chance of having Jesus cure your blindness? No, you would stay close to Jesus, just as those people did, even if you were faint with hunger.

Jesus knew how hungry these poor people were. After He had cured all of them, He said to His disciples, "I feel sorry for these people. They have been here three days without a thing to eat. If I send them home now,

they will faint on the way, because they are weak from hunger. Many of them are a long way from home."

The disciples said, "But where could we get food for them in this wilderness?"

Jesus asked, "How many loaves of bread do you have?"

They said, "Seven, and a few little fish." These were not large loaves, like ours, but small, about the size of a hamburg bun.

Jesus took the seven small loaves, and the little fish, and, lifting up His eyes to heaven, He thanked God for the food, as we also ought to do before we eat. Then He broke the seven loaves and the fish into pieces and gave them to the disciples to give to the people.

The hungry people took all the bread and fish they wanted, and ate till they were satisfied. Oh, how good that food tasted! After they had eaten, the disciples gathered up seven baskets of pieces that were left over.

Some of these people were seeing their friends for the first time in their lives, and their faces shone with happiness that they were no longer blind. There were people walking there who for years had been helpless cripples. There were deaf people who were listening to the voices of their friends for the first time. There were many who had come in pain and suffering. Now their happy faces showed that all their pain was gone.

The hearts of the people were filled with love for the Lord Jesus who had healed them! Was there ever such a happy picnic as that one held on the grass among the sweet-smelling flowers of Galilee?

Chapter 31

"WHO AM I?"

MATTHEW 16; MARK 8; LUKE 9

After a time Jesus again left the Sea of Galilee. He took His disciples for a long journey. They went straight north along the Jordan River for about thirty miles, till they came to the country of Caesarea Philippi. This was a place where they had never been before.

As they walked along, Jesus asked His disciples, "Who do people say that I am?"

The disciples answered, "Some say You are John the Baptist, some say You are Elijah come back to life, some say You must be some other of the prophets of long ago."

Then Jesus asked them a very important question. "Who do you think I am?"

Peter answered at once, "You are the Christ, the Son of the living God."

Jesus said, "Blessed are you, Peter, for it is My Father in heaven who has taught you this."

Jesus was happy to know that His disciples believed that He was the Son of God, the Christ anointed by God to be their long-promised Saviour. They had seen Him raise the dead, and walk on the water, and rule the storm. They had listened to His wonderful teaching. God had given them believing hearts which trusted in Jesus as their Saviour. And God will give you a believing heart if you are sorry for your sins and earnestly pray to Him to help you to trust in Jesus.

Jesus now began to explain to His disciples that soon He must go to Jerusalem. There the elders and chief priests would treat Him shamefully, and in the end they would kill Him; but three days after He had died, He would rise again from the grave.

Peter was shocked to hear that His beloved Master was going to suffer and die. He could not believe it. He knew that the Pharisees hated Jesus, but surely they would never dare to kill the blessed Son of God! Peter said, "No, no, that must never happen to You, Lord!"

Jesus turned to him and said, "Peter, what you want is to persuade Me to run away from the very thing I came into the world to do. You act like Satan when you do that. Satan also wants Me to give up the work which I came to do."

What was this work? Why did Jesus come down from heaven to be born as a little baby?

Jesus came to bear the punishment for our sins, so that we would not have to be punished for all the wicked things we have done. He came to die in our place.

Jesus knew that it was now near the time when He would have to suffer and die. He explained it ahead of time to His disciples, so that they would understand when it happened. He wanted Peter to realize that He had come into this world in order to die.

Jesus laid down this rule for His disciples, and for us: Whoever is willing to forget himself, and to live for Jesus, shall have eternal life. Jesus' friends must not always think about what they want, but they must try to be unselfish and to please Jesus.

Chapter 32

GLORY ON THE MOUNTAIN
MATTHEW 17; MARK 9; LUKE 9

Three of Jesus' disciples seemed to be nearer to Him than the others.

Peter was one of these three. It was he, you remember, who trusted Jesus enough to try to walk on the water to go to Him. It was Peter who said, "Thou art the Christ, the Son of the living God."

John, too, was very close to Jesus. He seemed to love and understand Jesus better than any of the other disciples. The Bible calls him "the beloved disciple." John wrote a part of the Bible that tells about Jesus; it is called The Gospel according to John. This book is so full of love to Jesus that many people like it better than any other part of the Bible.

James was John's brother. He was the third of the disciples who were closest to Jesus.

You remember that it was these three that Jesus took with Him when He raised the little daughter of Jairus from the dead. There were many other times when Jesus kept these three beside Him.

One day Jesus took Peter, James, and John with Him up on a very high mountain. There they were going to see something very strange and holy.

While they were there on the mountain, a change came over Jesus. His face shone as bright as the sun, and His clothes became dazzlingly white, like new-fallen snow. There was a heavenly majesty on His face. Moses and Elijah came down from heaven to talk to Him.

While Peter and James and John watched in amazement, a bright cloud covered the heavenly group. Out of the cloud came the voice of God Himself, saying, "This is My beloved Son, in whom I am well pleased. Listen to Him!"

If Peter and James and John had had any doubt whether Jesus was really the Son of God, they could not doubt any longer. They saw Him clothed with heavenly glory. They heard God the Father speaking from heaven, saying, "This is My beloved Son. Listen to Him!" The three disciples fell down on their faces and worshiped Jesus.

After a time Jesus came and touched the disciples, telling them not to be afraid. Looking up, the disciples saw that the cloud of glory and the two prophets were gone. Jesus stood there alone. On His face was a look of peace and light.

As they went down the mountain Jesus told the three disciples not to tell anybody what they had seen and heard until after He had risen from the dead. Indeed, the disciples did not want to shout the story out. They felt deep in their hearts that they had seen something very sacred. It was too precious to be spoken of lightly.

Never would the disciples forget what they had seen! Never again did Jesus seem to them only a man. They never forgot that glorious figure — His face shining like the sun, and His clothing so dazzlingly white that they could hardly look at Him. After this, to them Jesus was the Lord of glory.

Chapter 33

THE GOOD SAMARITAN
LUKE 10

One day a lawyer came to Jesus and asked, "Master, what must I do to have eternal life?"

Jesus answered, "What does the scripture say you must do?"

The lawyer answered, "The scripture says, 'You must love the Lord your God with all your heart, and with all your soul, and with all your strength, and with all your mind; and you must love your neighbor as yourself.'"

Jesus had made the man answer his own question. "You have answered right," He said. "Do this, and you shall live."

"But who is my neighbor?" the lawyer asked.

Then Jesus told a story, to show the lawyer what loving our neighbor means. This is the story He told:

There was once a man who went from Jerusalem to Jericho. The road to Jericho was rough and wild. Big rocks and rugged cliffs jutted out near the road. Robbers often hid among these rocks, and then sprang out upon lonely travelers and stripped them of everything they had.

As this man was traveling along, a band of robbers sprang out on him. They stole his money, tore off even his clothes, and beat him up so badly that he was nearly dead. Then they ran away, leaving him helpless by the roadside.

A little later a priest happened to come by. He saw the poor man lying by the road, but he did not try to help him. He did not even stop to see if he was alive, but crossed over to the other side of the road and went on his way.

Soon a Levite came along. He, too, saw the wounded man. He even went and looked at him. But he did not take the trouble to put his hand on the man's heart to see if it was still beating. He just looked at him curiously, and then he, too, crossed to the other side of the road and went on.

Last of all a Samaritan came along the road. You remember that the Jews hated and scorned the Samaritans. All his life this traveler had suffered from the hatred and scorn of the Jews. But he did not try to return evil for evil. He did not hurry past the wounded man. Instead he went over to where the poor man was lying. He felt to see if his heart was still beating, and he listened to see if he was still breathing.

When he found the traveler was alive, the Samaritan took some wine and washed his wounds. Then he poured some olive oil in them. After a while the wounded man opened his eyes. The Samaritan lifted him up onto his own donkey. Then, holding on to him, he walked beside him till they came to an inn.

At the inn the Samaritan put the wounded traveler into a bed and watched over him. The next day, when he had to go on, he gave money to the innkeeper and said, "Take care of him, and if you have to spend more than this, I will pay you back when I come this way again."

After telling this story, Jesus asked the lawyer, "Which of these three men do you think was a neighbor to the man who fell among the robbers?"

The lawyer said, "The man who showed mercy to him."

Then Jesus said, "Go, and do likewise."

Chapter 34

THE FEAST OF TABERNACLES
JOHN 7-9

For one week in every year the Jews held a feast in Jerusalem called the Feast of Tabernacles. This was like our Thanksgiving, a happy season of rejoicing and praising God for His goodness in giving a bountiful harvest. It was held in the fall of the year, about six months after the other great feast of the Jews, the Passover.

A great many of the Jews went to Jerusalem to keep the Feast of Tabernacles. Most of them hoped they would see Jesus there. Some of them were His friends. Some of them He had healed. Some were just curious to see this teacher about whom they had heard so much during the past two years. Others, who had listened to the Pharisees, said, 'He is not a good teacher, for He does not keep the laws of Moses. He deceives us.'

Before long Jesus Himself came to the feast. He went into the temple and began to teach. Some of the people who heard Him for the first time were amazed. "How can this man speak so well?" they asked. "Isn't He just a carpenter's son?"

Others said, "Isn't this the man our leaders are trying to kill? He is speaking boldly, and they do not say anything to Him. Perhaps the rulers know that this is truly the promised Saviour. He must be the Saviour, because He does so many wonderful miracles!"

When the Pharisees and chief priests heard what the people were saying, they were furious. They sent some of the temple police to arrest Jesus.

Jesus stood in the temple and cried to the people, "If any man is thirsty, let him come to Me and drink!" This was His way of saying that if any man has a longing to be good and to be a child of God, Jesus will give him the Holy Spirit to live in his heart, to teach him how to be God's child.

The police whom the Pharisees had sent to arrest Jesus stood and listened. They were thrilled by what they heard. "Why do the Pharisees want to arrest this man?" they asked. "Why, He is a good man. It must be they do not know who He is, or they would never have sent us to arrest Him!"

The police went back without Jesus. When the Pharisees and the priests asked, "Why did you not bring Him?" they answered, "There was never a man in all the world who spoke as this man does!"

When evening came, Jesus left the city and went to the Mount of Olives, where He spent the night. Early in the morning He came back to Jerusalem to the temple. All the people gathered around Him, and He sat down and taught them.

He began, "I am the light of the world. Whoever follows Me shall not walk in darkness, but shall have the light of life." It is still true that whoever follows Jesus has a life full of light and happiness.

Jesus continued, "If a man keeps My word, he shall not see death." Jesus was not speaking of physical death but of eternal death. But the people did not understand this. "Abraham and the prophets died," they said. "Do You think You are greater than Abraham?"

Jesus answered, "Abraham was glad to see My day."

"You are not yet fifty years old," sneered the Jews; "do You mean to say You have seen Abraham?"

"Before Abraham lived, I am," Jesus replied. Jesus *was* God before Abraham or any other man ever lived. He was God long before He came to earth as a baby in Bethlehem. But the Jews refused to believe that He was the Son of God. They were shocked and angry at His claims, and they picked up stones to throw at Him. But Jesus hid Himself, and went out of the temple, and so escaped from them.

As Jesus was walking along, He passed a man who had been blind all his life. Once again Jesus showed the power of God. Making a little clay, He put it on the blind man's eyes, and told him to go and wash it off in a pool near Jerusalem.

Without a question the man went and did as he was told. When he came back, he seemed like a different person. The sadness had vanished from his face, for now he could see! He looked so different that some of his neighbors were not even sure this was the man they had known all their lives. "Yes," he insisted, "I am the same man. The teacher called

Jesus put some clay on my eyes, and I washed it off, and now I see!"

The Jewish leaders did not believe this story. They asked the blind man's parents, "Is this your son who, you say, was born blind? How then can he now see?"

His father and mother answered, "We know that this is our son, and that he was born blind. But how he now sees, we do not know. He is grown up. Ask him." For they were afraid of the Jewish leaders, who had decided that anyone who said Jesus was the Saviour would be thrown out of the synagogue.

Finally the angry Jews drove the man who had been blind away. A little later Jesus found him. "Do you believe in the Son of God?" He asked him.

The man said, "Who is He, Lord, that I may believe on Him?"

Jesus answered, "You have seen Him; He is the very one who is now talking to you."

The man said, "Lord, I believe," and he worshiped Jesus. He quite forgot how badly the Jewish leaders had treated him. For no one who has found Jesus as his friend and Saviour can be sad.

Chapter 35
TWO SISTERS WHO LOVED JESUS
LUKE 10; JOHN 10

Do you know where Jesus stayed at night, and how He got His meals? He had no house of His own, and no money. Foxes have holes in the earth, and birds have nests, but our Saviour did not even own a place where He could lay His tired head at night.

Among those who loved and followed Jesus were some women who looked after Him. When He needed

a new coat, some friend gave Him one. Sometimes He ate and slept outdoors under the stars, with just His coat for a covering. Sometimes He visited some of His friends or followers and stayed with them overnight.

In the little village of Bethany, close to Jerusalem, there lived a family Jesus especially loved to visit. There were two sisters in this family,

Mary and Martha, and one brother, Lazarus. All three were very dear friends of Jesus, and He often visited them.

One day Jesus was staying with this family. Martha was working very hard to prepare a nice supper for Jesus; but Mary sat at His feet, listening to the wonderful words He was saying.

Martha was not pleased that Mary had left all the work to her. She said to Jesus, "Lord, don't You care that my sister has left me to do all the work alone? Tell her to come and help me."

"Martha, Martha," Jesus said, "you are working hard at things which are not very important. To listen to what I say is the most important thing of all. Mary has chosen that good part, and it shall not be taken away from her."

After visiting Mary and Martha and Lazarus, Jesus went back to Jerusalem to teach the people. As usual, He went to the temple. He walked back and forth in the beautiful open space called Solomon's porch, saying, "I am the good shepherd. The good shepherd gives His life for the sheep. The hired man, to whom the sheep do not belong, when he sees the wolf coming, runs away, and the wolf snatches the sheep. He runs away because he is a hired man, and he does not love the sheep. I am the good shepherd, and I lay down My life for the sheep."

Some of the Jews said to Him, "How long are you going to leave us in doubt? If you are really the Christ, anointed by God to be our Saviour, why don't you tell us plainly?"

Jesus answered, "I have told you, but you do not believe Me, because you are not My sheep. My sheep hear My voice, and I know them, and they follow Me. I will give them everlasting life."

Jesus meant that the people who followed Him and trusted in Him as their Saviour were His sheep. These words made the rulers very angry. They began to throw stones at Jesus again.

Jesus said, "I have done many good works among you. For which of these do you stone Me?"

The angry leaders replied, "We do not stone you for doing good works, but because you claim to be God, when you are only a man."

Jesus said, "You ought to believe Me when I say that I am the Son of God, because you see the works that I do."

Again the Jewish leaders tried to seize Jesus, but He escaped out of their hands. He did not stay in Jerusalem, because the Jews would not listen to His teaching. Crossing over the Jordan River, Jesus went to the place in the desert where John had been baptizing when he began to preach. Many people followed Him there. They were not like the rulers in Jerusalem. These people gladly believed in Jesus.

Chapter 36
THE FRIEND OF CHILDREN AND HIS PRAYER
MATTHEW 6, 19; MARK 10; LUKE 18

Some of the people who listened eagerly to Jesus wanted Him to bless their children. "That will be beauti-ful," they thought. "Our children will remember all their lives that the Saviour has blessed them." So they brought their little ones to Jesus so that He could bless them.

The disciples saw the women coming. They thought Jesus was too busy to bother with little children. "You shouldn't bring your children here," they objected. "Can't you see that the Lord is very busy? He hasn't time to talk to children."

Jesus had seen the mothers with their little ones. He was displeased that the disciples were sending the children away. He called the mothers back and spoke kindly to them. "Let the little children come to Me," he said. "Do not forbid them, for the kingdom of heaven belongs to just such as they are." Then Jesus took the little children in His arms, and laid His hands on their heads and blessed them.

The mothers went home happy. They never allowed their children to forget that day when the dear Saviour put His hands on their heads and blessed them.

One day Jesus was praying, as He often did. When He had finished, one of His disciples said, "Lord, teach us to pray, as John also taught his disciples." So Jesus taught them the beautiful prayer which we call the Lord's Prayer:

Our Father which art in heaven, Hallowed be Thy name. Thy kingdom come. Thy will be done on earth, as it is in heaven. Give us this day our daily bread. And forgive us our debts, as we forgive our debtors. And lead us not into temptation, but deliver us from evil. For Thine is the kingdom, and the power, and the glory, forever. Amen

What does this prayer mean?

Our Father means that God, the great creator and ruler of the world, loves us as a father loves his children.

Hallowed be Thy name means "May everyone in the whole world worship God."

Thy kingdom come means "May the time come when all the people in the world will love God."

Thy will be done on earth, as it is in heaven means "May the people on earth do what God wants them to, just as the angels in heaven do God's will."

Give us this day our daily bread asks God to take care of us, and give us food and whatever else we need.

And forgive us our debts as we forgive our debtors means "May the heavenly Father forgive us our sins as we forgive those who sin against us."

Lead us not into temptation means "Guide us so that we may be kept from doing wrong."

Chapter 37
THE LOST SHEEP AND THE SON WHO LEFT HOME
LUKE 15

One day Jesus was again talking to the crowds of people who followed Him wherever He went. Among the crowd there were many publicans and sinners.

Publicans, you remember, were tax collectors. All the people hated them because they worked for the Roman rulers, and because many of them were dishonest and made the people pay more taxes than they owed.

When these publicans and sinners listened to Jesus, they were sorry for their sins, and wanted to turn away from them. They crowded around Jesus to hear His kind and loving words. Some of them asked Him to stay for supper, so that they could speak to Him longer. Jesus was glad to talk to them.

Among the crowd there were also some of the proud scribes and Pharisees. These people were shocked to see Jesus talking to such sinful men, and even eating with them. They would never dream of having anything to do with such people!

Jesus knew what the Pharisees were thinking. He told a little story, or parable, to show them how mistaken they were:

If one of you has a hundred sheep, and loses one, does he not leave the ninety and nine in the wilderness, and go to find the one that is lost, and hunt until he finds it? When he has found it, he will carry it home on his shoulders, rejoicing. He will call his neighbors and friends together, and say to them, "Rejoice with me, for I have found my sheep which was lost!"

I say to you, there is more joy in heaven over one sinner who turns back to God, than over ninety-nine good people who have never been in danger of being lost. For your Father in heaven does not want to lose even one of His children.

By this story Jesus taught the proud Pharisees that God did not love them one bit more than He loved the publicans and sinners. Jesus came into the world to find and save *lost* sheep, and to bring them home to God. There is great joy in heaven when one sinner, any sinner, is sorry for his sins and turns back to God.

Jesus told the people another little story:

There was once a man who had two sons. One day the younger son said, "Father, give me my share of your money." So the father gave the boy the money which he had been saving for him.

Not long after that the younger son collected all his things together and went on a journey to a distant country. While he was there, he began to spend his money foolishly, in all sorts of wild and wasteful ways. Soon his money was all gone.

Then there came a terrible famine in that country. The people began to suffer from hunger. Only rich people could buy the little food that was left. The young man's money was all gone, so that he could not get anything to eat. All his new friends deserted him now that he had no more money.

After this, the young man asked a farmer to give him some work. He was sent out into the fields to feed the pigs. He was so hungry that he would have been glad to eat the husks that he fed the pigs, but nobody gave him even that much.

At last the young man thought to himself, "In my father's house even the hired servants have more than enough to eat, and here I am, dying of hunger. I will go back to my father, and I will say, 'Father, I know I have sinned both against God and against you. I am no longer worthy to be called your son. Make me one of your hired servants.'"

So the young man started out for home. His father saw him coming a long way off, and ran to meet him. He threw his arms around his son and kissed him.

The boy said, "Father, I have been a bad son. I have sinned against God and against you, and I am not worthy to be called your son any longer."

His father did not let him get any further. He said to his servants,

"Bring the best robe, and put it on him, and put a ring on his hand, and shoes on his feet. Bring the fatted calf and kill it, and let us eat and be merry. For my son was dead, and is alive again. He was lost, and is found."

By this story Jesus wanted to show the scribes and Pharisees that publicans and sinners could become God's children, even though they had sinned greatly. God is ready and glad to receive anyone who turns back to Him.

Chapter 38
JESUS WAKES LAZARUS FROM DEATH
JOHN 11

After the Jews in Jerusalem tried to stone Jesus, He went to the other side of the Jordan, about thirty miles from Jerusalem. While He was teaching there, something very sad happened in the home of His friends Mary and Martha. Their brother Lazarus became very sick. His sisters feared he was going to die. Hastily they sent a message to Jesus: "Lord, he whom Thou lovest is sick." At first Jesus did not do anything about it. For two days He stayed where He was. Then He said to His disciples, "Let us go back to Judaea."

"But, Master," they said, "the Jews there want to kill You. Are You going to go back there?"

Jesus answered, "Our friend Lazarus is sleeping. I go to awake him out of sleep."

"That is a good sign, Lord," the disciples said. "If he is sleeping, he will get well."

Then Jesus told them plainly, "Lazarus is dead."

Thomas, one of the twelve apostles, said, "Let us go with our Master, so that we, too, may die with Him if He is killed." For they loved their dear Lord so much that they could not bear to leave Him, even if it meant risking their lives.

The long walk back to Bethany took several days. When Jesus and His disciples finally reached Bethany, Lazarus had been buried for four days. Mary and Martha sat at home, mourning for their dead brother, while their friends tried to comfort them.

When Martha heard that Jesus was coming at last, she ran to meet Him. When she saw Him, she cried out, "Lord, if You had only been here my brother would not have died! And I know that even now whatever You ask of God, God will give to You!"

Jesus said to her, "Your brother will rise again."

"I know that he will rise again in the resurrection at the last day," Martha said.

Jesus answered, "I am the resurrection and the life. Everyone who believes in Me shall never die. Do you believe this?"

"Yes, Lord," Martha said, "I believe that You are the Christ, the Son of God, whom God promised to send into the world."

Martha knew that Jesus would comfort her sister. She ran home. Quietly, so that the visitors in the house would not hear, she said to Mary, "The Master has come, and He is asking for you."

Mary got up quickly and went to meet Jesus. Her friends thought that she was going to the grave to weep there. They followed her, in order to comfort her.

Jesus was still outside the town where Martha had met Him. Mary dropped down at His feet and sobbed, "Lord, if You had been here, my brother would not have died!"

When He saw Mary and all her friends weeping, Jesus felt very sad. "Where have you buried him?" He asked.

They said, "Lord, come and see." Jesus wept.

The friends and neighbors of the two sisters said, "See how He loved him!" Others asked softly, "Could not this man, who has opened the eyes of the blind, have kept Lazarus from dying?"

Lazarus was buried in a cave, with a big stone rolled across the opening. Jesus said, "Take away the stone."

"Lord, he has been dead four days!" Martha said. "By this time his body will have begun to decay."

Jesus asked, "Didn't I tell you that if you only believed you would see the glory of God?"

When the stone had been rolled away, Jesus lifted His eyes to heaven and said, "Father, I thank Thee that Thou hast heard Me. I know that Thou hearest Me always, but I said it so that those who are standing here may know that Thou hast sent Me."

Going close to the grave, Jesus called out in a loud voice, "Lazarus, come forth!"

At these words the dead man came out of the grave. His body was still wrapped in the linen cloths in which he had been buried.

"Take off the wrappings, so he can walk," Jesus said. Oh, how eagerly the people tore off the cloths and looked at their friend, alive and well.

Mary and Martha and Lazarus had been Jesus' true friends for a long time. Now their hearts were almost bursting with love and worship. The disciples, too, were filled with wonder. And how did the friends of Lazarus feel? They also believed that Jesus was truly the Son of God.

But when the priests and the Pharisees heard what had happened, they were very jealous. For they knew that now even more people would leave them to follow Jesus.

"Why don't we stop Him?" they said one to another. "He is doing many miracles, and if we do nothing about it, soon all the people will be following Him."

The high priest, Caiaphas, said, "The best way to keep Him from doing these things is to kill Him. It is better that one man die than that the whole nation be led astray."

From that day on they plotted to kill Jesus. They did not dare to arrest Him publicly because so many of the people loved Him.

But Jesus had gone to a place near the desert on the east side of the Jordan, and the priests looked for Him in vain. They commanded that if anyone knew where He was, he must tell the chief priests and the Pharisees, so that they could arrest Him.

Chapter 39
THE BLIND BEGGAR WHO CALLED TO JESUS
MARK 10; LUKE 18

While Jesus was teaching near the desert, the time for the Passover celebration arrived. This feast was held in the spring of the year, at about the time when we have our Easter.

For the last time Jesus prepared

to go to the feast with His disciples. For three years He had been teaching the people and healing the sick. He knew that His time on earth was nearly finished, and that the Jews in Jerusalem would soon seize Him and kill Him.

As He walked down the road with His disciples, He seemed anxious to hurry toward Jerusalem. The disciples could not understand why He was so eager to return to the city where the Jews had tried to kill Him. Before they had gone far, Jesus stopped and called them to come close. What He told them was so different from what they wanted and expected that they could not understand it.

He said, "You know that the prophets long ago wrote that when the Saviour would come, He would be mocked and killed. All the things written in the scripture are going to come true when we reach Jerusalem. The high priests and the scribes will arrest Me, and turn Me over to the Roman soldiers. They will mock Me, and spit on Me, and beat Me. In the end they will kill Me. But on the third day I will rise again from the dead."

The disciples had always hoped that Jesus would be a king in Jerusalem, just as David had been. Even when He told them plainly that He must suffer and die, they did not want to believe Him.

There were many people going to the feast on the road to Jerusalem. Some of them joined Jesus and His disciples. Jesus taught them, and healed the sick among them.

As they walked, they came to Jericho. Near the city gate a poor blind man named Bartimaeus sat by the roadside, begging. When he heard the voices of the crowd passing by, he wondered what was the matter. He asked someone who stood near, "What is happening? Why are so many people coming this way?"

"Jesus of Nazareth is passing by," the man answered.

Poor Bartimaeus trembled with hope and longing. Oh, if only Jesus would pass near him, and stop long enough to heal his blindness! But would Jesus see him in this crowd? How near was He? Oh, if he could only see how near Jesus was! The Lord might pass by without seeing him, and his one chance to be cured would be gone.

These thoughts flashed through the mind of the blind man. Then he called out, just as loudly as he could, so that Jesus would hear him even if He were not near: "Jesus, son of David, have mercy on me!"

He made such a noise with his shouting that the people were annoyed. They told him to keep still. But the blind man raised his voice even louder and shouted, "Jesus, Thou son of David, have mercy on me!"

Jesus heard his cry. He stopped and told the people to bring the blind man to Him. Someone said to Bartimaeus, "Be of good cheer! He is calling you." Bartimaeus got up quickly. In his excitement he dropped his coat on the ground and forgot all about it. Some kind person took his arm and led him to Jesus.

"What is it you would like Me to do?" Jesus asked.

"Lord, I would like to be able to see," Bartimaeus answered.

Jesus saw that Bartimaeus truly believed in Him. "Because of your faith in Me," He said, "you shall receive your sight."

At once Bartimaeus, who had been blind all his life, could see for the first time. With great joy he joined the crowd of people following Jesus and went along with them to Jerusalem.

Chapter 40

MARY'S GIFT
MATTHEW 26; MARK 14; JOHN 12

As Jesus and His followers traveled to Jerusalem, He taught them many things. At last they reached the Mount of Olives, which was opposite Jerusalem. Here was the little town of Bethany, and the home of Lazarus whom Jesus had raised from the dead. There was no one in Bethany so eager to see Jesus as Mary and Martha and their brother Lazarus.

In Bethany there lived a man named Simon. He had once suffered from leprosy, but Jesus had healed him. This man, too, was glad to see Jesus again. He made a fine supper for Jesus, and invited his friends and all the disciples. Lazarus was one of the guests, and Martha helped to serve the dinner.

In those days people did not sit in chairs at the table when they ate. The table was shaped like a large letter "U." The guests lay on couches, with their heads toward the table and their feet away from it.

During the meal Mary, the sister of Lazarus, came into the room, carrying a white alabaster jar. Inside the jar was a very expensive and sweet-smelling ointment called spikenard. This perfume was so costly that after it was put into the jar, the lid was sealed shut. The only way to get the perfume out was to break the jar. Since it was so very expensive, it was used only by rich people, or on important occasions.

Mary was certainly not rich, but she loved Jesus very dearly. She was so grateful to Him for raising her brother from the dead that she wanted to give Him the nicest thing that she could think of.

As Jesus was eating, Mary came up behind Him. She broke the jar, letting the fragrant perfume fall on His head. She put some of it on His feet and wiped them with her hair. The whole house was filled with the sweet smell.

The people who were eating supper looked at her in surprise. "Why was this expensive perfume wasted?" the disciples asked. Judas especially was angry. "Why wasn't it sold," he said, "and the money given to the poor?" Judas pretended that he cared about the poor, but that was not the real reason that he was angry. He was the one of the little group of disciples who took care of the money given to them, and he stole some of it. He had been a disciple for a long time. He had seen both the love and the power of Jesus. But he did not love the Saviour.

Jesus knew all this. He also knew about the love in Mary's heart, which made her want to do something for Him. He said to Judas, "She has done a good thing. You always have poor people among you. You can help them whenever you wish. But you will not always have Me with you. I shall soon leave you. I am going to die and be buried. By anointing Me with this perfume Mary has prepared My body for burial. Whoever preaches about Me in the whole world will also tell what Mary has done, in remembrance of her."

After dinner Jesus went to visit Mary and Martha and Lazarus. When they heard that He was in Bethany, many Jews came from Jerusalem, which was only a mile and a half away. They wanted to see Lazarus too, just as you and I would want to see and talk to any man in our town

24: THE LAST SUPPER

25: JESUS REDEEMS THE WORLD

who had died and been buried and then been brought back to life again.

Many of these people believed that Jesus was truly the Son of God. Even some of the chief rulers believed it, but they were afraid to say so openly, for the Pharisees had announced that if any man said that Jesus was the Christ, he would be thrown out of the synagogue. And because so many people believed because of Lazarus, who had been raised from the dead, the Pharisees planned to kill Lazarus too.

Chapter 41
THE KING COMES
MATTHEW 21; MARK 11; LUKE 19; JOHN 12

Many people had heard that Jesus was in Bethany, on His way to the feast. They came out from Jerusalem to meet Him, a whole crowd of men and women and little children, eager to see the great teacher.

Jesus sent two of His disciples into the village nearby. "Go into the village," He said, "and you will see a young colt tied, that no man has ever sat on. Unfasten him, and bring him to Me. If anyone asks you why you are taking the colt, tell him, 'The Lord has need of him,' and at once he will send him to Me."

The disciples went into the village, and they saw a young colt tied at the door of a house. As they were unfastening the colt, two or three people standing nearby said, "Why are you doing that?"

"The Lord needs him," the disciples answered.

"Oh, then you may take him," the men said.

And so the words of a prophet spoken five hundred years earlier were fulfilled. You can read this prophecy in the book of Zechariah, the ninth chapter, the ninth verse: "Rejoice greatly, O daughter of Zion; shout, O daughter of Jerusalem: behold, thy King cometh unto thee: He is just, and having salvation; lowly, and riding upon an ass, and upon a colt, the foal of an ass."

The disciples put their coats on the colt's back to soften it for Jesus. They were excited and happy because Jesus was riding into Jerusalem as the kings of Israel had always done when they came to the throne.

The great crowd of people who had come to meet Jesus were wild with joy. They wanted Jesus to be their king. They pulled off their coats and threw them on the ground to make a carpet for Him to ride over. Others cut down branches of palm trees and laid them in the road.

All the people shouted with joy, "Hosanna! Blessed is He that cometh in the name of the Lord! Blessed is the kingdom that cometh, the kingdom of our father David! Hosanna in the highest!"

When the parade reached Jerusalem, all the people came out of their houses and gazed in wonder at the crowd waving palm branches and shouting joyfully, "Hosanna! Hosanna to the son of David!"

"Who is this?" some of them asked. "Why are you shouting?"

The crowd answered, "This is Jesus, the prophet from Nazareth."

The Pharisees saw Jesus riding into the city like a king, with the crowd waving palm branches before Him, and throwing their coats on the road for Him to ride over. They heard the people shouting, "Hosanna in the highest! Hosanna to the son of David, who comes in the name of the Lord!"

They said to each other, "Don't you see how little good it does for us to try to stop Him? Look, all the people are following Him!" Some of them said to Jesus, "Master, make Your disciples stop this shouting."

But Jesus answered, "I tell you, that if the people stopped, the very stones would cry out in praise."

And so the Pharisees watched the parade move on to the temple, and all the people went on praising and glorifying God because the Saviour whom God had promised had come at last.

Chapter 42
THE ROMAN PENNY
MATTHEW 22, 26; MARK 12; LUKE 20

Jesus had only a few more days to spend with His friends on this earth. Every day He taught in the temple and healed the sick. Everyone was astonished at His teaching and His miracles.

The Pharisees were more determined than ever to kill Him. But they did not dare to harm Him, even when He taught openly in the temple. There were several reasons why they were afraid to arrest Jesus.

At this time the Jews did not have a king of their own, for they were not a free people. Almost the whole world had been conquered by the Romans, and had to pay taxes to Rome. The Jews were ruled by a Roman governor whose name was Pilate.

The Romans allowed the Jews to rule themselves in small matters, with the high priest as their judge. But if a man committed a serious crime, which had to be punished by death, he had to be brought to Pilate, the Roman governor. The high priest was not allowed to condemn anyone to death.

And so even though the Pharisees and priests wanted to kill Jesus because He healed people on the Sabbath, and called Himself the Son of God, they did not dare to harm Him.

They knew that Pilate did not care whether Jesus kept the Sabbath, or even whether He called Himself God. If they brought Him before the Roman governor, Pilate would say, "You cannot put a man to death for things like these."

And so the Jews tried to trick Jesus. They tried to get Him to say something against the Roman government, so they could tell Pilate He had broken the law.

One of them asked Him, "Is it lawful to pay taxes to Caesar?" Now the Jews hated their Roman rulers, and most of all they hated to pay taxes to Rome. The Pharisees thought that in order to please the people Jesus would say, "No, you must give your money to God." If He said that, they could tell Pilate Jesus told the people not to pay taxes to Rome, and Pilate would arrest Him.

But Jesus knew they were trying to trick Him. He said, "You are trying to get Me into trouble. Show Me a penny." Someone brought Him a Roman penny. On it was the head of Caesar. "Whose head is this?" Jesus asked. They answered, "Caesar's." Then Jesus said, "Give to Caesar the things that are Caesar's, and to God the things that are God's."

No one could find fault with this

answer. Even the Pharisees had to admit that no man had ever spoken as Jesus did. They were so awed by His heavenly dignity that they did not dare to arrest Him.

There was another reason why the priests and Pharisees let Jesus alone. They were afraid of the crowds of people who came every day to listen to Him as He taught in the temple. The majority of these people loved and believed in Jesus. Do you think that they would have let the Roman soldiers arrest Him? Indeed, no! They would have fought the soldiers, and there would have been a terrible uproar.

And so the priests and the scribes and the elders met in the palace of the high priest, Caiaphas. They tried to think of some way to take Jesus by surprise.

Chapter 43
THE LAST DAY AND THE GREAT SIN
MATTHEW 24-26

One day, instead of teaching in the temple, Jesus took His disciples out of Jerusalem, across the brook, and over to the Mount of Olives. He was going to be with them only a few more days, and there were some important things He wanted to tell them before He left them.

On the quiet mountainside they sat down together. One of the disciples said, "Tell us what the end of the world will be like, and how we can know when You are coming again."

And so Jesus told them about His *second* coming to earth. When He comes back to earth again, He will not be born in a stable. He will come as a king upon the clouds of heaven, and all His angels with Him. Everyone in the whole world will see Him, for He will come as the lightning which shines from one end of heaven to the other. No one knows when that day will come, not even the angels. Only God the Father knows.

All the nations will be gathered before Him as He sits on His throne of glory. Those who love and trust Him will be at His right hand, and the others at His left.

"And then," Jesus said, "the King shall say to those on His right hand, 'Come, you blessed of My Father, take the kingdom prepared for you from the foundation of the world. For I was hungry, and you gave Me food. I was thirsty, and you gave Me drink. I was a stranger, and you took Me into your house. I was naked, and you clothed Me. I was sick, and you visited Me. I was in prison, and you came to see Me.'

"Then they shall answer, 'Lord, when did we see You hungry, and feed You? Or thirsty, and give You a drink? When did we see that You were a stranger, and take You into our house? Or when did we see You naked, and clothe You? Or when did we see You sick, or in prison, and come to visit You?'

"And the King shall say, 'Truly, because you have done it to one of these My brothers, even the smallest of them, it is as if you did it to Me.'

"Then shall He say to those on His left hand, 'Depart from Me, you cursed, into everlasting fire prepared for the devil and his angels. For I was hungry, and you did not give Me anything to eat. I was thirsty, and you did not give Me a drink. I was a stranger, and you did not take Me into your house. I was naked, and you did not clothe Me. I was sick, and in prison, and you did not come to help Me.'

"And they also shall answer Him and say, 'Lord, when did we see You hungry, or thirsty, or a stranger, or naked, or sick, or in prison, and did not come to help You?'

"And the King shall say, 'Because you did not do it to one of the least of these My brothers, you did not do it to Me.'

"And these shall go away into everlasting punishment, but the good shall go into eternal life."

While Jesus spoke these words, there was one disciple who was not listening. Evil thoughts had come into the heart of Judas Iscariot. Judas did not love and trust Jesus. And when Satan whispered a wicked plan to him, he gladly listened. Satan suggested to Judas that he should sell and deliver Jesus over into the hands of the priests and Pharisees who were trying to kill Him.

Secretly Judas went to the high priest and said, "What will you give me if I bring you to Jesus when He is alone?" The council of priests promised to give him thirty pieces of silver.

Of course, neither Judas nor Satan could have harmed Jesus if He had not allowed them to do it. Jesus was truly the Son of God, and He was far more powerful than Judas or Satan.

It was not the jealousy of the priests, nor the greed of Judas, nor even the hate of Satan that brought the holy and sinless Jesus to His death. Jesus died because that was what He had come into the world to do. He died because He wanted to bear the punishment for our sins — the punishment which otherwise we would have had to pay ourselves. He died because He loved us. And if we love Him, and trust Him, He will save us from sin and death.

Chapter 44
IN THE UPPER ROOM
MATTHEW 26; MARK 14; LUKE 22; JOHN 13

All over Jerusalem the people were preparing for the Passover feast which was to be held that night.

Thirteen hundred years before, the Jewish people had been slaves in Egypt. When Pharaoh refused to let them go free, God sent ten plagues upon the Egyptians. In the last of these plagues the oldest son in every Egyptian house died. No one died in the homes of the Israelites. God had commanded the Jews to kill a lamb, and sprinkle its blood on the doorways of their houses. When God saw the blood, He "passed over" that house.

Every year at Passover time the Jews commemorated that night when the lamb was killed and its blood sprinkled on the doorway, the night when the lamb died instead of the first-born. But this Passover lamb did more than just point back to that night in Egypt. It also pointed forward to the time when God would send His own Son to die in the place of all those who trusted in Him. For Jesus was the true Lamb of God, who came into this world to die for our sins.

To celebrate this last Passover feast Jesus came to Jerusalem. On the day when the feast was to be held, the disciples asked Him, "Where shall we make the Passover supper ready?"

Jesus said to Peter and John, "Go into Jerusalem. A man with a pitcher of water will meet you. Follow him to the house where he is going. Say to the owner of the house, 'The Master says, "Where is the guest room, where I may eat the Passover with My disciples?"' He will show you a large upper room with couches and tables. There we shall celebrate the feast."

Peter and John went into Jerusalem, and found the room just as Jesus had said. There they prepared everything for the Passover supper.

This Thursday night was Jesus' last night on earth. The disciples did not know this, but they felt that He was soon going to leave them, and this made them sad. When it was evening, Jesus sat down with His twelve disciples in the upper room, to eat the Passover.

As they were eating, Jesus said, "I have wanted very much to eat this supper with you before I leave you." Then He said something which made them forget everything else. "One of you who are eating supper with Me will betray Me."

The disciples were shocked. Was one of them going to betray their beloved Lord, one of His own disciples who loved Him so much? How grieved they were at this thought! One of them asked sadly, "Is it I, Lord?" Another said, "Is it I?" And all the others asked, "Is it I?"

One of the disciples was lying on the couch next to Jesus with his head on Jesus' breast. It was John, the beloved disciple. Peter made a sign to him to ask Jesus who would do this wicked thing. John asked, "Who is it, Lord?"

Jesus answered, "It is the one to whom I am going to give this bread, when I have dipped it in the dish." Taking a little piece of bread, Jesus dipped it into the dish and gave it to Judas Iscariot. As He did this, He said, "Woe to that man who betrays Me! It would be better for that man if he had never been born."

You would think that after hearing these words of warning Judas would have turned back from the black deed he was planning. But Satan came into Judas' wicked heart and whispered that this very night was a good time to betray Jesus to the priests. All the people were in their own homes celebrating the Passover, and Jesus was alone with His disciples.

Jesus knew the thoughts in Judas' heart. He said, "What you are going to do, do quickly." Judas got up and went out into the night. None of the other disciples thought this was strange. They thought that perhaps Jesus had sent Judas to give something to the poor, because Judas carried the purse in which Jesus and the disciples kept the money they received.

But Jesus knew that Judas was going to betray Him, and that this was His last night on earth. He wanted to teach the disciples to remember always how He had died for them, to pay for their sins. He took some bread, blessed it, and broke it into little pieces. He gave each of them a piece, saying, "Take this and eat it. This is My body which is broken for you. Do this in remembrance of Me."

Then He took a cup of wine and gave thanks and said, "Drink ye all of it. This is My blood which is shed for many."

Since that night Christian people in all the world celebrate the Lord's Supper by eating bread and drinking wine in memory of the death of our dear Lord. The bread and wine are signs that we share in the forgiveness of sins which His death made possible. To those who truly love Jesus, and who come to Him to have their sins forgiven, the Lord's Supper is sacred.

Chapter 45
JESUS' LAST WORDS TO HIS DISCIPLES
MATTHEW 26; MARK 14; LUKE 22; JOHN 13-17

After the Passover supper Jesus said many things to comfort His beloved disciples before He left them. "Do not let your hearts be troubled," He said. "I am going to My Father. In My Father's house there are many beautiful places. I am going to prepare a place for you."

The disciples knew that these were the last words Jesus would teach them. How eagerly they listened!

"If you love Me, keep My commandments," Jesus said. "My commandment is that you love one another, just as I have loved you. No man can have greater love than this, that he gives his life for his friends. I am going to lay down My life for you.

"When I go to heaven, I will ask My Father to send you a Comforter to stay with you forever. He will send the Holy Spirit down into your hearts to strengthen you. When the Holy Spirit comes into your hearts, He will tell you about Me."

The disciples remembered these words. After Jesus returned to heaven, the Holy Spirit came to live in the hearts of those who love and trust Jesus, to strengthen and to teach them. For the Holy Spirit is God, just as Jesus and the Father are. These three are one God.

"You have been with Me from the beginning," Jesus said, "and you have heard all My words, and have seen all My works. Now I want you to go and tell all the world about Me.

I am going to leave you for a little while, and you will be sad. But soon I shall see you again, and then your hearts will be full of joy."

"What does this mean?" the disciples wondered. "Shall we see Him again in a little while?" For they did not yet understand that Jesus would rise from the dead.

Then Jesus lifted His eyes to heaven and prayed, "Father, the time has come for Me to leave the earth. I have finished the work which Thou gavest Me to do. I have given eternal life to those that love Thee. I have glorified Thee on this earth. But now I come to Thee. I pray that Thou wilt keep My disciples from all evil. And I pray not only for them, but for all the people in the world who will believe in Me."

After this, Jesus and His disciples sang a hymn. Then He led them out of the upper room. They passed through Jerusalem and over the brook Kidron to the Mount of Olives, where they had often gone together.

As they walked through the quiet night toward the mountain, Jesus said, "This very night every one of you will leave Me."

Peter cried, "Even if everyone else leaves You, I will never leave You."

Jesus said sorrowfully, "Peter, I tell you truly that this very night, before the rooster crows twice, you will say three times that you do not even know Me."

Peter exclaimed, "I will *never* desert You! Even if I should have to die, I would not deny You!" And each of the other disciples spoke in the same way; for they did not know what was going to happen that very night.

Chapter 46
THE KISS OF JUDAS
MATTHEW 26; MARK 14; LUKE 22; JOHN 18

On the slopes of the Mount of Olives there was a garden called Gethsemane where Jesus and the disciples often went. After the Passover supper Jesus led the way to this garden and said, "Sit here while I go and pray."

Taking Peter and James and John with Him, Jesus went a little further into the garden. He said to the three of them, "My soul is very sorrowful, even unto death. Stay here and watch with Me."

Then Jesus went a little distance away, about as far as one can throw a stone. He fell on the ground and prayed to His Father.

Jesus knew that He had come into the world to suffer and die for sin. But now that He faced that terrible suffering, He felt as if He could not stand it. He was not afraid to die. It was the anger of God against my sins and yours that Jesus dreaded. He prayed aloud, "O My Father, if it be possible, take away this suffering from Me! Nevertheless, not as I will, but as Thou wilt!"

In the great agony of His suffering Jesus' sweat was like great drops of blood falling down on the ground. After a time He rose up from His prayer and returned to His disciples. He found them sleeping. Sorrow had worn them out.

"Why do you sleep?" He asked. "Get up, and spend your time in prayer. Could you not watch with Me for one hour?"

A second time Jesus went away and prayed, "O My Father, if I must endure this suffering, Thy will be done!" A second time He returned to His disciples. They were asleep again, for their eyes were heavy. They did not know what to say to Him. They were ashamed that they could not keep awake when Jesus asked them to watch and pray with Him.

Jesus left them and went away again, and prayed the third time, "O My Father, if I must suffer, Thy will be done!" He had so wanted His disciples to pray with Him while He was in such agony. He was man as well as God, and He needed help in His suffering, just as all men do. But His disciples went to sleep instead of watching and praying with Him. So God sent an angel down from heaven to comfort Jesus.

After Jesus had prayed this prayer the third time, He came back to His disciples and said, "Get up. Let us be going, for the one who is going to betray Me is here."

Just then there appeared in the darkness of the garden a sudden flare of torches, lighting up the blackness of the night. In the light of the torches the disciples saw a band of soldiers and officers, with swords and sticks. And leading them was — Judas!

Judas had gone to the chief priests and Pharisees and said, "Now is the time to seize Jesus! He will be alone with His disciples in the garden, where He often goes. Give me some soldiers, and we will soon catch Him!"

As Judas showed the soldiers where the garden was, he said, "I will kiss Him, and you will know by that which one of them is Jesus." He went forward and said, "Master, Master," as if he were glad to see Jesus, and kissed Him.

Jesus knew that it was not friendship that was in Judas' heart. He said sorrowfully, "Judas, do you betray Me with a kiss?" Then, turning to the officers, He said, "For whom are you looking?"

The soldiers answered, "Jesus of Nazareth."

Jesus answered with simple dignity, "I am He."

The soldiers had not expected anything like this. They were awed and afraid. They stepped back and fell to the ground, not daring to touch Him. Jesus said again, "For whom are you looking?" And they said again, "For Jesus of Nazareth."

"I told you that I am He," Jesus said.

Peter saw that the soldiers had come to arrest Jesus. He was not going to stand by and let the soldiers capture his dear Lord. He pulled out his sword, swung it wildly, and struck off the ear of the high priest's servant.

But Jesus turned to Peter and said, "Put away your sword. Don't you know that if I pray to My Father, He will send Me more than twelve legions of angels to take care of Me? But how then shall the scripture be fulfilled?" Then Jesus touched the man's ear and healed it.

The soldiers closed in around Jesus. The disciples were overcome with terror. They ran away and left Him, for fear that they would be arrested too. Peter and John soon came back. They followed the soldiers at a distance.

Chapter 47
WHY PETER WEPT
MATTHEW 26; MARK 14; LUKE 22; JOHN 18

All the chief priests and scribes and elders were gathered together in the house of Caiaphas, the high priest. Toward this house the soldiers made their way from the garden, with Jesus bound in their midst. Peter and John followed at a distance, to see what would happen to their Lord.

John happened to be acquainted with Caiaphas, and he went into the house when Jesus was led inside. Peter did not dare to go in. He stood outside with the servants. After a while John noticed Peter standing there. He told the young girl in charge of the door to bring Peter in. The girl looked closely at Peter as he entered.

"Are you not one of this man's disciples?" she asked.

Peter was terribly afraid that the girl would tell the priests he was a follower of Jesus, and that he, too, would be arrested and killed. "No, I am not," he said.

Jesus had been taken to an upper room where all the priests and scribes were assembled. The two disciples waited with the servants in the outer hall. They could see Jesus through the open door, but they could not hear what was said in the room upstairs. The nights are often chilly in Palestine, and the hall of the high priest was cold. The servants had built a little fire to warm themselves while they waited. Peter went and sat down by the fire too.

Standing by the fire was a girl who looked at Peter curiously. She asked, "Aren't you one of His disciples?"

This was the second time someone had asked Peter about his connection with Jesus. He was more frightened than ever. "Truly, I am not," he said hastily.

About an hour later one of the high priest's servants, a relative of the man whose ear Peter had cut off in the garden, asked, "Didn't I see you in the garden with this man? I can tell by the way you talk that you also come from Galilee."

In his terror Peter began to curse and swear, saying, "Man, I don't know what you are talking about. I tell you, I don't know the man!" So

Peter denied three times that he had ever known Jesus!

It was now early morning. Just as Peter spoke this last time, a rooster crowed outside. Jesus turned around and looked at Peter. That look reminded Peter of what Jesus had said, "Before the rooster crows twice, you will deny Me three times." That look reminded Peter of how he had solemnly promised, "Even though everybody else deserts You, I will never desert You. I will go with You even to death."

Peter ran out of the palace. Oh, to think that he had denied his beloved Lord, and had done it after promising to go to prison and to death for Him!

Peter's heart was filled with grief. He went away by himself. He threw himself on the ground and put his head down on his arms. How could he have done such a thing? He would never, as long as he lived, forget the look Jesus gave him when he said that he never knew Him!

Peter wept bitterly!

Chapter 48
JESUS BEFORE THE HIGH PRIEST
MATTHEW 26, 27; MARK 14; LUKE 22

The soldiers had taken Jesus to an upstairs room where the priests and elders were gathered together to question Him. It was now late at night, and it was against the Jewish law for the court to meet at night. But the priests did not trouble themselves about the law. They could not wait till morning to question Jesus, for fear the people in the crowded city would hear of His arrest and storm the high priest's palace. They were determined to find something they could accuse Him of when they

took Him to the Roman governor Pilate, early the next morning. They wanted to make an accusation so serious that Pilate would have to condemn Jesus to death.

Many persons who had been bribed by the priests to lie about Jesus came into the judgment hall and made accusations against Him, but no two of them accused Him of the same thing. According to Jewish law at least two witnesses had to agree before a man could be sentenced.

No matter what His enemies said, Jesus was silent. At last the high priest stood up and said, "Why do you not answer what these men say against you?"

Still Jesus made no answer. Then the high priest said solemnly, "I say to you, in the name of the living God, to tell us whether you are the Christ, the Son of God?"

Jesus answered, "I am, and one day you shall see Me sitting at the right hand of God, and coming on the clouds of heaven!"

Triumphantly the high priest said to the others, "We no longer need any witnesses. You yourselves have heard him say that he is the Son of God. That is blasphemy! What is your judgment?"

They called out, "He is guilty of death!" For the priests refused to believe that Jesus really was God's Son. They thought He was speaking terrible blasphemy when He called Himself God. According to the law of Moses, any man who spoke blasphemy must be killed.

The high priest Caiaphas tore his clothes to show how shocked he was to hear a man call himself God. The other judges began to treat Jesus shamefully. They spit in His face. Some of their servants blindfolded Him and hit Him, saying, "Prophesy to us who it was that hit you!"

By this time the morning light was beginning to show in the sky. With hearts filled with hate, a great crowd of priests and scribes and elders went out through the city streets to bring Jesus to the house of Pontius Pilate, the Roman governor.

Among the crowd that followed was the traitor Judas, who had led the soldiers to Jesus in the garden. When Judas heard the high priest accusing Jesus, and realized that Jesus would be killed, he began to understand what a wicked thing he had done.

Taking with him the thirty pieces of silver which they had paid him, Judas went back to the priests and elders. "Take the money back!" he cried. "I have betrayed innocent blood! Jesus has not done anything wrong!"

But the priests replied coldly, "What do we care? That is your business." They refused to take the money back.

Then Judas saw that it was too late. They would not let Jesus go, no matter what he said. He threw the money on the floor and ran out of the city to a field. There he hanged himself on a tree.

The priests picked up the money from the floor. "What shall we do with it?" they wondered. "We cannot give it to the temple, because it is the price of blood." Finally they used it to buy a piece of land on which to bury strangers. They called this cemetery the Potter's Field. Afterward, when the people in Jerusalem heard what had happened, they gave the field another name. They called it the Field of Blood.

Chapter 49
WHY PILATE WASHED HIS HANDS
MATTHEW 27; MARK 15; LUKE 23; JOHN 18, 19

Early that morning Pilate saw a crowd of Jewish priests and elders coming toward his palace, bringing with them a prisoner who was bound. He came outside to talk to them, for the priests would not even go into the house of a Gentile, for fear they might become unfit to worship God through this contact with a heathen.

Pilate asked the priests, "Why are you bringing this man here? What has he done?"

They answered, "If he were not a criminal, we would not have brought him to you. We found this fellow teaching the people that they must not pay taxes to Caesar, and saying that he is Christ, a king."

Pilate went inside the judgment hall and called Jesus. "Are you the king of the Jews?" he asked Him.

Jesus answered, "My kingdom is not of this world. If My kingdom were an earthly kingdom, my servants would fight for Me so that I would not be arrested."

"Are you a king then?" Pilate asked.

"Yes," Jesus said, "I am a king. I came into this world to reveal the truth. Those who love the truth listen to Me."

"What is truth?" Pilate asked. He did not wait for an answer, for he did not believe Jesus could teach him anything. He went back outside where the priests and elders and other people were waiting. "You have brought this man to me to be judged," he said. "I have talked to him, and I can find no fault in him. He has done nothing deserving death."

The crowd set up a clamor. "He has been telling the people to rebel from Galilee through all the land."

When Pilate heard that Jesus came from Galilee, he decided to send Him to Herod, the king of Galilee, who was just then visiting in Jerusalem. It was this Herod, you remember, who put John the Baptist in prison and murdered him.

Herod was glad to see Jesus. He had wanted to see Him for a long time, because he had heard so many things about Him. Sometimes he wondered whether Jesus could possibly be John the Baptist come back from the dead. He hoped that Jesus would do a miracle to amuse him.

But Jesus refused to answer Herod's questions, or to work a miracle for his amusement. So Herod sent Him back to Pilate, saying he saw no reason why Jesus should be put to death.

Herod's reply made Pilate all the more sure that it would be wrong to kill Jesus. Pilate's wife also sent a message to him, saying, "Do not have anything to do with that good man. I have had a terrible dream about him."

So Pilate went out again to the Jews and said, "You have a custom that every year at the time of the feast I should release one prisoner to you. Shall I release the King of the Jews, or Barabbas?" Now Barabbas was a robber and a murderer.

Pilate knew that the chief priests had delivered Jesus to him because they were jealous that so many of the common people followed Him. He thought perhaps his offer would arouse the people to demand Jesus' release. But the priests persuaded the people to shout, "Not this man, but Barabbas! Not this man, but Barabbas!"

Pilate said, "Then what shall I do with Jesus who is called the Christ?"

The crowd yelled wildly, "Crucify him! Crucify him!"

"Take him yourselves and crucify him," Pilate said. "I don't find he has committed any crime."

The Jews answered, "We have a law, and by our law he ought to die, because he called himself the son of God!"

When he heard this, Pilate was afraid. What if Jesus really were the son of God? He went back into the judgment hall. He asked Jesus, "Where do you come from?" But Jesus answered not a word.

"Do you refuse to answer me?" Pilate asked. "Don't you know I have power to crucify you, and power to let you go?"

"You would have no power against Me," Jesus said, "if God did not give it to you."

Then Pilate brought Jesus outside, where the crowd was, and said, "I find no cause of death in this man. I will therefore whip him, and let him go."

Instantly they shouted, "If you let him go, you are not Caesar's friend! Whoever calls himself a king speaks against Caesar, the Roman emperor!"

Pilate saw that he could not stop them. He took a basin of water and washed his hands before all the crowd, as if he were washing away his guilt. "I am not to blame for killing this innocent man," he said solemnly. "You are to blame."

"We will bear the blame!" the people shouted. "His blood be upon us and upon our children!"

Then Pilate released the murderer Barabbas from prison, and he gave Jesus over to the soldiers to be crucified.

Chapter 50
CARRYING THE CROSS
MATTHEW 27; MARK 15; LUKE 23; JOHN 19

What joy the enemies of Jesus felt when they heard Pilate give the order for Jesus to be crucified! At last this troublesome fellow would be put out of the way!

The Roman soldiers bound Jesus to a post. They beat His back with a cruel knotted whip until Jesus' back was covered with blood. It was you and I who deserved to be beaten that way because of our sins, but Jesus bore it for us.

Then the soldiers began to mock and insult Him. Because He had said He was a king, they pretended to treat Him like a king. They dressed Him in a purple robe, the color which was reserved for kings. They took some thorny branches and twisted them together into a wreath. This they put on Jesus' head for a crown. In His hand they put a reed for a royal scepter.

When they had done all this, they kneeled down before Him, saying, "Hail, King of the Jews!" They spit on Him, and snatched the reed out of His hand and hit Him with it. It was you and I who deserved to be mocked, but Jesus bore this also for us. He bore it without a word. Seven hundred years before this the prophet Isaiah had said, "Surely He hath borne our griefs, and carried our sorrows."

After they had had their fun, the soldiers took the purple robe off Jesus. On His bleeding shoulders they put a heavy wooden cross and led Him away to be crucified.

Outside the city of Jerusalem there was a low hill called Calvary, where the Romans crucified condemned criminals. The soldiers led Jesus toward this hill, while a crowd of Jesus' enemies and a few of His friends followed.

It was a long way to Calvary, and the cross was heavy. Jesus was weakened from the pain and the loss of blood. As they came out of the city of Jerusalem, Jesus stumbled and fell under the heavy cross.

Just then a strong countryman named Simon happened to be coming into the city. When they saw that Jesus was too weak to carry His cross, the soldiers forced Simon to carry it for Him.

Where were all of Jesus' friends? Where were the great crowds who came to listen to Him teach in the temple, the people who only a week before had shouted, "Blessed is the King who comes in the name of the Lord!"?

Many of the Jews did love Jesus. But most of Jesus' friends did not know what was happening to Him. The priests had been careful to arrest Jesus when no one would know about it. It was evening when Judas came to the garden to betray his Master. Jesus had been kept in Caiaphas' house all night, and had been brought to Pilate's judgment hall in the very early morning. Even now it was only nine o'clock. Many people were quietly eating their breakfast, not knowing what was happening to Jesus.

Probably they planned to go to the temple a little later, and expected to hear Jesus teaching there as He had done on so many other days.

But soon the news spread through the city like wildfire, in every direction. "They have captured our Lord! They have arrested Him, and are going to kill Him at last! Hurry! *Hurry!* They are taking Him outside the city to crucify Him!"

Many of Jesus' friends came hurrying out of their houses and ran to Calvary. The women who had followed Jesus while He was teaching hurried along the same road that Jesus had stumbled over a little earlier. Among them was Mary, Jesus' own mother. Another was Mary Magdalene, one of the many people whom Jesus had cured.

John, the beloved disciple, had not left Jesus during the long night. He had seen the soldiers beat and mock his Lord. He stayed near Jesus all the way to Calvary.

At last the spot was reached. The soldiers dug a hole for the cross. The friends of Jesus watched helplessly, their hearts filled with grief.

Chapter 51
THE SUN BECOMES DARK
MATTHEW 27; MARK 15; LUKE 23; JOHN 19

The soldiers fastened to the top of the cross the title which Pilate had written, in Greek, and in Hebrew, and in Latin: *Jesus of Nazareth, the King of the Jews.*

Then they stretched Jesus out upon the cross. With heavy spikes they nailed His blessed hands and feet to the wooden beams. They raised the cross and set it in the hole which they had dug, and filled the hole with stones and earth so that the cross would stand upright. Two thieves

were crucified with Jesus, one on His right hand, and one on His left.

When they had finished all this, the soldiers divided up Jesus' clothes among the four of them. His coat was one piece, without any seams. So they said, "Let us not tear it, but cast lots for it, whose it shall be."

It is very painful to you and me to see our beloved Lord hanging there on the cross, with His blood dripping down. But even though it is painful, we need to look, for He hangs there because of what we have done. His blood is being shed to pay for our sins. He loved us so much that He chose to die in our place.

Even in His great suffering Jesus thought not of Himself but of others. The first words He uttered were a prayer: "Father, forgive them, for they know not what they do."

Around the cross Jesus' friends had gathered. The two whom Jesus loved most of all, His mother and the beloved disciple John, were standing close to the cross. He saw them there, and even in His pain He did not forget them. He said to His mother, "John shall be your son," and to John, "Take My mother to be your mother." From that very day John took her into his own house.

While Jesus' friends wept, there were many there who were glad to see Him die. The scribes and priests who had cried, "Crucify him!" had followed to Calvary. Now they jeered and mocked, "Save yourself, and come down from the cross, and then we will believe in you!"

"He saved others, but he cannot save himself," others sneered.

One of the thieves who hung beside Jesus joined in, saying, "If you are the Christ sent by God, save yourself and us!"

But the other thief said, "How dare you talk like this when you are soon going to die and appear before God? You and I deserve to die because of our wicked deeds, but this man has done nothing wrong." Then he said to Jesus, "Lord, remember me when You come into Your kingdom!"

Jesus answered, "Today you shall be with Me in heaven." And that is the promise Jesus gives to every dying one who puts his trust in our Saviour.

At noon God took away the light of day. For three dreadful hours, while Jesus hung on the cross, the darkness of night spread over all the land.

Jesus was suffering pain from the nails in His hands and feet, but He was also suffering a much deeper kind of pain. For during these three hours God Himself turned His back on His dearly beloved Son and left Him.

All His life on earth Jesus had loved God and served Him perfectly, without any sin. But now He had taken upon Himself all the sin that ever has been done or ever will be done in the whole world — your sin, and my sin, and the sin of every single person who puts his trust in Jesus as his Saviour. God gave Him the punishment you and I deserved to suffer. God separated Himself from Jesus so that Jesus felt only God's anger against sin and no longer His love for His Son. And that is the worst punishment any person can ever suffer.

In His anguish Jesus cried out, "My God, My God, why hast Thou forsaken Me?" Jesus was forsaken by God so that you and I would never be forsaken by God. It is no wonder that in those black hours the light of the sun was withdrawn and the whole earth was plunged in darkness.

Just before the end Jesus said, "I thirst." Someone kindly dipped a sponge into a dish of vinegar and raised it on a stick to Jesus' mouth.

It was almost over now. Jesus knew that His work was done. He cried out in a loud voice, "It is finished!" And then He said one last thing. "Father, into Thy hands I commend My spirit."

Then He died. The suffering was over. The work He had come to do was done. He had paid for our sins.

Just as Jesus died, God sent an earthquake. The ground trembled and shook, and great rocks were torn apart. The veil of the temple, which separated the place where God's glory shone above the cherubim from the rest of the temple, was torn from the top to the bottom. Now everyone could look into the Holy of Holies where, before Jesus paid for our sins, only the high priest could go, and he only once a year. For since Jesus has paid for sins, there is no longer any need for a veil to separate those who trust in Jesus from the holy God.

The captain of the Roman soldiers was astonished to see the greatness of the suffering Saviour, and the signs of God's anger in the three hours of darkness and the earthquake. "Truly, this was the Son of God!" he cried.

And the captain was right. It was truly the very Son of God who died there on the cross of Calvary. He died for us. He gave His very life to pay for our sins. As the prophet said long before, "He was wounded for our transgressions, He was bruised for our iniquities, and by His stripes we are healed" (Isaiah 53).

We may go to this same Jesus today with all our sorrows, and all our problems, and all our sins. He sees us, and hears us, and loves us. If we trust and love Him, we have new life — a joyous, happy life. For He takes away all our burdens.

Shall we not love and serve this wonderful Jesus, who finished the work of our salvation on the cross?

Chapter 52
THE STONE IS ROLLED AWAY
MATTHEW 27, 28; MARK 15; LUKE 23; JOHN 19

Among those who loved and trusted Jesus was a rich man named Joseph. Before this, Joseph had never dared to serve Jesus openly for fear of the priests. Now that Jesus was dead, Joseph went to Pilate and begged to be allowed to bury His body.

Another rich friend of Jesus was Nicodemus, the ruler of the Jews who, you remember, once came to talk to Jesus at night. Nicodemus brought a hundred pounds of spices such as the Jews used when a person was buried.

In a garden near Jerusalem was a new grave which Joseph intended to be used for his own burial when he died. It had been carved out of solid rock, like many Jewish graves. Here they laid Jesus' body. They rolled a great stone in front of the entrance.

By now it was sunset, and the Jewish Sabbath was about to begin.

Jesus' friends left the grave and went home with sad hearts. They did not really understand the promises Jesus had made that He would rise from the grave after three days. They only knew they had hoped so much that Jesus was the Saviour long promised by God, and now He was dead!

The next morning the chief priests and the Pharisees met in Jerusalem. They congratulated each other that at last they had gotten rid of Jesus. Suddenly one of them remembered that Jesus had said, "After three days I will rise again."

None of the priests believed that Jesus would really rise from the dead. But they were afraid His disciples might come at night and steal His body from the grave, and then tell the people that Jesus had risen from the dead.

So they hurried to Pilate's palace and said, "Sir, we remember that while that deceiver was yet alive, he said, 'After three days I will rise again.' Therefore we request that his grave be sealed, for fear his disciples steal him away by night and tell the people he has come back to life."

"You may have some soldiers to watch the grave, and you may seal the opening," Pilate replied. "Make it as sure as you can."

So the Pharisees and the priests hurried to the garden where Jesus was buried. They sealed the stone before the opening of the grave, and set some soldiers to watch and make sure it was not disturbed.

That Sabbath was a sad day for Jesus' disciples and the women who had followed Him from Galilee. They met together in an upper room, where the enemies of Jesus would not see them, and they talked sadly together about what had happened.

These people had loved Jesus dearly — more than they had ever loved anyone before. They had hoped He would set up a kingdom and rule over His people, as David had done long ago. But Jesus was dead. A dead man could not become their king!

All that day and night, while Jesus' friends wept together in the upper room, the watching soldiers guarded the grave. Just as the first faint streaks of dawn came into the sky on Sunday morning, all at once the earth began to tremble and shake

Big, wide cracks opened in the ground.

The soldiers were terrified. They were afraid that any moment the earth would open at their feet and swallow them up. While the earth quaked, a mighty angel of the Lord came down from heaven and rolled away the stone and sat on it. His face shone like lightning, and his clothes were as white as newly fallen snow.

Terrified, the soldiers fell to the ground like dead men. When at last they dared to look up, they saw that the grave was open, and empty! They ran to the city of Jerusalem, to tell the chief priests and the Pharisees about the angel, and the earthquake, and the empty grave.

Did the priests now at last believe in Jesus when they heard about the angel coming down from heaven to open His grave? No, no matter how many wonderful signs about Jesus were given to them, they refused to believe.

The priests did a most dishonest thing. They said to the soldiers, "Tell everybody that His disciples came and stole His body while you were sleeping. Say nothing about the angel. If you do this, we will pay you well. And if Pilate hears that you slept on duty, we will persuade him not to punish you." So the Pharisees bribed the soldiers to tell a wicked lie.

Chapter 53
VISITORS TO THE TOMB
MATTHEW 28; MARK 16; LUKE 24; JOHN 20

Mary Magdalene and several other women had also prepared spices to anoint Jesus' body on Friday night. All during the Sabbath they rested, as God had commanded.

Early on Sunday morning, before the sun was up, they hurried to the garden where Jesus had been buried. "Who will roll the stone away from the entrance?" they asked each other as they walked through the silent streets of the city. They knew that they would never be able to move such a heavy stone.

When they reached the garden, they were surprised to find that the stone had already been rolled away. They stooped down and went inside the grave. The tomb was empty! Jesus' body was not there!

The women did not know what to think. As they stood there wondering, two angels in shining white clothes stood beside them. The women were afraid, and bowed their faces to the ground.

"Do not be afraid," the angels said. "You are looking for Jesus who was crucified. He is not here. He is risen! Don't you remember that He told you that He would rise on the third day?"

Suddenly the women did remember. He had said just that! They ran all the way back to Jerusalem, to tell the disciples what they had seen. They burst into the upper room and said excitedly, "We found Jesus' tomb empty! And we saw a vision of angels, who said He is alive! But we did not see Him."

The disciples did not believe the story of the excited women. Had they not themselves seen Jesus' dead body? They completely forgot that Jesus had told them that He was going to die and be buried, and then rise again from the grave.

Peter and John wanted to go to the grave and see for themselves. The garden where Jesus had been buried was more than a mile away, but in their eagerness to find out if He could possibly be alive again, they ran all the way.

John ran faster than Peter, for he was younger. He reached the grave first. Stooping down to look in, he saw the linen cloths that had been wrapped around Jesus' body, but Jesus Himself was gone.

By that time Peter also came panting up. He went past John into the grave itself. There were the linen cloths, and the napkin that had been wrapped around Jesus' head lay in a place by itself.

John now followed Peter into the tomb. There were no angels to be seen, as the women had claimed there were. Slowly, sadly, not knowing what to think, they went back to Jerusalem.

Mary Magdalene could not stay away from the grave. She went back, and stood there with tears rolling down her cheeks. Indeed, she had done almost nothing but weep these three days. Jesus had been so good to her, and now He was dead! She had been so greatly frightened to see the angel that she could hardly remember what he had said. She did not understand that Jesus was actually alive again. His body was not in the grave, and she did not know where to look for it.

After a while she stooped down and looked into the grave. Two beautiful angels were sitting there, one at the head and one at the foot of the place where the body of Jesus had lain.

The angels said, "Woman, why do you weep?"

Mary answered, through her tears, "Because they have taken my Lord away, and I do not know where they have laid Him." As she turned around, Mary saw someone standing before her. It was Jesus. But Mary was so lost in her grief, and her eyes were so blurred by tears, that she did not even recognize Him. She thought that it was the gardener.

Jesus said to her, "Woman, why are you weeping? For whom are you looking?"

"Oh, sir," Mary said, "if you have carried His body away, tell me where you have put it, and I will take Him away."

Jesus answered with only one word: "Mary!"

When she heard that voice she so loved, Mary turned and looked straight at Jesus. "Master!" she cried. It was truly her dear Lord!

Mary was wild with happiness. While she looked at Him with love and joy, Jesus told her to go and tell His disciples that He was going to ascend to His Father in heaven.

How happy Mary was as she ran back to Jerusalem to the room where the disciples sat together, sorrowing! "He is alive!" she cried. "I have seen Him myself! He came and spoke to me in the garden. He told me to go back and tell you that He is risen from the dead! And soon He is going to ascend to His Father in heaven!"

The hearts of these disciples who loved Jesus had been so heavy with grief that they could hardly realize what Mary was saying. At last they began to remember that Jesus *had* told them all these things before they happened. They had not understood that Jesus is stronger even than death. They began to believe that Jesus is the Lord of life. Soon they would see Him again!

Chapter 54
THE RISEN LORD
MARK 16; LUKE 24; JOHN 20

On that first Easter Sunday two people were walking from Jerusalem to the little village of Emmaus, not far away. The name of one of them was Cleopas; the name of the other we do not know.

As they walked, they talked sadly about Jesus' death, and the strange story of the women who had gone to the grave early that morning. Suddenly Jesus came up and walked along with them, but they did not recognize Him. He asked, "What are you talking about that makes you so sad?"

"Are you a stranger in Jerusalem?" Cleopas asked in surprise. "Don't you know about the things that happened there these last three days?"

"What things?" Jesus asked.

"About Jesus of Nazareth," they said. "He was a wonderful prophet of God, both in what He taught and in the works He did. We had hoped that He was the promised Saviour of Israel. But our chief priest and rulers crucified Him. Today is the third day since these things happened." Both were sad at the thought.

Then they went on. "Some women went to His grave early this morning. They say that His body was not there, and that they saw a vision of angels who said He is alive. Some of us went ourselves to see, and found that His body was really gone. But we did not find Him!"

"O how foolish you are, and slow of heart to believe," Jesus said. "Don't you understand that all these things were written long ago in the scriptures? It was God's plan that the Saviour suffer and die for men, and afterward go up to heaven in glory."

And, starting at the beginning of the Old Testament, Jesus explained to them all the things which had been prophesied about Himself. He talked until they came to the town of Emmaus, where Cleopas and his friend were planning to stay. It was already evening, and they begged Jesus to spend the night with them.

After Cleopas and his friend had set out some food, the three of them sat down to supper. Jesus blessed the bread and gave it to them. All at once their eyes were opened, and they saw that it was Jesus Himself!

Even while they stared at Him with joy, He vanished out of their sight. For since He had risen from the dead Jesus could go anywhere without walking there. He could go through closed doors and into locked rooms.

Now Cleopas and his friend remembered how Jesus had talked to them as they walked together. "Did not our hearts burn within us while He talked to us along the road, and explained the prophets to us?" they said to each other. Eagerly they hurried back to Jerusalem to tell the others the marvelous news that Jesus had actually risen from the dead! It was six miles back to Jerusalem, but they did not care. It was dark already, but that did not stop them. They almost ran the whole way in their eagerness to tell the disciples the wonderful news.

The disciples were still sitting in the upstairs room in Jerusalem. They had shut the doors tight, for they were afraid that the priests would arrest them next. But they were no longer sad, for Jesus had appeared to Peter as well as to Mary.

Then Cleopas and his friend burst in with their story of meeting and talking to Jesus. While they were still talking, suddenly Jesus Himself stood in the middle of the room and said, "Peace be unto you!"

Instead of being wild with joy, the disciples were terrified. They thought He must be a ghost, because He had come in when the doors were locked. "Why are you frightened?" Jesus said. "And why do you think I am a ghost? Look at My hands and feet, and see that it is I Myself. Touch Me, and see that I have real flesh and bones. A ghost does not have a body, as I have."

Then the disciples saw His hands and feet, torn by the cruel nails of the cross, and they knew that this was indeed their own dear Lord. Their hearts were filled with joy and wonder.

"Have you anything here to eat?" Jesus asked. They gave Him a piece of a broiled fish, and He ate it to prove to them that He really was alive.

Then He asked, "Don't you remember that while I was still with you I told you I must suffer and die, as the prophets wrote in the scriptures?" And He began to explain all the prophecies about Himself in the Old Testament, as He had explained them to Cleopas and his friend on the road to Emmaus.

"I suffered and died," He said to them, "so that all who are sorry for their sins can be forgiven. Go and preach to all nations, beginning right here in Jerusalem. You who have been with Me and have seen all these things are to tell them to all the world. I will send the Holy Spirit to you. Stay here in Jerusalem until the Spirit comes to give you power."

The disciples listened with wonder and with joy. How could they be sad and afraid, now that their Lord was living again? Jesus was stronger than the death which had ruled all the world ever since Adam sinned. By rising from the dead Jesus brought eternal life to all who love and trust in Him.

Chapter 55

JESUS COMES TO HIS FRIENDS
LUKE 24; JOHN 20, 21

When Jesus appeared to the disciples in the upper room, one of them was not there. That one disciple was Thomas. When the others told Thomas they had seen the Lord, Thomas said, "Unless I see the print of the nails, and put my finger into the nail holes, and thrust my hand into the wound in His side, I will not believe."

Eight days later the disciples were again together in the same room with the doors shut. This time Thomas was with them. Again Jesus stood among them and said, "Peace be unto you!"

Turning to Thomas, Jesus said, "Reach out your finger, and put it into the nail holes in My hand. Reach out your hand and thrust it into My side, and be not faithless, but believing!"

Thomas could not doubt any longer. He said in awe, "My Lord, and my God!"

Jesus said, "Thomas, you have believed because you have seen Me. Blessed are those who have not seen, and yet have believed."

Now that Jesus had risen from the dead, He no longer spent all His time with the disciples. He came and went mysteriously, even going through closed doors. In this way He was preparing them for the time when He would return to His Father in heaven.

Sometimes when Jesus appeared, the disciples did not recognize Him at first. Some of them had gone back to Galilee, where they had lived before Jesus called them to be His disciples. Simon Peter was a fisherman. He and some of the other disciples took nets and rowed out on the lake to fish.

They fished all night without any success. In the morning, as they rowed back to shore, Jesus was standing on the beach, but they did not recognize Him.

He said to them, "Children, have you anything to eat?"

They answered, "No."

"Throw out your net on the other side of the boat, and you will find some fish," He said.

They did as He told them, and now their net was so full of fish they could not draw it up into the boat. They tugged as hard as they could, but they could not pull it in.

John understood this was a miracle. He said to Peter, "It is the Lord."

Peter could not wait for the boat to row to the shore. He jumped out into the shallow water, leaving the others to drag the net to land.

When the disciples reached shore, they saw a fire with fish frying on it, and some bread beside it. "Bring some of the fish you caught," Jesus said. They brought some of the fish. Then Jesus said, "Come and eat." So they sat down and ate. Not one of them dared to ask, "Who are you?" for they all knew it was the Lord.

After they had finished eating, Jesus said to Peter, "Peter, do you love Me?"

Peter answered, "Lord, You know that I love You."

"Feed My lambs," said Jesus. Then He asked again, "Peter, do you love Me?"

Peter said, "Yes, Lord, You know that I love You."

Jesus said, "Feed My sheep."

Then for the third time Jesus asked, "Peter, do you love Me?"

Peter was grieved that Jesus asked this question three times. He knew that Jesus was thinking of the three times Peter had denied Him on the night of the trial. He answered, "Lord, You know *all* things. You know that I love You."

Jesus did know that Peter loved Him. He answered, "Feed My sheep." Jesus had a great work for Peter to do, as you shall learn later.

Chapter 56
HOW JESUS LEFT THE EARTH
MATTHEW 28; MARK 16; LUKE 24; ACTS 1; I CORINTHIANS 15

Many times after He rose from the dead, Jesus appeared to His friends. Once when the eleven apostles were on a mountain in Galilee, where Jesus had promised to meet them, He appeared and told them what they must do after He had left them to go back to His Father in heaven. He said to them, "Go and teach all nations, and baptize them in the name of the Father, and of the Son, and of the Holy Spirit. Teach them to do all the things I have commanded you. And I will be with you always, even to the end of the world."

At another time Jesus appeared to five hundred of His friends who had gathered together to talk about Him. Later He visited His brother James, but the Bible does not tell us what He said.

Last of all Jesus appeared to His disciples in Jerusalem. They walked together to the place they had so often visited — the village of Bethany, on the Mount of Olives.

It was now forty days since that Sunday morning when Jesus rose from the dead. He had appeared to His friends eleven times since then. At last the time had come for Him to leave this earth and go back to live with His Father in heaven.

When they reached the Mount of Olives, Jesus told the disciples to wait in Jerusalem for the Holy Spirit to come. "Before many days," He said, "you shall be baptized by the Holy Spirit. He will give you power you do not have now. You must tell all the people in the world about Me — those who live in Jerusalem, and those in Samaria, and all those who live in the furthest parts of the earth."

These were the last words Jesus spoke to His disciples. He raised His hands to bless them. As they watched, they saw Him rise from the ground. Higher and higher into the blue sky He rose, until at last a cloud hid Him from their eyes, and they saw Him no more.

Wasn't that a glorious way for Jesus to go back to heaven? The disciples felt that it was. They stood looking after Him for a long time, trying to catch a last glimpse of Him.

While they were looking into the sky, two angels dressed in white appeared to them. "Why do you stand looking up into heaven?" the angels asked. "This Jesus, who has gone into heaven, will come back again, in the same way you have seen Him go."

The disciples knelt down and worshiped God. Then they returned to the upper room in Jerusalem where they had been living together. Much of their time they spent in prayer. For though Jesus had ascended to heaven, they still felt very close to Him, and loved to talk to Him.

Peter said to the others, "Judas has left us and has gone to his own place. We ought to choose another man who has been with us all the time, and has seen and heard all that Jesus has done and spoken, to take the place of Judas. In that way we will still be twelve apostles, sent out to tell all the world about Jesus and His resurrection from the dead."

The others agreed with Peter. They selected two men, named Joseph and Matthias, and prayed, "O Lord, Thou knowest the hearts of all men. Show us which one of these two men Thou hast chosen." Then they cast lots, and Matthias was chosen. After this he was counted among the apostles.

Another person who spent much time with the disciples was Mary, the mother of Jesus. His brothers, too, were often with them. They had not believed in Him at first, but now that He had risen from the dead, they felt very different.

When Jesus died, the disciples were grieved and bewildered. They had thought that He was the Son of God, but how could the Son of God die? Now that He was alive again, they began to understand that Jesus was God Himself. They realized that He could make them live forever too. They were not afraid any longer. They knew that Jesus could keep them from all harm.

Chapter 57
POWER FROM ABOVE
ACTS 2

Now that Jesus had gone back to heaven, the disciples spent much time together in prayer. One day, when they were all together in one place, they suddenly heard a sound like a mighty rushing wind. It seemed to fill the room where they were. And upon the head of each disciple there appeared something that looked like a tongue of fire.

People in Jerusalem heard the strange sound too, and came running. It was early in the morning — only nine o'clock — but a crowd of people soon gathered around the disciples, wondering what had happened, and wondering at the strange little flames of fire.

Meanwhile the disciples could feel that a wonderful change had happened to them. They felt new strength and power. The Holy Spirit of God had come, according to Jesus' promise. The little flames upon their heads were a sign that the Holy Spirit had come to live in their hearts.

The power of the Holy Spirit at once made the disciples strong and brave. They no longer wished to hide themselves for fear of what the Jews might do to them. They were eager to talk, eager to tell about Jesus. And now they began to talk in many different languages — languages which before they did not know how to speak

PART IX
The Early Church

— telling the wonderful works of God.

The crowd listened in astonishment. They said, "Are not these men from Galilee? How is it that we hear them speak, every one of us, in our own language?"

It is not surprising that the men marveled. In that crowd there were people from more than a dozen different countries. There were men from the east, from the countries near Persia. There were others from Egypt and the desert. There were men from the north, and some from faraway Rome. And each of them heard the apostles talking in his own language. This was a wonderful miracle of God, showing the people the great power of the Holy Spirit.

In every crowd there are some people who can think of something disagreeable to say. In this crowd, too, there were those who said, "Oh, these people are drunk. That is all that is the matter with them."

But Peter stood up and spoke boldly to them.

Peter had changed since the night when he said three times that he did not even know Jesus. He was no longer afraid, now that the Holy Spirit had come into his heart. He was never again going to be afraid to stand up for Jesus. Peter had be-

333

come the boldest of all the disciples; he had become their leader. He was going to fight for Jesus. Now he really would be glad to die for his Master to show his love — not in his own strength, but in the wonderful strength of God's Holy Spirit in his heart.

Peter said to the crowd, "You men of Judaea and Jerusalem, listen to me. These men are not drunk, as you seem to think. No, this is what was prophesied long ago in the scriptures by the prophet Joel, in these words: 'And it shall be in the last days, says God, I will pour forth of My Spirit upon all flesh: And your sons and your daughters shall prophesy. . . . And it shall be that whosoever shall call on the name of the Lord shall be saved.'

"Now this prophecy has come true. The Spirit of the Lord is being poured out upon us now. Listen to what I tell you.

"You know that Jesus of Nazareth was a man to whom God gave the power to do wonderful miracles. You seized Him and wickedly crucified Him. But God raised Him up from the grave, because it was not possible for death to hold Him. We know that He is living because we saw Him.

"Now He is on the right hand of God in heaven. It is He who has sent this Holy Spirit whose sign you see on our heads, and hear in the words we speak. Therefore you must know that God has made this same Jesus whom you crucified both Lord and Christ."

When the crowd heard these brave words, they were terribly troubled. They were afraid that God would punish them for killing Jesus. "What shall we do?" they asked desperately. Peter said to them, "Repent of your sins, and be baptized, every one of you, in the name of Jesus. God will forgive you, and will give you the Holy Spirit. Save yourselves from this wicked generation."

Peter and the other apostles began to baptize those who were sorry for their sins. All day long they baptized, and taught the people about Jesus.

At the beginning of that day there had been only about one hundred and twenty followers of Jesus in the city. How many do you think there were at the end of the day? More than three thousand!

Every day after that the disciples preached about Jesus in the temple and in the streets of Jerusalem. They wanted to teach everyone about Jesus, as He had commanded them to do while He was still on earth. And every day God added more people to the church.

Among these believers there was a spirit of love. Nobody called anything his own, for they all sold whatever they had and shared the money with the rest. And, as Jesus had commanded them, they often celebrated the Lord's Supper in remembrance of His death.

This was the beginning of the Christian church. Since then the story of Jesus has been told in nearly every land, and His followers have become so many that they cannot be numbered.

26: PHILIP AND THE ETHIOPIAN

27: PETER IS DELIVERED FROM PRISON

Chapter 58

THE LAME MAN IN THE TEMPLE
ACTS 3, 4

One afternoon Peter and John went together to the temple. At the Beautiful Gate, one of the entrances of the temple, a poor lame man was lying on a rug. This poor cripple had never walked in his whole life. He was helpless. Every day some of his friends carried him to the Beautiful Gate. People going in and out of the temple sometimes gave him a few coins, to pay for his food and clothes.

When this poor man saw Peter and John coming into the temple, he begged them to give him something. The two men stopped beside him. Peter said, "Look at us." The man looked up at them, thinking they were going to give him some money. Peter said, "I have no money to give you, but I will give you what I do have." He took hold of the man's hand, lifted him up, and said in a loud voice, "In the name of Jesus Christ of Nazareth, rise up and walk!"

Immediately the man's feet and ankle bones became strong. He walked with the apostles into the temple, running, and jumping up and down, and shouting, "God be praised! God be praised! I can walk!"

"How did it happen?" everyone was asking. "Who healed you?"

When Peter saw a crowd gathering, he said in a voice loud enough for all to hear, "Why do you look at us, as if we had cured this man by our own power? In this miracle God has glorified His servant Jesus. You brought Jesus to Pilate, and would not permit Pilate to let Him go. You asked the governor to give you a murderer instead. You killed the Prince of life. But God made Him alive again, and we have seen Him. This man has been completely healed through faith in the name of Jesus."

Then Peter changed his tone and said gently, "I know that you did this without realizing what you were doing. Repent, and be sorry, and God will blot out your sins. Someday Jesus will come again from heaven. Long ago God told Moses that He was going to send Jesus, and that everyone who did not listen to Him would be destroyed. So turn away from your sins, and God will bless you."

For days the chief priests had watched the crowds flocking to the temple to listen to the teaching of the apostles. "This is very bad," they had said to each other. "When we killed Jesus we thought that would be the end of this teaching. But these men keep preaching about Him and saying He is alive. We must do something to stop them."

When the chief priests heard about the healing of the lame man, they sent soldiers to arrest Peter and John, and put them in jail for the night. But the words which had been spoken in the power of the Holy Spirit could not be stopped. More and more people turned to Jesus, and they in turn told their friends about the Saviour they had found. There were already about five thousand people in Jerusalem who had been baptized in the name of Jesus, and it was not even two months since Jesus had gone back to heaven.

The next day the high priest assembled all the priests and rulers and scribes together in the courtroom. The two apostles were brought out of jail to be questioned. "Where did you get the power to cure this man?" the priests asked.

Peter's heart was filled with the Holy Spirit, and he spoke stirringly, "O rulers and elders, if you ask us how we cured the lame man, we will tell you. It was by the power of Jesus Christ of Nazareth, whom you crucified, and whom God raised from the dead. There is no other way to be saved except by Jesus."

How bold Peter had become, now that the Holy Spirit lived in his heart! He was no longer afraid to speak for his Lord.

The priests, who were well educated, were surprised to hear Peter and John speak so boldly, for they knew they were men who had not been to school. Although the rulers were proud of their wisdom, they did not know how to answer these uneducated men. They could tell that Peter and John must have been taught by Jesus. And the man who had been healed stood right there. There was no use trying to deny that this was a miracle.

They sent Peter and John out of the room for a few minutes so that they could talk among themselves. "What shall we do with these men?" they said. "It is plain that they have done a wonderful miracle. Everybody in Jerusalem knows it. But this teaching must not spread. We will tell them not to speak about Jesus to anyone. If they do, we will punish them."

They called Peter and John back and commanded them not to speak about Jesus any more. Peter was not afraid. He said, "Do you think we ought to obey you instead of God? We cannot help speaking about the things we have seen and heard."

The high priests did not know what to do. They did not dare to punish Peter and John for fear of the people. A crowd had gathered when the news spread that Peter and John had been arrested. Everybody was praising God because the crippled man had been healed.

They warned the apostles once more, and then let them go. Peter and John hurried to the other disciples and told them what had happened. All of them prayed together, "Lord, see how the rulers are threatening us! Help us not to be afraid, and to speak boldly. And now, Lord, give us power to work signs and wonders by the name of Thy holy servant Jesus."

When they had finished praying, the house where they were was shaken. They were filled with the Spirit of God, and praised the Lord.

Chapter 59
THE STORY OF A LIE
ACTS 5

Among these first members of Jesus' church there was a spirit of love. They lived like one big family, loving each other and taking care of each other. Those who had been rich sold their houses and lands and gave the money to the apostles, to give to whoever was in need. They felt that whatever they owned was not theirs, but God's, and that they must live together as children of God.

The Holy Spirit also filled the hearts of the people with courage. The apostles were given such power to preach about Jesus that many who heard them believed.

Among the believers was a man named Ananias and his wife Sapphira. They saw all the Christians selling their land and bringing the money to Peter. They wanted everybody to think they were just as generous. But they did not want to give all their money away.

So when Ananias and Sapphira sold some land which belonged to them, they brought Peter just part of the money they had received, not all of it. This was not wrong, of course. They did not have to sell the land at all. And if they did sell it, they did not have to give any of the money to Peter for the poor. They could have kept it all if they had wanted to.

What was wrong was that Ananias and his wife agreed to tell a lie. Ananias brought part of the money to Peter and said, "We have sold our land, and we are giving the poor every penny we received."

The Holy Spirit in Peter's heart told him this was a lie. Ananias had kept part of the money for himself. It was a dreadful thing that there was a liar in the church of Jesus Christ among all the believers who were filled with the Spirit of God.

Peter said sternly, "Ananias, why has Satan come into your heart, and told you to tell a lie? No one made you sell the land. After you sold it, the money belonged to you. You could have kept it all if you had wanted to. You are telling a lie to God, not to me."

As Peter spoke, God punished the liar. He fell down dead at Peter's feet. Some of the young men took up the body, wrapped it in linen cloth, and carried Ananias out to bury him.

About three hours later the wife of Ananias came in. She did not know that her husband was dead. Peter said to her, "Tell me, did you sell the land for so much, for the amount of money which your husband brought to me?"

Sapphira had agreed beforehand with her husband to tell the lie. "Yes," she said to Peter, "we sold the land for just that amount of money which my husband gave you."

Peter said, "How is it you and your husband have agreed together to lie to the Holy Spirit of God? The young men are just coming back from burying your husband. They will carry you out and bury you too."

As Peter spoke, Sapphira fell down dead. The young men came in. They saw her lying there dead at Peter's feet. They took her out and buried her beside her husband.

God sent this swift punishment to warn the people that He knows what we do, and we must live lives pleasing to Him. Everybody who heard what had happened was filled with fear.

Chapter 60
THE OPEN PRISON DOORS
ACTS 5

By the power of the Holy Spirit all of the apostles were able to work miracles and to heal people, as Jesus had done. Those who had sick friends brought them on beds and couches into the streets, so that the shadow of Peter might fall on them as he went by. And they were healed, every one of them.

Every day the apostles preached to the people. Those who believed talked to their friends and brought them to the Lord. As more and more people believed, the priests became more and more angry and alarmed. At last they sent soldiers to arrest all twelve of the apostles, and put them in prison.

That night the angel of the Lord came down from heaven, opened the prison doors, and brought the apostles out. The angel said, "Go and speak in the temple to all the people, and tell them about Jesus."

So early in the morning the twelve went back to the temple and began to talk to the people. They were not afraid of the priests. Had not God sent His own angel to rescue them the night before?

That morning the high priest called the council together, and sent the soldiers to bring the apostles from prison. The soldiers found the doors locked, and the guards still standing outside, watching. How astonished they were when they unlocked the gates and found nobody inside!

The soldiers hurried back to the priests with this strange news. "But how could they have escaped through locked doors?" the priests asked. "Why didn't the guards see them?"

Just then somebody came up and said, "Those men that you put in prison last night are standing in the temple teaching the people." The priests were more astonished than ever. How did the apostles dare to go on talking about Jesus after they had been thrown into prison?

The captain and some officers went to the temple to arrest the apostles again and bring them to the high priest. They did not treat the twelve roughly, for fear that the people would be angry and throw stones at them.

When Peter and the others were brought in, the high priest asked, "Did we not command you very strictly not to teach any more in the name of Jesus? Now you are filling the city with your teaching, and blaming us for killing him."

Peter answered, "We must obey God rather than men. God brought Jesus into the world, but you killed Him on a cross. God has set Him at His right hand in heaven. He is a Prince and a Saviour. He will make His people Israel sorry for their sins, and He will forgive them. God has sent the Holy Spirit into the hearts of all who believe, so that they may teach about Jesus."

These words made the rulers furious. They knew that they were responsible for Jesus' death, but it made them very angry when Peter called them murderers. They said to each other, "We will have to kill these men. That is the only way to stop their teaching."

Among them was a very wise man named Gamaliel. He said, "Put these men out of the room for a few minutes." When they were gone, Gamaliel said, "You must be careful what you do. You remember that about thirty-five years ago there was a man who gathered about four hundred followers and pretended he was important. Soon he was killed and his followers were scattered. After that, many people followed a man named Judas. But he also died. Let these men alone. If this teaching is from men, it will come to nothing. But if it is from God, you cannot overthrow it. If you try to, you will find you are fighting against God."

The rulers saw at once that this was wise advice. They decided to do as Gamaliel suggested. They called the apostles, and had them beaten. Then they warned them not to talk about Jesus any more, and let them go.

The apostles went out. Their backs were sore and bleeding, but their hearts were filled with great happiness. They were happy not because they had been freed, but because they had been beaten! They had been allowed to suffer for their dear Lord, who had suffered so much for them.

They did not obey the command not to speak about Jesus. Instead, they obeyed the angel who told them to teach in the temple. And every day more people believed.

THE MAN WHO LOOKED INTO HEAVEN

ACTS 6, 7

Although the high priest and the rulers hated the name of Jesus, yet there were some priests who believed. These men had not dared to follow Jesus openly when He was alive. But now that He had died and risen again from the grave, they understood that this must be the very Son of God.

There were many poor people in the church. Some of them were widows who had no way to earn any money. Every day the apostles gathered these people together and gave them some money or food. The rich shared what they had with the poor, and no one was in need.

As more and more people joined the church, there came to be so many poor people that the twelve apostles did not have time to take care of them all and to preach about Jesus too. And so they said to the believers, "It is better for you to choose seven good men to look after the care of the poor, while we give all our time to teaching."

When the seven men had been chosen, the apostles laid their hands on their heads and prayed. These seven spent their time helping the poor with food and money. One of the seven was Stephen. He taught and did miracles among the people, for his heart was filled with the Holy Spirit.

One day, as Stephen was teaching, some men began to argue with him. They were not willing to believe what he said, but he spoke with such wisdom that they could not prove he was wrong. As they argued with him, they became very angry. They tried to find some way in which they could get him in trouble.

They told lies about him, saying that he spoke against Moses and the temple. They stirred up a mob of people and came suddenly upon Stephen. They dragged him before the rulers and said, "We heard this man speak against Moses and against the temple."

The rulers looked at Stephen. They were amazed, for his face had a look of glory. It was like the face of an angel.

The high priest said to Stephen, "Are the things these men say true?"

Stephen answered, "Men, brothers, and fathers, listen to me." He told them how God had helped their fathers long ago. He reminded them how often their nation had refused to listen to God and to obey Him. They had left God and turned to worship idols. They had killed the prophets who told them about the coming of the Saviour. And when the Saviour came, they killed Him too! "You have always resisted God, just as your fathers did," Stephen accused them.

All this was true. The Jews had killed Jesus, just as their fathers had killed God's prophets. But when Stephen reminded them of this, the rulers and the mob grew angrier than ever. They shook their fists at Stephen, and screamed at him in a rage.

Stephen lifted up his eyes and

looked straight into heaven. He said, "I see the heavens opened, and Jesus standing at the right hand of God!"

The angry mob would not listen. Yelling and screaming, they ran at Stephen. They pushed and pulled him out of the city to stone him to death. So as to be able to throw more easily, they jerked off their coats and dropped them at the feet of a man named Saul (who was also called Paul). When Stephen knew that he was going to die, he raised his eyes to heaven and prayed, "Lord Jesus, received my spirit." As the stones came thick and fast, he kneeled down.

With a loud voice he cried, as Jesus had done on the cross, "Lord, lay not this sin to their charge!" Then he fell asleep. He woke up in heaven.

Stephen is called the first martyr, because he was the first one to die for Jesus. Since that time thousands have been killed because they loved the Lord. Even today, in some parts of the world, Christians are hated and persecuted.

As the members of the church buried Stephen, they wept that such a good man had been killed. But they knew that Stephen was happy because he was with Jesus.

Chapter 62
THE MAGICIAN WHO TRIED TO BUY GOD
ACTS 8

The hatred of the Pharisees and Jewish leaders for the followers of Jesus grew more and more violent. They did everything they could to stop the disciples from preaching. They went into people's houses. Anyone who was found praying to Jesus, or talking about Him, was arrested and thrown into prison.

Jerusalem became a very dangerous place for the Christians. They could not talk about Jesus without being in danger of arrest. Yet they could not be silent. Many of the believers left the city and moved to other places. Wherever they went, they told people about Jesus. Only the apostles themselves stayed in Jerusalem.

One of the seven men who had been chosen to take care of the poor was called Philip. He had been a friend of Stephen, the martyr. When the rulers of Jerusalem began to arrest the believers, Philip went down to the city of Samaria and taught the people there. He cured many sick people and worked many miracles, as Jesus had done.

The people of Samaria gladly listened to Philip, and many of them believed in Jesus. A few years earlier, you remember, Jesus Himself had talked to the Samaritans. The woman who came to draw water at the well told her friends about Him. Jesus stayed with them two days. Probably many of those who heard Philip remembered hearing and seeing Jesus. They became His disciples gladly now, and were baptized as members of the church.

In this city there lived a man named Simon, who was a magician. He pretended he was a very great man sent by God. For a long time all the people had looked up to him, because of the magic tricks he did.

Simon heard Philip preaching to the people about God. He saw him heal the sick. Simon, too, believed and was baptized. He stayed with Philip, watching the miracles he did.

The twelve apostles in Jerusalem

heard the good news that the Samaritans believed in Jesus. They sent Peter and John to Samaria to help Philip.

All the new believers in Samaria came together in a big meeting. Peter and John prayed that they might receive the Holy Spirit. Then as the new believers came forward, the apostles laid their hands on their heads, and the Holy Spirit came into their hearts.

Simon the magician looked on in wonder. He did not understand how the Holy Spirit came into people's hearts when Peter and John laid their hands on their heads. He was a magician, but he had never been able to do anything like this! Simon thought it was a kind of magic, like his own tricks. He brought money to the apostles and said, "Give me this power, too, that when I lay my hands on someone's head he may receive this Spirit."

Peter was horrified. Sternly he said, "May your money perish with you! This is the gift of God. It cannot be bought with money. You are not one of Jesus' followers if you think such a thing. Your heart is not right in the sight of God. Be sorry for your sin, and pray that God will forgive you."

Simon was frightened. "You pray to God for me," he begged, for he saw that the power of God cannot be bought with money.

Chapter 63
THE ETHIOPIAN WHO BELIEVED
ACTS 8

After preaching the gospel in many cities of the Samaritans, Peter and John went back to Jerusalem. Philip did not go with them, for the angel of the Lord spoke to him and said, "Arise and go toward the south, to the road which goes from Jerusalem to Gaza through the desert."

Leaving Samaria, Philip went toward the south on the road to Gaza. All around him was lonely desert country. He did not know why the Lord had sent him here, but he walked along willingly.

What should Philip see before long but a fine chariot drawn by two handsome horses in shining harness! In the chariot sat a black man, reading aloud to himself.

This man had come from Ethiopia, which is a country in Africa far away from the land of the Jews. He was very rich, for he was an important officer in the court of the queen of Ethiopia. He had charge of all her treasure — her gold and her silver and her jewels.

The Ethiopian was not a worshiper of idols. Somehow he had learned about the true God. He was returning now from a visit to Jerusalem, where he had worshiped God in the temple.

The book which he was reading was a part of the Old Testament he had bought in one of the shops in Jerusalem. It was the book of the prophet Isaiah. As he returned home, the Ethiopian was reading the prophecies and trying to understand them.

The Holy Spirit said to Philip, "Go and join this man in the chariot."

As Philip ran up to the man, he heard him reading out loud to himself the words of Isaiah. "Do you understand what you are reading?" Philip asked.

"How can I, unless someone explains it to me?" the Ethiopian answered. "Climb up into the chariot and tell me what it means."

So Philip climbed into the chariot. The man was reading the fifty-third chapter, the seventh verse, which says this about Jesus: "He was led as a sheep to the slaughter, and as a lamb before his shearer is dumb, so He opened not His mouth."

The Ethiopian said, "I do not understand this. Is the prophet speaking about himself, or about some other man?"

Then Philip explained that Isaiah was speaking about the death of Jesus. He told the Ethiopian all about Jesus and the wonderful things that had happened.

As they rode along, they came to a small pool or stream. The man said to Philip, "See, here is water. Why may I not be baptized?" Philip answered, "If you believe that Jesus is the Son of God, you may."

So the Ethiopian commanded the chariot driver to stop. Philip went down with him into the water and baptized him in the name of the Father, and the Son, and the Holy Spirit.

As they came up out of the water, the Spirit of the Lord caught Philip away, and the Ethiopian did not see him again. He went on down the road very happy. When he reached his home, he must have told all his friends about the wonderful things he had heard.

The Spirit of God took Philip to the seashore. All along the coast Philip preached to everyone he met.

The story of Jesus was spreading very far. The people who moved away from Jerusalem carried it with them wherever they went. The Ethiopian took it with him back to Africa. Before long it would go still further.

Chapter 64
THE LIGHT ON THE ROAD
ACTS 9

Among the Pharisees was a young man named Paul. Paul's parents were Jews who lived in Tarsus, a large city north of Jerusalem. Tarsus was not a Jewish city, and Paul's parents did not want him to grow up without knowing about God. So they sent him to school in Jerusalem. At this time the Jews lived in many cities outside their own land. Wherever they went, they built synagogues and worshiped God, just as they had done in their own country. As often as they could, they went back to Jerusalem for the feasts, and many sent their children there to school.

Paul had had a fine education in Jerusalem. His teacher had been that wise doctor of the law, Gamaliel, who had advised the Pharisees to let the Christians alone. Paul had studied the Old Testament until he knew it thoroughly. He was strict in keeping the law. Like the other Pharisees, Paul hated the followers of Jesus. He believed the Christians were teaching wrong things. He was certain that they were working against God, and that it was his duty to do all he could to stop them. He had held the coats of the men who stoned Stephen, and he had cheered them on. If he heard of people who believed in Jesus, he went into their houses and dragged them off to prison. The Christians hated and feared Paul, because he had had so many of them thrown into prison; and when they came to trial he always voted for the death penalty.

But even this did not satisfy Paul. He went to the high priest and said, "We *must* stamp out this new religion. Give me letters to the priests in Damascus. I will go there, and if I find any followers of Jesus there, I will bind them and bring them back to Jerusalem, so that you can imprison them."

The high priest gave him letters to the priests in Damascus, telling them to help Paul arrest the followers of Jesus. Paul set out, taking along with him some men to help in this work of tracking down the Christians.

Damascus is a very interesting place, one of the oldest cities in the world. It is more than a hundred miles from Jerusalem. It must have taken Paul several days to travel this far, even if he and his men rode on horses. Probably at night they stopped at inns along the road.

After traveling for several days, they were approaching Damascus. Suddenly a light streamed from heaven, brighter than the light of the sun. It was so startling and so blinding that they all fell to the ground. A voice came out of heaven, saying, "Paul, Paul, why do you persecute Me? It is hard for you to kick against the pricks."

Paul was very much frightened.

He trembled all over as he replied, "Who is speaking to me?"

The voice said, "I am Jesus of Nazareth. I am the one you are fighting against."

Jesus of Nazareth? Paul had been certain Jesus was dead. He had thought God was pleased with what he was doing. Now that he heard this voice from heaven, he realized that he had been wrong, and that he had been fighting against God Himself. He said, "Lord, what do You want me to do?"

Jesus answered, "Stand up, Paul. I have appeared to you to show you that you are not to fight against Me any more. You are to become one of My disciples, and tell everybody about Me. I will appear to you again and show you more about Myself. Go into Damascus, and there it shall be told you what you must do."

When the light disappeared, and Paul stood up, he found that he could not see. He had been blinded by the glory of the light that was brighter than the sun.

The men with him had seen the light and heard a voice, but they had not understood what the voice said. They had not been blinded, so they took Paul by the hand and led him into the city.

From that time on Paul was a changed man. He became a follower of Jesus.

Chapter 65
THE CHANGED MAN
ACTS 9

Down the streets of Damascus came a little procession. A group of men were carefully leading by the hand a well-dressed man who was blind.

The street they were walking along was called Straight Street because it

ran straight through the city. The men were looking for the house of a man named Judas. There they went in. If you had stopped them, they would have told you a strange story about a dazzling light which had appeared to them as they were coming into the city, and which had blinded their companion, Paul.

For three days Paul was blind. He sat in Judas' house without talking, eating, or drinking. His life had changed so suddenly and so completely that he needed to think about what had happened.

Like all the other Pharisees Paul had thought Jesus was only a man who deserved to be killed because He dared to claim He was God. He thought the disciples had made up their story about Jesus rising from the dead. But now he knew that the disciples of Jesus were right, and that Jesus was really the Son of God. When he heard Jesus speak from heaven, he knew that Jesus was God, that He was alive, that He had actually risen from the grave and conquered death.

Having had a very fine education in the school of the great teacher Gamaliel, Paul knew all the Old Testament prophecies about the Saviour promised by God. As he sat quietly in his blindness, thinking about what had happened, he realized that every one of those Old Testament prophecies had come true in Jesus.

In the same city of Damascus there lived one of Jesus' faithful disciples named Ananias. This man had heard of Paul. Somebody in Jerusalem had sent word to the disciples in Damascus, warning them that Paul was coming to arrest and imprison them.

One night the Lord appeared to Ananias in a vision and said to him, "Ananias!"

"Yes, Lord, I am here," he said.

God said, "Get up and go to the house of Judas who lives on Straight Street, and ask to see a man named Paul, who is praying to Me. He has had a vision in which he saw a man named Ananias coming and putting his hands on him to cure him of his blindness."

But Ananias was afraid. He said, "Lord, I have heard such dreadful things about this man! He has done terrible things to Your disciples in Jerusalem! He has come here to arrest all who are Your followers!"

The Lord said, "You do not need to be afraid of him now, Ananias. I have chosen him to be one of My special disciples. I have a great work for him to do. He is going to preach about Me to kings, and to the heathen, and to the children of Israel. Instead of arresting My followers, he himself is going to suffer great things for My sake."

Ananias was not afraid any longer. He went to see Paul and said, "Brother Paul, the Lord Jesus, who appeared to you along the road, has sent me to you so that you may be cured of your blindness, and may also be filled with the Holy Spirit. For God chose you to be His disciple, and to see Jesus and hear His voice, so you can tell all men what you have seen and heard."

Ananias put his hands on Paul, and the blindness left Paul's eyes, so that he could see again. At once he was baptized in the name of the Father, and of the Son, and of the Holy Spirit. The man who had come to arrest the followers of Jesus was now their brother and a member of Jesus' church!

Paul was weak and faint, for he had eaten nothing for three days. As soon as he had been given some food, he felt strong and well again. He was eager to go into the synagogue and begin to tell people what had happened to him.

Chapter 66

PAUL ESCAPES TWICE
ACTS 9

How surprised the Jews of Damascus were one morning! In wonder they listened to a man who was telling them about Jesus, the Saviour. Then they turned to each other and asked, "Isn't this the very same man who came here to arrest the followers of Jesus? Isn't this the man called Paul?" Many of those who listened to his preaching began to believe.

Paul was a well-educated man. He became one of the greatest preachers the world has ever known. He also wrote many of the books of the New Testament. God told him what to say. Paul was well prepared to work for God, and God used him to bring many people to belief in Jesus.

If sometimes you get tired of going to school and studying your lessons, remember Paul. Someday God may use you for some great work. God has work for all of us to do, and a child is serving God when he studies to prepare himself for the work God has for him.

Some of the Jews in Damascus believed in Jesus, but many others refused to believe that Jesus could be the promised Saviour. They expected the Saviour to be a king, with a great army to fight all the enemies of His people. Many Jews are looking for just such a Saviour even today. Like those of Paul's time, they will not believe that Jesus, who died on a cross, could be the Christ anointed by God to save them.

After Paul had been preaching in Damascus for some time, the unbelieving Jews became very angry, and wanted to kill him. They watched the gate of the city day and night to keep him from escaping. It was dangerous for Paul to stay in Damascus any longer. But it was equally dangerous for him to try to slip past those guarded gates.

At last some of the disciples thought of a plan. They got a large, strong basket, and tied ropes to the handles. One night they went to a place far away from the gate, where nobody was watching. They climbed on top of the high wall which surrounded the city. They let Paul down to the ground on the other side of the wall outside the city in the basket.

Paul made his way carefully through the fields. When he was far away from the city, he walked along the road toward Jerusalem, a hundred miles away. How different this journey was from his trip to Damascus! Then he was eager to put the disciples of Jesus in prison. Now he was fleeing to save his life because he, too, believed in Jesus.

When Paul reached Jerusalem, he went to Peter and John and the other apostles. He told them what had happened, and that he wanted to live with them, and to teach about Jesus. The apostles were afraid to receive him, because they remembered that he had arrested and killed so many of their friends.

Barnabas, one of the disciples, knew about the change in Paul's life. He told the apostles all about how Paul had seen Jesus on the road to Damascus, and how Jesus had spoken to him, and how earnestly Paul had preached about Jesus in Damascus. When the disciples heard this story, they gladly received Paul.

Paul lived in Jerusalem with the disciples, teaching about Jesus. Often he talked to the Greeks who lived in the city. But after a while the unbelieving Jews became angry at his preaching. Like the Jews in Damascus, they tried to kill him.

The apostles saw it was not safe for Paul to stay in Jerusalem. They went with him as far as the city of Caesarea on the seacoast. For safety Paul went still further north to the city of Tarsus, where he had been born, and lived there for a while.

Chapter 67

THE GOOD WOMAN WHO WAS BROUGHT BACK TO LIFE

ACTS 9

About forty miles from Jerusalem was a city called Joppa. It was a large and busy place, for it had a good harbor. Ships from all over the world docked here, to unload cargo, or to take on goods for other places.

There were many followers of Jesus in Joppa. Some of them had gone there because it was not safe for them to stay in Jerusalem. They had told others about Jesus, and now in this city, as in many others, there was a group of believers.

One of the disciples was a very good lady named Dorcas. She spent all her time helping people. The poor people and the widows loved her, because she was kind to them. When Dorcas became sick and died, all the disciples at Joppa were very sad.

It happened about that time that Peter was in a town a few miles away. He had been going from town to town, preaching about Jesus and healing the sick. The friends of Dorcas heard that Peter had healed a man who had been sick in bed for eight years. In their trouble they sent for him, and brought him to the room where Dorcas lay dead. The poor people whom Dorcas had helped stood there, weeping. They showed Peter the nice clothes Dorcas had made for them.

Peter made everybody leave the room. Then he kneeled down and prayed to God. After his prayer he turned to the bed and said, "Dorcas, arise!"

Dorcas opened her eyes as though she had only been asleep. When she saw Peter, she sat up. He took her hand and helped her get up. Then he called her friends and showed them that she was alive.

This was a miracle, like the wonderful things Jesus did when He was on earth. Jesus had promised that the Holy Spirit would enable the disciples to do miracles too. But there was a difference between the miracles Jesus did and those done by Peter and the other disciples. The wonderful works of Jesus were done by His own power, because He was the Son of God. Peter never pretended to cure people by his own power. He always said he healed by the power of Jesus.

After bringing Dorcas back to life, Peter stayed in Joppa for some time. He lived with a man called Simon, a tanner. Many people in the city heard what had happened, and believed in Jesus. Peter spent his time talking about his Lord. All the Jews who went to the synagogue heard him again and again.

Chapter 68
A LESSON PETER HAD TO LEARN
ACTS 10

None of the followers of Jesus thought of telling the Greeks and Romans and others who were not Jews about Jesus. Jews never had anything to do with heathen people, and even the believing Jews thought that Jesus had come just to save their own nation. The apostles did not yet understand what Jesus meant when He told them to go into all the world and preach to all peoples.

Not far from Joppa, where Peter was staying, was the city of Caesarea, on the seacoast. In Caesarea there lived a Roman soldier named Cornelius. He was a centurion, which means a captain over a hundred men.

Although Cornelius was a Roman and not a Jew, he had learned about the one true God. He taught his family and servants to pray to God and to worship Him. And he was very generous in helping the poor.

One day, about three o'clock in the afternoon, a strange thing happened to Cornelius. While he was praying, he had a vision. An angel said to him, "Cornelius!"

The brave soldier was frightened. He said, "What is it, Lord?"

The angel said, "God has seen your good works, and heard your prayers. He wants you to send to Joppa for a man called Simon Peter. He is staying by the seaside at the house of Simon, a tanner."

As soon as the angel had left, Cornelius called two of his servants and a faithful soldier who lived with him. He told them what the angel had said, and sent them to get Peter.

The next day a very curious thing happened to Peter. About noon, while the dinner was being cooked, he went up to the flat roof of the house. He was hungry, and he wished the dinner were ready. The rooftop was quiet, because it was separated from the rest of the house. As Peter waited, he prayed.

While he prayed, Peter had also a vision. He saw a great sheet let down from heaven by its four corners, like a kind of a bag. In it were all kinds of four-footed animals and wild beasts and creeping things and birds. He heard a voice saying, "Get up, Peter, kill some of these animals and eat them."

Peter was astonished. Many hundreds of years before, in the law of Moses, God had told the Jews to eat only certain kinds of animals, which were called clean. Sheep and goats and cows were clean, but pigs and lions and cats and many other kinds were called unclean, and the Jews were not allowed to eat them.

No matter how hungry he was, a Jew would not touch an unclean animal. So when Peter heard a voice saying, "Rise, Peter, kill and eat," he said, "Oh, no, Lord, for I have never eaten anything that is common or unclean."

The voice said, "What I have made clean, you must not call unclean."

This vision came three times. After the third time, the sheet went back up into the sky. While Peter was wondering what this could possibly mean, the three men sent by Cornelius arrived. They stood in front of the gate and called out, "Is Simon Peter staying here?"

The Holy Spirit said to Peter, "There are three men here looking for you. Arise, and go with them, for I have sent them."

Since it was late in the day, Peter

asked the men to stay overnight. In the morning he and some of his friends went with them.

Cornelius was waiting for them. He met Peter at the gate and fell down to worship him. Peter quickly pulled him to his feet and said, "You must not do that, for I am only a man like yourself."

When they came into the house, Peter was surprised to find a whole roomful of people. They were the family and friends of Cornelius. He had invited them to come and hear what Peter would say.

"You know," Peter began, "that a Jew does not visit anyone who is not a Jew. But God has showed me that I must not call any man common or unclean. I came when you sent for me, and now I would like to know why you asked me to come."

Cornelius answered, "Four days ago, as I prayed, an angel in bright clothing stood beside me. He told me to send for you. I am very glad that you have come. I have invited all my friends to hear what God has told you to tell us."

"I see now," said Peter, "that God does not love just the Jews, as I always supposed. Now I know that God loves those who love Him and try to serve Him, in every nation." He went on and told about Jesus, who died to save sinners.

As Peter spoke, the Holy Spirit came into the hearts of the people that were listening, and they began to speak in many different languages, as the apostles had done. At this sign Peter knew that these people, too, were now disciples of Jesus. He baptized them, and they became members of Jesus' church.

At last Peter understood what Jesus had meant when He said, "Go ye into *all* the world."

Chapter 69

A NEW CHURCH

ACTS 11, 12

When Peter went back to Jerusalem, the disciples there found fault with him. "We heard," they said, "that you visited men who were not Jews, and that you even ate with them. Why did you do that? You know it is against our law."

Then Peter told them about his vision — about the sheet which came down from heaven and the voice which said, "What God has made clean you must not call unclean." He told them about the angel which had spoken to Cornelius, and about the coming of the Holy Spirit into the hearts of the people in Cornelius' household.

"If God has taken these people into His church," Peter said, "it was only right for me to baptize them. God, who knows the hearts of all men, gave His Holy Spirit to them, just as He did to us. And who was I, that I could withstand God?"

When the disciples heard this, they saw that it was God's doing. They began to rejoice, for now they understood for the first time that Jesus was the Saviour of all men, not just of the Jews. Now they remembered that Jesus had said, "Go ye into all the world, and preach the gospel to every creature." And God had said to Abraham, "In thy seed shall all the nations of the earth be blessed."

When the disciples thought of the big world, reaching far, far away to foreign countries, they saw for the first time how wonderful it is that Jesus died to save men everywhere. They began to realize how big their work was.

You remember that after Stephen was killed, it was not safe for the disciples to stay in Jerusalem. Some of them settled in the city of Antioch, near the seacoast. The disciples there told their new neighbors about Jesus. Many of the Greeks who lived in the city believed.

When the church in Jerusalem heard that the Greeks were turning to God, they realized that here was a chance for them to obey Jesus' command to preach. They sent a man to help form a church in Antioch. This man was Barnabas, one of the very first disciples. He was one of those who had sold their land and given the money to the poor. Barnabas had become a great teacher in the church.

The people at Antioch were glad to have Barnabas come to preach to them. The new church grew so fast that soon it needed two ministers. Barnabas went to Tarsus, where Paul was living, and asked him to come and help. For a whole year the two disciples worked in Antioch.

It was at Antioch that the disciples were first called Christians, or followers of Christ. All over the world they are called by that name today.

While Paul and Barnabas were preaching in Antioch, things were not so happy in Jerusalem. Wicked King Herod, who ruled the land of the Jews, had come to Jerusalem. He was the nephew of the Herod who had killed John the Baptist, and even more cruel than his uncle had been.

To please the unbelieving Jews, Herod arrested James, one of Jesus' twelve apostles. Herod had James killed. The Jews were delighted. Now that Herod was on their side, they were sure that in a short time there would be no more Christians left in the world.

Chapter 70
THE ANGEL IN PRISON
ACTS 12

Herod saw how pleased the Jewish leaders were that he had killed James. So he sent his soldiers to arrest Peter too. He planned to keep him in prison until after the feast of the Passover, and then to kill him too.

Once when the disciples were put in prison by the high priest, they escaped, even though all the doors were locked. Herod decided that he would not let this happen again. He appointed sixteen soldiers to take turns guarding Peter, four at a time. To make it doubly sure, one of Peter's hands was chained to the soldier on his right side, and the other to the soldier on his left. Besides all this

the guards of the prison stood in front of the doors day and night. "There!" laughed Herod. "I'd like to see him get away now!"

What were the other disciples doing while Peter was in prison? They were praying to God to save him. Peter was praying too, though he was not afraid to die for Jesus.

For several days Peter was kept in prison. At last the Passover was over. The next morning Herod planned to bring Peter out of prison and kill him. That night many of the disciples met at the home of Mark, one of the believers, to pray that God would save Peter's life.

In the middle of the night, when all the guards were soundly sleeping, the angel of the Lord came into the prison. The angel went to Peter and touched him gently, saying softly, "Get up quickly, Peter." At these words the chains fell from Peter's hands.

The angel said, "Put your shoes on and dress yourself." Peter had been asleep, and he was not more than half awake now. He thought he must be dreaming, but he dressed himself and put on his shoes.

The angel said, "Put on your coat and follow me." Peter still thought it was a dream, but he put on his coat and followed without a word. The angel led him past the first guard, and then past the second guard.

A stone wall with a heavy iron gate surrounded the prison. When Peter and the angel came to the locked gate, it opened all by itself, and they went through. They were outside the prison. Peter was free!

As they walked through the street leading away from the prison, the angel disappeared. The streets were dark and quiet. Peter stood still, wondering whether he was awake or asleep. Soon the cold night air made him fully awake. He realized that he was not in prison, but in the streets of the city. And then he knew that God had sent an angel to rescue him.

Down the dark streets Peter walked till he reached the house of Mark, where a light shone. The Christians were still there praying, although it was the middle of the night. The door of the house was locked tight. In those dangerous times the disciples had to be very careful.

So when Peter came to Mark's house, he knocked loudly on the gate. A young girl named Rhoda came to find out who was there in the middle of the night. She was not going to open the door to strangers, who might be thieves, or perhaps soldiers come to arrest them all. She called, "Who's there?"

Peter answered, "It is I, Peter. Open the gate for me."

Rhoda recognized Peter's voice. In the excitement of her joy she forgot to open the gate. She left Peter standing outside, and ran into the house shouting, "It's Peter! It's Peter!"

They said to her, "You are out of your mind! Peter is in prison!"

"It is Peter! I know it is!" Rhoda said.

"Then it must be his ghost," they said.

But Peter kept on knocking. At last some of the others went to the gate. There was Peter, safe and sound! God had answered their prayers! How glad they were to see him!

They all began to talk at once, but Peter motioned to them to be quiet. He told them how God had sent His angel to set him free. His friends fell down on their knees and thanked God, who by His almighty power had rescued Peter from the hands of wicked Herod.

Peter knew it was not safe for him to stay in Jerusalem. While it was still dark he slipped quietly out of the city and went to another place where Herod could not find him.

As soon as daylight came, there was a great stir in the prison, because no one knew what had become of Peter. His guards were just as surprised as everyone else. They had not heard a sound. Nor had the guards on the outside of the gate seen anyone go out.

Herod was furious when he heard Peter had escaped. He asked the guards all sorts of questions. At last he said angrily, "I'll show them what happens to people who let my prisoners escape! Kill them all, every one of them!"

Soon after this Herod went back to his own capital city, Caesarea. He sat down on his throne, clothed in his royal robes, and made a speech. The people, who were afraid of him and wanted to please him at all costs, shouted, "It is the voice of a god speaking, and not the voice of a man!"

This pleased Herod, but it displeased God. At that moment the angel of the Lord struck Herod with a terrible disease. His servants had to carry him from his throne. Soon afterward this enemy of the Christians died.

Chapter 71
ON TO CYPRUS
ACTS 13

While the Christians in Jerusalem were living in fear of wicked King Herod, the church in Antioch was quietly growing stronger and stronger. More and more people learned about Jesus through the preaching of Paul and Barnabas.

At this time the Holy Spirit spoke to the church at Antioch, "I want Paul and Barnabas to leave this church and go to other heathen countries to preach to the people who have not yet heard about Jesus."

After the Christians in Antioch had prayed, and laid their hands on the heads of Paul and Barnabas, they sent them away. The two new missionaries — the first foreign missionaries there ever were — went to the coast and took a boat for the island of Cyprus. There were many Greeks living there.

The Greeks worshiped a great many gods, not just one great Creator of heaven and earth. They thought the gods were much like men, only a little stronger, and that they lived on a high mountain in the north of Greece. In Paul's time they still worshiped these gods, although they had given them Roman names.

The greatest god was Jupiter. Another, named Mercury, had wings on his feet and could fly very swiftly. Diana was the goddess of hunters. Venus was the goddess of love and beauty. There were many others, all of them very much like ordinary men and women.

The Greek people were artistic and well educated. They were famous for their schools and teachers. Some of them were so wise that even today the books they wrote are studied in our schools.

The Greeks had the most beautiful language in the world, and they wrote some of the loveliest poetry. Their artists made marble statues of their gods, shaped like beautiful men and women, which are among the greatest works of art the world has ever known.

Many of the wiser Greeks knew that their gods were not true gods. They tried and tried to find out about the one true God. But knowledge of God is something men cannot find by themselves. Even before the time of Abraham, God had told certain people about Himself. If God had not told us about Himself in the Bible, we, too, would be worshiping idols.

For many centuries the Jews had lived separate from other nations, because God did not want them to forget what He had told them about Himself. But after Jesus came, God wanted the disciples to go to all the nations of the world and teach them about the true God and His son, Jesus. That was why the Holy Spirit sent Paul and Barnabas to teach the Greeks.

Paul and Barnabas preached from one end of the island of Cyprus to the other. Then they took a boat again and sailed to Perga. From there they crossed the high mountains to another city called Pisidian Antioch, to distinguish it from the Antioch in Syria which they had just left.

In this city of Antioch Paul preached in the Jewish synagogue. Both Jews and Greeks came to hear him. They listened very closely. Afterward the Jews went home, but many Greeks stayed to beg Paul to speak to them again on the next Sabbath day.

On the next Sabbath almost the whole city came to hear Barnabas and Paul preach. When the Jews saw this big crowd, they were jealous and angry, and they began to contradict what Paul and Barnabas said. So Paul said, "Since you refuse to listen to our words, we will stop preaching to you, and preach only to the Greeks."

The Greeks were very glad. They listened carefully, and many of them became Christians. They told their friends what Paul had said about the true God, and soon all that country heard about Jesus and many more became Christians.

But the Jews remained angry. They made trouble for Paul and Barnabas, and drove them out of the city. So the two missonaries went to Iconium.

Chapter 72
WHY PEOPLE THOUGHT PAUL WAS A GOD
ACTS 14

In the synagogue of Iconium every Sabbath day two men got up to talk. Always they talked about the same thing — about the Son of God, Jesus, who had come to save His people. Many of the Jews and the Greeks in the city believed what the men said, but others did not. After a while those who did not believe began to make trouble for the missionaries. They even made a plan to stone them. But the two preachers, Paul and Barnabas, found out about it. They left Iconium and went on to Lystra.

At Lystra there was a man who had been a cripple all his life. He had been born with deformed feet and so had never been able to walk a single step, nor even to stand up. When this man heard Paul speak, he believed. Seeing this, Paul said to him, "Stand upright on your feet." At once the man jumped up. He stood without falling, and even walked.

When the people of the city saw this, they were sure Paul and Barnabas could not be ordinary men like themselves. They thought they must be gods come down to earth in the form of men, for they believed their gods often came to earth. And surely no mere man could heal a cripple!

Barnabas they called Jupiter, and Paul they called Mercury, because he did most of the talking. They started to worship Paul and Barnabas and wanted to offer sacrifices to them.

The priests of Jupiter brought some oxen decorated with wreaths of flowers to sacrifice to the missionaries.

When Paul and Barnabas realized what was happening, they ran among the people, calling out, "Sirs, do not do this! We are men like yourselves! We have come here to tell you to turn away from such foolishness. Turn away from idols, and believe in the one true God, who made heaven and earth and everything in them." But in spite of all that Paul and Barnabas said, they could hardly stop the people from offering sacrifices.

Some of the Jews who had wanted to stone Paul at Iconium had followed him to Lystra. They told the people bad and untrue things about Paul and Barnabas. The people quickly changed their minds, and decided that the two men were not gods but mischief makers. They threw stones at Paul. When they thought Paul was dead, they dragged his body out of the city to the fields and left it there.

Some of the Christians wept when they saw Paul treated so cruelly. They went over to him, and found to their surprise that he was still breathing. After a little while Paul opened his eyes. Though he was sore and bruised, he was able to get up and stumble into the city to the house where he was staying.

The next day he and Barnabas left Lystra and went on to Derbe. There they preached about Jesus, and were happy to find that many people believed.

Then they went back and visited the places where they had preached before. They had started a little church in each of these cities, and, now, upon their return, they appointed elders in each church.

At last they got on a ship and sailed back to Antioch, to the church which had sent them out. The disciples there called a meeting of all the Christians in the city, to listen to what Paul and Barnabas had to say about their missionary journey, and how God had turned many of the heathen to Jesus.

After this Paul and Barnabas stayed and preached in Antioch for several years.

The two largest churches were the one in Jerusalem, of which James, the brother of Jesus, was the leader, and the one in Antioch. But small churches were springing up everywhere in many countries.

Chapter 73
A NEW JOURNEY
ACTS 15, 16

A few years after this first missionary journey, Paul said to his friend Barnabas, "Let us make another journey, and visit all the new churches and see how they are getting along."

Barnabas wanted to take Mark along with them. You remember that it was at Mark's house that the Christians were gathered to pray the night Peter was released from prison by the angel.

Paul said, "We took Mark with us the first time, but he did not stay with us very long. He soon turned back. I don't think we ought to take him again."

They could not reach an agreement. Barnabas wanted to take Mark, who was his cousin, but Paul did not think it was wise to choose a companion who might turn back along the way.

At last they separated. Barnabas took Mark with him and sailed to the island of Cyrus. Paul chose Silas to go with him. They did not go to Cyprus. Instead of traveling by sea, as Paul had done before, they went by land across the mountains.

Soon Paul and Silas reached Derbe and Lystra, where churches had been founded on the first visit. One of the Christians here was a fine young man named Timothy. His father was a Greek, but his mother and his grandmother were Jews. They were good women, and had taught Timothy to love God. He had known the Old Testament well even from the time he was a child.

Paul loved this young man as if he had been his own son. He invited Timothy to go with him and Silas as their helper on their missionary trip, and Timothy was glad to join them.

Preaching wherever they went, the three missionaries traveled throughout the cities of that country. At last they came to Troas, a city on the seashore. While they were here, Paul had a vision one night. He saw a man standing before him who said, "Come over into Macedonia and help us." Paul knew the vision had been sent by the Lord because He wanted him to preach in a new country, to people who had never heard about Jesus.

Macedonia is a large country north of Greece, separated from Troas by the sea. The missionaries found a ship which would take them across the sea. For several days they sailed, and at last they came to the big city of Philippi. They stayed here for a few days.

Paul and his helpers were now completely surrounded by heathen people who worshiped idols. There were not enough Jews in Philippi to build a synagogue; for there had to be at least ten Jews before a synagogue could be built.

When the Sabbath day came, Paul went down to the riverside where some women were gathered together to pray. The missionaries sat down and talked to them about Jesus.

One of these women was a seller of purple dyes. Her name was Lydia. She had heard about the true God, and tried to worship Him as best she knew how. When she heard what Paul said about Jesus, the Son of God, her heart was opened. She became a Christian, and she invited the missionaries to stay at her house.

Chapter 74

THE POOR FORTUNE-TELLER

ACTS 16

In Philippi there was a young woman who was a fortune-teller. She was not in her right mind, for an evil spirit lived in her and made her say strange things. Many people believed that what she said was sure to happen. They asked her all sorts of questions about the future, and did whatever she told them.

Some men of the city had made this poor girl their slave. Every day she had to go out into the streets to tell people's fortunes for money. Her masters became rich through the money she brought back to them.

Whenever she saw Paul and Silas and Timothy in the streets, this poor girl followed them, calling out so that everybody could hear, "These men are servants of the Most High

God, and they come to tell us how to be saved."

Of course people stared at the young girl following three strangers and shouting after them. Everybody knew that she was not in her right mind. Those who did not believe in her fortune-telling laughed at the sight.

Paul did not like this at all. He knew that it was an evil spirit which spoke through the lips of the poor girl. And he did not want people to laugh at his teaching.

For many days the girl followed the missionaries, calling out after them. At last Paul turned and said to the evil spirit that was in her, "I command you in the name of Jesus Christ to come out of her!"

Immediately the evil spirit left her, and the girl was restored to her right mind. But now that the spirit had left her, she could not tell fortunes any more. When her owners found this out, they were very angry at Paul and Silas. They did not care about the poor girl. They were not glad that she was well again and happy. All they cared about was the money they would lose now that she would no longer tell fortunes.

"We don't want strangers to come here and interfere with our business," they said furiously. "We won't put up with it." Dragging Paul and Silas before the rulers of the city, they complained, "These men do not belong here. They are Jews, and they disturb our city. We do not want to follow Jewish customs. We are Romans, and we want to follow Roman customs."

As the men talked, the people in the marketplace became angry. Even the rulers became so angry that they tore the clothes off the missionaries and ordered them to be beaten.

After the beating Paul and Silas were thrown into prison, and the jailer was strictly warned to guard them carefully. Their feet were fastened in a wooden frame called the stocks, which held them so tightly that they could not take a single step. They could not even change their uncomfortable position, because their feet were held straight in front of them.

Poor Paul and Silas! Their backs were bleeding from the beating and smarting with pain. As night came, the prison grew dark. Paul and Silas could not sleep because of the pain. They could not even lie down, but had to sit with their feet straight out in front of them.

But when they remembered that they were suffering for Jesus, who had borne so much more for them, they were happy in spite of their pain. They lifted up their voices and prayed and sang songs of praise to God. The other prisoners listened in wonder. Who were these strange men who could sing even after they had been beaten and thrown into prison?

Chapter 75
THE JAILER WHO BELIEVED
ACTS 16

Although Paul and Silas had been thrown into prison for helping the poor girl, God had not forgotten them. He was taking care of them, just as He had taken care of Peter in prison in Jerusalem. His almighty power is far greater than any jailer's. No prison door in the world can remain closed against Him.

About midnight, when Paul and

Silas were singing, suddenly there was a great earthquake. Everything began to rock. The very foundations of the prison were shaken, and all the doors flew open. The stocks fell apart, and the prisoners found that their chains were broken. They were free!

The great earthquake woke up the prison warden. When he saw that all the prison doors were open, he thought all the prisoners had escaped. He knew that if they got away, he would be punished cruelly. The rulers of the city would surely kill him.

The jailer was a heathen, and he had never heard the commandment we know so well, "Thou shalt not kill." He thought it would be better to kill himself than to be tortured and executed because he had allowed the prisoners to escape.

Drawing his sword, he was about to drive it into his heart when Paul cried out, "Do not harm yourself, for we are all here. No one has tried to escape!"

When the startled jailer heard this, he called for a light, and ran into the prison. Trembling, he fell down before Paul and Silas, begging them to come out of the prison into his house. He felt that Paul and Silas must be servants of God, since they did not even try to escape when they had a chance. Surely, he thought, they must know the truth about God. "Sirs," he cried out to them, "what must I do to be saved?"

They said to him, "Believe on the Lord Jesus Christ, and you shall be saved, and all the members of your household too." Probably the jailer did not even know who Jesus Christ was. But Paul and Silas explained that Jesus was the Son of the true God, who had come into the world to die on the cross for the sins of all who put their trust in Him, and that

He had risen on the third day, and was now in heaven at God's right hand.

While Paul was explaining this, the jailer's whole household gathered to hear these words of life. The jailer, his wife and his children, and all his servants were baptized that very night, and there was great joy in his house.

Then the jailer brought cool water and carefully washed the ugly cuts where Paul and Silas had been beaten. He told his servants to bring food. The two prisoners were very hungry, for they had not eaten for a long time.

When morning came, the rulers sent word to the jailer to let the prisoners go. But Paul and Silas refused to leave. They had been badly treated although they had broken no law. They had been punished without a trial, and this was against the law.

In those days there were certain persons who were Roman citizens even though they had not been born in Rome. Some of them had bought this right, and others had received it as a gift in return for some great service they had done the emperor. Roman citizens had many privileges other people did not have. No Roman citizen could be beaten or put in prison unless he had first been tried and found guilty.

Paul was such a Roman citizen. Probably he had inherited this privilege from his father. The rulers of Philippi thought Paul was just a Jew. They did not dream he was a Roman citizen and that they had broken the law by having him beaten and imprisoned.

When the rulers sent word that Paul and Silas should be released, Paul said, "They have beaten us openly, without any trial, even though we are Roman citizens. They have thrown us in prison. And now do they send word for us to leave quietly and secretly? If they want us to leave, they themselves must come and bring us out publicly!"

When the rulers heard that Paul and Silas were Roman citizens, they were terrified. They hurried down to the jail and begged Paul and Silas to forgive them, and to come out and leave their city.

So Paul and Silas went back to Lydia's house. They called all the Christians together and told them what had happened. After comforting them, they said good-bye to them and left the city.

The two missionaries had lived in Philippi for a long time. A few years later Paul wrote a letter to the church there, where he had so many friends. You will find that letter in your Bible.

Chapter 76
FROM CITY TO CITY
ACTS 17

After Paul and Silas left Philippi, the two missionaries visited other cities in Macedonia. At last they came to Thessalonica. There they stayed with a man named Jason.

In that city there was a synagogue of the Jews. Paul and Silas went there to preach on the Sabbath, instead of preaching on the street corners or by the river, as they did in many of the heathen cities.

For three Sabbath days they preached in the Jewish synagogue. Many people came to hear Paul — not only Jews, but also Greeks. A great many of the Greeks were glad to hear about the one true God, and about Jesus Christ who loved them. When they heard the story of how Jesus suffered and died for the sins of the world, and rose again from the grave, and ascended to heaven, they were glad to turn away from the idols which were made by men's hands.

But some of the Jews in the city did not believe what Paul said. They were angry and jealous when they saw how many people listened to him. Some of the rough fellows of the town gathered together in a mob.

They screamed and yelled and made such a noise that they set the whole city in an uproar. The mob came to Jason's house, and wanted to seize Paul and Silas and Timothy.

But the three missionaries were not there just then. So the mob seized Jason and some other Christians instead, and dragged them before the city rulers. "These men," they cried, "who have turned the world upside down, have now come here also. Jason has taken them into his house. They do things against our emperor Caesar, and they say there is another king named Jesus."

The rulers saw that they must calm this rough mob. They made Jason and the others promise not to make any trouble, and then let them go. Since Paul and Silas and Timothy had not been found, no action could be taken against them.

The Christians knew it would not be safe for Paul and his friends to stay there any longer. They sent them away that night to Berea. The people of that city were more noble than those of Thessalonica. They listened eagerly to Paul, searching the scriptures daily to see if the things

Paul told about Jesus had been foretold by the prophets long ago.

Many Greek men and women of Berea turned from their idols to the living God. But when the trouble-some Jews in Thessalonica heard that Paul was preaching in this nearby city, they came to stir the people up against him. Paul's friends thought it would be better for him to leave.

Chapter 77
ABOUT THE UNKNOWN GOD
ACTS 17, 18

This time Paul went to Athens. You probably know that Athens is the greatest city of Greece. It is big and beautiful, but in Paul's time it was even more splendid than it is now. It was filled with great marble temples, in which the people worshiped. The Greeks made marble statues of their gods. Some of the statues which once stood in Greek temples were found many years later. You will find copies and pictures of them all over the world, for many people believe they are the most beautiful statues ever made.

When Paul walked through the beautiful city, and saw these idols on every side, he knew the Athenian people did not know about the one true God. He felt very sorry for them, and he wanted to tell them about Jesus. At last he came to the Jewish synagogue. For though Athens was a Greek city, many Jews and people from other nations lived there.

Paul went into the synagogue, and began to talk to the Jews there. Every day after that he went to the marketplace and preached to all who would listen to him.

The people of the city liked to hear about new ideas. In Athens there lived some of the wisest men the world has ever known. They spent their time teaching in the streets and the marketplace. It was no new thing for the people to hear men talking on the street corners.

The wise men of the city came to see Paul and to hear what he was teaching. Some asked, "What does this babbler say?" Others, who had heard him speaking about Jesus and the resurrection, said, "He seems to be teaching about some strange gods."

The people were so much interested in what Paul was saying that they brought him to the hill of Mars, where they could listen to him without interruption from the noise of the buying and selling that was going on in the marketplace. They asked him politely, "Will you tell us about this new doctrine you are preaching? You bring strange things to our ears, and we would like to know what these things mean."

So Paul stood on Mars' hill, and said to them, "You men of Athens, I see that you are very religious. For as I passed through your city, and saw the gods that you worship, I found one altar that said, 'To the Unknown God.' You are worshiping one God you do not know. That is the God that I am preaching about.

"He is the God that made the world and all the things that are in the world. Because He is the Lord of heaven and earth, He does not need to live in temples that are made with men's hands. He does not need to have us give Him food, or any of the things which you sacrifice to your idols. For He is the one who gives life and breath and all things to us.

28: THE RIOT AT EPHESUS

29: PAUL'S DEFENCE BEFORE AGRIPPA

"Some of your own poets have said, 'We are the children of God.' If we are the children of God, we ought not to think that God is a statue of stone or silver or gold, made by men's hands. In the past you did not know any better, so God overlooked your ignorance. But now God wants everyone to repent of his sins. He has chosen Jesus Christ to judge the world, and He has given you sure proof by raising Jesus from the dead."

When Paul spoke about the resurrection from the dead, some of the people began to make fun of him, because they did not believe such a thing was possible. Others said, "We want to hear more about this." And some of them believed.

Leaving Athens, Paul went to Corinth, another Greek city. He stayed there two years, living with a Jew named Aquila and his wife Priscilla. They were tent makers, as Paul was, and they worked on their tents together. Every Sabbath Paul preached to Jews and Greeks about Jesus.

Several years later Paul wrote two letters to the Christians at Corinth. These letters became part of the New Testament, and are called First and Second Corinthians.

From Corinth Paul crossed the sea again and went to Ephesus. But he did not stay there, for he wanted to get to Jerusalem. He promised he would come back if it was God's will, and he sailed away. He stopped at many of the new little congregations to visit them and to strengthen them.

Chapter 78
THE RIOT OF THE STATUE-MAKERS
ACTS 19

Paul kept his promise and came back to Ephesus after a while. This time he stayed for more than two years. He founded a Christian church there. And there God performed many miracles through Paul, healing the sick and driving out evil spirits. The church at Ephesus grew strong and big.

In Ephesus there was a magnificent temple of Diana, the goddess of hunting. In the temple there was a great statue of the goddess. The people of the city thought this statue had been dropped down to them from heaven. This temple was famous, and many people came from far away to worship there. Before going home, many of them bought a little silver statue or image of Diana to take back with them.

The men who made these statues became very rich, for all the people thought they had to have a statue of their goddess in their homes.

Demetrius, the leader of the silversmiths, saw that if Paul went on preaching that idols were not gods at all, soon nobody would want to buy their images. So he called a meeting of all the silversmiths and said to them, "You know that we get our money by making these images. You see and hear that not only here in Ephesus but through all of Asia Minor this Paul has been telling people that idols made by men's hands are not really gods at all. If this continues, soon nobody will want to buy our images of Diana. Before long the temple of our goddess, where all Asia and the world worship now, will be laughed at."

The very idea of this alarmed the silver workers, and they cried out in anger, "Great is Diana of the "Ephesians!" They made such a noise that soon the whole city was filled with confusion. The mob caught some of Paul's companions and rushed with them into the open-air amphitheater. Paul wanted to go to the amphitheater too, but his friends held him back, for they were afraid he might be injured.

In the theater there was a great crowd, some shouting one thing and some another. Most of them did not know what the excitement was all about.

A man called Alexander came up to the platform and tried to talk to the people. He motioned with his hand for them to listen, but when the crowd saw that he was a Jew, they raised their voices and shouted, "Great is Diana of the Ephesians! Great is Diana of the Ephesians! Great is Diana of the Ephesians!" For almost two hours they kept this up, shrieking and screaming.

After they had yelled their throats hoarse, the chief officer of the city managed to get them quiet. When they could hear him talk, he said to them, "You men of Ephesus, who does not know that our city contains the temple of the great goddess Diana, and the image which fell down from heaven? Since no one can deny this, you ought to be quiet, and do nothing foolish. These men you have brought here have not done any harm. If Demetrius and the others have a quarrel with anyone, let them go to the courts about it, and not make a riot here. We are going to get in trouble with the Roman authorities because of this uproar, for there is no good reason for it." When he had said this, he dismissed the crowd.

After the crowd had gone home, and the city was quiet again, Paul called the disciples together to say good-bye to them. There were many Christians, for he had been there for almost three years. And so once more Paul set out on his journey.

Chapter 79
THE YOUNG MAN WHO FELL ASLEEP
ACTS 20

From Ephesus Paul went to Macedonia and then to Greece. He visited all the places where he had been before, where churches had been started. He did not stay long anywhere, for he was eager to be in Jerusalem on the day of Pentecost, which, you remember, was the day when the Holy Spirit had first come down from heaven into the hearts of the disciples.

Finally he came to the city of Troas on the seashore. There he stayed for a week, preaching and teaching. When Sunday came, all the Christian people of the city met in a large room on the third floor of a building to listen to Paul. They were very eager to hear him, for the only way they could learn more about Jesus was by hearing Paul or one of the other apostles preach. The new Christians could not go home and take down their Bibles and read over the things which they had forgotten. The New Testament had not yet been written. They just had to try hard to remember everything Paul told them.

Paul had a great deal to say, for he did not expect to return again to preach in the church at Troas. After he had been to Jerusalem, he hoped to go to Rome to preach about Jesus, and then after that to Spain, still further away. And so he kept on preaching until it was past midnight, and the people listened eagerly to every word.

Since the room was crowded, one young man had perched himself on a window sill to listen. Near the end of the long sermon, the young man fell asleep. Before anyone could catch him, he tumbled backward out of the third-story window, and fell all the way to the ground.

Paul ran down the stairs as fast as he could, but the young man was dead when he got there. Paul threw himself on the young man's body and held him tight. He said to the people, "Don't be troubled. He is alive again." At first they could hardly believe it, but then they saw that it was true. God had given Paul power to bring the dead young man back to life.

The people went upstairs again. They had communion together, celebrating the Lord's Supper by eating the bread and drinking the wine in memory of the broken body and poured-out blood of the Lord Jesus, as He had commanded His followers to do.

Paul stayed and talked to them all night long, until daylight came. Then at last he said good-bye and went down to the ship that was to take him away. In it he sailed around the coast of Asia Minor. He did not have time to stop at all the places he had visited on his first trip.

On this journey Paul was joined by a man who stayed with him on the rest of his journeys. He was a doctor, and a very good man. His name was Luke.

It was now almost thirty years since Jesus had gone back to heaven. His disciples had been preaching all that time, and there were many Christian churches far and wide, with thousands of members.

So far nothing had been written down about Jesus. But now the apostles realized that they must write down all that they knew about Him. Otherwise, after they were dead, there would be no one who knew just how it all had happened.

Matthew, who, you remember, had been a tax collector, wrote the story of the life of Jesus, and this became the first book of our New Testament. Mark, who had accompanied Paul and Barnabas partway on their first missionary journey, did the same. Luke wrote another. Like Mark, he was not one of the twelve apostles, but he had followed Jesus, and he knew about the life of Jesus from the beginning. Besides writing this story about the life of Jesus, Luke wrote an account of what the apostles did after Jesus died. He could do this very well, because he traveled with Paul for many years. This book written by Luke is called The Acts of the Apostles.

A long time after these first books were written, John, the beloved disciple, wrote another account of the life of Jesus.

And Paul wrote letters to the churches he loved so dearly. The Christians in these churches read Paul's letters in church on Sundays, just as we sometimes do. These letters are God's Word, for God told Paul what to write.

God helped every one of these men to write. He told them exactly what to say, because He wanted these books to be part of the Bible, without any mistakes in them. God's telling the writers what to say we call inspiration.

The whole Bible is God's book, although it was written by many different men at different times. Everything in it was put there by God.

Chapter 80

BACK TO JERUSALEM
ACTS 20, 21

As Paul and his friends sailed around the coast of Asia they soon came near Ephesus, where Paul had preached for a long time and where he had founded a church. Since Paul was in a hurry to get to Jerusalem in time for Pentecost, he could not stop at Ephesus. Still, he wanted to see his friends, the members of the church. So he sent word to them to come to the seashore to meet him.

When they came, he said to them, "I am going to Jerusalem, and I do not know what is going to happen to me there. Everywhere I go, the Holy Spirit tells me I shall have trouble in Jerusalem, that I shall be arrested and suffer. But I will not stop on that account, not even for fear of losing my life. For it is my joy to preach about Jesus and the grace of God. Now I know you will never see me again. Do not forget what I taught you the three years I was with you. And God will take care of you."

When Paul had said this, he kneeled down on the seashore and prayed with them. They all wept, sorrowing most of all because he said they would not see him again. They took him to his ship, and after the last sad good-byes, Paul sailed away.

The ship sailed around the coast of Asia, stopping at many places. At last it reached Caesarea. In this city there lived a man of whom you have heard before — Philip, the man who talked to the Ethiopian from Africa on the road through the desert. Philip was the minister of the church in Caesarea. He had four daughters who were a great help to him, for they were all prophetesses to whom God spoke.

While Paul was staying at Philip's house, a prophet from Jerusalem arrived. Taking Paul's girdle, he tied his own hands and feet with it and said, "The Holy Spirit told me that just so the Jews in Jerusalem will bind the hands and feet of the man who owns this girdle."

Luke writes in his book, "When we heard this, we begged Paul not to go to Jerusalem, but he answered, 'Why are you weeping and breaking my heart? I am ready not only to be bound, but also to die for the Lord Jesus at Jerusalem.' So when we saw he would not be persuaded, we stopped trying and said, 'The Lord's will be done!' "

Paul had to travel only a little way to get to Jerusalem. The Christians there were very glad to see him. "The next day," says Luke, "we went to see James." This James was the brother of Jesus. He had been made head of the church in Jerusalem. All the elders of the Jerusalem church gathered at his house to greet Paul. For a long time they had had no news of his missionary journeys.

Paul told them all the things God had done among the heathen in Asia and in Greece — how he had preached and founded churches in Antioch, Iconium, Lystra, Philippi, Corinth, Ephesus, and Troas. He told them how he had been stoned at Lystra, and beaten and put in prison at Philippi; and how much trouble he had had in Ephesus because of the heathen goddess Diana and her images; and how God had delivered him out of all his troubles.

When James and the others heard how many heathen had turned to the Lord through Paul's preaching, they glorified and thanked God.

Chapter 81
AN UPROAR IN THE TEMPLE
ACTS 21

One day, after Paul had been in Jerusalem for about a week, he went into the temple to worship God. Some of the Jews saw him there. They knew that Paul had been walking around in Jerusalem with some Greek friends, and they suspected he had brought them into the temple with him. The Jews had a very strict law that any foreigner who entered God's holy temple must die. Paul knew this, and he had been careful not to bring any of the Greek Christians into the temple.

But Paul's enemies thought they had caught him in a crime. They called out, "Men of Israel, help! This is the man who has been teaching everywhere against the law of Moses, and against our temple. Now he has brought Greeks into our temple, and has made the holy place unclean!"

When the people heard this, they ran to the spot quickly, and dragged Paul out of the temple to the outer court. Then they quickly shut the doors, so that no more Greeks could enter the building. For they believed Paul had really taken his Greek friends into the temple. They were so angry at this that they wanted to kill him. Soon a mob gathered and shouted, "Kill him! Kill him!"

Just above the temple and to one side was the fortress where the Roman soldiers were stationed. Somebody quickly ran to tell the chief captain that a great mob was gathering, and that all Jerusalem was in an uproar.

It was the chief captain's business to keep order in Jerusalem. As soon as he heard that the whole city was upset, he took several hundred soldiers and ran down the steps to the temple court as fast as he could.

The Jews saw the soldiers coming, so they stopped beating Paul. The first thing the captain did was to put two chains on Paul, something like our handcuffs, so that he could not escape. Then he turned to the wild mob and said, "Who is this man, and what crime has he committed?"

Some yelled one thing, and some another. They all shouted together, making such a noise and confusion that the chief captain could not understand a word they said. At last he commanded the soldiers to take Paul inside the fortress.

The Jews pushed and shoved wildly, screaming, "Away with him! Away with him!" The soldiers could not get Paul through the crowd and up the stairs. At last they had to lift him up on their shoulders and carry him to the fortress.

As they were about to take him inside, Paul said in Greek to the chief captain, "May I speak to you?"

The chief captain was astonished to hear Paul speak Greek. "Can you speak Greek?" he said. "Aren't you the Egyptian who some time ago led four thousand murderers into the wilderness?"

"No, I am not an Egyptian," Paul said. "I am a Jew. I beg you, let me speak to the people."

So Paul stood at the top of the stairs. All around him were the soldiers with their spears, to protect him from the crowd. He beckoned with his hand to the people to be quiet, so that he could talk. Then Paul started to talk in Aramaic. When they heard him speak their own language, the people finally quieted down.

Paul looked over the crowd of angry Jews who had pulled him out of the temple yelling, "Kill him!" Now they were listening to hear what he had to say.

Paul began very politely. "Men, brothers, and fathers, I am a Jew. I was born in Tarsus, but I went to school here in the city of Jerusalem. The great Gamaliel was my teacher. I was very strict about all the Jewish laws, just as you are. I hated the Christians, just as you do. I hunted them down and had them arrested and put in prison. I even persecuted them to death.

"The high priest knows these things. He gave me letters to the priests in Damascus, so that I could arrest any Christians I found there, and bring them here to be punished.

"But something wonderful happened to me on the way to Damascus. When I had almost reached the city, about noon, suddenly a great light from heaven shone round about me. I was so startled and frightened that I fell to the ground. I heard a voice saying to me, 'Paul, Paul, why do you persecute Me?'

"I answered the voice and said, 'Who are You, Lord?' He answered, 'I am Jesus of Nazareth. You are persecuting Me.'

"Those who were with me saw the light, but they did not hear the voice. I said, 'What shall I do, Lord?' And the Lord said to me, 'Get up, and go to Damascus. There you will be told what you shall do.'

"But I could not see because of the glory of the light. It had blinded me, and those who were with me had to lead me by the hand. So I came to Damascus, and after I had been there three days, a man came to see me. He said, 'Brother Paul, receive your sight.' So my blindness went away, and I saw him.

"This man said to me, 'You are not to fight against the Christians any more, for they are God's people. God wants you to become a Christian, for He has chosen you to see Jesus and to hear His voice. You are to go to all the world and tell them about Jesus. Now get up, and be baptized, and wash away your sins.'

"After this, I came to Jerusalem. While I was praying here in the temple, the Lord said to me, 'Hurry and leave Jerusalem, for the people here will not listen to you. I will send you far away to preach to the heathen.' "

The crowd listened quietly till Paul spoke about the heathen. Then they became angry, for they did not believe that God wished to save anybody except the Jews. They thought that only the Jews were God's people. They did not remember that God had said, "All the earth is Mine."

So when Paul said that God had sent him to preach to the heathen, the crowd began to yell, "Away with him! Away with him! Away with such a fellow from the earth, for it is not fit that he should live!"

When the chief captain saw this, he commanded the soldiers to bring Paul into the fortress, and to give him a beating. For it was a Roman custom to torture a prisoner into confessing what crime he had committed.

The soldiers led Paul into the fortress and began to bind his hands and feet with strips of leather. Paul asked them, "Is it lawful to beat a man who is a Roman citizen?"

When the soldier in charge heard

this, he hurried to the chief captain and said, "Be careful what you do, for this man is a Roman citizen."

This was disturbing news, for it was against the law to beat a Roman citizen unless he had already been tried and found guilty of some crime. The chief captain went at once to Paul. "Is it true that you are a Roman citizen?" he asked.

Paul answered, "Yes."

"I am too," answered the captain. "But I had to pay a great sum of money to buy this privilege."

Paul said, "I was born a Roman citizen."

When the captain heard this, he quickly took off the chains that bound Paul. He was afraid he would be in serious trouble because he had put chains on a man who was a Roman citizen.

Chapter 83
A WICKED OATH
ACTS 23

In Paul's day only a Roman citizen had a right to be tried and to defend himself when he was accused of a crime. Other people were beaten, to make them confess. But when a Roman was tried, the man who accused him had to come and tell his complaint. Then the prisoner was given a chance to defend himself.

Since Paul was a Roman, the captain commanded the chief priests, who had said Paul should not be allowed to live, to come to the judgment hall and tell what they had against him.

When Paul entered the hall where he was to be tried, he looked at the crowd of people. At once he noticed that some of them were Pharisees and some were Sadducees. The Pharisees believed that all the Old Testament was God's Word, but the Sadducees believed only in the first five books of Moses. The Sadducees did not believe that people live again after they have died, nor that there are any angels. Because of these different beliefs, the two groups hated each other bitterly.

Paul knew this. When he saw that these bitter enemies had joined together to accuse him, he called out,

"Men and brothers, I am a Pharisee, and the son of a Pharisee, and I am accused here because I believe in the resurrection from the dead."

Immediately a fight arose among the Jews. The Pharisees took Paul's part. "Why, this man is all right," they said. "Perhaps an angel or some spirit really did speak to him on the road to Damascus. Let's not fight against God!"

The Pharisees tried to get hold of Paul, shouting, "This man has done no wrong. He says an angel has spoken to him." At the same time the Sadducees tried to snatch him from the Pharisees, yelling, "There are no such things as angels." Between them there was such shouting and fighting that the chief captain was afraid Paul would be pulled to pieces. Finally he commanded the soldiers to take Paul away from them by force, and bring him back into the fortress.

That night the Lord came and stood by Paul, and comforted him, saying, "Do not be afraid, Paul. I will not let the people of Jerusalem kill you. I am going to send you to Rome to preach about Me there." These words were a great comfort to Paul. Now he knew that no matter what might happen the Lord would save him from the angry Jews.

The Jews were furious that Paul was safe in the Roman fortress, out of their reach. More than forty of them plotted together. They swore they would not eat or drink until they had killed Paul. Then they went to the chief priests and elders and said, "We have bound ourselves by a terrible curse that we will not eat or drink till we have killed Paul. Tell the chief captain tomorrow that you have some questions you want to ask Paul. Persuade him to bring Paul down to the judgment hall. We will be hiding, and we will kill him before he ever reaches the place of judgment."

What do you think would happen today if a band of men came to the governor with such a scheme? They would be thrown into prison before they knew what was happening to them. They would be tried for attempted murder.

This is just what would have happened to the forty men if the priests had been good men. But they were not. Instead of arresting the forty plotters, the priests made a bargain with them. They were only too glad to find some people who would kill Paul for them.

Chapter 84
HOW PAUL WAS SAVED
ACTS 23

God was taking care of Paul. He was not going to let the Jews kill him, as they had planned. A son of Paul's sister heard the wicked plan of the forty Jews. He went right into the fortress and told his uncle Paul.

Paul called one of the guards and said, "Bring this young man to the chief captain, for he has something to tell him." The soldier led the young man to the captain and said, "Paul, the prisoner, called me, and told me to bring this young man to you, because he has something to say to you." Then the guard went away, leaving them alone.

Paul's nephew said to the captain, "The chief priests and elders have made an agreement with some rough men. Tomorrow they will ask you to bring Paul down, as if they wanted to ask him some questions. The rough men will be lying in wait, and just as soon as he comes down they will kill him. When they ask you, O captain, to bring Paul down, do not do so. For there are more than forty of them in the plot, and they have sworn a solemn oath not to eat or drink till they have killed Paul."

The captain said, "You did right to come and tell me. I will look after Paul. You keep still about what you have told me. Don't say a word to anyone." Then he let the young man go.

At once the captain began to make arrangements to protect Paul. He called two centurions, each an officer over a hundred soldiers. "Get two hundred soldiers ready," he commanded, "to go to Caesarea tonight at nine o'clock. Take two hundred spearmen along, too, and seventy horsemen. Take animals for everyone to ride on, so you can make good time. Bring Paul safely to Governor Felix at Caesarea."

Caesarea was the governor's capital city, and it was heavily garrisoned with Roman soldiers. Wicked Herod, who was governor when Peter was thrown into prison, you remember, had had his palace there. He was dead now, and Felix was Roman governor in his place.

The chief captain sent along with the centurions a letter to Felix:

This man, Paul, was caught by the Jews. They were getting ready to kill him, but I heard he was a Roman citizen, and so I came with the soldiers and rescued him.

When I asked the Jews what he had done, they said he had broken some of their Jewish laws, but I found he had done nothing worthy of death or imprisonment.

Hearing that the Jews were plotting to kill him, I am sending him to you. I have also told the Jews to come down to Caesarea to accuse him, if they have any fault to find with him.

The two centurions took the letter and the soldiers. At nine o'clock they started out, all four hundred and seventy of them, with Paul safely in the middle of the troop, riding on horses or donkeys, and traveling as fast as they could.

When morning light came, they were a long way from Jerusalem, and it was safe to let most of the soldiers go back. Only the seventy horsemen went the rest of the way with Paul.

At last they reached Caesarea, and the centurions gave the letter to Felix. The governor read the letter. Then he said to Paul, "I will hear your case when the priests and elders come to accuse you."

Chapter 85
THE TRIAL
ACTS 24

Five days after Paul reached Caesarea safely, the high priest Ananias and the elders came down to accuse him before the court. Governor Felix brought Paul out, to find out what he had done to make the Jews so angry.

The Jews had brought with them a man who was a fine public speaker. He began by addressing the governor in flattering words:

"Most noble Felix, we are very thankful to you that you are such a good governor, and that our whole nation lives in peace under your wise administration. But we do not want to tire you with long speeches, and so we beg you to listen to just a few words.

"This man is an annoying fellow. He stirs up trouble wherever he goes. Besides this, he is a ringleader of the Nazarenes, or Christians. He has defiled our holy temple. We were going to punish him for that, but your captain came with his soldiers and took him by force out of our hands. If you examine him, you will find these things are true."

All the Jews nodded their heads and said, "Yes, all this is true."

Then the governor motioned to Paul that it was his turn to speak. Paul was glad to be able to defend himself before Felix. This man had a Jewish wife and knew a great deal about the Jews and their religion which most Romans did not understand.

Paul began, "I am glad to speak for

myself, for I know that you have been a judge of this nation for many years. It is not true that I was making trouble in the city, and they cannot prove what they say. But it is true that I am a follower of Jesus, and that I believe everything found in the books of the law and the prophets. The only fault they can find with me is that I cried out to them, 'I believe in the resurrection from the dead.'"

When he had listened to Paul's defense, Felix was sure that he had not done anything wrong. Felix had heard many things about the Nazarenes, as the Christians were called by the Jews, and he hoped he could perhaps find out more from Paul. Felix sent the high priests and elders back to Jerusalem. "When the chief captain comes down," he said, "I will settle this case." Meanwhile Paul was kept in Caesarea, with a soldier to guard him. All his friends were allowed to come and see him. There was a large Christian church in Caesarea, which Paul had visited on his way to Jerusalem. Many Christians came to see Paul, and Luke the doctor stayed near him too.

A few days after the Jews had returned to Jerusalem, Felix, and his wife Drusilla, who was a Jewess, sent for Paul. They wished to hear more about Jesus and the new group called Christians.

Paul talked very seriously to Felix and Drusilla. The governor was very much interested. But when Paul began to speak about the great judgment day which is coming, Felix trembled in terror. He said to Paul, "That is enough for this time. When it is convenient, I will send for you again, and will be glad to hear more."

Felix often sent for Paul, for he was very much interested in what Paul said. But he did not become a Christian, nor did he settle Paul's case one way or the other. He kept Paul in prison because he hoped Paul would offer him a bribe in exchange for his freedom. But Paul did not offer a bribe.

After two years Felix was recalled to Rome, and another governor, named Festus, arrived. Felix left Paul in prison because he knew this would please the Jews. Paul had been in prison now for more than two years, but he had not been idle. He was permitted to see his friends and other visitors. In many ways Paul managed to tell people about Jesus, even though he was no longer able to "go into all the world."

Chapter 86
THE APPEAL TO CAESAR
ACTS 25

Paul was still a prisoner when Festus became governor. After spending three days in his palace at Caesarea, the new governor went up to Jerusalem.

The high priest and the elders had not forgotten about Paul though two years had passed since those forty men had sworn that they would not eat or drink till they had killed Paul. Surely they must have broken their oath long ago, for they could not live without eating or drinking that long!

Now that there was a new governor, the priests again tried to get rid of Paul. They asked Festus to send him to Jerusalem to be tried. They planned to hide along the road and kill Paul.

Perhaps the old governor, Felix, had warned Festus not to let Paul go to Jerusalem. At any rate, Festus refused to listen to their suggestion. He said he was going to keep Paul in Caesarea. If any of the Jews wished to accuse him of anything, they could come down to Caesarea and accuse him there.

When Festus returned to Caesarea, about ten days later, some of the Jews went with him to accuse Paul.

The next day Festus commanded that Paul be brought into the judgment hall. The Jews at once began to accuse Paul of many things he had never done. None of the things they said could be proved.

Then it was Paul's turn to speak. He said, "I have not done anything wrong against the law of the Jews, nor against the temple, nor against the Roman emperor."

Festus wanted to make a good impression as the new governor and so he tried to please the Jews if he could. He asked Paul, "Will you go up to Jerusalem to be judged about these things?"

Paul knew that he would never reach Jerusalem alive, for he knew the Jews would hide along the road and kill him. He also knew that as a Roman citizen he had certain rights. If he did not think he was getting a fair trial, he could demand to be tried by the highest judge of all, the emperor, in Rome.

So when Festus asked him if he would go to Jerusalem to be tried there, Paul answered, "I stand at Caesar's judgment seat. I have done nothing wrong to the Jews, as you

very well know. They cannot prove any of these things of which they accuse me. I appeal to Caesar."

Now that Paul had appealed to Caesar, Festus was obliged to send him to Rome, whether he wanted to or not. So he answered, "Since you have appealed to Caesar, unto Caesar you shall go."

A few days later King Agrippa and his wife Bernice made a visit to Caesarea to greet the new governor Festus. Agrippa ruled the land east of the Jordan River for the Romans. He was a son of the king Herod who put Peter in prison. Although this king was a Jew, he worshiped idols as well as the true God, and he was more anxious to please his Roman masters than to rule his Jewish subjects well.

Festus said to King Agrippa, "There is a man here who was left a prisoner by Felix. When I went up to Jerusalem, the Jews there told me they wanted to have him killed. I told them it is not the custom of the Romans to condemn anyone until he has a chance to speak for himself.

"So when the Jews came down here to Caesarea, I commanded the prisoner to be brought to the judgment hall. When the Jews began to accuse him, they did not have anything important to say. They accused him only of some offense against their own religion, and about somebody named Jesus who was dead, though Paul said He is alive. I did not think such questions were very important, and I asked Paul if he would go down to Jerusalem to be judged. But Paul appealed to Caesar, and so to Caesar he shall be sent."

Agrippa said, "I should like to hear this man myself."

"Very well," said Festus. "You shall hear him tomorrow."

Chapter 87
A KING IS ALMOST PERSUADED

ACTS 25, 26

In the judgment hall of the Roman governor all the important people of Caesarea were gathered together. Some of them had come because they wanted to see King Agrippa, who was visiting the governor. Others wanted to hear the prisoner Paul defend himself before Agrippa and Festus. Perhaps Philip and some of the other Christians were there, too, to listen to Paul. King Agrippa and his wife Bernice put on their finest clothes and came to the judgment hall with much display of their importance. They knew that Paul was a learned man and a fine speaker.

Then Paul was brought in. Because he was a prisoner, he was chained to his guard. Governor Festus stood up before the people. Turning first to King Agrippa, and then to the crowd, he said, "King Agrippa, and all men present here, you see this man Paul, who, the Jews say, ought not to live any longer. But I found he has done nothing worthy of death, and he himself has appealed to Caesar. So I have decided to send him to Rome. But I do not like to send him to the emperor when I have no definite complaint to make against him. It seems unreasonable to send a prisoner and not to send along a list of the crimes of which he is accused. I have brought him out here for you to hear, King Agrippa, so that perhaps, when you have heard him, you can tell me what to write to the emperor."

As Festus sat down, King Agrippa said to Paul, "You may speak for yourself."

King Agrippa was different from the other people before whom Paul had spoken. Since he himself was partly Jewish, he understood the Jewish customs and religion, and would be able to judge of Paul's defense.

Paul began, "I think myself happy, King Agrippa, that I am to speak before you, because I know that you understand all the customs of the Jews. So I beg you to hear me patiently.

"All the Jews know what kind of man I have been all my life. They know that I was a Pharisee, and that I lived a very strict life. It is because I believe that Jesus Christ is the one so long promised to our fathers that they find fault with me. But why should it seem strange that God should raise the dead?

"I used to think that those who believed in Jesus of Nazareth were wrong, and I did many things against the Christians. I shut up many of them in prison, and when they were sentenced to death voted against them. I was so furious against them that I even followed them to strange cities. I went to Damascus with letters from the high priest, to arrest all the Christians I could find there.

"As I was traveling to Damascus, about the middle of the day, O king, I saw a light from heaven brighter than the sun shining round about me and about those who were with me. When we had all fallen to the earth, I heard a voice speaking to me in the Aramaic language, 'Paul, Paul, why do you persecute Me? It is hard for you to kick against the pricks.' Then I said, 'Who are You, Lord?'

"He said, 'I am Jesus, whom you are persecuting. I have appeared to you to make you one of My servants. I will send you to the heathen, to open their eyes, and to turn them from darkness unto light, and from the power of Satan to God, so that they may have their sins forgiven, and may go to heaven, together with all those who trust in Me.'

"O King Agrippa, I was not disobedient unto this heavenly vision, and I did what Jesus told me to do. I preached, first in Damascus, and then in Jerusalem, and then to the heathen. That is the reason why, when the Jews caught me in the temple, they tried to kill me. But God has kept me from being hurt, and I still go on preaching just what Moses and the prophets prophesied — that Jesus should suffer, and that He should rise again from the dead."

When Paul had finished, the new governor, Festus, cried with a loud voice, "Paul, you are out of your head! You have studied so much that you have gone crazy!"

Paul answered, "I am not crazy, most noble Festus. I am speaking truth and soberness. For King Agrippa knows all about these things that I have been saying. I am sure that he knows, for none of these things was done in a corner secretly."

Turning to Agrippa, Paul said, "King Agrippa, do you believe the prophets? I know that you believe them."

"Paul, you have almost persuaded me to be a Christian," answered the king.

Paul said, "I would to God that not only you, but all those who hear me today, were Christians, just like me, except for these chains!"

The king arose to leave the hall. He and Festus went to one side by themselves and said, "This man has done nothing worthy of death or chains." And Agrippa said to Festus, "This man might have been set free if he had not appealed to Caesar."

Chapter 88
PAUL SETS OUT FOR ROME
ACTS 27

Since Paul had appealed to Caesar, it was decided that he should be sent to Rome. Luke went with him. He has written all about the journey, which was a very exciting one.

Paul and some other prisoners were put in the charge of a Roman centurion named Julius. The prisoners were going to be well guarded on their trip, for the centurion had one hundred soldiers.

Luke wrote, "We started out from Caesarea by boat. The first day we stopped at Sidon. Julius the centurion was very kind to Paul, and let him go on shore here to see his friends. Then we got back on the ship, and sailed near the island of Cyprus. It was hard sailing, for the wind blew the wrong way."

This was long before there were any power boats. There were only rowboats and sailing boats. When the wind blew from the wrong direction, or when it blew too hard, the sailors had a difficult and dangerous time guiding the boat. Besides this, the sailors had no compass, as we have, to point to the north. When they were out of sight of land, the only way they could tell directions was by the sun in the daytime, or by the stars at night. When they could not see the sun or the stars because it was cloudy or stormy, they could not tell which way they were going.

Luke wrote, "We had to sail very slowly for many days, because the wind was against us. But at last we came to the island of Crete and stopped at Fair Havens.

"We waited there for better weather, so that we could sail more safely. For many days we waited, but the weather kept getting worse instead of better. At last Paul said, 'Sirs, I am sure that if we try to go on with our voyage at this time of year, we will have serious trouble. Our ship will be destroyed, and the grain the ship is loaded with will be lost, and we will be in great danger of losing our lives. We had better stay here till the winter is over and good weather comes.'"

In the winter the Mediterranean is a stormy sea, and it was not possible to sail across it during those months. They had already been delayed so much by the unfavorable winds that the shipping season was about to close.

Luke goes on with the story: "But the centurion listened to the owner of the ship rather than to Paul. Fair Havens was not a very comfortable place to spend the winter. They decided to try to go a little further to a town called Phoenix, which was on the other side of the island.

"After a few days the stormy weather let up. The sun came out, and a south wind blew softly. They thought it would be safe to leave Fair Havens and to try to get to Phoenix.

"When we had left the harbor and sailed along the coast of the island, a terrible wind sprang up. It was a real hurricane. We were too far from the island of Crete to turn back now. The wind was so terrible we could not manage the ship at all. We could only let her go where she was driven.

"The sky turned black as night. The rain poured down in sheets. The lightning streaked across the sky. The hurricane howled and shrieked, and the waves ran mountain high.

"Our ship was tossed to and fro. We were lifted to the crest of a mounting wave, only to be dropped into its trough the next moment. We did everything we could to make the ship lighter. We threw overboard everything we could lay hands on. We helped the sailors pull down the sails, and the masts, and the tackle, and toss it into the sea.

"Day after day the storm kept on. Day after day the tempest raged. No sun or stars appeared in the sky. We gave up all hope of escaping alive.

"Then Paul stood up among us and said, 'Sirs, you should have listened to me, and not sailed away from Crete. But now do not give up hope, for none of you will die, but only the ship will be lost. For this night the angel of my God stood by me and said to me, "Do not be afraid, Paul, for God will save you, for you must go to Rome to stand before Caesar. And God will save all those in the ship with you for your sake." So be of good cheer, for I know that what God says is true, but we must first be cast upon an island.'"

Chapter 89

THE SHIPWRECK
ACTS 27

Luke goes on with the story of Paul's journey to Rome:

"We had now been driven to and fro by the terrible storm for two weeks. One night, as the wind was driving us about in the sea, the sailors thought we were near some land. They dropped a line in the sea to measure the depth of the water, and found that it was only twenty fathoms deep. Soon they dropped another line into the sea, and this time it was only fifteen fathoms deep.

"Then we knew we must be near to some land. There was great danger that we would strike rocks near the shore and be dashed to pieces. So we cast four anchors out into the sea to keep the ship from crashing on the rocks.

"It was a dark night, and the waves were high. We could not see any land, but we knew that it must be near because the water was not deep. We longed for the light of day to come.

"The sailors tried to save themselves by letting a little boat down into the sea. They were going to try to row to shore, leaving us to perish with the ship. They hoped that in the darkness of the night the captain of the ship would not see them.

"But Paul saw them letting the boat down, and he said to the centurion, 'If the sailors leave the ship, you will all be drowned.' So the captain stopped the sailors in their attempt. The soldiers cut away the ropes, and let the boat drop down into the sea and drift away.

"As day was about to dawn, Paul said to all the men on the ship, 'I beg you to eat some food, for it is now fourteen days since you have tasted anything. It will be far better for you to eat. Not a hair shall fall from the head of any one of you.'

"With these words Paul took some bread. Looking up to heaven, he gave thanks to God, and ate it. When the men saw Paul so calm and cheerful, they were encouraged, and they, too, ate some food.

"Counting all of us in the ship, there were two hundred and seventy-six men. When everyone had eaten as much as he wanted, the sailors tried to make the ship lighter, so that it would float in shallow water. They threw the grain with which the ship was loaded into the sea.

"When daylight came, we saw a strange new land. Close to us there was a little bay with a smooth beach. We decided to try to drive the ship into the bay and land on the beach.

"First of all the sailors loosened the ship from the four anchors they had let down the night before. Then they raised the mainsail to the wind and headed the ship toward the shore. They found a place where the waters ran in toward the shore, and they let the waves carry the ship with all their force.

"Soon the ship ran aground. The front part stuck fast in the sand and could not be moved, but the back was broken up by the violent pounding of the wild waves.

"The soldiers advised the centurion to kill all the prisoners, for fear they would swim away and escape. The centurion, however, wanted to save Paul, as he knew he was a good and innocent man. So he commanded that all who could swim should jump into the sea and swim ashore.

"The waves were pounding on the

ship. Those who could not swim were afraid to stay on her, and they were still more afraid to jump into the raging sea. But the ship was breaking up so fast that at last they found the courage to jump overboard.

"Some of them managed to climb onto boards, and some onto broken pieces of the ship. And so all of them reached the shore safely."

Chapter 90
THE RESCUE
ACTS 28

After telling about the shipwreck, Luke writes:

"When we were all safe ashore on the island, we looked around. We soon discovered that we were on the island of Melita. The people there were very kind to us. They built a big fire to warm us. We were soaking wet and almost frozen from being in the sea so long. It was still raining, and very cold.

"As Paul gathered a bundle of sticks to burn in the fire, a poisonous snake came out from among them and fastened on his hand. The native people, when they saw the deadly snake on Paul's hand, whispered among themselves, 'This man must be a murderer. Even though he has escaped drowning in the sea, now justice has finally caught up with him. The poison will surely kill him.'

"But Paul shook off the snake into the fire, and felt no harm. The natives watched him closely for a long time, waiting to see his hand swell up, expecting him to fall down dead. When nothing happened to him, they changed their minds and said that he must be a god come down to earth in the form of a man.

"The chief of the island was a man named Publius. His house was near the place where we had been cast up on the shore. He took care of us for three days very kindly.

"This man had an old father who was very sick. Paul went to see the old man. Laying his hands upon him, he prayed, and the man was made well again. When the natives on the island found that Paul could heal the sick, they brought others to be healed, and all were made well.

"We stayed on this island for three months, till winter was over. The people treated us with great respect, and afterward, when we left, they gave us freely all we needed.

"At last we found another ship, whose name was the *Twin Brothers*. She was on her way from Egypt to Rome, and had stayed in the island all winter to wait for good weather. We boarded this ship and continued our journey.

"Landing at Syracuse in Sicily, we stayed there three days. When a south wind blew, we went on and came to a city on the coast of Italy. There we found that we had Christian friends. We left the ship and stayed with them seven days. After this we went on toward Rome, traveling by land.

"The Christians at Rome had heard of our arrival. They came to meet us at the Market of Appius and the Three Taverns. Oh, how happy Paul was to see them! He thanked the Lord, and was much encouraged.

"At last we came to Rome, and our long journey was ended. The centurion sent the prisoners to the captain of the guard in Rome. Paul was not put in prison. He was allowed to

374

rent a house and live there, with only one soldier staying with him as his guard. His friends were allowed to visit him freely. But he had to wear a chain which fastened him to his guard, and this chain was very heavy and uncomfortable.

"After he had been in Rome for three days, Paul sent for the leaders of the Jews there. They had not heard anything about the trouble in Jerusalem, but they were glad to talk to Paul, for they had heard many things about the Christians. And so Paul talked to them for a long time about Jesus, the promised Saviour. Some of the Jews believed him, but others would not listen.

"Paul lived in Rome for two years, preaching to everyone who came to see him, before the emperor was ready to hear his case."

Chapter 91
THE HERO OF FAITH
II CORINTHIANS 11, 12

After Paul and Luke reached Rome, Luke's story ends. We know nothing more about Paul with certainty, except that he died bravely as a soldier of Jesus.

In all the years since then there has been no greater preacher and missionary than Paul. He spent his life telling people about Jesus. He founded churches all over Asia Minor and Greece. Once he talked about going to Spain, but we do not know whether he ever got there.

Paul wrote many letters to the churches he had founded, explaining about Jesus. We, too, can read some of these letters, for they became parts of the New Testament. The Holy Spirit of God helped Paul, telling him what to write. Like the rest of the Bible, Paul's letters are God's words to us.

Paul was a great hero. He endured great suffering for the Master he loved so dearly. Five times he was cruelly beaten. Each time he was given the worst beating the law allowed. Three times he was beaten with rods. Once he was stoned and left for dead. Four times he was shipwrecked, and once he was in the water a whole day and a night before being rescued. Just think of being on the sea for such a long time, kept afloat only by some broken piece of the ship! Often the men to whom Paul preached became so angry that they acted like wild beasts who wanted to tear him to pieces.

But many beautiful, wonderful things happened to Paul, too, which strengthened him for his work. Jesus spoke to him right from heaven on the road to Damascus. God stood by him and spoke to him many times, bringing him messages of comfort and hope.

Once Paul was taken right up to heaven. It was all so wonderful that he could never tell if he was really taken to heaven, or if he only saw it in a vision. But he knew that he had actually seen the glories of heaven, and had heard words so wonderful that there were no human words to describe them.

Although Paul was glad to work and fight for Jesus in this world, he often longed to go to heaven to be with Jesus, for he said this was far better. Near the end of his life he said, "I have fought the good fight. I have finished the course. I have kept the faith. Henceforth there is laid up for me a crown of righteousness, which the Lord, the righteous Judge, shall give me at that day." Soon afterward this splendid soldier of the cross was killed in Rome. For so many years already he had been homesick for heaven, and now at last he saw his Saviour face to face.

Probably Peter also died in Rome at about the same time; he was killed by the wicked emperor Nero. There is a legend that when Peter was about to die, he asked that he might be crucified with his head at the bottom of the cross, because he felt that he was not worthy to die in the same way his beloved Lord had died.

Like Paul, Peter wrote some of the books of the New Testament. They are the letters which we call I and II Peter.

Luke wrote The Gospel according to Luke and The Acts of the Apostles.

Matthew wrote a story about the life of Jesus, and Mark wrote another. James, the brother of Jesus, wrote a book called James. Judas, the son of Alphaeus, wrote a letter called Jude.

John, the beloved disciple, wrote a book about the life of Jesus, and he also wrote three letters, I John, II John, and III John.

John was the youngest of the twelve apostles, and the one who lived the longest. Toward the end of his life he was arrested. Instead of being sent to prison, he was exiled on a lonely little island called Patmos. While John was on this island, he wrote the last book of the Bible, called The Revelation of St. John. It tells us about the things that will happen at the end of the world, and about heaven.

No one knows for sure who wrote the book of Hebrews. Some people think that Paul wrote it, and some think Apollos did, for the Bible says that he was "an eloquent man, and mighty in the scriptures."

All these writers were inspired by God. That means that God told them what to say. The New Testament is God's book, just as the Old Testament is. Together they form the Bible, which is the Word of Life.

Chapter 92
THE VISIONS OF THE APOSTLE JOHN
REVELATION 1, 5, 7, 20-22

When the apostle John was an old man, he was sent to the little island of Patmos. He was a prisoner there, a lonely exile. He could not go away again for the rest of his life.

While John was there, he had many wonderful visions. He wrote them down in the book of Revelation, which became the last book of the Bible. It tells us about heaven.

John saw Jesus as He looks in heaven. His head and His hair were white as snow, and His eyes were like a flame of fire. John fainted and

fell down, because he was afraid. But Jesus laid His hand on John and said to him, "Do not be afraid. I am He that liveth and was dead, and, behold, I am alive forevermore. Write the things which you shall see in these visions."

John saw a great white throne upon which God sat. He saw the dead, small and great, standing before God. Even the sea gave up the dead which were in it, and all men were judged according to the things which they had done. Whoever was not found written in the Book of Life was cast out of heaven into the lake of fire.

John saw Jesus looking like a lamb that had been killed, and heard a new song sung in heaven: "Thou art worthy, for Thou wast slain, and hast purchased to God with Thy blood men of every tribe and tongue and people and nation."

John heard the voice of many angels around the throne, saying, "Worthy is the Lamb that hath been slain, to receive power, and riches, and wisdom, and might, and honor, and glory, and blessing."

And every creature in heaven and on the earth and under the earth and in the sea, and all things in them said, "Unto Him that sitteth on the throne, and unto the Lamb, be the blessing, and the glory, and the dominion forever and ever."

In another vision John saw a great multitude, so great that no man could count it, men out of every nation and tribe and people, standing before the throne and before the Lamb, dressed in white robes, with palms in their hands. One of the elders asked him, "Who are these in the white robes? Where do they come from?" And John said, "Sir, you must know, but I do not."

Then the elder answered, "These are they who have come out of great troubles, and they have washed their robes and made them white in the blood of the Lamb. That is why they are before the throne of God, and serve Him day and night in His temple. And God Himself shall live among them. They will never be hungry any more, nor thirsty. The sun will not smite them with its heat. For the Lamb will feed them, and will lead them to living fountains of water. And God Himself shall wipe away all tears from their eyes."

Last of all John wrote, "I saw a new heaven and a new earth: for the first heaven and the first earth are passed away. . . . And I heard a great voice out of the throne, saying, 'Behold, the tabernacle of God is with men. And He shall dwell with them and be their God. And God shall wipe away every tear from their eyes. And death shall be no more. Neither shall there be mourning, nor crying, nor pain any more.'

"And there came to me one of the angels, and he carried me away in the spirit to a mountain great and high, and showed me the holy city, new Jerusalem, coming down from God out of heaven.

"And the city was pure gold, like transparent glass. The foundations of the wall of the city were adorned with all kinds of precious stones. The twelve gates were twelve pearls, and the street of the city was pure gold.

"And I saw no temple therein, for the Lord God Almighty and the Lamb are the temple thereof. And the city had no need of the sun to shine on it, for the glory of God lighted it up, and the lamp thereof is the Lamb. And all the nations which are saved shall walk in the light of the city. And there shall be no night there. There shall in no wise enter into it anything unclean, but only those whose names are written in the Lamb's Book of Life.

"And he showed me a river of water of life, bright as crystal, proceeding out of the throne of God and of the Lamb. In the midst of the street, and on this side of the river, and on that, was the Tree of Life, bearing twelve manner of fruits, yielding its fruit every month. And the leaves of the tree were for the healing of the nations.

"And there shall be no curse any more. The throne of God and of the

Lamb shall be in it. His servants shall serve Him, and they shall see His face, and His name shall be on their foreheads.

"And there shall be no night there, and they need no lamp, for the Lord God shall give them light. And they shall reign forever and ever.

"I John saw these things and heard them. And I heard the Holy Spirit saying, 'Come! Let him that is thirsty come. Let him take of the water of life freely.'

"And the Lord said, 'Surely I come quickly!' And I answered, 'Even so, Lord Jesus, come quickly!' "

Some Words Explained

No attempt has been made to give an exhaustive theological definition of these words, but only to clarify their meaning as they are used in this book.

ALABASTER A beautiful, clear stone, often made into bottles for expensive perfumes.

ANGELS Messengers of God, often sent to earth to help His people. Angels are spirits without a body.

ANOINT To pour on oil as a sign that God has chosen the person anointed for some special work, and that God will give him whatever he needs to perform that work.

APOSTLES Followers of Jesus sent out by Him to tell others that Jesus has died for the sins of those who trust in Him, and has risen from the dead.

ARCHANGELS Angels of very high rank.

ARK (1) A boat, as Noah's ark. (2) The gold-covered box placed in the Holy of Holies in the tabernacle or temple. The tablets on which God wrote the Ten Commandments, a dish of manna, and Aaron's rod which budded were kept in the ark.

ASHERAH A Canaanite goddess, or her image made of wood.

ATONE To make payment for sin.

BAPTIZE To dip in or sprinkle with water, as a solemn sign that the person baptized has been washed from his sins and given a new heart by God. In baptism we are united to Jesus in His death, so that we die to our sins and rise with Him to a new life.

BLASPHEMY The use of God's name in an insulting or dishonorable way.

BLESSED Favored by God, and therefore desirable and happy.

CAESAR The title of the Roman emperor.

CAST LOTS A way of discovering God's will, or the will of idols, by shaking stones in a container, and then taking one out. Casting lots by God's people was always accompanied by prayer that God would direct the outcome.

CENSER A small shovel on which hot coals were carried in the temple service. Often incense was placed on the coals, so that the fragrance rose with the smoke.

CENTURION A captain in the Roman army who had one hundred soldiers under him.

CHERUBIM Heavenly beings sent by God to guard the Tree of Life in the Garden of Eden, and the Mercy Seat on the ark in the tabernacle.

CHRIST The one anointed by God to be our Saviour, called the Messiah in the Old Testament.

COLT A young horse or donkey.

COMFORTER The Holy Spirit, one of the three persons in God. The Comforter was sent to the disciples to teach and strengthen them after Jesus ascended to heaven.

COVENANT A solemn agreement which God makes with man.

CREATED Made out of nothing by God.

CURSE, CURSED Condemned by God, and therefore separated from all that is desirable and happy.

DENARIUS A small Roman coin made of silver, equal to one day's wages for a laborer.

DISCIPLES Followers of a teacher.

DOCTORS OF THE LAW Men who spent all their time studying and explaining the law of Moses.

ELDERS (1) Persons who were leaders because of their age and experience.
(2) Men appointed by the apostles to rule the church, in the book of Acts.

EPHOD A tunic, or smock, worn by the priests when they served in the temple.

ETERNAL Always the same, without beginning and without end.

FAITH Believing what God tells us, and trusting in His promises, especially in the promise of salvation through the death of Jesus.

FAST, FASTING To refrain from eating as a way of showing outwardly our inner sorrow for sin, or as a prayer to God in time of special crisis.

FATHOM The distance between the hands when the arms are outstretched, about six feet.

FATTED CALF A calf which has been especially fattened to be served at feasts or celebrations.

FOAL A young horse or donkey.

FRANKINCENSE A sweet-smelling perfume given by the wise men to the baby Jesus.

GIRDLE A belt or sash.

GLEAN To gather up the grain which the harvesters drop and which is left in the fields.

GOSPEL The good news of the coming of Jesus to die for our sins.

GRACE The undeserved goodness of God toward man.

HANDMAID A woman slave.

HOLY Perfectly good, separated from all sin. Only God is perfectly holy.

HOSANNA "Save, we pray Thee!" used as a shout of welcome and praise.

IMMORTAL Something or someone that cannot die.

INSPIRATION God's guidance of those who wrote the Bible so that what they wrote is true.

JEALOUS (as used of God in the Ten Commandments) The fact that God is unwilling to share the love and trust of His people with other gods.

KINGDOM OF HEAVEN The rule of God, both in this world and in the next.

LAVER A basin in which the priests washed themselves before offering sacrifices to God.

LAWYER A man who spent all his time studying and explaining the law of Moses.

LEGION A unit of the Roman army consisting of about 6,000 soldiers; hence any very large number.

LEVITES Members of the tribe of Levi (one of Jacob's twelve sons) who helped the priests in the wor-

380

ship service of God in the tabernacle and the temple.

LORD'S SUPPER The eating of broken bread and drinking of poured-out wine as a solemn sign that we remember the death of Jesus for our sins.

MANGER A feed trough for animals.

MARTYR Someone who dies for Jesus. Stephen was the first Christian martyr.

MASTER The name the disciples gave to Jesus because He was their teacher.

MERCY SEAT The golden cover of the ark, where the presence of God among His people was shown by a dazzling light. The Mercy Seat was protected by the wings of the cherubim on the cover.

MIRACLE An act which can only be done by the almighty power of God, for whom all things are possible.

MORTAL Something or someone who will die.

MYRRH A fragrant spice given by the wise men to the baby Jesus.

NAZARENES The name used by the Jews for the early Christians because Jesus came from Nazareth.

NAZARITE Someone especially set aside for God's service. To show his dedication the Nazarite did not drink wine or cut his hair.

PARABLE A story told by Jesus to illustrate a spiritual truth.

PASSOVER The Jewish feast which celebrated God's rescue of the Israelites from slavery in Egypt. On the night of their departure, a child died in every Egyptian home, but God "passed over" the houses of the Israelites when He saw the blood of a lamb on the door.

PHARISEES One of the two main groups of the Jewish leaders at the time of Jesus. The Pharisees were very strict about observing not only God's law but also the hundreds of interpretations and additions they had added to the law.

PRIEST Someone appointed by God to serve in His temple and to offer sacrifices for the sins of the people.

PROPHET A person sent by God to carry God's message to men.

PUBLICANS Jews who collected taxes for the Romans.

REPENT To be sorry for one's sins and to turn away from them.

RESURRECTION The raising up of both body and soul from death. Jesus' resurrection is a pledge that all who trust in Him will also someday rise from the dead, body as well as soul.

RULER OF THE FEAST The man in charge of a wedding, similar to our master of ceremonies.

RULER OF THE SYNAGOGUE The man who arranged the services in the synagogue, and who looked after the building.

SACKCLOTH Rough clothing worn as a sign of grief.

SADDUCEES One of the two main groups of the Jewish leaders at the time of Jesus. The Sadducees were less strict about the letter of the law than the Pharisees, and more willing to compromise with the Roman rulers. They did not believe in angels or in the resurrection. Most of the high priests were Sadducees. They bitterly opposed Jesus because He interfered with the traders in the temple.

SAMARITANS   People of a mixed race who occupied the northern part of Palestine after the ten tribes were carried into captivity. They accepted only the five books written by Moses, and their religion was a mixture of the worship of God and of idols. There was bitter hatred between the Jews and the Samaritans.

SANCTIFY (the temple). To make holy and especially set aside for the worship of God.

SATAN   The leader of the wicked angels, or devils, who rebelled against God.
Satan tempted Adam and Eve in the Garden of Eden, and he tempted Jesus at the beginning of His teaching.

SCEPTER   The decorated rod carried by a king as a symbol of his authority.

SCRIBES   (1) In the Old Testament, a secretary or public writer. (2) In the New Testament, a man who made it his business to study and interpret God's law.

SCRIPTURE, SCRIPTURES   The name the Jews at the time of Jesus gave to the writings in the Old Testament.

SERAPHIM   Angels with six wings who surround the throne of God.

SHEARER   The man who cuts the woolly fleece off a sheep.

SPIKENARD   A very expensive and fragrant perfume imported from India.

STOCKS   Wooden frames in which the feet of prisoners were fastened.

SWADDLING CLOTHS   Narrow strips of cloth in which the Jews wrapped new-born babies.

SYNAGOGUE   A building where the New Testament Jews assembled to hear God's Word and to pray. Sacrifices were offered only in the temple in Jerusalem, not in the synagogues. A synagogue was set up wherever there were ten Jewish men living.

TABERNACLE   A meeting place in a tent which the Israelites made at God's command while they traveled through the desert.

TANNER   A man who treated animal skins to make them into leather.

VOW   A solemn promise made to God.

PALESTINE DURING THE TRIBAL PERIOD

+ MT. HERMON

PHOENICIA

ARAM

Leontes River

MEDITERRANEAN SEA

ASHER

NAPHTALI

DAN

• Tyre

Hazor •

LAKE HULEH
(SEMECHONITIS)

Merom •

Acco •

SEA OF CHINNERETH

Yarmuk River

ZEBULUN

Kishon River

MT. CARMEL

ISSACHAR

MANASSEH

• Dor

Megiddo •

• Beth-shean

• Ramoth-gilead

ISRAEL

• Jabesh-gilead

MANASSEH

AMMON

Samaria •

+ MT. EBAL

MT. GERIZIM + • Shechem

GAD

Jordan River

EPHRAIM

Succoth •

Jabbok River

Joppa •

Adamah •

THE DIVIDED MONARCHY

Bethel •

• Rabbath-ammon

Beth-horon •

• Ai

• Gilgal?

Ekron •

DAN

Jericho •

• Abel-shittim

• Gibeon

Ashdod •

Aijalon •

BENJAMIN

Gilgal? •

• Heshbon

Jarmuth •

Jerusalem •

Ashkelon •

• Gath

REUBEN

Eglon •

• Lachish

• Hebron

SALT SEA
(DEAD SEA)

Gaza •

JUDAH

SIMEON

Arnon River

• Beer-sheba

MOAB

JUDAH

PHILISTIA

Brook Zered

EDOM

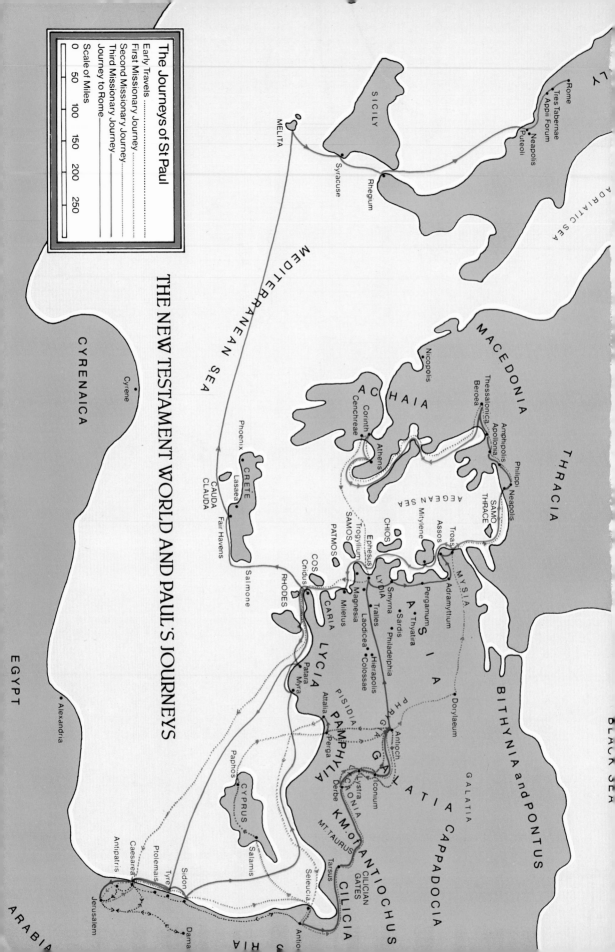